OXFORD PAPERBACK REFERENCE

The Oxford Dictionary of Philosophy

SEE WEB LINKS

Some entries in this dictionary have recommended web links. When you see the symbol at the end of an entry go to the dictionary's web page at http://www.oup.com/uk/reference/resources/philosophy, click on **Web links** in the Resources section and select the entry from the alphabetical list, then click straight through to the relevant websites.

Simon Blackburn is Professor of Philosophy at the University of Cambridge. He was previously Edna J. Koury Distinguished Professor of Philosophy at the University of North Carolina. He was a Fellow and Tutor of Pembroke College, Oxford from 1969 to 1990. The author of *Spreading the Word* (1984) and *Essays in Quasi-Realism* (1993), he edited the journal *Mind* from 1984 to 1990. Recent books include *Think* (1999), *Being Good* (2001), *Lust* (2004), *Truth* (2005), *Plato's Republic* (2006), and *How to Read Hume* (2008).

The Oxford Dictionary of
Philosophy

SECOND EDITION REVISED

SIMON BLACKBURN

OXFORD
UNIVERSITY PRESS

Great Clarendon Street, Oxford OX2 6DP

Oxford University Press is a department of the University of Oxford.
It furthers the University's objective of excellence in research, scholarship, and education by publishing worldwide in

Oxford New York

Auckland Cape Town Dar es Salaam Hong Kong Karachi
Kuala Lumpur Madrid Melbourne Mexico City Nairobi
New Delhi Shanghai Taipei Toronto

With offices in

Argentina Austria Brazil Chile Czech Republic France Greece
Guatemala Hungary Italy Japan Poland Portugal Singapore
South Korea Switzerland Thailand Turkey Ukraine Vietnam

Published in the United States
by Oxford University Press Inc., New York

First published 1994
First issued as an Oxford University Press paperback (with a new Chronology) 1996
Second edition 2005
Second edition revised 2008

British Library Cataloguing in Publication Data
Data available

Library of Congress Cataloging in Publication Data
Data available

Typeset by SPI Publisher Services, Pondicherry, India
Printed in Great Britain
on acid-free paper by
Clays Ltd., St Ives plc

ISBN 978-0-19-954143-0

4

Contents

Preface to the Second Edition

It is now eleven years since the first edition of this Dictionary was published, and time moves on. When I was writing the original edition there were few comparable works to help the job of compilation and selection. In the intervening years, a great many have appeared, some of admirable weight and authority. Now, as well, the resources of the web are everywhere, and bring both a blessing and a curse: the blessing of instant access to information which, only little more than a decade ago, required ferreting out of patchy libraries and archives, but the corresponding curse of overload. A good curator, it is said, knows what to destroy, but it is hard for a dictionary writer to opt out of the arms race of adding the obscure and the marginal, the exotic and the antiquarian, when there is so little cost to doing so. My own criteria remain roughly as they did for the first edition, although I have allowed myself a fair amount of expansion where I became persuaded that the original was a little too sparse. But I have tried to keep the likely needs of the user in mind, and at least some of those needs are better met with reasonable brevity than massive prolixity. The historian Macaulay says of some unfortunate that the great weight of his learning had quite extinguished his slender faculties, but as before I have been more concerned to light up the faculties than to add to the learning. And, as before, this is my excuse for refracting so much through my own interests and judgments, rather than packaging the entries of others.

Finally, as in the case of the first edition, I owe thanks to many colleagues who patiently dealt with questions, and also to correspondents, who wrote, usually with tact and courtesy, raising issues or even, alas, pointing out infelicities or actual errors. On this account I would like to thank Lars Bergstrom, Brian Bix, Denny Bradshaw, Keith Burgess-Jackson, John Corcoran, Solomon Feferman, Thomas Meeks, Desiderio Mucho, Jan Österberg, and John Warfield. Angela Coventry began the major job of revising and updating the headword list, and it was extended and completed by my wife Angela, without whom the work of revision would by now have barely started. Any remaining mistakes are, of course, my own, and all I can do is hope that they are tending towards zero with time, and then by way of self-protection direct my readers to the two quotations from the wise Dr Johnson in the following Preface to the First Edition.

SIMON BLACKBURN

Cambridge, Feb 2005

Preface to the First Edition

Philosophy is human thought become self-conscious. Its topics are life, the universe, and everything; it can include all the categories of religious, artistic, scientific, mathematical, and logical thought. This dictionary of philosophy is a record of some of the terms that excite such reflection, and some that have been found helpful in conducting it.

Johnson writes in the Preface to his great *Dictionary of the English Language* that:

> when the nature of things is unknown, or the notion unsettled and indefinite, and various in various minds, the words by which such notions are conveyed, or such things denoted, will be ambiguous and perplexed.

Philosophy by its nature inhabits such areas of ambiguity and perplexity, places where, in Russell's phrase, we meet only uncertain patches of meaning. Philosophers make their reputations by contesting meanings: success often consists in showing that predecessors misunderstood the categories of experience, reason, proof, perception, consciousness, virtue, or law. Such discussions are intricate and lengthy. Philosophies, like movements of thought in general, demand lengthy statement and resist swift definition. Thus the distinguished historian of ideas A. O. Lovejoy records that, in 1824, two citizens of the French village of La Ferté-sous-Jouarre, MM. Dupuis and Cotonet, began the enterprise of discovering what Romanticism is, by collecting the definitions given by eminent authorities. The endeavour, they recorded, cost them twelve years of suffering and ended in disillusion.[1] In the same paper, Lovejoy confidently tells us that over sixty senses of the word 'nature' can clearly be distinguished. With such dismal examples before us, brevity may seem impossible, and any attempt at an overview an insult to the abundant complexities.

No dictionary-sized explanation of these terms can substitute for the full explorations. A dictionary entry on virtue or quantum mechanics cannot substitute for an education in ethics or physics. What I have attempted to do is to indicate where the central explorations are headed, and the points of dispute that have attracted reflection. Naturally, this means that my own interests and assessments are not always disguised. Other topics are not themselves subject to such disputes. It is not, for example, seriously contested what Newcomb's paradox is, or the axiom of choice. Here a more magisterial treatment is possible, and this I have given.

Any acquaintance with the history of philosophy shows how closely its concerns fuse with those of subjects that go under different academic headings: literature, physics, psychology, sociology, and theology. Indeed, the separation of philosophy as a discipline can seem to be an artefact of academic administration, rather than a reflection of a clear division between using a concept and thinking about it. I have therefore been free in introducing terminology from other sciences where such terminology is heavily embedded in philosophical discussion. For example, in the contemporary literature, someone thinking about the ethics of abortion may come across casual mention of zygotes and meiosis, just as surely as they may come across the doctrine of double effect or the acts/omissions doctrine. Someone interested in physical reality may need to know the content of Bell's theorem or the Einstein–Podolsky–Rosen thought experiment, and in such matters I have attempted to help. Similarly I have tried to be generous with thinkers from neighbouring subjects and traditions, although inevitably there is a certain amount of arbitrariness. Addison, Blake, and Pope were probably as significant philosophical thinkers as many people included here, but they fell just outside the range; Carlyle, Coleridge, and Dante get in. I have been particularly concerned to include the great scientists whose work infused major changes in philosophy: Boyle and Faraday, as well as Galileo, Newton, Darwin, and Einstein.

However, I have been moderately sparing with contemporaries. My criterion was, in effect, whether the name might occur as a point of reference without explanation, as in a Quinean theory of meaning, a Davidsonian view of interpretation, or Lewis's view of possible worlds. This may mean that persons associated with particular doctrines gain entries, when equally distinguished, or even better, philosophers remain less well-exposed, and I trust that this sugars the pill for anyone disappointed at not being included. We must all reflect that new stars appear in the intellectual firmament, and old ones disappear.

Most of the conventions used in the work are self-explanatory. I have tried to design it as a playground for browsers and a resource for anyone interested in general intellectual movements, as

[1] A. O. Lovejoy, *Proceedings of the Modern Language Assocation of America*, 34 (1924), 229.

well as a simple work of reference. Hence there is extensive cross-referencing; indeed the tracing of influences and predecessors, often across apparent divisions within the subject, is my principal excuse for undertaking the enterprise myself, rather than relying on self-contained, 'packaged', entries from experts in different areas. The first mention of a useful cross-reference in an entry is asterisked, and related topics picked up by '*see*' and '*see also*'. I have used standard simplifications for the transliterations of Arabic, Chinese, Hebrew, Parsi, and Sanskrit, believing that all transliteration schemes are artificial, and that more readers are put off by the proliferation of accents and diacriticals than are helped by them. I have, however, kept the macron for long vowels in Greek words, as in *epochē* or *aretē*, since this is a well-established convention in contemporary philosophical literature. Alphabetization is surprisingly tricky, and the rule is that where there are complications, entries are ordered by what occurs before the first comma. Thus we have self-intimating; selfish gene; self-refuting ...; and fact, facticity, factive, fact/value .... 'St' and 'Mc' are alphabetized as Saint and Mac. For modern European languages other than English, original titles are given, and the titles of published translations, with dates of translation where it was felt that this information was useful (for example, in signalling how quickly or how slowly a work was disseminated in English).

I owe thanks to many people who have saved me from error: Benjamin Arnold, Julia Annas, George Boolos, Andreas Edmüller, Roderick Long, Keith Simmons, and Paul Teller gave me extensive advice, and I have also received assistance from Bernard Boxill, Ned Block, Edward Craig, Daniel Dennett, Luciano Floridi, Allan Gibbard, Rosalind Hursthouse, Jay Rosenberg, Galen Strawson, and Ralph Walker. Ruth Opochinsky, Robert Michels, and Andrew Mills provided invaluable research assistance. The huge editing job was undertaken by my wife, Angela Blackburn, whose patience has been beyond praise. I owe thanks to MIT Press for permission to reproduce the diagram in the entry on 'connectionism' which is adapted from Paul Churchland's *Matter and Consciousness* (1984). In this reprint a number of minor errors in the original edition have been corrected. I am very grateful to colleagues and students for help in identifying these. Any errors that remain are of course my own responsibility. Here, again, I can only echo Johnson:

> It is the fate of those who toil at the lower employments of life, to be rather driven by the fear of evil, than attracted by the prospect of good; to be exposed to censure, without hope of praise; to be disgraced by miscarriage, or punished for neglect, where success would have been without applause, and diligence without reward. Among these unhappy mortals is the writer of dictionaries ...

SIMON BLACKBURN

Chapel Hill 1994

abandonment Term used by *existentialists to dramatize the sense of loss that comes from realizing that there is no external source of moral authority, such as a God.

Abbagnano, Nicola (1901–90) Leading Italian *existentialist. Born in Salerno, Abbagnano studied in Naples and taught at Turin. His 'philosophy of the possible' condemned other existentialists for either denying human possibility (because all our efforts are futile in a hostile and meaningless universe) or exaggerating it, imagining us capable of things which actually lie outside our potential. In his later work he tended to adopt a more naturalistic and scientific approach to philosophy, although still condemning the 'myth of security' implicit in a complacent scientific world view. His major works include the monumental three-volume *Storia della filosofia* ('History of Philosophy', 1946–50) and *Possibilità e libertà* ('Possibility and Liberty', 1956).

Abderites Term for the two earliest *atomists, *Democritus and *Leucippus, both of whom came from Abdera in northern Greece.

abduction Term introduced by *Peirce for the process of using evidence to reach a wider conclusion, as in inference to the best *explanation. Peirce described abduction as a creative process, but stressed that the results are subject to rational evaluation. However he anticipated later pessimism about the prospects of *confirmation theory, denying that we can assess the results of abduction in terms of probability.

Abduh, Muhammad (1849–1905) Egyptian philosophical theologian, notable for attempting to reconcile Islam with elements in the modern world. His work *The Theology of Unity* was translated into English in 1966.

Abelard, Peter (Abaelard, Abailard) (1079–1142) French scholastic philosopher. Born near Nantes, Abelard lived a hectic life, quite apart from the misfortune he incurred as a result of his romance of 1118 (for the details of which, *see* HÉLOÏSE). He was educated at Chartres and Paris, and lived as monk and abbot at a succession of monasteries. He survived an attempt on his life at a Breton monastery in 1132. A controversial figure, he found his work condemned in 1121, and his scepticism about the legends of St Dionysius forced him to leave the Abbey of St Denis. In 1125 he became Abbot of St Gildas, and later returned to Paris. His work was denounced by *Bernard of Clairvaux, who described him as having sweated to prove that Plato was a Christian, but only proved himself a heretic. He was again censured in 1140, but he died in one of the daughter monasteries of the Abbey of Cluny.

Abelard wrote extensively on the problem of *universals, probably adopting a moderate *realism, although he has sometimes been claimed as a *nominalist. He wrote commentaries on *Porphyry and other authorities. His *Scito te Ipsum* ('Know Thyself') is a treatise on ethics holding that sin consists entirely in contempt for the wishes of God; action is therefore less important than states of mind such as intention. Consistently with this, his theory of the *atonement is that it is simply a supreme example for us to follow. Abelard lived at a time when a new sense of the clash of classical authorities was becoming evident; translations revealed discrepant opinions and generated the disputatious atmosphere in which Abelard flourished. His *Sic et Non* ('For and Against') is a collection of contradictions from scripture and early writings, coupled with his own rules for resolving disputes. It provided the initial programme for the scholastic method. Abelard's contributions to logic have been the object of recent admiration, while his hymns include *O quanta qualia* ('Oh how great and glorious are those sabbaths').

ab esse ad posse valet consequentia From the fact that something exists, it follows that it is possible.

abhidharma Books containing the key categories of *Buddhist philosophy.

abninivesha Sanskrit term for self-love, or the desire for self-preservation. Since this is a form of bondage it stands in the way of spiritual freedom, and has a generally negative overtone.

abortion Termination of the life of a foetus, after conception but before birth. The event may be intentionally induced or natural, although it is intentionally induced abortion that is the topic of moral philosophy. The issues divide conservatives or 'pro-life' supporters, who regard deliberately induced abortion as impermissible, and liberals or 'pro-choice' supporters, who regard the action as permissible in a variety of cases. The liberal attitude may extend to almost any case in which a mother wishes an abortion, or may involve a variety of restrictions, including the age of the foetus. Moderates restrict the permissible cases, but the debate has not been notable for moderation. Issues arising include the nature of personhood, and its beginning; the extent of the right to life; the fragile notion of the sanctity of life; the way in which conflicting rights should be treated; and the political and social issues of who has the right to decide moral and legal policy and to enforce it.

SEE WEB LINKS

- An archive of related religious, medical, and legal debates
- A UN review of abortion policies around the world

Abrabanel, Isaac (1437–1508/9) Spanish Jewish philosopher and commentator on *Maimonides.

Abrabanel, Judah (*c.*1463–*c.*1523) Son of Isaac Abrabanel, and also known as Leone Ebreo. His *Dialoghi d'amore* (*Dialogues of Love*) explore the mystical relation of love and desire, and the way in which love infuses and maintains the cosmic order. They were influential in Italian Platonist and Neoplatonist circles in the Renaissance.

Absolute, the *See* ABSOLUTE IDEALISM.

absolute idealism 19th-century version of *idealism in which the world is equated with objective or absolute thought, rather than with the personal flux of experience, as in subjective idealism. The doctrine is the descendant of several ancestors, including the *Parmenidean One, the theological tradition of an unconditioned and unchanging *necessary being responsible for the contingent changing world, *Spinoza's pregnant belief that there is just one world with the characteristics of facts and things on the one hand and of ideas on the other, the *transcendental idealism of *Kant, and the emergence of activity and the will as the main determinants of history. Other influences include a dynamic conception of nature as an organic unity tending towards a goal of perfection, a belief that this process is mirrored in the spiritual education of the individual, and the belief shared by many German thinkers at the end of the 18th century that ordinary thought imposes categories and differences that are absent from the original, innocent immersion of humankind in nature, and due to be transcended when this ideal unity is recaptured.

Talk of the Absolute first appears in *Schelling's *System des transzendentalen Idealismus* of 1800. The idea of a Spirit sweeping through all things was by then an integral part of the *Romantic movement, deeply influencing such metaphysically-minded poets as *Shelley and *Coleridge. *Hegel complained that Schelling's Absolute was, like Kant's *noumenon, unknowable, and in his hands the Absolute became that being which is progressively manifested in the progress of human history, a definition that has been taken to fit many things, including ordinary human self-consciousness. The idealist elevation of self-consciousness, first seen in *Fichte, undoubtedly encourages this equation. But human self-consciousness cannot be the only ingredient in the Absolute, since Hegel also held the doctrine that the merely finite is not real. Apart from Fichte few have been satisfied that human consciousness is the spirit that is responsible for the entire cosmos. *Green wrote of Wordsworth looking to 'the open scroll of the world, of the world, however, as written within and without by a self-conscious and self-determining spirit' (*Works*, iii. 119), and such a spirit transcends the human mind. In any event, the culminating point of history is one at which 'mind knows mind', or final self-conscious freedom is grasped. Hegel also insists on *holism, implying that a mind capable of knowing any truth must have the capacity to know all truth, since partial and divided truth is dead or non-existent.

The most influential exponent of absolute idealism in Britain was *Bradley, who actually eschewed the label of idealism, but whose *Appearance and Reality* argued that ordinary appearances were contradictory, and that to reconcile the contradiction we must transcend them, appealing to a superior level of reality, where harmony, freedom, truth and knowledge are all characteristics of the one Absolute. An essential part of Bradley's case was a preference, voiced much earlier by *Leibniz, for categorical, *monadic properties over relations. He was particularly troubled by the relation between that which is known and the mind that knows it. The consolations of progress and unity with the universe prompted the not wholly hostile verdict by *James that the Absolute was the banisher of cosmic fear, and the giver of moral holidays. Absolute idealism was a major target of *realists, *pragmatists, and of *Russell and *Moore in much of their writing at the beginning of the 20th century, although it continued to be influential for another twenty years.

absolute theory of space Theory that space is itself a kind of container, so that objects have a position or motion or acceleration in relation to space itself rather than purely in relation to each other. In his famous 'bucket' *thought experiment

*Newton noted that water spinning in a stationary bucket would creep up the sides, while the water stays flat if it is stationary, and the bucket is spinning. Newton concluded that to explain this asymmetry we must assume not just relative motion between objects but absolute motion with respect to space. The strongest such notion involves the idea of space as an existing thing with points which persist through time. Absolute motion is then change of place with respect to these points. However, to explain inertial effects such as the bucket experiment, one needs only a weaker notion of absolute space, relative to which there is absolute acceleration, but for which different inertial motions are all relative.

absolutism In political theory, the view that there are no restrictions on the rights and powers of the government. In moral theory, the view that there are inviolable moral standards or absolutes, which cannot, therefore, be the result of potentially variable human desires or policies or prescriptions. *See also* CATEGORICAL IMPERATIVE.

abstract/concrete Many philosophies are nervous of a realm of abstract entities, such as numbers and *universals, as opposed to empirical objects and stuff located at places and times. *Nominalism is the general programme of showing that mention of abstract objects is not what it appears to be, but a misleading way of talking about more ordinary objects. Friends of abstract objects say that there is nothing wrong with referring to them, but we must not make the mistake of imagining them to be especially large or spread-out kinds of concrete object. Another dispute concerns whether, when we do such things as see an edition of the morning paper, or admire a computer program, or hear a word, we literally see or hear abstract objects, which are therefore elements of our experience. *See also* PLATONISM, UNIVERSALS.

abstract ideas Concept that was the focus of dispute between *Locke and *Berkeley. Locke had highlighted the problem of the way in which a particular idea, as it might be of a person or a cow, comes to stand for just the right class of things: persons or cows in general. His solution was to postulate an *abstraction of the general kind away from the particular qualities of examples, until eventually we have an idea of the right degree of generality: one that encompasses all and only persons, or cows. Berkeley took the greatest exception to this account, arguing instead that all ideas are perfectly particular, and only become general in the use we make of them. His animosity arose partly because he believed that the doctrine of abstraction enabled Locke to deceive himself that we can make sense of things that are actually unintelligible: objects with no colour, inanimate causes, and qualities of things dissociated from the sensory effects they have on us.

abstraction Supposed process of forming an idea by abstracting out what is common to a variety of instances: a process stressed, for example, by *Aquinas in his moderate solution to the problem of *universals (*abstrahentium non est mendacium*: abstraction is not lying). The problem is that unrestricted abstraction leads one to suppose that qualities such as substance, causation, change, and number may apply not only to the sensible bodies that give rise to our ideas of them, but also in a spiritual realm or other domain quite outside the reach of experience. *Locke is vehemently attacked by *Berkeley for this and related errors. *See also* ABSTRACT IDEAS.

absurd Any belief that is obviously untenable (*see also* *REDUCTIO AD ABSURDUM*). In *existentialism, a term for the pointless or meaningless nature of human life and action.

Abunaser *See* FARABI.

Academy of Athens Teaching college founded by *Plato, around 387 BC. Although knowledge of its organization is fragmentary, it appears to have favoured a teaching method based on discussion and seminars. The fundamental studies were mathematics and dialectic. It is customary to distinguish the Old Academy (Plato and his immediate successors) and the New Academy (beginning with *Arcesilaus). The distinction is first made by *Antiochus of Ascalon. The Old Academy included *Aristotle, *Speusippus, *Eudoxus, *Xenocrates, and *Theaetetus of Athens. It was largely preoccupied with mathematical and cosmological themes arising from the late work of Plato, although at some point ethical interests also emerged. There is a sharp break with Arcesilaus, who produced the sceptical New Academy which maintained a running battle with the teaching of the *Stoics. The last head of the sceptical Academy was *Philo of Larissa, who went to Rome *c.*87 BC when Mithridates VI of Persia threatened Athens, thereby ending the Academy as an institution. The rehabilitation of dogmatic Platonic themes after Antiochus of Ascalon (*c.*79 BC: *see also* MIDDLE PLATONISM) was not properly the doing of the Academy, but paved the way for the emergence of *Neoplatonism.

SEE WEB LINKS

- A brief history of the Academy
- An introduction to the Academy and its site

Academy of Florence Circle gathered around *Ficino between 1462 and 1494, in a villa at Careggi put at their disposal by Cosimo de' Medici.

It was a central intellectual influence in the Italian Renaissance, its main activities being the translation, study, and reinterpretation of Platonic and Neoplatonic writings.

SEE WEB LINKS

- A biography of Marsilio Ficino, including his role in the Academy

acatalepsy Incomprehensibility. The impossibility of things being grasped by us, supposedly demonstrated by *sceptical arguments.

acceptance Is accepting a proposition the same thing as believing it? Whilst there is no general distinction signalled by the words, philosophers have been led to distinguish acceptance from belief for various reasons. The *lottery paradox may be approached by saying that whilst one accepts that an arbitrary ticket will not win, one cannot be said to believe that it will not, thereby avoiding the pitfall of having an inconsistent set of beliefs. In the philosophy of science a variety of anti-*realist positions may counsel one to accept a scientific theory, for instance in order to predict and control nature, or in the spirit of open-minded conjecture, without going so far as to believe it. The central difficulty in such recommendations is defining exactly what one is supposed not to do; in other words, saying what is distinctive about belief as opposed to the supposedly lesser and legitimate acceptance. *See* CONSTRUCTIVE EMPIRICISM.

access *See* PRIVILEGED ACCESS.

accessibility relation *See* MODAL LOGIC, POSSIBLE WORLDS.

accident In Aristotelian metaphysics an accident is a property of a thing which is no part of the *essence of the thing: something it could lose or have added without ceasing to be the same thing or the same substance. The accidents divide into *categories: quantity, action (i.e. place in the causal order, or ability to affect things or be affected by them), quality, space, time, and relation.

accident, fallacy of the *See* *A DICTO SIMPLICITER AD DICTUM SECUNDUM QUID*.

accidentalism Theory that the flow of events is unpredictable, or for *Epicureans, that mental events are specifically unpredictable. *See also* CHAOS, DETERMINISM, LIBERTARIANISM, TYCHISM.

accidie State that inhibits pleasure and prompts the rejection of life; one of the *Seven Deadly Sins. *Aquinas associates it with turning one's back on things, through depression or self-hatred, and nicely defines it as a torpor of spirit which prevents one from getting down to anything good (*Summa Theologiae*, IIa 35.1). Often it is translated as sloth, which is actually quite different. *See also* APATHY.

Achilles and the Tortoise *See* ZENO'S PARADOXES.

acosmism Denial of the reality of the material world. The term was originally applied or misapplied to *Spinoza, but in the nineteenth century was also used to characterize the other-worldliness of Christianity.

acquaintance and description Distinction in our ways of knowing things, highlighted by *Russell and forming a central element in his philosophy after the discovery of the theory of *definite descriptions. A thing is known by acquaintance when there is direct experience of it. It is known by description if it can only be described as a thing with such-and-such properties. In everyday parlance, I might know my spouse and children by acquaintance, but know someone as 'the first person born at sea' only by description. However, for a variety of reasons Russell shrinks the area of things that can be known by acquaintance until eventually only current experiences, perhaps my own self, and certain universals or meanings qualify. Anything else is known only as the thing that has such-and-such qualities. *See also* LOGICAL ATOMISM.

acrasia *See* *AKRASIA*.

action What an agent does, as opposed to what happens to an agent (or even what happens inside an agent's head). Describing events that happen does not of itself permit us to talk of rationality and intention, which are the categories we may apply if we conceive of them as actions. We think of ourselves not only passively, as creatures within which things happen, but actively, as creatures that make things happen. Understanding this distinction gives rise to major problems concerning the nature of agency, of the *causation of bodily events by mental events, and of understanding the *will and *free will. Other problems in the theory of action include drawing the distinction between an action and its consequences, and describing the structures involved when we do one thing 'by' doing another thing. Even the placing and dating of action can give rise to puzzles, as in cases where someone shoots someone on one day and in one place, and the victim then dies on another day and in another place. Where and when did the murder take place?

action at a distance Contested concept in the history of physics. Aristotelian physics holds that every motion requires a conjoined mover. Action can therefore never occur at a distance, but needs a medium enveloping the body, and which parts before its motion and pushes it from behind (*antiperistasis). Although natural motions like free fall and magnetic attraction (quaintly called 'coition') were recognized in the post-Aristotelian period, the rise of the *corpuscularian philosophy again banned 'attractions', or unmediated actions at a distance: the classic argument is that 'matter cannot act where it is not'. Cartesian physical theory also postulated 'subtle matter' to fill space and provide the medium for force and motion. Its successor, the aether, was postulated in order to provide a medium for transmitting forces and causal influences between objects that are not in direct contact. Even *Newton, whose treatment of gravity might seem to leave it conceived of as action at a distance, supposed that an intermediary must be postulated, although he could make no hypothesis as to its nature. *Locke, having originally said that bodies act on each other 'manifestly by impulse and nothing else' (*Essay*, 1st edn., ii. viii. 11), changes his mind by the 4th edition, and strikes out the words 'and nothing else', although impulse remains 'the only way which we can conceive bodies operate in'. In the *Metaphysical Foundations of Natural Science* *Kant clearly sets out the view that the way in which bodies repulse each other is no more natural, or intelligible, than the way in which they act at a distance; in particular he repeats the point half-understood by Locke, that any conception of solid, massy atoms requires understanding the force that makes them cohere as a single unity, which cannot itself be understood in terms of elastic collisions. In many cases contemporary *field theories admit of alternative equivalent formulations, one with action at a distance, one with local action only.

active euthanasia *See* EUTHANASIA, ACTIVE/PASSIVE.

activism The doctrine that action rather than theory is needed at some political juncture; an activist is therefore one who works to make change happen.

act–object ambiguity Ambiguity between an actual action, and the upshot of an action. This ambiguity is visible in words like 'observation': an observation may be a process that takes time and is performed by someone, or it may be the piece of information that is the upshot of such a process. Many philosophers of mind believe that a similar ambiguity distorts thinking about experience, and especially perception. Perception should be thought of in terms of an active process of engagement with the world, rather than the presence of an object (a display) in the theatre of the mind.

act–object psychology An approach to the mind that distinguishes between the experienced mental nature of a state of mind and its intended object, or what it is directed towards. It was felt by *Meinong and others that the distinction had been ignored by *Brentano. *See also* INTENTIONALITY.

acts, mental Things that agents do, but within their own minds, or not by means of bodily movements. Notably these include trying, willing, and perhaps even private thinking. They seem to be things that do not just happen, perhaps inside our brains, but of which we are the authors. The problem is to understand what this means. *See also* ACTION, VOLITION.

acts/omissions doctrine The doctrine that it makes an ethical difference whether an agent actively intervenes to bring about a result, or omits to act in circumstances in which it is foreseen that as a result of the omission the same result occurs. Thus suppose I wish you dead. If I act to bring about your death I am a murderer, but if I happily discover you in danger of death, and fail to act to save you, I am not acting, and therefore according to the doctrine not a murderer. Critics reply that omissions can be as deliberate and immoral as commissions: if I am responsible for your food and fail to feed you, my omission is surely a killing. 'Doing nothing' can be a way of doing something, or in other words, absence of bodily movement can also constitute acting negligently, or deliberately, and depending on the context may be a way of deceiving, betraying, or killing. Nevertheless, criminal law often finds it convenient to distinguish discontinuing an intervention, which is permissible, from bringing about a result, which may not be, if, for instance, the result is death of a patient. The question is whether the difference, if there is one, between acting and omitting to act can be described or defined in a way that bears general moral weight. *See also* DOUBLE EFFECT, TROLLEY PROBLEM.

SEE WEB LINKS

- Notes on the doctrine and related ethical issues, with a bibliography

actual In *modal logic the actual world is the world as it is, contrasted with other *possible worlds, representing ways it might have been. The central problem is to understand how the actual state of the world is to be characterized, except in terms that themselves make reference to alternative possibilities.

actualism Sometimes known as actual idealism. For one usage *see* GENTILE. The term also applies in contemporary works to the view that only the actual world is real, with other *possible worlds regarded as not themselves existing, but as wrongly thought to exist because *modal idioms are useful instruments of thought about the real world. *See also* FICTIONALISM, MODAL REALISM.

actuality and potentiality The contrast between what is actually, or really, the case, and what could have been or could come to be the case. One of the major problems of *scholastic thought is understanding what reason God might have for actualizing a particular possibility rather than none at all, or some alternative. Questions that arise include why there is something and not nothing, and whether this is the best of all possible worlds. *See also* POTENTIALITY; SUFFICIENT REASON, PRINCIPLE OF.

actualization For something to be actualized is for it to be made real, or made part of the actual world. In theology it may be important that God has no potential that is not actualized, since this would imply a change away from present perfection to something different and worse, or away from present imperfection to something better, neither of which is acceptable.

act utilitarianism Version of *utilitarianism associated especially with *Bentham, according to which the measure of the value of an act is the amount by which it increases general *utility or happiness. An act is to be preferred to its alternatives according to the extent of the increase it achieves, compared to the extent the alternatives would achieve. An action is thus good or bad in proportion to the amount it increases (or diminishes) general happiness, compared to the amount that could have been achieved by acting differently. Act utilitarianism is distinctive not only in the stress on utility, but in the fact that each individual action is the primary object of ethical evaluation. This contrasts it with varieties of indirect utilitarianism, as well as with ethical systems that accord priority to duty or personal virtue.

Adams's thesis Hypothesis due to Ernest Adams (*The Logic of Conditionals*, 1975, p. 3) that the probability of an indicative conditional of the form 'if p is the case then q is' is a conditional probability; that is, the probability of 'if p then q' should equal the ratio of the probability of (p & q) to the probability of p.

adaptation In biology, a characteristic of an organism that arose through its being naturally selected for its current use (*see* DARWINISM). This is contrasted with an exaptation or feature that is co-opted for a use: an exaptation is a feature that will have arisen by natural selection, but for another use than the one that it currently has. A nonaptation is a feature that exists without promoting fitness for survival at all.

Adelard of Bath (*c.*1070–*c.*1145) English Benedictine remembered as a conduit for the introduction of Arabic astronomy and philosophy to the West.

ad hoc hypothesis Hypothesis adopted purely for the purpose of saving a theory from difficulty or refutation, but without any independent rationale.

ad hominem argument *See* *ARGUMENTUM AD*.

adhyatman (Sanskrit, related to the self) Hindu writings, doctrines, or exercises relating to the self. *See* *ADVAITA*, *ATMAN*.

adiaphora (Greek, indifferent) In *Stoic philosophy things such as knowledge, power, pleasure, and health, in which value may be found but not quite in the way it is found in *virtue, which alone is good or 'chosen'. The distinction bears some relationship to Kant's distinction between the overriding and necessary value of a morally good will, and the genuine but lesser attractions of other things.

a dicto secundum quid ad dictum simpliciter (Latin, from the qualified statement to the unqualified) The fallacy of taking out a needed qualification: 'If it is always permissible to kill in war, then it is always permissible to kill.' Also known as the converse fallacy of the accident.

a dicto simpliciter ad dictum secundum quid (Latin, from the statement unqualified to the statement qualified) The (alleged) fallacy of arguing from a general to a particular case, without recognizing qualifying factors: 'If people shouldn't park here, they shouldn't park here to help put out the fire.' With forms of proposition other than generalizations, more evidently invalid arguments might bear this name: 'If some snakes are harmless, then some snakes in this bag are harmless.' Also known as the fallacy of the accident.

ad infinitum Latin, to infinity.

Adorno, Theodor Wiesengrund (1903–69) German sociologist and political thinker. Adorno was a leading member of the *Frankfurt school, whose general stance he shared. His work belonged mainly to sociology, and was especially concerned with the contradictions and distortions imposed upon people by the post-Enlightenment world, with its sacrifice of life to instrumental, technological reasoning. Perhaps his best-known general work is *The Authoritarian Personality* (1950), describing the rigid, conformist personality-type, submissive to higher authority and bullying towards inferiors. Adorno's celebration of paradox and ambiguity, as well as his pessimistic take on the *Enlightenment, have been influential in postmodernist literary and cultural criticism. Other works include *The Dialectic of Enlightenment* (1941) and *Negative Dialectics* (1966).

advaita (Sanskrit, non-duality) The doctrine of the Vedantic school associated with *Shankara, that asserts the identity of **brahman* and **atman*; the empirical world is one of **phenomena bene fundata* and, like the self, is entirely a manifestation of God.

adverbial theory An adverbial theory of perception takes the *act–object ambiguity of experience to warrant thinking of perception in terms of action. The object of perception then becomes not a true object, but an adverb describing how the action is performed. Thus instead of 'I see a blue patch' we would have 'I see bluely', describing how the process or activity of seeing is taking place. It is often objected that the adverbs required become too complex, and obviously gerrymandered: 'I see a blue patch to the right of a red patch' becomes something like 'I see red-right-bluely' and without surreptitiously mentioning the patches it is hard to see how we could give meaning to the complex adverb involved.

adverbs If John swam fast, then it follows that John swam. But how do we understand this inference? In *first-order logic, the natural suggestion is that there is an individual, an event which was a swimming by John, and was fast. But now suppose John's swimming was also a crossing, and although John swam fast his crossing was not fast (most people cross by much faster means). Then the one event was a swimming and a crossing, and fast and not fast, which sounds like a contradiction. The question for logic and semantic theory is whether adverbs are to be regarded as predicates of special individuals such as events, or as predicate modifiers.

Aenesidemus of Cnossos (1st c. BC) Sceptical philosopher and defender of *Pyrrhonism, for the most part known through his influence on *Sextus Empiricus, and through the account of his teaching in *Diogenes Laertius. A radical, he broke away from the *Academy to return to the purer scepticism of Pyrrho. He is principally known for the ten tropes (*tropoi*) whereby we set up inconsistent but equally defensible claims about matters of fact. These tropes were canonized by Sextus Empiricus as the foundation of late Hellenic *scepticism. They include (i) the different ways different animals perceive things; (ii) the differing perceptions of different peoples; (iii) the way the different senses give differing judgements; (iv) the ways in which circumstances such as drunkenness or sobriety affect perception; (v) the differences brought in by distance and perspective; (vi) the way in which the intervening medium (air, or the constitution of the eyeball) affects perception; (vii) the way in which substances may look one way when combined and a different way when scattered or combined differently; (viii) the pervasive influence of the specific relationship between the perceiver and that which is perceived; (ix) the different importance and capacity for surprise that the same events assume for different perceivers; and (x) the way in which differences between people prevent us from thinking of ourselves as perceiving universal moral laws. A different set of eight *tropoi* put similar sceptical obstacles in front of knowledge of causal relationships. Almost all versions of scepticism and *relativism rely upon some version of one or more of the ten tropes.

Aesop (6th c. BC) Greek teller of fables, or stories with a satirical and moral twist. The life of Aesop is itself a fable: he is traditionally supposed to have been hunchbacked and ugly (which may be a symbol of racial stereotyping), to have been the slave of a philosopher, Xanthus of Samos, and to have gained his freedom only to fall foul of the citizens of Delphi, who were anxious to protect the reputation of their oracle against him and threw him off a cliff. Xanthus and his wife are represented as particularly prone to losing their dignity in the presence of Aesop, who is therefore a symbol of the subversive role of low, popular, folk wisdom in contrast to so-called high culture and philosophy. His fables were particularly popular in the late Renaissance, attracting commentaries from philosophers including *Valla and *Erasmus, and later on *Lessing.

aesthetic (Greek, sense perception) *Kant keeps the ancient Greek usage, in which anything treating of sense perception may be called an aesthetic. The word had earlier been restricted by *Baumgarten to the perception of *aesthetic properties or values in particular.

aesthetic attitude The attitude of detached and disinterested, but engaged, contemplation often supposed to be appropriate to understanding the aesthetic value of a work of art. The centrality of an aesthetic attitude is stressed in *Kant's *Critique of Judgement*.

aesthetic detachment *See* AESTHETIC ATTITUDE.

aestheticism Doctrine associated with late 19th-century writers and artists, including Walter Pater, James McNeill Whistler, and especially Oscar Wilde. It holds that the appreciation of art and beauty is the highest aim of human life, and

a

especially that the pursuit of such experience is not constrained by ordinary moral considerations. Art itself serves no ulterior moral or political purpose. The 'Aesthetic Movement' was a useful reaction against the didactic religious and moral art of the time and helped artists and critics to concentrate upon the formal and internal qualities of works of art. The movement had its exaggerated side, parodied by Gilbert and Sullivan in the opera *Patience* (1881).

aesthetic properties *See* AESTHETIC VALUES.

aesthetics The study of the feelings, concepts, and judgements arising from our appreciation of the arts or of the wider class of objects considered moving, or beautiful, or sublime. Aesthetic theory concerns itself with questions such as: what is a work of art? What makes a work of art successful? Can art be a vehicle of truth? Does art work by expressing the feelings of the artist, communicating feeling, arousing feeling, purging or symbolizing feeling? What is the difference between understanding a work of art, and failing to do so? How is it that we take aesthetic pleasure in surprising things: tragedies, or terrifying natural scenes? Why can things of very different categories equally seem beautiful? Does the perception of *beauty have connections with moral virtue, and with seeing something universal or essential, and is the importance of aesthetic education and practice associated with this? What is the role of the imagination in the production or appreciation of art? Are aesthetic judgements capable of improvement and training, and thence of some kind of objectivity? The classical origin of many of these questions is found in *Plato. The dialogues *Ion*, *Symposium*, and *Phaedrus* are centrally concerned with the place of beauty in the order of things, and the preoccupation surfaces in many other places, including in the context of Plato's famous dismissal of artists from the ideal Republic (*see* MIMESIS). *Aristotle's discussion in the *Poetics* centres on the nature of tragedy, and engendered the idea of *catharsis, or the purging of emotion as the deep effect of witnessing tragic drama. In the modern period aesthetics emerged as a separate topic in the work of *Baumgarten, *Lessing, *Hutcheson, *Hume, and especially *Kant. In the *Critique of Judgement* Kant addresses the question of how judgements of beauty are possible, when they are incapable of proof or of any reduction to rule, and are so intimately concerned to express the pleasure of the subject. His solution lies in the consciousness of the harmony of understanding and imagination, and, since this harmony can be felt by any rational being, judgements of taste can be demanded of others. They thereby achieve their necessary objectivity.

SEE WEB LINKS

- A list of internet resources on aesthetics, including bibliographies
- An audio discussion with three philosophers about the nature of art

aesthetic values Those features of a work that contribute to its success and importance as a work of art: the features upon which its significance or beauty *supervene. They include the form, content, integrity, harmony, purity, or fittingness of works. In philosophical aesthetics it has proved hard to define these features in usefully specific, objective, terms; they are in any event qualities whose apprehension pleases and satisfies us.

aether The 'luminiferous' aether was the medium that pervaded all space, and in which electromagnetic waves existed, postulated by 19th-century physics. *See* ACTION AT A DISTANCE.

aetiology (Greek, description of a cause) The assigning of causes. Hence, the chain of causes leading up to an event, particularly in medical science.

aeviternity *Eternity, thought of as an infinite past and future totality, in which events are contained in a matrix, like flies in amber.

affective Its affective quality is the feature of an experience which renders it pleasurable or desirable, or the reverse, or which gives it a distinctive emotional tone.

affirmative action Action designed to give special support to disadvantaged members of a community, for example by allowing them easier access than others enjoy to benefits such as education, jobs, or housing. This may be thought of as rectifying past injustice, or as instrumental in smoothing out historically entrenched inequalities. It is controversial since it involves what may appear to be procedural injustices of its own.

affirmative and negative propositions Intuitively there may be a difference between asserting that something is the case and 'merely' denying that something is the case. But there is no good logical or philosophical way of making the distinction. Modern logic allows that there is frequently an equivalence between positive-looking and negative-looking statements. Whether an assertion comes out positive or negative will depend on the way things are put and upon the menu of terms available: x is not married can be said as x is single; x is not guilty can be said as x is innocent, and so on. Not (p & not-q) (negative?) is equivalent to $p \rightarrow q$ (positive?) and not-not-p (negative?) is equivalent to p (positive?).

affirming the antecedent Arguing, validly, that from *p*, and if *p* then *q*, it follows that *q*. *See* MODUS PONENS.

affirming the consequent Arguing invalidly that from if *p* then *q* and *q*, it follows that *p*; e.g. arguing from 'if she is studying mathematics then she is not studying English' and 'she is not studying English' to 'she is studying mathematics'.

a fortiori (Latin, from the stronger) Phrase used for 'all the more' or 'even more so': if all donkeys bray, then *a fortiori* all young donkeys bray.

after-image Image seen after the cessation of a prolonged or intense stimulation of the eye. After-images are frequently cited as examples of purely 'mental' things which are yet coloured, disproving the claim that only real expanses of space can be coloured. Caused by the temporary decrease of sensitivity of the receptors that have been stimulated, they have the complementary colour to the original light.

agapē Greek term used particularly by Christian writers to signify fraternal and filial *love, as opposed to *eros* or sexual love. In the early Church the *agapē* was a feast at which fellow religionists celebrated their sense of solidarity.

agathon (Greek, the good) In *Aristotle, a life that involves the exercise of the highest faculties, fulfilling a person's **telos* or end. In other philosophies the good is identified with pleasure, or virtue, or the absence of desire, or conformity to duty. *See also* ETHICS, *EUDAIMONIA*, *SUMMUM BONUM*.

agent One who acts. The central problem of agency is to understand the difference between events happening in me or to me, and my taking control of events, or doing things. *See* ACTION, DETERMINISM, FREE WILL, WILL.

agent-causation A presumed special category of causation whereby agents initiate sequences of events when they act, without the initiation being itself causally determined. *See* DETERMINISM, FREE WILL, LIBERTARIANISM (METAPHYSICAL).

agent-centred morality In ethics, the view that the personal situation of agents, together with their personal desires and projects, gives rise to genuine moral restrictions and goals. The view opposes the impartial, impersonal, or public aspect of traditional moral thinking, including *utilitarianism, which seeks to minimize the agent's perspective in favour of that of a general point of view, an ideal observer, or an objective sum of all affected utilities. *See also* AGENT-NEUTRAL/AGENT-RELATIVE, STOICISM, UNIVERSALIZABILITY.

agent-neutral/agent-relative Agent-neutral reasons are those that apply to anyone in a situation, regardless of any special relationship to the individuals or other elements involved. By contrast an agent-relative reason would apply to a person only because of such a relation. So, for example, anyone should have a reason of general benevolence to help others in distress, but I would have a special reason to help if it is my children who are in distress. A good deal of moral theory concerns the nature of the balance between these two sorts of reasons.

age of reason *See* ENLIGHTENMENT.

agglomeration Principle of *deontic logic, named by Bernard *Williams. It states that if one ought to do A and ought to do B, then one ought to do both A and B. If it is accepted, it puts pressure on the principle that 'ought implies can', since arguably there may arise occasions on which, for instance, I ought to repay A, and ought to repay B, but cannot repay both A and B.

agnoiology (Greek, ignorance) The study of ignorance. An increasingly important branch of *epistemology.

agnosticism The view that some proposition is not known, and perhaps cannot be known to be true or false. The term is particularly applied to theological doctrines.

agreement, method of *See* MILL'S METHODS.

Agricola, Rudolph (1444–85) Renaissance humanist. His major work was *De inventione dialectica*, on rhetoric and dialectic in classical literature.

Agrippa (1st/2nd c. AD) Shadowy Roman sceptic. His legacy is the five 'tropes', partly a variation on the ten tropes of *Aenesidemus, but adding a stress on the implicit infinite regress in every proof, arising because the premises have to be proved in turn, and further insisting that all attempts to halt the regress will involve either blatant circularity, or arbitrary dogmatism. The uncomfortable three options are known as Agrippa's trilemma.

Agrippa of Nettesheim (Henricus Cornelius) (1486–1535) Occultist, humanist, and heterodox writer who contributed to revival of scepticism, criticized the subjection of women and witch-crazes, and contributed to the legend of Dr Faustus.

ahamkara (Sanskrit, 'I-maker') In Hindu philosophy, the faculty responsible for the unfolding or manifestation of a 'self'.

a

ahanta (Sanskrit, unchangeable, eternal) The indestructible nature of the divine or the truly real.

ahimsa (Sanskrit, non-injury) The ethical principle forbidding injury to all living creatures, subscribed to by many Hindus and Buddhists. It enjoins vegetarianism, pacifism, and in a pure form requires taking extraordinary precautions, such as sweeping the path before one walks on it, or straining liquid one drinks in case one inadvertently injures a living thing. Politically its most famous expression was Mahatma *Gandhi's non-violent movement of passive resistance to British rule in India.

AI *See* ARTIFICIAL INTELLIGENCE.

aitia (Greek, cause) Explanatory factors; reasons contributing to things being as they are. *See* CAUSES: MATERIAL, FORMAL, EFFICIENT, FINAL.

Ajdukiewicz, Kazimierz (1890–1963) Formal philosopher and logician, who held posts in Lvov, Warsaw, and Poznan. Ajdukiewicz was one of the leaders of the Polish school of *analytical philosophy, whose interests included the formal representation of language, translatability, and *convention.

akolasia (Greek, uncorrected) The vice of excess, when desires are not corrected by reason. In *Aristotle, the temperate person avoids this vice, indulging desires only to the correct extent.

akoluthic (Greek, following after) Term applied to a sense experience which supposedly carries as part of its content the fact that it follows later than some previous event. The existence of such experiences would explain why we can now see an event as the ending of a process whose earlier phases are not given to us in perception any more. In grammar an anacoluthon (Greek, not following after) is a sentence split so that one part does not follow from another (e.g. 'The fact is, let's go').

akrasia (Greek, incontinence) The condition in which while knowing what it would be best to do, one does something else. The phenomenon intrigued *Plato and *Aristotle, because if we accept the Socratic equation between knowing a thing to be good and desiring it, then it becomes difficult to see how *akrasia* is possible. Yet the phenomenon evidently exists. Less optimistic philosophies find it equally hard to see how strength of will is possible. *Akrasia* is commonly translated as weakness of will, although that properly includes general irresolution or infirmity of purpose, which is rather different.

alaya-vijnana (Sanskrit, storehouse-consciousness) In Buddhist thought, the continuation of consciousness as the development of potential, even during periods of apparent unconsciousness.

Albert of Saxony (1360–90) Medieval logician and founder of the University of Vienna.

Albert the Great (Albertus Magnus) (*c.*1200–80) The dominant scholastic of the 13th century, and teacher of *Aquinas. An encyclopaedic figure, known as the *Doctor Universalis*, Albert was prominent in the attempt to synthesize newly discovered Aristotelian and Platonic learning with the Christian tradition. He wrote commentaries on *Aristotle and many others, and showed an especial sympathy with the empirical approach to nature. His works include the *Summa de Creaturis* (trs. as *Handbook of Doctrine concerning Creatures*) and the *Summa Theologiae* or handbook of theology.

SEE WEB LINKS

- A biography of Albertus Magnus

alchemy The medieval combination of chemistry, philosophy, and secret lore aimed at transmuting base metals into gold (by means of the philosopher's stone), and discovering the universal cure for disease and mortality.

Alcinous (*c.*2nd c. AD) Author of a 'handbook of Platonism' which is a useful source for the history of Platonism in its time.

Alcmaeon of Croton (5th c. BC) A younger contemporary of *Pythagoras, and known as a physician. He is supposed to have recognized the brain as the seat of consciousness, a view accepted by *Plato on the grounds that the highest faculty should be seated in the highest part of the body, i.e. the head, but rejected by *Aristotle, who thought that the brain functioned as a refrigerator.

Alemanno, Yohanan ben Isaac (1433/4–after 1503/4) Synthesizing figure of the Italian Renaissance and the principal Jewish influence on the *Academy of Florence.

aleph The first letter of the Hebrew alphabet, used with subscripts to designate the sequence of transfinite numbers, $\aleph_0$, $\aleph_1$, $\aleph_2$. *See* CANTOR'S THEOREM, DENUMERABLE/NON-DENUMERABLE.

alethic (Greek, *alētheia*, truth) The alethic modes or modalities are the necessity, contingency, or impossibility of something being true.

Alexander, Samuel (1859–1938) Australian philosopher who studied philosophy at Oxford and experimental psychology at Freiburg. He was professor of philosophy at Manchester from 1893 to

1924. His main philosophical work was the two-volume *Space, Time, and Deity* (1920). Although a *realist who held that we had knowledge of a mind-independent world, Alexander nevertheless held an evolutionary picture of the world as moving towards an unrealized ideal or deity, a view more typical of the rival *absolute idealism.

Alexander of Aphrodisias (*fl.* 3rd c. AD) *Peripatetic philosopher. Alexander began lecturing at Athens around 200. He was an Aristotelian, singularly free from the mystical religious Platonism characteristic of the time (*see* MIDDLE PLATONISM). His own doctrines included denial of the reality of time and of the immortality of the soul, but it is as a commentator on *Aristotle that he is primarily known.

Alexander of Hales (*c.*1185–1245) Influential Franciscan theologian and writer on logic, known as 'Doctor Irrefragabilis' (irrefutable doctor). Alexander taught the independence of theology, based on revelation, and philosophy, based on reason.

Alexandrian School The school of *Platonism coupled with Christian elements that flourished in Alexandria for the two centuries before the city was captured by Arabs in 642. Its most famous member was *Hypatia.

al-Farabi *See* FARABI.

Algazel *See* GHAZALI.

algebra *See* BOOLEAN ALGEBRA.

algebraic number A real *number that is the root of a polynomial equation. All rationals are algebraic (they are all roots of equations bx = a where a, b are integers). Reals that are not algebraic are called transcendental numbers.

al-Ghazali *See* GHAZALI.

algorithm (derived from the name of the Islamic mathematician Al-Khowarizmi) A set of rules or instructions that will result in the solution of a problem. An algorithm gives a decision procedure, or computable method for solving a problem. Although an algorithm will solve the problem, it may not do so efficiently, and in the theory of computation algorithms may be measured for their efficiency and their behaviour in various circumstances, for example across average cases and unfavourable cases. *See also* CHURCH'S THESIS, DECISION PROBLEM, RECURSIVE, TURING MACHINE.

alienans An adjective that appears to be qualifying a subsequent description, but in fact functions to deny or leave open the question of whether the description applies: a fake parrot, an alleged criminal, a near victory.

alienation A pivotal concept in the philosophical writings of *Hegel, *Feuerbach, and *Marx, and subsequent writings in both idealist and Marxist traditions. Alienation (German *Entfremdung*, also translatable as estrangement) is centrally the idea of something being separated from or strange to something else: I am self-alienated in so far as I cannot understand or accept myself; thought is alienated from reality in so far as it inadequately reflects it; I am alienated from my desires in so far as they are not authentically my own, but assail me as it were from without; I am alienated from the results of my labour in so far as they become *commodities; and I may be alienated from my society in so far as I feel controlled by it, rather than part of a social unity that creates it. In Hegel the progress towards the *Absolute is one of the growth of self-consciousness, itself a process of 'dealienation' whereby what is separate and falsely objectified regains its unity through self-creation and self-consciousness (although finite minds, the agency of this growth, alienate themselves in activity and in the 'objectification' of their material and social products). In Feuerbach, by contrast, the absolutist trappings of Hegelian alienation are abandoned, and the concept is replaced by self-alienation, a condition to be overcome by the self-consciousness that proper relations with our own activities and products brings. Marx's use of the concept is sometimes thought to separate his early, Hegelian, period from the later writings, but there seems little doubt about his permanent attachment to the idea of a human nature as self-alienated so long as the communist transformation of society has not taken place. *See also* ANOMIE, AUTHENTICITY, *DASEIN*, FALSE CONSCIOUSNESS.

aliorelative Irreflexive (*see* RELATION).

al-Kindi *See* KINDI.

all *See* QUANTIFIER.

Allais paradox A paradox in decision theory. Suppose you are offered a choice between two gambles:

Gamble 1: $500,000 with probability of 1
Gamble 2: $2,500,000 with probability 0·1; $500,000 with probability 0·89; $0, with probability 0·01.

Many people will prefer the first option. Now suppose you are offered a choice between another two gambles:

Gamble 3: $500,000 with probability 0·11; $0 with probability 0·89

Gamble 4: $2,500,000 with probability 0·1; $0 with probability 0·9.

Many people will take the second. The problem is that this pair of preferences is not consistent with

a

any *expected utility function. For from the first choice we have it that

$$U(\$500{,}000) > 0{\cdot}1U(\$2{,}500{,}000) + 0{\cdot}89U(\$500{,}000) + 0{\cdot}01U(\$0)$$

and from the second choice we have it that

$$0{\cdot}1U(\$2{,}500{,}000) + 0{\cdot}9U(\$0) > 0{\cdot}11U(\$500{,}000) + 0{\cdot}89U(\$0)$$

but these are inconsistent: by the first equation

$$0{\cdot}11U(\$500{,}000) - 0{\cdot}01U(\$0) > 0{\cdot}1U(\$2{,}500{,}000)$$

but by the second equation the inequality is reversed.

Although the paradox can be used to attack the *sure thing principle, another approach is to use it to educate choices, so that if one genuinely prefers gamble 1 to gamble 2, one learns to reverse the initial feeling that gamble 4 is a better choice than gamble 3.

SEE WEB LINKS

- An account of the paradox's theoretical context, with links to related issues
- A bibliography of scholarly articles on the paradox and related issues

allele (contraction of Greek *allelomorph*, of another form) Two or more *genes that can occur as alternatives, and code for different versions of the same heritable characteristic (e.g. different eye colour). Sometimes the alternative characteristics themselves are referred to as alleles.

allographic Term introduced by *Goodman to describe works of art such as pieces of music or literary texts where there can be multiple copies, each of which is equally an instance of the work. The contrast is with those such as paintings where only one instance is the work, and copies would be either reproductions or forgeries. These are called autographic. *See also* TYPE–TOKEN AMBIGUITY.

Almegest *See* PTOLEMAIC SYSTEM.

al-Razi, Abu Bakr *See* RAZI.

al-Razi, Fakhr Al-Din *See* RAZI.

al-Sijistani, Abu Sulaiyman Muhammad *See* SIJISTANI.

als ob (German, as if) *See* VAIHINGER.

alter ego A second self; the way in which a friend is to be regarded, according to Aristotle (*Nicomachean Ethics* 1166[a] 32, 1169[b] 7).

alterity Term used in postmodern writings for the 'otherness' of others, or sometimes the otherness of the self. *See* ALIENATION.

alternation *See* DISJUNCTION.

Althusser, Louis (1918–90) French Marxist, noted for dismissing the early work of *Marx in favour of the later emphasis on *dialectical materialism. This is seen through a *structuralist filter, whereby interlocking combinations of political, economic, ideological, and theoretical structures and practices form objective determinants of resulting social forces. Althusser's true Marx is therefore anti-empiricist, anti-humanist, and anti-historicist. Even in its time this reinterpretation was severely criticized as divorcing Marx from the sphere of political activity. Althusser's reputation declined after he murdered his wife (Hélène Rytmann, a sociologist) in 1980 and was confined to a psychiatric hospital. However the view of the apparently active subject as nothing more than the locus of conflicting social forces remains extremely influential. Althusser's works include *Pour Marx* (1965, trs. as *For Marx*, 1969) and *Lire le Capital* (1965, trs. as *Reading Capital*, 1970).

altruism Term coined by *Comte for the disinterested concern for the welfare of another, as an end in itself. Questions include the reality of altruism (*see* EGOISM), and its value. While altruism is frequently thought to be a cornerstone of Christian ethics, as a category it is unknown in Greek thought. It was energetically attacked by *Nietzsche as entailing an unhealthy suppression or devaluation of the self, although in fact there is no evidence that altruistic personalities in general have particularly low self-esteem. In evolutionary theory behaviour is defined as altruistic only if it decreases the fitness of the animal, and there is the corresponding question of how such behaviour could exist and sustain itself.

SEE WEB LINKS

- An account of Comte's concept and its influence
- An audio debate on altruism between two philosophers and a biologist

ambiguity Having more than one meaning. The simplest case is *lexical* ambiguity, where a single term has two meanings. A sentence or grammatically complex construction can be ambiguous without any of the words in it being so, because of *structural* ambiguity: 'All the nice girls love a sailor' can bear at least three meanings for this reason (there is one particular sailor loved by all; to each nice girl her own sailor whom she loves; to each nice girl any sailor is lovable). *See also* ACT–OBJECT AMBIGUITY, AMPHIBOLY, SYSTEMATIC AMBIGUITY, TYPE–TOKEN AMBIGUITY.

ambiguous middle, fallacy of The flaw in a *syllogism due to an *ambiguity in the middle term: e.g. 'all men are rakes; all rakes are useful in the garden, so all men are useful in the garden'.

Ambrose, St (*c.*340–97) Ambrose was put forward as Bishop of Milan before being baptized; after his ordination he became a staunch defender of the privileges of the Church, and at one point excommunicated the Emperor Theodosius for a massacre. He opposed the Arian heresy, wrote on Christian ethics (*De Officiis Ministrorum* depends to some extent upon *Cicero), and was attacked by *Hobbes.

Ammonius Saccas (*fl.* 200–50) Alexandrian Platonist, and teacher of *Plotinus and *Origen (not to be confused with an earlier Ammonius, who taught *Plutarch). Little is known of Ammonius, who seems to have belonged to the *Neo-Pythagorean underground, and stood at some remove from orthodox philosophy of his time. Attempts to reconstruct his teaching by finding common elements in Plotinus and Origen have not been successful.

amoral Having no morality, or having no implications for morality. The amoralist either ignores or deplores the ways in which morality governs human lives.

amor fati (Latin, love of fate) The stoical or fatalistic acceptance of the determined or predetermined course of events.

amphiboly (Greek, *amphibolos*, not regular speech) A sentence whose grammatical structure permits different interpretations, e.g. 'She suffered a bad taxpayer's dream' (dream of a bad taxpayer? Bad dream of a taxpayer?). In *Kant a transcendental amphiboly is the confusion of an object of *pure understanding with appearance.

ampliative argument Term used by *Peirce to denote arguments whose conclusions go beyond their premises (and hence amplify the scope of our beliefs). Inductive arguments and arguments to the best *explanation are not deductively valid, but may yield credible conclusions. Most reasoning takes us to conclusions that go beyond our data, in ways that interest us.

anagoge (Greek, leading up, raising) An uplifting allegorical interpretation of a text. Also in the theory of the *syllogism, direct reduction to a figure of the first kind.

analogy A respect in which one thing is similar to another. The analogical extension of terms is the way in which a term covers similar things: people, bottles, and rivers have mouths. Shops, boxes, verdicts, ports, strings of a violin, questions, roads, and books may all be open, but in analogical senses. Analogy butts upon literal meaning, but also upon *metaphor, and thus forms a perplexing phenomenon in the philosophy of *language (*see also* RULE-FOLLOWING CONSIDERATIONS). Arguing by analogy is arguing that since things are alike in some ways, they will probably be alike in others. Its famous uses in philosophy include the argument to *design and the argument by analogy to the existence of *other minds: if you behave like me, and I have such and such mental states when I so behave, then by analogy you probably do so too. But: 'How can I generalize the one case so irresponsibly?' (*Wittgenstein). In medieval philosophy an important question was whether we can make statements about God only by analogy. *See also* CAJETAN, METAPHOR, MODEL (SCIENCE).

analysandum That which is to be the target of *analysis.

analysans That which provides the *analysis.

analysis The process of breaking a concept down into more simple parts, so that its logical structure is displayed. At its most elementary this may be revealed by a dictionary definition ('to be a vixen is to be a female fox'). But *analytic philosophy, as practised by *Russell, the early *Wittgenstein, and *Moore, took the successes of logic at the beginning of the 20th century to open the way to a general programme, in which the meaning or *truth conditions of propositions would be displayed by a process that revealed hidden logical structure beneath the surface form of statements (*see* LOGICAL ATOMISM, LOGICAL FORM). Philosophical analysis would provide a scientific, objective approach to traditional problems. Just as a mathematician can provide a definition of a complex notion, revealing its identity in terms of a sequence of simpler operations, so the philosopher should be able to identify the nature of a complex concept in terms of simple constituent ideas and operations. The programme of analysis reached its zenith with the early work of the *logical positivists, and especially *Carnap, although it influenced almost all Anglo-American philosophy for the first half of the 20th century, and much of it beyond that.

Although the ideal of analysis had a profoundly healthy effect on philosophy, by insisting on rigorous attention to meaning at all stages of philosophizing, the original confidence in the method proved over-optimistic. First, it turns out that remarkably few interesting concepts admit of uncontroversial analyses. Secondly, it is plausible that there is good reason for this, in that concepts gain their identity not so much through internal structure, as through their place in a larger theory or network of doctrines and practices with which they are associated (*see* HOLISM). Thirdly, apart from *empiricist or *atomistic doctrine, there is no principled way of determining where a process of analysis ought to stop, or even, perhaps, determining in which direction it ought to set out. Finally, the test for a successful analysis, namely the display of a complex structure that is actually *synonymous with the original concept, is uncertain in its application, and rather than being an objective arbiter of philosophical doctrine, will be contested in the light of such doctrines.

analysis, paradox of The paradox that if a philosophical *analysis is correct, then, since it substitutes one term or phrase for another with the same meaning, it must be trivial. If we present an analysis in the form 'to be an F is to be a G', then if the sentence is true it should mean the same as the sentence 'to be an F is to be an F' which is clearly trivial. The challenge is to show how such a claim could be conceptually illuminating.

analytic, transcendental *See* TRANSCENDENTAL ANALYTIC.

analytic(al) philosophy The philosophy that takes the process of *analysis to be central to philosophical method and progress. The common idea of analytical philosophers was that the surface form of a language may conceal hidden logical structure, and may mislead us as to that structure. This could be revealed by a process that would itself solve philosophical problems, or alternatively show them to be the offspring of the delusive surface forms of ordinary language. Confidence in the method of analysis was fostered by the early successes of *Frege and *Russell in reducing mathematics to logic, and by the insights afforded by the theory of *definite descriptions. The practitioners of analytical philosophy also included *Moore and *Carnap. For reasons why the initial confidence faltered, *see* ANALYSIS.

analytic/synthetic A contrast originally introduced by *Kant between types of proposition. An analytic proposition is one where the concept of the predicate is 'contained in' the concept of the subject. 'All brothers are male' is an example. A synthetic proposition is one where this is not so, and which is therefore apt for providing substantial information. Kant's definition is only preliminary, in that not all propositions are of subject–predicate form, and the notion of 'containment' is left metaphorical. But his goal of defining a class of propositions that are importantly trivial can be pursued in ways drawing on modern logic. Thus we might define a proposition to be analytic if it has the form of a *tautology, or valid formula of elementary logic, or can be represented as having that form by substitution of synonyms for synonyms. For example, if we substitute 'male and sibling' for 'brother', then 'all brothers are male' is of the form 'all things that are F and G are F', and this is a valid formula of the *predicate calculus.

The point of Kant's division is that we might not be too disturbed, philosophically, if everything that can be known **a priori* is analytic: analytic truths are so trivial as barely to count as knowledge at all. But if we can know synthetic propositions *a priori* the question of how such knowledge is possible becomes urgent. Part of the programme of *logical positivism was to show that all *a priori* propositions are, at bottom, analytic. The entire distinction was queried in one of the most famous papers of modern philosophy, *Quine's 'Two Dogmas of Empiricism' (1950), which attacks the idea that we have a reasonable criterion for synonymy, on which the definition depends.

anamnesis (Greek, recollection) In *Plato, the recollection of knowledge, possibly obtained in a previous state of existence. The topic is most famously broached in the dialogue *Meno*, and the doctrine is one attempt to account for the 'innate' unlearned character of knowledge of first principles. *See also* BEAUTY, LEARNING PARADOX, LOVE, *TABULA RASA*.

anangkē Greek, necessity or fate.

anaphora Anaphora in general is used of co-referential relations, where one element in a sentence takes its meaning or reference from another. In 'John said that it would rain, but I don't believe it' the last 'it' refers back to what John said. In the study in linguistics known as government–binding theory, specific terms like 'himself' or 'each other' form noun phrases that are necessarily dependent upon an antecedent. Some anaphoric relations are felicitously symbolized by the use of *bound variables. Cataphora arises when a word is to be interpreted in terms of what is still to come: forward-looking anaphora.

anarchism The doctrine associated with *Godwin, *Bakunin, *Proudhon, and others, that human communities can and should flourish without government. Voluntary cooperation should replace the coercive machinery of the state; government itself corrupts the natural sentiments of people. Anarchists may differ about the nature of the revolution that should destroy state power, but historically have tended to be associated with advocating violent opposition to the state. This makes them sound to be allies of the *left, but the *libertarian aspects of the doctrine also chime in with the *right.

anattavada The *Buddhist doctrine that there is no soul. The Buddha taught that nothing is permanent or unchangeable, and (as *Hume later insisted) when we look inside ourselves we find only fleeting mental events, but no substance which endures through time.

Anaxagoras of Clazomenae (*c.*500/499–428/7 BC) The first philosopher to teach in Athens, although indicted probably *c.*450, on charges of impiety, and for holding an astronomical theory that included the view that the sun is a red hot body, larger than the Peloponnese, from which the moon derives its light. He was exiled and died in honour at Lampsacus. Surviving fragments are few, and the interpretation of his philosophical system controversial. He assigned a fundamental cosmological role to mind both as the initiator of motion and as the animating principle of plants and animals. His most characteristic doctrine is that there is 'a portion of everything in everything', meaning that whatever a thing changes into is in some imperceptible way already present in it before the change; Anaxagoras also held that all qualities are present in all things although only those that are preponderant will emerge. Things are *homoiomereiai* (things with like parts) of each other. The principle of homoeomereity has been subject to multiple interpretations, but the idea that change is a matter of passing on something that is already present had a lasting influence in the metaphysics of *causation, especially in biology.

Anaxarchus (4th c. BC) A follower of Democritus and teacher of *Pyrrho. He accompanied Alexander the Great on his travels to the east, and was greatly esteemed by him. It is he whom Pyrrho is supposed not to have recognized, having trained himself to a sceptical distrust of the senses, when Anaxarchus was floundering in a bog.

Anaximander of Miletus (*c.*610–*c.*547/6 BC) The first Greek philosopher and astronomer whose thought is known in any detail. Anaximander constructed the first precise geometrical model of the universe, and produced maps of both the earth and the heavens. His inventions included the *gnomon* or upright pointer of the sundial used for tracking hours and seasons. Philosophically he is remembered for the quasi-theological conception of the **apeiron* or the boundless, limitless, imperishable, and eternal surrounding, which is also the **archē* or beginning of the cosmological process. The conception is an improvement on the cosmology of *Thales, in that Anaximander sees that the attempt to find one kind of matter, out of which everything else in all its variety is made, must end not with water or fire or some other particular kind of matter, but with something independent of both structure and form: something about which nothing can be said. Out of the *apeiron* worlds are produced by a conflict of opposites, itself an 'injustice' for which things pay restitution to one another.

Anaximenes of Miletus (*fl. c.*546 BC) The junior member of the Miletian school, and probably a pupil of *Anaximander. His astronomy was relatively unsophisticated, but he is remembered for the doctrine that one primary substance, *aer*, produces all others either by being rarefied into fire or condensed into wind, cloud, water, earth, and stone. This is the first physical account in the western tradition of different substances as modifications of one primary stuff. The phenomenon that impressed Anaximenes was that breath can blow warm (when it is rarefied, i.e. the mouth is open) or cold (when it is compressed, or hissed out). *See also* ATOMISM, *MATERIA PRIMA*.

ancestral relation Intuitively, a relation that stands to another as 'ancestor of' stands to 'parent of': an ancestor is a parent, or parent of a parent, and so on. The formal definition of the ancestral is due to *Frege. Suppose, to simplify, we allow that y is one of its own ancestors. Then the ancestors of y form a set that fulfils two conditions: the initial condition that y is a member, and the closure condition that all parents of members are members. So x is an ancestor of y if x belongs to all sets satisfying those two conditions. Formally this may be put $(\forall z)((y \in z)\ \&\ (\forall u)(\forall w)(u \in z\ \&\ Pwu \rightarrow w \in z) \rightarrow x \in z)$. This says that all classes satisfy this condition: if y belongs, and if, for anything at all, if it belongs then its parents do, then x belongs. It is notable that this definition can only be given by *quantifying over classes. With ancestor defined in this way, the ancestral of a relation is that relation that stands to it as ancestor does to parent. The class of numbers greater than a given number is the ancestral of the successor relation. *See also* PEANO'S POSTULATES.

and *See* CONJUNCTION.

Anderson, John (1893–1962) Scottish philosopher who was a professor at Sydney from 1927 until 1958. Anderson was the most influential philosopher practising in Australia in his time, both professionally and in the social and political debates of the day. He held a modern world view based on scientific realism and materialism, atheism, and empiricism. His ethics and politics were based upon a fierce concern for independence. His essays were published as *Studies in Empirical Philosophy* (1962) and his writings on education as *Education and Inquiry* (1980).

andreia (Greek, manliness, courage) One of the four *cardinal virtues.

androcentrism In *feminist theory, undue emphasis on masculinity, or the male point of view.

a

androgyny Combining male and female features; hermaphroditism. Also in *feminist writing, the absence of socially reinforced differences of behaviour supposedly characteristic of either gender.

Andronicius of Rhodes (1st c. BC) A leading member of the *Lyceum largely responsible for establishing and conserving the corpus of works of *Aristotle. None of his own writings survive.

a necesse ad esse valet consequentia (Latin, it is valid to infer from what is necessary to what is) A fundamental tenet of *modal logic.

angst (German, dread, despair, anguish; French, *angoisse*) Term introduced by *Kierkegaard to indicate general dread or anxiety, arising especially from the lack of purpose, concern, or meaning in the universe. *See also* NOTHING.

anguish In the philosophy of *Sartre, an inescapable sense of deep and total responsibility for one's own choice and action.

animal rights The view that animals have *rights, for instance to decent treatment, is more controversial than the view that we ought to behave decently towards them. This is because to some thinkers the notion of a right involves the ability to make a claim against someone, or the consciousness of choice, or the possession of rationality, or the ability to enter into reciprocal relationships. If these connections hold, then not only animals but infants and the mentally retarded will be denied rights, and their needs and our obligations towards them must be discussed in other terms. The expanding animal rights movement has sought to assimilate our moral discrimination against animals to discrimination on grounds of gender or race: *see* SPECIESISM.

SEE WEB LINKS

- A list of internet resources on animal rights
- A survey of related religious, medical, and legal debates

animal spirits *Descartes held that nervous transmission was mediated through a fine 'air or spirits' that pass messages to the brain and eventually, through the pineal gland, to the soul.

animal thought In the philosophy of mind as well as ethics the treatment of animals exposes major problems. If other animals differ from human beings, how is the difference to be characterized: do animals think and reason, or have thoughts and beliefs? In philosophers as different as *Aristotle and *Kant the possession of reason separates humans from animals, and also alone allows entry to the moral community. For *Descartes, animals are mere machines, and even lack consciousness or feeling. In the ancient world the rationality of animals is defended with the example of Chrysippus' dog. This animal, tracking a prey, comes to a crossroads with three exits, and after sniffing two of them and failing to find the scent, dashes down the third without pausing to pick up the scent, reasoning, according to *Sextus Empiricus: 'the animal went either by this road, or by that, or by the other; but it did not go by this or that, therefore he went the other way.' The 'syllogism of the dog' was discussed by many writers, since in *Stoic cosmology animals should occupy a place on the great *chain of being somewhere below human beings, the only terrestrial rational agents. *Philo Judaeus wrote a dialogue attempting to show against *Alexander of Aphrodisias that the dog's behaviour does not exhibit rationality, but simply shows it following the scent; by way of response Alexander has the animal jump down a shaft (where the scent would not have lingered). *Plutarch sides with Philo. *Aquinas discusses the dog (*Summa Theologiae*, IaIIae 13. 2, 3), and scholastic thought in general was quite favourable to brute intelligence (it was not uncommon for animals to be made to stand trial for various offences in medieval times). In the modern era *Montaigne uses the dog to remind us of the frailties of human reason; *Rorarius undertook to show not only that beasts are rational, but that they make better use of reason than people do. James I of England defends the syllogizing dog, and Henry *More and *Gassendi both take issue with Descartes on the matter. *Hume is an outspoken defender of animal cognition, but with the rise of the view that language is the essential manifestation of mentality, animals' silence began to count heavily against them, and they are completely denied thoughts by, for instance, *Davidson. Dogs are frequently shown in pictures of philosophers, as their assiduity and fidelity is a symbol of what is needed in the hunt for wisdom. *See also* INSTINCT.

anima mundi (Latin, the soul of the world) In Platonism the supposed spirit that permeates and animates all material nature. *See* PANPSYCHISM.

animism *See* PANPSYCHISM.

Anniceris (*fl.* c.320–280 BC) Minor Cyrenaic philosopher, who developed a sophisticated hedonism, with a stress on the pleasures of virtuous living that in some respects anticipates *Epicurus.

anoetic (Greek, not perceived, not conscious) Preconscious or subliminal states of mind. *See also* NOETIC.

anomalous monism A doctrine in the philosophy of mind associated with *Davidson. In his influential paper 'Mental Events' (1970), Davidson asked how the following three propositions could be made consistent: (i) mental events cause physical events, (ii) where there is causation there is lawlike regularity, (iii) there is no lawlike regularity connecting the mental and the physical. His solution was to identify mental events with physical events (hence *monism), but to deny that the classification of events as mental gave us a description apt for framing lawlike generalizations (hence anomalous, or not lawlike). Critics have charged that on this account the fact that a physical event falls under a mental description has no bearing on its causal powers, which are there in virtue of its purely physical nature, so that the causal power of the mental is not really protected by the combination. But the charge has in turn been rebutted, with defenders pointing out that it is no insult to the causal power of a hurricane that there are no laws framed in terms of hurricanes and what they do.

anomie (French, deriving from Greek, no law) A state of breakdown and chaos. The term is particularly associated with *Durkheim, for whom *anomie* characterizes periods of loosening of social norms, when the loss of authority tends to release moral bonds, produce unlimited desires, and cause increased rates of suicide. *Anomie* characterizes social states and is not the same as the fundamentally psychological notion of *alienation, although like that it may be a relatively permanent condition of fragmented modern societies.

anosognosia Failure to be aware of a defect or deficit. We normally take it that, for instance, seeing colours and being aware of ourselves as seeing colours go together. In anosognosia a subject may be unable to see colours, but not notice that the capacity has gone. The most extreme case is probably Anton's syndrome, or the denial of blindness by those who have lost their sight.

Anschauung (German, intuition) *See* INTUITION.

Anscombe, Gertrude Elizabeth Margaret (1919–2000) English philosopher. Educated at St Hugh's College, Oxford, where she read classics and philosophy (Greats), Anscombe graduated in 1941, in which year she married the philosopher P. T. *Geach. Anscombe became a research Fellow of Somerville College in 1946, and remained as tutor until 1970, when she became professor in Cambridge, retiring in 1986. A staunch Roman Catholic, she combined an Aristotelian concern with the actual nature of the phenomena of mind and morality, with the attention to language characteristic of post-war Oxford philosophy. Works include *Intention* (1957), and *An Introduction to Wittgenstein's Tractatus* (1959). Her translation of the *Philosophical Investigations* (1953) of *Wittgenstein was a landmark of modern philosophy.

Anselm, St (1033/4–1109) Medieval philosopher and theologian. Born in Aosta in Northern Italy, Anselm became a Benedictine, and was Archbishop of Canterbury from 1093, although he spent many of the following years in exile. He staunchly defended the rights of the Church, and in theology the rights of reason, which he saw as a buttress to faith rather than a source of scepticism. His two principal theological treatises are the *Monologion* ('Soliloquy') and the *Proslogion* ('Discourse'). The former contains versions of the *cosmological argument and argument from the existence of goodness to the existence of a supreme good. The latter contains the famous *ontological argument for the existence of God. Anselm also wrote many dialogues concerned with particular problems in logic and theology: *De Veritate* ('Of truth'), *De Libertate Arbitrii* ('Of free choice'), and *De Grammatico* contain linguistic and analytical investigations that justify his claim to be the father of *scholastic philosophy. His *Cur Deus Homo* ('Why was God man?') interprets the *atonement in terms of satisfaction due to the outraged majesty of God, which remains one of the main competing explanations available to Christian theology.

SEE WEB LINKS

- A biography of Anselm
- A list of internet resources on Anselm

antecedent *See* CONDITIONAL.

anthropic principle A controversial principle that allows explanation of some feature of the observed universe, by pointing out that did it not obtain we would not be here to be remarking on it. For example, if we ask why the universe began some fourteen thousand million years ago, the anthropic principle allows the answer that this is about the amount of time it takes for the physical and then chemical and biological complexity to develop, that ends up with persons capable of appreciating the age and asking the question (compare: why do I always see roads when I go driving?). The strong anthropic principle postulates many different universes with different structures, fundamental constants, and histories. But only ones like ours allow for us, so the answer to the question of why we find various features is, again, that we are only here because of them. To sceptics, the strong principle offends against *Ockham's razor in its proliferation of universes, and it serves to shut off proper requests for more substantive explanations.

SEE WEB LINKS

- A list of internet resources on the anthropic principle, including a bibliography
- A discussion of the anthropic principle, with links to related material

anthropocentric (Greek, man + centre) Any view magnifying the importance of human beings in the cosmos, e.g. by seeing it as created for our benefit. An account of a property such as that of a colour is anthropocentric if it incorporates an element relating possession of the property to the state of some human observer in some conditions.

anthropology In philosophical usage, a general theory of human nature, sometimes thought to be the necessary foundation of history and all social sciences. The philosophy of anthropology considers such issues as *translation, the interpretation of magic and religious ritual, and *cultural relativism.

anthropomorphism The representation of Gods, or nature, or non-human animals, as having human form, or as having human thoughts and intentions. Sometimes this is avowedly metaphorical, the problem being to understand for what it is a metaphor.

anthroposophy (Greek, wisdom about man) The Christian and occultist movement associated with Rudolph *Steiner stressing the cultivation of spiritual nature and the way to gain spiritual awareness of a higher world.

antilogism An inconsistent set of sentences, particularly the triad formed by the conjunction of the premises with the denial of the conclusion of a valid *syllogism.

antinomianism The belief held by various sects, but particularly by radical protestant movements of the 16th and 17th centuries, that certain chosen Christians are by faith or by predestination unable to sin, and are hence set free from the requirement to obey any moral law. Antinomianism is frequently associated with unconventional lifestyles and sexual practices.

antinomy A *paradox. In *Kant's first *Critique* the antinomies of pure reason show that contradictory conclusions about the world as a whole can be drawn with equal propriety. Each antinomy has a thesis and a contradictory antithesis. The first antinomy has as thesis that the world has a beginning in time and is limited in space, and as antithesis that it has no beginning and no limits. The second proves both the infinite divisibility of space and the contrary; the third shows the necessity, but also the impossibility of human freedom, and the fourth proves the existence of a necessary being and the lack of existence of such a being. The solution to this conflict of reason with itself is that the principles of reasoning used are not 'constitutive', showing us how the world is, but 'regulative', or embodying injunctions about how we are to think of it. When regulative principles are taken outside their proper sphere of employment, as they are when theorizing about the world as a whole, contradiction results. Kant also presents an antinomy of practical reason in his *Critique of Practical Reason* and two antinomies of judgment (aesthetic judgment) in his *Critique of Judgment*.

Antiochus of Ascalon (*c*.130–68 BC) Eclectic Hellenistic philosopher. Antiochus maintained the essential agreement of the opposed schools of philosophy of his time. His decisive break with *Philo of Larissa arose from his conviction that the *scepticism of the *Academy of Athens was a departure from the true Platonic ideas of the old Academy, which could in turn be reconciled with *Stoicism, and the views of the *Peripatetics. He is known as an influence on *Cicero, and as the founder of *Middle Platonism.

antiperistasis Term used by *Aristotle for the theory of motion that denies that there is a void, and denies the existence of any force except impulsion. The idea is to eliminate mysterious 'attractions' from nature. In nature there can be 'pushes' but no 'pulls'. The flight of projectiles, magnetic attraction, and the suction of fluids are among the phenomena the theory must explain. The view goes back to *Empedocles, and is adopted by *Plato in the *Timaeus*. In the 17th century the term became used more for the equally Aristotelian doctrine that contrary qualities 'repel', tending both to intensify one another, and to flee from one another. The common example is heat and cold, but *Boyle mentions the theory that water forms spherical drops because as wetness flees from dryness it attempts to squeeze into the smallest possible surface area. *See also* ACTION AT A DISTANCE, FIELD.

antiphasis The result of asserting and denying the same proposition; a contradiction.

Antiphon (*c*.480–411 BC) Athenian orator and *Sophist. Scholars have disagreed whether there are two Antiphons or whether, as is now generally believed to be the case, the orator is identical with the Sophist. The oratorical Antiphon had a distinguished public career, mainly composing speeches for others. He was the brains of the oligarchic conspiracy, and when that failed was condemned to death, although his own speech in his defence was regarded as the best of its kind ever made. The sophistical Antiphon is mentioned by *Xenophon and *Aristotle as an opponent of *Socrates.

anti-realism *See* REALISM/ANTI-REALISM.

Antisthenes (*c*.445–*c*.360 BC) A devoted follower of *Socrates, but also considered (e.g. by *Diogenes Laertius) to be an important influence on the first famous *Cynic, *Diogenes of Sinope. He shared much of Socrates' ethical teaching, but with a rather hearty penchant for those states of self-sufficiency that are the result of effort and exertion. He is cited by *Aristotle as having held a theory of language according to which there is no such thing as contradiction or definition, so he might leave the impression of an energetic country clergyman, although he lived a life of great self-denial.

antisymmetric A *relation is antisymmetric if whenever R*xy*, and R*yx*, then $x = y$.

antithesis (Greek, set against) The proposition that is the contradictory of a thesis. In *dialectical materialism the reaction to a change or process. From the process and the reaction together emerges the synthesis that transcends both.

antonym A word of opposite meaning: real/unreal, good/bad are antonyms.

anxiety A general, and sometimes neurotic, state of fear or dread. *See* ANGST.

apatheia (Greek, not suffering) In *Stoicism, not having any *pathē* means not having any feelings based on mistaken beliefs, including *emotions. Such mistakes involve thinking that the object of the feeling is sufficiently important to compete with virtue. So *apatheia* is not simply lack of feelings, but having feelings that deny virtue its all-important role.

apathy Although it is the particular enemy of teachers and sports coaches, apathy often gets a good philosophical press, especially in ethical systems that regard desire and worldly interest as low and unworthy. *Plato recognizes the need for passion or *eros* even in the advanced contemplative state of the philosopher, but *Hindu, *Buddhist, *Stoical, and some Christian traditions have all looked askance at desire, equating the **summum bonum* with a kind of torpid vacuity. *Hobbes shrewdly points out that while we live we have desires and Alexander Pope sides with the energetic: 'In lazy Apathy let Stoics boast, Their Virtue fix'd; 'tis fix'd as in a frost' (*An Essay on Man*, ii). However, like Stoics and Buddhists, *Kant found apathy to be particularly excellent: bliss is a state of 'complete independence from inclinations and desires' and this freedom is both itself a virtue and presupposed by other virtues. *Aquinas, however, recognizes the desolation involved in turning away from what is good, and classifies it as a leading or capital sin. *See* *ACCIDIE*, *ATARAXIA*, AUTONOMY/HETERONOMY, LOVE.

apeiron (Greek, boundless) Hence in Greek philosophy the infinite, or formless, and the flux of opposites which need *peras* or a principle of order to be rendered intelligible.

aphaeresis (Greek, taking away) Taking away or abstracting from some feature or another. In *Neoplatonism, abstracting from the lower to gain a conception of the highest being.

aphasia The disruption or total loss of the faculty of speech, often resulting from local damage to the left hemisphere of the brain. In ancient *scepticism *aphasia* is the silence enjoined on us after we have suspended judgement on things.

apocatastasis (apokatastasis) (Greek, restoration) In theology, the restoration of things after the millennium or final day of doom.

apodeictic (apodictic) (Greek, showing what to prove) *Necessarily true, or provable, or possessing certainty beyond dispute.

apodosis The consequent of a *conditional.

Apollonian/Dionysian Contrast introduced by *Nietzsche in *The Birth of Tragedy* (1872) between the spirit of order, rationality, and intellectual harmony, represented by Apollo, and the spirit of ecstatic, spontaneous will to life, represented by Dionysius. In later writings Apollo became, confusingly, more identified with Christian virtues, leaving a calm classicist such as *Goethe oddly classified as a Dionysian figure.

apologetics In theology, the attempt to show that a faith is either provable by reason, or at least consistent with reason. More generally, the attempts to defend a doctrine.

apophasis (Greek, assertion, proposition) Aristotelian term for a categorical statement. These may be divided into two kinds, a *kataphasis* or positive proposition and an *apophasis* or negative proposition. Apophatic theology is the view that we can only say what God is not, never what God is.

aporia A serious perplexity or insoluble problem. The Socratic method of raising problems without providing solutions is sometimes called the aporetic method. *Deconstruction is often credited with uncovering the concealed aporetic nature of texts upon which it is practised.

a posteriori *See* *A PRIORI/A POSTERIORI*.

appearance/reality One of the pivotal contrasts in philosophy, which from its earliest times has contrasted the world of 'mere' appearance—often argued to be contradictory, confused, a mere shadow of something greater—with what is real, and therefore (perhaps) of more value, timeless, eternal, and when it can be apprehended as it is, a fount of understanding and wisdom. The contrast is central to many Eastern philosophies, to Plato, and in religious form in Christianity. It is also prominent in *Kant, where the phenomenal world is conditioned by the mind's perceptual powers, in contrast to the *noumenal world which is not, but which therefore remains unknowable. In reaction many modern philosophies have tried to overcome the dichotomy. It gains its purchase mainly from the phenomena of illusions, where the way we take things to be indeed contrasts with how they are (*see* ILLUSION, ARGUMENTS FROM). But, it is argued, illusion is essentially a local matter, only identifiable against a contrasting background of veridical perception. Equally, to know or to describe how things appear is essentially parasitic on being able to know or describe how things are. Such arguments have an ancestor in *Aristotle, who considered that our words gain their sense only by contact with what is real. In modern writings they are found in Wilfrid *Sellars, J. L. *Austin, and *Wittgenstein, while an earlier and amusing anticipation is chapter 4 of *The Twilight of the Idols* by Friedrich *Nietzsche.

apperception Term introduced by *Leibniz for the mind's reflective apprehension of its own inner states. *Kant distinguishes empirical apperception, which is consciousness of the ordinary, changing self, and transcendental apperception. This is the unchangeable consciousness that unifies experience as that of one subject, and is thereby the ultimate foundation of the very possibility of experience and thought.

appetitive Pertaining to appetites; our appetitive nature is our nature in respect of our appetites and desires. Appetition in the philosophy of *Leibniz is the quasi-psychological *nisus making up the principle of change in *monads.

a priori/a posteriori A contrast first between propositions. A proposition is knowable *a priori* if it can be known without experience of the specific course of events in the actual world. It may, however, be allowed that some experience is required to acquire the concepts involved in an *a priori* proposition. Something is knowable only *a posteriori* if it cannot be known *a priori*. The distinction gives one of the fundamental problem areas of *epistemology. The category of *a priori* propositions is highly controversial, since it is not clear how pure thought, unaided by experience, can give rise to any knowledge at all, and it has always been a concern of *empiricism to deny that it can. This is often pursued by suggesting that all *a priori* propositions must be empty of real content (*see* ANALYTIC/SYNTHETIC). The two great areas in which real *a priori* knowledge seems possible are logic and mathematics, so empiricists have commonly tried to show either that these are not areas of real, substantive knowledge, or that in spite of appearances the knowledge that we have in these areas is actually dependent on experience. The former line tries to show that all *a priori* propositions are in some sense trivial, or matters of notation or conventions of language. The latter approach is particularly associated with *Quine, who denies any significant split between propositions traditionally thought of as *a priori*, and other deeply entrenched beliefs that occur in our overall view of the world.

Another contested category is that of *a priori* concepts, supposed to be concepts that cannot be 'derived' from experience, but which are presupposed in any mode of thought about the world: time, substance, causation, number, and the self are candidates. The need for such concepts, and the nature of the substantive *a priori* knowledge to which they give rise, is the central concern of *Kant's *Critique of Pure Reason*.

Apuleius (*c.*AD 125–80) The Latin writer, born in Madaura in Africa, had some claim to being a *Middle Platonist. He is principally remembered for the *Metamorphoses* or the *Golden Ass*, a narrative punctuated with many digressions that formed an important source of allegories and myths during the Renaissance.

Aquinas, St Thomas (*c.*1225–74) Born in the castle of Roccasecca in the kingdom of Naples in Southern Italy, into the family of the counts of Aquino, Aquinas was brought up in the Benedictine monastery of Monte Cassino. At the age of fourteen he was sent to complete his studies at the university of Naples, one of the few universities of the time where a full range of Aristotelian doctrine was studied. Here he became influenced by, and at the age of twenty joined, the Dominican order. He studied in Paris, and then Cologne, under *Albert the Great, and returned to Paris in 1251/2. He subsequently resided at Orvieto, Rome, Viterbo, Paris again, and Naples, constantly writing and engaging in the doctrinal and philosophical debates of the day. His works include numerous translations and commentaries on *Aristotle, theological writings, and the two major texts for which he is best known, the *Summa contra Gentiles* ('Against the Errors of the Infidels'), a 'text-book' for missionaries, and the *Summa Theologiae*, begun in 1266, and universally acknowledged to be the crowning achievement of medieval systematic theology.

Throughout his writings Aquinas's major concern is to defend a 'naturalistic' or Aristotelian Christianity, in opposition not only to sceptics but also to the surrounding tendency to read Christianity in *Neoplatonic terms, derived largely from *Augustine, and also channelled to the 13th century through such writers as *Avicenna. Aquinas takes issue with the *occasionalism of the Neoplatonists, which reduces mankind to spectators of the world order in which all causality is ultimately an expression of God's will; like Aristotle he is concerned to protect the notion of a genuine human agent who is the responsible author of his or her own actions. The human being is a composite, but not a queer amalgamation of two things, a soul in a body like a sailor in a ship, as *Plato is supposed to have held. Like Aristotle, Aquinas held that it is meaningless to ask whether a human being is two things (soul and body) or one, just as it is meaningless to ask whether 'the wax and the shape given to it by the stamp are one' (*De Anima*, 412 b 6). On this analogy the soul is the form of the body. Life after death is possible only because a form itself does not perish (perishing is loss of form), and is therefore in some sense available to reactivate a new body. It is therefore not I who survive bodily death, but I may be resurrected if the same body becomes reanimated by the same form. It is notable that on Aquinas's account a person has no privileged self-understanding. We understand ourselves, as we do everything else, by sense experience and abstraction, and knowing the principles of our own lives is an achievement, not a given. In the theory of knowledge Aquinas holds the Aristotelian doctrine that knowing entails some similarity between knower and known; a human's corporeal nature therefore requires that knowledge start with sense perception. The same limitation does not apply to beings further up the chain of being, such as angels.

In the domain of theology Aquinas deploys the distinction emphasized by *Eriugena between reason and faith. Although he lays out proofs of the existence of God (*see* FIVE WAYS) he recognizes that there are doctrines, such as that of the Incarnation and the nature of the Trinity, known only through revelation, and whose acceptance is more a matter of moral will. God's essence is identified with his existence, as pure actuality. God is simple, containing no potential. But we cannot obtain knowledge of what God is (his *quiddity), and must remain content with descriptions that apply to him partly by way of analogy: what God reveals of himself is not himself.

After a brief period in 1277 in which several of his views were condemned, the Dominicans officially imposed his teachings on that order. He was canonized in 1323, with the difficulty that his life did not display the necessary miracles being met by Pope John XXII who said that every question he answered was a miracle. His synthesis of Aristotelian philosophy and Christian doctrine was eventually to provide the main philosophical underpinnings of the Catholic church.

SEE WEB LINKS
- A biography of Aquinas
- Bibliographies of writings by or on Aquinas

Arcesilaus (*c.*316–242 BC) The founder of the middle *Academy of Athens, and the first to break with the older Platonic cosmologies in favour of *scepticism. The running battle between the Academy and the *Stoics started with his attack on the basis of Stoical reason in *phantasia katalēptikē* ('apprehensive perceptions'). His own attempt to avoid the paralysis that, according to the Stoic counterattack, followed upon sceptical suspension of judgement, was to rely upon some commonsensical, but probably undefended, notion of that which is *eulogon* or reasonable. *See also* CARNEADES.

archē (Greek, beginning) In *Presocratic thought, the fundamental, underlying source of the being of all things.

archetype (Greek, first pattern) The original model whose nature determines how things are formed. In *Plato the *forms are at least sometimes archetypes. In many seventeenth-century philosophers, including *Descartes and *Locke, archetypes are the patterns or properties of things of which resemblances are formed in the mind, either by perception or by thought. In *Berkeley and *Malebranche, archetypes become the original ideas in the mind of God, replicated in our own minds. According to *Jung the collective unconscious contains archetypal images and symbols, ready to manifest themselves in one form or another, for instance in dreams. An ectype is the impression or copy of an archetype.

Archimedean (mathematical) A number series is Archimedean if: $(\forall x)(\forall y)(\exists n)(0 < x < y \rightarrow y < nx)$. Well-behaved numbers are Archimedean: take any two numbers, however far apart they are, then there is some number that you can multiply the smaller by to give a result greater than the larger. Non-standard analysis introduces *infinitesimals of which this is not true.

Archimedean point Metaphor derived from Archimedes's alleged saying that if he had a fulcrum and a lever long enough, he could move the earth. The Archimedean point is a point 'outside' from which a different, perhaps objective or 'true' picture of something is obtainable. It might be a view of time from outside time, a view of science from elsewhere, a view of spatial reality from nowhere. Philosophers of a sceptical or anti-realist bent, as well as *deflationists and minimalists, often claim that such an alleged standpoint is

a

merely fantastical, and the alleged objectivity of the view mythical.

architectonic Term associated with *Kant, denoting the systematic structure or architecture of our knowledge. All our knowledge belongs to a possible system, and a goal of philosophy is to uncover the nature of the system, including the place in it that is occupied by philosophical reflection itself.

Archytas (*fl.* 400–350 BC) Late Greek disciple of *Pythagoras, better known as a distinguished mathematician than a philosopher. He was also responsible for getting Plato rescued from the court of Dionysus of Syracuse in 361.

Arendt, Hannah (1906–75) Political philosopher. Born in Hanover into a Jewish family, Arendt studied in the German existentialist tradition of *Jaspers and *Heidegger with whom she had a notorious affair which, in one form or another, survived her awareness of Heidegger's involvement with the Nazis. She moved to Paris in 1933, and escaped the Nazi occupation to America in 1940. Her first major work was *The Origins of Totalitarianism* (1951), and other books include *On Revolution* (1963) and *On Violence* (1970). She is best remembered for the idea of the 'banality of evil', arising from reflections on the trial of Adolph Eichmann in 1963.

SEE WEB LINKS

- Arendt's personal library at Bard College, with links to other Arendt sites, collections, and events

aretē (Greek, the goodness or excellence of a thing) The goodness or virtue of a person. In the thought of *Plato and *Aristotle virtue is connected with performing a function (*ergon*), just as an eye is good if it performs its proper function of vision. This is its **telos* or purpose (*see also* TELEOLOGY). *Aretē* is therefore identified with what enables a person to live well or successfully, although whether virtue is then just a means to successful life or is an essential part of the activity of living well becomes controversial. According to Aristotle the various virtues consist in knowing how to strike a *mean between opposing vices of excess and defect. Greek thought also paves the way for the Christian ideal that the fullest development of *aretē* for human beings consists in a self-sufficient life of contemplation and wisdom. The Sanskrit word *kusala* is used in *Buddhism to represent the same association of goodness with the skill of being a good human being.

argument To argue is to produce considerations designed to support a conclusion. An argument is either the process of doing this (in which sense an argument may be heated or protracted) or the product, i.e. the set of propositions adduced (the premises), the pattern of inference, and the conclusion reached. An argument may be deductively *valid, in which case the conclusion *follows from the premises, or it may be persuasive in other ways. *Logic is the study of valid and invalid forms of argument. *See also* INDUCTION, FALLACIES, PROOF.

argument from analogy *See* ANALOGY; DESIGN, ARGUMENT FROM OR TO; OTHER MINDS.

argument of a function *See* FUNCTION, LOGICAL.

argumentum ad ... The traditional classification of fallacies of reasoning describes many of them as involving an 'argument to ... '. They include: *A. ad ignorantiam*: arguing that a proposition is true because it has not been shown to be false, or vice versa. *A. ad baculum* (literally, arguing to a cudgel): supporting a conclusion by highlighting the dire consequences of not believing it (supposedly a fallacy, but *pragmatism insists that similar considerations underlie all processes of belief formation). *A. ad hominem*: attempting to disprove what a person holds by attacking the person (less commonly, supporting a person's contention by praising the person), or, more generally, arguing in a way that may or may not be forceful against a particular person's position, but does not advance matters for those who do not hold that person's particular combination of beliefs. It should be noticed that in some contexts, such as deciding whether to accept a person's testimony, *ad hominem* description of the person, for instance that they are notorious liars, may well be relevant. *A. ad misericordiam* (to pity): an argument trading on the sympathies of people. *A. ad populum*: an argument appealing to the prejudices of the people. *A. ad verecundiam*: appealing to an authority outside its legitimate area; illicitly trading on reverence and respect, as in celebrity endorsements.

Although processes of argument fall into these and other errors, it is difficult to separate improper from proper uses of arguments that might be described in these ways. For instance, appeal to sympathy, or popular belief, or authority might in some circumstances be quite legitimate. Except for *argumentum ad hominem*, the terms are not commonly used.

Arian heresy The doctrine denying the true divinity of Christ, named after the Alexandrian priest Arius (*c.*250–*c.*336). It maintained that the Son was not eternal, or of one nature with God, but was a dependent instrument created for the redemption of the world. In 325 the General Council of Nicaea under *Athanasius defined and affirmed the doctrine of the coeternity and coequality of God and the Son. This doctrine of **homoousion* requires some confidence that we know, for example, how to count whether things are of one or two substances.

Aristippus of Cyrene (*c.*435–350 BC) A companion of *Socrates, whose grandson via his daughter Arete was one of the founders of the *Cyrenaic school. *Diogenes Laertius leaves a memorable portrait of Aristippus as a wealthy, discriminating, and extravagant hedonist. The grandson was known as *matro-didactus* (mother-taught), suggesting a high degree of ability in Arete.

aristocracy Rule by a privileged class. In classical Greece an appealing alternative to monarchy, the rule of one person, or democracy, rule by the mob. The aristocracy is defended also by *Burke, in his *Reflections on the Revolution in France* as the repository of tradition, honour, responsibility, and education, dedicated to stability and the guardian of necessary virtues that have stood the test of time. In the contemporary world, similar claims are made for CEOs, company directors, and retired judges and civil servants of the right kind.

Ariston of Chios (early to mid 3rd c. BC) A pupil of *Zeno of Citium and early Stoic. He developed an uncompromising ethic based on the notion of the virtuous person and denying any feature of ethics not discernible from such an agent's point of view.

Aristotelianism Aristotle's influence originally survived through his own school, the *Lyceum. His works were collected and edited by Andronicus of Rhodes, and commentaries continued until Justinian closed the pagan schools in AD 529. *Avicenna and *Averroes contributed to the rebirth of Aristotelian studies in the West, which after mild attempts at suppression at the beginning of the thirteenth century burgeoned until Aristotle became 'the philosopher', the fountainhead and authority for the great medievals such as *Albert the Great and especially *Aquinas. However, the *Schoolmen were more interested in defending the truth of Aristotle's dynamical and physical system, which they saw as substantially compatible with Christianity, than in promoting the empirical and scientific method that he championed, with the result that to the scientific revolution of the seventeenth and eighteenth centuries Aristotle was regarded as little but an obstacle: the author of fossilized and dogmatic scholastic nonsense. Even at this low point Aristotle's moral and psychological insights fared better than his metaphysical and physical speculations, while his logic, although generally regarded as superseded by modern *propositional and *predicate calculus, is still admired and trawled for substantive insights.

Aristotle (384–322 BC) Along with *Plato the most influential philosopher of the western tradition, Aristotle was born at Stagira in Macedonia, the son of Nicomachus, the court physician to the Macedonian king Amyntas II. At the age of 17 he entered Plato's *Academy in Athens, and remained there until Plato's death. When the Academy under *Speusippus turned to mathematical and speculative pursuits, Aristotle accepted the invitation of Hermias to reside at Assos. Upon the death of Hermias (whose niece, Pythias, he married) in 345, Aristotle went to Mytilene on the island of Lesbos. To this period belong many of his zoological researches. Between 343/2 and 340 he acted as tutor to the young Alexander the Great, at the invitation of his father Philip of Macedon. In 335 he returned to Athens, and on the outskirts of the city in a grove sacred to Apollo Lyceus he founded a school, the *Lyceum (where was the *peripatos* or covered walk from which his followers, the Peripatetics, took their name). Here he conducted and organized research on many subjects and built the first great library of antiquity. On the death of Pythias he lived with Herpyllis, by whom he had a son, Nicomachus. On the death of Alexander in 325 anti-Macedonian feeling in Athens caused Aristotle to retire to Chalcis where he died in 322. He is described as having been bald, thin, with a lisp, and of a sardonic disposition.

The works known in his lifetime include dialogues modelled on those of Plato, but these are now lost. It is also known that he accumulated an immense collection of natural and historical observations during his headship of the Lyceum, but these too are mainly lost. The extant corpus is nearly all preserved through the edition of *Andronicus of Rhodes, made in the 1st century BC. The principal works of philosophical interest are (a) logical works (these form the *Organon*): *Categories, On Interpretation* (*De Interpretatione*), *Prior Analytics, Posterior Analytics, Topics, Sophistical Refutations* (*De Sophisticis Elenchis*); (b) works on physics: *Physics, On the Heavens* (*De Caelo*), *On Generation and Corruption* (*De Generatione et Corruptione*); (c) psychology and natural history: *On the Soul* (*De Anima*), *On the Parts of Animals* (*De Partibus Animalium*), *On the Movement of Animals* (*De Motu Animalium*), *On the Generation of Animals* (*De Generatione Animalium*), and shorter works collected as the *Parva Naturalia*; (d) ethics: *Nicomachean Ethics, Eudemian Ethics, Magna Moralia, Politics, Rhetoric,* and the *Art of Poetry*. Finally, (e) the general investigation of the things that are: the *Metaphysics*.

The scale of Aristotle's researches, and their central place in the subsequent history of philosophy, mean that his work defies brief description. His relationship to Plato is complex, with scholars on the whole repudiating the idea of a development away from an originally accepted Platonism, even to the point of detecting a swing towards Plato in the later metaphysics. The traditional contrast is between Plato's otherworldly, formal, and **a priori* conception of true knowledge (**noēsis*), as opposed to Aristotle's intense concern for the observed detail of natural phenomena, including those of thought, language, and psychology. Thus while Plato is the patron saint of *transcendental theories of knowledge and especially of ethics, Aristotle is concerned to protect knowledge of the plural and multifarious world we live in. His ethics, which he regarded as a branch of the natural history of human beings, shows a subtle (some would say, unequalled) appreciation of the complexities of human motivation. Aristotle, like *Kant, had a passion for categories, and as well as inventing the study of *logical form may be said to have laid down the division of the sciences we habitually use, not to mention the categories that have organized virtually all subsequent philosophical thought (*substance/*accident, *potential/*actual, *matter/*form, and the different categories of *causes). His orderly mind showed the same instinct for the *mean that is celebrated in his moral philosophy. He avoids all extremes, and typically does justice to each side of the divisions that split philosophers into warring camps. Aristotle was the central figure in Arabic and medieval philosophy. His fundamentally animistic conception of nature as a kind of plant or striving organism, his distinction between celestial phenomena and sublunary nature, and his conception of perception as a literal sharing of form with that which is perceived, all dominated European thought until the upheavals that produced the *Galilean world view in the 17th century. His reputation declined somewhat before that period, when the attempts of both warring Protestants and Catholics to appropriate his thinking led to a general revulsion from *scholasticism. In the 20th century his reputation was frequently refurbished, and he remains a pivotal figure in political theory, ethics, and aesthetics, while his logic and even some of his metaphysical doctrines received renewed attention in the late 20th century and the new millennium. (*See also* ACCIDENT, CATEGORIES, ESSENCE, SYLLOGISM, VIRTUE.)

SEE WEB LINKS

- A biography of Aristotle, including his influence on science and philosophy
- Essays on the principal topics in Aristotle with select bibliography and online sources

arithmetic The study of the natural numbers, which are 0, 1, 2, 3 ... and their successors. Arithmetic is characterized by *Peano's postulates. Philosophical questions include the nature of our knowledge of those postulates; the nature of the numbers, which are apparently the objects of which arithmetic treats; and the relation of arithmetic to empirical science. *See also* ABSTRACT/CONCRETE, CONVENTIONALISM, FORMALISM, LOGICISM.

arithmetization *See* GÖDEL NUMBERING.

Arius Didymus (1st c. BC) Known mainly as a source for *Stoic and Aristotelian ethics in the Hellenistic period, and also for earlier physics. He was the teacher of the Roman emperor Augustus, and wrote a consolation to Livia, his wife, on the death of Drusus, their son.

arkhe *See* ARCHĒ.

Arminius, Jacobus (1560–1609) Dutch theologian, remembered for defending a doctrine of free will against that of *predestination.

Armstrong, David Malet (1926–) Forthright Australian *materialist, and together with J. J. C. *Smart the leading Australian philosopher of the second half of the 20th century. Armstrong defends an uncompromising scientific materialism, together with a *functionalist theory of mind. However, he sees scientific laws as describing necessitation relations between *universals, about which he is a realist, but of an Aristotelian rather than a Platonist persuasion. He defends the view that every true proposition requires something to make it true, a 'truthmaker', and therefore holds an *ontology of states of affairs, reminiscent of *Wittgenstein's *Tractatus*, especially in that it is the combinatorial properties of states of affairs that underlie the theory of necessity and possibility. Books include *Perception and the Physical World* (1961), *A Materialist Theory of the Mind* (1968), *Belief, Truth and Knowledge* (1973), *What is a Law of Nature?* (1983) and *A World of States of Affairs* (1997).

Arnauld, Antoine (1612–94) French theologian and philosopher, and possibly the most distinguished and rigorous 17th-century thinker after *Descartes. Arnauld was a *Jansenist, and the turbulent controversies of the time led to his losing his doctorate and being forced into exile in Belgium in 1679. With Pierre Nicole he was the author of *La Logique, ou l'art de penser* ('Logic, or the art of thinking'), otherwise known as the *Port-Royal Logic*. His other main philosophical work is the *Traité des vraies et des fausses idées* (trs. as *On True and False Ideas*, 1990), which is a sustained attack on *Malebranche.

Arnauld particularly disliked Malebranche's *representationalism, and the view that 'we see all things in God'. At times he seems to espouse a direct *realism about perception, although the Cartesian mistrust of the senses may make his position seem closer to that of *Berkeley, who also holds that we directly perceive what really exists. The dispute became acrimonious, with Malebranche dwelling on Arnauld's heresies, and Arnauld getting Malebranche's *Treatise on Nature and Grace* placed on the Index of prohibited books.

arrow paradox *See* ZENO'S PARADOXES.

Arrow's theorem Sometimes (inappropriately) called Arrow's paradox. The most famous theorem in the logic of social choice or voting, proved by Stanford economist and 1972 Nobel prizewinner Kenneth Arrow, in his *Social Choice and Individual Value* of 1951. The theorem (properly entitled the general possibility theorem) shows the impossibility of a *social welfare function satisfying some very weak constraints. These in essence are: (i) it must work from any possible set of individual orderings of alternatives; (ii) it must satisfy the *Pareto principle, that if each person prefers *x* to *y* then society must prefer *x* to *y*; (iii) for any subset of the alternatives, only the individuals' preferences over the alternatives in the subset of alternatives are to count; and (iv) non-dictatorship: there must be no individual whose preferences alone dictate the preferences of the society, no matter what are the preferences of other individuals. The *voters' paradox is a simple example of the kind of inconsistency that arises. Subsequent work has often enlarged the basis on which a function might be constructed, for instance by taking account not only of preferences themselves, but of strength or propriety of preference. *See also* SEN.

art, philosophy of The philosophy of art is distinguished from the wider topic of *aesthetics only by confining attention to the aesthetic appreciation of deliberately produced works of art. A central problem is therefore that of defining what feature distinguishes such works from works of entertainment, craft works, things produced for other purposes, things in nature, or for that matter random effusions billed as instances of 'self-expression'. Although thus demarcating art proper may seem to be a pointless quest, the category retains great moral and political importance, for instance in distinguishing erotica from *pornography. Other problems surround the relation between art and truth, and also that between art and morality. There are philosophical difficulties as well about the difference between a work of art and a forgery, the nature of aesthetic response and its relation to imagination, the general difficulty of describing the importance of art in life, and the nature of the emotional response appropriate to different works of art.

artificial intelligence (AI) The science of making machines that can do the kinds of thing that humans can do. Topics of research have included speech recognition, visual recognition, and the more familiar problem solving and game-playing. Modelling a psychological phenomenon on a computer is a way of showing how the phenomenon is possible in a physical world, and is also a way of bringing out the complexities involved in apparently simple tasks. A central concept in much AI research is that of a representation, with programs designed to construct, adapt, and link representations in the production of intelligent responses. This research has been responsible for a considerable retreat from dogmatic *behaviourism, in which the idea of mental manipulations was thought to be unscientific, since it is exactly the storage and manipulation of representations of the world that is demanded in the problems AI approaches. Strong AI is the philosophical thesis that appropriately programmed computers have minds in exactly the same sense that we do. Weak AI is the methodological belief that the best way to explore the mind is to proceed as if this were true, without commenting on the legacies of *dualism that lead to discomfort with the strong thesis. *See also* CHINESE ROOM, CONNECTIONISM, FRAME PROBLEM, TURING TEST.

SEE WEB LINKS

- An audio discussion of AI by two scientists and a philosopher
- A dynamic library of internet resources on AI

artificial language *See* FORMAL SYSTEM.

artificial life While processes of self-organization, reproduction, learning, adaptation, and evolution are in nature confined to the biological sphere, they can be duplicated in principle in computer simulations, either in virtual realities such as computer games provide, or in principle in the design of sufficiently complex hardware. The study of such systems promises to throw light on the natural processes underlying natural living things.

ascetic (Greek, hermit, also one who exercises) In the early Church one who practised rigorous self-discipline, abstinence, and austerity. The association of religious excellence with extreme self-mortification is found in *Jainism, and some types of *Buddhism.

a

ascriptivism Term due to P. T. *Geach for the view (which he attacked: *see* FREGE–GEACH ARGUMENT) that in asserting that someone was responsible for an act we are not describing the causal antecedents of the act, but rather taking up a stance towards the act and the agent, such as expressing preparedness to hold the agent to some kind of account. The view is parallel to varieties of *non-cognitivism in ethics.

aseity (Latin, by or of itself) The God-like characteristic of being absolutely independent of other things. *See* *PERSEITY.*

a-series of time Term due to *McTaggart for the ordering of events in respect of past, present, and future. McTaggart's proof of the unreality of time argues first, that this ordering is essential to capturing the nature of time (*see* B-SERIES), and secondly, that it involves a contradiction, since being past, present, and future are incompatible properties, yet each event has to have all three: any event will eventually have been each of future, present, and then past. It is sometimes thought that this is no more contradictory than a house being both near (to me) and far (from you). But the heart of McTaggart's complaint is that distinctions of tense belong to one or another changing perspective, yet there is something improper about thinking of reality itself as essentially perspectival.

SEE WEB LINKS

- McTaggart's 'The Unreality of Time'
- A list of internet resources on McTaggart's philosophy, including a bibliography

assertion The action of putting forward some statement or proposition as true. Also, the statement or proposition thus put forward. *Frege noticed the crucial point that what is asserted can also be put forward not as assertion, but as a supposition or hypothesis, as possibly true, and so on. This is not true, for instance, in animal signalling systems. *See also* ASSERTORIC, FREGE–GEACH ARGUMENT.

assertion sign The sign ⊢ was used by *Frege to put in front of sentences that are being asserted as true, as opposed to sentences that are involved in some process of reasoning, but are not themselves put forward as true. This use was superseded in modern logic by the use of the sign to denote the provability relation within a system. $\{A_1 \ldots A_n\} \vdash B$ means that B may be proved from the premises $\{A_1 \ldots A_n\}$. $\vdash B$ means that B may be proved from no assumptions at all, i.e. is a *theorem of the system.

assertoric An assertoric context is one in which an assertion is made by the use of a sentence, as opposed to one in which a sentence occurs, but no commitment to its truth is expressed. Thus a straightforward assertion of 'They were here last Sunday' contrasts with 'If they were here last Sunday, then they will not come today', since in the latter example the sentence 'they were here last Sunday' is embedded, but it is not asserted that they were here last Sunday.

associationism *See* ASSOCIATION OF IDEAS.

association of ideas The pattern in which different items in consciousness occur together or in succession. According to associationism, laws of such association would play the same role in the study of conscious processes as *laws of nature do in the study of natural phenomena. The first attempt to isolate the properties in virtue of which ideas follow one another is that of *Aristotle, *De Memoria et Reminiscentia* (part of the shorter natural works, trs. as *Of Memory and Reminiscence*, ii. 451 b 18–20).

Connections whereby one idea leads to another can be seen as sources of delusion (e.g. in *Hutcheson, and to some extent in *Locke) or as an essential constructive mechanism of the human mind (e.g. in *Hume). Associationism, or the belief that there should be such laws, for instance depending on the similarity of ideas or their contiguity in time or place, is an important element in the philosophy of *Hartley and especially *Hume. It is appealing to empiricists in substituting natural processes for the apparently less tractable processes involved in complex trains of reasoning, or the use of imagination or analogies. It is later developed by *Bain, J. S. *Mill, and *Condillac, but the rise of *behaviourism and more sophisticated views about the relationship between consciousness and underlying processes have largely discredited the goal.

assumption A *proposition is treated as an assumption when it is added to a stock of *premises of an *argument. The conclusion is then conditional upon that assumption, unless the assumption can be discharged, or shown to be unnecessary, in the course of the argument.

assurance game Game-theoretic structure also known as the stag hunt, deriving from *Rousseau's example in *A Discourse on Inequality*. In an assurance game, it is best for everybody, individually and socially, if all cooperate. But each fears that the others may not play their part and is then motivated to defect. In Rousseau's example, instead of continuing to play a role in the stag hunt, which requires cooperation, individual hunters allow themselves to be distracted by the lesser game of a hare, which can be caught by an individual, each reasoning that they would be worst off of all if they ignored the hare and stood by the cooperative enterprise, while the others let themselves be distracted. Not being sure of the cooperative dispositions of the others, they may themselves rationally defect, and the social and individual optimum is missed. In an assurance game, the cooperative solution is a *Nash equilibrium, since nobody can do better for themselves by defecting from it. Nevertheless with enough suspicion of the others, one may maximize expected utility by defecting.

	Cooperate A	Chase Hare A
Cooperate	3	2
B	3	0
Chase Hare	0	1
B	2	1

Astell, Mary (1666–1731) English feminist and philosopher, influenced by John *Locke and *Malebranche. Her works include *A Serious Proposal to the Ladies* (1694), *Some Reflections on Marriage* (1700), *Letters Concerning the Love of God* (1695) and *The Christian Religion as Professed by a Daughter of the Church of England* (1705).

asymmetric A *relation R is asymmetric if when R*xy* it is not the case that R*yx*.

asymptotic A line is asymptotic to a curve if the distance between the line and the curve tends to zero as the distance along the curve tends to infinity.

ataraxia The state of tranquillity or imperturbability, freedom from anxiety, considered to be one of the desirable results of an immersion in *scepticism, and by *Epicureans to be part of the highest form of happiness.

Athanasius (*c*.297–373) Early Christian father, and early opponent of the *Arian heresy and proponent of **homoousion*.

atheism Either the lack of belief that there exists a god, or the belief that there exists none. Sometimes thought itself to be more dogmatic than mere agnosticism, although atheists retort that everyone is an atheist about most gods, so they merely advance one step further.

SEE WEB LINKS

- A list of internet resources on atheism
- An audio discussion of the arguments for and against God's existence

Atheismusstreit *See* FICHTE.

atman In *Buddhism the self or soul, conceived of as lying behind the empirical self, and in *Hindu thought an eternal unity, identified with **brahman*. The *Buddhist doctrine of *anatman* (*anatta*) denies the existence of the *atman*, holding that there is no ongoing owner of the fleeting perceptions and attributes that make up our lives. Although this doctrine is often applauded as a precursor of the *bundle theory of the mind or self, the matter is complex, for Buddhism makes a distinction between the surface self, or false self, and the true self that can be discovered by spiritual exercise. For the bundle theorist there can be no application for this notion of spiritual depth.

atomic formula/sentence Technically, an atomic formula is one with no *logical constants. An atomic sentence is an atomic formula with no free *variables. Intuitively, it is the kind of sentence on the basis of which one might start to construct logical complexity: a sentence consisting of a name and a *monadic predicate (Bill snores) or a number of names and a relational predicate (Bill loves Mary).

atomism A philosophical doctrine at least as old as *Democritus, and plausibly viewed as an attempt to combine an *a priori* conviction of the unchangeable and immutable nature of the world with the variety and change of things as we know them. This is the conviction that to understand complexity and change at one level it is necessary to find underlying unity at another level. In early Greek atomism quantitative change arises from the shifting configurations and quantities of atoms, which are themselves eternal, impenetrable, identical in nature, and unchanging. After *Aristotle, atoms were allowed to be subject to change: what is unchanging was not necessarily corpuscular in nature.

The revival of atomism in the 17th century owed more to the rise of empirical science. *Descartes produced the first serious departure from Democritus and Aristotle, identifying matter and extension, but differentiating corpuscles only in terms subject to mechanical and mathematical treatment (velocity, mass). *Leibniz was the most persistent critic of 17th-century atomism. Atoms offend against the principle of *sufficient reason, for there could be no reason why a particular atom occupies a particular position rather than any other. But on more physical grounds Leibniz held that they involve discontinuities in nature (density changes discontinuously at their boundaries); that their own cohesion would require a perpetual miracle; and that no theory of their inelastic collisions is tenable. His arguments were revived and turned into a positive *field theory by *Boscovich in the following century. Leibniz also held that whatever had extension was divisible, so that true atoms, the indivisible foundation stones, become quasi-mental things, with some of the qualities of the soul.

Further developments of atomism were hindered by the absence of a chemistry that could find a workable criterion of the difference between elements and compounds, and this was first delivered by the chemists Lavoisier (1743–94) and Dalton (1766–1844). The complexity of atoms in the chemical sense is now attested by the proliferation of subatomic particles. What remains of philosophical and methodological interest is the extent to which each level of complexity is to be understood by postulating some identical and unchanging constituents at a lower level, as Democritus originally supposed.

SEE WEB LINKS

- An introduction to ancient Greek atomism
- A summary of the debates over Democritus's atomism

atomism, logical *See* LOGICAL ATOMISM.

atonement In Christian theology, the sacrificial death of Christ as some kind of payment for the sins of mankind. Various theories attempt to make sense of a perfect deity directing a sacrifice of this kind. They include: (a) the idea that the event is the payment of some kind of a ransom to the forces of evil. But since the Son is rejoined with his Father, the forces of evil appear to have been cheated, and this seems incompatible with justice. (b) The Satisfaction theory (*Anselm). The sacrifice restores God's honour, insulted by sin. But the way this restoration works remains obscure, especially as the insult goes on. (c) The Acceptance theory (*Duns Scotus). God freely decides to accept this event as a repayment of our dues to him. But then why not freely decide to accept something less traumatic, such as the sacrifice of a sheep? (d) Jesus suffers as a substitute for us. But the morality of using substitutes or scapegoats is particularly unedifying. (e) The Ethical Message or Example (*Abelard). Jesus is sent to exemplify for us the perfect life. It seems strange, however, to deliver the message in one particular place and time, and especially one with such fragile means of recording the event. The matter is not rendered easier by the doctrine of the identity of the Son and the Father (*see HOMOOUSION, HOMOIOUSION*), and Christian theology continues to address the issue.

attitude An evaluative response, usually contrasted with simple belief by its more direct connection with motivation and behaviour. An attitude is a state whose essence is contentment or active discontent with some way the world is, rather than a simple cognition of the way the world is. Significant disputes arise when it is asked if some response, such as the evaluation of something as good or bad, is better seen as expressing attitude than belief. *See* EMOTIVISM, ERROR THEORY, EXPRESSIVISM, QUASI-REALISM.

attribution theory The theory that attempts to explore the factors governing the ways in which people explain the doings of others and themselves. The way people attribute behaviour to external causes is itself subject to social circumstance, or personality factors, and often designed to preserve self-esteem, diminish one's own responsibility, exaggerate the malevolence of others, and so forth.

attributive An attributive adjective is one that logically qualifies a subsequent adjective, and cannot be separated from it. Thus something may be a large mouse and a small mammal (i.e. large for a mouse, small for a mammal). If the qualified adjective is suppressed, ambiguity may result. The doctrine is frequently advanced that the adjective 'good' is attributive, implying a subsequent kind or qualification. If this is right it may make no sense to talk simply of a good thing or good state of affairs, and this is often regarded as undermining some of the attraction of *utilitarianism. *See also* ALIENANS.

aufheben (German, to supersede, to cancel) In the philosophy of *Hegel, dialectical progress occurs when each of a thesis and its antithesis are *aufgehoben*, or overcome by a synthesis that builds only on the good bits of each. Often used as a knowing way of presenting a theory that overcomes and abolishes previous dualities or dichotomies.

Aufklärung German term for the *Enlightenment.

Augustine of Hippo, St (354–430) Major Christian philosopher and theologian and the key figure in the transition from pagan to specifically Christian philosophy. Born at Tagaste in North Africa of a pagan father and a Christian mother (St Monica), Augustine studied rhetoric at Carthage, and taught in Rome and Milan. After periods believing in *manichaeanism, *scepticism, and *Neoplatonism, he converted to Christianity in 386, at the age of 31. Augustine found the theology of Christianity prefigured in Neoplatonism: what Christianity added was the specific belief in the incarnation and consequent salvation. Christianity thus succeeded in showing people how to live, where unaided philosophical reflection failed. In 395 he was appointed coadjutor of Bishop Valerius, and a year later became the Bishop of Hippo in North Africa. Of the two works by which he is best remembered, the *Confessions* were written around 400, and the *City of God*, occasioned by the fall of

Rome to Alaric in 410, was written in the years from 413 to 427.

Augustine's philosophy was always at the service of his theology, although containing fine discussions of metaphysics, particularly of *time and *free will, and of ethics. As a bishop he fought three major heresies: those of the manichaeans, the Donatists, and the *Pelagians. Against the first, Augustine argues that the universe is wholly good, and that evil is only the privation or absence of that which is good. In the case of moral evil, this is the result of free will (*see* FREE WILL DEFENCE). The Donatist schism arose because members of the African church refused to accept a bishop who had been consecrated by someone (a *traditor* or betrayer) low enough to surrender his bible during the persecutions conducted by the Emperor Diocletian. Augustine in response forges the doctrine of one Church and the efficacy of the sacraments. Philosophically some of his most important doctrines emerge in the third controversy, with the Pelagian heresy, against which the steely Augustine affirms the reality of the Fall, and of *original sin as the hereditary moral disease that we all bear, only curable by God's grace. This teaching confirms the predestination of the elect, for grace is a gift that is given rather than earned. It was left to *Calvinism to add the predestination of the damned (*see* HELL). Augustine's writing was much admired by *Wittgenstein, and his *Confessions* provide the archetype for all subsequent autobiography.

SEE WEB LINKS

- A biography of Augustine
- A list of internet resources on Augustine's philosophy

Augustinian view of language The view that *Wittgenstein attributes to *Augustine, at the very beginning of the *Philosophical Investigations*. On this view individual words name objects, and sentences are combinations of names. Wittgenstein goes on to argue that the position fails to differentiate kinds of word, and embodies an over-simple conception of language use.

Aurelius, Marcus (AD 121–80) Roman emperor from 161 until his death. His philosophical fame rests on the reflections and aphorisms collected in the twelve books of his *Meditations*. These breathe the highest *Stoic principles, without any great philosophical originality but with a particular personal intensity.

Aurobindo Ghose (1872–1950) Indian mystic and spiritual leader. His philosophical writings attempt to synthesize evolutionary science with a mystical view of the supreme reality or *Brahman.

Aussonderungsaxiom *See* SEPARATION, AXIOM OF.

Austin, John (1790–1859) British philosopher of law. Born in London, after a brief career in the army Austin was called to the Bar in 1818. With his wife, Sarah Taylor, he was closely associated with *Bentham and his circle. When the university of London was founded in 1826 he was offered the chair of jurisprudence, and his first series of lectures became his masterwork, *The Province of Jurisprudence Determined* (1832). In this year, however, he gave up the chair for financial reasons. Austin is known as the first and most rigorous exponent of an imperativist conception of law. Law is the command of the sovereign backed by sanctions; the sovereign is the person or institution whom the people have the habit of obeying. The model has been relentlessly attacked, for instance for failing to account for the persistence of legal authority and for the role of the law in providing a framework that enables people to do things. But it properly focuses upon the difference between law as it is and law as it should be (about which Austin was a *utilitarian), and it brings to the forefront the central and permanent question of the underlying relationship between law and political power.

Austin, John Langshaw (1911–60) British linguistic philosopher. Austin was educated and taught at Oxford, where he worked all his life except for a distinguished period in the Intelligence service during the Second World War. He had a classical and scholarly background, and his translation of *Frege's *Grundlagen der Arithmetik* in 1950 was the first and seminal introduction of Frege to English-speaking philosophers. Austin was the major figure of the movement known as *linguistic philosophy, or Oxford or 'ordinary language' philosophy, and he was frequently, but unfairly, charged with believing that ferocious attention to the niceties of everyday language exhausted the proper method of philosophy. In fact his method was more Aristotelian, holding that close attention to the concepts and distinctions that have become embodied in the language is the beginning, if not the end, of philosophy, whilst airy recommendations about how we *should* think about something frequently fall short of the skill and delicacy with which we *do* think about it. The major works illustrating his method arose out of papers and lectures, and were published after his death. They include *Sense and Sensibilia* (1962), *How to Do Things with Words* (1962), and the collected *Philosophical Papers* (1961). His work on the way language actually works pioneered the theory of *speech acts, as well as introducing many of its terms, such as *locutionary act and *illocutionary act.

autarkia (Greek, self-sufficiency) According to most Greek schools of philosophy, especially the

*Cynics and the *Stoics, independence of external events and happenings is a mark of true **eudaimonia*. A person at the mercy of events is not truly free. This denial of our inevitable dependencies may seem noble but may also seem fantastical.

authenticity The condition of significant, emotionally appropriate living. Contrasted, especially in *Heidegger, with inauthenticity: a state in which life, stripped of purpose and responsibility, is depersonalized and dehumanized. *See also* ALIENATION.

authoritarian personality Concept explored by *Adorno, and supposed to characterize the adherents of *fascism. The authoritarian personality is intolerant, bigoted, dominating, attracted to regimes of command and submission, and impatient of subtlety of any kind.

authority A person, institution, or organization is said to have authority when the power it exercises is supposed legitimate, that is, authorized by some system of *norms to which the speaker assents. The emergence of such norms in human society is a complex matter, with convention, habit, custom, and tradition playing different roles. *Social contract theory is one kind of solution to the problem of the basis of authority; the evident *utility of some rule-governed systems is another. While it is common to find scepticism about particular claims to authority, the idea that human co-ordination (and hence even communication) could exist without it is usually regarded as fanciful.

autological A word that applies to itself: 'short' is a short word; 'English' an English word. *See* GRELLING'S PARADOX, HETEROLOGICAL.

automaton Sometimes, a machine that imitates the behaviour of a conscious agent without itself being one. On this definition we ourselves are not automata, but the theory of how we differ from an automaton is not obvious (*see* BEHAVIOURISM, FUNCTIONALISM, MIND–BODY PROBLEM). More widely, any machine running according to a program may be thought of as an automaton, and the question whether that includes us is then open. *See also* TURING TEST.

autonomy/heteronomy Autonomy is the capacity for self-government. Agents are autonomous if their actions are truly their own. The necessity of this moral liberty appears in *Rousseau, and is a cornerstone of *Kant's ethical theory, in which possessing autonomy of the will is a necessary condition of moral agency. The difficulty in the concept is that our desires, choices, and actions are all partly caused by factors outside our control, including those factors originally responsible for our characters. So true autonomy can easily seem to be a myth. Yet the concept is important, since it is plausible to hold that only agents acting autonomously are responsible for their actions. But this idea also leads to quicksands: autonomy is often contrasted with the state of being 'enslaved' by bad desires. But if only the autonomous can be held responsible it will quickly follow that nobody is responsible for bad actions. Proposals for defending the concept include describing agents as autonomous when they are under the influence only of reason, when they can identify with the motivations prompting their action, or when they are capable of acting so as to change their motivations if they cannot identify with them. Agents are heteronomous if their will is under the control of another. It should be noted that the pair is not exhaustive: an agent may fail to be autonomous because of external factors that do not include control by another, but only other kinds of constraint and compulsion.

In the ethics of *Kant the terms are more specific. Autonomy is the ability to know what morality requires of us, and functions not as freedom to pursue our ends, but as the power of an agent to act on objective and universally valid rules of conduct, certified by reason alone. Heteronomy is the condition of acting on desires, which are not legislated by reason. The centrality of autonomy is challenged by ethical theorists, including many *feminists, who see it as a fantasy that masks the social and personal springs of all thought and action. *See also* AUTHENTICITY, DETERMINISM, FREE WILL, LIBERTARIANISM (METAPHYSICAL).

autonomy of ethics The view that ethics 'stands on its own feet', i.e. does not derive its authority from a non-ethical source, such as a divine command, the dictates of pure reason, or the facts of nature.

autonymy The use of an expression, usually in quotation marks, to refer to itself. 'London' refers to the six-letter term or word 'London', not to the city.

autotelic The author of its own goals, self-propelling.

Avempace (Ibn Bajja) (1085/90–1139) Disciple of *al-Farabi, born in Saragosa. He is remembered mainly for his political philosophy. Unlike al-Farabi, he thought the philosopher could attain the highest point of human wisdom without living in a virtuous city, i.e. while solitary. All existing human society is imperfect, which is why cities need doctors, judges, and so forth, but they also need 'weeds' or idiosyncratic thinkers, among which might be those who followed the solitary life of perfection.

Avenarius, Richard (1843–96) German philosopher and from 1877 professor at Zurich. His masterwork, the *Kritik der reinen Erfahrung* ('Critique of Pure Experience', 2 vols., 1888–90), expounded a particularly rigorous kind of positivism, known as empirio-criticism, which rejects the dualism of perception and the external world in favour of a *monism in which all knowledge and thought is confined to pure experience. The system is reminiscent of *Hume and, like Hume, Avenarius adds various laws of thought in order to explain the phenomena of cognition. His view was remembered partly because of the attack on its idealist tendency by *Lenin, in his *Materialism and Empirio-Criticism* (1908).

Averroës (Ibn Rushd) (1126–98) The most distinguished and influential Islamic Aristotelian, Averroës was born in 1126 in Cordoba, and was educated in law and various sciences. He lived partly in Marrakesh, and became a judge in Seville in 1169. Towards the end of his life he fell into disgrace, but although exiled for a short time was restored to favour, and died in Marrakesh. The majority of his works were commentaries on the writings of Aristotle. Averroës wrote with the intention of rescuing Aristotle from Neoplatonic and religious impurities, especially as found in the works of *Avicenna. In particular, whereas for Avicenna existence is an accident of essence, or in other words the *universal or *form precedes the individual thing, for Averroës individual substances are the primary existents, and the distinction between them and their essence is the work of the mind. He also criticized Avicenna's *cosmological argument, holding instead that only physical arguments, such as that showing the need for a prime mover, can prove the existence of physical things. Averroës was much concerned with improving and expanding upon Aristotle's doctrine of the intellect and the soul, holding a curious doctrine of a universal and immaterial passive intellect, common to all, and providing what is common, and immortal, in human beings. Because he held non-Christian doctrines, including the eternity of the world, the absence of individual providence, and the doctrine of merely collective immortality, Averroës became associated with the doctrine of *double truth, the slightly underhand way of reconciling theology and philosophy, although he himself never subscribed to such a view. As well as his 38 commentaries on Aristotle, he wrote the *Incoherence of the Incoherence* against the anti-rationalism of *Ghazali, works on medicine, a commentary on Plato's *Republic*, and treatises on religion.

Avicebron *See* IBN GABIROL.

Avicenna (Ibn Sina) Abu Ali Al-Husayn (980–1037) Leading Islamic philosopher and *Neoplatonist. Avicenna was born in Bukhara, and educated in literature, law, logic, and mathematics, as well as science and metaphysics. A child prodigy, by the age of sixteen he was an accomplished physician; however, although he read Aristotle's *Metaphysics* forty times, he claimed that it was not until he also absorbed *al-Farabi's *On the Objects of Metaphysics* that he finally understood it. The end of the Samanid dynasty in 999 saw the beginning of various wanderings and allegiances to different courts, and he eventually died in Isfahan. He wrote between 100 and 200 works on diverse subjects, mostly in Arabic but also in Persian. His major philosophical work, *The Healing*, became known to medieval western philosophy through *Ghazali's summary and through translations into Latin. Avicenna represents a Neoplatonic version of Aristotelianism, a strand of thought considered immensely influential on 13th-century scholasticism, although eventually eclipsed by a less Augustinian, purer Aristotelianism filtered through his western Islamic counterpart, *Averroës.

One of his arguments concerning the nature of the soul postulates a full-grown man suddenly coming into existence although suspended in empty space, with eyes covered and limbs separated. This 'flying man' would have no sensation, but nevertheless be aware of his being and his self. The argument anticipates the **cogito* of *Descartes. Avicenna believed that being was an accident of essence, and that contingent beings require necessary causes sustaining their existence. This version of the *cosmological argument was the one accepted by *Aquinas. It is in the theological domain, where he espouses doctrines of creation as a kind of emanation, and of celestial substances as kinds of intelligence, that Neoplatonism surfaces in his work.

avidya (Sanskrit, ignorance) Ignorance of the true nature of reality that keeps us in bondage to *karma.

avowals A *speech act thought of as an expression of a state of mind rather than a description of anything. *Wittgenstein took utterances such as 'I am in pain' or 'I intend to have lunch' not as descriptive of inner, mental states, but as behaviour symptomatic of such states.

awareness, sense *See* CONSCIOUSNESS, EXPERIENCE.

axiarchism The view that values rule or explain the natural order. Things are as they are because that is the way they ought to be. More generally, any view that sees the unfolding of events as subject to a moral causality is a species of axiarchism. *See*, for example, KARMA.

axiology The study of values.

a

axiom A *proposition laid down as one from which we may begin; an assertion that is taken as fundamental, at least for the purposes of the branch of enquiry in hand. The axiomatic method is that of defining a set of such propositions, and the *proof procedures or *rules of inference that are permissible, and then deriving the *theorems that result. It may be thought to be a hallmark of a particularly rigorous or 'scientific' approach to theories to demand that they should be axiomatized; on the other hand a willingness to rethink and challenge even accepted axioms has its own value.

axiomatic method *See* AXIOM.

axiom of choice *See* CHOICE, AXIOM OF.

axiom of comprehension *See* COMPREHENSION, AXIOM OF.

axiom of consistency *See* CONSISTENCY, AXIOM OF.

axiom of extensionality *See* EXTENSIONALITY, AXIOM OF.

axiom of infinity *See* INFINITY, AXIOM OF.

Ayer, Alfred Jules (1910–89) English philosopher and left-wing intellectual. Born of a Swiss father and Belgian mother, Ayer was educated in Britain. After graduating from Oxford in 1932 he studied in Vienna for a year, before returning to teach at Oxford. His exposure to the *logical positivists produced the scintillating and iconoclastic *Language, Truth, and Logic* (1936), which introduced positivism to the wider English-speaking public. It was followed by the *Foundations of Empirical Knowledge* in 1940. After the Second World War Ayer held chairs at University College London, from 1946, and at Oxford from 1959. *The Problem of Knowledge* (1956) has been an influential introduction to that topic. In later years Ayer turned increasingly to the history of philosophy, producing volumes on *Moore and *Russell, *pragmatism, *Hume, and *Voltaire. His philosophy was infused with the empiricism of Hume and the logic of Russell, and inherited both the strengths and weaknesses of those thinkers. Ayer also played a prominent intellectual role in British political life, writing for a wider public and espousing a variety of liberal causes with notable flair and wit. The definitive biography is by Ben Rogers (2002).

Babbage, Charles (1792–1871) English mathematician and mechanical inventor. Babbage has become famous posthumously because he foresaw many of the fundamentals of computing. He designed a 'difference engine' and an 'analytical engine' for the computation of mathematical tables, his machines working on a store (memory) according to a 'mill' or set of operations 'programmed' by punch cards. He also wrote a ninth *Bridgewater treatise, challenging *Hume on miracles.

Bachelard, Gaston (1884–1962) French philosopher of science, largely self-taught, who from 1940 to 1955 was the professor of history and philosophy of science at the Sorbonne in Paris. Bachelard propounds a view of science not as a gradually increasing total body of truth, but as an active dialogue between reason and experiment, in which scientific facts become as much the creation of the rational mind as one of its discoveries. The *philosophie du non* or 'philosophy of negation' in which his conception of scientific progress is encapsulated bears some affinities with the *falsificationism of *Popper, at least in so far as on both theories the scientist stands prepared to dispose of elements of his structure when recalcitrant experience forces him to do so, the result being an increasing consolidation of theory. However, Bachelard's own works explore the dynamics of the imagination from within a psychoanalytic framework. His work was also an influence on *Kuhn, whilst his romantic view of the enquirer extended to works on psychoanalysis, symbol, dream, and poetry, in which realms a person's secret being resides, beyond the reach of thought, laws, and human values. His voluminous works include *La Psychanalyse du feu* (1937, trs. as *The Psychoanalysis of Fire*, 1964).

backward causation The common notion of one event causing another naturally inclines us to think of the cause as earlier and the effect as later. It is, however, unclear why the causal order must in this way comply with the temporal order. The possibility of a cause succeeding its effect in time clearly opens up baffling problems, but none seem to render the idea self-contradictory, and it has been floated as a way of treating some of the phenomena of *quantum mechanics. *See also* CAUSATION.

Bacon, Francis (1561–1626) English statesman and philosopher. As a philosopher of science Bacon is the first notable example of the *empiricist tendency of English thought, but perhaps more importantly the prophet and protector of the dawning scientific revolution. He was a precocious child born into a leading family, and rapidly rose in the law, although not without questionable incident, as when at the behest of Elizabeth I he prosecuted the Earl of Essex, one of his earliest and principal patrons. His legal philosophy was one of absolute duty to the sovereign, which cannot have hindered his rise to the position of Lord Chancellor. In 1620, however, he was disgraced for bribery and spent his remaining years in seclusion. His collected works run to fourteen volumes, and include *Essays* (1597), *The Advancement of Learning* (1605), the *Novum Organon* (1620), and the *New Atlantis* (published posthumously, 1660).

Bacon was the first writer to try to delineate the proper methods of successful science, to enable science to become a craft or industry producing benefits for humanity rather than the haphazard pursuit of occasional eccentrics. Although the 'Baconian method' is sometimes identified with simple *induction by enumeration (the generalizing from instances of phenomena to experimental laws), in fact Bacon provided a sophisticated taxonomy of scientific methods, in most respects anticipating such later results as *Mill's methods, and certainly including an understanding that the search for laws was an imaginative and intellectual rather than a mechanical empirical exercise. His work included a running battle against the false approaches of metaphysics, and against superstition (his own attitude to religion certainly included some sceptical elements, and he regarded the whole matter as unimportant compared to science: 'the research into final causes, like a virgin dedicated to God, is barren and produces nothing'). *Diderot said of Bacon that his work amounted to a map of what men had to learn; he has often been described in terms of a prophet standing on the edge of the promised land of scientific knowledge. *See also* BACONIAN METHOD, IDOLS OF THE MIND.

b

SEE WEB LINKS

- Summaries of Bacon's life and works, with links to other sites
- An archive of Bacon's writings

Bacon, Roger (*c.*1214–92) English philosopher and scientist, known as *Doctor Mirabilis* ('marvellous doctor'). A member of the Franciscan order, Bacon began his career studying the previously forbidden works of *Aristotle. However, he mixed his admiration for science with a relatively uncritical interest in *Neoplatonic, astrological, and occult learning. His principal work is the *Opus Maius* ('Greater Work') detailing the causes that have hindered the progress of philosophy. Shorter works include the *Opus Minus* ('Lesser Work') and *Opus Tertius* ('Third Work'). Bacon's writings show remarkable prescience, particularly in his use of mathematics, his investigations into the science of optics, and a stress on correct use of experience and language, but his work is generally regarded as uneven in quality, mingling uncritical respect for authority with real philosophical and scientific insight. However, he is credited with inventing spectacles. In 1277 Bacon's work was condemned by the Franciscan order for 'suspect novelties' and Bacon is said to have been imprisoned for a time.

Baconian method The method of *induction advocated by Francis *Bacon, especially in Part II of the *Novum Organon*. The aim of science is to establish laws; for this purpose an exhaustive enumeration of instances of phenomena, together with the way in which they vary, and the occurrence of negative instances, must be made. Experiments then test the results that emerge. The method is a forerunner of *Mill's methods. It is sometimes erroneously supposed that the Baconian method is confined to simple enumeration of instances selected in a mechanical fashion, and generalization therefrom.

bad faith The condition highlighted by *Sartre, in which one averts one's gaze from facts, or options and choices, that at some level one knows to exist, but about which it is more convenient to be ignorant. *See also* SELF-DECEPTION.

Bain, Alexander (1818–1903) Scottish philosopher. The self-taught son of a weaver, Bain eventually enrolled in Marischal College, in Aberdeen, and became a radical follower of J. S. *Mill. He was appointed professor of logic and rhetoric at Aberdeen in 1860, and in 1876 founded the journal *Mind*. His main works are *The Senses and the Intellect* (1855), *The Emotions and the Will* (1859), and the later *Manual of Rhetoric* (1870). He is remembered as an *associationist, although in many respects he rejected associationist psychology, and his most original work is probably that on the will. His thought that a belief is but a preparation for action is respected by both *pragmatism and *functionalism.

Bakhtin, Mikhail Mikhailovich (1895–1975) Russian literary theorist and philosopher. An influential opponent of large-scale systems or theories in literary studies, Bakhtin highlighted the contingent, messy, unfinished unfolding of events, especially as they are revealed in the great realistic novels of the nineteenth century. His leading idea was that of the dialogue, an open-ended and indefinitely extensible form, a process that can never be reduced to a single system. His most important work was *Problems of Dostoevsky's Poetics*, originally written in Russian in 1963.

Bakunin, Mikhail Aleksandrovich (1814–76) The most celebrated 19th-century *anarchist, Bakunin was born in Russia of a cultivated and politically committed family. He studied in Moscow, where he came under the influence of the ideas of *Fichte and of the 'new Hegelian' movement, with its emphasis on transformation through revolutionary destruction, a notion that held a permanent romantic appeal for Bakunin. After taking part in various of the 1848–9 revolutions in Europe, Bakunin was imprisoned in Russia, until he contrived to escape and return to Europe by way of the United States in 1861. In 1865 he established the International Brotherhood, a revolutionary and anarchistic society, in Naples. His political philosophy derives much from *Proudhon, although he abjured the individualism of the latter, and was committed to collective ownership of the means of production. His disagreements with *Marx stemmed from his prophetic view that putting the power of the state in the hands of the workers was as bad as putting it anywhere else. Bakunin's principal writings were topical and practical in their intent. They include the *Appeal to the Slavs* (1848), and the *Revolutionary Catechism* (1865), which was the manifesto of the International Brotherhood.

bald man paradox *See* SORITES PARADOX.

Balguy, John (1686–1748) English moral philosopher and theologian. Balguy is remembered principally for his two-part work *The Foundation of Moral Goodness* (1727–8) in which he opposes the *sentimentalism of *Hutcheson, in favour of a rationalist moral theory along the lines of *Cudworth and *Clarke, based on the divinely ordained and rationally discernible fitness of right conduct and virtue.

ball of wax example The example *Descartes uses in the second *Meditation* to show what is essential to bodies. The ball of wax brought near to the fire changes in its sensible properties, but remains the same substance. The only property abiding through all the other changes is extension, which is therefore confirmed as the one essential property of matter.

Bañez, Domingo (1528–1604) Spanish theologian, sometime spiritual adviser to St Teresa of Avila, and commentator on Aristotle and Aquinas. He was an important opponent of Molinism (*see* SCIENTIA MEDIA).

Barbara *See* SYLLOGISM.

barber paradox A village has a barber in it, who shaves all and only the people who do not shave themselves. Who shaves the barber? If he shaves himself, then he does not, but if he does not shave himself, then he does. The paradox is actually just a proof that there is no such barber, or in other words, that the condition is inconsistent. *See also* RUSSELL'S PARADOX.

Barcan formula A fundamental thesis in quantified *modal logic, first isolated by the 20th-century American philosopher Ruth Barcan *Marcus. It was originally the *schema that $\Diamond(\exists x)Ax$ strictly implies $(\exists x)\Diamond Ax$ (informally: if possibly something is A, then something is possibly A). Adding this to a standard modal logic is equivalent to adding $\Diamond(\exists x)Ax \rightarrow (\exists x)\Diamond Ax$ or $(\forall x)\Box Fx \rightarrow \Box(\forall x)Fx$, and either of these may be called the Barcan formula. Informally the latter means that if everything is necessarily F, then necessarily everything is F. The formula has been criticized on the grounds that when we consider possible worlds with different objects in them, then although the antecedent might be true of the actual world, the consequent may be false. For instance, it may be possible that there should be things of a different species from any actual living organism, but not possible of any living organism that it should be of a different species.

bargaining theory The branch of *game theory that treats the rational strategies whereby agreements can be reached, for example on the price to be paid for a commodity.

Bar Hayya, Abraham (*c.*1016–*c.*1136) Jewish writer based in Spain and influenced by Arabic Platonism and Aristotelianism. His leading work was *The Meditation of the Sad Soul.*

Barth, Karl (1886–1968) Protestant theologian, and professor at Bonn and Basel. His doctrines include the denial of the possibility of attaining any knowledge of God by the use of reason (i.e. denial of *natural theology), and renewed stress on the corruptions of sin. Although Barth's outlook on this world was bleak, he also allowed the possibility of redemption for everyone, unlike other *Calvinists. The movement he represents is called crisis theology, or dialectical theology. His principal work was *Die Kirkliche Dogmatik* (*Church Dogmatics*).

Barthes, Roland (1915–80) French literary theorist and philosopher, whose work in *semiotics made him one of the founding fathers of the more general applications of *structuralism, although his own journey took him from Marxism and existentialism, through structuralism to *post-structuralism. He pioneered the study of the meanings behind symbols of mass culture, media, advertising and fashion. His writings include *Mythologies* (1957–72, trs. under the same title, 1972), and *Critique et vérité* (1966, trs. as *Criticism and Truth*, 1987).

base and superstructure The metaphor used by *Marx and *Engels to characterize the relation between the economic organization of society, which is its base, and the political, legal, and cultural organization and social consciousness of a society, which is the superstructure. The sum total of the relations of production of material life 'conditions the social, political, and intellectual life process in general' (Marx, Preface to *A Contribution to the Critique of Political Economy*). The way in which the base determines the superstructure has been the object of much debate, with writers from Engels onwards concerned to distance themselves from the reductionist and mechanistic implications that the metaphor might suggest. It has also been pointed out that relationships involved in production are not merely economic, but involve political and ideological relations. The view that all causal power is centred in the base, with everything in the superstructure merely *epiphenomenal, is sometimes called economism. The problems are strikingly similar to those that arise when the mental is regarded as *supervenient upon the physical, and it is then disputed whether this takes all causal power away from mental properties.

basic action Many actions are done by doing other things: I buy the house by writing the cheque, which I do by signing my name, which I do by writing the individual letters. The idea of a basic action is of that which I just do, but not by doing anything else. It should not be identified with making things happen further and further back in the nervous system: if a person can make a physiological event happen in the brain stem or upper body, it would be by doing such macroscopic things as clenching the fist or blinking, in a situation in which these actions have the effect on the nervous system. This is just to say that the order of explanation of events in terms of actions is not the same as the neurophysiological order of these occurrences.

basic statements *See* PROTOCOL STATEMENTS.

Bataille, Georges (1897–1962) Bleak French essayist and thinker. Bataille's unsystematic work can be characterized as a kind of follow-on from *Nietzsche, concentrating upon the absence of God, the disappearance of the stable subject, and the non-existence of values and identities in modern life. The principal notion is that of 'expenditure', a squandering of force that has no other end but the process itself. Works included *The Inner Experience* (1943) and *Theory of Religion* (1948).

Baudrillard, Jean (1929–2007) French sociologist and critical theorist. A guru of *postmodernism, Baudrillard was best-known as a critic of contemporary culture. His polemical works include *Forget Foucault* (1977, trs. 1989) and *The Gulf War Did Not Take Place* (1991, trs. 1995). The latter is not, as it may sound, a piece of revisionist history, but a meditation on the way in which listeners and viewers are trapped in a maelstrom of stories, scripts, paradigms, and icons determining how the media present events, to the extent that they in effect live in a *virtual reality.

Bauer, Bruno (1809–82) German theologian and leader of the 'young *Hegelians', who became a radical atheist and influence on *Marx.

Baumgarten, Alexander Gottlieb (1714–62) German aesthetician. Baumgarten was born in Berlin and educated at Halle, where he became professor before moving in 1740 to a chair at Frankfurt. He taught a modified *Leibnizian system, very much in the spirit of *Wolff. He is remembered for his introduction of the term 'aesthetics' in the sense, which it retains in *Kant, of the attainment of knowledge by means of the senses. But he also wrote on aesthetics in the narrow sense, insisting on the 'confusion' inherent in the particular experience of beauty, and the importance of 'sensitive representations' as a mode of knowledge independent of reason but not its inferior. His works include the two-volume *Aesthetica* (1750–58).

Bayesianism In statistical theory, Bayesians believe that *Bayes's theorem is fundamental to the assignment of probabilities to hypotheses, and to the rational process of updating credence, or degree of belief in a hypothesis, as new evidence comes in. Non-Bayesians believe its application is extremely limited, often citing the abstract and artificial nature of the prior probabilities that are required. Non-Bayesians usually believe that the process of statistical testing can produce the rational rejection and acceptance of hypotheses of statistical significance with no involvement of prior attitudes. *See also* PERSONALISM.

SEE WEB LINKS

- An introduction to Bayesianism and its applications, with a bibliography
- A list of internet resources on Bayesian statistics

Bayes's theorem Theorem in probability theory. Thomas Bayes (1702–61) was an English clergyman, whose *An Essay towards Solving a Problem in the Doctrine of Chances* occurs in two memoirs presented by *Price (Bayes having died), in *Philosophical Transactions* of 1763 and 1764. Bayes gave a result for the probability that the chance of an event on a single trial is within a certain interval, given the number of times the event has occurred and the number it has failed. But the form in which his theorem is remembered is as an expression for the posterior probability of a hypothesis (its probability after evidence is obtained). This is a product of (i) its probability before the evidence, or prior probability, and (ii) the probability of the evidence being as it is, given the hypothesis, divided by (iii) the prior probability of the evidence (often expressed as the probability of the evidence considered in the light of all the different possible hypotheses).

Bayle, Pierre (1647–1706) French philosopher and sceptic. Born of Protestant parents in the south-west of France, Bayle was educated at Toulouse, became Catholic, lapsed, fled to Geneva, and then became professor in the Protestant academy at Sedan in northern France from 1675 to 1681, in which year he again fled from religious persecution to Holland. He lived in Rotterdam for the rest of his life, writing and corresponding with the philosophers and theologians of his time. His personal experience made him an impassioned defender of religious toleration, and an opponent of pretensions of reason in theological and metaphysical matters. Much of his energy was spent undermining the orthodox *Calvinism of his time, represented by his one-time teacher, Jurieu, ostensibly on behalf of a true Calvinism based on revelation, but arguably in favour of religious *scepticism. His attitude is captured in the remark quoted by Gibbon: 'I am most truly a Protestant; for I protest indifferently against all systems and all sects.' Bayle's critical and sceptical attitudes gained full expression in his masterpiece, the *Dictionnaire historique et critique* (1695–7, trs. as *An Historical and Critical Dictionary*, 1710). In this work, the 'arsenal of the Enlightenment', Bayle combines historical treatments of religious and philosophical figures (most notably secondary and neglected ones) with a pervading scepticism. The dictionary is often witty and profane, and in its own time was notorious for advocating the complete separation of religion and morality, and for gleefully depicting the immoral lives of many people important to the Church. But its more substantial philosophical content made the *Dictionary* a sourcebook for all 18th-century discussions of difficulties with the *Cartesian world view. It contains many of the arguments later deployed by *Berkeley and *Hume, and is undoubtedly the most important contribution to scepticism since *Sextus Empiricus. Famous articles included those on *Pyrrho, *Rorarius (which heads an attack on *Leibniz's theory of pre-established harmony), and *Zeno of Elea (*see* BAYLE'S TRILEMMA).

SEE WEB LINKS

- A list of internet resources on Bayle, including bibliographies

Bayle's trilemma In his famous article on *Zeno of Elea in his *Dictionnaire historique et critique*, *Bayle represents a latter-day Zeno arguing against motion by arguing against the existence of spatial extension. There are three possible theories of spatial extension: (i) space is made of mathematical points, (ii) space is 'granular', made of finite atoms, (iii) space is made of parts that are divisible *in infinitum*. These three exhaust the possible theories, but none of them is tenable. The first demands that a quantity of things with no extension eventually makes up an extension, which is absurd. The second forbids us from recognizing the atoms as having parts, such as left-hand and right-hand edges, but this we must do. The third, Aristotelian, theory improperly shelters behind the notion of a purely potential infinity, forgetting that spatial (and temporal) extension is actual; it also forgets that space is continuous, i.e. its parts touch each other, whereas between any two elements of an infinite series of the kind proposed there is an infinite number of other elements. No two elements touch, any more than any two fractions are 'next to' one another. A modern mathematical treatment of the paradoxes (e.g. Adolf Grünbaum, *Philosophical Problems of Space and Time*, 1963) may be used to show how the first option is tenable since, as it is defined set-theoretically, the sum of any finite or infinite number of dimensionless points need not necessarily be zero. We can assign zero length to unit point sets, and differing finite lengths to the unions or sums of those sets that make up a finite interval. However, the solution requires that we are happy co-ordinating the fundamental points of space with the point sets of the theory, and the way in which space becomes describable in these terms, or in other words the ontological problem that Bayle (or Zeno) is posing, may be felt not to have been addressed. *Kant makes the divisibility of space the subject of the second *antinomy, and a crucial part of his *idealist argument that it is we who organize experience spatially, rather than the world which is constituted of a spatial manifold. *See also* ZENO'S PARADOXES.

Beattie, James (1735–1803) Scottish moralist and theologian. Called by *Hume 'that silly, bigoted fellow Beattie', he was one of Hume's most persistent and virulent critics. He was part of the 'common sense' school centred on Aberdeen, whose most distinguished member was Thomas *Reid. His principal work was *An Essay on the Nature and Immutability of Truth* (1771).

beauty The central place of beauty in *Plato's thought is witnessed in the Dialogues *Phaedrus* and *Symposium*. The perception of beauty induces **anamnesis*, a recollection of previous acquaintance with the universal, the real, or, in a word, the *forms. Beauty is capable of higher and higher manifestations, and once apprehended it induces *eros*, or the passion that drives the soul towards a spiritual ascent, a journey of knowledge combined with *love (*Symposium*, 210A) culminating eventually in a purely intellectual apprehension of beauty, goodness, justice, and wisdom. The connection between physical and intellectual beauty is mediated through the notion of light: there is an intrinsic analogy between the light of reason (or the Good) and the light of the sun, and between physical and intellectual vision. The divinization of light is as old as *Zoroastrianism, reappears in *Heraclitus' conception of the first principle as fire, and is developed in *Neoplatonism, from whence it passes to the medievals. For *Plotinus beauty is not confined to the good or the perfect. The entire sensory world is beautiful, because it is via the embodiment of spiritual forms that light infuses the world of matter. In *Augustine beauty has the function of manifesting the divine: the non-human part of creation wants to make known (*innotescere*) the nature of the divine. In beauty fullness of form radiates from an object; a thing is as it should be in the highest degree (Augustine here connects the Latin for form, *forma*, with beautiful, *formosa*). All creation radiates in this way, and is a reflection or *speculum* of the Divine beauty. The medieval celebration of light and colour, culminating in the poetry of *Dante, marks the continued power of this idea. In the modern era, beauty has become a contested concept in *aesthetics, in the sense that some theorists have seen it as dispensable, and an obstacle to the perception of more detailed aesthetic values such as being sublime, harmonious, graceful, dainty, winsome, elegant. For others it remains the central, unifying concept appropriate to pleasure derived from the senses or from intellectual contemplation. Things of almost any category (persons, elements of nature, and also geometrical figures and mathematical proofs) may be beautiful, and experiencing them as such retains the Platonic associations with value and goodness, and with the 'revelation' of something deep, just as much as with the pleasure that is felt. Discovering how there can be a concept subject to these constraints is the topic of *Kant's *Critique of Judgement*.

Beauvoir, Simone de (1908–86) French *feminist philosopher and novelist. Born in Paris, de Beauvoir studied at the Sorbonne, and became famous when she wrote the classic study of women's oppression *Le Deuxième Sexe* (1949, trs. as *The Second Sex*, 1953). This is the first influential work of feminist philosophy to distinguish between biological sexual difference and the socially imposed categories of gender. Before that her concern was to develop a non-solipsistic, social *existentialism, in which an individual's freedom is only achieved in communication with others equally free. De Beauvoir's long association with *Sartre is not usually regarded as an example of this equality. It culminated in *Les Cérémonies des adieux* (1981, trs. as *Adieux: a Farewell to Sartre*, 1984), an account of the last years of Sartre's life published a year after his death. Autobiographical writings include *Mémoires d'une jeune fille rangée* (1958, trs. as *Memoirs of a Dutiful Daughter*, 1959) and *Une morte très douce* (1964, trs. as *A Very Easy Death*, 1964).

Beccaria, Cesare (1738–94) Italian economist, criminologist, and social reformer. Beccaria's work *Dei delitti e delle pene* (*On Crimes and Punishments*) of 1764 is an early work to have *utilitarianism as its basic principle. It had an immense impact on *Enlightenment circles throughout Europe. He argued for a deterrent and protective theory of punishment, the abolition of the death penalty, and mitigation of the intensity of punishment.

becoming *See* CHANGE.

beetle in the box In the *Philosophical Investigations* §293, *Wittgenstein asks us to imagine a situation in which everyone has a box into which they alone can look. Their activities can include talking about the thing, a beetle, they find in the box, but, claims Wittgenstein, the nature of what is inside the box has no place in the language. That is, it does not matter whether what each person has in their box is the same as that of others, or different, or even whether the box is empty. The nature of what is inside the box 'cancels out'. The example and the claim are part of Wittgenstein's attack on the 'inner theatre' or *Cartesian concept of our own privileged access to our mental states. But the analogy seems imperfectly adapted to Wittgenstein's purpose, since in the beetle case there is a sameness or difference of beetle, whether or not the people can communicate it (for this is how the case is specified), and this appears to accord well with the Cartesian theory that Wittgenstein opposed. Such theories are frequently happy with the *ineffable nature of private mental occurrences. But the example comes at the end of Wittgenstein's extended treatment of the *private language argument, which may be thought to have already closed off the possibility of any such theory.

begging the question The procedure of assuming what is at issue in an argument. Although the charge is commonly made, there is no logical definition of those kinds of argument that beg the question. In the widest sense, any *valid argument might be thought to beg the question, since its premises already 'contain' its conclusion. Yet valid arguments can and do move reasonable people to accept their conclusions. The best definition is that an argument begs the question if it contains a definite premise or move that would not be accepted by any reasonable person who is initially prone to deny the conclusion.

behaviourism In psychology behaviourism, associated with *Watson and such researchers as Ivan Pavlov (1849–1936), was first of all a methodological view, counselling the avoidance of introspection and the *subjective in favour of the scientific measurement of behaviour and its causes. In later hands, particularly those of B. F. Skinner (1904–1990), the view became identified with a simplistic vision of the springs of human action, and with the prospect of control of action by relatively simple manipulation of the stimuli and patterns of reinforcement that are allowed to impinge on an agent. Skinner's belief that the explanation of behaviour through belief, intention, and desire is somehow unscientific, or the preserve of 'mentalists', has also lost ground to the development of *cognitive studies.

Philosophically the doctrine of behaviourism is that mental states are *logical constructions out of dispositions to behaviour, or in other words, that describing the mental aspects of a person is a shorthand for describing the various dispositions to behaviour that the person possesses. The most influential work promoting this point of view was *The Concept of Mind* (1949) by *Ryle which urged behaviourism as the best defence against the *Cartesian myth of the '*ghost in the machine'. The extent to which *Wittgenstein, writing the

Philosophical Investigations at the same time, intended to promote a behaviourist doctrine is subject to dispute. Like other *reductionist doctrines behaviourism fell foul of the difficulty of providing workable analyses, notably because of the *holism of the mental, or the fact that how a person behaves is not a function of one belief or one desire, but of a whole field or network of beliefs and desires. The modification to take care of this turns behaviourism into its more popular modern successor, *functionalism.

behaviour therapy An offspring of *behaviourism, in which underlying cognitive states are ignored, but behaviour is itself rewarded or punished with different stimuli, in order to encourage or suppress it.

being Everything real and nothing unreal belongs to the domain of Being. But there is little useful that can be said about everything that is real, especially from within the philosopher's study, so it is not apparent that there can be such a subject as Being by itself. Nevertheless the concept has a central place in philosophy from *Parmenides to *Heidegger. The central question of 'why is there something and not nothing?' prompts logical reflection on what it is for a *universal to have an instance, and a long history of attempts to explain contingent existence by reference to a necessary ground. In the tradition since *Plato this ground becomes a self-sufficient, perfect, unchanging, and eternal something, identified with the Good or God, but whose relation with the everyday world remains obscure (*see* COSMOLOGICAL ARGUMENT, ONTOLOGICAL ARGUMENT, PRINCIPLE OF PLENITUDE). Modern logic gives little comfort to these speculations, and prompts suspicion that the question of why there is something and not nothing is either ill-formed or profitless, since any intelligible answer will merely invite the same question. A central mistake in the area is to treat Being as a noun that identifies a particularly deep subject-matter. This is parallel to treating *Nothing as a name of a particular thing, perhaps an object of dread or fear. The modern logical treatment of these notions by means of *quantifiers and *variables provides a defence against this error and others. The less abstract part of the study of being concerns the kinds of things whose existence we have to acknowledge: abstract entities, possibilities, numbers, and so on, and disputes over their reality form the subject of *ontology.

being, hierarchy of *See* CHAIN OF BEING, PLENITUDE.

being in-itself/for-itself A contrast heralded in the phenomenology of *Husserl and *Heidegger, and central to *Sartre's work *Being and Nothingness.* Being for-itself (*pour-soi*) is the mode of existence of consciousness, consisting in its own activity and purposive nature; being in-itself (*en-soi*) is the self-sufficient, lumpy, contingent being of ordinary things. The contrast bears some affinity to *Kant's distinction between the perspective of agency or freedom and that of awareness of the ordinary phenomenal world.

belief To believe a proposition is to hold it to be true. The philosophical problem is to understand what kind of state of a person constitutes belief. Is it, for example, a simple disposition to behaviour? Or a more complex state that resists identification with any such disposition? Is verbal skill or verbal behaviour essential to belief, in which case what is to be said about prelinguistic infants, or nonlinguistic animals? An evolutionary approach asks how the cognitive success of possessing the capacity to believe things relates to success in practice. Further topics include discovering whether belief differs from other varieties of assent, such as *acceptance, discovering whether belief is an all-or-nothing matter, or to what extent degrees of belief are possible, understanding the ways in which belief is controlled by rational and irrational factors, and discovering its links with other properties, such as the possession of conceptual or linguistic skills.

belief, ethics of *See* CLIFFORD.

Bell's theorem Bell's Interconnectedness theorem, proved by the physicist John Bell in 1964, asserts that no local model of reality can do justice to the facts of *quantum behaviour. A local model of reality is one in which all causal connections propagate by signals that travel at less than the speed of light. Bell showed that quantum mechanics describes correlations that cannot be explained by a local model. The theorem considers a set-up which is a variation on that of the *Einstein–Podolsky–Rosen thought experiment, and proves that if reality is local, we would expect certain defined measurements to show a certain inequality (the Bell inequality). But in fact the experimental results are otherwise, suggesting a conflict with relativity theory, which appears to require locality. Interpreters disagree whether the conflict is real—for example, perhaps one should say that the correlations are unexplained brute facts.

bellum omnium contra omnes Latin: the war of all against all, a phrase especially associated with Thomas *Hobbes's description of the *state of nature.

benevolence General desire for the good of others, and disposition to act so as to further that good. Moral philosophers may be more or less optimistic about the intensity and scope of such desire, or its general presence in human nature. *See* ALTRUISM, EGOISM.

b

Benjamin, Walter (1892–1940) A leading literary critic and member of the *Frankfurt school. Benjamin is remembered for his analyses of the material conditions governing literary and artistic production.

Bentham, Jeremy (1748–1832) English philosopher of law, language, and ethics. Born in London, Bentham was educated at Oxford, and studied law, for which he developed a profound mistrust. His major preoccupation became the flimsy theoretical foundations of law and the abuses to which the law gives rise. His first important publication, *A Fragment on Government* (1776), was a small part of his enormous *Comment* on the *Commentaries* of the jurist Blackstone, the classic statement of the conservative legal theory that was one of Bentham's principal aversions. The main theoretical work Bentham published during his lifetime was the *Introduction to the Principles of Morals and Legislation* (1789). Bentham was the founder of *utilitarianism, and made famous the formula that the proper end of action is to achieve the greatest happiness of the greatest number. Much of his work tried to elaborate that doctrine and to show how utilitarianism could be developed into a calculus of pleasures (a hedonic or *felicific calculus) whereby the effects of actions could be judged and right policy thereby identified. Utilitarianism was to provide a coherent and rational foundation for social and legal policy, whereas such fictions as natural *rights, the *social contract, and natural law served only to introduce incoherent and indefensible systems privileging some set of 'intuitions'. Bentham's concern with law included a far-reaching critique of the abstractions and fictions within which law is often couched, and a penetrating understanding of the ways words force attitudes on the things they denote. He promoted a generally *nominalistic and *pragmatic theory of language, while his conception of definition by paraphrasis anticipates *Frege in holding that the fundamental unit of meaning is not the individual word, but the sentence in which it occurs.

Bentham exercised enormous influence as the leader of a like-minded group of 'philosophical radicals', a group that included James and John Stuart *Mill. He founded the *Westminster Review* as a counterpoise to the more conservative journals of the time, and was also the founder of University College London, where his embalmed body, topped by a wax head, is still revealed on special occasions.

SEE WEB LINKS

- Website of the Bentham Project at University College London, with a biography, bibliographies, and images of Bentham
- Biography of Bentham with a list of on- and offline resources

Bentley, Richard (1662–1742) Pugnacious Yorkshire classicist. The great textual critic and controversial Master of Trinity College, Cambridge, is known to philosophy through the first Boyle lectures of 1692, entitled 'A confutation of atheism' and intended both to introduce *Newton's mechanics, and to use it as a springboard for *natural theology, especially in refutation of atheists such as *Hobbes. A second series of lectures given two years later is now lost. Bentley's other philosophical work is *Remarks on a late Discourse of Freethinking*, an answer to the *deist Anthony *Collins.

Berdyaev, Nikolai (1874–1948) A Russian thinker better known for the religious consequences he drew from his metaphysics than for his philosophical thought itself. Berdyaev was forced to resign from his chair at Moscow in 1922, and worked in Paris until his death. He taught a doctrine of communal religion, in which spiritual and creative freedom is achieved, ideally, in communion with others.

Bergmann, Gustav (1906–87) Austrian philosopher and junior member of the *Vienna circle, who taught at Iowa for many years. Bergmann tried to develop a systematic *ontology, opposed to materialism, and based on the properties of momentary particular things. These include relations and *intentionality. Books included *Meaning and Existence* (1959) and *New Foundations of Ontology* (1992).

Bergson, Henri-Louis (1859–1941) French philosopher and evolutionist. Born in Paris, in 1900 Bergson became professor at the Collège de France, and held the post until 1921. His fluent and accessible works with their uplifting spiritual content led to many honours in France, and the Nobel prize for literature in 1927. Bergson's philosophy was hostile to materialism and mechanism, and while embracing evolution saw it as driven by a creative force or original impetus of life (the **élan vital*) rather than the blind operation of natural selection. His 'dynamism' focuses upon the continuous nature of experience, and the artificial nature of the divisions we impose with the intellect; the flow of life becomes the prime datum falsified by mechanistic and scientistic philosophies. This flow is an active, melting process or 'pure' time, quite different from the abstract time of natural science. This difference recurs in Bergson's analysis of memory, which retains the whole of the past in the present, with the brain acting as a kind of censor, selecting only those apprehensions of the past that are useful for the present occasion. In an analogous manner the theories of natural science, which purport to be complete theories of reality, are better seen as partial and limited reflections of the way the mind functions. In spite of the sweep of Bergson's philosophy the spiritual, indeed rhapsodic, aspect of his work has not stood the test of time, nor does the spiritual interpretation of evolution fare well against modern developments. His books included *Matière et mémoire* (1896, trs. as *Matter and Memory*, 1911), *Le Rire: essai sur la signification du comique* (1900, trs. as *Laughter: an Essay on the Meaning of the Comic*, 1921), and *L'Évolution créatrice* (1907, trs. as *Creative Evolution*, 1911).

Berkeley, George (1685–1753) Irish *idealist. Born at Kilkenny in Ireland, Berkeley entered Trinity College, Dublin in 1700. In 1707 he became a Fellow of the College and two years later published *An Essay towards a New Theory of Vision* (his *Philosophical Commentaries* were unpublished notes of the years before 1709). This was followed by the first (and only extant) part of *A Treatise concerning the Principles of Human Knowledge* (1710) and the *Three Dialogues between Hylas and Philonous* (1713), which was an attempt to explain the doctrines of the earlier work in a more readily understood form. Berkeley moved to London and spent much of the next decade travelling in France and Italy. However, the fact that he was in London in 1715 seems to disprove the story that it was a fit of apoplexy, brought on by arguing with Berkeley, that carried off the philosopher *Malebranche. In 1721 Berkeley published *De Motu* ('On Motion') attacking *Newton's philosophy of space, a topic he returned to much later in *The Analyst* of 1734. In 1724 he entered with enthusiasm on a project for founding a College in Bermuda, for the Christian education of both colonial and indigenous people of America. With his new wife he set sail westward in 1728, arriving and settling in Rhode Island. While there he corresponded with the American philosopher Samuel *Johnson, and wrote *Alciphron*, which was eventually published in 1732. Government support promised for his educational project never materialized, and Berkeley returned to London in 1732, and was made Bishop of Cloyne in 1734. Thenceforth his publications concerned the well-being of the people of his diocese, although *Siris* (1744) contains discussions of the philosophy of nature, as is promised by its full title (*A Chain of Philosophical Reflexions and Inquiries concerning the Virtues of Tar-Water, and divers other subjects connected together and arising from one another*). He died in Oxford.

Berkeley is notorious for his immaterialism, or apparent denial of the reality of any external world, with the consequent shrinking of reality down to a world of minds and their own sensations or 'ideas'. The theme of the impossibility of 'inert senseless matter', and the merits of a scheme based on a pervading, all-wise providence whose production is the conceptual world, the world of ideas, that make up our lives, runs through all Berkeley's writing. What he saw and emphasized with great rigour was the impossibility of bridging the gap opened up by the *Cartesian split between mind and matter. Berkeley's target is the comfortable, common-sense view of mind as entirely different from matter, yet in satisfactory contact with a material world about which it can know a great deal. He deploys many of the arguments of ancient *scepticism, and others found in Malebranche and *Bayle, to undermine this synthesis, showing that once the separation of mind from the material world is as complete as *Descartes makes it, the hope of knowing or understanding anything about the supposed external world quite vanishes. A relationship of resemblance, for example, whereby our ideas can be taken to resemble qualities in things that give rise to them, is unknowable and unintelligible. Unlike Cartesian scepticism, which stresses the bare possibility of things not being as we take them to be, Berkeley urges the actual inconsistencies within the conceptual scheme left by Cartesianism, that entrap such thinkers as *Locke (and, arguably, common sense itself). His way out is not to advocate scepticism, which he consistently regards with extreme repugnance, but to reformat the relation between mind and the world so that contact is re-established. Unfortunately this introduces subjective idealism, in which what the subject apprehends as the world is just the relationship between the subject's own mental states (plus an uneasy relationship with archetypes of the subject's ideas in the mind of God). In promoting his system Berkeley makes brilliant use of the sceptical problems that will bedevil alternatives, as well as of the problems faced by particular elements of the conceptual scheme he opposes: problems of causation, substance, perception, and understanding. Although his system has proved incredible to virtually all subsequent philosophers, its importance lies in the challenge it offers to a common sense that vaguely hopes that these notions fit together in a satisfactory way.

SEE WEB LINKS

- An audio discussion of Berkeley by three philosophers
- A list of internet resources on Berkeley, including bibliographies

Berlin, Isaiah (1909–97) British political philosopher and historian. Born in Latvia and educated at Corpus Christi College, Oxford, Berlin held Fellowships at All Souls and New College, before becoming President of Wolfson College, Oxford, from 1966 to 1975. He is best known in political philosophy for the distinction between negative and positive liberty, drawn in his *Two Concepts of*

Liberty (1959): that is, although any statement about liberty ought to specify both what one is free to do (positive) and what one is free from in doing it (negative), nevertheless different political philosophies give the one much more importance than the other. Thus *liberalism dwells on the virtues of being free from legal and social constraint; *idealist and *Hegelian theories stress that the most important kinds of freedoms and opportunities can only exist in a structured society, so that the constraints needed to produce such societies may be a necessary means to the best ends. Berlin also energetically opposed the value-free, *historicist view of history of *Marxism, notably in *Historical Inevitability* (1954).

Bernard, St (1090–1153) The founder of the abbey of Clairvaux in France, and the major force behind the Cistercian order, Bernard is remembered in philosophy principally for his opposition to *Abelard, although he also wrote *De Gratia et Libro Arbitrio* ('Of Grace and Free Will') which links him with *Augustine. His mystical and unanalytic approach to problems of faith is remembered in his title of *Doctor Mellifluus* ('the sweet-sounding doctor').

Bernard of Chartres (*fl.* 1114–26) Influential teacher of classical philosophy, especially Plato. Only fragments of Bernard's works survive. He is best known for the saying that he and others were 'dwarves sitting on the shoulders of giants'.

Bernoulli's theorem Title used for the 'law of large numbers' in probability theory, proved by Jakob Bernoulli (1654–1705). The theorem provides the best-known link between probability and the frequency of occurrence of events in a sequence of trials. It is thus fundamental to the epistemology of probability. Bernoulli showed that if we have a sequence of n trials, on each of which an outcome has probability p, then the most probable number of times the event occurs is pn (or the nearest integer to this); furthermore for any small number e, the probability that the frequency of occurrence falls within the interval $np \pm e$ increases with n, and approaches 1 as n approaches infinity.

Berry's paradox The phrases of a language that refer to numbers can be ordered, alphabetically and according to length. There will be a definite set of integers named by those phrases of less than any given length. In particular there will be some integer which is the least integer not nameable in fewer than nineteen syllables. But this phrase 'the least integer not nameable in fewer than nineteen syllables' then names this number, yet itself contains fewer than nineteen syllables. Berry's paradox is of the same family as the *Liar and other semantic paradoxes.

Bertrand's box paradox There are three boxes, one with two gold coins, one with one gold and one silver, one with two silver. A coin drawn at random is gold. What is the probability that the other coin in the same box is gold? The coin came either from the first box, or the second; there is no reason for preferring either, so the chance should be a half. But the coin picked was either the first in the first box, or the second in the first box, or the one gold coin in the second box. Two of these three possibilities give it that the other coin in the same box is gold, so the probability is ⅔.

Bertrand's paradox Paradox described in the *Calcul des probabilités* (1889) of the French probabilist J. Bertrand (1822–1900). What is the probability that a chord drawn at random in a circle is longer than the side of an equilateral triangle whose three corners touch the circle? It is longer if its midpoint falls nearer the circumference than the centre of a radius bisecting it, so the probability is ½. Keeping one end of the chord fixed, it is longer if the angle at which it is drawn is within the 60° arc of the triangle, so the probability is ⅓. Or, it is longer if its midpoint lies in the area of the inner circle with radius one half of the original; this circle occupies one quarter of the area of the original, so the chance is ¼. Bertrand used the paradox to show that there is no unique best way of applying the *principle of indifference to such a case.

best, principle of the *See* BEST OF ALL POSSIBLE WORLDS.

best explanation, inference to *See* EXPLANATION.

best of all possible worlds The celebrated view of *Leibniz, parodied by *Voltaire in *Candide*, that the actual world is the best of all possible worlds: anything else would be inconsistent with the omnipotence and benevolence of the Creator.

Beth's definability theorem A theorem for classical *first-order logic. A theory implicitly defines a non-logical term T if any two *models of the theory with the same domain, and the same extensions for other primitive terms, have the same extension for T. Beth's theorem states that a non-logical term T is implicitly defined by the theory if and only if an explicit definition of the term (one giving necessary and sufficient conditions for its application in terms of other primitives) is deducible from the theory. It therefore connects the proof theory of such a logic to its *model theory.

Bhagavad Gita (Sanskrit, *gita*, song, *Bhagavat*, of the blessed one) The poem forming the part of the Indian epic the *Mahabharata*, composed between the 5th century BC and the 2nd century AD, in which Krishna, as a charioteer, explains to Arjuna ('Everyman') the nature of human life and its purpose, and the way to achieve the good life.

bhakti (Sanskrit, worship) The devotion due to God, the blessed one (*Bhagavat*).

biconditional A proposition of the form 'if p then q and if q then p'. It is standardly written p iff q.

bijection *See* FUNCTION, LOGICAL.

binary operation A *function of two arguments. Addition is a binary operation, i.e. $x+y$ is a function from the two numbers x, y, to a third number, which is their sum.

binary relation A relation with two terms, expressed by a two-place predicate.

bioethics The branch of ethics that investigates problems specifically arising from medical and biological practice. These include problems of the nature and distribution of treatment; the sphere of authority of the patient, the physician, and others; the scope and limits of confidentiality; the limits of acceptable intervention and experimentation (*see* ABORTION, EUTHANASIA); and the propriety of genetic research and its applications.

SEE WEB LINKS

- A list of internet resources on bioethics
- An archive of writings on medical ethics

biology, philosophy of As a special science biology prompts the general philosophical problem of how its explanations relate to those of underlying chemistry, or even fundamental physics. Biology also raises acute questions of its own. One is whether the theoretical taxonomies or principles of classification of living things into species and families reflect real differences, or are reflections of conventions. Another focus of philosophical interest is the notion of a biological *function. The notion of the function of an organ has sometimes been dismissed as a remnant of the Aristotelian notion of a final *cause, although currently most writers are optimistic about defining it in terms of a trait that is responsible for the differential evolutionary success of the organisms possessing it. Among other controversial questions is that of biological reductionism, or the attempt to explain psychological, social, and cultural phenomena in biological terms. *See also* EVOLUTION, SOCIOBIOLOGY.

bit Abbreviation of 'binary digit'. The amount of information obtained by asking a yes-or-no question; a computational quantity that can take on one of two values, such as false and true or 0 and 1.

bivalence, principle of (bivalence, law of) The law of classical logic that every proposition is either true or false: that is, there are just two values a proposition may take. More than other basic laws of logic, its status and truth have proved highly controversial, because of problems associated with vagueness, because it seems incompatible with *constructivism, and because of the problems raised by the *semantic paradoxes.

black box theory An understanding of something entirely in terms of its function. This leaves on one side the question of what the mechanism is that enables it to perform that function. The thing is treated as a black box whose workings are invisible. A black box theory of science, for example, would treat a scientific theory simply as a formalism, or a mere device for delivering predictions from data; a black box theory of the mind would take it that the mind is exhaustively understood once we know which inputs yield which outputs.

Blackstone, William (1723–80) English jurist educated at Pembroke College, Oxford, and subsequently Vinerian Professor of Law at Oxford. His historical treatise on the common law, *Commentaries on the Laws of England*, was first published in four volumes over 1765–9. He is remembered in philosophy chiefly as a central target of Jeremy *Bentham.

blindsight The phenomenon in which a patient has no conscious visual experience in some direction, yet functions much better than a blind person could in various tasks involving the spatial location of objects in that region. Philosophically, the syndrome illustrates the complexities of mental processes that may occur somewhere below the conscious threshold.

Bloch, Ernst Simon (1885–1977) German Marxist philosopher, notable for a doctrine of hope, or utopianism, that attempted to incorporate religious strivings into a fundamentally materialist world view. His major work was the eclectic mixture *The Principle of Hope* (1959).

block universe theory of time The view that reality is in some sense timeless. It is completely captured by description in terms of *McTaggart's *b-series, or in other words reference to present, past, and future is inessential to the true scientific and metaphysical world view.

Our propensity to think in those terms is explained away as the result of subjective, perspectival pressures.

b

Blondel, Maurice (1861–1949) French Christian existentialist, interested in human action and its primacy to thought as an indicator of the divine.

Bobbio, Norberto (1909–2004) Foremost Italian philosopher of law and politics. He taught jurisprudence at the University of Camerino, then at Siena, and was appointed to a chair at Padua in 1940. In 1948, he became professor of legal philosophy at Turin, where he remained until 1972. A *positivist in spirit, his works included *A Theory Of Judicial Norms* (1958), *A Theory Of The Legal Order* (1960), and studies of Locke, Kant, and legal positivism. Between 1955 and 1970, he also published three collections of essays. These writings had a similar place in Italian academic legal circles to the work of H. L. A. *Hart in English jurisprudence.

Bodin, Jean (*c.*1529–96) French political philosopher. Bodin advocated absolute sovereignty as the only effective guarantee of peace in the State, a doctrine anticipating *Hobbes. His main work was *Six livres de la république* (1576/7).

body The body is often contrasted unfavourably with the mind, and in Pythagorean, Indian, and Christian traditions bodily residence is a kind of penance compared with the full joy of purely spiritual existence. However most 20th-century philosophy has acknowledged, at least in principle, that embodiment is a necessary condition of a mental life: our bodies are not just parts of the world external to our minds. A proper account of the nature of our perception of our own bodies, and the place of our bodies in perceiving other things, has been most resolutely pursued by *phenomenologists, particularly by *Merleau-Ponty (*Phenomenology of Perception*, 1962, Part 1). In this approach perception of the body and by means of the body is not passive reception of experience from a point of view 'inside' the head, but an active, living synthesis of movement and awareness of space: 'experience of one's own body runs counter to the reflective procedure which detaches subject and object from each other.'

Boehme (Behmen), Jacob (1575–1624) German mystic, whose vision of God as the undifferentiated Absolute (the *Ungrund*), and opposition to formal and biblical statements of religious doctrine, influenced both the Quakers and German *Romantics, particularly *Schelling. The unromantic Dr Johnson remarked of him that if Jacob saw the unutterable, Jacob should not have attempted to utter it.

Boethius, Anicius Manlius Severinus (*c.*475/80–525/6) Roman philosopher and theologian. Born in Rome of an aristocratic family, the son of a consul (and father of two more), Boethius served as consul and the principal minister for Theodoric the Ostrogoth, who ruled Italy from 493 to 526. However, he fell out of favour, was exiled and imprisoned at Pavia, and executed a year later. It was while he was in prison that he wrote his masterpiece, *De Consolatione Philosophiae* (*On the Consolations of Philosophy*), but before that he had written extensively on mathematics, science, logic, and theology. His translations included *Aristotle's *Categories, Prior Analytics, Posterior Analytics, Topics*, and *Sophistical Refutations*, whilst his translation of *Porphyry's *Introduction* (*Isagoge*) to the *Categories* of Aristotle, together with his own commentaries, became the standard textbook for medieval logic, and initiated the enduring medieval controversy over the nature of *universals. His own solution to the problem as it is raised by Porphyry, that universals 'subsist in sensible things, but they are understood apart from bodies', is Aristotelian, although there is also evidence that he inclined towards a more robust *Platonism.

The *Consolations of Philosophy*, one of the most influential books of the Middle Ages, is a dialogue between Boethius, who writes in prose, and a personified Philosophy, who answers in verse. It divides into discussions of the fundamental purpose of the universe, the unreliability of fortune and the false promise of many ways of trying to achieve happiness, the goodness of God, and the compatibility of human freedom with his foreknowledge. This last leads Boethius to investigate the nature of time and the nature of God. The work is not, however, Christian in spirit, but more concerned with God as an abstract or Platonic idea: Boethius inclines to a kind of *pantheism in which those who are happy or blessed participate in God. Its classical calm and freedom from sectarianism and superstition, coupled with the circumstances of its composition, give the *Consolations* an unmistakable moral authority.

SEE WEB LINKS

- A biography of Boethius
- A list of internet resources on Boethius, including a bibliography

Bogdanov, Alexandr Alexandrovich (1873–1928) Significant early theorist of Bolshevism, whose work was attacked by *Lenin in 1909. He sought to combine *Marxism with the empiriocriticism of *Avenarius and *Mach.

Bohr, Niels (1885–1962) Danish physicist and Nobel prizewinner, remembered philosophically as the founder of the *Copenhagen interpretation of *quantum theory. This *anti-realist interpretation of the quantum world accorded with Bohr's more general views of the *perspectival and partial nature of complementary understandings of the world.

Boltzmann, Ludwig (1844–1906) Austrian physicist and philosopher of science. Boltzmann sought to integrate physics with the philosophy of science, opposing both the *a priori*, uninformed speculations of philosophers, and the philosophically indifferent approaches of many physicists. His emphasis on the open-ended hypothetical nature of theorizing strikingly anticipates the *falsificationism of *Popper, whilst his connection between the direction of time and the increasing entropy of a universe in which some states can be achieved in more ways than others, is still one of the major contributions to the problem of *time's arrow.

SEE WEB LINKS

- A biography of Boltzmann, with a bibliography
- A summary of Boltzmann's scientific contributions, with links to related issues

Bolzano, Bernard (1781–1848) Moral philosopher and epistemologist. Born in Prague of Italian and German parents, Bolzano became a doctor of mathematics in 1804, and a priest a year later. In his own time he was influential as a socialist and *utopian moral philosopher. His logical work is based on a strong sense of there being an ontological underpinning of science and epistemology, lying in a theory of the objective entailments making up the structure of scientific theories.

Bonaventure, St (*c.*1217/21–74) Italian Franciscan theologian, later dubbed *Doctor Seraphicus* ('the seraphic doctor'). He is remembered in philosophy as an opponent of the rationalism prevalent in the theology of his time, and an upholder of the necessity of revelation and return to a spiritual union with God.

boo-hooray theory Pejorative name for the *emotivist theory of ethics.

Boole, George (1815–64) English mathematician and logician. Born in Lincoln and educated locally, Boole worked as a schoolmaster until he gained recognition as a mathematician, and became professor at Queen's College, Cork, Ireland, in 1849. His pamphlet *The Mathematical Analysis of Logic* (1847) pioneered the assimilation of logic to mathematics, or the algebra of classes. The work was continued in *An Investigation of the Laws of Thought* (1854). Boole also published many works in pure mathematics, and on the theory of probability. His name is remembered in the title of *Boolean algebra, and the algebraic operations he investigated are denoted by Boolean operators.

Boolean algebra A Boolean algebra is a system consisting of a set S and two operations, $\cap$ and $\cup$ (cap and cup), subject to the following axioms. For all sets a,b,c, that are members of S:

1 $a \cap (b \cap c) = (a \cap b) \cap c$.
Also $a \cup (b \cup c) = (a \cup b) \cup c$
(associativity)
2 $a \cap b = b \cap a$.
Also $a \cup b = b \cup a$ (commutativity)
3 $a \cap (b \cup c) = (a \cap b) \cup (a \cap c)$.
Also $a \cup (b \cap c) = (a \cup b) \cap (a \cup c)$
(distributivity)
4 There belong to S two elements, 0 and 1, with the properties
$a \cup 0 = a$; $a \cap 1 = a$ (identity)
5 For each set a in S there exists a set a′ with the properties that $a \cup a' = 1$, $a \cap a' = 0$ (complementation).

The propositional calculus can be represented as a Boolean algebra, with $\cap$ representing &, $\cup$ representing $\vee$, and 1 = T, 0 = F. The Boolean operators are then the *truth functors, such as &, $\vee$, and $\neg$. A Boolean search is a search for things meeting a condition defined with these operators.

SEE WEB LINKS

- An historical introduction to Boolean algebra
- An online tutorial on Boolean algebra

borderline case A case falling within the grey area or twilight zone of application of some term. Within classical logic it is not easy to understand and formalize the pervasive possibility of such cases. *See* SORITES PARADOX, VAGUENESS.

Borgès, Jorge Luis (1899–1986) Argentinian writer whose imaginative works often centred on philosophical themes of memory, time, authenticity, and fate. The first collection of these stories was *The Garden of Forking Paths* (1941) followed by *Artifices* and retitled *Ficciones* in 1944. Borges was a founding figure of the 'magical realist' movement in South American fiction, and of *postmodernism in literature.

Bosanquet, Bernard (1848–1923) English *absolute idealist. Bosanquet was educated and taught at Oxford, left in order to involve himself in charity work in London, and finally held the chair of moral philosophy at St Andrews, Scotland. He held a view of the individual as a social entity whose realization involved absorption into the

b

social and cultural activities of others. The priority of social wholes, and their necessity to the full existence of a single individual, is a reversal of classical liberal priorities, described by Bosanquet as based on the 'pathos and bathos of sentimentalism'. His works include *Knowledge and Reality* (1885), *Logic* (1888), *History of Aesthetics* (1892), numerous translations from German, and works on social and ethical issues.

Boscovich, Roger Joseph (1711–87) Jesuit mathematician and scientist. Born in Dubrovnik of Serbian and Italian parents, Rudjer Josip Bošković was educated at Rome, and became professor of mathematics at the Collegium Romanum in 1740. He contributed extensively to different branches of mathematics and physics, but his philosophical fame rests on *Philosophiae Naturalis Theoria Redacta ad Unicam Legem Virium in Natura Existentium* ('A Theory of Natural Philosophy Reduced to a Single Law of the Actions Existing in Nature', 1758, trs. as *Theory of Natural Philosophy*, 1922). In this work Boscovich rejects the corpuscular theory that bases physics on the actions of impenetrable, inelastic, solid, massy atoms. Instead, following some of Leibniz's objections to this conception, he develops a theory of *puncta*, or point particles, interacting with each other according to an oscillatory law. There is nothing to the existence of a point particle except the kinematic forces with which it is associated. Boscovich's views were influential on scientists such as Michael *Faraday and James Clerk Maxwell and provided a forerunner of modern *field theories. *See also* ACTION AT A DISTANCE, CORPUSCULARIANISM, FIELD.

bound variable A *variable x is bound in a formula if it is within the scope of a *quantifier (in *first order logic, $(\forall x)$ or $(\exists x)$). Intuitively this means that as the formula is evaluated and x in this occurrence is assigned to an object, the quantified expression in which it occurs is evaluated with respect to that object. If a variable is not bound it is free. In $(\forall x)(Fx \rightarrow Gx)$ all the variables are bound. In $(\forall x)(Fx \rightarrow Gx)$ & Gx the final occurrence of the variable x is free, so the expression is an open sentence or *predicate. To turn it into a closed sentence one must either replace the variable with a constant or closed term referring to a thing, or extend the scope of the initial quantifier, or introduce another quantifier: $(\forall x)(Fx \rightarrow Gx)$ & $(\exists x)(Gx)$, for example.

Bourbaki, Nicolas The pseudonym for a group of French mathematicians that since 1939 has produced a multi-volume rigorous axiomatic treatment of mathematical structures.

bourgeoisie/proletariat The bourgeoisie is defined by *Engels as the class of capitalists, who own the means of social production and are the employers of wage labour. In this sense the bourgeoisie does not include the intermediate middle class, whose labour is supervisory and intellectual. The proletariat or working class is in *Marxism the political force that will destroy capitalism and effect the transition to socialism. Marxists associated with the *Frankfurt school came to deplore the non-revolutionary conservatism of western working classes and their gradual absorption into a growing middle class, and to put faith in other sources of revolution. The terms in their Marxist senses may appear somewhat dated, as society has changed so that the means of production are no longer generally owned by individuals, but by corporations, pension funds, and so forth, with a wider dispersion of shares. However, the extent to which this change disguises a concentration of real power in the hands of a few owners is also debated.

Boyle, Robert (1627–92) Irish scientist. Born the fourteenth son of the first earl of Cork, Boyle was able to pursue an independent life devoted to scientific and academic matters. He was the most important British chemist of his time, whose work on gases is remembered in Boyle's law. He was an important figure in the 17th-century rejection of Aristotelian emphases on *final causes, believing that all the properties of materials can be explained by the size, shape, and motion of particles, and the textures to which their associations give rise. His major work was *The Sceptical Chemist* (1661), but he wrote widely not only on chemical but on philosophical and theological matters. His *General History of the Air* was published in 1692. His conception of the qualities of things, and the division between primary and secondary qualities, was a major influence on *Locke.

bracketing Term used by *Husserl to describe the process of thinking away the natural interpretation of an experience in order to concentrate on its intrinsic nature or phenomenology. Also known as *epochē*.

Bradley, Francis Herbert (1846–1924) British *absolute idealist. Educated at Oxford, Bradley was awarded a Fellowship at Merton College that gave him complete leisure for his studies and writing: it is said that he only visited Oxford during the vacations. He was the major British absolute idealist, owing much to the influence at Oxford of *Green. His *Ethical Studies* (1876) is a polemical and fertile attack on *utilitarianism, largely on the grounds that the self-sufficient individual that it requires does not exist: individuals gain their identities only through community, and to realize oneself is to contribute to social and other ideals. Bradley's logic was similarly an attack on the basis of empiricism in the atomistic relation of experiences and thoughts to things, which he rejected in favour of an acquaintance with general properties and universals. The metaphysical picture to which this leads is one that celebrates unity and wholeness as attributes of the real, with anything partial and dependent upon division, in the way that thought is, regarded by contrast as flawed and contradictory. Truth as formulated in language is always partial, and dependent upon categories that themselves are inadequate to the harmonious whole. Nevertheless these self-contradictory elements somehow contribute to the harmonious whole, or Absolute, lying beyond categorization. Although absolute idealism maintains few adherents today, Bradley's general dissent from empiricism, his *holism, and the brilliance and style of his writing continue to make him the most interesting of the late 19th-century writers influenced by *Hegel. His battles with the new realism of *Russell and *Moore, and the complex relationship he had with *pragmatism, mark a major crux in the history of philosophy. His major works include *Ethical Studies* (1876), *Principles of Logic* (1883), and *Appearance and Reality* (1893). Collections of his essays include *Essays in Truth and Reality* (1914) and *Collected Essays* (1935).

Bradwardine, Thomas (*c.*1300–49) One of the 'Oxford Calculators'. He is remembered mainly by historians of medieval science as an influential mathematician. His principal work was *De proportionibus velocitatum in motibus* ('On the Ratio of Velocities in Motions'). In philosophy he wrote *De futura contingentibus* ('On Future Contingents').

brahman In the *Upanishads the ground of all being; that in virtue of which everything else exists; the ultimate reality, which makes possible time, space, and the natural order. As in *Parmenides, this is an unchangeable, eternal unity, lying beyond all limitation and hence all description. *See also* ATMAN.

brain The brain contains something over 10^{11} neurons, each connected to something over three thousand others; this makes something over 10^{14} connections. If each connection is capable of ten different 'weights' or levels of activation, then the number of distinct brain states possible is 10 to the power of 10^{14}. By comparison, the number of elementary particles in the universe is estimated at a miserly 10^{87}. The progress of neuroscience in understanding brain function increases the urgency of reconciling the scientific view of a person as a conglomerate of connected cells, with the personal view of a unified, conscious, single self subject to experiences and capable of rational and voluntary action. If this reconciliation cannot be managed, then either the scientific view drives out the personal view (*see* ELIMINATIVISM), or we end with some kind of *dualism whereby the mental is different from and additional to the physical. Reconciling approaches include *functionalism and *physicalism, both hoping to show how mental explanation of events is a consistent supplement to their physical explanation, not a rival to it.

brain in a vat An updated version, due to *Putnam, of *Descartes's thought experiment with the *malin génie* (*see* METHOD OF DOUBT). We are invited to consider the sceptical possibility that our experience is actually produced by a brain suspended in a life-preserving medium (a vat) and stimulated electrically in such a way as to give us the delusive experience of living the life with which we are familiar. One reaction is to deny that this is even a bare logical possibility; another is to argue that even if it is a bare logical possibility, we know that it is not the way things are. A controversial argument of Putnam's attempts to show that the hypothesis that I am a brain in a vat self-destructs, since if I were one, were I to put it to myself 'I am a brain in a vat', I would not be referring to brains and vats, and hence would not express appreciation of my true situation.

brain transplants A kind of *thought experiment frequently used to unsettle our theories of *personal identity. Two persons, A and B, enter a scrambling device, after which A (or the person looking like A, and with A's old body) emerges with B's brain installed, and vice versa. Which person is now A: the person looking like the old A, or the person controlled by the old A's brain, and therefore possessing old A's memories and personality? Variations on the case exist. Reactions include definite verdicts in favour of each candidate, but also dismissal of the case either as one that our everyday conception of identity does not cover, or as improperly transgressing the facts of neurophysiology and scientific possibility.

Braithwaite, Richard Bevan (1900–90) Cambridge philosopher of science and probability. His major work *Scientific Explanation* (1955) takes a forthright empiricist line, derived from *Hume and *Ramsey, in the philosophy of probability and causation. His inaugural lecture 'The theory of games as a tool for the moral philosopher' was an early example of this application of *game theory.

Brentano, Franz Clemens (1838–1917) German philosopher and psychologist. His teaching at the universities of Wurzburg and Vienna may be regarded as the foundation of the *phenomenological movement in philosophy.

b

Brentano became a priest in 1864 but left the Church in 1873. His major work was *Psychologie vom empirischen Standpunkt* (1874, trs. as *Psychology from an Empirical Standpoint*, 1973) which rehabilitates the medieval concentration upon the 'directedness' or *intentionality of the mental as a fundamental aspect of thought and consciousness. Brentano also wrote on theological matters, and on moral philosophy, where the directedness of emotions allows a notion of their correct and incorrect objects, thus permitting him a notion of moral objectivity.

Brentano's thesis The thesis proposed in Brentano's *Psychology from an Empirical Standpoint* (1874) that it is the *intentionality or directedness of mental states that marks off the mental from the physical.

Bridgewater Treatises Series of eight influential treatises published between 1833 and 1836, demonstrating the power, wisdom, and goodness of God, especially in the light of modern science. *Whewell wrote one, and *Babbage wrote a 'Ninth Bridgewater Thesis' challenging *Hume on miracles.

Bridgman, Percy William (1882–1962) American physicist and Nobel prizewinner (1946). Bridgman wrote extensively on the philosophical implications of modern physics. He is inseparably linked with *operationalism, or the view that each scientific concept is defined in terms of a set of empirical operations. However, he later modified this stark, and some say stifling, doctrine by allowing indirect connections between concepts and experience. Works include *The Logic of Modern Physics* (1927) and *The Nature of Physical Theory* (1936).

Brillat-Savarin, Jean Anthelme (1755–1826) French lawyer, politician, and gourmet whose masterpiece, published in the last year of his life, was *Physiologie du Gout, or Méditations de Gastronomie Transcendante* ('The Physiology of Taste, or Meditations on Transcendental Gastronomy'), the only philosophical meditation on cooking.

British empiricists Title conventionally given to the trio *Locke, *Berkeley, and *Hume. There were others of an *empiricist bent before these (such as *Ockham, or Francis *Bacon, or *Hobbes), and the extent to which *Locke, in particular, is an empiricist is distinctly debatable.

Broad, Charlie Dunbar (1887–1971) English philosopher. Educated at Cambridge, Broad became a life Fellow of Trinity College, and was professor of moral philosophy at Cambridge from 1933 to 1953. His interests spanned almost the entire field of philosophy, and his extensive writings include works on relativity theory, ethics, the history of philosophy, and parapsychology. He maintained a traditional respect for the central problems of modern philosophy, and his lucid works exhibit a scrupulous attention to the variety of possible solutions and their difficulties. The attitude gave him a wry scepticism of philosophical fashions, particularly those associated with the more impressionistic approach of the later *Wittgenstein. A characteristic expression of his stance was that on the issue of life after death we can only wait and see, or alternatively, which is no less likely, wait and not see. His main works include *Mind and its Place in Nature* (1925) and the two-volume *Examination of McTaggart's Philosophy* (1933–8).

Brouwer, Luitzen Egburtus Jan (1881–1966) Dutch mathematician and the founder of mathematical *intuitionism. Brouwer's first philosophical work, *Leven, Kunst und Mystiek* ('Life, Art and Mysticism', 1905), argued that logic was derivative from mathematics, and mathematics dependent upon a temporal intuition, in which there is a 'falling apart of the life moment into two qualitatively distinct things'. This Kantian association between the experience of time and that of plurality was associated in Brouwer with rejection of the *logicist approach to the foundations of mathematics, and a *constructivist modification of classical mathematical practice. The logical importance of this has become separated from the Kantian elements in Brouwer's thought. Brouwer's writings are translated in *Collected Works* (1975–6).

Bruno, Giordano (1548–1600) Gifted Italian philosopher, astrologer, poet, and magus, who lived a hectic career in various European cities, largely promoting a *hermetic creed based on supposed Egyptian sources and allied with the recent discoveries of *Copernicus. The extent to which the magical and animistic elements of his thought are mere throwbacks, or are brilliant foreshadowings of such thinkers as *Leibniz, is debated. He unwisely placed himself within reach of the Inquisition, by whom he was eventually burned.

Brunschvicg, Léon (1869–1944) A commanding presence in French philosophy for the first half of the 20th century, Brunschvicg espoused an idealist and neo-Hegelian philosophy, which sought to interpret the progress of self-consciousness in terms of the emergence of the natural sciences. He was equally well-known as a scholar and philosopher of mathematics, responsible for bringing *Frege and *Russell to the attention of French philosophers.

brute fact Brute or bare facts are supposed to obtain without doing so in virtue of any other facts obtaining. *Supervening facts and *institutional facts by contrast obtain because other facts do.

There is no generally agreed list of (absolutely) brute facts, although it is possible to say that some facts are brute relative to others.

Bryson of Heraclea (early 4th c. BC) Greek *sophist criticized by Aristotle for a mathematical construction that may have been perfectly sound, closing in on the area of a circle by considering it as lying between the areas of convergent sequences of external and internal polygons. He also upset Aristotle by claiming that there is no such thing as obscene or indecent language.

b-series of time The ordering of events as earlier or later than one another, with no reference to their place in the past, present or future. *See* A-SERIES OF TIME.

Buber, Martin (1878–1965) Jewish religious thinker and *existentialist. Born in Vienna, Buber eventually settled in Palestine, and became the first President of the Israeli Academy of Science and Humanities. His most important work was *Ich und Du* (1922, trs. as *I and Thou*, 1970). In Buber's approach religion creates reciprocal relationships of dialogue between one subject and another, and these are sharply distinguished from objective relations between subject and thing. Buber interpreted religious experience in terms of perpetual encounter and dialogue with another personal subject, rather than in terms of knowledge modelled upon scientific knowledge of an extra 'thing' in the universe. The idea has been immensely influential in modern theology. *See also* RELIGION, PHILOSOPHY OF.

Buchmanism Better known as moral rearmament, the evangelical movement founded by Frank Buchman (1878–1961), an American Lutheran minister. It promoted a strenuous personal moral philosophy of purity and anti-communism.

Buddhism The philosophical system formed in India in the 5th century BC by Siddhartha Gautama (usually 563–483 BC; an alternative date of death based on Chinese sources is 368 BC), the Buddha or enlightened one. Buddhism teaches salvation through escape from **samsara*, the endless cycle of birth and rebirth. The state of enlightenment or *nirvana is a state of liberation from the passions and frustrations of ordinary living, a radiant state of living in the present, obtained by following the Way, or the *eightfold path. Two main kinds of Buddhism are recognized. Theravada (or Hinayana, lesser vehicle) Buddhism is found mainly in Thailand, Laos, Cambodia, and Sri Lanka. Mahayana Buddhism is found in Nepal and the countries surrounding and including China. Theravada Buddhism is conservative and simple in its forms; Mahayana or greater vehicle Buddhism includes more elaborate rituals, scriptures, and a gallery of saints (bodhisattvas).

The Buddha's own awakening came with realization that neither the way of meditation, nor that of asceticism, provides a way to awareness of a 'Self' conceived of as a permanent, unchanging object of yogic contemplation (*see ATMAN*). Buddhism therefore rejects the desire to constitute oneself as a single ego or self, on which point it is sometimes acknowledged as a precursor of the *bundle theory and the *no-ownership theory of the self. Rejecting this desire is the beginning of enlightenment. Buddhism rejects any concept of permanent substance, either mental or physical, in favour of a metaphysics of transient states and events. It equally rejects anything resembling the god of monotheistic religions. Philosophically however Buddhism, as much as Christianity, has a long history of diverse schools, representing different attitudes to reality, mind, scepticism, and experience. *See also* EIGHTFOLD PATH, FOUR NOBLE TRUTHS, *MADHYAMIKA*, YOGACARA, ZEN.

Buffier, Claude (1661–1737) French Jesuit whose aim was to show how experience requires interpretation in terms of an external world, thereby countering the sceptical tendencies inherent in the philosophies of *Descartes and *Locke. He is often classed as a kind of precursor of Thomas *Reid and the common-sense school. His various treatises and essays are collected as *Oeuvres philosophiques* (1843).

Bultmann, Rudolf (1884–1976) German religious thinker who worked mainly at Marburg, and was influenced by *Heidegger. He is famous for a 'demythologizing' approach to religion, arguing that Christianity needs no commitment either to the historical claims of the Bible or to the myths that may be found there. Although Bultmann does not embrace it, the natural consequence of this seems to shrink religious commitment to a purely personal stance lacking the objective ambitions of traditional religion.

bundle theory of the mind or self The view, particularly associated with *Hume but anticipated in *Buddhism, that we have no reason to think in terms of a single unified self that owns a variety of experiences or states; we only have access to the succession of states themselves. The enduring self is then a fiction, or a figment of the imagination. However, Hume confessed himself dissatisfied with his own account of the matter (*Treatise*, 1st Appendix). The problem is that the idea of one determinate self, that survives through life's normal changes of experience and personality, seems to be highly metaphysical. But if we avoid it we seem to be left only with the experiences themselves, and no account of their unity in one life, or, as it is sometimes put, no idea of the rope around the bundle. A tempting metaphor is that from individual experiences a self is 'constructed', perhaps as a fictitious focus of the narrative of one's life that one is inclined to give. But the difficulty with the notion is that experiences are individually too small to 'construct' anything, and anything capable of doing any constructing appears to be just the kind of guiding intelligent subject that got lost in the flight from the metaphysical view. *See also* ATMAN, PERSONAL IDENTITY.

Burali-Forti's paradox The first paradox discovered in the modern theory of sets. Every well-ordered set has an ordinal number assigned to it. These ordinals can be compared: of any two, either they are equal, or one is smaller and one is larger. They therefore form a well-ordered set. The ordinal of this set must be greater than any ordinal within the set. Let S be the set of all ordinals. Since it is well-ordered it has an ordinal number, w, that must be greater than any element in the set. But S was the set of all ordinals, and must include w.

Burckhardt, Jakob Christoph (1818–97) Swiss cultural historian. Philosophically he was an opponent of *Hegel's view of history as essentially progressive, as well as a conservative opponent of democracy and industrialization. His best-remembered work is *The Culture of the Renaissance in Italy* (1860, trs. 1878).

burden of proof If in some situation there is a proper presumption that something is true, anyone seeking to prove its opposite is said to bear the burden of proof. A certain amount of philosophical jockeying consists in trying to shift the burden of proof.

Buridan, John (*c.*1300–after 1360) French *scholastic philosopher. Buridan was educated under *Ockham and taught at Paris, where he was also rector of the university. Little is known directly of Buridan's life, although it is known that he climbed Mont Ventoux considerably before Petrarch, and it was rumoured that he was tossed into the Seine in a sack for dallying with the Queen of France. He was a logician rather than a theologian, and pursued issues of formal logic for their own sake rather than for the sake of doctrinal argument. In addition to his writings in philosophy and logic, he contributed extensively to the science of his time, and his ethics shows a teleological bent related to *Cicero and *Seneca rather than to the more authoritarian and *deontological ethics of Ockham. In logic his *Consequentiae* and *Sophismata* contain discussions of modal logic and of paradoxes of self-reference which still hold considerable interest.

Buridan's ass The creature who, placed midway between two identical bales of hay, starved to death, since there was no reason for moving one way rather than the other. The ass is not referred to in the *Sophismata* of *Buridan, but was probably an example used to refute him, since he held that choice is always delayed until reason has decided in favour of one course of action against another. A similar example of a dog is found in *Aristotle, *De Caelo* (295 b 32).

Burke, Edmund (1729–97) Irish thinker and politician. After his education at Trinity College, Dublin, Burke lived by writing in London, until becoming a Member of Parliament in 1766. His first important work, *Philosophical Inquiry into the Origin of Our Ideas of the Sublime and the Beautiful* (1756), marked a very early *Romantic turn away from the 18th-century aesthetic of clarity and order, in favour of the imaginative power of the unbounded and infinite, and the unstated and unknown. Although he supported both Irish and American revolution, his later work *Reflections on the Revolution in France* is a masterly attack on the danger of airy political abstractions, and a defence of the preservation of traditional aristocratic liberties, rights, and privileges.

business ethics The branch of *ethics that analyses problems and dilemmas created by business practices: for example, the social responsibilities of the firm, the proper limits of acceptable competition, the weighing of conflicting obligations to stockholders and clients, and the extent and limits of company loyalty.

Butler, Joseph (1692–1752) English moral philosopher. Born of a Presbyterian family, Butler was educated at Oriel College, Oxford, and became a minister of the Church of England, where he rose to be Bishop of Durham, as well as the spiritual adviser of Queen Caroline and George II. His moral philosophy is contained in his *Fifteen Sermons* (1726), while his theology is contained in *The Analogy of Religion* (1736). His moral philosophy is an attempt to ground ethics on a proper understanding of human nature, and as such continues the tradition of *Aristotle, *Hobbes, and *Shaftesbury. Butler's refutation of ethical *egoism is a classic of moral thought. He carefully distinguishes self-love, benevolence, and the impact of conscience, although the authority of the last of these remains unclear. Butler has been well described as 'Aristotle clad in a diaphanous mantle made of Christianity'.

Butler, Samuel (1835–1902) English writer and critic. An unsystematic thinker who spent much time discussing and attacking Darwin's view of evolution, Butler is remembered philosophically mainly for *Erewhon* (1901), a satire of ethics in which the hero visits a country where values are inverted: for instance, sickness is a crime, but crime treated merely as a sickness.

Cabanis, Pierre-Jean-Georges (1758–1808) French doctor and writer on the mind and human nature. In his *Rapports du physique et du moral de l'homme* ('The Connections between the Physical and the Moral in Man') of 1802, Cabanis promoted a materialist and physiological understanding of the mental operations of human beings.

cabbala *See* KABBALA.

Caird, Edward (1835–1908) Scottish *absolute idealist, Professor at Glasgow and Master of Balliol College, Oxford. Like *Hegel, Caird believed that the aim of philosophy was to overcome philosophical oppositions and dualisms, thereby seeing everything as a part of the larger whole, or Absolute. His main work was *The Critical Philosophy of Kant* (1889).

Cajetan, Thomas (1468–1534) Italian *scholastic philosopher and commentator on *Aquinas. His work *De Nominum Analogia et de Conceptu Entis* (trs. as *The Analogy of Names and the Concept of Being,* 1953) is an extended discussion of the role of analogy in the theory of knowledge, and thence in theology. In this it anticipates more modern attempts to exploit metaphor for the same purpose.

calibration paradox Someone who forecasts events with a probability (such as a weather forecaster) may be more or less well calibrated in the following sense. Consider the sequence of days for which he predicts rain with 0.1 probability. It may rain on 0.1 of them, or more, or less. If the frequency of rain on such days corresponds to the probability he offers, for every probability, then he is perfectly calibrated. This would be a remarkable success, and it would be quite irrational for anyone to have such confidence in their own abilities that they expect to be so successful. But the paradoxical theorem (discovered in 1962 by Pratt, a Harvard statistician, and rediscovered by Dawid, in London) states that an agent with a view about his own calibration must assign 1 (corresponding to certainty) to the proposition that he is perfectly calibrated, on pain of having an incoherent set of probabilities. The situation bears some analogy to that of the paradox of the *preface, where modesty induces inconsistency.

Callicles The character, probably based upon a real person about whom nothing more is known, in Plato's dialogue *Gorgias,* who advocates the doctrine that might is right, voicing contempt for the conventional restraints of morality.

Calvinism The rigorous form of Protestantism founded by the French reformer and theologian John Calvin (1509–64) distinguished by belief in the Bible as the rule of faith, denial of human freedom since the Fall, and particularly emphasis on the arbitrary *predestination of some to salvation and others to damnation. Calvinism was the creed of the Huguenots, and found congenial soil in Scotland. *See also* ELECTIVE AFFINITY, PROTESTANT WORK ETHIC.

Cambridge change A thing changes in a sense associated with *Russell (hence, at Cambridge) if it satisfies a description at one time that it does not satisfy at another. However, some such changes are 'merely' Cambridge changes: if you outgrow me, then I satisfy the description of being as tall as you at one time, and I do not satisfy the description at another. So, by the Cambridge criterion, I have changed, but I need have undergone no robust or substantial change, for I may have stayed at exactly the same height. The term was introduced by P. T. *Geach (*Logic Matters,* 1972); a possible application of the notion is to make the unchanging (substantial) nature of God compatible with his (merely Cambridge) changing relations to the temporal world.

Cambridge Platonists A small group of mid-17th century thinkers centred on Cambridge, whose members included Ralph *Cudworth, Henry *More, and Benjamin *Whichcote. The problems they addressed included the rise of low-church 'enthusiasm', the increasing influence of the Godless system of *Hobbes, and the decreasing prestige of Aristotelian logic and science. The solution was an increased reliance on themes from *Plato, including a general sympathy with mysticism and especially a belief that ethics rests upon absolute standards of right and wrong, divine revelation.

Campanella, Tommaso (1568–1639) Italian Dominican, Renaissance magus, prophet, poet, and astrologer, as well as a speculative philosopher. Campanella rejected Aristotelianism in favour of an understanding of reality in terms of heat and cold. He also thought that all things in nature are endowed with sense and that nature has a mental aspect, usable by the magician.

Campbell, George (1719–96) Scottish minister principally remembered for his *The Philosophy of Rhetoric* (1776), in which he considered classical rhetoric from the standpoint of the nature of the human mind. He had earlier written *A Dissertation on Miracles* (1762) seeking to rebut *Hume on the topic.

Campbell, Norman Robert (1880–1949) British physicist and philosopher of science. He is remembered for his account of scientific theories, arguing that as well as theoretical postulates and principles connecting them with empirical laws, theories require models or analogies, for example in mechanical terms, without which they would remain mere formalisms, offering no understanding of their subject matter. His major work was *Physics: the Elements* (1920).

Camus, Albert (1913–60) Algerian-born French novelist and thinker, and winner of the 1957 Nobel Prize for literature. His work explores the themes associated with *existentialism, in particular the experience of 'absurdity' or metaphysical nihilism, and the moral reactions that the experience demands, which comes in various combinations of stoicism and rebellion. Camus's novels include *L'Étranger* (1942, trs. as *The Stranger*, 1946, and also as *The Outsider*) and *La Peste* (1947, trs. as *The Plague*, 1948). Two major essays explaining the philosophical and metaphysical basis of his themes are *Le Mythe de Sisyphe* (1942, trs. as *The Myth of Sisyphus*, 1955) and *L'Homme révolté* (1951, trs. as *The Rebel*, 1953).

Canguilhem, Georges (1904–96) French historian and philosopher of science, who succeeded *Bachelard as head of the Institut d'Histoire et Sciences et des Techniques at the University of Paris. He extended Bachelard's work into the history and philosophy of biological science. His emphasis on the life of concepts independently of particular theories involving them, and his historically orientated epistemology greatly influenced *Foucault. His principal work was *The Normal and the Pathological* (1943, revised 1966).

canonical A canonical derivation in logic is one satisfying some set of conditions that are laid down: thus it may be important to show that if there is a derivation of B from A, there is a particular kind of derivation, en route to showing some result of *proof theory. More widely the term may refer to a derivation which mirrors the structure of what is proved, as opposed to an indirect derivation that does not. A canonical description of a sentence would be one that revealed its basic structure or showed how the sentence is built by transformations from a basic structure.

Cantor, Georg (1845–1918) German mathematician and founder of *set theory. Born in St Petersburg, Cantor studied at Berlin under Weierstrass, and taught at the university of Halle from 1872. His celebrated *diagonal argument proving the different cardinality of the reals and the rationals was first used in a paper of 1874. This demonstrated the existence of infinite sets of differing cardinality: the fundamental result of the modern theory of sets. Cantor's work was much misunderstood, and attacked by his contemporaries for its unfettered use of the notion of a completed infinity. Although suffering from problems of mental health, he devoted the major part of the remainder of his academic career to the mathematical (and philosophical) defence of the world of mathematical objects that he had opened up. He was also the first to pose and to attempt to prove the *continuum hypothesis.

Cantor's paradox The contradiction arising if we compare for size the set of all sets, and its own *power set. By *Cantor's theorem the power set must be bigger (contain more members). But it is itself a subset of the set of all sets, and so cannot be bigger. The paradox shows that the collection of all sets cannot itself be a set-theoretic object.

Cantor's theorem Fundamental theorem of *set theory, proved by *Cantor in 1891. It is usually split into two parts. Cantor's theorem says that the set of real numbers is non-*denumerable. Cantor's power set theorem shows that the *power set of any set is always greater than the set itself. Cantor proved both results by a *diagonal argument. *See also* CONTINUUM, NUMBER, SET THEORY.

capabilities The capabilities approach to welfare propounded by contemporary philosophers Martha *Nussbaum and Amartya *Sen uses the number of basic capabilities enabled by a political and social system as a measure of the quality of life. This contrasts with using preference satisfaction or simple utility as the same measure. Capabilities include those of self-determination, the pursuit of friendship, education, and other human exercises of dignity. The approach underpins a universalist liberal ethic, overcoming cultural *relativism and blunting charges of *paternalism.

capacity Another term for a thing's potentiality (*see* ACTUALITY AND POTENTIALITY).

capitalism Mode of socioeconomic organization in which a class of entrepreneurs and entrepreneurial institutions provide the capital with which businesses produce goods and services and employ workers. In return the capitalist extracts profits from the goods created. Capitalism is frequently seen as the embodiment of the market economy, and hence may result in the optimum distribution of scarce resources, with a resulting improvement for all; this optimism is countered by pointing to the opportunity for *exploitation inherent in the system.

Cardano, Girolamo (1501–76) Italian mathematician, scientist, doctor, and philosopher. One of the great exemplars of the Renaissance ideal of the 'universal man', Cardano embraced a fundamentally *Neoplatonist view of the world. Mathematics, rather than sense experience, would be the key to unlocking esoteric knowledge of the whole unified world. His *Opera omnia* were published in ten volumes in 1663, while his autobiography, written in 1575, is a valuable document in Renaissance history. *See also* LIBERTINS.

cardinality The cardinality of a set is the *cardinal number that measures the number of its members.

cardinal number An object associated with a class of equinumerous sets, that is, sets that may be put into a *one-to-one correspondence with each other. Intuitively, the number that measures the size of a set.

cardinal virtues The Platonic cardinal virtues are courage, temperance, wisdom, and justice.

Carlyle, Thomas (1795–1881) Writer and social prophet. Carlyle was born in Ecclefechan in Scotland, but uneasily lost his *Calvinist faith, and became influenced by German *Romanticism. He translated Goethe's *Wilhelm Meister's Apprenticeship* in 1824, and published the *Life of Schiller* the following year. *Sartor Resartus* (1833–4) reflects Carlyle's debt to the German movement, and the themes of anti-democratic Romanticism, invoking the dynamic as opposed to the mechanical, and the personal, moral force of the 'strong just man' as against the degraded masses and the plod of everyday events, dominate much of his difficult and mannered work. The manuscript of Carlyle's *History of the French Revolution* (1837) was accidentally used to light a fire by one of J. S. *Mill's servants when Carlyle was visiting him, but he rewrote it. He was a friend of *Emerson and greatly influenced the *New England transcendentalists. Samuel *Butler said that it was very good of God to let Carlyle and Mrs Carlyle marry one another, and so make only two people miserable instead of four.

SEE WEB LINKS

- A biography of Carlyle
- A list of internet resources on Carlyle

Carnap, Rudolf (1891–1970) German *logical positivist. Carnap left Vienna to become professor at Prague in 1931, and fled Nazism to become professor in Chicago in 1935. He subsequently worked at Los Angeles from 1952 to 1961. Carnap was probably more influential than any other thinker in combining a basic *empiricism with the logical tools provided by *Frege and *Russell, and it is in his works that the main achievements (and difficulties) of logical positivism are best exhibited. His first major work was *Der logische Aufbau der Welt* (1928, trs. as *The Logical Structure of the World*, 1967). This *phenomenalistic work attempts a *reduction of all the objects of knowledge, by generating *equivalence classes of sensations, related by a primitive relation of remembrance of similarity. This is the solipsistic basis of the construction of the external world, although Carnap later resisted the apparent metaphysical priority here given to experience. His hostility to metaphysics soon developed into the characteristic positivist view that metaphysical questions are pseudo-problems. Criticism from *Neurath shifted Carnap's interest towards a view of the unity of the sciences, with the concepts and theses of special sciences translatable into a basic physical vocabulary whose *protocol statements describe not experience but the qualities of points in space–time. Carnap pursued the enterprise of clarifying the structures of mathematical and scientific language (the only legitimate task for scientific philosophy) in *Logische Syntax der Sprache* (1934, trs. as *The Logical Syntax of Language*, 1937). Refinements to his syntactic and semantic views continued with *Meaning and Necessity* (1947), while a general loosening of the original ideal of reduction culminated in the great *Logical Foundations of Probability*, the most important single work of *confirmation theory, in 1950. Other works concern the structure of physics and the concept of entropy.

Throughout his work Carnap continued his hostility to metaphysics, believing that questions such as whether numbers exist merely raise a choice, that can be settled either way, of the framework of description that we are to adopt. Because his views are both forthright and developed Carnap has been a convenient target for critics of the structures that positivism tended to impose upon linguistic and scientific thought. However, his massive range and insistence on precision in philosophy made him one of the 20th century's most influential philosophers.

C

Carneades (*c.*214–129 BC) The most prominent member of the later *Academy after *Arcesilaus. Carneades was a distinguished *sceptic, famous (especially through the report by *Cicero) for impressive speeches at Rome on two successive days in either 155 or 156 BC, the first defending justice and its immutable nature, and the second opposing it in favour of expediency. Conservative Romans were duly shocked, and demanded the speedy return of the Athenian delegation in order to protect Roman youths from the influence of the philosophers. His philosophical originality lay in admitting a concept of the plausible (*to pithanon*), perhaps better thought of as what is acceptable or that which is better to act upon. He needed to fend off the charge that scepticism leads to total paralysis, by defining the kind of reasoning that, in spite of scepticism, remains a suitable basis for action. In this his difficulty anticipated that of later philosophers of science such as *Popper, of how to make room for action based on reasonable opinion, given the rejection both of any *foundation in certainty and of any increase in the probability of hypotheses via evidence. Carneades voiced a robust rejection of *natural theology, anticipating arguments that only re-entered the western tradition with *Hume and *Kant.

Carroll, Lewis *See* DODGSON.

Cartesian Adjective derived from the Latin name of René *Descartes: Renatus Cartesius.

Cartesian circle *See* METHOD OF DOUBT.

Cartesian doubt *See* METHOD OF DOUBT.

Cartesian dualism The view that mind and body are two separate substances; the self is as it happens associated with a particular body, but is self-subsistent, and capable of independent existence.

Cartesian ego The self conceived as *Descartes presents it in the first two *Meditations*: aware only of its own thoughts, and capable of disembodied existence, neither situated in a space nor surrounded by others. This is the pure self or 'I' that we are tempted to imagine as a simple unique thing that makes up our essential identity. Descartes's view that he could keep hold of this nugget while doubting everything else is criticized by *Lichtenberg and *Kant, and most subsequent philosophers of mind. *See also* ATMAN, AVICENNA, BUNDLE THEORY OF THE MIND OR SELF.

Cartesian product The Cartesian product of two sets, A and B (written A × B), is the set of all *ordered pairs whose first member is an element of A, and whose second member is an element of B.

Carvaka One of the unorthodox schools of Hindu thought, characterized by a generally sceptical and materialistic reaction to the *Vedas. Carvaka bears a resemblance both to Greek *scepticism and to early *atomism.

Cassirer, Ernst (1874–1945) German *Neo-Kantian, who resigned as Rector of Hamburg University in 1933, and subsequently taught at various universities in England and the United States. His main ambition was to develop Kant's work into a general theory of culture. This involved a general theory of symbolization, and Cassirer, although influential in his time in many areas, is best remembered for his work on varieties of 'symbolic forms', presented in his major work *Die Philosophie der symbolischen Formen* (1923–9, trs. as *The Philosophy of Symbolic Forms*, 1953–7).

casualism The doctrine that all things and events happen by chance.

casuistry (Latin, *casus*, a case) The approach to ethical problems in which the circumstances of cases affect the application of general rules; a casuist is one who distinguishes and marshals the relevance of different cases and rules. The *Resolutiones morales* (1659) of the Spanish 'prince of casuists' Antonio Diana (1585–1683) discusses some 20,000 cases. The term is often used pejoratively, implying the multiplication of doubtful distinctions, and their use to defend apparently self-serving and conflicting moral verdicts. Casuistry as a discipline declined in the 17th century with the rise of Protestant and pietistic approaches to religion and morality. However, '*situation ethics' provides the ground for the re-emergence of attention to the special circumstances of any object of a moral verdict.

catastrophe theory Mathematical theory pioneered by the French mathematician René Thom, treating abrupt changes or discontinuities.

categorematic *See* SYNCATEGOREMATIC.

categorial grammar A type of formal grammar that works with a fixed number of basic categories, such as the sentence and the noun or noun phrase. A categorial grammar may serve as the basis for more powerful rules, such as those of *Montague grammars.

categorical/hypothetical imperative A pair contrasted in *Kantian ethics. A hypothetical imperative embeds a command which is in place only given some antecedent desire or project: 'If you want to look wise, stay quiet.' The injunction to stay quiet only applies to those with the antecedent desire or inclination; if one has no desire to look wise the injunction or advice lapses. A categorical imperative cannot be so avoided: it is a requirement that binds anybody, regardless of their inclinations. It could be represented as, for example: 'Tell the truth! (regardless of whether you want to or not).' The distinction is not always signalled by presence or absence of the conditional or hypothetical form: 'if you crave drink, don't become a bartender' may be regarded an absolute injunction applying to anyone, although only activated in the case of those with the stated desire.

In *Grundlegung zur Metaphysik der Sitten* (1785), Kant discussed five forms of the categorical imperative: (i) the formula of universal law: 'act only on that *maxim through which you can at the same time will that it should become universal law'; (ii) the formula of the law of nature: 'act as if the maxim of your action were to become through your will a universal law of nature'; (iii) the formula of the end-in-itself: 'act in such a way that you always treat humanity, whether in your own person or in the person of any other, never simply as a means, but always at the same time as an end'; (iv) the formula of autonomy, or considering 'the will of every rational being as a will which makes universal law'; and (v) the formula of the Kingdom of Ends, which provides a model for the systematic union of different rational beings under common laws.

A central object of the study of Kant's ethics is to understand these expressions of the inescapable, binding requirement of the categorical imperative, and to understand whether they are equivalent at some deep level. Kant's own applications of the notion are not always convincing (*see*, for example, SEX). One cause of confusion in relating Kant's ethics to theories such as *expressivism is that it is easy, but mistaken, to suppose that the categorical nature of the imperative means that it cannot be the expression of a sentiment, but must derive from something 'unconditioned' or 'necessary' such as the voice of reason.

categorical proposition In Aristotelian logic, a proposition of one of the four forms: all S is P; some S is P; no S is P; some S is not P. Also, a proposition that is not a *conditional. As with the *affirmative and negative, modern opinion is wary of this distinction, since what appears categorical may vary with the choice of a primitive vocabulary and notation. Apparently categorical propositions may also turn out to be disguised conditionals: X is intelligent (categorical?) = if X is given a range of tasks she performs them better than many people (conditional?). The problem is not merely one of classification, since deep metaphysical questions arise when facts that seem to be categorical and therefore solid, come to seem by contrast conditional, or purely hypothetical or potential. *See also* FIELD.

categories A permanent concern of philosophers has been to discover whether the most general categories of thought, such as space, time, reality, existence, necessity, substance, property, mind, matter, states, facts, and events, are absolute and universal, to be found in any mode of thought, or whether they are relatively parochial and in principle changeable. In the *Categories* and the *Topics* *Aristotle lists ten categories: substance, quantity, quality, relation, place, time, posture, state, action, and passion, but he seems not to have been wedded to the idea that this classification was definitive. He held that any 'uncombined' term in a sentence stands for one of these (*see also* PARONYM). Other terms are auxiliary terms, later called *syncategorematic expressions or ones that together with categorical expressions make up a sentence. These include prepositions and logical connectives. In *scholastic thought Aristotle's list becomes substance, quantity (the way a body is made up of others, and owes its extension to theirs), the acting and being acted upon of a body (its activity and passivity), qualities arising from the disposition of constitutive parts, spatial and temporal properties, and relations.

*Kant's passion for system led him to a fourfold division with three categories in each. Under quantity we have unity, plurality, and totality; under quality we get reality, negation, and limitation; under relation we have inherence and subsistence, causation and dependence, and reciprocity between agent and patient; under modality we have possibility, existence, and necessity. Few have had Kant's faith that this is an exhaustive and principled division. In the modern era *Frege's logic gives us a clearer view of the fundamental ways in which information is constructed, and his analysis of language suggests the highly general division of concept and object, but by itself it does not speak to the problems of classification within these categories. A new twist was added by *Wittgenstein's *Tractatus Logico-Philosophicus* (1921) in which it is suggested that the fundamental categories of a language show themselves, but their structure and relations are amongst the things that cannot be said. The problem remains of finding a fundamental classification of the kinds of entities recognized in a way of thinking. *See also* DISPOSITION.

category mistake A notion prominent in the work of *Ryle. A category mistake arises when things or facts of one kind are presented as if they belonged to another. Someone would make a category mistake if after being shown all the battalions and regiments she wished to be shown the army. Ryle believed that a *Cartesian theory of mind depended on the category mistake of *reifying mental events, instead of seeing mental descriptions as just one kind of description of persons and their dispositions. Thinking of beliefs as in the head, or numbers as large spatial objects, or God as a person, or time as flowing, may each be making category mistakes.

C

catharsis In *Aristotle, the cleansing (purifying, purging) of feelings such as pity and fear by feeling them in an aesthetic context, such as the theatre. The aim of tragedy is to achieve this purification. According to the younger *Freud a psychological disorder could be relieved by a process of catharsis when the original traumatic event was re-enacted, although he later held that other repressive factors might inhibit this outcome.

causal chain The sequence of events leading up to some final effect, where each member of the sequence causes its succeeding member to come about. While the notion applies to identifiable cases (the stumble causes the fall that causes the fracture that causes the visit to hospital ...), it is not clear that causation in general can be analysed into linear chains of discrete events. Amongst classical problems is that of time: if the earlier event precedes the later, how can it be causally efficacious after it has ceased to exist? But if simultaneous, how do we find the chain stretched back in time?

causal law A *law of nature framed in terms of a causal relation between two distinct kinds of events, or two distinct features of a system. *See also* CAUSAL NEXUS, CAUSATION.

causal nexus (Latin, *nectere*, to bind) The bonding or link between a cause and its effect. The ancient *sceptics, subsequent *occasionalists, and, most famously, *Hume argue that no such link is perceptible or imaginable: we can see that events do follow one upon another, but we cannot see that they must do so, or frame any notion of the necessary connection. The idea that causation is a matter of discrete events joined by links is highly problematic: what links the event to its link? Is the link to be thought of as a third partner? What is the temporal relationship between the first event, the link, and the later event?

causal principle The principle that every event has a cause.

causal regress, infinite *See* FIRST CAUSE ARGUMENT.

causal theory of identity The theory that the relation that unifies successive states into being states of a single thing is their causal linkage, whereby the later states are effects of the earlier ones.

causal theory of knowledge/justification The view that an agent knows that something is so when there is some appropriate causal connection between the fact that it is so, and the agent's belief. The clearest example is direct perception, where the fact that there is a chair in the room causes my visual state of seeing that there is, and hence causes my knowing that there is. Difficulties include identifying the appropriate relation, extending the idea to less direct cases, especially those involving such apparently non-causal things as abstract objects, and accommodating examples where there may be a causal connection, but it would be most unreasonable of the agent to believe that there is. *See also* DEVIANT CAUSAL CHAIN.

causal theory of meaning The view that the link between words and the world, whereby words mean what they do, is a causal link. The theory is aired in *Kripke's *Naming and Necessity* for the special case of proper names. A plausible way of thinking of the link between the name 'Plato' and the philosopher Plato is that there was an original naming of the philosopher with a term, which is itself an ancestor of the word we use, and a reference-preserving linkage causally responsible for our present use of the term. Even in this case there are difficulties over what makes for a reference-preserving link, and extending the theory to other kinds of term, such as those designating *natural kinds, is not straightforward.

causal theory of perception (causal theory of memory) The view that to perceive an object is to be in a state that has some appropriate causal relationship to it, or that to remember an event is to stand in a similar causal relationship to its original occurrence. Whilst the basic idea is widely accepted, it proves difficult to pin down exactly the kind of relationship that counts as appropriate, for *deviant causal chains may connect us with things that we nevertheless do not perceive or remember.

causal uniformity, principle of A combination of the principle of the *uniformity of nature, with the view that the laws of nature are causal laws, prescribing which events have which effects. *Russell held that the mathematical nature of the laws of modern physics shows that science needs to postulate a uniformity of nature, but without couching the uniformities in terms of causation.

causa sui (Latin, cause of itself) The (problematic) property possessed only by God, of being his own cause, i.e. independent of any other ground, yet containing within himself a sufficient explanation of his own being. *See also* COSMOLOGICAL ARGUMENT, ONTOLOGICAL ARGUMENT, PERSEITY.

causation One of the central problem areas of metaphysics. Causation is the relation between two events that holds when, given that one occurs, it produces, or brings forth, or determines, or necessitates the second; equally we say that once the first has happened the second must happen or that the second follows on from the first. However, it is not clear that only events are related by causation: *Kant cites the example of a cannonball stationary on a cushion, but causing the cushion to be the shape that it is, and this suggests that states of affairs or objects or facts may also be causally related. In any case the central problem is to understand the element of necessitation or determining of the future. Events, *Hume thought, are in themselves 'loose and separate'; how then are we to conceive of the power that one has to constrain others? The relationship seems not to be perceptible, for all that perception gives us (Hume argued) is knowledge of the patterns that events do actually fall into, rather than any acquaintance with the connections determining the patterns. It is clear that our conception of everyday objects is largely determined by their causal powers, and all our action is based on the belief that these causal powers are stable and reliable. But although scientific investigation can give us wider and deeper reliable patterns, it seems incapable of bringing us any nearer to the 'must' of causal necessitation. Particular examples of puzzles with causation, quite apart from the general problem of forming any conception of what it is, include: how are we to understand the causal interaction between mind and body? How can the present, which exists, owe its existence to a past that no longer exists? How is the stability of the causal order to be understood? Is *backward causation possible? Is causation a concept needed in science, or dispensable? *See also* CONSTANT CONJUNCTION.

SEE WEB LINKS

- A bibliography of online philosophical papers on causation

cause, immanent In *scholastic theory, a kind of cause that lies within, as opposed to causation from external factors. *See also* *CAUSA SUI*.

causes: material, formal, efficient, final Four kinds of causation distinguished by *Aristotle. If we think of an example of something that is produced by an agent, such as a statue, then the material cause is the substance or material that constitutes the statue; the formal cause is the pattern or blueprint determining the form of the result; the efficient cause is the agency producing the result; and the final cause is that for the sake of which the result is produced, i.e. the end towards which the production is directed. Whilst the notions may be clear enough in such a case, their wider applicability is much more doubtful. There are clearly events (e.g. a lightning flash) that we think of as caused, yet which are not made of material, not made according to a blueprint, not the result of agency (at least where that is intelligent agency), and apparently purposeless. Aristotle's generally *teleological approach to nature almost certainly led him to see the categories as more widely applicable than we do.

causes/reasons *See* REASONS/CAUSES.

cave, myth of *See* MYTH OF THE CAVE.

Cavell, Stanley (1926–) Walter M. Cabot Professor of Aesthetics and General Theory of Value at Harvard University from 1963 to 1997. His diverse publications cover film theory, literary theory, painting, and music, as well as epistemology, and essays on philosophers from Wittgenstein to Heidegger and Derrida. They include *Must we Mean What we Say?* (1969), *The Claim of Reason* (1979), and *Themes Out of School* (1984). He was the recipient of a 'Genius Award' from the MacArthur Foundation in 1992.

Cavendish, Margaret (1623–73) Prolific writer whose topics included science and its philosophy. She moved from Epicurean *atomism to a more organic view of the material world, raising problems for the notion of inert matter. Her works include *Philosophical Letters* (1664), *Observations on Experimental Philosophy* (1666), and *Grounds of Natural Philosophy* (1668). Virginia Woolf said of her: 'though her philosophies are futile, and her plays intolerable, and her verses mainly dull, the vast bulk of the Duchess is leavened by a vein of authentic fire.'

Celsus (late 2nd c. AD) Middle Platonist and author of a comprehensive polemic against Christianity, *The True Doctrine*, known primarily through *Origen's response, *Against Celsus*.

central state materialism The philosophy of mind that identifies mental events with physical events occurring in the brain and central nervous system. It is thus a form of *physicalism. The two forms most commonly distinguished are token–token identity theory, and *type–type identity theory.

certainty and doubt We take a proposition to be certain when we have no doubt about its truth.

We may do this in error or unreasonably, but objectively a proposition is certain when such absence of doubt is justifiable. The *sceptical tradition in philosophy denies that objective certainty is often possible, or ever possible, either for any proposition at all, or for any proposition from some suspect family (ethics, theory, memory, empirical judgement, etc.). A major sceptical weapon is the possibility of upsetting events that cast doubt back onto what were hitherto taken to be certainties. Others include reminders of the divergence of human opinion, and the fallible sources of our confidences (*see* AENESIDEMUS). *Foundationalist approaches to knowledge look for a basis of certainty, upon which the structure of our systems of belief is built. Others reject the metaphor, looking for mutual support and *coherence, without foundations. *See also* EPISTEMOLOGY.

ceteris paribus (Latin, other things being equal) A disclaimer frequently needed to qualify otherwise overstated claims, which are thereby qualified to apply only across a normal range of cases. By extension, ceteris paribus laws or generalizations are ones applying only when other things are equal.

chain of being The *Great Chain of Being* is the title of a book by the American philosopher and historian of ideas A. O. *Lovejoy, in which he explored the *Neoplatonic and medieval notion of a hierarchy of actual existent things, ordered from the lowest, up through all possible intermediate gradations, including men, angels, and eventually culminating in God. The great literary celebration of this kind of hierarchy is the *Divina Commedia* of *Dante. The notion connects to the view that it would be an inexplicable defect in the created universe if any real possibilities went unactualized. *See also* PLENITUDE, SUFFICIENT REASON.

chance Chance is frequently regarded as unreal, a mere reflection of human ignorance, due to be eroded by the onset of deterministic science. In ancient and medieval philosophy chance could be contrasted with divine purpose, and until the 18th century the concept was of little application, since nothing is strictly due to chance when God's purpose is shown in all creation. The equally ancient opposition between chance and science was eroded after the rise of statistics and probability theory in the 17th century. Probability became the 'guide of life' providing the tools with which to assess chances in insurance and gambling, discovering causal connections, finding rates of mortality, crime, and marriage, even before the onset of probabilistic theories in physics, such as statistical mechanics and then *quantum mechanics. The problem of interpretation is that of deciding whether probabilities measure something 'real' or whether they merely reflect the beliefs of reasonable persons faced with various quantities of data (*see* PERSONALISM). The widespread view that quantum mechanics is irreducibly probabilistic, so that quantum events do not merely manifest superficial randomness overlaying a deterministic basis, is the main stimulus to attempts to give theories of what chance 'really is', or of how fundamental laws of nature can have a probabilistic form. One difficulty lies in seeing how two universes that are the same in respect of the events that occur, might yet differ in the chance with which those events came about.

change The central problems for a philosophy of change are the relationship of change to *time, and the relationship of both of them to us. Although change is a fundamental element of the perceived world, a permanent theme in both eastern and western philosophies is an other-worldliness according to which the restless everyday world of changing things and events must be regarded as unreal in comparison with a more fundamental immutable reality. The first expression of this in the western tradition occurs in *Parmenides. The arguments of *Zeno of Elea against motion are usually interpreted as partly a defence of Parmenidean monism. The backlash came with *Heraclitus, whose vision of the world as eternally in flux nevertheless found something contradictory in the notion: 'we step and we do not step into the same river, we are and we are not.' The idea that there is a contradiction in the notion of change was defended in modern times by *McTaggart (*see* A-SERIES), who also thought that reality had to be conceived of as essentially static, with apparent change an artefact of a mental perspective. The idea that the changing, decaying world is a reflection of an eternal, incorruptible, and changeless world is central to Christian metaphysics, and finds expression in Kant's doctrine that time is merely the form of inner sense, imposed by the mind. In *absolute idealism, notably that of *Bradley, there is the same doctrine that change is contradictory and consequently unreal: the Absolute is changeless. A way of sympathizing a little with this idea is to reflect that any scientific explanation of change will proceed by finding an unchanging law operating, or an unchanging quantity conserved in the change, so that explanation of change always proceeds by finding that which is unchanged. The metaphysical problem of change is to shake off the idea that each moment is created afresh, *ex nihilo*, and to obtain a conception of events or processes as having a genuinely historical reality, really extended and unfolding in time, as opposed to being composites of discrete temporal atoms. A step towards this end may be to see time itself not as an infinite container within which discrete events are located, but as a kind of *logical construction from the flux of events. This relational view of time was advocated by *Leibniz and a subject of the debate between him and Newton's absolutist pupil, *Clarke.

Chang Tsai (1020–77) Major *Neo-Confucian figure who provided a metaphysical basis for ethics, deriving from the unity of creation. Underlying all phenomena is material force (**chi*), which in turn he identifies with the *Tao (Way) of Taoism and with the Supreme Ultimate (*t'ai chi*) of the Book of Changes. The virtue of the sage is to understand and accept this fundamental unity.

chaos **1.** Historically, the contrast is between chaos, or the unordered, unformed, undifferentiated beginnings of things, and the *cosmos, which is the ordered universe (*see also* LOGOS). The concept is thus implicit in early Greek *cosmogony. **2.** In modern science, chaotic systems are ones in which an arbitrarily small difference in the initial conditions can produce arbitrarily large differences in later states. The common example is that the atmosphere may be such that the flapping of a butterfly at a point and a time may determine whether or not there occurs a hurricane at a different point some time later. The possibility of such systems forces a distinction between thinking of a system as *deterministic and thinking of it as completely predictable in principle. Chaotic systems can be deterministic, but are not predictable, for however accurate a measurement of the state at a time, a variation smaller than any it can detect may be responsible for a difference in the eventual outcome.

character A person's character is the sum total of dispositions to action (including thinking and saying). An action is (apparently) out of character if it does not conform to the pattern the person has so far exhibited, although it may then be an indication of a more complex character than hitherto appeared. In *virtue ethics, character is the prime object of appraisal, and actions are derivatively good or bad, right or wrong, in so far as they would have been the actions of a virtuous person.

characteristica universalis (Latin, universal language) The ideal language, projected by *Leibniz, in which logical relations would be so transparent that, when people used the language, there would be no irresoluble dispute, but only the need to 'calculate'. The idea is of a language whose categories and combinations accurately mirror the structure of reality itself, with no potentially misleading human perspective contaminating it. The lustre of this ideal has waxed and waned: it gains when a new notation (e.g. that of the calculus, or of modern *logic) sweeps away old confusion, but loses ground when it appears that any language must be a reflection of possibly muddled ways of life, rather than an independent source of rational Enlightenment.

charisma In the analysis of *Weber, the charismatic leader exercises power through a certain quality whereby he or she is set apart from ordinary people, and becomes irrationally treated as almost superhuman. Charismatic leadership arises only at periods or places where traditional norms of reason and forms of authority are weak, and the leader fills the vacuum. *See also* FASCISM.

charity, principle of Principle especially highlighted by *Davidson as governing the interpretation of others. In various versions it constrains the interpreter to maximize the truth or rationality in the subject's sayings. For Davidson it follows that there is no sense in conceiving of a system of thought of which most propositions are false, so the principle forms a surprising buttress against *scepticism. *See also* HUMANITY, PRINCIPLE OF.

Charron, Pierre (1541–1603) French Catholic priest who presented *Montaigne's thought in didactic form in order to defend Catholicism against Calvinists and others. In his *On Wisdom* (1603) he argues that *Pyrrhonian scepticism leaves faith as our only recourse. He also set forth a naturalistic moral theory based on Stoic ideas.

chastity Either complete abstinence from sexual activity, especially in females, or the virtuous exercise of it to just the right extent, for instance in the Catholic *natural law tradition, solely in marriage, and solely in order to produce children.

***ch'eng* (*cheng*)** Chinese term meaning 'sincerity', applied to the ultimate metaphysical principle, the true or real.

Cheng Hao (1032–85) and **Cheng Yi** (1033–1107) Brothers who played a pivotal historical role in establishing mature *Neo-Confucianism. Of the two, Cheng Hao was the more mystical and introspective; Cheng Yi emphasized extending knowledge of the world through investigation.

Chernyshevski, Nikolai Gavrilovich (1828–89) Russian political theorist, Hegelian and materialist, who spent much of his life imprisoned in Siberia. He was an inspiration to engaged liberal intellectuals, admired by Plekhanov and Lenin, and in official Soviet ideology regarded as the greatest Russian philosopher before Marx.

***chi* (*ch'i*, *Qi*)** (Chinese, breath, vital spirit, force) The vital force, in particular as it is expressed in the combination of passive and active principles (*yin and yang). In some Chinese philosophy *chi* plays something of the role of Aristotelian *form, being what distinguishes and individuates particular things, and what is lost with the death or dissolution of anything. In *Confucianism it also refers to whatever is material or corporeal. *Chi* is frequently opposed to *li* or principle.

C

chicken Game theoretic example derived from a frightening game allegedly played by Los Angeles teenagers. The two players drive cars straight at each other. They will crash fatally if neither swerves. If one swerves, he is 'chicken' and loses face, while the other can triumph and gloat over him. If each swerves, neither wins any kudos, but each survives. The options can be represented in a matrix:

	Swerve A	Drive on A
Swerve B	A: 2, B: 2	A: 3, B: 1
Drive on B	A: 1, B: 3	A: 0, B: 0

This differs from the more famous *prisoners' dilemma, in that the outcome of both driving on is collectively and individually the worst, whereas in the prisoners' dilemma the worst outcome for an individual is to stay quiet while the other confesses. In his *Common Sense and Nuclear Warfare* (1959) Bertrand *Russell compared the 'mutually assured destruction' of the nuclear deterrent to this game: 'As played by irresponsible boys, this game is considered decadent and immoral, though only the lives of the players are risked. But when the game is played by eminent statesmen, who risk not only their own lives but those of many hundreds of millions of human beings, it is thought on both sides that the statesmen on one side are displaying a high degree of wisdom and courage, and only the statesmen on the other side are reprehensible.'

chiliagon (Greek, *chilioi*, 1000 + *gonia*, angle) A closed plane figure with 1000 internal angles (thus almost indistinguishable from a circle). Chiliasm is the doctrine that Christ will come again and reign for 1000 years, a form of *millenarianism.

chimera (chimaera) A wild fancy. In Greek mythology, a fire-breathing monster with a lion's head, a goat's body, and a serpent's tail.

Chinese Classics A group of 13 texts of divination, history, philosophy, poetry, ritual, and lexicography that from the time of the Song dynasty defined the orthodox *Confucian tradition.

SEE WEB LINKS

- Downloadable texts and translations of the Confucian classics
- Discussion of the core doctrines of Confucianism as expounded in the Chinese Classics

Chinese room A *thought experiment introduced by the American philosopher J. R. Searle in 'Minds, Brains, and Programs' in the journal *Behavioral and Brain Sciences* (1980). We suppose that I am locked in a room and given a large batch of Chinese writing, although I know no Chinese. But I am also given, in English, instructions for returning particular batches of Chinese ('answers') in response to other batches ('questions'). I do this by manipulating uninterpreted batches of Chinese script, recognized purely by its shape. Searle's claim is that 'as far as the Chinese is concerned, I simply behave like a computer; I perform computational operations on formally specified elements'. The point of the thought experiment is to suggest that in this example I have everything that *artificial intelligence can put into me by way of a program. Yet it is obvious that I do not understand Chinese. The conclusion is intended to undermine the thesis of 'strong AI' that appropriately programmed computers have understanding, or cognitive states, or that their programs can help explain human cognition.

The thought experiment has been heavily criticized, most forcibly on the grounds that it is the overall system (not just I myself, in the middle, shifting paper) that is appropriately compared to a programmed computer, but also on the grounds that the strong AI research program is entitled to develop ways of bringing symbols into further interaction both with the environment, and with behaviour of the machine, and that these together generate a better model of the cognitive subject. Searle's own response insists that anything characterized as a thinker must have appropriate causal powers, but also suggests, surprisingly, that such powers essentially require biology or 'wetware' rather than hardware.

Chisholm, Roderick Milton (1916–99) Influential American philosopher and teacher, who spent virtually his entire career at Brown University. His work is characterized by scrupulous and often elaborate attention to detail. He was among the first to develop an *adverbial theory of perception, and to bring *Brentano to the attention of American philosophers. Works include *Perceiving: A Philosophical Study* (1957), *Person and Object: A Metaphysical Study* (1976), and *The First Person: An Essay on Reference and Intentionality* (1981).

choice The philosophical crux is whether choice is a process in which different desires, pressures, and attitudes fight it out and eventually result in one decision and action, or whether in addition there is a 'self' controlling the conflict, in the name of higher desires, reason, or morality. The attempt to add such an extra to the more passive picture (often attributed to *Hume) is characteristic of *Kantian ethics, and is a particular target not only of Humean, but also of much feminist and postmodernist writing. *See also* FREE WILL, NEWCOMB'S PARADOX, VOLITION, WILL.

choice, axiom of The axiom of *set theory asserting that if S is a set of *disjoint, non-empty sets, then there exists a set containing exactly one member from each member of S. The axiom is problematic because it asserts the existence of an object that there may be no way of constructing, and thus offends against mathematical *constructivism.

Chomsky, Avram Noam (1928–) American linguist, philosopher, and political activist. Born in Philadelphia, Chomsky was educated at the University of Pennsylvania under the linguist Zellig Harris, and after a period at the Society of Fellows at Harvard was awarded his doctorate there in 1955. He has taught at the Massachusetts Institute of Technology since 1955. Arising from his dissertation, his book *Syntactic Structures* (1957) is widely regarded as the most significant contribution to theoretical linguistics of the second half of the 20th century. Chomsky believes that the speed with which children master their native language cannot be explained by learning theory, but requires acknowledging an innate disposition of the mind, an unlearned, innate, and universal grammar, supplying the kinds of rule that the child will *a priori* understand to be embodied in examples of speech with which it is confronted. In computational terms, unless the child came bundled with the right kind of software, it could not catch on to the grammar of language as it in fact does. *Cartesian Linguistics* (1966) makes plain the anti-empiricist, rationalist implications of this idea. Critics such as *Ryle complained that the argument pays too little attention to the realities of imitation and practice in the learning process, and seeks to fill the gap only with 'clouds of biological glory', but Chomsky's nativism is still the ruling paradigm in linguistics and psychology. Outside linguistics Chomsky was well-known for his opposition to the American war in Vietnam, and was at the time the leading dissident academic critic of the United States government. He has continued to be the best-known radical and dissident voice of his time in the United States. *See also* GENERATIVE GRAMMAR, INNATE IDEAS.

Chomsky hierarchy A series of increasingly complex and comprehensive classes of formal languages. The simplest are finite state languages, followed by *context-free, context-sensitive, recursive, and recursively enumerable languages. The descriptions refer to the type of formal *grammar (and hence the type of computational program) needed to generate the sentences of the language.

Christine de Pizan (1365–*c*.1430) Venetian-born poet, political theorist, and advocate for women, and probably the first European woman known to have made a living by writing. Her verse *Letters on the Romance of the Rose* attacked Jean de Meung's popular *The Romance of the Rose* as immoral and misogynistic. Her *City of Ladies* (1405) describes a utopian city for women inhabited by powerful, educated, and influential women both of antiquity and of her own time.

chromosome The threadlike bodies in the nucleus of a cell that contain the strands of DNA which carry *genes. In sexual reproduction, chromosomes pair up and divide in ways which randomly allocate genes to the resulting *gametes, ensuring inherited diversity in the resulting progeny.

Chrysippus (*c*.280–207 BC) The third leading *Stoic after *Cleanthes, and possibly the most productive philosopher of all time, having written 705 books, none of which survive (however, ancient books were relatively short; *see also* DEWEY). Chrysippus was originally a pupil of *Arcesilaus, and was converted to Stoicism by Cleanthes. He enjoyed a considerable reputation as a logician, and there is some evidence that he commanded the fundamental idea of a *truth-function, which then lay dormant until the 20th century. He also held a cognitive theory of the *emotions, which he thought consisted in judgements of the value of things.

Chrysippus' dog *See* ANIMAL THOUGHT.

Chu Hsi (1130–1200) Chinese philosopher and scholar. His systematization and collection of the work of *Confucius and *Mencius gave rise to the *Four Books on which subsequent Chinese education was largely based.

chung* or *shu In *Confucianism, conscientiousness and altruism. *Chung* means the full development of the virtuous self, and *shu* means the extension of that mind to others. *See also* ALTRUISM, *EUDAIMONIA*, FRIENDSHIP.

Church's theorem Theorem due to the American mathematician and philosopher Alonzo Church (1903–95) stating that the theorems of the *predicate calculus do not form a general recursive set. Given *Church's thesis, this means that there is no decision procedure or algorithm for deciding whether an arbitrary formula of the first-order predicate calculus is a theorem of the calculus.

Church's thesis The thesis that every *effectively computable function is general recursive. A thesis rather than a theorem, because the notion of effective computability remains intuitive rather than mathematically defined. The thesis is generally believed, since a number of notions, including *Turing computability, coincide in identifying this class of functions, and nobody has yet found something that is effective, intuitively, but not recursive.

Cicero, Marcus Tullius (106–43 BC) The Roman orator and statesman is philosophically important partly as a transmitter of Greek ideas in Latin, but also for the unity of philosophy and *rhetoric that he sought to promote. Rhetoric enables the statesman, educated to wisdom by philosophy, to prevail by gaining the consent of a free citizenry. Cicero was an eclectic who had sympathy with *Stoicism, the *Peripatetics, and the *scepticism of the *Academy, but was opposed to the system of *Epicurus. He exercised a considerable influence on thinkers of the *Enlightenment, and notably on *Hume.

SEE WEB LINKS

- Plutarch's biography of Cicero (translated by Dryden)
- A list of internet resources on Cicero, including a bibliography

Cieszkowski, August von (1814–94) Polish economist and philosopher. A leading Young *Hegelian, and one of the first to develop the notion of *praxis or revolutionary political practice infused with theory.

circle, vicious A definition is viciously circular when the term to be defined reappears in the definition, or where the notion that is being defined is implicitly contained in the definition. The definition '"*x* is good" means that we think that *x* is good' is an example of the former. The definition '"*x* is good" means that ideal people like *x*' is an example of the latter, since although the word 'good' does not recur, it seems hidden in the notion of an ideal (= maximally good) person. Reasoning is condemned as viciously circular when the conclusion is improperly concealed in the premises, or is improperly needed to get the conclusion itself from the premises (*see also* BEGGING THE QUESTION). It is extremely hard to say when such concealment is vicious, since there is one sense in which in any *valid argument the conclusion is concealed in the premises. Controversial cases of circular reasoning in philosophy include *Descartes's alleged appeal to God to certify that the clear and distinct ideas that enabled him to prove the existence of God did not deceive him, and the use of the fact that *induction has worked well in the past as an argument for supposing that it will work well in the future. For *Russell's particular use of the concept, *see* VICIOUS CIRCLE PRINCIPLE.

circle, virtuous A virtuous circle is a circular definition or argument whose circularity does not matter for the purpose at hand. For example, in the definition '*x* is boring if and only if *x* seems boring to most people in standard conditions', the term 'boring' reappears, but the definition may have some limited use for all that, depending upon the purposes for which the equation is needed. *See also* CIRCLE, VICIOUS.

circular reasoning/definition *See* CIRCLE, VICIOUS.

citizenship In political theory citizens, as opposed to subjects, are thought of as the free and equal participants in the democratic government of the body politic. *See* DEMOCRACY, REPUBLICANISM.

citta-matra (Sanskrit, consciousness only) The doctrine defended in *Yogacara Buddhism, that maintains that there is no reality outside the mind. A variety of *idealism.

civil disobedience The political tactic of disobeying a law deliberately, in order to bring about some change. The disobedience should ideally be public, non-violent, and committed by activists willing to face the penalties of the law.

SEE WEB LINKS

- A summary of the moral arguments for and against civil disobedience
- Thoreau's classic 'Civil Disobedience', annotated and with links to other internet resources

civil society In Hegel, forms of social association intermediate between the family and the state.

Cixous, Hélène (1937–) Algerian-born French academic and feminist. In 1974 Cixous became director of the Centre de Recherche en Études Féminines at the university of Paris at Vincennes. She is particularly associated with the use of psychoanalytic themes in feminist literary theory. Although closely identified with the 'Psych et Po' (psychology and politics) movement in literary Paris of the 1960s and 1970s, unlike *Kristeva she believes in a special form of female or bisexual writing, akin to song, forward-looking, and reflecting the multiple nature of female libido and sexuality. She has analysed the role of myth in representing the patriarchal order, and has written fictions and plays. Her works include *Dedans* (1969, trs. as *Inside*, 1986), *Révolutions pour plus d'un Faust* (1975), and *Le Livre de Prométhéa* (1983).

clairvoyance *See* PARANORMAL.

Clarke, Samuel (1675–1729) English theologian and rationalist. Clarke studied at Cambridge, and became rector of St James, Westminster, where he was an influential minister. He is remembered as a *natural theologian, whose cosmological proof of the existence of God was delivered in the Boyle lectures of 1704 ('A Demonstration of the Being and Attributes of God'). His derivation of the basis of morality from right reason alone was presented the following year ('A Discourse concerning the Unchangeable Obligations of Natural Religion'). Both provided convenient targets for the naturalistic philosophers of the *Enlightenment. He is mainly remembered for his defence of *Newton (a friend from Cambridge days) against *Leibniz, both on the question of the existence of absolute space and on the question of the propriety of appealing to a force of gravity. The exchange has been collected as *The Leibniz–Clarke Correspondence* (1956). Clarke had the last word (publishing his fifth reply after Leibniz's death) but Leibniz won the argument. In his *Lettres philosophiques* (1734), *Voltaire describes Clarke as a 'veritable reasoning machine'.

class, logical Sometimes used as a synonym for *set. But a class is contrasted with a set in classical set theory. A class of things may answer to a condition but not form a set, if various restrictions designed to avoid the *logical paradoxes are not met. Intuitively this usually means that the class may never be treated as a completed totality. But in some set theories classes are completed totalities, but are too big to be sets: paradox is avoided by not allowing them to be members of other sets. *See also* SEPARATION, AXIOM OF.

class, social A grouping separating a society into subsets defined in terms of status, privilege, place in the processes of economic production, access to power and *authority, and sometimes an individual's self-definition in such terms. In a complex society various measures of class may come apart: for example, the traditional upper class may be relatively impoverished.

classicism The aesthetic and cultural perspective guided by admiration for what are perceived as classical qualities: order, maturity, harmony, balance, moderation. The central models for works striving to achieve these qualities are the literary, artistic, and architectural works of ancient Greece and Rome. In the 18th century the pursuit of these ideals became codified in terms of rules of decorum deriving from *Aristotle's *Poetics* and Horace's *Art of Poetry*. The Augustan age in England stretched from the time of Dryden to the middle of the 18th century, and included many self-conscious attempts to imitate the poets of the Augustan age in Rome (Virgil, Horace, Ovid, Propertius). In philosophical writing Hume is the most self-consciously Augustan of the great philosophers. In the late 18th century the more idiosyncratic, free, unfettered spirit of *Romanticism rebelled against what became perceived as the artificial restrictions of classicism.

class paradox *See* RUSSELL'S PARADOX.

class struggle *Marx wrote in the *Communist Manifesto* that 'the history of all hitherto existing society is the history of class struggles'. But the statement needs qualification in its application to societies in which there were gradual gradations of rank rather than classes sharply defined by their different relationships to the modes of economic production. A critical issue for modern Marxism is whether there is a gradual intensification of class struggle in developing capitalist societies, or whether the *embourgeoisement* of the working classes undermines their revolutionary role. *See also* BOURGEOISIE/PROLETARIAT.

Cleanthes (*c.*331–232 BC) *Stoic philosopher, and second head of the Stoic school. Coming between *Zeno of Citium, the founder, and *Chrysippus, the 'second founder' of the Stoic school, Cleanthes has usually been accorded a relatively minor position. However, his *Hymn to Zeus* contains an elaboration of Stoic physics, explaining the flux in terms of a principle of 'tension' (*tonos*) in the underlying substance of the world. He represents the pantheism of Stoicism, and the conception of ideal life as one lived in accordance with nature. He is himself recorded as a patient and gentle person, undeserving of his nickname 'the ass'.

clear and distinct ideas Term used by *Descartes to signify the particular transparent quality of ideas on which we are entitled to rely, even when indulging the *method of doubt. The nature of this quality is not itself made out clearly and distinctly in Descartes, but there is some reason to see it as characterizing those ideas that we just cannot imagine false, and must therefore accept on that account, rather than ideas that have any more intimate, guaranteed, connection with the truth.

Clement of Alexandria (AD *c.*150–*c.*215) Titus Flavius Clemens was born in Athens of pagan parents, converted to Christianity, and studied and later taught at Alexandria. His *Protrepticus* or 'Address to the Greeks' (*c.*190) was designed to prove the superiority of Christianity to pagan cults and ways of life, and is a copious (but biased) source of information about the pagan mysteries. He supported a fusion of Platonism and Christianity and saw pagan philosophy and the Old Testament as preparation for Christianity which is an ascent to perfect **gnosis* with Christ as **logos*.

Cleomedes (*c.* 2nd c. AD) Writer of a Greek treatise on astronomy, 'Elementary Theory of the Heavens', valuable for what it preserves of earlier mathematical and philosophical writers, notably *Posidonius and *Eratosthenes.

Clifford, William Kingdon (1845–79) Cambridge mathematician and essayist. He is remembered in philosophy for the spirited essay 'The Ethics of Belief' (1879) defending an uncompromising religious agnosticism: 'It is wrong, always, everywhere, and for anyone, to believe anything on insufficient evidence.' The essay brought an attempted rebuttal by William *James, in his essay 'The Will to Believe' (1897), which itself, however, looks too much like a defence of wishful thinking to be convincing.

SEE WEB LINKS

- A biography of Clifford, including his contributions to science, mathematics, and philosophy
- James's 'The Will to Believe', with commentaries on their debate

clinamen (Latin, inclination) In the *atomism of *Epicurus, the 'swerve' of atoms responsible for introducing indeterminacy into an otherwise deterministic system.

Clitomachus (186/7–110/09 BC) Academic *sceptic and pupil of *Carneades. He allegedly wrote over 400 books, mainly recording the arguments of Carneades, and became head of the Academy in 127/6. *Cicero reports him as insisting that Carneades never abandoned the counsel of strict suspension of judgement, the fundamental sceptical aim, although his defection from this standard had been rumoured.

clock paradox Also known as the twins paradox or two-clock paradox. An apparent paradox of special and general *relativity theory. The time dilation effect in the special theory of relativity is that clocks at rest in different *inertial frames observe each other to run slow. The alleged consequence is that if we consider a universe of two adjacent clocks at rest with respect to each other, which are then separated and subsequently reunited, after this event each will be slow relative to the other (i.e. each will show less time to have elapsed than the other), which is a contradiction. The argument is that in a universe with no independent objects providing a frame of reference, there is no fact of the matter which clock should be considered to be the one that has moved. The flaw in the reasoning is that if a clock goes on a journey then there is no inertial frame in which it is at rest throughout the interval: it needs to accelerate outwards and accelerate back. Whichever clock does this will indeed show that less time has elapsed when reunited with another clock with no past history of acceleration, for this is a physical effect consequent upon accelerating with respect to space. However, the clock paradox does show that this real acceleration does not *supervene upon the symmetrical properties of the two clocks, in the universe of which they are the only constituent masses.

Asymmetric ageing as a consequence of changes in velocity is a well-confirmed empirical consequence of general relativity theory. In general relativity theory, space involves a dynamic field created by gravitational mass, and movement relative to it is a physical state with its own consequences.

clocks, image of the two Image used by *Leibniz to illustrate the principle of *pre-established harmony.

closed A *set is closed with respect to an operation if the result of applying that operation to a member of the set is itself a member of the set.

closed formula (closed sentence) A formula in which all the *variables are *bound.

Coase theorem Informal theorem due to University of Chicago economist and Nobel prizewinner Ronald Coase. It states that if there are zero transaction costs, the socially efficient outcome will occur regardless of legal entitlement. In other words if rights can be bought and sold rational agents will trade them for money in such a way as to maximize returns. In jurisprudence as influenced by economics, this can be used to argue that rights should be allocated to those willing to pay the highest price for them. The implication is taken to be that the market can take care of matters such as the costs to be borne by businesses that harm the environment.

Cockburn, Catherine (1679–1749) A precocious dramatist, whose plays were mainly written and performed while she was a teenager, Cockburn's first philosophical work (1702) was an anonymous defence of *Locke, against the charge of materialism brought against him by Thomas Burnet (1635–1715). In 1747 she published a defence of the rationalistic moral system of *Clarke; her collected prose works were published in 1751.

coextensive Two predicates are coextensive if they apply to exactly the same things.

cogito ergo sum (Latin, I think therefore I am) *See* METHOD OF DOUBT.

cognition Cognitive processes are those responsible for knowledge and awareness. They include the processing of experience, perception, and memory, as well as overtly verbal thinking.

cognitive achievement word *See* SUCCESS WORD.

cognitive architecture The structures that determine mental processing; the shape of mental mechanisms responsible for cognitive achievements. *See also* COGNITIVE PLURALISM.

cognitive dissonance Term introduced by the American psychologist Leon Festinger (1919–89), whose *Theory of Cognitive Dissonance* (1957) directed interest to the ways in which the drive to reduce 'dissonance', or the sense that something is wrong in one's system of beliefs, may lead to surprising strategies of belief formation or retention.

cognitive meaning The cognitive aspect of the meaning of a sentence. This is thought of as its content, or what is strictly said, abstracted away from the *tone or *emotive meaning, or other *implicatures generated, for example, by the choice of words. The cognitive aspect is what has to be understood to know what would make the sentence true or false: it is frequently identified with the *truth condition of the sentence.

cognitive pluralism The view that different people, or groups of people, may have different *cognitive architectures, therefore being disposed to reason differently or form and revise beliefs and desires differently.

cognitive psychotherapy A process of improving one's take on a situation, by taking advantage of available and relevant information, and representing it in an ideally vivid way. The process is identified by Richard Brandt in *A Theory of the Good and the Right* (1979); according to Brandt rational moral norms are those that would be chosen by anyone motivated by attitudes that survive such a process.

cognitive science The scientific study of processes of awareness, thought, and mental organization, often by means of computer modelling or *artificial intelligence research.

Cohen, Hermann (1842–1918) German Neo-Kantian and Jewish philosopher, and founder of the Marburg School. Cohen defended Kantian views of the *a priori*, but without leaving a place for the *noumenal. He found Kantian respect for the moral subject implicit in the Judaic tradition, and in later years became a major influence on Jewish thought. His principal legacy is *Die Religion der Vernunft aus den Quellen des Judentums* (1919), trs. as *Religion of Reason out of the Sources of Judaism* (1972).

coherence theory of truth The view that the truth of a proposition consists in its being a member of some suitably defined body of other propositions: a body that is consistent, coherent, and possibly endowed with other virtues, provided these are not defined in terms of truth. The theory, though surprising at first sight, has two strengths: (i) we test beliefs for truth in the light of other beliefs, including perceptual beliefs, and (ii) we cannot step outside our own best system of belief, to see how well it is doing in terms of correspondence with the world. To many thinkers the weak point of pure coherence theories is that they fail to include a proper sense of the way in which actual systems of belief are sustained by persons with perceptual experience, impinged upon by their environment. For a pure coherence theorist, experience is only relevant as the source of perceptual beliefs, which take their place as part of the coherent or incoherent set. This seems not to do justice to our sense that experience plays a special role in controlling our systems of belief, but coherentists have contested the claim in various ways. *See also* CORRESPONDENCE THEORY OF TRUTH.

coherentism *See* COHERENCE THEORY OF TRUTH, FOUNDATIONALISM.

Coleridge, Samuel Taylor (1772–1834) The English poet is important in the history of philosophy as one of the main conduits by which both the work of *Kant and German *Romanticism were introduced into England. Coleridge visited Germany in 1798 and began a period of intense study and assimilation of thinkers including Kant and *Schelling. Like them, Coleridge propounded a view of individual spiritual salvation far removed from simple *Enlightenment and *utilitarian confidence in social engineering and material progress.

collective Term used by the mathematician Richard von Mises (1883–1953) in *Probability, Statistics, and Truth* (1957; 1st German edn, 1928) for a sequence of events constituting a 'mass phenomenon' or sufficiently large repetition of an underlying cause, to form the basis for an attribution of probability. A large number of tosses of an identical coin, or large number of persons taking a certain drug, or large number of molecules in a gas in a certain state, may afford the basis for a probability judgement: that heads is 0.5 probable, that the chance of a heart attack is 0.1, or that the chance of a collision with another molecule in a certain time has a certain value. Treated mathematically a collective may be regarded as an infinite sequence of events, on each of which the chance of some attribute occurring is identical. The mathematical collective is an idealization of empirically given collectives, which have only finite numbers of members. *See also* FREQUENCY THEORY OF PROBABILITY.

collective/distributive Taking a class of things collectively is contrasted with taking them separately or distributively. Not knowing which is meant can be fatal. Article II of the American Bill of Rights states that 'a well-regulated militia, being necessary to the security of a free state, the right of the people to keep and bear arms shall not be infringed', and is unfortunately ambiguous over whether what is being created is the right of the citizens collectively to keep and bear arms (i.e. to organize themselves militarily, or to sustain a militia), or the right of each individual separately, and not well regulated, to amass his or her own arsenal. In other parts of political philosophy the distinction surfaces when we know what each person prefers individually, but are unable to construct a unique *social welfare function telling us what 'they' prefer as a whole or collectively. *See also* ARROW'S THEOREM, GENERAL WILL, PRISONERS' DILEMMA.

collective goods Goods that benefit every individual belonging to some group, and where it is hard to exclude any individual from that benefit. For example, the benefit of having a defence force, or law and order. Since an individual cannot be excluded from these benefits, there is a motive for agents to *free ride on the supply of these goods by others.

collective unconscious The term in the psychology of *Jung for the inherited deposit of the past experience of the human species, preserved in the unconscious of each of us in the form of *archetypes or symbolic figures and myths. These determine the shape of our imaginings and dreams, and in periods of crisis may recur with great emotional intensity to point out our destinies.

collectivism The political theory that regards the collective as the fundamental unit of social authority; it is usually opposed both to liberal *individualism, and to the larger authority of the state. A collective is a self-governing association of individuals. An absolutist form of collectivism holds that no institution or person which is part of it can have rights against the collective. *See also* TOTALITARIANISM.

Collier, Arthur (1680–1732) English parish priest whose *Clavis Universalis* ('universal key') of 1713 propounds an *immaterialism strikingly similar to that of *Berkeley. There is uncertainty over the extent to which Collier may have been indebted to Berkeley.

Collingwood, Robin George (1889–1943) English philosopher and historian. Born in the Lake District, Collingwood enjoyed a dual career as Roman historian and philosopher. He became a Fellow of Pembroke College, Oxford, in 1912, and professor of philosophy in Oxford in 1934. At the beginning of his career Collingwood tended towards *idealism, being more in sympathy with *Bradley and *Croce than with the realists *Russell or *Moore, whose careless readings of historical philosophers particularly irked him. His historical work gave him a special interest in the activity of understanding and interpreting the past, an activity that he saw as continuous with our self-understanding and self-interpretation. It is not achieved by theorizing, but by the empathetic identification of the problem as it must have appeared to the subject, and a reliving of the deliberation that must then have ensued (*see also* SIMULATION THEORY, *VERSTEHEN*). Collingwood anticipates themes in the later *Wittgenstein by stressing how the meaning of sentences is given by the practical problems and questions to which they provide answers. He also emphasizes that the **a priori* is a doubtful and shifting historical category, and especially stresses the *Hegelian insight that people essentially discover themselves first as members of communities, not as self-sufficient individuals. This removes any first-person *privileged access in the philosophy of mind. Towards the end of his career, in the *Essay on Metaphysics* (1940), Collingwood argued for a full-blooded identification of metaphysics with history. The proper subject of metaphysics becomes the descriptive study of the 'absolute presuppositions' of the thought and science of a particular age. His major contributions include *Speculum Mentis* (1924), *The Principles of Art* (1938), and *The Idea of History* (1946).

Collins, Anthony (1676–1729) Collins is celebrated primarily as an early 'free-thinker' or atheist, with his *Discourse of Free-thinking* (1713) being the best-remembered of his works. However, he wrote extensively on other philosophical issues, combining deterministic and materialist elements of *Hobbes, *Spinoza, *Bayle, and *Locke. Other works include *Philosophical Inquiry* (1717).

colour Colour is the most prominent example of a secondary quality (*see* PRIMARY/SECONDARY QUALITIES). Philosophical opinion has always been divided over whether to allocate colour (and smell, taste, and sound) to the physical world, or to regard them as holding their 'residence entirely in the sensitive body; so that if the animal were removed, every such quality would be abolished and annihilated' (*Galileo, *Opere complete*, vol. iv). The *atomists and *Epicureans of the ancient world held the latter view, and it returned to popularity with the rise of 17th-century science. More accurately, we can distinguish at least five general families of philosophical position: (i) colours of things are the microphysical structures responsible for the different reflectances of light of different wavelengths by their surfaces; (ii) colours are the powers or dispositions bodies have, in virtue of these structures, to affect our visual experience in particular ways; (iii) colours are properly qualities of experience itself, displaced or projected onto external things; (iv) colours are complex dispositions of the perceiving subject, differentially triggered by different surfaces; (v) colours are to be identified with complex neurological events. The last two are a subjective mirror image of the first two positions. Many of these suggestions face well-aired problems: whether they are even consistent with the fact that colours are visible, for example, and whether they make them intersubjectively accessible. Mixed and more complex theories are also found. Recent colour science has highlighted the extremely complex function of energies at different parts of the electromagnetic spectrum that result in things being perceived as one colour or another. Such work, emphasizing the active role of the brain in generating a definite experience from the complex flux, has tended to favour theories on the more subjective side of the fence, but the topic is currently wide open, even to the point of some theorists craving a pre-Galilean, Aristotelian, innocent confidence that the world is, in itself, coloured just as we take it to be. One interesting constraint on a successful theory of colour is its ability to explain various necessities: that yellow is a bright colour, that there cannot be transparent white, nor a grey flame. *See also* PRIVATE LANGUAGE ARGUMENT, QUALIA.

comedy Narratives or performances that emphasize the ridiculous and the absurd in human life, or that expose pretensions and hypocrisy, causing laughter and delight. Comedy tends to get a bad press compared to the loftier and nobler genre of *tragedy, but arguably contains as much or more *wisdom, substituting the earthy facts of existence for the inflated ideals of tragedy. *See also* LAUGHTER.

commensurable Two things are commensurable if they can be ordered by some single measure. There is often a real problem about knowing whether this is so: deciding whether two persons' *utilities or states of happiness can be measured one against the other, for example. In the philosophy of science two theories are said to be commensurable if the claims of one can be framed in the language of the other. When two theories are incommensurable there may be no neutral standpoint from which to make an objective assessment of the merits of the one versus those of the other.

commitment In some philosophies of mind a commitment may be thought of as functioning slightly differently from a belief. One may be committed to a proposition in the sense of relying on it, or using it to structure explanation and prediction, but entirely in an *instrumentalist spirit, and therefore without supposing it to be true. *See* CONSTRUCTIVE EMPIRICISM. Moral and aesthetic opinions may also be called commitments, and opposed to beliefs by being thought of as expressions of attitude. *See* EMOTIVISM, PROJECTIVISM.

commodity A commodity is the form a product takes when the material means of existence are organized through exchange. Commodities have two values: their immediate use in satisfying some need or desire, and their use as vehicles of exchange. Money is simply a measure of the second kind of value, enabling different goods to be commensurated in the market. Commodity fetishism is, in *Marxist thought, the process whereby the products of labour come to appear to have an independent value separated from the labour of the people who created them. The role commodities have in exchange disguises the way that their value ought to be entirely derivative from the labour that produces them. In the analysis of *Lukács all human relationships come to be treated as commodities, a species of false consciousness characteristic of capitalist ideology.

common consent arguments An argument that since something is commonly supposed to be so, then it is so. Clearly invalid in general (e.g. it might commonly be supposed that the earth is flat, when it is not), but more compelling in special cases. For example if a society commonly supposes that a construction is grammatical, or that a term has a certain meaning, this may entail that the construction is grammatical, or that the word does have that meaning. The place of common consent, like common sense, in *epistemology is not easy to establish. *See also* HERBERT OF CHERBURY.

common good Especially in *Thomistic and *Neo-Thomistic ethics, the common good is the common goal of all those who promote justice in a community, the common source of fulfilment of those who share in the just arrangements. The view is based on *Aristotle's notion of us as essentially social and political animals, only capable of flourishing when involved in doing things together, rather than exclusively concerned with private ends.

C

common law Law as founded in custom and precedent. It is therefore neither the creation of a sovereign nor dictated or invented by legal dictation, but handed down in a continuous process of interpretation and reinterpretation of the significance of previous custom. It is more reverenced by social conservatives such as *Blackstone or *Burke, and by lawyers themselves, than by reformers such as *Bentham.

common notions In *Stoicism, the trustworthy common basis of knowledge.

commons, tragedy of the The structure christened by the biologist Garrett Hardin in *Science* in 1968, whereby if a good such as a village common or an area of fishing is held in common by a society, there will be a tendency to over-use or exploit it. Each individual gains the full benefit of herding an extra animal, or taking an extra cargo of fish, whereas any loss is borne across the community. Any individual can also argue that if the others exploit the resource he had better do so as well; if the others do not, then it will do no harm for him to take a little more. The inevitable outcome is the eventual destruction of the resource.

SEE WEB LINKS

- Hardin's 'The Tragedy of the Commons', with updates and responses
- A list of internet resources on Hardin's work

common sense In early modern writing (e.g. *Descartes) the faculty responsible for coordinating the deliveries of the different senses. In this meaning the objects of common sense are the 'common sensibles', i.e. qualities such as extension and motion that can be detected by more than one sense. Later the term loses any special meaning, coming to refer just to the sturdy good judgement, uncontaminated by too much theory and unmoved by *scepticism, that is supposed to belong to persons before they become too philosophical. *Ryle once suggested that *Locke invented common sense, and *Russell added that none but Englishmen have had it ever since. The term became prominent in philosophy after *Moore argued in 'A Defence of Common Sense' that no philosophical argument purporting to establish scepticism could be more certain than his common-sense convictions. Moore's knowledge that he had a hand was more certain than any philosophical premises or trains of argument purporting to show that he did not know this. *See also* COMMON SENSE SCHOOL.

common sense school Title for a school of Scottish philosophy, whose most distinguished member was Thomas *Reid, but which was widely disseminated by teachers, especially in the United States. It stood for opposition to Hume, and what was seen as Hume's scepticism. If philosophy throws the basic tenets of common sense into doubt, then it is the philosophy that is mistaken and not the common sense. *See also* MOORE.

communication The transmission of information. Problems in the philosophy of communication include the question of whether communication is essential to thought, whether we can do better than thinking of words as mere vehicles for independent thoughts or ideas, and what distinguishes a primitive signalling system, such as animals may possess, from full-fledged meaningful language. *See also* GRICE.

communism A socio-economic system based on communal ownership and production of goods, communal self-government, and sometimes communal living. The slogan 'from each according to his ability, to each according to his need' encapsulates the disappearance of market mechanisms of exchange.

communitarianism A model of political organization that stresses ties of affection, kinship, and a sense of common purpose and tradition, as opposed to the meagre morality of contractual ties entered into between a loose conglomeration of individuals. The contrast was originally offered by the German sociologist F. Tönnies (1855–1936) in his *Gemeinschaft und Gesellschaft* (1887, Engl. trs. published as *Community and Association*, 1955, and *Community and Society*, 1957). *See also* COMMON GOOD.

commutative An operation or *function is commutative if its value is not affected when its arguments are exchanged. Addition is commutative, since $x + y = y + x$. Division is not commutative, since $x/y \neq y/x$.

commutative justice *See* JUSTICE, COMMUTATIVE.

compactness theorem Theorem in *first-order logic stating that if every finite subset of an infinite theory T has a model, then the theory as a whole has a model. The result follows from the *completeness theorem for first-order logic.

compatibilism *See* FREE WILL.

compatible Two propositions are compatible if they can both be true together, i.e. they are not mutually inconsistent.

competence/performance Distinction highlighted by *Chomsky, between the knowledge that we have of the language we speak, and the actual use we make of that knowledge. Competence might be modelled as the system of grammatical and semantical rules that identify a language, and in some sense guide the speaker who knows the language, whereas performance is the widely variable and idiosyncratic use an individual may then make of that system. The distinction is similar to that drawn by *Saussure between *langue* and *parole*. The notion of competence is sometimes extended to cover implicit knowledge of other conventional but rule-governed matters, such as the forms of fiction or poetry.

complement The complement of a *set S is the class of objects that are not members of S. In standard set theory the complement of a set cannot itself be a set: only those things not in the set but meeting some further restriction can form a set. *See* SEPARATION, AXIOM OF.

complementarity principle Sometimes the principle that various physical magnitudes come in conjugate pairs subject to the *Heisenberg uncertainty principle. Also the principle formulated by Niels *Bohr in 1927, that electrons and other denizens of the quantum world can be described as particles or described as waves, but that there is no way of integrating these complementing descriptions into one consistent theory.

completeness Intuitively, a logical system is complete if everything that we want can be derived in it. Thus a formalization of logic is complete if all logically valid forms of argument are derivable in the system; a system designed to codify mathematical reasoning is complete if all mathematical truths can be derived in it, and so on. Although put like this the notion seems to be entirely informal, more precise definitions can be given. A logical system is complete in the sense introduced by *Gödel if and only if all valid well-formed formulae are theorems of the system. In a stronger sense a system is complete if for any well-formed formula A, either A is a *theorem, or the system would become inconsistent if A were added as an axiom. *See* GÖDEL'S THEOREM(S), MODEL THEORY.

complex idea A doctrine of *empiricism is that the mind is furnished with its raw materials through perception. In imagination and thought we can build new ideas, but only by recombining the elements already given. Such new ideas would therefore be complex, and the basic elements from which they are built are the simple ideas.

complex number *See* NUMBER.

composite idea *See* COMPLEX IDEA.

compositionality A language is compositional if the meaning of a complex expression is derivable from the meaning of its parts and the way in which they are combined. A compositional *semantics would exhibit a way to derive the meaning of every well-formed construction (sentence) of a language from its composition. It was influentially argued by *Davidson that it is only because languages are compositional that they are learnable.

composition/division, fallacies of The fallacy of composition is one of arguing that because something is true of members of a group or collection, it is true of the group as a whole. For example, in *Utilitarianism*, J. S. *Mill appears to argue that since each person desires just their own happiness, people together desire the common happiness. (The correct conclusion has to be that nobody desires the common happiness—the premise of the argument tells us that each person desires just his or her own.) The fallacy of division is the converse fallacy of arguing that if something is true of a group, then it is also true of individuals belonging to it. *See also* COLLECTIVE/DISTRIBUTIVE.

compossibles *See* INCOMPOSSIBLE.

comprehension Term introduced by *Arnauld in *Port-Royal Logic*, for the attributes determining whether a term applies. Now superseded by *intension.

comprehension, axiom of The unrestricted axiom of *comprehension in set theory states that to every condition there corresponds a set of things meeting the condition: $(\exists y)\ (y = \{x : Fx\})$. The axiom needs restriction, since *Russell's paradox shows that in this form it will lead to contradiction. For the classical repair *see* SEPARATION, AXIOM OF.

compresence The special relationship between experiences or thoughts when they occur together within one moment of consciousness.

compulsion An irresistible pressure to act in some way. The key philosophical and legal problem with this concept is to distinguish compulsion from pressures that are in fact not resisted but in some appropriate sense could have been. Hard determinism typically maintains that there is no basis for this distinction, but most thinking about responsibility and agency acknowledges it in some form. *See* DETERMINISM, FREE WILL.

computable functions Intuitively, any *function for which there is an effective procedure or *algorithm for calculating a solution. Mathematically, a function whose value can be computed by a *Turing machine.

computer Any device capable of carrying out a sequence of operations in a defined manner. The definition of the operations is called the program. An analog computer performs computations by manipulating continuous physical variables, such as voltage and time. A digital computer operates on discrete quantities, most often represented as 'on-off', indicating whether the value of a *binary variable is 0 or 1. Numbers and information are then represented by the binary system. Philosophically the excitement generated by computers has been in exploring the extent to which mental operations are well-represented as computations. *See also* ARTIFICIAL INTELLIGENCE, CHINESE ROOM, CONNECTIONISM, TURING MACHINE, VON NEUMANN MACHINE.

Comte, Auguste (1798–1857) French philosopher and social theorist. Born in Montpellier, France, Comte was educated at the École Polytechnique, and became Secretary to *Saint-Simon in 1817; after 1826 he supported himself by teaching mathematics and giving private lectures. He believed that human society goes through stages such as the theological/military, and the scientific/industrial, as well as a transitional or metaphysical stage, which was where he conceived the Europe of his own time to be. He also delineated three stages, the theological, the metaphysical, and the positive, in the evolution of each science. Against the rationalism of *Descartes he believed that each science has its own method, and that its development is contingent on the historical level which it has achieved; Comte therefore stands as a figurehead for thinkers who value the historical and empirical study of science above an *a priori* or rationalistic attempt to dictate the way sciences ought to be. Although Comte is regarded as the founder of *positivism, in his hands it had less to do with *empiricism, than with a positive, i.e. affirmative, attitude to the study of social relations: it was Comte who coined the term 'sociology'. After his six-volume *Cours de philosophie positive* (1830–42, trs. and condensed by Harriet Martineau as *The Positive Philosophy of Auguste Comte*, 2 vols., 1853), Comte suffered a nervous breakdown, although he also managed to write the four-volume *Système de politique positive* (1851–4, trs. as *The System of Positive Polity*, 1875–7). In his later years he devoted his efforts to establishing a religion of humanity, with a calendar of saints including Adam *Smith, Frederick the Great, and himself as Pope.

SEE WEB LINKS

- A brief biography of Comte
- A list of internet resources on Comte, including a bibliography

conation (Latin, trying) Conative aspects of the mind are those associated with the initiation of action.

conatus In *Spinoza the endeavour of anything to persist in its own being, which we are aware of as the drive to self-preservation.

conceive To hold in the mind, or form an idea of something. It is important to distinguish it from conjuring a mental picture or rehearsal of the sensory awareness of a thing.

concept A concept is that which is understood by a term, particularly a predicate. To possess a concept is to be able to deploy a term expressing it in making judgements: the ability connects with such things as recognizing when the term applies, and being able to understand the consequences of its application. The term 'idea' was formerly used in the same way, but is avoided because of its associations with subjective mental imagery, which may be irrelevant to the possession of a concept. In the semantics of *Frege, a concept is the reference of a predicate, and cannot be referred to by a subject term. *See also* CONCEPT AND OBJECT.

concept and object Distinction in *Frege's philosophy of language, explored in 'On Concept and Object' (1892). Frege regarded predicates as incomplete expressions, in the same way as a mathematical expression for a function, such as sine ... or log ... , is incomplete. Predicates refer to concepts, which themselves are 'unsaturated', and cannot be referred to by subject expressions (we thus get the paradox that the concept of a horse is not a concept). Although Frege recognized the metaphorical nature of the notion of a concept being unsaturated, he was rightly convinced that some such notion is needed to explain the unity of a sentence, and to prevent sentences from being thought of as mere lists of names.

conceptual analysis *See* ANALYSIS.

conceptualism The theory of *universals that sees them as shadows of our grasp of concepts. Conceptualism lies midway between out-and-out *nominalism, holding that nothing is common to objects except our applying the same words to them, and any *realism which sees universals as existing independently of us and our abilities.

conceptual role semantics *See* INFERENTIAL ROLE SEMANTICS.

conceptual scheme The general system of concepts which shape or organize our thoughts and perceptions. The outstanding elements of our everyday conceptual scheme include spatial and temporal relations between events and enduring objects, causal relations, other persons, meaning-bearing utterances of others, and so on. To see the world as containing such things is to share this much of our conceptual scheme. A controversial argument of *Davidson's urges that we would be unable to interpret speech from a different conceptual scheme as even meaningful; we can therefore be certain *a priori* that there is no difference of conceptual scheme between any thinker and ourselves. Davidson daringly goes on to argue that since *translation proceeds according to a principle of *charity, and since it must be possible for an omniscient translator to make sense of us, we can be assured that most of the beliefs formed within the common-sense conceptual framework are true. *See also* SAPIR–WHORF HYPOTHESIS.

conclusion The result or proposition arrived at by a process of reasoning.

concomitant variations, method of *See* MILL'S METHODS.

concrete *See* ABSTRACT/CONCRETE.

concrete universal A key conception in the philosophy of *Hegel, that certifies the reality of categories. A category is a synthesis of two opposed abstractions (e.g. becoming is a synthesis of being and not-being) and in turn will be one member of a pair of opposites: the *dialectical progress of history unites or sublates the pair under a yet higher category. The only absolutely concrete universal is reality as a whole: an all-embracing system of thought. British *absolute idealists, such as *Bosanquet and *Bradley, supposed that if the concrete universal is substantial and real it ought to be identified with individual things.

concretion, principle of In the philosophy of *Whitehead, the principle that drives things towards actualizing their form, or towards emerging and advancing into more complex forms.

concupiscence (Latin, *concupiscere*, to desire, covet) In theological ethics, concupiscence comes in three grades: it may cover first, the whole range of appetite and desire; secondly, that desire which is not deliberate, but a spontaneous reaction of the appetitive part of a person; and thirdly, that which actively opposes free and rational decision. In this last sense concupiscence is a thoroughly bad thing. The *Pelagian heresy contained the view that concupiscence is innocent, and is enthusiastically countered by *Augustine, who founded the tradition of identifying concupiscence with fleshly lust, and hence as the vehicle for transmitting *original sin.

Condillac, Étienne Bonnot de (1715–80) French philosopher of mind. Born in Grenoble, and originally trained for the priesthood, Condillac became one of the leading followers and interpreters of the *empiricist philosophy of *Locke, and of the scientific revolution of *Newton (it is said that although he wore a cassock until the end of his life, he celebrated Mass only once). His *Essai sur l'origine des connaissances humaines* (1746, trs. as *An Essay on the Origin of Human Knowledge*, 1756) was followed by the *Traité des sensations* (1754, trs. in *Philosophical Writings*, 1982) which attempted to answer the charge of subjective *idealism brought against him by *Diderot. In it, Condillac develops an early *phenomenology of exterior perception, showing how sensation is not an inert presence, but part of an active involvement with the external world. It is through the development of kinaesthetic and tactile sensation, and the sensations of pressure and physical opposition, that the concept of an external world arises. The sensation of touch is the teacher of the other senses.

condition, necessary/sufficient If p is a necessary condition of q, then q cannot be true unless p is true. If p is a sufficient condition of q, then given that p is true, q is so as well. Thus steering well is a necessary condition of driving well, but it is not sufficient, for one can steer well but drive badly for other reasons. Confusion may result if the distinction is not heeded. For example, the statement that A causes B may be interpreted to mean that A is itself a sufficient condition for B, or that it is only a necessary condition for B, or is perhaps a necessary part of a total sufficient condition. Lists of conditions to be met for satisfying some administrative or legal requirement frequently attempt to give individually necessary and jointly sufficient sets of conditions.

conditional Any proposition of the form 'if p then q'. The condition hypothesized, p, is called the antecedent of the conditional, and q the consequent. Various kinds of conditional have been distinguished. The weakest is that of *material implication, merely telling us that either not-p, or q. Stronger conditionals include elements of *modality, corresponding to the thought that 'if p is true then q must be true'. Ordinary language is very flexible in its use of the conditional form, and there is controversy whether conditionals are better treated semantically, yielding different kinds of conditionals with different meanings, or pragmatically, in which case there should be one basic meaning, with surface differences arising from other *implicatures. *See also* ADAMS'S THESIS, COUNTERFACTUAL CONDITIONAL, MATERIAL CONDITIONAL, STRICT IMPLICATION.

conditional probability Term for the *probability of one event given, or conditional upon, another. The process of conditionalizing is one of taking the probability of an event e′ occurring after another event e has occurred, to have the value that the conditional probability of e′ upon e was, before e occurred. *Personalist theories of probability justify the process as required by coherence over time. The view that the process is central to rational belief formation and modification is characteristic of the Bayesian school of statistics. *See also* ADAMS'S THESIS, DUTCH BOOK.

conditional proof, rule of The rule in a deductive system that if $A_1 \ldots A_n \vdash B$ then $A_1 \ldots A_{n-1} \vdash A_n \rightarrow B$.

conditioning According to *behaviourism in psychology, conditioning is the way in which new connections between stimulus and response are learned, and therefore forms the basic pattern of learning. It comes in two forms. In classical or Pavlovian conditioning (known as type S) an animal such as a dog comes to associate a neutral signal with one which already produces a result, with the consequence that the hitherto neutral stimulus itself produces the result. In the famous case, after becoming associated with food in the mouth (the unconditioned stimulus), the bell (the conditioned stimulus) stimulates the dog to salivate (the conditioned response). In instrumental or operant conditioning (type R) the animal learns to do something to produce the result. The essential behaviourist claim is that this kind of association has its own laws, and can be studied without postulating that the animal has come to know something or expect anything. The claim is that the relationship between stimulus and response is essentially simple and passive, depending only on the temporal contiguity between the stimulus and the reward. Nor is there any need to postulate *cognition in the animal. This claim is not, however, borne out in experience: for example, whether an animal performs some learned action on a stimulus can vary with the varying degree to which it now wants the likely result of that action.

conditio sine qua non Latin, a condition without which not; a necessary condition.

Condorcet, Marquis de (1743–94) French mathematician and social theorist. Condorcet was educated by Jesuits, and became the permanent Secretary of the Académie des Sciences, for which he was qualified by his mathematical writings, in 1776. The eulogies (*Éloges*) for dead members that he composed are quintessential documents of the French *Enlightenment. Condorcet believed in the progress and perfectibility of mankind, aided by the application of mathematical methods to the moral and political sciences. His *Essai sur l'application de l'analyse à la probabilité des décisions* ('Essay on the Application of Analysis to the Probability of Majority Decisions', 1785) was an early example of a long French tradition of mathematical treatment of the social sciences (*see also* INVERSE METHODS, LAPLACE, RULE OF SUCCESSION, VOTERS' PARADOX). His other major work is the optimistic, indeed visionary, *Esquisse d'un tableau historique des progrès de l'esprit humain* (1795, trs. as *Sketch for a Historical Picture of the Progress of the Human Mind*, 1795), often cited as being one of the targets of *Malthus.

configurationism *See* GESTALT.

confirmation, paradoxes of *See* GOODMAN'S PARADOX, HEMPEL'S PARADOX.

confirmation theory The theory of the measure to which evidence supports a theory. A fully formalized confirmation theory would dictate the degree of confidence that a rational investigator might have in a theory, given some body of evidence. The grandfather of confirmation theory is *Leibniz, who believed that a logically transparent language of science would be able to resolve all disputes. In the 20th century a fully formal confirmation theory was a main goal of the *logical positivists, since without it the central concept of verification by empirical evidence itself remains distressingly unscientific. The principal developments were due to *Carnap, culminating in his *Logical Foundations of Probability* (1950). Carnap's idea was that the measure needed would be the proportion of logically possible states of affairs in which the theory and the evidence both hold, compared to the number in which the evidence itself holds (*see also* RANGE THEORY OF PROBABILITY). It therefore demands that we can put a measure on the 'range' of possibilities consistent with theory and evidence, compared with the range consistent with the evidence alone. Among the obstacles the enterprise meets is the fact that while evidence covers only a finite range of data, the hypotheses of science may cover an infinite range. In addition, confirmation proves to vary with the language in which the science is couched, and the Carnapian programme has difficulty in separating genuinely confirming variety of evidence from less compelling repetition of the same experiment. Confirmation also proved to be susceptible to acute paradoxes (*see* GOODMAN'S PARADOX, HEMPEL'S PARADOX). Finally, scientific judgement seems to depend on such intangible factors as the problems facing rival theories, and most workers have come to stress instead the historically situated sense of what looks plausible, characteristic of a scientific culture at a given time. *See also* LIMITED INDEPENDENT VARIETY, PRINCIPLE OF.

Confucianism The practical philosophy derived from the teachings of *Confucius, influential in China and other Far Eastern countries. Confucianism was the state orthodoxy in China until the revolution of 1911. It teaches that harmony is found by following the right actions of piety and respect, religious ritual, and righteousness. Developed by followers such as *Mencius, it emphasizes human goodness (and the right to rebel against those who stand in its way, such as unjust rulers), while its veneration of literacy, scholarship, poetry, ceremony, and music aligns it with the Platonic and Aristotelian ideals of contemplation and wisdom. *See also* CHINESE CLASSICS.

SEE WEB LINKS

- A list of internet resources on Confucianism, including bibliographies
- An audio discussion of Confucianism by three philosophers

Confucius (551–479 BC) (Chinese, *K'ung fu-tzu*, venerable master Kung) Born in poverty in Shantung, Confucius rose to become a major administrator in his native state. In 496 BC he began a period of wandering with the intention of persuading the various rulers he came among to practise his moral doctrines. Settling once more he became the most celebrated teacher of poetry, history, and moral philosophy of Chinese history. His sayings were collected by pupils in the *Lun Yü* or *Analects*, which form the principal source for his philosophy.

Confucius lived at a time of gross civil disorder, as rival warlords shared out the power of the crumbling Chou dynasty. His philosophy is aimed at injecting moral principle into the exercise of political power: to substitute government by virtue for government by force. By cultivating humanity (*jen*), a person becomes great in personal and public life, and when all individuals do this, happiness will be achieved. Doing this requires observing the rules of propriety (*li*) embedded in social life, so Confucianism also stands for a defence of the moral significance of the extant traditional forms of social order. *Li* is the principle that channels respect for each other and for the world, and regulates human nature. The Way (*tao*) is to live within the structures of the social order. adopting the virtues appropriate to a son, mother, ruler, etc.

conjunction The conjunction of two propositions, *p*, *q*, is the proposition *p* & *q*. It is true if, and only if, each of *p*, *q* is true. The medievals were interested in whether there exist different kinds of conjunction subject to a weaker condition, since while a book is a conjunction of the assertions it contains, it seems harsh to say that it is wholly false if one of them is false. *See also* TRUTH-FUNCTION.

connected *See* ORDERING RELATION.

connectionism The view that one of the most impressive and plausible ways of modelling cognitive processes is by means of a connectionist or parallel distributed processing computer architecture. In such a system data is input into a number of cells at one level. These are each connected to a middle layer of cells, or hidden units, which in turn deliver an output.

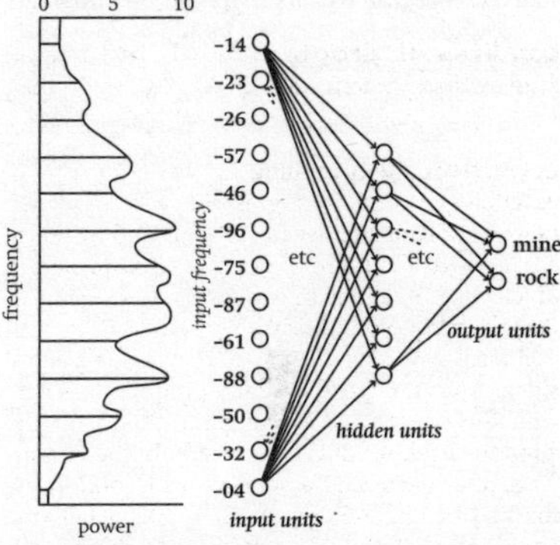

Such a system can be 'trained' by adjusting the weights a hidden unit accords to each signal from an earlier cell. The training is accomplished by 'back propagation of error', meaning that if the output is incorrect the network makes the minimum adjustment necessary to correct it. Such systems prove capable of producing differentiated responses of great subtlety. For example, a system may be able to take as input written English, and deliver as output phonetically accurate speech. Proponents of the approach also point out that networks have a certain resemblance to the layers of cells that make up a human brain, and that like us, but unlike conventional computing programs, networks degrade gracefully, in the sense that with local damage they go blurry rather than crashing altogether. Controversy has concerned the extent to which the differentiated responses made by networks deserve to be called recognition, and the extent to which non-recognitional cognitive functions, including linguistic and computational ones, are well approached in these terms.

connective In formal logic a connective is an element of a sentence that joins parts in such a way that the logical properties of the whole are a defined function of the logical properties of the parts. The most familiar connectives are those expressing the *truth-functions.

C

connotation/denotation Pair of terms associated with J. S. *Mill, and marking much the same distinction as the currently more usual intension/extension. The denotation of a singular term is the object to which it refers, and of a predicate the set of objects satisfying it. The connotation is the abstract meaning, or principle or condition whereby something is picked out as denoted by the term.

conscience The consciousness humans have that an action is morally required or forbidden. In the Christian tradition the nature of this awareness and its status as knowledge is a central problem. On the one hand it is sinful to act against one's conscience; on the other hand conscience can deceive, since we can be mistaken about what is required or forbidden. *Aquinas puts the problem thus: 'if obeying and disobeying a mistaken conscience are both bad, it seems that men with mistaken consciences are caught in a trap, and cannot avoid sin' (*Summa Theologiae*, IaIlae 19.6). The solution is to distinguish between errors of conscience that are voluntary or blameworthy and ones that are involuntary: in the former case we are responsible, in the latter we only do wrong unknowingly. The problem of the authority of conscience became urgent with the rise of Protestant ethics, in which it plays the role hitherto reserved for the independent authority of the Church. Critics of the notion include *La Mettrie and *Nietzsche, both of whom regarded a bad conscience as a kind of malady.

consciousness Possibly the most challenging and pervasive source of problems in the whole of philosophy. Our own consciousness seems to be the most basic fact confronting us, yet it is almost impossible to say what consciousness is. Is mine like yours? Is ours like that of animals? Might machines come to have consciousness? Is it possible for there to be disembodied consciousness? Whatever complex biological and neural processes go on backstage, it is my consciousness that provides the theatre where my experiences and thoughts have their existence, where my desires are felt and where my intentions are formed. But then how am I to conceive the 'I', or self that is the spectator, or at any rate the owner of this theatre? These problems together make up what is sometimes called 'the hard problem' of consciousness. One of the difficulties in thinking about consciousness is that the problems seem not to be scientific ones; *Leibniz remarked that if we could construct a machine that could think and feel, and blow it up to the size of a mill and thus be able to examine its working parts as thoroughly as we pleased, we would still not find consciousness (*Monadology*, para. 17), and drew the conclusion that consciousness resides in simple subjects, not complex ones. Even if we are convinced that consciousness somehow emerges from the complexity of brain functioning, we may still feel baffled about the way the emergence takes place, or why it takes place in just the way it does.

The nature of conscious experience has been the largest single obstacle to *physicalism, *behaviourism, and *functionalism in the philosophy of mind: these are all views that, according to their opponents, can only be believed by feigning permanent anaesthesia. But many philosophers are convinced that we can divide and conquer: we may make progress not by thinking of one 'hard' problem, but by breaking the subject up into different skills and recognizing that rather than a single self or observer we would do better to think of a relatively undirected whirl of cerebral activity, with no inner theatre, no inner lights, and above all no inner spectator.

SEE WEB LINKS

- An audio discussion of consciousness by three philosophers
- A list of internet resources on consciousness

consent A central concern of *liberal political theory is to determine the place of consent in the legitimation of social and political practices. Coercion, exploitation, fraud, deception, and perhaps more general categories of treating people as means, all imply a lack of someone's consent to what has happened. Conversely, just or permissible transactions imply either the actual or potential consent of affected parties. In order to remove the obvious problem that a person may be bound by the laws of a country when there has been no episode of actual consent, a doctrine of tacit consent was developed by *Locke. More common now is a concept of potential consent, that is, of a situation being such that an appropriately placed subject would or could rationally consent to it. It is possible to envisage the entire moral and political framework built upon the idea of those interactions to which a person could rationally consent, although the development of this theme requires a view of the motivations as well as the knowledge, rationality, and situation of the agent. *See also* CONTRACTARIANISM, RAWLS.

consequence (logical) A proposition is a logical consequence of others when it is impossible that they should be true and it false. *See* MODEL THEORY, PROOF THEORY.

consequent *See* CONDITIONAL.

consequential characteristics *See* SUPERVENIENCE.

consequentialism The view that the value of an action derives entirely from the value of its consequences. This contrasts both with the view that the value of an action may derive from the value of the kind of character whose action it is (courageous, just, temperate, etc.), and with the view that its value may be intrinsic, belonging to it simply as an act of truth-telling, promise-keeping, etc. The former is the option explored in *virtue ethics, and the latter in *deontological ethics. Consequentialism needs to identify some kinds of consequence whose value is not derivative from actions, but resides, for example, in states of pleasure or happiness, thought of as ends towards which actions are means. Opposition to this way of looking at ethics may begin with wondering whether self-standing states of this kind exist, given that generally we take satisfaction and pleasure in acting, and it is not possible to separate the pleasure as an end from the action as a mere means. Critics also point out the way in which much ethical life is 'backward looking' (seeing whether an action is a case of breaking a promise, abusing a role, betraying a trust, etc.) rather than exclusively 'forward looking' as consequentialism requires. *See also* PLEASURE, UTILITARIANISM, UTILITY.

consequentia mirabilis (Latin, marvellous consequence) Name given by medieval logicians to the principle that if a statement follows from its own negation it must be true.

conservation principles The principles in physical theory asserting that some quantity, such as mass, momentum, energy or momentum-energy, is invariant over time.

conservatism Originally in *Burke an ideology of caution in departing from the historical roots of a society, or changing its inherited traditions and institutions. In this 'organic' form it includes allegiance to tradition, community, hierarchies of rank, benevolent paternalism, and properly subservient underclasses. By contrast, conservatism can be taken to imply a **laissez-faire* ideology of untrammelled *individualism that puts the emphasis on personal responsibility, free markets, law and order, and a minimal role for government, with neither community, nor tradition, nor benevolence entering more than marginally. The two strands are not easy to reconcile, either in theory or in practice.

consilience A concept in philosophy of science first described by *Whewell, especially in his *Philosophy of the Inductive Sciences* (1840). Whewell highlighted the process whereby *inductions 'tie together' facts by the formation of new ideas. Thus separate pieces of evidence may tie together to support a conclusion whose total credibility is then greater than that given by any individual piece of evidence. A good hypothesis not only predicts facts of diverse kinds, but shows that underneath the diversity there is a fundamental unity. Although Whewell is perhaps over-optimistic in thinking that there is one 'right' unifying conception to be found in any branch of science, the virtues he points out are extremely important.

consistency, axiom of The statement that a given set of sentences is consistent. In formal studies, there are significant questions of when such an axiom can itself consistently be added to a set of sentences, or proved within a background formal language and deductive system.

consistent/inconsistent Intuitively a group of propositions is consistent if they could all be true together. In formal logic various other notions are defined. A system is consistent if it does not yield both a formula and its negation, or consistent if not all *well-formed formulae are provable. See also OMEGA-COMPLETE, OMEGA-CONSISTENT.

constant A term in a *logical calculus to which any *interpretation assigns a fixed meaning, unlike a variable or schematic letter.

constant conjunction Two events A and B are constantly conjoined if whenever one occurs the other does. The constant conjunction theory of *causation, often attributed to *Hume, is that this relationship is what is meant by saying that the one causes the other, or that if more is intended by talking of causation, nevertheless this is all that we can understand by the notion.

Constant de Rebecque, Henri Benjamin (1767–1830) Swiss-born political philosopher and politician. Educated partly in Edinburgh, Constant was a long-time intimate of Madame de *Staël. He consistently opposed political extremism and despotism. In opposition to *Rousseau he contrasted the 'liberty of the ancients' in the collective life of the polity, with the 'liberty of the moderns', or the individualistic liberty of individuals in modern commercial and market-dominated society. He was a founding figure of modern liberal theory. Principal writings include *Principes de politique* (1810), and a multi-volume history of religion, *De la religion* (1824–31).

constative Term used by J. L. *Austin to denote a *speech act with which one declares something to be the case, as opposed to performing other things.

constitution In political theory, the written or unwritten laws or conventions that govern the powers and limits of political authority in the state.

constitutive/regulative Distinction used by *Kant to reconcile the conflict of reason with itself, as illustrated in the *antinomies of pure reason. Regulative principles are *maxims of thought, deriving from our interest in 'a certain possible perfection' of knowledge of an object. Constitutive principles determine the way things must be, and derive from insight into their nature. When a maxim, such as everything must have a cause, is taken to apply constitutively and universally, antinomies develop. The distinction was taken over by the 20th-century American philosopher J. R. Searle, to describe the way rules (such as those of chess) may not only regulate the activity, but actually constitute it.

constraint One proposal for solving the problem of *free will and *determinism is that we distinguish between acting when caused to do so, which if determinism is correct always happens, and acting under constraint, i.e. when restrictions on our options exist. The suggestion is that while constraint interferes with freedom, causation does not, and should not be regarded as a kind of constraint.

construct *See* CONSTRUCTIVE, LOGICAL CONSTRUCTION.

construction (social) *See* SOCIAL CONSTRUCTION.

constructive A constructive proof is one that enables one to give an example, or give a rule for finding an example, of a mathematical object with some property. A non-constructive proof might result in us knowing that an example exists, but having no idea how to define it. The axiom of *choice in *set theory is the classical non-constructive existence axiom: it tells us that a certain set exists, whether or not there is any prospect of finding a condition defining membership in it. Similarly the definition of a function to take the value 0 if every even number is the sum of two primes, and 1 if this is not so, is classically a definition enabling us to assert that there is a number that is the value of the function, although we cannot identify which. The view that such a definition is inadmissible and that mathematics should confine itself to constructive proofs and definitions is known as constructivism. Constructivism will be suspicious of indirect existence proofs, because showing that a contradiction follows from denying that some object exists need not of itself show us how to identify the object. Constructivism frequently involves suspicion of the idea of a completed infinite set, thought of as a self-standing object of investigation, as a finite set would be.

constructive empiricism A position in the philosophy of science associated with the 20th-century Canadian philosopher Bas van Fraassen (*The Scientific Image*, 1980). Constructive empiricism divides science into observation statements and theory statements. It holds that the latter are capable of strict truth and falsity, but maintains that the appropriate attitude is not to believe them, but only to accept them at best as empirically adequate. It is often regarded as a variety of *pragmatism or *instrumentalism, although more orthodox varieties of those positions deny that theoretical statements have truth-values. A related view is held by *Vaihinger, who, however, thinks that we can be sure that theoretical statements are actually false.

constructivism (ethical) The view that in moral thought we do not apprehend an independent moral reality, but construct a system of principles or norms governing right action. The view may suppose that such construction is constrained, for instance by considerations of rationality, or by human nature, or it may permit a *pluralism or *relativism allowing that many such constructions are possible.

constructivism (mathematics) The doctrine that mathematics should confine itself to *constructive proofs.

constructivism (social) *See* SOCIAL CONSTRUCTIVISM.

consubstantial Of one and the same *substance. A concept especially necessary in Christian theology, as providing the unity between the three persons in the Trinity. *See* ATHANASIUS, *HOMOOUSION*.

contemplation A curious view common to Indian ethics, *Plato, *Aristotle, and much of the western tradition, holds that the **summum bonum* or supremely valuable state of mind lies in the right kind of contemplation: contemplation of the form of the good, or reflection upon the virtues. The idea is found in the Christian conception of beatitude as the eternal contemplation of a certain vision, and in the *Kantian view that the ideal state is one free of desire and inclination (*see* APATHY). Less mystical philosophies point out that contemplation is apt to decay into emptiness without the continual stimulus of desires, fresh action, and fresh problems.

content That which is expressed by an utterance or sentence: the proposition or claim made about the world. By extension, the content of a predicate or other sub-sentential component is what it contributes to the content of sentences that contain it. The nature of content is the central concern of the philosophy of *language. *See also* CONTENT, WIDE AND NARROW; MEANING.

content, wide and narrow What a person expresses by a sentence is often a function of the environment in which he or she is placed. For example, the disease I refer to by a term like 'arthritis' or the kind of tree I refer to as a 'beech' will be defined by criteria of which I know next to nothing. This raises the possibility of imagining two persons in rather different environments, but in which everything appears the same to each of them (*see* TWIN-EARTH). The wide content of their thoughts and sayings will be different if the situation surrounding them is appropriately different: 'situation' may here include the actual objects they perceive, or the chemical or physical kinds of object in the world they inhabit, or the history of their words, or the decisions of authorities on what counts as an example of one of the terms they use. The narrow content is that part of their thought which remains identical, through the identity of the way things appear, regardless of these differences of surroundings. Partisans of wide (sometimes called broad) content may doubt whether any content is in this sense narrow; partisans of narrow content believe that it is the fundamental notion, with wide content being explicable in terms of narrow content plus context.

context In linguistics, context is the parts of an utterance surrounding a unit and which may affect both its meaning and its grammatical contribution. A context-free grammar is one where the rules apply regardless of context; a context-sensitive grammar is one where this is not so. Context also refers to the wider situation, either of speaker or of the surroundings, that may play a part in determining the significance of a saying. Sometimes the term *co-text* is used for the narrow purely linguistic context.

contextualism (aesthetics) The view that a work of art can only be understood in the context of its historical or cultural circumstances, or in the light of other works by the same artist or in a surrounding tradition. The opposed position is *isolationism.

contextualism/formalism (ethics) Formalism is the doctrine that morality should be structured by a set of abstract principles of a high degree of generality: that morality should aspire to be a kind of geometry of rights, duties, and goods. Opposition to this view maintains that the primary focus of ethics is the concrete situation, so that ethical judgement is not the application of general rules, but is akin to aesthetic judgement in demanding attention to the details of the individual case, and in delivering verdicts that cannot be ratified by the mechanical application of antecedent rules, nor automatically extended to new cases. An extreme version of formalism is represented by *Kant, and contextualism by a number of philosophers including *Aristotle (*see PHRONĒSIS*), *Aquinas, and *Hegel (*see SITTLICHKEIT*). Contextual judgement is represented as demanding virtues, sympathies, appreciations, and perhaps intuition and tact. *Feminism has tended to embrace the contextualist wing of this debate, applauding intuitive, tactful sympathy with individual cases as opposed to the abstraction and rule-worship supposed to characterize male practical reasoning. *See also* CASUISTRY, SITUATION ETHICS.

contiguity, law of In *Leibniz, the principle that there are no discontinuous changes in nature: '*natura non facit saltum*', nature makes no leaps. Leibniz was able to use the principle to criticize the mechanical system of *Descartes, which would imply such leaps in some circumstances, and to criticize contemporary *atomism, which implied discontinuous changes of density at the edge of an atom. *See also* ACTION AT A DISTANCE.

contiguous Literally, placed next to or touching. According to *Hume the contiguity of events is an important element in our interpretation of their conjunction as causal.

continence *See AKRASIA*.

continental philosophy Inaccurate term used, often polemically, to refer to the writings of philosophers influenced by European political philosophers such as *Hegel, *Marx, or *Heidegger, by *phenomenology and *existentialist schools, or by *post-structuralist French philosophy. Writing in this vein is often politically engaged and aspires to large-scale *praxis and social critique. It is also infused with various examples of writing that does not aspire to any great clarity, which indeed it is apt to mistrust. Generally contrasted with *analytical philosophy, thought to be more the preserve of Anglo-American and Australian philosophers, although a great many practitioners of that themselves originated in Europe.

contingency *See* NECESSARY/CONTINGENT.

continuity Mathematically a class is densely or compactly ordered if between any two distinct members there is always another not identical with either of them. A class is continuously ordered if every non-empty subset that has an upper bound has a *least upper bound; intuitively, there are no leaps. (One might say that some philosophical writing appears to confuse density with continuity.) A *function f is continuous at a point c if $f(x) \to f(c)$ as $x \to c$.

continuum The linear continuum is the set of 'points' on a line. The great achievement of Cantorian *set theory was to provide a purely mathematical treatment of this set, without invoking undefined notions like nearness or distance.

C

continuum hypothesis The hypothesis proposed by *Cantor that there is no set with a *cardinality greater than that of the natural numbers but less than the cardinality of the set of all subsets of the set of natural numbers (the *power set of that set). The generalized continuum hypothesis is that the cardinality of any power set of an infinite set is the next highest cardinality after that of the set itself. *Gödel proved in 1938 that the continuum hypothesis is consistent with classical set theory; the American mathematician Paul Cohen proved in 1963 that its negation is so too, i.e. the hypothesis is independent of the other axioms.

contract, social *See* SOCIAL CONTRACT.

contractarianism A contractarian approach to problems of ethics asks what solution could be agreed upon by contracting parties, starting from certain idealized positions (for example, no ignorance, no inequalities of power enabling one party to force unjust solutions upon another, no malicious ambitions). The idea of thinking of civil society, with its different distributions of rights and obligations, as if it were established by a *social contract, derives from *Hobbes and *Rousseau. The utility of such a model was attacked by *Hume, who asks why, given that no historical event of establishing a contract took place, it is useful to allocate rights and duties as if it had; he also points out that the actual distribution of these things in a society owes too much to contingent circumstances to be derivable from any such model. Similar positions in general ethical theory (sometimes called contractualism) see the right thing to do as one that could be agreed upon in a hypothetical contract. *See also* CONSENT, RAWLS.

contradiction The *conjunction of a proposition and its *negation. The law of non-contradiction provides that no such conjunction can be true: not (*p* & not-*p*). The standard proof of the inconsistency of a set of propositions or sentences is to show that a contradiction may be derived from them.

In *Hegelian and *Marxist writing the term is used more widely. A contradiction may be a pair of features that together produce an unstable tension in a political or social system: a 'contradiction' of capitalism might be the arousal of expectations in the workers that the system cannot requite. For Hegel the gap between this and genuine contradiction is not as wide as it is for other thinkers, given the equation between systems of thought and their historical embodiments.

contradictory A contradictory position is one from which a *contradiction follows.

contrapositive The contrapositive of a conditional 'if *p* then *q*' is the conditional 'if not-*q* then not-*p*'. The two forms are equivalent. The contrapositive of a generalization 'all As are B' is the equivalent 'all non-Bs are non-A'. This equivalence is exploited in *Hempel's paradox.

contrary Two propositions are contrary if only one of them can be true, but they may both be false. 'He is in his forties' and 'he is in his fifties' are contraries, since he cannot be both, but he might be a different age again, in which case both are false. *See* SQUARE OF OPPOSITION.

contrary-to-fact conditional *See* COUNTERFACTUAL CONDITIONAL.

convention The influential analysis of David *Lewis suggests that a regularity holds as a matter of convention when it solves a problem of *coordination in a group. This means that it is to the benefit of each member to conform to the regularity, providing the others do so. Any number of solutions to such a problem may exist. For example, it is to the advantage of each of us to drive on the same side of the road as others, but indifferent whether we all drive on the right or the left. One solution or another may emerge for a variety of reasons. It is notable that on this account conventions may arise naturally; they do not have to be the result of specific agreement. This frees the notion for use in thinking about such things as the origin of language or money or of political society itself. *See also* CONVENTIONALISM.

conventionalism A theory that magnifies the role of decisions, or free selection from amongst equally possible alternatives, in order to show that what appears to be objective or fixed by nature is in fact an artefact of human *convention, similar to conventions of etiquette, or grammar, or law. Thus one might suppose that moral rules owe more to social convention than to anything imposed from outside, or that supposedly inexorable *necessities are in fact the shadow of our linguistic conventions. In the philosophy of science, conventionalism is the doctrine often traced to *Poincaré that apparently real scientific differences, such as that between describing space in terms of a Euclidean and a non-Euclidean geometry, in fact register the acceptance of a different system of conventions for describing space. Thus one can no more ask whether Euclidean geometry is true than whether the metric system is true. Poincaré did not hold that all scientific theory is conventional, but left space for genuinely experimental laws, and his conventionalism is in practice modified by recognition that one choice of description may be more convenient than another. More recent *holistic approaches to theories and to meaning find it impossible to separate out the objective or empirical from the conventional or linguistic (*see also* QUINE). The disadvantage of conventionalism is that it must show that alternative, equally workable conventions could have been adopted, and it is often not easy to believe that. For example, if we hold that some ethical norm such as respect for promises or property is conventional, we ought to be able to show that human needs would have been equally well satisfied by a system involving a different norm, and this may be hard to establish.

convention T Convention or principle laid down by *Tarski as a 'material adequacy condition' governing the enterprise of giving a definition of the *truth-predicate for a language. A theory satisfies the requirement only if every instance of the schema 'S is true if and only if *p*' is derivable within it. Here S is a description of a sentence of the *object language, and *p* is its translation into the *metalanguage. The leading idea is that our characterization of the language will be incomplete unless we can derive such a biconditional for any sentence that the object language can frame. If we were left unable to say under what conditions some sentence would be true, we would not have a full account of the ways the object language can put together sentences. Tarski expresses this by saying that we would not have an adequate definition of the truth-predicate for the language. He believed that because of the *semantic paradoxes no language can define its own truth-predicate. To fully describe the semantics of a language therefore means ascending to a higher language, or metalanguage, containing terms not expressible in the original language on pain of contradiction. Convention T became centrally important to philosophers working on *Davidson's programme of giving a semantically sound description of natural languages. It remains controversial just how legitimate this appropriation of Tarski's ideas is: the shift in focus that has worried certain philosophers is sometimes put by saying that whereas Tarski took translation for granted, and sought to understand truth, Davidson takes truth for granted, and seeks to understand translation.

conversational implicature *See* IMPLICATURE.

converse The converse of a *relation R*xy* is that relation R′ such that R′*yx* iff R*xy*. 'Child of' is the converse of 'parent of'. The converse of a conditional 'if *p* then *q*' is the very different conditional 'if *q* then *p*'.

converse fallacy of the accident *See* *A DICTO SECUNDUM QUID AD DICTUM SIMPLICITER.*

conversion Term used in the theory of the *syllogism for a transformation in which the original predicate is made the subject of a proposition, and vice versa. Conversion is sometimes straightforward (with an E or an I proposition): 'some As are B' is equivalent to 'some Bs are A'. But 'all As are B' can only be converted with a shift in the figure, being deemed equivalent to 'some Bs are A'.

Conway, Lady Anne Finch (1631–79) Anne Finch was the daughter of Sir Henry Finch, Speaker of the House of Commons. She studied *Descartes at an early age, and through her brother, a student at Cambridge, became acquainted with Henry *More. She taught herself mathematics, astronomy, and geometry, continuing her studies after her marriage in 1650 to Edward, Viscount Killulagh, later 1st Earl of Conway. She became interested in the *kabbala and developed a theory of nature as an integrated mental and material order, in which individual monads developed from lower to higher forms. She joined the Quakers in 1670. From 1671 to 1675 she put her vitalist philosophy into notebooks, which were published in Latin and in English in 1692 as *The Principles of the Most Ancient and Modern Philosophy, Concerning God, Christ, and the Creation, that is, Concerning Spirit, and Matter in General.* She was an acknowledged influence on *Leibniz, who may have adopted the term *monad from her.

cooperative principle A convention suggested by *Grice directing participants in conversation to pay heed to an accepted purpose or direction of the exchange. Contributions made without paying this attention are liable to be rejected for other reasons than straightforward falsity: something true but unhelpful or inappropriate may meet with puzzlement or rejection. We can thus never infer from the fact that it would be inappropriate to say something in some circumstance that what would be said, were we to say it, would be false. This inference was frequently made in *ordinary language philosophy, it being argued, for example, that since we do not normally say 'there *seems* to be a barn there' when there *is* unmistakably a barn there, it is false that on such occasions there seems to be a barn there.

coordination problem A situation in which the interests of agents coincide, and the aim is to try to reach an outcome in which those interests are satisfied. Informally, this is a situation in which each person has an interest in doing something that chimes in with what the others do. For example, we may each have an interest in meeting at dinner time, but face the problem that neither of us is sure in which part of the town the other will be. Going to the only restaurant, expecting the other to reason that this is the salient thing to do and to go there likewise, would be a solution to the problem. The problem would not be so easy if there were several restaurants, or if an element of competition entered, whereby my interests are better served by one choice (e.g. a restaurant near me) and yours by a different choice (one near you). More formally, a solution requires finding an equilibrium, meaning that no agent can do better by unilaterally doing something else given the choices of the others. A proper equilibrium is one which each agent likes better than any other equilibrium. Much social action, including perhaps inventing language and society, requires solving coordination problems. *See also* CONVENTION, GAME THEORY, NASH EQUILIBRIUM, PRISONERS' DILEMMA.

coordinative definitions Term used by the German-born American philosopher of science Hans Reichenbach (1891–1953), in *The Philosophy of Space and Time* (1957), for the coordination of a concept of physical theory with an actual physical process. For example, the metre may be coordinated with a standard rod in Paris, or in geometry a straight line may be coordinated with the path of a light ray, or the path of a light ray in a certain kind of space. Reichenbach thought that since there is no way of knowing whether objects maintain their size when transported to different regions of space, the assumption that they do takes on the status of a convention or definition, and is part of what coordinates the concepts with which we measure space with physical space itself.

Copenhagen interpretation The anti-*realist interpretation of *quantum mechanics championed by the physicist Niels Bohr (1885–1962) who worked in Copenhagen, and the subject of extended debate with *Einstein. According to Bohr, there is no deep quantum reality, no world of electrons and photons. There is only description of the world in these terms: quantum mechanics affords us a formalism that we can use to predict and manipulate events described in everyday languages, or the language of classical physics, but it is misguided or senseless to postulate a quantum reality answering to the description. Problems such as the wave-particle duality, or the problem of *Schrödinger's cat, suggest that there is no reality behind our observations.

SEE WEB LINKS

- An introduction to the Copenhagen interpretation
- An online exhibition on the history of the Copenhagen interpretation

Copernican revolution *Copernicus made the perceived revolution of the heavens into a function of the actual revolutions of the perceiver. In the Preface to the *Critique of Pure Reason* (2nd edn, B xvi), *Kant uses this as an analogy to describe how progress in metaphysics requires attributing the apparent temporal, spatial, and causal order of the world to the structure of the perceiving mind.

Copernicus, Nicolaus (1473–1543) Polish astronomer. The first developed heliocentric theory of the universe in the modern era was presented in *De Revolutionibus Orbium Coelestium*, published in the year of Copernicus's death. The system is entirely mathematical, in the sense of predicting the observed position of celestial bodies on the basis of an underlying geometry, without exploring the mechanics of celestial motion. Its mathematical and scientific superiority over the *Ptolemaic system was not as direct as popular history suggests: Copernicus's system adhered to circular planetary motion, and let the planets run on 48 epicycles and eccentrics. It was not until the work of *Kepler and *Galileo that the system became markedly simpler than Ptolemaic astronomy.

copula In traditional logic a *proposition not only contains a *subject and a *predicate, but also a coupling device or copula (is, are, is not, are not) binding them together. It is generally held that very different things are covered by the notion, such as the 'is' of predication (rain is wet), that of identity (Marilyn Monroe is Norma Jean), and that of composition (this statue is marble). The need for a copula arises from a picture in which all the other elements of a proposition are complete 'terms', so they need some glue to bind them together into a sentence. Since *Frege it has been more common to think of the predicate in a subject-predicate sentence on the model of an expression for a mathematical *function, which needs no coupling device to bind it to its argument. No such connection has to be postulated, any more than there is a connection between the square function and 2 in the expression 2^2.

Cordemoy, Géraud de (1626–84) French lawyer and tutor to the future Louis XV. Cordemoy was one of the most important followers of *Descartes of his time. In his *Le discernement du corps et de l'âme* (1666) he defends a dualist philosophy, but modifying Descartes's physics by the introduction of discrete indivisible atoms. He also wrote on the origins of language, *Le discours physique de la parole* (1668).

coreferential Two terms are coreferential when they refer to the same thing.

corollary A straightforward consequence of a *theorem.

corporeal Bodily: our corporeal nature is our bodily nature.

corpuscularianism The variety of atomism especially associated with *Boyle, and expounded in his *Sceptical Chemist* (1661) and *The Origin and Form of Qualities* (1666). Boyle held that all material substances are composed of minute corpuscles, themselves possessing shape, size, and motion. The different properties of materials would arise from different combinations and collisions of corpuscles: chemical properties, such as solubility, would be explicable by the mechanical interactions of corpuscles, just as the capacity of a key to turn a lock is explained by their respective shapes. In Boyle's hands the idea is opposed to the Aristotelian theory of elements and principles, which he regarded as untestable and sterile. His approach is a precursor of modern chemical *atomism, and had immense influence on *Locke. However, Locke recognized the need for a different kind of force guaranteeing the cohesion of atoms, and both this and the interactions between such atoms were criticized by *Leibniz. *See also* ACTION AT A DISTANCE, FIELD.

corrective justice *See* JUSTICE, RETRIBUTIVE.

correspondence theory of truth *Aristotle said that a statement is true if it says of what is that it is, and of what is not that it is not (*Metaphysics* Γ, iv. 1011). But a correspondence theory is not simply the view that truth consists in correspondence with the *facts, but rather the view that it is theoretically interesting to realize this. Aristotle's claim is in itself a harmless platitude, common to all views of truth. A correspondence theory is distinctive in holding that the notion of correspondence and fact can be sufficiently developed to make the platitude into an interesting theory of truth. Opponents charge that this is not so, primarily because we have no access to facts independently of the statements and beliefs that we hold. We cannot look over our own shoulders to compare our beliefs with a reality apprehended by other means than those beliefs, or perhaps further beliefs. Hence we have no fix on 'facts' as something like structures to which our beliefs may or may not correspond. *See also* COHERENCE THEORY OF TRUTH, FACTS, IDENTITY THEORY OF TRUTH, PRAGMATIC THEORY OF TRUTH, REDUNDANCY THEORY OF TRUTH, SEMANTIC THEORY OF TRUTH.

corrigible A proposition is corrigible when it is capable of correction by new evidence or new theoretical changes. It is widely held that all propositions are in theory corrigible, although some may be so established that there is no realistic possibility of new evidence upsetting them.

corroboration In the philosophy of science of *Popper there is no definable measure of the extent to which evidence confirms a hypothesis (*see* CONFIRMATION THEORY). Instead, hypotheses face the tribunal of experience by surviving efforts to falsify them. The degree of corroboration of a hypothesis by evidence is then a function of the stringency of the test the evidence provides, and hence a measure of the success of the hypothesis in surviving it. Critics have complained that corroboration in this sense is an empty notion, since it provides no reason to trust the hypothesis on any future occasion. *See* FALSIFIABILITY, VERISIMILITUDE.

cosmogony A theory of the origin of the universe, whether religious, mythical, or scientific.

cosmological argument An influential argument (or family of arguments) for the existence of God. Its premises are that all natural things are dependent for their existence on something else; the totality of dependent beings must then itself depend upon a non-dependent, or necessarily existent, being, which is God. Like the argument to *design, the cosmological argument was attacked by *Hume and *Kant. Its main problem is that it requires us to make sense of the notion of necessary existence. For if the answer to the question of why anything exists is that some other thing of a similar kind exists, the question merely arises again. So the 'God' that ends the question must exist necessarily; it must not be an entity of which the same kinds of question can be raised. The other problem with the argument is that it unfortunately affords no reason for attributing concern and care to the deity, nor for connecting the necessarily existent being it derives with human values and aspirations.

cosmology The study of the origin and structure of the universe.

cosmos (Greek, *kosmos*, order; cf. cosmetic) The whole world, especially conceived as ordered and law-governed, whether by destiny, fate, justice, divine command, or rational necessity. *See* *LOGOS*.

counterexample A counterexample is an example that refutes a claim about some subject-matter. Switzerland is a counterexample to the claim that all countries with armed citizens are dangerous. Notice that it is not a counterexample to the claim that some countries with armed citizens are dangerous. Much philosophy proceeds by finding counterexamples. For example, the claim that if you have promised someone to be at a place at a time, you must be there, could be countered with the example of a situation in which the person you promised has died in the meantime. In some developments of logic a counterexample set is made by combining the premises of some argument with the negation of the conclusion, and seeing if a contradiction can be derived. If it can, then the original argument was valid.

counterfactual conditional Sometimes known as subjunctive conditionals, although the terms do not exactly coincide. A counterfactual is a conditional of the form 'if *p* were to happen *q* would', or 'if *p* were to have happened *q* would have happened', where the supposition of *p* is contrary to the known fact that not-*p*. Such assertions are nevertheless useful: 'if you had broken the bone, the X-ray would have looked different', or 'if the reactor were to fail, this mechanism would click in' are important truths, even when we know that the bone is not broken or are certain that the reactor will not fail. It is arguably distinctive of laws of nature that they yield counterfactuals ('if the metal were to be heated, it would expand'), whereas accidentally true generalizations may not. It is clear that counterfactuals cannot be represented by the *material implication of the propositional calculus, since that conditional comes out true whenever *p* is false, so there would be no division between true and false counterfactuals.

Although the subjunctive form indicates a counterfactual, in many contexts it does not seem to matter whether we use a subjunctive form, or a simple conditional form: 'if you run out of water, you will be in trouble' seems equivalent to 'if you were to run out of water, you would be in trouble'. In other contexts there is a big difference: 'if Oswald did not kill Kennedy, someone else did' is clearly true, whereas 'if Oswald had not killed Kennedy, somebody else would have' is most probably false.

The best-known modern treatment of counterfactuals is that of David *Lewis, which evaluates them as true or false according to whether *q* is true in the 'most similar' possible worlds to ours in which *p* is true. The similarity-ranking this approach needs has proved controversial, particularly since it may need to presuppose some notion of the same laws of nature, whereas part of the interest in counterfactuals is that they promise to illuminate that notion. There is a growing awareness that the classification of conditionals is an extremely tricky business, and categorizing them as counterfactual or not may be of limited use.

counter-induction A strategy reversing the normal logic of *induction, by taking the way things are within our experience as a guide to how they will not be outside our experience. It proves surprisingly hard to formulate a consistent counter-inductive strategy. For example, a red tomato has not been yellow so the strategy might be to predict that it will be yellow. But it has also not been blue, but one cannot also predict that it will be blue, because it is inconsistent to predict that it will be both yellow and blue.

counterpart theory The view endorsed by David *Lewis, that identical entities do not exist in different possible worlds, and that statements that appear to require that they do are evaluated by thinking of a counterpart in other worlds. Thus 'if you had touched the wire you would have been electrocuted' will be true if, in a possible world like this in virtually every respect, except that you touch the wire, you are electrocuted. But 'you' as it occurs in this analysis no longer refers to you, but to a 'counterpart you' who touches the wire. The doctrine bears some resemblance to the metaphysically-based view of *Leibniz that if a person had any other attributes than the ones he has, he would not have been the same person. Leibniz thought that when I ask what would have happened if Peter had not denied Christ, I am asking what would have happened if Peter had not been Peter, for denying Christ is contained in the complete notion of Peter. But he allowed that by the name 'Peter' might be understood 'what is involved in those attributes [of Peter] from which the denial does not follow'. A controversial argument against counterpart theory associated with *Kripke asks why it should matter to me not to have touched the wire, if all you can tell me is that if I had done so, a counterpart of me would have been electrocuted.

counting The procedure of uniquely associating one number with each element of a set in order to arrive at a measure of the set. Along with *measurement, counting is the procedure whereby mathematics is applied. Hence its objectivity is a principal datum for any philosophy of mathematics.

count noun A noun indicating a kind that can be counted; you can count the books or tables in a room, but not the stuff or the matter. *See also* MASS NOUN, SORTAL.

courage An action is courageous if it is an attempt to achieve an end despite penalties, risks, costs, or difficulties of sufficient gravity to deter most people. Similarly a state such as cheerfulness is courageous if it is sustained in spite of such difficulties. A courageous person is characteristically able to attempt such actions or maintain such states. For *Aristotle, courage is dependent on sound judgement, for it needs to be known whether the end justifies the risk incurred. Similarly, courage is not the absence of fear (which may be a vice), but the ability to feel the appropriate amount of fear; courage is a *mean between timidity and overconfidence.

Cournot, Antoine Augustin (1801–77) French mathematician and economist, founding figure of econometrics. Cournot maintained a synthesis of empiricism and rationalism, seeing the world as subject to principle, but also as manifesting the objective existence of chances deriving from the intersection of different independent chains of unfolding events. His main philosophical work was the *Essai sur les fondements de nos connaissances et sur les caractères de la critique philosophique* (1861), trs. as *An Essay on the Foundations of our Knowledge* (1956).

Cousin, Victor (1792–1867) French historian of philosophy and educationalist. Cousin was a philosophical eclectic, merging influences from Thomas *Reid, *Kant, and *British empiricism with French traditions. As minister of education under Louis-Philippe he was influential in setting the course of philosophical education in France for much of the 19th century. His own works include *Fragments philosophiques* (1826).

Couturat, Louis (1868–1914) French mathematician, historian of ideas, and celebrated interpreter of *Leibniz. Couturat's doctoral thesis was a defence of completed *infinite collections. This work led to an interest in Leibniz, and Couturat's *La Logique de Leibniz* (1901) placed Leibniz's logical work at the heart of his metaphysical system. Couturat's rationalism and admiration for Leibniz's ideal of a **characteristica universalis* resulted in his spending his later years prosecuting the goal of an international language.

covering law model *See* EXPLANATION.

Craig's theorem A theorem in mathematical logic, held to have implications in the philosophy of science. The logician William Craig at Berkeley showed how, if we partition the vocabulary of a formal system (say, into the T or theoretical terms, and the O or observational terms), then if there is a fully *formalized system *T* with some set S of consequences containing only O terms, there is also a system *O* containing only the O vocabulary but strong enough to give the same set S of consequences. The theorem is a purely formal one, in that *T* and *O* simply separate formulae into the preferred ones, containing as non-logical terms only one kind of vocabulary, and the others. The theorem might encourage the thought that the theoretical terms of a scientific theory are in principle dispensable, since the same consequences can be derived without them.

However, Craig's actual procedure gives no effective way of dispensing with theoretical terms in advance, i.e. in the actual process of thinking about and designing the premises from which the set S follows. In this sense *O* remains parasitic upon its parent *T*.

Crates of Thebes (*c*.365–285 BC) Greek *Cynic, and the principal pupil of *Diogenes of Sinope. He led a wandering life devoted to poverty, yet is represented as universally respected and beloved: people wrote welcomes to him on their doors. Given the Cynic's principled opposition to conventional forms and usages (*see* HIPPARCHIA) one should pause and admire the tolerance of ancient societies.

Cratylus (5th c. BC) Greek philosopher, sometimes thought to have been a teacher of *Plato before *Socrates. He is famous for capping the doctrine of *Heraclitus that you cannot step into the same river twice by adding that you cannot step into the same river once: the river is changing and gone even as a single event of stepping occurs. The point is that reality is utterly particular (one individual event, one moment of time, one individual thing after another). Any adequate thought would have to match the flux with change of its own, so any attempt to categorize reality is like trying to cage the winds. He is also represented in Plato's dialogue *Cratylus* as holding a doctrine of the 'right name' of things, although the proper conclusion of his views was that the flux cannot be captured in words. According to *Aristotle (*Metaphysics* Γ, iv. 1010) he eventually held that since 'regarding that which everywhere in every respect is changing nothing could truly be affirmed', the right course is just to stay silent and wag one's finger. Plato's theory of *forms can be seen in part as a reaction against the impasse to which Cratylus was driven.

creatio ex nihilo (Latin, creation from nothing) The doctrine that only a free act of the Creator was needed to bring into existence the natural universe.

creation *See* FIRST CAUSE ARGUMENT.

creationism 1. The doctrine that a new soul is created afresh for each person: opposed to *traducianism. **2.** In the philosophy of biology, the belief that perceived difficulties or gaps in the scientific theory of *evolution by natural selection are well filled by positing Divine intervention, to create new species, and certainly to create people. Even when it does not depend upon misunderstanding the theory of evolution, the doctrine is unscientific because it simply postulates a God-sized cause for whatever gap is currently of interest: this leads to no *falsifiable predictions or unification of knowledge. *See also* INTELLIGENT DESIGN.

credo quia absurdum est Also known as Tertullian's dictum or paradox. Literally (Latin), I believe because it is absurd: that is, the very impossibility of a proposition becomes (mostly in theology) a kind of motivation for belief in it. Only certain absurd propositions have such magnetism.

credo quia impossibile est Alternative form of the above.

credo ut intelligam (Latin, I believe in order to understand) A formula of *Anselm's implying that the intelligibility of Christian doctrine can only become evident after belief in it. The idea, especially frustrating to atheists, has echoes in the doctrine associated with the later work of *Wittgenstein, according to which immersion in a way of life is necessary for understanding its specific structures and guiding concepts.

Crescas, Hasdai ben Abraham (*c.*1340–*c.*1412) Jewish philosopher and theologian. Crescas was the first European thinker to oppose Aristotelian cosmology, arguing instead for an infinitely extended cosmos. He opposed the extreme rationalism of *Maimonides, and his emphasis on the emotional side of religious observance was influential on such Renaissance figures as *Ficino and *Bruno, and later upon *Spinoza. Works include *The Light of the Lord*.

crisis theology *See* BARTH.

criterion 1. A sufficient condition of something else. **2.** A condition that may not be sufficient for another, but can be seen *a priori* to provide good evidence for it. Thus the fact that someone is behaving appropriately may not guarantee logically that he or she is in pain, but it may be *a priori* true that it is excellent evidence for it. The latter usage is attributed (controversially) to *Wittgenstein. It fits with a generally *holistic view of language, with assertions tied to each other by semantic forces of different strengths, rather than by straightforward logical relations.

criterion of identity *See* INDIVIDUATION, PRINCIPLE OF.

critical idealism Term sometimes used for the philosophy of *Kant, but more particularly for the philosophy of the French philosopher Léon *Brunschvicg, which incorporated the historical emphasis of *Hegel, viewing history as a 'progress of consciousness'.

critical legal studies Term covering a loose agglomeration of theories and views of the nature of law, inspired by *critical theory, and originally by social theorists such as *Marx or *Weber, but then by more radical *postmodern theorists from *Nietzsche to *Foucault and *Derrida. The general stance is that since texts, including legal documents, admit of multiple readings, legal decisions are not so much constrained by rational responses to texts and precedents, but manifestations of social and political forces acting upon legal agents.

critical realism Any doctrine reconciling the real, independent, objective nature of the world (*realism) with a due appreciation of the mind-dependence of the sensory experiences whereby we know about it (hence, critical). In critical, as opposed to naïve, realism the mind knows the world only by means of a medium or vehicle of perception and thought; the problem is to give an account of the relationship between the medium and what it represents. The position was associated especially with R. W. Sellars (1880–1973), whose *Critical Realism* (1916) was in part a reaction against the supposed simplistic realism of *Russell and *Moore. In 1920 a number of philosophers including *Lovejoy and *Santayana contributed to *Essays in Critical Realism*, which served as a manifesto of the school.

critical theory The title is specifically applied to the philosophical approach of the *Frankfurt school. This owed its philosophical background to *Hegel and to *Marx, seeing social and cultural imperfections as defects of rationality, and comparing them with an ideal to which the progress of reason, embodied in pure and undistorting social arrangements, would ideally tend. Critical theory works dialectically, that is by searching out '*contradictions' in social arrangements in which, for example, certain groups are systematically excluded from power or from the free access to information that structures rational debate (*see also* HABERMAS).

More generally, critical theory may describe any attempt to understand practices of criticism, interpretation, and historical understanding of social action, including especially that of writing. An increased self-consciousness about the role of the critic, and the different social and historical circumstances that interfere with communication and *translation, is characteristic of *postmodernism, and this topic has been expressed in a variety of literary forms. However, it may be doubted whether the resulting reflections are always either critical or theoretical in any sense recognized in the philosophy of *science. *See also* Derrida, Foucault.

Croce, Benedetto (1866–1952) Italian philosopher and historian. Born in the Abruzzi, Croce studied in Rome from 1883 (when his parents were killed in an earthquake) until 1886, when he took up residence in Naples, where he lived the rest of his life. In 1903 he founded the journal *La Critica*, to which he contributed extensively. After the First World War, Croce became involved in Italian public life, firstly as a senator, and then after 1925 as a leading intellectual opponent of *fascism. His opposition was expressed largely in historical and aesthetic writing in the period. In 1944, at the end of the fascist years, he served briefly as a cabinet minister.

Croce's philosophy showed a retreat from an early *realism towards a *Hegelian preoccupation with the nature of spirit, as revealed in historical and artistic activity. His aesthetics is centrally concerned with the way in which 'intuition' as a non-cognitive and emotional state nevertheless generates genuine cognition or understanding. This understanding is the point of art, which is therefore sharply separated from mere amusement or instruction (a doctrine which greatly influenced *Collingwood). Logic balances aesthetics by studying concepts rather than intuitions. These stand to each other in a dialectical relationship reminiscent of *Kant, but Croce does not allow that concepts can be the building-blocks of a true, Kantian science. Truth is not found in science, which Croce regards in an *instrumentalist spirit, and still less in the delusions of metaphysics and religion, but only in historical judgements. Like Hegel and *Gentile, Croce identifies philosophy with the historical study of the development of concepts. In ethics Croce kept a sensitive distance from the dangerous Hegelian notion of the nation-state as the organic unity responsible for the development of the spirit, instead finding the highest realization of understanding in the self-conscious, free exercise of historical enquiry. His philosophy has been titled the 'Philosophy of Spirit'. Its best-known expressions are *Estetica* (1902, trs. as *The Aesthetic as the Science of Expression and the Linguistic in General*, 1992), *Logica* (1905, trs. as *Logic as the Science of the Pure Concept*, 1917), *Filosofia della pratica* (1909, trs. as *Philosophy of the Practical*, 1967), and *Teoria e storia della storiografia* (1917, trs. as *Theory and History of Historiography*, 1921).

crucial experiment An experiment held to decide with certainty between two rival hypotheses about some matter. Famous examples include Eddington's observation of the bending of light rays by the sun during the eclipse of 1919, held to decisively uphold general *relativity against *Newtonian mechanics, or the observation of weight gain during combustion, held to decide for the theory that combustion is oxidation and against the view that it consists in loss of phlogiston. In practice experiments require a great deal of scene-setting and agreement on what would count as an *ad hoc hypothesis before they play such a decisive role, so that rational disagreement on whether one or another rival is really refuted is both possible in theory and often found in practice.

Crusius, Christian August (1715–75) German theologian and philosopher. Crusius was professor of philosophy at Leipzig, and is principally remembered as one of the targets of *Kant, particularly in his *Dreams of a Spirit-Seer* (1766). Crusius himself was a *pietist, whose opposition to *Wolff lay in admitting moral and other intuitive principles into the foundations of knowledge, without over-concern about their origin and authority. However Crusius also rejected the traditional arguments, especially the *ontological argument for the existence of God, and stressed the limits of human understanding, as well as the impossibility of underpinning it by purely logical and mathematical means. In these respects and others he was an important influence on Kant.

Cudworth, Ralph (1617–88) The foremost *Cambridge Platonist, whose major works were *The True Intellectual System of the Universe* (1678) and *A Treatise Concerning Eternal and Immutable Morality* (published posthumously, 1731). The former, although massive, is only the first third of a projected larger work. Cudworth was educated at Emmanuel College, Cambridge. In 1645, as a supporter of the Puritans, he was made Master of Clare College, Cambridge, which he left after a crotchety reign in 1650, only to return to Cambridge as Master of Christ's College in 1654. The major aim of Cudworth's metaphysical work was to refute both materialism and *hylozoism. He held that the mind cannot be the merely passive recipient of atomic impacts, and its independent reality is certified by its agency in the world. Cudworth developed the importance of agency in nature with an Aristotelian doctrine of 'plastic natures' or inner directive principles, which guide the formation of living things, and themselves have purposes, and operate even upon the soul, but are not conscious. This doctrine attracted a good deal of discussion, by *Bayle (who found it atheistic in tendency), by *Leibniz, and in the **Encyclopédie*.

Cudworth believed that ethics is given in eternal and immutable truths, apprehended by reason. However, in his moral psychology the emphasis is not upon the kind of conformity with reason later associated with *Kant, but upon the question of whether we act out of love or out of self-interest.

Cudworth's daughter was Damaris, Lady *Masham.

cultural relativism *See* CONSTRUCTIVISM, RELATIVISM.

culture The way of life of a people, including their attitudes, values, beliefs, arts, sciences, modes of perception, and habits of thought and activity. Cultural features of forms of life are learned but are often too pervasive to be readily noticed from within.

Culverwel, Nathanael (*c*.1618–*c*.1651) Although educated at Emmanuel College surrounded by *Cambridge Platonists, Culverwel retained a *Calvinist temper, and maintains a distance from the unfettered celebration of reason characteristic of the Platonists. His principal work is *An Elegant and Learned Discourse of the Light of Nature*, composed about 1646 but published posthumously.

Cumberland, Richard (1631–1718) A Cambridge figure and staunch Protestant, who is reported to have fallen into a dangerous fever when James II attempted to reintroduce Roman Catholicism into England. Cumberland's philosophical reputation, however, rests upon *De Legibus Naturae* ('Of the Laws of Nature', 1672), which was the first significant attempt to refute *Hobbes's view of law as founded upon nothing more than the will of the sovereign. Cumberland's work is unsystematic and diffuse, but influenced subsequent rationalists such as *Clarke, and also contains anticipations of *utilitarianism.

Curry's paradox The paradox is generated by a conditional: (C) If (C) is true, then *p*, where *p* is an arbitrarily chosen proposition—say, one which is just plain false. Classically we can now argue: suppose (C) is true. Then, if (C) is true then *p*. So *p*, by *modus ponens. So, by the rule of *conditional proof, we can infer (Q): if (C) is true, then *p*. That is, we have obtained (C), and hence (C) is true. Now, since we have (C) is true, and we have (Q), we can infer *p* by modus ponens. That is, we have proved any arbitrary proposition by logic alone. The paradox is sometimes attributed to the mathematicians Kleene and Rosser, and sometimes called Löb's paradox. It is noteworthy as clearly arising from a vicious self-reference, but not involving negation. *See also* SEMANTIC PARADOXES.

curve-fitting problem The problem of finding the curve that best fits a number of data points. The philosophical interest lies in justifying any particular trade-off of simplicity, accuracy, and boldness, that may commend itself. The problem of *induction can be represented graphically as a curve-fitting problem.

custom A pattern or habit of action. A custom may exist without any specific basis in reason, but can itself form the basis for rational action, if the custom gives rise to a *norm of action. *See* CONVENTION.

cut elimination theorem Also known as the *Hauptsatz*. A theorem stating that a certain type of inference rule is not needed. The idea was anticipated by J. Herbrand and the theorem was proved for classical logic by G. Gentzen.

cybernetics (Greek, *kybernētēs*, pilot, governor) The science of communication and control systems.

Cynics (Greek, *kynikos*, dog-like) The 'dog philosophers', probably called after the nickname of *Diogenes of Sinope, their most prominent member and founder. In the ancient world, dogs were symbols of lack of shame. For Cynics the virtuous life consisted in an independence achieved by mastery over one's desires and needs: happiness demands that one desires nothing and hence lacks nothing. To encourage people to renounce the desires engendered by civilization and convention the Cynics waged a crusade of antisocial mockery, hoping to show by their own example the hollow illusions of social life. For some of the results *see* CRATES, DIOGENES, HIPPARCHIA.

Cyrenaics The school of *hedonistic philosophy founded by *Aristippus of Cyrene, and flourishing at the end of the 4th century BC. The central doctrine was that the goal or end of action must be the particular pleasure of the moment, the 'strong sensations' of physical pleasures, which are the basic facts given in our lives. Reason is cultivated purely in order to maximize the attainment of such pleasures for the agent. The Cyrenaic attitude anticipated the more subtle analysis of *Epicurus, and must have been a relief from the relentless high-mindedness of *Plato and *Aristotle.

daimon In *Plato's *Symposium*, something intermediate between the human and the divine, although in previous Greek thought just the divine, not personalized as any one particular God. The need for intermediaries between the sublunar world of change and happenstance, and the supralunary or timeless celestial world, becomes a staple of *Middle Platonism and *Neoplatonism. A *daimon* can also refer to one's self, or an aspect of oneself: this is the usage that survives in phrases like 'Van Gogh's artistic demon'.

d'Alembert, Jean le Rond (1717–83) French mathematician and philosopher. Although he achieved his distinction as a mathematician, in philosophy d'Alembert is remembered as one of the greatest figures of the French *Enlightenment. Together with *Diderot he was the moving force behind the **Encyclopédie*. His own philosophy placed total faith in natural science, although like *Locke before him he tempered his *empiricism with confidence in a rational structure to both the natural and the ethical domain. There is some evidence that d'Alembert progressed from a tentative theism, based upon the distinct nature of intelligence and the impossibility of it emerging in a purely material universe, to an atheistic and materialist view of the world. There are many testimonies to his virtuous and philosophical character, and *Hume entirely entrusted to him the conduct of his dispute with *Rousseau.

Damascius (*c.*462–*c.*550) Greek Neoplatonist philosopher, last head of Athenian *Academy before its closing by Justinian in 529. *See also* NEOPLATONISM.

Dante Alighieri (1265–1321) Italian poet and philosopher. Born in Florence, Dante sought the consolations of philosophy after the death in 1290 of his beloved Beatrice Portinari, who was the wife of the painter Simone de Bardi. Active in the political life of Florence, Dante was sent to Rome as an envoy to the papal court in 1301, and while absent was condemned to exile. He never returned to Florence, but died an honoured guest of Guido da Polenta, the ruler of Ravenna.

Dante's principal conventional philosophical work is the *Convivio*, or *Banquet* (1304–8), intended as a series of fourteen treatises of which only four are complete. *De Monarchia* (*c.*1313) contains Dante's political theory. But it is his masterpiece, the *Divina Commedia*, begun possibly as early as 1307, and finished just before his death, that is universally acknowledged as the literary embodiment of the moral, religious, and philosophical ideals of the late 13th and early 14th centuries. The poem divides into three parts. In the first, the *Inferno*, Dante visits the circles of Hell, with their increasingly wicked moral transgressors (the scale goes from *apathy, which is scarcely damned at all, to the basest treachery). The punishments do not increase in severity in step with the faults, but represent the kind of retribution or loss that a particular vice brings: for example, the lovers Paolo and Francesca are ceaselessly whirled in a storm. In the *Purgatorio* the poet encounters the repentant sinners who await redemption, and in the last circle of this, the earthly paradise, he is reunited with the dead Beatrice, who in the *Paradiso* introduces him to the ascending circles of beauty and light, culminating in the vision of God. In the heaven of the sun (light) Dante encounters the souls of twelve wise men, who are *Albert the Great, *Aquinas, the Venerable Bede, *Boethius, *Dionysius the Pseudo-Areopagite, Gratian, Isidore of Seville, Peter Lombard, Paul Orose, Richard of Saint Victor, *Siger of Brabant, and Solomon. Perhaps surprisingly, given that it is *Augustine's equation of light with spiritual excellence that infuses the whole poem, it is Aquinas, who thought that light could only be predicated metaphorically of spiritual substances, who guides him at this point. In accordance with Dante's Christianized *Neoplatonism, the heaven of the sun is above the heaven of the moon, where live those who could not quite keep their vows of chastity, above the heaven of Mercury, where there are those who tried to acquire glory by good deeds, and of Venus, where dwell those who loved intensely in their lives. But it is below the heaven of Mars (reserved for martyrs), of Jupiter (just and wise princes), of Saturn (contemplatives and mystics), of the fixed stars (saints, Apostles, and the blessed), and well below the Crystalline heaven, or *primum mobile*, where Dante encounters the angelic hierarchies, and finally the Empyrean, where, losing Beatrice, he is able with the help of the Virgin Mary and St *Bernard to direct his gaze at the point source of light, the love which moves the sun and the stars, God himself.

The structure of the poem is that of a moral allegory of fall and redemption. If Dante's immediate philosophical ancestors are Aquinas and Augustine, it is also clear that the poem fuses themes from *Plato, Neoplatonism, and the Islamic tradition, especially that of *Avicenna. *See also* BEAUTY, LOVE.

SEE WEB LINKS

- A list of internet resources on Dante, including bibliographies
- A multimedia archive on Dante's *Divina Commedia*

Danto, Arthur C. (1924–) Philosophy professor at Columbia University (1966–87) whose major works include *Nietzsche as Philosopher* (1965). He is however best known as a philosopher of art, and art critic, and especially for the concept of the 'artworld', an ingredient in the *institutional theory of art. Other works include *The Transfiguration of the Commonplace* (1981), *Encounters and Reflections: Art in the Historical Present* (1990), and *Embodied Meanings: Critical Essays and Aesthetic Meditations* (1994).

dao *See* TAO.

darshana (Sanskrit, vision) The schools of Hindu thought crystallized in the Sutra period (400 BC–AD 500). As usually counted there are six orthodox schools accepting the authority of the *Vedas, which can be divided into three pairs. These are the *Nyaya and *Vaisheshika; *Samkhya and *Yoga; *Mimamsa and *Vedanta. In each case the first member of the pair may be regarded as a codification or methodology for the metaphysical system represented by the second. Characteristic doctrines are described under the separate headings. There are three unorthodox schools: *Buddhism, *Jainism, and *Carvaka.

Darwin, Charles Robert (1809–82) English naturalist. Darwin was born in Shrewsbury and studied medicine at Edinburgh, then Cambridge. His naturalistic observations came to maturity on the famous voyage of the *Beagle* (1831–6). During the subsequent twenty years Darwin consolidated his scientific reputation while living the life of a country gentleman of scientific interests, breeding and observing domestic animals, especially pigeons, and working out the details of the theory of evolution. It was only in 1858 that, prodded by reading the essay *On the Tendency of Varieties to Depart Indefinitely from the Original Type* sent to him by Alfred Russell Wallace (1823–1913), he prepared a joint paper with Wallace, to be read to the Linnaean Society. *The Origin of Species by Means of Natural Selection* followed in 1859. Darwin's work is the foundation of modern biology. In itself it affords a rich field not only for philosophers of science interested, for example, in the relationship between theory and observation, or in the place of *falsification in science, but also to those interested in the sociology of *paradigms, and the various factors that affect the climate of ideas. Darwin's other claim to philosophical attention arises from *The Expression of the Emotions in Man and Animals* (1872).

SEE WEB LINKS

- An archive of Darwin's complete works, with a biography

Darwinism Belief in the theory of *evolution by natural selection. Core Darwinism has been defined by the biologist Richard Dawkins as 'the minimal theory that evolution is guided in adaptively nonrandom directions by the nonrandom survival of small random hereditary changes'. The theory in its original form took wing from the observation of *Malthus that although living organisms produce multiple offspring, adult populations remain relatively stable in number. Darwin realized that the different chances of survival of differently endowed offspring could account for the natural evolution of species. Nature 'selects' those members of a species best adapted to the environment in which they find themselves, much as human animal breeders may select for desirable traits in their livestock, and thereby control the evolution of the kind of animal they wish. In the phrase of *Spencer, nature guarantees the 'survival of the fittest', although the phrase is misleading in suggesting that an original species, from which others evolve, may not itself continue to occupy some niche to which it is well enough adapted. *The Origin of Species* was principally successful in marshalling the evidence for evolution, rather than providing a convincing mechanism for genetic change, and Darwin himself remained open to the search for additional mechanisms, whilst also remaining convinced that natural selection was at the heart of it. It was only with the later discovery of the *gene as the unit of inheritance that the synthesis known as 'neo-Darwinism' became the orthodox theory of evolution in the life sciences. *See also* CREATIONISM, EVOLUTIONARY ETHICS, INTELLIGENT DESIGN, SOCIOBIOLOGY.

Darwin machine A model for the brain that treats it as a flexible instrument in which the function of groups of neurons is selected by the pressure on the organism to adapt to the surrounding world. Such functions will include recognizing repeating patterns in the external environment and the body of the agent, and initiating appropriate routines in response.

Dasein (German, existence, being there) Being in the world, characterized by *Heidegger in terms of *affective relationships with surrounding people and objects. This primary mode of being is falsely split, in the *Cartesian tradition, into a self-contained inner world and an independent outer world, bearing only problematic relations to one another. *See* AUTHENTICITY.

datum (Latin, what is given) A piece of evidence considered as fixed for the purpose in hand. What is taken as a datum may change as changes of theory and evidence arise. Something would be absolutely a datum if it were *incorrigible, but many theorists of knowledge tend to be nervous about regarding anything as absolutely given, for although some things may serve as a basis for particular enquiries, this does not protect them from eventual challenge. *See* EPISTEMOLOGY, PROTOCOL STATEMENTS, VERIFICATION; *see also* SENSE DATUM.

Davidson, Donald Herbert (1917–2003) American philosopher. Born in Springfield, Massachusetts, and educated at Harvard, Davidson held posts at a number of universities before becoming professor at Berkeley in 1981. His writings were a major influence on philosophy of mind and language in the latter half of the 20th century. Davidson introduced the position known as *anomalous monism in the philosophy of mind, instigating a vigorous debate over the relation between mental and physical descriptions of persons, and the possibility of genuine explanation of events in terms of psychological properties. Following but enlarging upon the work of *Quine on language, Davidson concentrated upon the figure of the *radical interpreter, arguing that the method of interpreting a language could be thought of as constructing a *truth definition in the style of *Tarski, in which the systematic contribution of elements of sentences to their overall meaning is laid bare. The construction takes place within a generally *holistic theory of knowledge and meaning. A radical interpreter can tell when a subject holds a sentence true, and using the principle of *charity ends up making an assignment of truth conditions to individual sentences. Although Davidson is a defender of the doctrines of the *indeterminacy of radical translation and the *inscrutability of reference, his approach has seemed to many to offer some hope of identifying meaning as a respectable notion, even within a broadly *extensional approach to language. Davidson is also known for rejection of the idea of a *conceptual scheme, thought of as something peculiar to one language or one way of looking at the world, arguing that where the possibility of translation stops so does the coherence of the idea that there is anything to translate. His papers are collected in *Essays on Actions and Events* (1980), *Inquiries into Truth and Interpretation* (1983), *Subjective, Intersubjective, Objective* (2001), and *Problems of Rationality* (2004).

SEE WEB LINKS

- An interview with Davidson about his life and works
- Q & A between Davidson and some eminent philosophers

de *See* TE.

death Since death is the cessation of life, it cannot be experienced, nor be a harm, nor a proper object of fear. So, at least, have argued many philosophers, notably *Epicurus and *Lucretius. A prime consideration has been the symmetry between the state of being dead, and the state of 'being' not yet in existence. On the other hand death is feared, and thought of as a harm (even if it is instant: it is not the process of dying that makes the difference). The alternative, *immortality, sounds better until the detail is filled in, when it can begin to sound insupportable (*see* MAKROPOULOS CASE). The management of death is one of the topics of *bioethics.

death of God The assertion that God is dead, but that we have to vanquish his shadow, first occurs in *Nietzsche's *The Gay Science*, iii. 108. At 125 Nietzsche tells of the madman who hails it as the greatest achievement of mankind, to have killed God and turned the churches into tombs and sepulchres of God. But people do not listen to the madman for 'the deed is still more distant from them than the most distant stars—*and yet they have done it themselves*'.

death-of-the-author The idea associated with French critic Roland *Barthes that a text should be regarded as self-standing, a field for the interplay of signs. The idea is not that things like *Pride and Prejudice* grow on trees, but that information or speculation about the author and the author's intentions is irrelevant to reading it. *See* INTENTIONAL FALLACY.

death with dignity A catchphrase for the ethical movement opposing the assumption that the doctor's authority can extend to keeping patients alive regardless of their actual wishes, or what they would wish were they rationally aware of their situation.

deceit The intentional attempt to mislead people. It gives rise to questions of definition (separating it from such neighbours as exaggeration, irony, parody) and to questions of justification.

Many moral traditions separate the deliberate lie from the equally deliberate failure to tell the whole truth, it being thought that the former, an act, is worse, other things being equal, than the latter (*see* ACTS/OMISSIONS DOCTRINE). However, since each may involve the same end and the same strategy of manipulation of other people's opinion and action, the difference is difficult to defend in all cases. The absolutist position on lying is defended by *Kant: it is an unconditional duty to tell the truth, come what may. *Constant urged against him that we only have a duty to tell the truth to those who have a right to the truth. He and others urge that while in a perfect world there would be no lying, deceit may be justified when one is faced with the evil or the incompetent, or the need for self-defence in the face of injustice, or the need to promote sufficiently important goods. The difficulty is to defend a departure from the absolutist position that does not justify lying for the sake of mere expediency.

decidability *See* DECISION PROBLEM.

decision problem The problem of finding an *algorithm or decision procedure for deciding whether an arbitrary well-formed formula of a logical system is a theorem of the system. A positive solution is a proof that such a procedure exists; a negative solution is a proof that there can be no such procedure. *Truth-tables provide a decision procedure for the *propositional calculus, whereas *Church's theorem is a negative solution for the first-order *predicate calculus with identity.

decision procedure *See* ALGORITHM.

decision theory The theory of choices made when each option is associated with a risk, or expectation of gain or loss, where the expectation is a function of the probability of some outcome and the total gain or loss involved. Decision theory may be pursued with the aim of finding results about how decisions ought to be made (normative decision theory) or with the aim of finding out how they are actually made (empirical decision theory). *See* DOMINANCE, EXPECTED UTILITY, GAME THEORY.

deconstruction A sceptical approach to the possibility of coherent meaning initiated by the French philosopher *Derrida. Derrida is self-consciously evasive, but the drift is that there is no privileged point, such as an author's intention or a contact with external reality, that confers significance on a text. There is only the limitless opportunity for fresh commentary or text (a linguistic version of the *idealist belief that we cannot escape the world of our own ideas). However, a deconstructionist reading of a text subverts its apparent significance by uncovering contradictions and conflict within it. The very use of a term (e.g. 'male' or 'free') may suppress or marginalize an opposite ('female', 'oppressed') which, by being excluded, is somhow regarded as having had its rights trampled upon. Sometimes, since it is impossible to say very much without using terms upon which this trick can be pulled, or therefore to take up a significant vantage point above a text, it is supposed that deconstruction leaves everything as it was; its attempt to think the unthinkable proceeds with puns and jokes as much as by recognizable argument. The apparently wilful obscurity of much deconstructionist writing has tended to outrage more orthodox philosophers. *See* DERRIDA, *DIFFÉRANCE*, POSTMODERNISM, POSTSTRUCTURALISM.

Dedekind, Julius Wilhelm Richard (1831–1916) German mathematician. He is remembered in the philosophy of mathematics both for the celebrated construction of real numbers by means of the *Dedekind cut, and for first providing the axiomatization of arithmetic by means of what are unfairly known as *Peano's postulates. His works are collected in *Essays on the Theory of Numbers* (1963).

Dedekind cut (Dedekind section) It has been known since the Greeks that there is no ratio of numbers, a/b, that is equal to the square root of 2. But there is no maximum ratio whose square is less than 2, and no minimum ratio whose square is greater than 2. The German mathematician Richard Dedekind in 1872 pointed out that each real *number corresponds to a 'cut' like this in the class of ratios. This means that if we are given the set of rationals, we can construct reals in terms of sets of them: the set of rationals whose square is less than 2 is an open set that can represent the square root of 2. Mathematicians including *Russell and *Whitehead were thus able to identify a real with the class of all ratios less than it. This has the disadvantage that rational numbers are no longer a subset of the reals, but there are other ways of using Dedekind's insight and preserving a uniform treatment for rational and irrational reals.

deduction A process of reasoning in which a conclusion is drawn from a set of *premises. Usually confined to cases in which the conclusion is supposed to *follow from the premises, i.e. the inference is logically *valid. *See also* LOGICAL CALCULUS, MODEL THEORY, PROOF THEORY. In spite of his own claims, Sherlock Holmes's methods were not typically deductive, but rather exercises of *abduction.

deduction theorem The theorem provable about some logical systems, that if a conclusion C can be proved from a set of premises $A_1 \dots A_n$, then there is a proof of $A_n \rightarrow C$ from $A_1 \dots A_{n-1}$.

deductive closure principle A principle in the logic of knowledge that has found general favour. It states that if S knows that *p*, and knows that *p* entails *q*, then S knows that *q*. Knowledge is preserved over known entailment. The principle was challenged by Robert *Nozick, relying on some odd features of the logic of *counterfactual conditionals, but the challenge is not generally thought successful.

deep/surface structure *See* GENERATIVE GRAMMAR.

de facto/de jure (Latin, of fact/of right) The contrast between a matter of fact and one of right. For example, the *de facto* authority of a brigand over his followers is contrasted with *de jure* authority of a constitution or sovereign. A central problem of the philosophy of *law is to discover which kinds of fact account for the emergence of *de jure* authority.

defeasible Capable of being overturned by further events. At law a judgement is defeasible if a higher court may overturn it. A *proposition is defeasible if further evidence may render it doubtful.

deferred ostension *See* OSTENSIVE DEFINITION.

de Finetti, Bruno (1906–85) Italian mathematician and philosopher. Born in Innsbruck, and educated at Milan, de Finetti worked on many different branches of mathematics, in Milan, in Rome, and from 1931 in the Assicurazioni Generali di Trieste, as an actuary and administrator. In 1961 he assumed the chair of mathematics of probability in Rome. He published over three hundred mathematical and scientific articles. Philosophically he is remembered alongside *Ramsey as the pioneer of the subjective view of probability, since developed into the school of statistical thought known as *personalism. De Finetti's first work dealing with the topic was *Probabilismo: saggio critico sulla teoria della probabilità e sul valore della scienza* (1931). He is best-known in the English-speaking world for *La Prévision: ses lois logiques, ses sources subjectives* (1937, trs. as *Foresight: its Logical Laws, its Subjective Sources*, 1967), and the two-volume *Teoria della probabilità* (1970, trs. as *Theory of Probability*, 1974). De Finetti was an uncompromising *error theorist: he places probability in the same category as the aether or fate, and prefaces the latter work with the remark 'my thesis is simply this: probability does not exist'. Surprisingly, he ends his *Probabilismo* text by connecting the freedom given by rejecting this superstition with the exhilarating liberations of *fascism. *See also* REPRESENTATION THEOREM.

definiendum That which is to be defined. The defining phrase or sentence is the *definiens*.

definiens *See* DEFINIENDUM.

definist fallacy The illicit insistence on defining a term in a way that is favourable to one's own side of an argument. Thus a *libertarian may insist on defining taxation as theft by the state, or a pro-life supporter may insist on defining a foetus as an unborn person. The term may also be used for the allegedly Socratic fallacy of supposing that unless a term can be defined it means nothing (*see* SOCRATIC PARADOX).

definite description A description of a (putative) object as the single, unique, bearer of a property: 'the smallest positive number'; 'the first dog born at sea'; 'the richest person in the world'. In the theory of definite descriptions, unveiled in the paper 'On Denoting' (*Mind*, 1905), *Russell analysed sentences of the form 'the F is G' as asserting that there is an F, that there are no two distinct Fs, and that if anything is F then it is G. A legitimate definition of something as the F will therefore depend on there being one and not more than one F. To say that the F does not exist is not to say, paradoxically, of something that exists that it does not, but to say that either nothing is F, or more than one thing is. Russell found the theory of enormous importance, since it shows how we can understand propositions involving the use of empty terms (terms that do not refer to anything or describe anything) without supposing that there is a mysterious or surrogate object that they have as their reference (*see* SUBSISTENCE). So, for example, it becomes no argument for the existence of God that we understand claims in which the term occurs. Analysing the term as a description, we may interpret the claim that God exists as something like 'there is a unique omnipotent, personal creator of the universe', and this is intelligible whether or not it is true.

Formally the theory of descriptions can be couched in the two definitions:

$$\text{The F is G} = (\exists x)((Fx \,\&\, (\forall y)(Fy \rightarrow y = x)) \,\&\, Gx)$$
$$\text{The F exists} = (\exists x)(Fx \,\&\, (\forall y)(Fy \rightarrow y = x))$$

See also ACQUAINTANCE AND DESCRIPTION.

definition *See* ANALYSIS, IMPLICIT DEFINITION.

deflationary theories of truth Theories of truth that aim at showing that truth is not a 'robust' or metaphysically heavyweight property. The general idea is that there may be nothing to say about truth in general. But if you provide any sentence, such as 'ducks quack', it is possible to say what its truth consists in, namely ducks quacking. The original theory of this kind is the *redundancy theory of truth. One elaboration gives us *disquotational theories of truth. *See also* PROSENTENTIAL THEORY OF TRUTH.

degree The degree of a predicate is the number of terms with which it must be combined to give a well-formed sentence. If the number is one, the predicate is monadic (e.g. '... is a man'), if two then it is dyadic or binary ('... is brother of ... '), and so on. In classical formal language the degree or 'adicity' of a predicate is fixed, but there is no theoretical bar to predicates of variable adicity ('... cooked supper together').

degrees of perfection argument The fourth of the *Five Ways of *Aquinas. Its premises include: (i) some things are better and more noble than others; (ii) comparative terms describe varying degrees of approximation to a superlative; (iii) whatever is the best is the most fully in being, or most real; (iv) whenever things possess some property in common, the one most fully possessing it causes it in the others. Hence, there is something which 'causes in all other things their being, their goodness and whatever other perfections they have. And this we call God.' The argument presupposes a concept of *causation as a kind of gift of reality. This idea survived until the 17th century, but is no longer attractive. In addition, the second premise is clearly faulty (one number may be greater than another, but there is no greatest number; similarly one automobile may be better than another without there being a perfect automobile). In so far as the argument depends upon an association of value with degrees of reality, and thence with causation, it is probably best seen as a version of the *cosmological argument.

de gustibus non disputandum Latin, matters of taste are not to be disputed.

deictic Adjective from deixis (*see* INDEXICAL).

deism Historically, a term referring to the doctrine of 'natural religion' emerging in England and France in the late 17th and early 18th centuries, according to which while reason (particularly the argument to *design) assures us that there is a God, additional revelation, dogma, or supernatural commerce with the deity are all excluded. Supplication and prayer in particular are fruitless: God may only be thought of as an 'absentee landlord'. Leading deists included *Herbert, John *Toland (1670–1722), whose *Christianity not Mysterious* (1696) was an influence on *Berkeley, and Anthony *Collins (1676–1729), as well as *Shaftesbury and, arguably, *Locke. The belief that remains is abstract to vanishing point, as witnessed in *Diderot's remark that a deist is someone who has not lived long enough to become an atheist.

deixis *See* INDEXICAL.

Deleuze, Gilles (1925–95) Sorbonne-educated and based in Paris for most of his career, Deleuze started as a historian of philosophy, writing about Hume, Spinoza, and Nietzsche. Later work, particularly in collaboration with Félix *Guattari, has branched into psychoanalysis, politics, film and literary theory. He stands for a general opposition to 'essentialism' in favour of a *holistic and *process orientated conception of the world. In conjunction with this goes a view of the philosopher as someone who creates concepts with which to approach this flux, rather than someone whose role is confined to examining handed-down forms of thought. His many books include *Empirisme et subjectivité* (1953, trs. as *Empiricism and Subjectivity*, 1991), *Nietzsche et la philosophie* (1962, trs. as *Nietzsche and Philosophy*, 1983), and with Guattari *Capitalisme et Schizophrénie 1. L'Anti-Oedipe* (1972/3 trs. as *Anti-Oedipus—Capitalism and Schizophrenia*, 1985), *Qu'est-ce que la philosophie?* (1991, trs. as *What Is Philosophy?*, 1996).

deliberation *See* CHOICE.

delusion Generally, any false opinion that a person persists in may be called a delusion. In the philosophy of perception, delusions such as hallucinations are sometimes distinguished from more everyday illusions, such as the bent appearance of a stick in water, or a mirage. Mirages and standard illusions are public and repeatable. They are cases in which a certain kind of stimulus naturally gives rise to an incorrect interpretation. A delusion, by contrast, is thought of as a private perceptual derangement.

de Maistre, Joseph Marie (1753–1821) Savoyard conservative and opponent of the *Enlightenment; the inspiration for countless French monarchists and Catholics. De Maistre came from an aristocratic background, was educated by Jesuits, and trained as a lawyer. He regarded the French revolution as a divine punishment for France's hospitality to the Enlightenment, and advocated a return to an absolute monarchy, sanctified by the infallible Pope, the guarantor of morality and stability in Europe. Books included *Du pape* (1821), trs. as *On the Pope* (1850) and *Essai sur le principe générateur des constitutions politiques* (1814), trs. as *Essay on the Generative Principle of Political Constitutions* (1847). The somewhat disorganized *Les Soirées de St*

Petersbourg (1821), trs. as *St. Petersburg Dialogues* (1993), contains a withering attack on *Locke, and a panegyric on the role of the executioner in society.

demarcation problem The problem of defining a line separating genuine science, thought of as properly responsive to evidence and experiment, from pseudo-science, which is not. *See* FALSIFIABILITY, POPPER.

Demetrius Lacon (2nd c. BC) Not a major figure even in antiquity, he yet enjoys the unusual distinction of being an *Epicurean from Sparta.

demiurge (Greek, craftsman) The intermediary that makes the physical world, in the cosmology of *Plato's *Timaeus*.

democracy (Greek, rule by the people) In Greek thought, rule by the citizens in general (nevertheless excluding women and of course slaves) in contrast to government by the rich and aristocratic. In modern society the sovereignty of the people in general, expressed not directly by a vote on individual questions, but through representatives. Questions arise whether various mechanisms ensure that decision-making authentically answers to the people, or serves their interest (*see also* GENERAL WILL). The problem of delimiting a democratic constitution encounters these and other difficulties; critics suggest that political democracy is hollow unless accompanied by power in other spheres, and especially the area of economics.

democracy, paradox of The problem (not a true paradox) facing a democrat who recognizes the right of people to follow a majority decision with which he or she disagrees. The problem can generate a *moral dilemma, although in practice we have little difficulty in accommodating the two different pressures.

Democritus of Abdera (*c.*460–*c.*370 BC) Along with *Leucippus, the founder of classical *atomism. He was known as very widely travelled, and was called the laughing philosopher. There is a legend, related by Tertullian although denied by *Plutarch, that in order to retain his cheerfulness (*euthumia*, the ultimate end recommended by his ethical system) he blinded himself, so as to put an end to his desire for women (*see* ULYSSES). The atomism proposed by Democritus and Leucippus was a response to the *Eleatic arguments against motion. The Eleatics argued that what is real is both single and motionless, since motion is impossible without empty space (*see also* ZENO'S PARADOXES) and plurality is impossible without empty space to separate the different unities. By allowing empty space, the atomists could avoid the Eleatic conclusion, but the individual atoms retain the characteristics that *Parmenides attributed to the whole of unchanging reality. They are indivisible, homogeneous, solid, and unchanging, but they may differ from each other in shape and size. They are infinite in number, exist in empty space (the *void), and are in eternal motion. When enough atoms exist in a region of space they form a vortex, with a mass of heavier atoms at the centre attracting others; the speed of the motion ignites such masses and causes the celestial bodies. The arrangements and conglomerations of atoms produce the world we experience; this world is, however, only one of the infinite number of worlds that different arrangements of atoms produce. The soul is made of particularly fine atoms, but is a composite and hence as perishable as the body. Perception is the result of **eidola* or thin films of atoms being shed from the surfaces of objects and interacting with the atoms of the soul.

The magnificent vision of the universe that Democritus conjures up, with its mechanism and its total absence of purpose and design, was too much for *Plato and *Aristotle, and only wholeheartedly embraced by *Epicurus, until it was rediscovered in the 17th century and formed the basis of modern science.

demonstration In contemporary usage, a *logically valid *proof from *axioms or other accepted premises. It is extremely important that in the period between *Descartes and J. S. *Mill a demonstration is not this, but a chain of 'intuitive' comparisons of ideas, whereby a principle or maxim can be established by reason alone. It is in this sense that *Locke believed that theological and moral principles are capable of demonstration, and *Hume denies that they are, and also denies that scientific enquiry proceeds by demonstrating its results. *See also* MATTER OF FACT, PROOF, RELATIONS OF IDEAS.

demonstrative reasoning *See* LOGIC.

demonstratives *See* INDEXICAL.

De Morgan, Augustus (1806–71) English mathematician and logician. De Morgan was born in India and educated at Trinity College, Cambridge, and became first professor of mathematics at the university of London, being appointed to his chair at the age of 21. He wrote widely on mathematics and astronomy. His *Essay on Probabilities* (1838), *Formal Logic* (1847), and *Syllabus of a Proposed System of Logic* (1860), together with the informal *Budget of Paradoxes* (1872), represent his work in logic and scientific method. He was a pioneer ahead of his time in the development of *formal logic, writing that 'every science that has thriven has thriven upon its own symbols: logic, the only science which is admitted to have made no improvements in century after century, is the only one which has grown no symbols'. De Morgan was a pioneer in recognizing the close affinities between logic and algebra, in recognizing the importance of a doctrine of predication, and in opening up the logic of relations. He corresponded widely, and was an acknowledged influence on *Hamilton and *Peirce.

De Morgan's laws The equivalences (i) not-(A or B) if and only if not-A and not-B, and (ii) not-(A and B), if and only if not-A or not-B, are known as De Morgan's laws, although De Morgan himself gave the equivalent statements in *Boolean algebra. Each equivalence is a *theorem of the *propositional calculus.

demythologizing Removing the mythical element; particularly, a mode of biblical interpretation associated with *Bultmann that takes the mythical elements of the Bible not as descriptions of the real world, but as metaphors or indirect assertions about human life.

Dennett, Daniel Clement (1942–) American philosopher of mind. Dennett was educated at Harvard and Oxford, and teaches at Tufts University. His conception of our understanding of each other, in terms of taking up an 'intentional stance' which is useful for prediction and explanation, has been widely discussed. Debate concerns whether we can usefully take up the stance towards inanimate things, and whether the account does sufficient justice to the real existence of mental states. Dennett has also been a major force in illustrating how the philosophy of mind needs to be informed by work in surrounding sciences. Works include *Content and Consciousness* (1969), *Brainstorms* (1978), *Elbow Room* (1984), *The Intentional Stance* (1987), *Consciousness Explained* (1991), and *Darwin's Dangerous Idea* (1995).

denotation That which is *denoted, or referred to by a term. *See* CONNOTATION/DENOTATION.

denote To refer. *Russell sometimes uses the term so that what he called complexes, or something more like concepts, are what denote, and what they denote is whatever falls under them. *See* DEFINITE DESCRIPTIONS, REFERENCE.

denoting phrase The term with which *Russell introduced his famous paper 'On Denoting' (*Mind*, 1905): denoting phrases include *definite and indefinite descriptions (a man, some man, any man, the present King of England ...) regardless of whether anything is actually denoted by them. In the theory of definite descriptions, and in standard modern logic, the form of sentences containing such phrases is given by means of the *quantifiers.

dense order *See* CONTINUITY.

denumerable/non-denumerable A denumerable set is one whose *cardinality is that of the natural numbers. A set is non-denumerable if it is of greater cardinality than this. *Cantor's theorem proves the existence of such sets. A finite set is of lesser cardinality than the natural numbers, and an enumerable or countable set is either denumerable or finite.

deny To reject. *Frege argued influentially that denial is not a separate activity from assertion, but that to deny a proposition is to assert that it is false, or to assert its *negation.

denying the antecedent To argue invalidly that given that if p then q, and given not-p, we can infer not-q. 'If she is in Barbados she is in the Caribbean; she is not in Barbados, so she is not in the Caribbean.'

denying the consequent To argue validly that, given that if p then q and given not-q, we can infer not-p. 'If the leg is broken this will hurt; it does not hurt, so the leg is not broken.'

deontic (Greek, fitting, correct) In ethics, the deontic categories are those of obligation and permission.

deontic logic A *logical calculus created by adding operators 'Op' (it ought to be the case that p) and 'Pp' (it is permissible that p) to a basic system such as the *propositional calculus, together with rules of inference for them. A deontic logic will study inferences between these forms, telling for instance whether $Op \ \& \ p \rightarrow q$ yield Oq, or whether $Op \rightarrow \neg O \neg p$. Principles such as these have proved controversial and there is no one 'classical' system of deontic logic. *See also* GENTLE MURDER, PARADOX OF.

deontic paradoxes *See* GENTLE MURDER, PARADOX OF.

deontological ethics Ethics based on the notion of a duty, or what is right, or rights, as opposed to ethical systems based on the idea of achieving some good state of affairs (*see* CONSEQUENTIALISM) or the qualities of character necessary to live well (*see* VIRTUE ETHICS). The leading deontological system is that of *Kant.

depiction The relation whereby one thing depicts another is important both in *aesthetics and in understanding mental imagery. At first sight mere resemblance might be supposed to be sufficient. But if A resembles B then B resembles A, whereas if a picture depicts a sitter, the sitter does not also depict the picture. Depiction may therefore be more a matter of the intention of the creator, or the interpretation given to a work by the audience. This in turn raises the question of whether anything can depict anything, if it is taken to do so, or whether an element of convention constrains how works are taken.

depth grammar *See* GENERATIVE GRAMMAR.

de re/de dicto (Latin, of a thing/of a statement) A contrast between two ways of interpreting sentences that may, or may not, be about a particular thing. *Quine's example is 'I want a sloop', which may mean that there is a particular sloop I want, or which on the other hand may be true although I have no particular sloop in mind, when it just signals the desire for 'relief from slooplessness'. The contrast can be given in the *predicate calculus as that between: $(\exists x)(x$ is a sloop & I want to own $x)$ and 'I want it that: $(\exists x)(x$ is a sloop & I own $x)$'. The former can only be true if I am related to a specific thing, whereas the latter apparently relates me only to a statement, which I wish would become true but which could be made true by different things. Many contexts invite this ambiguity: 'Jane said that the smallest girl in the class was taller than one of the others' would impute a contradiction to Jane taken *de dicto*, but leaves her rationality unchallenged taken *de re*. *Russell's example was the conversation: 'I expected the ship to be longer than it is'; 'No, it is just as long as it is.' Knowledge *de re* is knowledge of a particular thing, that it is thus and so; knowledge *de dicto* is knowledge that something is the case where what is known could in principle be 'realized' by different things.

Derrida, Jacques (1930–2004) Controversial French *postmodernist and leader of the *deconstructionist movement. Born in Algeria, Derrida was a philosophy teacher for more than twenty years at the École Normale Supérieure in Paris. The notion of deconstruction was first presented in the introduction to his 1962 translation of Husserl's *Origin of Geometry*. Derrida urged the importance of the unconscious rhetorical aspects of works, arguing that attention to the incidentals often subverts the principal doctrines of a text: the process of deconstruction is one of showing how the author's ostensible message is undermined by other aspects of its presentation. In *De la grammatologie* (1967, trs. as *Of Grammatology*, 1976), Derrida argued against the 'phonocentrism' that privileges speech above writing by imagining that the presence of the author affords a fixed point of meaning and intention. This desire for a 'centre' generates familiar oppositions (subject/object, appearance/reality, etc.) which need to be overcome and dismissed. Instead the endless possibility of interpretation and reinterpretation opens up a receding horizon within which meaning is endlessly deferred, although the reader as much as the author is a creator of any provisional significance that is eventually found (*see also* GADAMER).

Derrida's work emerged from the tradition of *Husserl and *Heidegger, and although it has proved catching in some circles, it is not easily assimilated by people used to normal expressions of thought. In an article 'Reiterating the Differences: A Reply to Derrida' John Searle gave an exasperated deconstruction of a tissue of confusions he found in one of Derrida's most famous essays, 'Signature Event Context'. Derrida replied with a blizzard of text which did little to clarify the issue in *Limited Inc.* (1977). *See also* DECONSTRUCTION, *DIFFÉRANCE*, POSTSTRUCTURALISM.

de Ruggiero, Guido (1888–1948) Italian historian of philosophy, and professor at Messina and Rome. He made his name with the thirteen-volume *Storia della filosofia* (1918–48). *Collingwood translated his *Storia del liberalismo europeo* (1925) as *History of European Liberalism*.

Descartes, René (1596–1650) French mathematician and founding father of modern philosophy. Born in La Haye, near Tours, Descartes was educated at the new Jesuit college at La Flèche, before reading law at Poitiers. In 1618 he enlisted at his own expense in the Dutch army of Maurice of Nassau, in order to have the leisure to think. His interest in the methodology of a unified science is supposed to have been stimulated by a dream 'in a stove-heated room' when he was serving at Ulm in 1619. In the subsequent ten years he travelled widely, returning to Holland in 1628. Little is known of his private life, but the death of his illegitimate five-year-old daughter Francine in 1640 is known to have been a devastating blow. His first work, the *Regulae ad Directionem Ingenii* (1628/9), was never completed. In Holland, between 1628 and 1649, Descartes first wrote, and then cautiously suppressed, *Le Monde* (1634), and in 1637 produced the *Discours de la méthode* as a preface to the treatise on mathematics and physics in which he introduced the notion of Cartesian coordinates.

His best-known philosophical work, the *Meditationes de Prima Philosophia* (*Meditations on First Philosophy*), together with objections by distinguished contemporaries and replies by Descartes (the *Objections and Replies*), appeared in 1641. The authors of the objections are: first set, the Dutch theologian Johan de Kater; second set, *Mersenne; third set, *Hobbes; fourth set, *Arnauld; fifth set, *Gassendi; and sixth set, *Mersenne. The second edition (1642) of the *Med-*

itations included a seventh set by the Jesuit Pierre Bourdin. Descartes's penultimate work, the *Principia Philosophiae* (*Principles of Philosophy*) of 1644, was designed partly for use as a theological textbook. His last work was *Les Passions de l'âme* (*The Passions of the Soul*), published in 1649. In that year Descartes visited the court of *Kristina of Sweden, where he contracted pneumonia, allegedly through being required to break his normal habit of late rising in order to give lessons at 5:00 a.m. His last words are supposed to have been 'Ça, mon âme, il faut partir' ('So, my soul, it is time to part').

Descartes's theory of knowledge starts with the quest for certainty, for an indubitable starting-point or foundation on the basis alone of which progress is possible (*see* METHOD OF DOUBT). This is eventually found in the celebrated 'Cogito ergo sum': I think therefore I am. By locating the point of certainty in my own awareness of my own self, Descartes gives a first-person twist to the theory of knowledge that dominated the following centuries in spite of various counter-attacks on behalf of social and public starting-points. The metaphysics associated with this priority is the famous Cartesian dualism, or separation of mind and matter into two different but interacting substances. Descartes rigorously and rightly sees that it takes divine dispensation to certify any relationship between the two realms thus divided, and to prove the reliability of the senses invokes a 'clear and distinct perception' of highly dubious proofs of the existence of a benevolent deity. This has not met general acceptance: as *Hume drily puts it, 'to have recourse to the veracity of the supreme Being, in order to prove the veracity of our senses, is surely making a very unexpected circuit'.

In his own time Descartes's conception of the entirely separate substance of the mind was recognized to give rise to insoluble problems of the nature of the causal connection between the two (*see* OCCASIONALISM). It also gives rise to the problem, insoluble in its own terms, of *other minds. Descartes's notorious denial that non-human animals are conscious is a stark illustration of the problem. In his conception of matter Descartes also gives preference to rational cogitation over anything derived from the senses. Since we can conceive of the matter of a *ball of wax surviving changes to its sensible qualities, matter is not an *empirical concept, but eventually an entirely geometrical one, with extension and motion as its only physical nature. Descartes's thought here is reflected in *Leibniz's view, held later by *Russell, that the qualities of sense experience have no resemblance to qualities of things, so that knowledge of the external world is essentially knowledge of structure rather than of filling. On this basis Descartes erects a remarkable physics. Since matter is in effect the same as extension there can be no empty space or *void; since there is no empty space motion is not a question of occupying previously empty space, but is to be thought of in terms of vortices (like the motion of a liquid).

Although the structure of Descartes's epistemology, theory of mind, and theory of matter have been rejected many times, their relentless exposure of the hardest issues, their exemplary clarity, and even their initial plausibility, all contrive to make him the central point of reference for modern philosophy.

SEE WEB LINKS

- A biography of Descartes, including his influence on science and philosophy
- A list of internet resources on Descartes, including bibliographies

description, knowledge by *See* ACQUAINTANCE AND DESCRIPTION.

descriptions, theory of *See* DEFINITE DESCRIPTIONS.

descriptive meaning It may seem plausible to split the meaning of some terms into two components, descriptive and evaluative. Saying that someone is courageous or temperate would partly be describing them, and partly offering a positive evaluation of what is described. The two-part analysis is, however, controversial, partly because it proves hard to separate out the descriptive meaning in the absence of the evaluation, and partly because often one side or the other seems not to be fixed as part of the conventional meaning of the term, but more by a moral consensus. *See also* THICK TERMS.

descriptivism The view contrasted with *prescriptivism by *Hare, according to which the meaning of an evaluative term is given without the element of command, or approval, or pressure on action, but is simply thought of as a paraphrase of the natural descriptions of the things to which it applies. The problem is that the element of evaluation seems to have thereby got lost. *See* NATURALISTIC FALLACY, OPEN QUESTION ARGUMENT.

desert The term denotes the idea that how a person ought to be treated depends on a fact about their actions, or their character: a proportioning of happiness to virtue, or unhappiness to vice. Treating persons as they deserve is then the exercise of justice. Problems include the distinction between moral and non-moral desert, and the question of whether the variations of treatment have a fundamental place in ethics, or whether they are to be justified, for instance on *consequentialist grounds. *See also* FREE WILL.

design, argument from or to The argument that the world (meaning the entire universe) sufficiently resembles a machine or a work of art or architecture, for it to be reasonable for us to posit a designer whose intellect is responsible for its order and complexity. The argument is avowedly an argument by *analogy, claiming that since the universe and (say) a clock resemble each other in some respects, they probably resemble each other in the further respect of being the product of design. The argument was used by the *Stoics, and had immense appeal in the 18th century, but it was overwhelmingly attacked by *Hume in the *Dialogues Concerning Natural Religion*, and by *Kant in the *Critique of Pure Reason*. The argument clearly invites a vicious regress, since the universe plus a designer seems an even more wonderful example of organization, and ought to lead us to postulate a designer-of-designers. If it is felt natural that a designer can 'just exist' (*see* PERSEITY) then it has to be asked why the cosmos cannot also 'just exist'. The argument to design also runs into moral trouble; since the nature of the deity is evidenced by his or her creation, we should not attribute more concern for goodness or justice to him or her than we find in the normal running of things (*see also* EVIL, PROBLEM OF). The theory of *evolution by natural selection has further undermined the effect of one of the main examples of design in nature that was often adduced, namely the adaptation of the organs and faculties of animals to their environments. However, physicists and cosmologists, impressed by the 'fine-tuning' of the forces that apparently govern the universe, are still prone to imagine that recourse to a guiding intelligence affords some explanation. *See also* INTELLIGENT DESIGN.

designate To refer to or *denote.

designated value The valuation that *valid formulae get in an intended *interpretation of a *logical calculus. *See* MODEL THEORY.

designator A term that designates. *See* DEFINITE DESCRIPTION, RIGID DESIGNATOR, SINGULAR TERM.

desire The standard model of human motivation, sometimes called the 'Humean' theory of motivation, is that it takes a desire and a belief. Belief by itself will not suffice, unless the objects of belief interact with the agent's desires. They must be things towards which there is some attraction or aversion. Some say that if desires are thought of as conscious states of mind, this is untrue. On the other hand, if they are thought of as no more than interpretations certified by the agent's behaviour, then perhaps the model is trivial. But *functionalism rescues the Humean theory, seeing 'desire' as a respectable theoretical category, identified by its role in systematizing the explanation of agents. Salient questions include whether we always do what we desire to do, whether we can control our strongest desires, and how motivation by desire compares with motivation by principle. Major philosophies of life, including *Buddhism and *Stoicism, have presented the overcoming of desire as an ideal. *See* APATHY, LOVE, *SUMMUM BONUM*.

despair *See* ABANDONMENT, ANGST.

destiny *See* FATALISM.

detachment In logic, the rule allowing inference from a formula A, and another read as 'if A then B', to the formula B. Another term for modus ponens.

determinable/determinate A contrast relating the more general ('colour') to the more specific ('red'). It was originally introduced by W. E. *Johnson. In one usage, the contrast differs from that of genus to species, in that the specific difference identifying a determinate is itself a modification of the determinable. Thus what differentiates red from blue is just colour, whereas many different properties may differentiate a member of one species, for instance of animal, from those of another.

determinism The doctrine that every event has a cause. The usual explanation of this is that for every event, there is some antecedent state, related in such a way that it would break a law of nature for this antecedent state to exist yet the event not to happen. This is a purely metaphysical claim, and carries no implications for whether we can in principle predict the event (*see* CHAOS). The main interest in determinism has been in assessing its implications for *free will. However, *quantum physics is essentially indeterministic, yet the view that our actions are subject to quantum indeterminacies hardly encourages a sense of our own responsibility for them. *See also* DILEMMA OF DETERMINISM, LIBERTARIANISM (METAPHYSICAL).

determinism, biological The view that our genetic inheritance not only influences, but constrains and makes inevitable our development as persons with a variety of traits. At its silliest the view postulates such entities as a gene predisposing people to poverty, and it is the particular enemy of thinkers stressing the parental, social, and political determinants of the way we are. *See also* GENE.

deus ex machina (Latin, god from the machine) The phrase refers to the theatrical device whereby a supernatural agency is introduced to solve the dramatic situation; hence, any artificial, introduced, external, and *ad hoc solution to a problem.

deus sive natura (Latin, god or nature) The slogan of *Spinoza's pantheism: the view that god and nature are interchangeable, or that there is no distinction between the creator and the creation.

deviant causal chain A notion used to test and refine *causal theories of perception, action, meaning, and memory. Suppose it is suggested that for me to remember an event it is enough (a) that I witnessed it, and (b) that this was the original cause of my present thought about it. Then a deviant causal chain might be that I witnessed the event, because of that wrote about it in my diary, and on now reading the diary think about the event. A causal chain is in place, but it is not enough to establish that I remember the event; it is consistent with this story that I have forgotten it entirely. Ingenious deviant causal chains include objects causing hallucinations that match the appearance of the object, thoughts causing spasms causing events that match those that would have occurred had the thought given rise to an intention to act, and many others.

Dewey, John (1859–1952) American educator, social reformer, and philosopher of *pragmatism. Dewey was born in Burlington, Vermont, and had a relatively undistinguished academic career, until he enlisted at Johns Hopkins, America's first graduate university, in 1881. At this time he was influenced by *Hegel, and his writings never lost an enthusiasm for the dynamic, the vital, and the progressive. His work took on a steadily more practical bent when in 1894 he became chairman of the department of philosophy, psychology, and education in Chicago. Here he remained for ten years before removing to Columbia, where the *Journal of Philosophy* became largely a house magazine for discussions about and by Dewey. His work as a psychologist and educational thinker crystallized a reaction against the excessively formal and rigid educational practices of the time. Dewey recognized that the child is an active, exploring, inquisitive creature, so the task of education is to foster experience infused by skills and knowledge. Dewey's enormous influence owed more to his skill at expounding the pragmatic, scientific, and democratic progressiveness of the America of his time than to accurate or technical philosophical argument. But his development of the *pragmatism of *James and *Peirce remains influential. In his hands enquiry is a self-corrective process conducted in a specific historical and cultural circumstance; it requires no foundation in certainty or 'the *given', and knowledge is just that which is warranted through enquiry. Dewey expressed his views in a torrent of books and articles: the centennial bibliography of his work contains more than 150 pages.

SEE WEB LINKS

- A list of internet resources on Dewey
- Bibliographies of writings by or on Dewey

dharma (Sanskrit, carrying or holding) In *Buddhism, the factors of existence. Originally not so much an ethical concept as one of cosmological theory, *dharma* bears some relationship to the Greek **logos*, meaning the principle or law governing the universe, and in particular the cycles of rebirth. It became associated with the teachings of the Buddha and the sphere of temporal (non-religious) duty and custom, and from here is extended to cover aspects of character that make up a personality. As in the ethics of *Kant, it is also associated with concern for others as extensions of oneself. This ethical notion of *dharma* is prominent in the Buddhist contribution to *Hindu thought.

Dharmakirti (7th c. AD) Indian philosopher and logician of the *Yogacara school of *Buddhism. Dharmakirti was a perceptual idealist, but his principal influence was to establish the basis of logical relations in reality. His major work was the *Pramanavarttika* or 'Explanation of the Touchstones'.

diachronic (Greek, through time) Processes are diachronic, and the nature of their existence as extended in time is sometimes contrasted with that of events (instantaneous) or even objects (*see* ENDURANCE/PERDURANCE).

diagonal procedure The method first used by *Cantor to show that there cannot be an enumeration of the real numbers. Any real number can be written as an infinite decimal. So we imagine a correspondence with the natural numbers, giving us some real as the first, another as the second, and so on. Given such a list, Cantor defines a real number that differs from the first real in the first decimal place, the second in the second place, and so on for every listed real. Thus if the decimal expansion of the first real is written as the sequence of digits $x_{01}\ x_{02}\ x_{03}\ldots$ and the reals are laid out in order:

$$\begin{array}{lllll} \mathbf{x_{00}} & x_{01} & x_{02} & x_{03} & \cdots \\ x_{10} & \mathbf{x_{11}} & x_{12} & x_{13} & \cdots \\ x_{20} & x_{21} & \mathbf{x_{22}} & x_{23} & \cdots \\ x_{30} & x_{31} & x_{32} & \mathbf{x_{33}} & \cdots \end{array}$$

We then consider the diagonal (highlighted) real $x_{00}\ x_{11}\ x_{22}\ldots$ and define a non-terminating decimal that differs in each place: e.g. let $y_{nn} = 5$ if $x_{nn} \neq 5$, and $y_{nn} = 6$ otherwise. This then is a real that was not on the original list, for it differs from the nth real on the list in the nth place. The construction refutes the thesis that we had enumerated all the reals. Diagonal arguments are one of the most powerful tools of set theory and *metamathematics. They also bear a close relationship to arguments of the *Liar family: an explicit use of diagonal reasoning occurs in *Richard's paradox.

dialectic (Greek, *dialektikē*, the art of conversation or debate) Most fundamentally, the process of reasoning to obtain truth and knowledge on any topic. According to the different views of this process, different conceptions of dialectic emerge. Thus in the *Socratic method dialectic is the process of eliciting the truth by means of questions aimed at opening out what is already implicitly known, or at exposing the contradictions and muddles of an opponent's position. In the middle dialogues of *Plato, however, it becomes the total process of enlightenment, whereby the philosopher is educated so as to achieve knowledge of the supreme good, the *form of the Good. For *Aristotle, dialectic is any rational inference based on probable premises. In *Kant, dialectic is the 'logic of illusion', or the misuse of logic to deliver the appearance of solid belief. It is one of the jobs of true philosophy to reveal the places where reason transgresses its proper boundaries, producing the illusions of transcendental metaphysics (*see* ANTINOMY, PARALOGISM). In *Hegel, dialectic refers to the necessary process that makes up progress in both thought and the world (which are identified in Hegel's idealism, although the idea that processes in the world unfold in a way that mirrors the processes of reason is as old as *Heraclitus). The process is one of overcoming the contradiction between thesis and antithesis, by means of synthesis; the synthesis in turn becomes contradicted, and the process repeats itself until final perfection is reached. *See also* DIALECTICAL MATERIALISM.

dialectical materialism The dominant philosophical strain of *Marxism, combining materialism as an embracing philosophy of nature and science, with the *Hegelian notion of dialectic as a historical force, driving events onwards towards a progressive resolution of the *contradictions that characterize each historical epoch. The combination was perhaps first fully developed by *Engels, in *Anti-Dühring* (1878). Human thought itself aims to mirror the uniform but contradictory character of external reality. Plekhanov and *Lenin interpreted dialectical materialism as implying that the nature of the world coincided with the ideals of the revolution, and the heady belief that history itself guarantees the victory of one's own cause or party has proved one of the more widely alluring consolations of philosophy.

dialectical school A branch of the *Megarian school of classical philosophy, whose principal member was *Diodorus Cronus. The central concern was logic and paradox, and the school was an influence on *Stoic logic.

dialectical theology *See* BARTH.

dialetheia A contradiction. Dialethic logic is logic that studies *formal systems that may include divisions between valid and invalid arguments involving contradictions.

diallelon (Greek, through or by means of one another) Term used by Sir William *Hamilton for a circular argument or definition. *See* CIRCLE, VICIOUS.

dianoia Knowledge in general. In *Plato, knowledge of a kind that falls short of the highest kind, **noēsis*. *Dianoia* describes knowledge of mathematical and technical subjects. *See also* LINE. It is subdivided in Aristotle into real theoretical knowledge, *technē*, or knowhow, and **phronēsis*, or practical and moral wisdom.

dichotomy A division into two.

dichotomy paradox Another title for the paradox of the racecourse. *See* ZENO'S PARADOXES.

dictum de omni et nullo The principle of *Aristotle that whatever is affirmed or denied of an entire class or kind may be affirmed or denied of any part of it. The principle is supposed to validate the four moods of the first figure of the *syllogism, and motivated the reduction of the other three figures to this one.

Diderot, Denis (1713–84) The principal editor of the **Encyclopédie*, and together with *Voltaire the leading figure of the 18th-century *Enlightenment in France, enjoying a long and eventful career dedicated to the acquisition and dissemination of learning. Diderot was an outspoken champion of the modern, secular, and scientific world view in an age where free-thinking was still dangerous in France. His philosophical works include *Le Neveu de Rameau* (composed in the 1760s, pub. in German, 1805, trs. as *Rameau's Nephew*) and *Le Rêve de d'Alembert* (composed in 1769, pub. 1782, trs. as *D'Alembert's Dream*), both of which breathe a delightful spirit of conversational play and banter, while in fact discussing with great seriousness the foundations of ethics and the nature of animal creation, albeit in the light of the speculative biology of the time. He burned what he believed to be the only manuscript of the latter work, in the presence of *d'Alembert, who had been asked to seek its destruction by the *saloniste* Julie de l'Espinasse, who appears in the story. Fortunately, unknown to Diderot, an additional copy had been made.

différance Term introduced by *Derrida, combining the French for 'difference' and 'deferral'. It is used to suggest both the *Saussurean emphasis on meaning as the function of differences or contrasts within a network of terms, and also the endless deferral of any final fixed point or privileged, meaning-determining relationship with the extra-linguistic world.

difference, method of *See* MILL'S METHODS.

difference principle The principle chosen by rational people from behind the *veil of ignorance, in *Rawls's *A Theory of Justice.* The principle requires that social benefits and burdens are allocated in such a way as to make the position of the least well-off as good as it can be. *See also* ORIGINAL POSITION.

differentia The distinguishing characteristics, differentiating a *species from other species within the same *genus.

Digby, Kenelm (1603–65) Colourful Catholic alchemist, philosopher and interpreter of 17-century *corpuscularianism. Digby's brilliance took him through a celebrated marriage to Venetia Stanley, naval engagements, diplomatic missions, duels, exile, and eventually to becoming a founding member of the Royal Society. The *Private Memoirs of Sir Kenelm Digby, Gentleman of the Privy Chamber to King Charles the First* is now but a literary curiosity. His philosophical reputation hinges on *Two Treatises: in the one of which, the nature of bodies, in the other, the nature of man's mind, is looked into* defending the immateriality and immortality of the soul, published in Paris in 1644.

dignity While in ordinary thought dignity is something some people have more than others, and undignified moments are a pitfall for all of us, in moral philosophy, especially that of *Kant, dignity is more often considered as a universal attribute, an offshoot of the capacity for self-consciousness and practical reason. The capacity for self-legislation and the control of the will by the *categorical imperative belongs to all of us, and is the foundation of the right to respect and to treatment as an end rather than as a means.

dilemma The simplest form of a dilemma is an argument of the form: 'If *p* then *q*, if not-*p* then *q*, so in any event *q*.' More complex forms were traditionally distinguished. A constructive dilemma is of the form: 'If *p* then *r*, if *q* then *r*, but either *p* or *q*, so *r*.' A destructive dilemma is of the form: 'If *p* then *q*, and if *p* then *r*, but either not-*q* or not-*r*, so not-*p*.' The two conditional premises of a dilemma are called its horns. Escaping between the horns of the dilemma is denying the disjunction '*p* or *q*'; taking it by the horns is denying one of the conditionals. The notion generalizes to trilemmas, in which there are three horns (*see*, for example, BAYLE'S TRILEMMA). For other dilemmas *see* EUTHYPHRO DILEMMA, MORAL DILEMMAS, PRISONERS' DILEMMA.

dilemma of determinism It is often supposed that if an action is the end of a *causal chain, i.e. determined, and the causes stretch back in time to events for which an agent has no conceivable responsibility, then the agent is not responsible for the action. The dilemma adds that if an action is *not* the end of such a chain, then either it or one of its causes occurs at random, in that no antecedent events brought it about, and in that case nobody is responsible for its occurrence either. So whether or not *determinism is true, responsibility is shown to be illusory. *See also* FREE WILL, LIBERTARIANISM (METAPHYSICAL).

dilemmas, moral These arise when on the face of it you ought to do each of two incompatible actions. That is, each seems obligatory but you can at best do one of them. There is dispute over whether it is right to say that you ought to do one, ought to do each, or ought to do neither. Saying you ought to do both transgresses against the principle that ought implies can. One option is that you ought to do neither, following the analogy that if two runners are first equal, then neither is an outright winner. But it has been argued against this, by *Williams, that there is properly a psychological 'remainder' of guilt or the need to make reparation, suggesting that the neglected action was obligatory after all.

Dilthey, Wilhelm (1833–1911) German philosopher, literary critic, and historian. Dilthey taught at a variety of universities, and succeeded *Lotze at the university of Berlin in 1882. He is especially remembered for his studies in the methodology of the social sciences, or *Geisteswissenschaften*. For Dilthey these are distinguished from natural science by the use of a method of understanding, or **Verstehen*, whereby we comprehend the meaning of a human expression, such as words or actions. In his earlier writings *Verstehen* is thought of as the reliving (*nacherleben*) of the mental states of others, inferred by analogy and on the basis of a knowledge of our own experiences. However, the subjective and psychological basis of this process was replaced in later years, when *Verstehen* becomes not the semi-scientific attempt to find the idea or mental modification that caused an expression, but rather the location of the expression in an objective framework of human meaning, to which context, language, and cultural climate all contribute. These are 'objectifications of life', and the object of study in the various human sciences. In this sense the process of *Verstehen* is never complete, since different aspects of the way in which meanings 'hang together' (*zusammenhängen*) can always be uncovered. Dilthey never completed a systematic treatise. His *Einleitung in die Geisteswissenschaften* ('Introduction to the Social Sciences') of 1883 was the first volume of an uncompleted work. His voluminous writings on many aspects of history, biography, the study of culture, and philosophy were collected as the *Gesammelte Schriften* ('Collected Writings') of which more than eighteen volumes exist. He was a major influence on methodological reflections in sociology, particularly through *Weber, on subsequent *hermeneutics, and latterly on discussions of the epistemology of '*folk psychology'.

SEE WEB LINKS

- A list of internet resources on Dilthey
- Bibliographies of writings by or on Dilthey

Ding an sich (German, thing in itself) In *Kantian metaphysics the thing in itself exists independently of us, unfiltered by the forms of sense. It is not in space or time, and cannot be known. *See* NOUMENON.

Diodorus Cronus (late 4th–early 3rd c. BC) The most famous member of the *dialectical school. His principal surviving contribution is his *master argument.

Diogenes Laertius (? 3rd *c.* AD) Greek biographer. Diogenes is not a serious philosopher, but his book *Lives of Eminent Philosophers* is a major biographical source for all classical Greek and Roman philosophers until the 3rd century AD, when it is presumed that Diogenes Laertius lived. He has been counted as making reference to 365 books by 250 authors, and it is in his quotation of lost material that he is regarded as most reliable. *Nietzsche, himself a considerable classicist, wrote of Diogenes that he is 'by accident the clumsy watchman guarding treasure whose value he does not know'.

Diogenes of Apollonia (5th c. BC) Diogenes is principally known for combining detailed empirical work, especially in biology, with the ambitious cosmological speculations characteristic of the *Presocratics. He believed that everything was made of different combinations of the same basic stuff, aer, which had conscious and purposive attributes, and whose condensation and rarefaction created the different substances we know.

Diogenes of Sinope (*c.*400–325 BC) The founder of the *Cynics, Diogenes lived in Athens and perhaps Corinth. He may have been taught by *Antisthenes, but it was his life and influence that gave the Cynics their importance. He taught that the right way of life was to have the simplest possible needs and to satisfy them in the most direct way. In particular, whatever is natural is honourable and decent, and can therefore be done in public without any shame. Conventions contrary to this openness should be ignored. The ethic is not just one of self-sufficiency, but more one of self-mastery born of a healthy contempt for one's own pleasures and pains, and especially born of impatience with the conventions and hierarchies of a presumably corrupt society: 'Aristotle breakfasts when it pleases the king; Diogenes, when it pleases Diogenes.'

Dionysian *See* APOLLONIAN/DIONYSIAN.

Dionysius the Pseudo-Areopagite (*c.*AD 500) Also known as Pseudo-Dionysius and Pseudo-Denys or Denis. A mystical theologian, confusedly identified in the early Middle Ages with Dionysius the Areopagite whose conversion is described by St Paul (Acts 17: 34). The Pseudo-Dionysian writings aim at a synthesis between Christianity and *Neoplatonism, and the mistaken belief that they both originated at the time of the Apostles contributed to their authority. Man approaches God by leaving behind perception and reason, and entering an obscurity from which he will be rescued by a 'ray of divine darkness', and brought to knowledge of the being that in its total unity transcends all description. The 9th-century translation by *Eriugena provided the rhetorical model for much subsequent mystical writing.

Diotima of Mantinea A priestess whose teaching on the subjects of beauty and love is reported by *Socrates in the *Symposium*. The historicity of Diotima has usually been doubted, although there are what appear to be bronze bas-relief representations of her dating from the 4th century BC, and her key doctrines differ tellingly from those of *Plato.

direction of fit A concept deriving from G. E. M. *Anscombe's influential book *Intention*. Anscombe introduced two ways of using a shopping list: one as a set of instructions of what to put in the basket, but the other, as might be used by a detective spying on a shopper's movements, as a record of what has gone into the basket. In the first case the goal is to have the basket fit the list, but in the second to have the list fit the basket. The concept is used to differentiate mental states like desires or intentions, which conform to the first model, from representations and beliefs, which conform to the second. There is controversy over which direction of fit moral commitments exhibit.

direct realism *See* REALISM.

dirty hands argument The justification often given for acting badly, that if we don't do it, someone else will (and reap the reward). For example, if we don't sell arms to an evil regime, and thereby earn a living, someone else will; so we might as well do it.

disanalogy *See* ANALOGY.

disappearance theory Any theory that, whilst purporting to give an account of some phenomenon, actually has the consequence that it does not exist. Various theories of mind are charged with this defect. For example, a view that approaches the question what it is to think by examining what it is for an interpreter to attribute thought, faces a potentially vicious *regress when it is asked for an account of what it is for the interpreter to be thinking. *See also* ELIMINATIVISM.

disconfirmation A piece of evidence disconfirms a theory if it puts a particular difficulty in front of it, or diminishes its acceptability or probability.

discourse (Latin, *discursus*, a running from one place to another) A continuous stretch of language containing more than one sentence: conversations, narratives, arguments, speeches. Discourse analysis is the social and linguistic description of norms governing such productions, and may include (in critical linguistics) focus upon the social and political determinants of the form discourse takes; for instance, the hidden presuppositions that the persons addressed are of a certain class, race, or gender.

discourse ethics *See* HABERMAS.

discourse semantics An extension of *semantics to include an analysis of the relation between a sentence and the context or discourse in which it is embedded. For example, the reference of pronouns or other *indexical elements within a sentence may only be derived from its relation to surrounding sayings.

discovery, logic of The idea that there is any such thing as a 'logic' of scientific discovery has been a frequent object of attack, especially by philosophers of science influenced by Sir Karl *Popper. There is usually thought to be no authoritative *confirmation theory, telling how bodies of evidence support a hypothesis. Instead science proceeds by a *hypothetico-deductive method, or method of conjectures and refutations.

discrimination Distinguishing or differentiating. One of the principal abilities underlying any kind of cognition. However, in moral and political philosophy, the term is often confined to the unfavourable treatment of particular groups of individuals, on prejudiced and irrelevant grounds. Confusing these two senses can lead to the view that almost any description of people is politically incorrect.

disembodiment The state of a person supposed to continue to exist after their bodily death. *See* IMMORTALITY.

disenchantment Term associated with *Weber, for the eradication of values, emotions, traditions, in favour of strict means–end rational calculation. According to Weber this process involves social beings using knowledge for the purpose of controlling the world, although its actual effect may be the confining cage of bureaucratic management.

disjoint Two sets are disjoint if they have no member in common.

disjunct One of the pair of propositions in a *disjunction.

disjunction The statement that at least one of two propositions is true: it thus corresponds to '*p* or *q*'. Inclusive disjunction allows that both may be true; exclusive disjunction that one but not both is true. In the *propositional calculus disjunction is treated as a *truth function.

disjunction elimination The rule permitting one to infer: 'either A or B; if A then C, if B then C' to C.

disjunction introduction The rule permitting one to infer 'A so either A or B' (or equally, 'B, so either A or B').

disposition A thing has a disposition to become F in a situation G if it is such that were G to come about, it would become F. Dispositions, potentials, or powers are thus certified by the outcomes that would arise in specified circumstances. Dispositional properties are frequently contrasted with categorical ones, thought of as underlying them, and permanently present, whereas dispositions are only realized or manifested in the circumstances specified. Thus a chemical substance is soluble in water if it is such that, were it placed in water, it would dissolve, and the categorical basis of this disposition will be the nature and configuration of its molecules. This way of thinking accords better with a *corpuscularian or *atomistic philosophy than with modern physical thinking, which finds no categorical basis underlying the notions like that of a charge, or a *field, or a probability wave, that fundamentally characterize things, and which are apparently themselves dispositional. The distinction between dispositional and categorical properties is also threatened by the reflection that even solidity and shape, perhaps the best candidates for categorical properties, seem susceptible to a dispositional treatment: solidity in a body is its disposition to exclude other bodies from the region of space that makes its shape. *See also* COUNTERFACTUAL CONDITIONAL, FINKISH.

disquotational theory of truth The simplest formulation is the claim that expressions of the form 'S is true' mean the same as expressions of the form S. Some philosophers dislike the idea of sameness of meaning, and if this is disallowed, then the claim is that the two forms are equivalent in any sense of equivalence that matters. That is, it makes no difference whether people say 'Dogs bark' is true, or whether they say, dogs bark. In the former representation of what they say the sentence 'Dogs bark' is mentioned, but in the latter it appears to be used, so the claim that the two are equivalent needs careful formulation and defence. On the face of it someone might know that 'Dogs bark' is true without knowing what it means (for instance, if he finds it in a list of acknowledged truths, although he does not understand English), and this is different from knowing that dogs bark. Disquotational theories are usually presented as versions of the *redundancy theory of truth.

distributed *See* DISTRIBUTION OF TERMS, SYLLOGISM.

distribution (probability) *See* RANDOM VARIABLE.

distribution of terms In the classical theory of the *syllogism, a term in a categorical prop-osition is distributed if the proposition *entails any proposition obtained from it by substituting a term which denotes only a subset of the items denoted by the original. For example, in 'all dogs bark' the term 'dogs' is distributed, since it entails 'all terriers bark', which is obtained from it by such a substitution. In 'not all dogs bark' the same term is not distributed, since it may be true while 'not all terriers bark' is false.

distributive justice *See* JUSTICE, DISTRIBUTIVE.

distributive laws *See* DE MORGAN'S LAWS.

disvalue The opposite of value: the amount of harm or demerit attaching to some outcome or action or character trait.

divided line *See* LINE, IMAGE OF THE.

divine attributes In the monotheistic traditions God is usually presented as being all-good, all-knowing, and all-powerful, the creator of the universe, but also eternal or timeless. If God is to be found by some of the classical arguments, then he must also possess necessary existence, or *perseity. *See also* RELIGION, PHILOSOPHY OF.

divine command Theories of ethics that ground the nature of ethical demands in the fact that they represent the commands of God. The classic philosophical problem in front of such an account, apart from the fragile access we have to any such commands, is the *Euthyphro dilemma. The social problem generated by the account is that in periods of declining religious belief, people become unable to attach importance to moral concerns either: 'If God is dead, everything is permitted.'

divine foreknowledge *See* FOREKNOWLEDGE.

division, fallacy of *See* COMPOSITION/DIVISION.

doctor Doctors of the medieval Church were theologians of outstanding merit and saintliness. The original four were Gregory the Great, *Ambrose, *Augustine, and Jerome. In *scholastic times outstanding teachers were also given doctoral epithets. *Aquinas is the angelic doctor, *Bonaventura the seraphic doctor, Roger *Bacon the marvellous doctor, *Duns Scotus the subtle doctor, *Albert the Great the universal doctor, *Bernard the mellifluous doctor.

Dodgson, Charles Lutwidge (1832–98) English mathematician, logician, and humorous writer, better known as Lewis Carroll. Educated at Christ Church, Oxford, Carroll spent his entire career there as a mathematician. He wrote upon the theory of voting and various mathematical and logical issues, as well as filling *Alice in Wonderland* (1865), *Alice through the Looking Glass* (1871), and *The Hunting of the Snark* (1876) with play upon logical, philosophical, and semantic themes. Humpty Dumpty exhibits a form of the *Euthyphro dilemma in his views on his authority over his words; the White Knight delves deep into the problem of names; the White King takes *nobody to be a person; the Snark is a *topic-neutral object of a quest (sometimes identified with the *Absolute); and throughout the humour depends upon pushing logical and philosophical reasoning to absurdity. Carroll's paper 'What the Tortoise said to Achilles' (*Mind*, 1895) presents the classic statement of the need for *rules of inference as well as *axioms in formal systems.

SEE WEB LINKS

- A biography of Dodgson, including his contributions to mathematics and logic
- A list of internet resources on Dodgson

Dōgen Kigen (1200–53) The founder of the Japanese Sōtō school of *Zen Buddhism. Dōgen was a poet as well as a philosopher, and has been interpreted as a *panpsychist. He understands all things as already in a state of enlightenment, and developed sophisticated views of time and consciousness.

dogma In general, a belief held unquestioningly and with undefended certainty. In the Christian Church, a belief communicated by divine revelation, and defined by the Church. Dogmatism is one possible reaction to *scepticism: it selects some set of propositions and insists, apparently arbitrarily, that they be not doubted.

domain The domain of a *quantifier is the set of things that serve as possible values for its *variable. The domain of a *relation is the set of things that bear the relation to something else.

dominance In *decision theory, one choice dominates another if it is at least as good under all outcomes and better under some. This is commonly put by saying that it can win and cannot lose. *Pascal's wager may be viewed as an attempt to show that setting about believing in God is a dominant strategy when the decision problem is how to conduct your religious life. *See also* NEWCOMB'S PARADOX, PRISONERS' DILEMMA.

doomsday argument Suppose the human race is to exist a long time. Then you would be one of the first people. But it is very improbable that an arbitrary person is among the set occupying the very first segment of any population. It is more probable that one is not in such a segment, so it is more probable that the human race is not to exist a long time. The argument is not generally accepted.

Dostoevsky, Fyodor (1821–81) The great Russian novelist is 'philosophical' in the sense that his writings explore deep themes of psychology, politics, and religion. They are often cited as '*existentialist' in their general tendency, and are also important to literary theorists and critics interested in the polymorphous and diverse forms which literary production can take. *See* BAKHTIN.

double aspect theory The view that instead of thinking of mind and body as things, whose relations with each other are then problematic, we should recognize that the one subject, a person, may be described equally in mental or physical terms, which then denote different aspects of the same entity. An attractive alternative to Cartesian *dualism, it nevertheless faces the difficulty of avoiding an equally daunting dualism of properties, with similar problems about how these different properties interact.

double effect, principle of A principle attempting to define when an action that has both good and bad results is morally permissible. In one formulation such an action is permissible if (i) the action is not wrong in itself, (ii) the bad consequence is not that which is intended, (iii) the good is not itself a result of the bad consequence, and (iv) the two consequences are commensurate. Thus, for instance, I might justifiably bomb an enemy factory, foreseeing but not intending the death of nearby civilians, whereas bombing the civilians intentionally would be disallowed. The principle has its roots in Thomist moral philosophy (*see* AQUINAS). Its applications include the problem of removing (thereby killing) a life-threatening foetus. All the clauses of the definition are highly controversial, but the second especially gives rise to deep problems about the relation between action, consequence, and intention.

double-mindedness Term used by *Kierkegaard to signify the doing of the right thing for the wrong reason: out of fear of punishment, hope of reward, pride, or other motivations.

double negation The result of negating the negation of a proposition. In classical *propositional calculus, $\neg\neg p$ is equivalent to p. In *intuitionistic logic this is not so; we cannot infer p from $\neg\neg p$.

double truth The notion, formally condemned several times in the 13th century, that something may be false philosophically yet true theologically. The doctrine would have been an attempt to reconcile Aristotelian metaphysics with revealed religion, but it is not clear that any major figure adopted it. *Averroës, whose followers were charged with the view, held that there was but one truth, although many modes of access to it.

doubt The state of neither believing nor disbelieving a proposition; a suspension of judgement. Classically *scepticism has advocated that we doubt either everything, or as much as possible, or in more local forms, propositions of some particular kind.

doubt, Cartesian *See* METHOD OF DOUBT.

doxa (Greek, belief) Opinion, frequently contrasted with real knowledge in classical philosophy.

doxastic logic The logic of belief.

doxography The practice of recording the opinions of other philosophers, practised by classical philosophers and historians. The term is due to the work by the classicist Hermann Diels, *Doxographi Graeci* (1879).

dravya (Sanskrit, substance) Different Indian schools differ over the numbers and kinds of substance, with *Buddhism denying that there are any substances, so that only momentary states or events exist in their own right.

dread *See* ALIENATION, ANGST.

dreams Dreams are not merely the succession of visual images, but rather experiences of living in a world of events, actions, and emotions. The widespread belief in the significance of dreams, either as prophecies or divine messages, or as especially valuable indicators of psychological truths, as in the work of *Freud and *Jung, has little empirical support. Although actual dreams have a nature and a content that is parasitic upon normal experience, since the things in our dreams are persons and objects of a kind with which we are generally familiar, philosophically dreams have been a convenient image of the possibility of total dissociation between what a subject experiences, and how things are in the real world. Hence they form a central metaphor in epistemology; one of the first questions in philosophy is sometimes posed as 'How do I know I am not now or always dreaming?' (*See* METHOD OF DOUBT.) Dreams also provide a test case for philosophers trying to deny the reality of private experience knowable only to the subject.

dualism Any view that postulates two kinds of thing in some domain is dualistic; contrasting views according to which there is only one kind of thing are *monistic. The most famous example of the contrast is mind–body dualism, contrasted with monism in the form either of idealism (only mind) or more often physicalism (only body or matter). Cartesian dualism is the cluster of views about mind and body associated with *Descartes. Other dualisms include those of form and content, of concepts and intuitions, freedom and causation, being and becoming, reason and passion. In every case there are philosophers who insist that the way forward is to transcend these dualisms.

DuBois, William Edward Burghardt (1868–1963) American black activist and social philosopher. Born in Maryland, Dubois was educated at Fisk University, Tennessee, and Harvard. He taught at Wilberforce College, the University of Pennsylvania, and then at Atlanta College from 1897 to 1910, when he became director of research for the National Association for the Advancement of Colored People and editor of their journal *Crisis*. DuBois argued that African Americans should conserve their cultural differences, while insisting on equal opportunities for development. If successful, coloured people could overcome results of racial prejudice such as the 'double consciousness' that prevented them from achieving true self-realization. He gradually lost faith in moral suasion, becoming a communist in 1961, and died in Ghana. His books include *The Philadelphia Negro: A Social Study* (1899), *Soul of Black Folk* (1903), and *Color and Democracy* (1945).

Ducasse, Curt John (1881–1969) French-born American philosopher, and teacher at Brown (1926–58) where his students included Roderick *Chisholm. Ducasse is best-known for attacking *Hume on *causation, and for his *adverbial theory of perception, subsequently developed by Chisholm, but also for wide-ranging and systematic philosophical views within the analytical tradition. His books included *Philosophy as a Science* (1941), the more popular and polemical *Art, The Critics, and You* (1944), and *Nature, Mind and Death* (1951).

du Châtelet-Lomont, Gabrielle-Émilie (1706–49) French astronomer, mathematician, and long-time mistress of *Voltaire. She tried to combine Leibnizian metaphysics with Newton's empirically based science in her *Institutions de physique* (1740), but was best-known as a proponent of Newton's system against the Cartesian physics then prevailing in France, and for translating Newton's *Principia* into French (1756).

duck-rabbit The visually ambiguous figure originally used by the psychologist J. Jastrow, and published in his book *Fact and Fable in Psychology* (1900).

The figure is discussed by *Wittgenstein in *Philosophical Investigations*, Pt. II, sec. xi.

d

Duhem, Pierre Maurice Marie (1861–1916) The French physicist is remembered philosophically for his *La Théorie physique: son objet, sa structure* (1906, trs. as *The Aim and Structure of Physical Theory*, 1954). Duhem's conception of science is that it is simply a device for calculating: science provides a deductive system that is systematic, economical, and predictive, but not one that represents the deep underlying nature of reality (Duhem, a conservative and Catholic, thought that such representation was only achieved by rational thought). Duhem is further remembered for stressing the *holistic character of verification and falsification in science. *See also* DUHEM THESIS.

Duhem thesis Sometimes called the Quine-Duhem or Duhem–Quine thesis. The thesis that a single scientific hypothesis cannot be tested in isolation, since other, auxiliary hypotheses will always be needed to draw empirical consequences from it. The Duhem thesis implies that refutation is a more complex matter than might appear. It is sometimes framed as the view that a single hypothesis may be retained in the face of any adverse empirical evidence, if we are prepared to make modifications elsewhere in our system; although strictly speaking this is a stronger thesis, since it may be psychologically impossible to make consistent revisions in a belief system to accommodate, say, the hypothesis that there is a hippopotamus in the room when visibly there is none.

Dühring, Eugen Karl (1833–71) Originally trained as a lawyer, Dühring taught philosophy and economics in Berlin. He combined a materialism derived from *Feuerbach with a scattered variety of utopian and metaphysical reviews. He is remembered chiefly as the named target of *Engels's tract *Anti-Dühring* of 1878.

Dummett, Michael Anthony Eardley (1925–) British philosopher of logic and language. Born in London and educated at Oxford, Dummett was a Fellow of All Souls, and from 1979 to 1992 held the chair of logic at Oxford. Dummett has been one of the most influential British philosophers of the second half of the 20th century. His work centres upon the philosophy of language and the philosophy of mathematics, and shows a marked sympathy with *verificationist and *constructivist ideals. Almost single-handedly he kept the flame of mathematical *intuitionism alive as philosophically interesting, while his massive works in the philosophy of language inspired continuing interest in the relationship between evidence, or assertibility, on the one hand, and truth on the other (*see also* REALISM/ANTI-REALISM).

Dummett is also known for an uncompromising re-evaluation of the western tradition, viewing writings before the rise of *analytic philosophy as fatally flawed by having taken *epistemology to be fundamental, whereas the correct approach, giving a foundational place to a concern with language, only took wing with the work of *Frege. Critics have queried whether Frege's thought was thus born 'unfertilized by external inferences', and have objected there is more than a passing concern with meaning in *Plato, *Aristotle, the *Nyaya school of Indian philosophy, and many others. Equally, the supposedly pure investigation of language in the 20th century often kept some dubious epistemological and metaphysical company.

Dummett's works include *Frege: Philosophy of Language* (1973), and the collections of essays *Truth and Other Enigmas* (1978) and *The Seas of Language* (1994). Rather different interests are met in *The Game of Tarot* (1980), an exploration of the game designed to discredit what Dummett regards as the irrational theories and pseudo-history of occultists, and *Style and Grammar*, an explanation of the correct way to write lucidly (1993).

Duns Scotus, John (*c*.1266–1308) Franciscan philosopher and theologian. It is known that John Duns, the Scot, was ordained in 1291, but his earlier life is largely uncertain. He lectured in Cambridge and Oxford, then Paris, where he became regent master of theology, and he died in Cologne. His early death interrupted the production of his commentary on the *Sentences* of Peter *Lombard. Scotus was primarily a metaphysician concerned with the nature and reality of God, with such transcendental categories as being, existence, the one, the true, and the good, and with the relations between such notions as causation, matter and form, dependency, and finitude. Amongst his preoccupations was that of the principle of individuation or distinctness, separating one horse from other horses, or me from other men. Scotus supplements the traditional Aristotelian kinds with a **haecceitas* or 'thisness': a uniquely individuating concept under which only one object falls. Scotus was a realist about *universals, and his emphasis on the unique individual and its importance in metaphysics and knowledge is reflected in ethics in the primacy he accords to individual freedom, again in reaction to a *fatalistic view of the problem of God's omnipotence and foreknowledge. Like *Anselm, Scotus locates freedom in our ability to turn from desire and towards justice. Scotus has been admired by such different thinkers as *Peirce and *Heidegger; he was dubbed the *doctor subtilis*, but as applied to his followers the word 'dunce' (short for Dunsman) reflects the low esteem into which *scholasticism later fell amongst humanists and reformers.

duration *See* TIME.

Durkheim, Émile (1858–1917) French sociologist. Durkheim was educated in philosophy at the École Normale Supérieure in Paris, and gained his first university post at Bordeaux in 1887. He held a chair at the Sorbonne from 1902 until his death. Although his writings concern sociology and its practice rather than philosophy, they are philosophically important through their resolute hostility to methodological *individualism. Durkheim mounted a sustained campaign for a distinct, proper, self-contained level of analysis in which social facts are conceived as having their own power and their own identity, and therefore make proper objects of study in their own right: 'social facts are to be explained by other social facts.' Any association of individuals creates its own level of fact, irreducible to a mere aggregate of individual psychological facts. His most famous work, *Le Suicide* (1897, trs. as *Suicide*, 1952), shows that this apparently personal and psychologically subjective act is in fact sociologically determined and a reflection of social pressures and currents. Durkheim also believed that awareness of this would create the scientific basis for proper social intervention and improvement. His work on the prohibition of incest and on totemism is sometimes hailed as an ancestor of *structuralism, although his assumption that some forms of human life are primitive or 'elementary' compared with our own has occasioned substantial criticism. In his later years he studied religion as the most characteristic manifestation of social life; this work culminated in *Les Formes élémentaires de la vie religieuse* (1912, trs. as *The Elementary Forms of Religious Life*, 1915).

SEE WEB LINKS

- A list of internet resources on Durkheim
- Translations of Durkheim's writings

Dutch book A set of beliefs held with various degrees of confidence is open to a Dutch book if, were a subject forced to bet in accordance with these degrees of confidence, he could be made to lose whatever happens. For example, if I am confident that *p* but also confident that not-*p*, then in acting out that confidence I should accept a small stake from you in return for a large payout if not-*p*, thereby acting out my confidence that *p*, and similarly accept a small stake in return for a large payout if *p*, acting out my confidence that not-*p*. I then lose whatever happens. A semi-Dutch book is sometimes defined as a combination of bets where the subject may lose, but cannot win. For *personalists following *de Finetti and *Ramsey, avoiding a Dutch book is the key conception of coherence, on which the logic and mathematics of probability judgements depends. A problem in developing the approach has been that of extending the notion of coherence to dynamic situations, in which an adjustment to previous confidences must be made in the light of new evidence. *See* CONDITIONAL PROBABILITY.

duty That which one must do, or that which can be required of one. The term carries implications of that which is owed (due) to other people, or perhaps to oneself. Universal duties would be owed to persons (or sentient beings) as such, whereas special duties arise in virtue of specific relations, such as being the child of someone, or having made someone a promise. Duty or obligation is the primary concept of *deontological approaches to ethics, but is constructed in other systems out of other notions. In the system of *Kant a perfect duty is one that must be performed whatever the circumstances; imperfect duties may have to give way to the more stringent ones. In another usage, perfect duties are those that are correlative with the rights of others; imperfect duties are not. Problems with the concept include the ways in which duties need to be specified (a frequent criticism of Kant is that his notion of duty is too abstract). The concept may also suggest a regimented view of ethical life, in which we are all forced conscripts in a kind of moral army, and may encourage an individualistic and antagonistic view of social relations.

Dworkin, Ronald (1931–) American philosopher of law. Born in Worcester, Massachusetts, Dworkin was educated at Harvard and Oxford. He was Professor of Jurisprudence at Oxford (1969–98), at New York university since 1975, and Quain Professor of Jurisprudence at University College, London (1998–). He is known for his defence of 'legal realism', here meaning the integral place that moral and pragmatic considerations play in legal decision-making, in opposition to what he sees as their exclusion by legal positivism and by the work of his predecessor at Oxford, H. L. A. *Hart (*see* LAW, PHILOSOPHY OF). Although he is described as a realist about legal truth, Dworkin's system may also be described as constructivist, since it approaches the nature of legal truth through the method of an ideal or perhaps romanticized judge 'Hercules'. This fictional character is sensitive to both morality and settled law, and above all to the theory that best explains settled law, and it is his procedures that give us our conception of legal method and legal truth. A liberal and a Democrat, Dworkin bases constitutional rights on a fundamental right of all people to equal concern and respect; applications of this include defences of reverse discrimination (this may be tough on those who are denied schools or jobs because of such policies, but the 'right to be treated as an equal' need not imply a right to equal treatment). On the other hand, Dworkin defends other freedoms, such as the right to produce and consume *pornography, against the objection that its existence displays lack of equal concern and respect for women. His books include *Taking Rights Seriously* (1977), *A Matter of Principle* (1985), *Law's Empire* (1986), and *Life's Dominion: An Argument about Abortion, Euthanasia, and Individual Freedom* (1993).

d

dyadic A dyadic *relation is a two-place relation.

dynamic logic A logic for analysing actual processes of computation. It includes a representation of the idea that after *every* terminating computation according to some program something is true, and after *some* terminating computation according to a program something is true. These give operations analogous to the necessity and possibility operators of *modal logic.

dynamis/energeia The former refers to the powers inherent in things. In *Aristotle it becomes a potential in contrast to *energeia* which is the actualization of the potential.

dyslogistic *See* EULOGISTIC/DYSLOGISTIC.

dystopia A negative *utopia: a place where instead of all being well, all is not well. Aldous Huxley's *Brave New World* and George Orwell's *1984* are the best-known fictional examples.

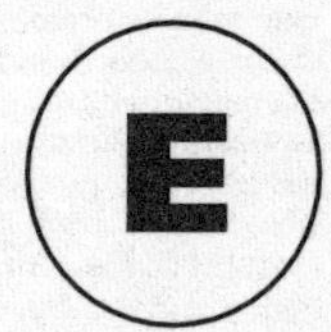

Eckhart, Johannes von Hochheim (Meister Eckhart) (*c.*1260–1328) German Christian mystic. A member of the Dominican order, theologian and professor of the university of Paris, Eckhart wrote highly influential sermons and meditations in vernacular German. His message is strikingly *pantheistic in tone, talking of passing beyond God to a 'simple ground', or 'still desert' without any distinctions, out of which all things were created. He stressed the *scintilla animae* or spark of the soul which enables us to know God. It was all too much for the 14th century, and the year after Eckhart's death twenty-eight of his theses were condemned by Pope John XXII, seventeen being heretical, and eleven being merely ill-sounding, rash, and suspected of heresy. There are moves to have him reinstated.

eclecticism (Greek, *eklegein*, to choose) An eclectic position in philosophy or religion is one that seeks to combine the best elements of other views.

Eco, Umberto (1932–) The well-known Italian author is a prolific and learned writer on the theory of interpretation. He earned his doctorate in 1954 for a thesis on Thomas Aquinas, and the medieval world remains a favourite subject, but alongside a career as a journalist Eco developed an academic niche in the study of signs or semiotics, becoming professor at Bologna in 1971. While sensitive to the position which much postmodern theory accords to the reader, Eco has typically drawn back from an 'anything goes' approach. He has attacked *deconstructionism and its happy adoption by writers such as Richard *Rorty, in favour of a more 'contractarian' relationship between author and reader. *Foucault's Pendulum* (1989) is a long allegory of the dangers of unbridled tendencies to multiply meanings. More academic works include *The Limits of Interpretation* (1990) and *Kant and the Platypus* (1997), while historically orientated works include *The Search for the Perfect Language* (1993). *See also* READER RESPONSE THEORY.

ecofeminism A movement in which humanity's unfortunate domination over nature is seen as analogous to men's equally unfortunate domination over women—an alliance that adds resonance both to ecological and feminist concerns.

ecology The science which investigates interacting systems of biological organisms.

economic man *See* HOMO ECONOMICUS.

economics, philosophy of The basic questions of economics blend with those of political philosophy and ethics. Perhaps the most fundamental concern is whether we can compare and measure different levels of well-being in economic terms, given that the sources of value are diverse, and only partially concerned with economic activity. Other problems include the difficulties of achieving a *social welfare function, and of understanding the conception of the free economic agent who exercises choices in the market. *See also* LABOUR THEORY OF VALUE, MARX, PROTESTANT WORK ETHIC, SMITH.

economism *See* BASE AND SUPERSTRUCTURE.

ecstasy (Greek, standing outside) A state in which normal sense experience is suspended and the subject becomes joyfully conscious of higher things, although what the subject is aware of is then not typically communicable.

ectype *See* ARCHETYPE.

education, philosophy of The enquiry into the ideas that dominate educational theory and policy. The central questions are what it is worthwhile or necessary to teach, and what are the best ways of doing it. Different views about human nature will influence answers to both questions. Rival metaphors include that of the young mind as an empty pot that needs filling up, versus the mind as an unexercised athlete that needs practice. The focus has often been Plato's question whether virtue can be taught, and this quickly spreads to include intellectual virtue. Plato's paradox from the Meno that you cannot understand what you do not know and therefore cannot set about discovering it is usually felt to be soluble (*see* LEARNING PARADOX), but in practice education remains bedevilled by the fact that people missing it do not know what they are missing.

The solution from the right is coercion and discipline; that from the left is to worry whether education involves *discrimination, or indeed trespasses against the equal rights and dignity of the ignorant and stupid. Eminent philosophers who have written at length about education include Plato and Aristotle, Locke, Rousseau and Mill, and in the 20th century, Dewey.

Edwards, Jonathan (1703–58) American philosopher and theologian. Born in Connecticut, Edwards was educated at Yale, and showed an early passion for philosophy and theology. His uncompromising *Calvinism survived exposure to the works of *Locke, and in metaphysics led to an idealism quite similar to that of *Berkeley, with the ordinary world no more than the set of impressions afforded to us by God. In ethical matters Edwards retained the view that any virtue people acquire is through the free gift of God, and that no unaided effort can improve the fallen condition of humanity. Edwards played a major role in the 'Great Awakening' or New England born-again movement of the mid-18th century. The sovereignty of God, the depravity of humankind, and the reality of hell are all on display in his most famous sermon, 'Sinners in the Hands of an Angry God' (1741).

effect *See* CAUSATION, LAW OF EFFECT.

effective procedure A procedure that results in a solution to a problem in a finite number of steps. Another term for an *algorithm.

efficient cause *See* CAUSES: MATERIAL, FORMAL, EFFICIENT, FINAL.

effluxes, theory of The *Presocratic theory that perception is a matter of physical objects emitting some pattern of themselves, that, meeting a corresponding efflux from the body, brings about perception. *Epicurus later holds that effluxes enter into 'pores' in the body. *See* *EIDOLA*.

egalitarianism The doctrine that moral and political life should be aimed at respecting and advancing the *equality of persons.

ego The thinking, active self; the self conceived of as the organizing and continuing subject of experience and the author of action. In *Kant there is a distinction between the empirical ego, given in ordinary self-consciousness, and the transcendental or pure ego, which cannot be known but must be presupposed for our experience to have the unity that it needs in order to be experience at all. In *Freudian psychology the ego is the conscious self, occupying a beleaguered middle ground between the disreputable demands of the id, and the repressive discipline of the superego. *See also* CARTESIAN EGO, PERSONAL IDENTITY.

egocentric particular Term for a *token-reflexive, or what is more commonly called an *indexical, expression.

egocentric predicament The problem originally described in an article of the same name (*Journal of Philosophy*, 1910) by the American philosopher R. B. Perry (1876–1957). The predicament is the fact that we are each limited or confined to our own perceptual world. This may seem either highly significant and tragic, or tautologous.

egoism Egoism is usually considered in two forms. Psychological egoism is the view that people are always motivated by self-interest. Ethical egoism is the view that whether or not people are like this, they ought to be like this; usually this is advanced in the form that rational behaviour requires attempting to maximize self-interest. Psychological egoism is usually thought to depend upon confusions, such as reasoning from 'all my actions need a motive which is mine' (true) to 'a state of myself is the object of all my motives' (false, or at any rate not proven). Critics such as Joseph *Butler also emphasize that without other objects of desire a life spent absorbed in one's own pleasure cannot well get off the ground (*see* HEDONISM, PARADOX OF). We need something independent to spark the pleasure. Ethical egoism is often argued to be self-defeating, in that a society of egoists do worse for themselves than a society of altruists (*see* PRISONERS' DILEMMA). Another fundamental objection is that it is inconsistent with the nature of trust and friendship that each party should be motivated solely by self-interest. Yet the ethical egoist gives no reason why these goods should be given up in favour of an egoistic conception of rational behaviour. *See also* ALTRUISM, FRIENDSHIP.

eidetic images (Greek, *eidos*, form, appearance) Usually imagery is a weak source of knowledge. Visual images are vague, and cannot be scrutinized (or rotated or interrogated) like real pictures. However, some persons, mainly children, have the ability to form what seem to be more vivid, stable, and informative images, often producing powers of total recall after brief exposure to a scene. These are known as eidetic images.

eidetiker Person with the power of forming *eidetic images.

eidola In the theory of *effluxes, the intermediaries that flow out of objects as the first part of the process resulting in perception.

eidos (Greek, form) Term used by Plato for the abstract *forms or ideas.

eightfold path According to the last of the *four noble truths of Buddhism, the eightfold path is the key to release from suffering. Its elements are (i) the right or perfect view of the four noble truths, and of the nature of the self (**atman*); (ii) perfect resolution in favour of renunciation and **ahimsa*; (iii) perfect speech, i.e. avoidance of lying and slander; (iv) perfect conduct; (v) perfect livelihood, i.e. avoidance of harmful professions; (vi) perfect effort; (vii) perfect mindfulness or control of thought; and (viii) perfect concentration, or attainment of the contemplative ideal. The eightfold path is not a linear progression, but a separation of the different elements needed to live a life released from suffering.

eikasia The lowest stage of knowing according to *Plato's image of the *line. Also the state of the prisoners in Plato's *myth of the cave: benighted and unenlightened they see only shadows of copies of things.

Einfühlung (German, empathy) In *Husserl, a primary mode of awareness of the experience of other people.

Einstein, Albert (1879–1955) German physicist and discoverer of the theory of *relativity. Born in Ulm, Einstein received his scientific education in Zurich. After an undistinguished career as a student he found employment in the Patent Office in Bern, and it was from here that in 1905 he published the papers that laid the foundation of his reputation, on the photoelectric effect, on Brownian motion, and on the special theory of relativity. In 1916 he published the general theory. In 1933 Einstein accepted the position at the Princeton Institute for Advanced Studies which he occupied for the rest of his life. Einstein maintained profound philosophical interests, and frequently emphasized the importance to his work of the philosophical thought of his predecessors, especially *Hume and *Mach. In his later years his reflections on the nature of the world as it is described by *quantum mechanics occasioned prolonged discussion with the Danish physicist Niels *Bohr. Einstein's conviction that quantum mechanics could not possibly be the last word about the nature of physical reality was frequently felt to be conservative, but the project that occupied him, the search for a field theory that would unify the four fundamental physical forces, has recently sprung back into prominence. Einstein's belief that fundamental physics should concern the 'marble' of space, time, and geometry, rather than the 'wood' of arbitrary proliferations of particles, is again congenial to many physicists.

SEE WEB LINKS

- An online exhibit on Einstein, with links to other resources
- An archive of Einstein's writings

Einstein–Podolsky–Rosen thought experiment Thought experiment introduced in 1935 by these three authors in their *Physical Review* paper 'Can Quantum-Mechanical Description of Physical Reality be Considered Complete?' Suppose two quantum systems 1 and 2 that briefly interact, and are then separated and in no kind of physical contact. Then a measurement on system 1 for property P will yield some definite value, p_1, for 1. Corresponding to this can be calculated a value of P, p_2, for system 2. Similarly if we measured a property Q yielding a value q_1 for 1, we can calculate the value q_2 for 2. So definite magnitudes can be assigned to properties of 2 from measurements that do not affect 2. But if we now consider conjugate pairs (*see* HEISENBERG UNCERTAINTY PRINCIPLE), such as the position and momentum of a particle, this makes the existence of states of 2 depend upon which processes of measurement we choose to carry out on 1, although there is no signal betwen them. Attributing an antecedent determinate nature to 2 that can be revealed by a measurement on 1 contradicts the Heisenberg uncertainty principle, if that is taken to apply to reality itself, rather than to mere indeterminacies of measurement. The contentious conclusion of the paper was that the quantum mechanical description of physical reality is not complete. *See also* BELL'S THEOREM.

élan vital The life force. The term is used by *Bergson to denote a mysterious force, unknown to natural science, that drives life; as such it has been generally discredited, due to the successes of the life sciences. *See* VITALISM.

Eleatics Philosophical school agreed to have started with *Parmenides of Elea in the 6th century BC. Its other members were *Zeno, whose defence of the Parmenidean doctrine of the one indivisible and unchanging reality is the best-remembered work of the school (Zeno himself may have rejected both unity and plurality), and *Melissus.

Eleatic stranger (Eleatic visitor) The figure in Plato's dialogues the *Sophist* and *Statesman* who represents the problems that *Parmenides and the *Eleatics had with non-being, and the possibility of saying what is false.

elective affinity Term used by *Weber to describe the match between aspects of Protestantism, and those of the ethos of capitalism. The one provides the soil in which the other can flourish, although nobody need be consciously aware of the relationship.

elenchus (Greek, cross-examination) The dialectical or *Socratic method of eliciting truth by cross-examination; hence sometimes the elenctic method. *See also* IGNORATIO ELENCHI.

eliminative induction In eliminative induction a number of possible hypotheses concerning some state of affairs is presumed, and rivals are progressively eliminated by new evidence. The process is an idealization, since in practice no closed set of initial theories is usually possible. *See* LIMITED INDEPENDENT VARIETY, PRINCIPLE OF; MILL'S METHODS.

e

eliminativism The view that the terms in which we think of some area are sufficiently infected with error for it to be better to abandon them than to continue to try to give coherent theories of their use. Eliminativism should be distinguished from scepticism, which claims that we cannot know the truth about some area; eliminativism claims rather that there is no truth there to be known, in the terms with which we currently think. An eliminativist about theology simply counsels abandoning the terms or discourse of theology, and that will include abandoning worries about the extent of theological knowledge. Eliminativists in the philosophy of mind counsel abandoning the whole network of terms mind, *consciousness, *self, *qualia, that usher in the problems of mind and body. Sometimes the argument for doing this is that we should wait for a supposed future understanding of ourselves, based on *cognitive science and better than any our current mental descriptions provide; sometimes it is supposed that *physicalism shows that no mental descriptions of ourselves could possibly be true.

Elis City of the Peloponnese of Greece, deserving immortal fame because, in honour of its native son *Pyrrho, it passed a law exempting all philosophers from taxation.

elitism The view that the formation of elites in some sphere is desirable, and that the status and privileges of existing elites are worth protecting. *Plato is the most famous advocate of the view that government is the job of those who are superior in wisdom, but since people are unlikely to recognize those wiser than themselves, this is not the usual result of *democracy.

Elizabeth of Bohemia (1618–80) The daughter of Frederick, the Elector Palatine and King of Bohemia, and Elizabeth Stuart, the daughter of James I of England. Elizabeth is known in philosophy through her extensive correspondence with *Descartes. After an early conversion to Catholicism she refused the throne of Bohemia, and her philosophical interests led her to avoid marriage; in 1667 she retired to the Protestant convent of Herford in Westphalia, where she eventually became abbess, running a tolerant and liberal regime. Her questions to Descartes reveal an acute philosophical intelligence, particularly in probing the inadequacy of the Cartesian explanation of how immaterial substance (the mind) can generate motion in material substance (the body), and in questioning elements of Descartes's ethics.

ellipsis An expression in which material essential to the meaning is omitted, but where the intended sense can be deduced or guessed from the context. An elliptical argument is called an *enthymeme.

Elster, Jon (1940–) Norwegian social and political philosopher, currently Robert K. Merton professor of social sciences at Columbia University. Elster has ranged widely over political philosophy, rational choice theory, and game theory, with a particular concern for the complexities of human decision-making. His many publications include *Ulysses and the Sirens* (1979), *Sour Grapes* (1983), *Making Sense of Marx* (1985), *The Cement of Society* (1989), *Solomonic Judgements* (1989), *Nuts and Bolts for the Social Sciences* (1989), *Local Justice* (1992), and *Ulysses Unbound* (2000).

emanationism The attempt made by *Plotinus, and foreshadowed in *Plato, to understand creation as an overflow, radiating out from the supreme principle or God, somewhat as light emanates from a light source without in any way diminishing it. In *Neoplatonism the doctrine is associated with *pantheism.

embodiment A key concept for some schools of *phenomenology, and in particular for *Merleau-Ponty. The subjective experience of one's own body is different from the objective or scientific picture of a body in physiological terms. The specific ways we experience ourselves as embodied thus become prime data for theorizing about knowledge and experience.

emergent properties *See* SUPERVENIENCE.

Emerson, Ralph Waldo (1803–82) The son of a Unitarian clergyman, Emerson was born in Boston, and educated at Harvard. Although he studied philosophy extensively, he was not a critical or systematic thinker, but rather a channel for many religious, literary, and philosophical currents of the early 19th century. Meetings with *Coleridge and Wordsworth in 1833, and a continuing friendship with *Carlyle, enthused Emerson with a fusion of the Protestant doctrine of self-reliance with the romantic doctrine of the primacy of personality, to both of which were added reverence for the genius and hero. To these in turn were added elements of *absolute idealism, whereby the final flowering of spirit would reveal the unity of mind and nature, but Emerson also showed a *pragmatist streak, emphasizing the practical effects of ideas and principles. This heady cocktail, allied with his sage's contempt for contemporary civilization, gave Emerson a huge following, addressed in a vast number of essays and lectures and through his journal *The Dial*, the organ of *New England transcendentalism.

eminently *See* FORMALLY AND EMINENTLY.

emotion The typical human emotions include love, grief, fear, anger, joy. Each indicates a state of some kind of arousal, a state that can prompt some activities and interfere with others. These states are associated with characteristic feelings, and they have characteristic bodily expressions. Unlike moods they have objects: one grieves over some particular thing, or is angry at something. Different philosophical theories have tended to highlight one or other of these aspects of emotion. Pure arousal theory imagines a visceral reaction triggered by some event, which stands ready to be converted into one emotion or another by contextual factors. Theories based on the feel or *qualia of an emotion were put forward by writers such as *Hume and *Kant, but the approach meets difficulty when we consider that an emotion is not a raw feel, but is identified by its motivational powers, and their function in prompting action. The characteristic expression of emotion was studied extensively by *Darwin, resulting in the classic *The Expression of the Emotions in Man and Animals* (1872). In 1884 *James published what became known as the *James–Lange theory of emotion whose main contention is that we feel as we do in virtue of the bodily expressions and behaviour that we are prompted towards, rather than the other way round: 'our feeling of the changes as they occur *is* the emotion'. Again it is not clear how such a theory would accommodate the directed, cognitive side of emotions that have a specific object, rather than being simply the experience of bodily change. Directly opposing this some philosophers have put forward a purely cognitive theory of the emotions, derived from *Stoicism, seeing them simply as judgements: fear of the dog is no more than the judgement that it is dangerous or a threat to one's well-being. The Stoics thought that as judgements the emotions were typically false, but modern cognitive theories tend to be more generous to them, often influenced by the idea that our capacity for emotions is often an admirable moral adaptation. Other questions concern the cultural variability of emotion, and the dependence of some emotions, but not all, on the existence of linguistically adequate modes of expression and self-interpretation.

emotive meaning The emotive meaning of a term is the attitude or other emotional state that is conventionally taken to be expressed by a straightforward use of it. Thus a derogatory term conventionally expresses some kind of contempt or hostility to some class of people. Terms like 'firm', 'stubborn', and 'pig-headed' apply to more or less the same class of people for more or less the same reason, but convey different appreciations. Other terms like 'super!' or 'wow!' have nothing but an emotive function, but most terms with which we communicate approval or disapproval have *descriptive aspects as well. *See also* PARADIASTOLE, THICK TERMS.

emotivism (emotive theory of ethics) The view that ethical utterances serve to express emotional or *affective states, rather than to state truths or falsehoods. The emotive theory was first presented in the 20th century in *The Meaning of Meaning* (1923) by C. K. Ogden and I. A. Richards. But precursors include *Berkeley's view of the non-representative character of much language, the *sentimentalist tradition in British ethical theory, and *projective theories of various parts of discourse. It was a popular way of dealing with the non-empirical yet non-logical character of ethics among the *logical positivists. Its problems include accounting for the way ethical assertions appear to be capable of truth and falsity, and identifying the characteristic states they supposedly express. *See also* EXPRESSIVISM, NON-COGNITIVISM, QUASI-REALISM.

empathy Translation of the German term **Einfühlung*: the state of being emotionally and cognitively 'in tune with' another person, particularly by feeling what their situation is like from the inside, or what it is like for them. Sometimes we feel what it *should* be like for someone else, for instance by feeling embarrassed for someone making a fool of themselves, although they are unaware of it. Empathy may or may not precede *sympathy. The place of empathy both in our understanding of other persons and in our ethical responses is much debated: *see* SIMULATION THEORY, *VERSTEHEN*. Less centrally, empathy is invoked in the suggestion that some *aesthetic experiences have us feeling as if we ourselves are part of the object, as when we tense our muscles while we look at a flying buttress.

Empedocles of Acragas (*c.*495–*c.*435 BC) Greek *Presocratic philosopher. Empedocles was a native of Acragas (Agrigento) in Sicily, and attained a remarkable personal and religious importance, being a poet, orator, scientist, statesman, miracle worker, and in his own eyes a god. The legend that he died by throwing himself into Mount Etna witnesses the semi-divine status that he managed to achieve. In his principal philosophical poem, *On Nature,* he replaces the *Parmenidean One with a universe whose changes were the recombination of four basic and permanent elements, air, earth, fire, and water, mixing and separating under the influence of two forces, attraction (Love) and repulsion (Strife). The universe moves through cycles according to whichever one of these is predominant. He also proclaims the *Pythagorean doctrine of the pre-existence and immortality of the soul and the contingency of its bodily existence: souls are condemned to the cycle of birth and rebirth by a fall from heavenly grace. His other main poem, *Purifications,* associates his cosmology and doctrine of the soul with a theological system in which Love, or a principle of organization, is present throughout the universe. Empedocles also held a doctrine of the evolution of the species. The exact way in which he reconciled the natural and the theological elements of his philosophy is controversial, but the doctrine of the four elements was taken over by *Aristotle and thence by the medievals.

empirical In a wide sense, an empirical belief is one capable of being confirmed or disconfirmed by sense experience. More narrowly, the term may be restricted so that the confirmation must avoid the use of intermediate theory, since otherwise the belief becomes theoretical in contrast with empirical. In this sense an empirical quality of things is one that can be represented in sense experience, as opposed to an inferred or postulated theoretical property. A purely empirical theory trades only in empirical qualities. *See* EMPIRICISM.

empiricism The permanent strand in philosophy that attempts to tie knowledge to experience. Experience is thought of either as the sensory contents of consciousness, or as whatever is expressed in some designated class of statements that can be observed to be true by the use of the senses. Empiricism denies that there is any knowledge outside this class, or at least outside whatever is given by legitimate theorizing on the basis of this class. It may take the form of denying that there is any **a priori* knowledge, or knowledge of necessary truths, or any innate or intuitive knowledge or general principles gaining credibility simply through the use of reason; it is thus principally contrasted with *rationalism. An empiricist account of our concepts will hold that they depend upon experience: '**nihil in intellectu nisi prius in sensu*' (nothing in the intellect that was not previously in the senses). Some philosophers such as *Aquinas have held this principle without denying that reason can apprehend knowledge, provided it uses the materials afforded by the senses. One of the main problems for empiricism is to accommodate the way in which thought does not just derive from experience, but provides us with *categories with which to organize it. The necessity for such addition (and its legitimacy) is the central theme of the *Critique of Pure Reason* of *Kant. Radical empiricism, as espoused by *James, holds that the relations between experiences that are implied in their organization are themselves objects of observation. The key problems for empiricism include avoiding a picture according to which the subject knows nothing but experiences of the present moment (*scepticism), demarcating the legitimate basis of theory in observation, defending the view that observation is itself free of non-empirical elements, describing legitimate ways of using observation in building a picture of the world, and explaining or explaining away knowledge that appears to have no basis in experience, notably mathematical, logical, or other *a priori* knowledge. *See also* MYTH OF THE GIVEN.

empirio-criticism *See* AVENARIUS.

empty set The *set that has no members (there is only one, since sets are different only if they have different members). The existence of this set as a mathematical object can be puzzling if one is (incorrectly) inclined to visualize a set as a kind of heap.

enantiomorphs *See* INCONGRUENT COUNTERPARTS.

Encyclopédie The great 18th-century French enterprise, the *Encyclopédie* was designed as a synoptic description of the branches of human knowledge. The leading figures behind the enterprise were *Diderot and *d'Alembert, and contributors included *Holbach, *Montesquieu, *Rousseau, and *Voltaire, sometimes known collectively as the Encyclopedists. The work is a bible of the *Enlightenment, philosophically very much in the tradition of *Locke and *Bayle. Its anticlerical, humanistic tone led to its temporary suppression by royal decree in 1759, but publication continued from 1751 to 1777. It required the collaboration of 140 contributors, with nearly the same number of writers and engravers. Eventually the 32 volumes included 21 volumes of text, containing 70,000 articles, and 11 volumes of plates. The work was reprinted five times before 1789.

SEE WEB LINKS

- An article on the *Encyclopédie* and its influence
- An audio discussion of the *Encyclopédie* by three experts

end in itself Something desired or aimed at or valued purely for its own sake, rather than as a means to anything else. *See also* GOOD WILL, *SUMMUM BONUM*.

endoxon (Greek, accepted opinion) In some systems of epistemology, including that of *Aristotle, it is permissible or compulsory to start from accepted opinions (*endoxa*) rather than engaging on a fruitless search for some firmer foundations, for instance in private experience.

ends and means The end of an action is that for the sake of which it is performed; the means is the way in which the end is to be achieved. The distinction arises in connection with various moral principles (you may not do evil for the sake of good; who wills the end wills the means; people must always be treated as ends, never merely as means) and its application is not always clear. For example, could you treat someone as a mere means if they want to be so treated, and you respond to that want? *See* DOUBLE EFFECT, PRINCIPLE OF; MEANS–ENDS REASONING.

endurance/perdurance Terminology introduced by the Australian philosopher Mark Johnston for an older contrast, and described by David *Lewis in *The Plurality of Worlds*. Something perdures if and only if it persists by having different temporal parts, or stages, at different times, though no one part of it is wholly present at more than one time. It endures if and only if it persists by being wholly present at more than one time. Perdurance corresponds to the way a play is extended in time: Act I is not present when Act II is. The question then is whether it is better to think of ordinary objects as perduring or enduring.

The issue is ancient, in that many philosophers have been tempted to think of the persistence of bodies, especially in motion, as a succession of new entities, or re-creations at different places. *Leibniz puts the doctrine especially clearly in a letter to Princess *Sophie: 'the duration of things or the multitude of momentary states is the collection of an infinity of strokes of God, of which each one at each instant is a creation or reproduction of everything, without a continuous passage, narrowly speaking, from one state to the next.'

energeia In *Aristotle, the actualization of a potential. *See* DYNAMIS/ENERGEIA.

energeticism The physical view that energy is the fundamental element in all physical change. It was propounded by the chemist Wilhelm Ostwald (1853–1932), but rebutted by Ludwig *Boltzmann and Max Planck.

energy The capacity of something to generate work, itself defined as the product of force times distance. In the 17th century dispute arose between the *Cartesians, who held that energy should be measured by mass times velocity (later separately identified as momentum), and *Leibniz, who held that it was proportional to mass times the square of the velocity. Later potential energy, stored in a system such as a mass at a height, or a coiled spring, became distinguished from the original idea of kinetic energy. More subtle concepts of energy evolve in special and general *relativity theory.

Engels, Friedrich (1820–95) German social philosopher and collaborator of *Marx. Born in the Rhineland of prosperous, factory-owning parents, Engels already had good liberal credentials when he came to Manchester in 1842, partly as agent for the family firm. In the following years his writings attracted the approval of Marx, and the affinity was confirmed by the impassioned *Lage der arbeitenden Klasse in England* (1845, trs. as *The Condition of the Working Class in England*, 1845). Engels collaborated with Marx on *The Communist Manifesto* (1848). He is generally credited with shaping two of the major philosophical components of Marxism: *historical materialism and *dialectical materialism. His most mature philosophical work is *Anti-Dühring* (1878), a materialist rebuttal of the work of Eugen *Dühring, one of Marx's rivals for influence in German socialist circles. Another late work, *The Origin of the Family, Private Property, and the State* (1884), is a communist, and feminist, attack on the subordination of women in the patriarchal family. Engels was the main supporter of Marx and his family, but also the editor of Marx's works, so that the task of separating their respective contributions to Marxist doctrine is daunting.

SEE WEB LINKS

- A list of internet resources on Engels, including bibliographies
- Translations of Engels's writings

Enlightenment The period of European thought characterized by the emphasis on experience and reason, mistrust of religion and traditional authority, and a gradual emergence of the ideals of liberal, secular, democratic societies. In England the movement can be discerned in the 17th century with the writings of Francis *Bacon and *Hobbes, and in France with the new emphasis on unaided reason in the work of *Descartes. But the 18th century saw the full flourishing of the Enlightenment, especially in France (*see* *ENCYCLOPÉDIE*), Scotland (*see* HUME, SMITH), and Germany, where the critical philosophy of *Kant is both a kind of culmination, and also a portent of the succeeding *Romantic period. Although it is difficult to find positive doctrines common to all these thinkers, the Enlightenment is associated with a materialist view of human beings, an optimism about their progress through education and science, and a generally *utilitarian approach to society and ethics. However, the Constitution of the United States, which is not a utilitarian document but one based on an ethic of natural *rights, is frequently cited as a concrete embodiment of Enlightenment ideals. It has been fashionable in *postmodernist circles to talk of the Enlightenment as having had a project, and one which has failed, but the meaning of this criticism remains unclear. *See also* OPTIMISM AND PESSIMISM, PERFECTIBILITY.

SEE WEB LINKS

- A list of internet resources on the Enlightenment, including classic writings
- A history of the Enlightenment

Enneads *See* PLOTINUS.

en-soi *See* BEING IN-ITSELF/FOR-ITSELF.

ens rationis (Latin, a being of reason) In medieval thought, another term for an intentional object or object of thought, as opposed to self-subsistent or independent objects. *See also* INTENTIONALITY.

ens realissimum (Latin, the most real being) A term for God, reflecting the belief that reality, like goodness, comes in degrees, and that there must be a limiting, ultimately real entity.

entailment The relationship between a set of premises and a conclusion when the conclusion *follows from the premises, or may validly be inferred from the premises. Many philosophers identify this with it being logically impossible that the premises should all be true, yet the conclusion false. Others are sufficiently impressed by the paradoxes of *strict implication to look for a stronger relation, which would distinguish between valid and invalid arguments within the sphere of necessary propositions. The search for a stronger notion is the field of *relevance logics.

entelechy (Greek, to have perfection) In *Aristotle, the realization of the potential of a thing, or the mode of being of a thing whose *essence is fully realized, as opposed to being merely potential. In later usages the entelechy became treated as the informing spirit that gives life to something; sometimes as well the active power generating motion in material things.

enthusiasm Term used pejoratively, especially in the 17th and 18th centuries, for irrational and disturbed states of religious fervour, especially as found among Puritans, evangelicals, and low-church born-again zealots. *Hume gives the definitive Enlightenment verdict: 'A gloomy, hare-brained enthusiast, after his death, may have a place in the calendar; but will scarcely ever be admitted, when alive, into intimacy and society, except by those who are as delirious and dismal as himself.' Hume distinguishes enthusiasm from *superstition, which is associated more with high-church and Catholic practice.

enthymeme An argument in which one of the premises is not explicitly stated.

entity A real thing. Entity realism is the term associated with the contemporary Canadian philosopher Ian Hacking, whereby the issue of scientific *realism is not one of the truth or falsity of scientific theories, but of the real existence of the things which scientists manipulate.

entrenchment A predicate is entrenched if it is true as a matter of historical fact that it has been used to formulate true predictions. *Goodman argued that this is the only property separating well-behaved, 'projectible' predicates from badly-behaved but syntactically simple predicates that can be defined. *See* GOODMAN'S PARADOX.

entropy A property of a closed thermodynamical system (i.e. one considered in terms of interchanges of heat and other forms of energy) corresponding to the degree to which the particles of the system are randomly arranged. Entropy is a measure of the disorder in the system. The second law of *thermodynamics states that entropy always increases.

enumerable *See* DENUMERABLE/NON-DENUMERABLE.

enumerative induction The method of reasoning that enumerates cases in which some regularity has obtained, and on that basis alone predicts its reoccurrence. It is usually contrasted unfavourably with more theoretical reasoning, or with approaches that consider variations in circumstances and possible causal explanations. *See* ELIMINATIVE INDUCTION, MILL'S METHODS.

envelope paradox *See* TWO-ENVELOPE PARADOX.

environmental ethics Most ethics deals with problems of human desires and needs: the achievement of happiness, or the distribution of goods. The central problem specific to thinking about the environment is the independent value to place on such things as preservation of species, or protection of the wilderness. Such protection can be supported as a means to ordinary human ends, for instance when animals are regarded as future sources of medicines or other benefits. But many would want to claim a non-utilitarian, absolute value for the existence of wild things and wild places; it is in their very independence of human lives that their value consists. They put us in our proper place, and failure to appreciate this value is not only an aesthetic failure but one of due humility and reverence, a moral disability. The problem is one of expressing this value, and mobilizing it against utilitarian arguments for developing natural areas and exterminating species more or less at will. *See also* NATURE, SUBLIME.

eo ipso Latin, by that very fact.

epapogē (Greek, *induction) An ampliative procedure of arguing from the particular to the general, originally identified by *Aristotle.

ephemeral, fallacy of the The mistake made by a transitory being who believes in the immutability of things. The fallacy is so named in *D'Alembert's Dream* by *Diderot, who gives the lovely illustration from *Fontenelle of the rose, who said that so far as any rose could remember, no gardener had ever died. A parallel problem afflicts *creationists who cannot see, and therefore do not credit, the ceaseless processes of geological change.

Epictetus (*c.*AD 55–135) The most influential teacher of *Stoicism of his time, Epictetus was born a slave in Asia Minor. He was given his freedom around the year 68, but was banished from Rome by Diocletian around 90. He was lame for much of his life. It is known that he was extremely popular, and respected, and lived a life of the utmost simplicity, in accordance with Stoic doctrine. His teachings or *Discourses* survive only through notes taken by his pupil Flavius Arrianus. They include an emphasis on submissiveness, humility, and charity, but also upon the ability and duty of a person to mould his or her character in the effort to achieve self-government and independence of external circumstance.

SEE WEB LINKS

- Bibliographies of writings by or on Epictetus
- A list of internet resources on Epictetus

Epicureanism In common usage, a way of life based on sensual enjoyment. However, this is not the recommendation of *Epicurus, who advocated the pursuit only of pleasures that can be controlled and enjoyed in moderation: pleasures of friendship, peace, and aesthetic contemplation. More properly Epicureanism is any philosophy combining the central doctrines of Epicurus.

Epicurus (341–270 BC) Greek philosopher. Epicurus was born on the island of Samos, but moved to Athens in 307/6 BC, where he established a secluded community called the 'Garden'. His doctrines are known mainly through the account in *Diogenes Laertius, and through *Lucretius' poem *De Rerum Natura*, which is believed to be a faithful representation of his thought. Epicurus followed the *atomistic metaphysics of *Leucippus and *Democritus, in particular allowing for empty space, an infinite number of atoms, and the infinite number of worlds their changing combinations produce. Epicurus also had a doctrine of the survival of the fittest in order to account for the evolution of species without appeal to the final *causes of *Aristotle. However, room is made for gods, although they have no concern at all for this cosmos, and in particular play no role either as first causes or as providing ends for existence. *Free will is allowed by the 'swerve' or *clinamen of atoms in their courses. Another interesting doctrine is that of the *prolepsis* or way in which experience becomes general, by allowing us to anticipate the kind of object to which terms refer (*prolepsis* is therefore a solution, or perhaps a labelling, of the difficulty that later bedevilled the *British empiricists, of how words become general in their significance).

The aim of all philosophy is, however, to enable us to live well, which is not to live in the hedonistic trough the word Epicureanism now suggests, after centuries of propaganda against the system. Rather, practical wisdom, attained through philosophy, is needed to attain the pleasant life, which consists in a preponderance of *katastematic* pleasures, capable of indefinite prolongation, over merely *kinematic* or volatile sensory pleasures. *Katastematic* pleasures are capable of variation but not of increase, so that one who lives longer does not thereby obtain more of them than one who lives less long, and this is important to the Epicurean attitude towards death. As with other Greek ethical philosophies, **ataraxia* is the summit of the *katastematic* pleasures, and requires understanding the limits of life and removal of the fear of death, cultivation of friendships, and the removal of unnecessary desires and false gratifications.

SEE WEB LINKS

- A biography of Epicurus
- An archive of writings by or on Epicurus

epigone An acolyte or undistinguished follower of some teacher.

Epimenides Epimenides the Cretan is supposed to have said that all Cretans are liars. If he spoke truly, then what he said was false, and vice versa. *See* LIAR PARADOX.

epiphany The manifestation of God's presence in the world. A spiritual or mystical revelation.

epiphenomenalism The view that some feature of a situation arises in virtue of others, but itself has no causal powers. In the philosophy of mind this means that while there exist mental events, states of consciousness, and experiences, they have themselves no causal powers, and produce no effect on the physical world. The analogy sometimes used is that of the whistle on the engine, that makes the sound (corresponding to experience), but plays no part in making the machinery move. Epiphenomenalism is a drastic solution to the major difficulty of reconciling the existence of mind with the fact that according to physics itself only a physical event can cause another physical event. An epiphenomenalist may accept one-way causation, whereby physical events produce mental events, or may prefer some kind of parallelism, avoiding causation either between mind and body or between body and mind (*see* OCCASIONALISM). A major problem for epiphenomenalism is that if mental events have no causal relationships it is not clear that they can be objects of memory, or even awareness. *See also* BASE AND SUPERSTRUCTURE, PRIVATE LANGUAGE ARGUMENT.

epiphenomenon An incidental product of some process, that has no effects of its own. *See* EPIPHENOMENALISM.

epistemic logic The search for a systematization of inferences depending upon 'it is known that *p*' (K*p*). The usual backbone of such systems, for example in the work of *Hintikka, is the idea of epistemically possible worlds, or worlds left open by a piece of information. This enables 'known' and 'unknown' to be seen as analogous to the 'necessary' and 'possible' of *modal logic, and similar questions arise, such as whether we should adopt the principle that $Kp \rightarrow KKp$. Particular problems emerge in the interaction of K with names and quantifiers, since it induces *intensional contexts: it may be known that the murderer is dangerous but not known that the postman is dangerous, although the postman is the murderer.

epistemic privacy *See* PRIVILEGED ACCESS.

epistemic relativism The thesis that what may be a proper claim to know something when made by one group or culture may be otherwise when made by a different group or culture. In some cases this is harmless and banal (people who have looked and seen may know things that people who have not do not know). In other cases it can be highly contentious, as when there are claims made for specific cultural, religious, or female ways of knowing things, unavailable to outsiders.

epistemics Equivalent to *epistemology.

epistemology (Greek, *epistēmē*, knowledge) The theory of knowledge. Its central questions include the origin of knowledge; the place of experience in generating knowledge, and the place of reason in doing so; the relationship between knowledge and certainty, and between knowledge and the impossibility of error; the possibility of universal *scepticism; and the changing forms of knowledge that arise from new conceptualizations of the world. All of these issues link with other central concerns of philosophy, such as the nature of truth and the nature of experience and meaning. It is possible to see epistemology as dominated by two rival metaphors. One is that of a building or pyramid, built on foundations. In this conception it is the job of the philosopher to describe especially secure foundations, and to identify secure modes of construction, so that the resulting edifice can be shown to be sound. This metaphor favours some idea of the 'given' as a basis of knowledge, and of a rationally defensible theory of confirmation and inference as a method of construction (*see also* FOUNDATIONALISM, PROTOCOL STATEMENTS). The other metaphor is that of a boat or fuselage, that has no foundations but owes its strength to the stability given by its interlocking parts. This rejects the idea of a basis in the 'given', favours ideas of coherence and *holism, but finds it harder to ward off *scepticism.

The problem of defining knowledge in terms of true belief plus some favoured relation between the believer and the facts began with *Plato's view in the *Theaetetus* that knowledge is true belief plus a *logos*. For difficulties *see* GETTIER EXAMPLES. For further issues *see* CONFIRMATION THEORY, EMPIRICISM, FEMINISM, NATURALIZED EPISTEMOLOGY, PROTOCOL STATEMENTS, RATIONALISM, RELATIVISM, RELIABILISM.

epochē Greek, the suspension of belief that is one of the goals of sceptical argument. *See also* BRACKETING.

equality In social philosophy, a central but controversial ideal. In *Aristotle equality of treatment is contingent upon the subjects of the treatment being equal 'in the relevant respects'. The question of which respects are relevant gives a spectrum ranging from extreme egalitarian approaches, in which virtually nothing forfeits equality of treatment, to elitist ones, in which many things do so. Kantian ethics discerns the equal right of all human beings to treatment as ends in themselves as a foundation of all morality, but the application of this ideal is controversial, since it is unclear what counts as a departure from respect for persons as ends in themselves (persons may clearly be treated sometimes as means, as when someone is quarantined to prevent the spread of an infection, but must not be treated as mere means, or perhaps means in themselves). In political theory the question is whether equalities of social, political, and economic situation are possible, and whether the attempt to create such equalities infringes other values such as liberty, or even undermines too many of the economic and cultural conditions for stable society.

equipollence Equally powerful, used especially in the context of Greek scepticism, where the arguments on each side of a question are often supposed to cancel each other out.

equivalence, material Two propositions *p*, *q* are materially equivalent to one another when *p* is true if and only if *q* is true, or in other words they share the same *truth-value.

equivalence relation (equivalence class) A *relation which is transitive, symmetric, and reflexive divides its field into exclusive classes of things. Within each class everything bears the relation to everything else, and nothing bears it to anything in a different class. 'Of the same height as' or 'having the same number of members as' are equivalence relations that divide the field of people into classes of equally tall people, and sets into different classes depending on how many members they have. Defining an equivalence class of things at the same point on the scale is the fundamental operation in establishing any kind of measure of a property or quantity. In mathematical logic an early definition of a cardinal number (*Frege's) was as an equivalence class of equinumerous classes.

equivalent Having the same value. *See also* EQUIVALENCE RELATION.

equivocate To make a statement that is capable of being taken in more than one way, with the aim of exploiting the ambiguity.

Er, myth of *See* MYTH OF ER.

Erasmus, Desiderius (*c.*1466/9–1536) One of the earliest and greatest *humanists of the Northern Renaissance. Erasmus was educated in Holland, possibly at Deventer, and entered the Augustinian priory of Steyn, near Gouda, in 1487. He was ordained in 1492. For a short while he studied theology in Paris. Travel to England in 1499 put him in touch with Thomas *More and other humanists. Living the life of a travelling scholar, Erasmus published collections of classical proverbs, his *In Praise of Folly* in 1509, and in 1516 a new and more accurate Greek edition of the New Testament. Although his satires upon religious practice and the complexities of *scholastic theology, together with his preference for the early, simpler, beliefs of the Church, made him an inspiration for the new movement of reform, Erasmus had little confidence that the unaided powers of men were capable of forging new utopias. He withdrew from the political arena, and in 1524 broke with *Luther, in his work *De Libero Arbitrio* ('On Free Will'). The moderation, and moderate scepticism, of Erasmus had no place in the increasingly divisive splits within the Church, but his classical learning and attitudes were widely influential in the centuries following. He died in Basel, preparing to return to the Netherlands.

erastianism The doctrine that the State is ascendant over the Church in ecclesiastical matters. It is named after the Swiss theologian Thomas Erastus (1524–83).

erasure In *deconstructionist writing a word is used under erasure (French, *sous rature*) if it is necessary to use it, but it is only doubtfully intelligible. The device is akin to placing inverted commas around a word to show that its use is suspicious, e.g. Locke's concept of 'substance'.

Erfahrung *See* ERLEBNIS.

ergo Latin, therefore.

Erinyes In Greek mythology, dark forces of the earth, representing the power of retribution and revenge, especially in the family. In the tragedian Aeschylus, daughters of the night. In the play cycle the *Oresteia* they eventually become the Eumenides, or kindly ones, signifying their role in maintaining civic stability. *See also* JUSTICE, RETRIBUTIVE; REVENGE.

eristic (Greek, conflict) Reasoning that aims not at truth but at victory over an opponent or at making a weaker position prevail.

Eriugena, Johannes Scottus (Erigena) (*c.*810–*c.*877) Also known as John the Scot, Eriugena was born in Ireland, achieved a remarkable degree of learning, and taught at the court of Charles the Bald. He is important as a translator and transmitter of Greek thought, the translator of *Dionysius the Pseudo-Areopagite and other writers, and arguably the most important thinker in the Christian world between *Augustine and *Anselm. He defended the reality of *free will (*Pelagianism) against one Gottschalk, a monk, but the reliance on reason that he shows was condemned by two councils, although John himself escaped censure. His greatest work is *De Divisione Naturae* ('Of the Division of Nature'). In this he shows a pronounced tendency towards *pantheism and *Neoplatonism: God becomes the one unchanging, universal reality in which creation participates, himself beyond human categories, and knowable only by what he is not.

Created beings are themselves disclosures or manifestations of the divine principle, and their goal is reabsorption in God. Eriugena's distinction was to insist on a reconciliation between reason and Christian theology. The theology that results is of doubtful orthodoxy, although certainly influential on later Neoplatonic Christians such as *Dante.

Erlebnis German philosophical term for experience. In post-Romantic German philosophy the term took on the connotation of 'lived', non-conceptualized, and sometimes ineffable, experience, akin to the stream of *qualia of some theorists of consciousness. It can be contrasted with *Erfahrung*, which denotes more ordinary perception of interpreted fact. Elementary experiences form the basis of *Carnap's early construction of the world of empirical objects.

eros *See* LOVE.

erotetic (Greek, *erōtēsis*, a questioning) Pertaining to questions. Erotetic logic studies the logic and pragmatics of questions and answers.

error theory Term due to the 20th-century philosopher J. L. Mackie, describing a theory according to which everyday thought in some area is sufficiently infected by mistaken philosophical views to be widely in error. Mackie believed that ordinary moral thinking involved belief in an objective, rationally compelling property of 'to-be-doneness' in things, but that this belief cannot be defended. An error theory stands directly opposed to the *Wittgensteinian view that ordinary language is perfectly in order as it is, and that only philosophical thought about it gives rise to confusion. The principal problem confronting an error theory is to say how our thinking ought to be remedied to free us of the error. One suggestion is wholesale *eliminativism, counselling us to abandon the area entirely; other less radical moves would counsel various cleaning-up operations. *See also* QUASI-REALISM.

eschatology (Greek, *eschatos*, the last) The formation of ideas about the end of life, or the end of the world, and in Christian theology, the last judgement and resurrection.

esoteric Hidden from all but a small circle of initiates. The idea that Plato, Aristotle, or almost any great philosopher was concealing the 'true' doctrine from all except initiates is well-received in a world which likes codes, conspiracies, and cryptograms; it flatters would-be insiders, and acts as a general excuse to interpret writers as meaning the opposite of what a natural reading of their works would suggest. *See also* STRAUSS, LEO.

ESP Extrasensory perception. *See* PARANORMAL.

esse est percipi (Latin, to be is to be perceived) The fundamental tenet of the subjective *idealism of *Berkeley.

essence (Latin, *esse*, to be) The basic or primary element in the being of a thing; the thing's nature, or that without which it could not be what it is. A thing cannot lose its essence without ceasing to exist, and the essential nature of a natural kind, such as water or gold, is that property without which there is no instance of the kind. *Locke contrasted real essences, in something like this sense, with the *nominal definition provided by a description of the common properties of a thing. Throughout Greek, scholastic, and some modern philosophy there have been many proposals of ways for finding the essences of things, and views about what science would be like if we did know them. The distinction between essential and accidental properties is rejected by *holistic approaches to science, such as that advocated by *Quine. *See also* ESSENTIALISM, HAECCEITY, QUIDDITY.

essentialism The doctrine that it is correct to distinguish between those properties of a thing, or kind of thing, that are essential to it, and those that are merely *accidental. Essential properties are ones that it cannot lose without ceasing to exist. Thus a person wearing a hat may take off the hat, or might not have been wearing the hat, but the same person cannot cease to occupy space, and we cannot postulate a possible situation in which the person is not occupying space. If we agree with this (it is not beyond debate, which illustrates the difficulty with essentialism), occupying space is an essential property of persons, but wearing a hat an accidental one. The main problem is to locate the grounds for this intuitive distinction. One suggestion is that it arises simply from the ways of describing things, and is therefore linguistic or even *conventional in origin. Contrasted with this (the nominal essence) is the *Lockean idea that things themselves have underlying natures (real essences) that underlie and explain their other properties.

Essentialism is used in feminist writing of the view that females (or males) have an essential nature (e.g. nurturing and caring versus being aggressive and selfish), as opposed to differing by a variety of accidental or contingent features brought about by social forces. *See also* DETERMINISM (BIOLOGICAL).

essentially contested concepts The idea promoted by W. B. Gallie that some concepts admit of no one authoritative definition, because they are essentially the focus of different accounts, especially different moral attitudes. Concepts of which this is true might include persons, justice, equality, and others about which moral and political disagreement is apt to be endemic.

eternal return (eternal recurrence) The image of cycles in which the universe returns to re-enact exactly the same course of events is common to many religions, and was a theme of much Greek thought, including that of the *Stoics. Usually recurrence is thought of in terms of events that cycle in a common-sense, linear time, but the possibility of time itself cycling was also considered. The contradiction that in that case the 'later' events would be numerically identical with the earlier, so that everything happens only once after all, was noticed by Eudemus of Rhodes, a pupil of *Aristotle. A doctrine of recurrence was held by *Plotinus and *Origen. The notion of endless recurrence was embraced by *Nietzsche in 1882, and is explored in the notebooks making up *The Will to Power*. It is not clear whether for Nietzsche the cycle is scientifically probable, but it provides a litmus test for success in life: if we succeed in giving the right style to our actions we can joyously affirm their return, but otherwise we cannot.

eternity The totality of time, conceived of as having no beginning and no end. The central philosophical dispute is whether eternity should be contrasted with time, not to be thought of as an especially long quantity of time, but as instead involving a kind of timelessness. Thus eternal objects, such as numbers, enjoy a timeless existence. *Plotinus and the *Neoplatonist tradition insist on a non-temporal interpretation of God's existence. *Boethius makes the distinction between sempiternity (everlastingness) and eternity: 'For our "now", as if running, creates time and sempiternity, whereas the Divine "now" stays not moving, but standing still, and creates eternity' (*De Trinitate*, 4. II). Such timelessness is beyond description, but its apprehension is the goal of mystical contemplation.

ether *See* AETHER.

ethical constructivism The *anti-realist view of *ethics that supposes that there do exist ethical truths, but that these are somehow constituted by human practices, including our emotions and reactions, policies and cultural habits.

ethical formalism The view, especially associated with *Kant, that the form of a maxim or principle of action can be constrained sufficiently by consistency considerations to yield substantial ethical directives.

ethical naturalism The attempt to place ethical properties and ethical thought in the natural world. In the form discussed and supposedly refuted by *Moore, this is the view that the meaning of an ethical predicate ('... is good') is identical with that of a predicate displaying the features in virtue of which the object is good, e.g. '... is such as to create happiness' if one operates a *utilitarian standard. Moore attacks this with the *open question argument. Other positions calling themselves naturalism may abandon the claim about identity of meaning, but still hold that ethical properties are identical with natural properties, rather as we hold that water is H_2O, even if the two terms mean something different. Most widely, naturalism includes any belief that the nature of ethical thinking is exhaustively understood in terms of natural propensities of human beings, without mysterious intuitions, or operations of conscience, or divine help.

ethical objectivism The view that the claims of ethics are objectively true; they are not 'relative' to a subject or a culture, nor purely subjective in their nature, in opposition to *error theories, *scepticism, and *relativism. The central problem is finding the source of the required objectivity.

ethical relativism The view that the truth of ethical claims is relative to the culture or way of life of those who hold them. It thus generalizes to all of ethics what may reasonably be supposed true of matters of etiquette, summed up in the tag 'when in Rome, do as the Romans do'. The doctrine is not easy to formulate although its spirit appeals especially to people afraid of the imperial ambitions which they detect in Western liberalism.

ethics (Greek, *ethos*, character) The study of the concepts involved in practical reasoning: good, right, duty, obligation, virtue, freedom, rationality, choice. Also the second-order study of the objectivity, subjectivity, relativism, or scepticism that may attend claims made in these terms. For the kinds of problems encountered, see under the special terms. For a possible distinction between ethics and morality, *see* MORALITY.

ethics, applied The subject that applies *ethics to actual practical problems, such as those of *abortion, *euthanasia, the treatment of *animals, or other environmental, legal, political, and social problems. *See also* BIOETHICS, BUSINESS ETHICS, ENVIRONMENTAL ETHICS. Practitioners of practical ethics are sometimes called ethicists.

ethnology Cultural anthropology. The techniques whereby anthropologists observe and come to understand the lives of different cultures have philosophical problems, since they raise the question of how much is genuinely observed, and how much is read into the alternative way of life by anthropologists who, inevitably, have to interpret it in terms that they themselves understand. *See also* CONCEPTUAL SCHEME, INDETERMINACY OF TRANSLATION, SAPIR–WHORF HYPOTHESIS.

ethnomethodology The study of common social knowledge, in particular as it concerns the understanding of others and the varieties of circumstance in which it can take place.

Eubilides Philosopher of the school of *Megara, sometimes supposed to have been the discoverer of the paradox of the *Liar.

e

Euclid (*fl.* *c.*300 BC) Greek geometer. One of the greatest mathematicians, Euclid lived under Ptolemy I and taught at Alexandria. His *Elements* contain thirteen books: six on plane geometry, three on the theory of numbers, one on irrationals, and three on solid geometry. Euclidean geometry is the greatest example of the pure *axiomatic method, and as such had incalculable philosophical influence as a paradigm of rational certainty. It had no competitor until the 19th century when it was realized that the fifth axiom of his system (parallel lines never meet) could be denied without inconsistency, leading to Riemannian spherical geometry. The fifth chapter of Euclid's *Elements* is attributed to the mathematician Eudoxus, and contains a precise development of the real numbers, work which remained unappreciated until rediscovered in the 19th century. *See also* GEOMETRY.

eudaimonia (Greek, happiness, well-being, success) The central goal of all systems of ancient ethics; according to *Aristotle, the 'best, noblest, and most pleasant thing in the world'. *Eudaimonia* is a place-holder waiting for further specification, and different ethical theories will fill it out differently. Aristotle conceives of it as the active exercise of the powers of the (virtuous) soul in conformity to reason. *Eudaimonia* is usually translated as happiness or well-being, but it has some of the same connotations as 'success', since in addition to living well it includes doing well. For example, it can be diminished by events that happen after the subject's death, and it is not a state that children can possess. It is complete and self-sufficient, to be attained for no other end than itself, so it includes all other ends that are pursued for themselves. It therefore includes pleasure, but goes beyond it. In Bk x of the *Nicomachean Ethics* Aristotle extols the life of study as the essential realization of *eudaimonia*. *See also* *SUMMUM BONUM*.

eudaimonism Ethics as based on the Aristotelian notion of **eudaimonia* or human flourishing. While closely allied to *virtue ethics, the approach is different when the Greek equation between acting virtuously and flourishing is broken. Eudaimonism can also vary in so far as different conceptions arise of what it is to truly flourish. Thus the *Cyrenaics stress sensual pleasure; the *Stoics place emphasis on detachment from worldly goods, such as health and friendship; *Aquinas puts more emphasis on happiness as the eternal contemplation of God; and so on.

Eudemus of Rhodes (late 4th c. BC) Pupil of *Aristotle who had a strong claim to succeed as head of the *Lyceum. Theophrastus was preferred. His name is coupled with that of Theophrastus in important innovations in modal logic and he wrote widely on rhetoric, physics, astronomy, and theology; the attribution of *Eudemian Ethics* to him rather than to Aristotle is now rejected.

Eudoxus of Cnidus (*c.*408–*c.*355 BC) Greek pupil of *Plato's, and outstanding geometer and cosmologist. Eudoxus invented a general theory of proportion able to handle incommensurables, also a mathematical theory of the limit enabling avoidance of infinitesimals. He constructed a mathematical model of the heavens, based on advanced mathematics but poor observational data.

eulogistic/dyslogistic Distinction used by *Bentham between the favourable way of putting something, and the unfavourable way of putting the same thing: 'What is the difference between that *luxury* which the world condemns, and that *prosperity* which the world admires?' *See also* EMOTIVE MEANING, PARADIASTOLE.

euthanasia, active/passive Euthanasia is the action of directly causing the quick and painless death of a person, or omitting to prevent it when intervention was within the agent's powers. It is usually understood that euthanasia is performed only with the intention of relieving suffering, and where death is perceived as the greater good or lesser evil for the patient. Active euthanasia means acting to bring the death about, passive euthanasia means not preventing it (*see* ACTS/OMISSIONS DOCTRINE). Although medical codes more commonly allow doctors to follow the passive option than they allow them to actively intervene to cause death, there are problems of drawing the distinction in particular cases. There is also the unpleasant possibility that the passive withholding of treatment may condemn the patient to a lingering and painful death, which an active intervention would have prevented. Euthanasia is something many people would wish for themselves if life were to become unbearable, although it is frequently opposed. One set of worries concerns its expansion to form a climate in which old people are encouraged to go quietly, and to feel guilty about hanging on. It is also opposed on the curious grounds of respect for life. In many systems of law it would be illegal to give a suffering person a painless death when, if a cat or dog were in the same condition, it would be illegal not to do so.

SEE WEB LINKS

- A survey of related religious, medical, and legal debates
- Video lectures on euthanasia and related issues

Euthyphro dilemma The dilemma explored in *Plato's dialogue *Euthyphro*. Are pious things pious because the gods love them, or do the gods love them because they are pious? The dilemma poses the question of whether value can be conceived as the upshot of the choice of any mind, even a divine one. On the first option the choice of the gods creates goodness and value. Even if this is intelligible it seems to make it impossible to praise the gods, for it is then vacuously true that they choose the good. On the second option we have to understand a source of value lying behind or beyond the will even of the gods, and by which they can be evaluated. The elegant solution of *Aquinas is that the standard is formed by God's nature, and is therefore distinct from his will, but not distinct from him.

The dilemma arises whatever the source of authority is supposed to be. Do we care about the good because it is good, or do we just call good those things that we care about? It also generalizes to affect our understanding of the authority of other things: mathematics, or *necessary truth, for example. Are truths necessary because we deem them to be so, or do we deem them to be so because they are necessary?

evaluative An evaluative proposition or commitment is one that attributes value or the reverse to something. The philosophical difficulty is to describe what is specific to this kind of attribution. *See also* ATTITUDE, FACT/VALUE DISTINCTION.

Evans, Gareth (1946–80) English philosopher. Evans had a meteoric career at Oxford, energetically developing a fusion of the Kantian metaphysics of Peter *Strawson with the new insights into reference provided by Saul *Kripke and others. His principal work was *The Varieties of Reference* (1982).

event A change or happening. The central debate in the philosophy of events is whether they are to be thought of as individuals, like objects, capable of date and place and capable of being described in different ways, or whether they are more like propositions or *facts, whose identity depends essentially on the concepts in which they are framed. On the former model it may prove easier to understand how events can cause things, and how one event (e.g. a commotion in the brain) may be identical with another (e.g. being struck by a thought). The latter model assimilates events to facts, so that just as it can be a fact that the admiral did not arrive, his non-arrival can be a significant event (not at all a non-event) which may have its own causes and effects. Similarly there can exist disjunctive events (John's going to India or China) or quantificational events (Mary's finding a job, i.e. there being some job-finding by Mary).

evidence That which raises or lowers the probability of a proposition. The central question of *epistemology is the structure of this process and its ultimate rationale.

evil, problem of The problem of reconciling the imperfect world with the goodness of God. The problem has two forms. One is whether it is consistent to hold that an omnipotent, omniscient, and perfect creator could have made a world in which pain and evil form a prominent part of life, and possibly of life after death (*see* HELL). This is purely a logical question, and frequently if callously answered by citing the supposed extra goodness that a tincture of evil makes possible (*see also* FREE WILL DEFENCE). The second and more robust version of the problem is whether, even if such saving hypotheses restore consistency to the theistic position, it could ever be reasonable to take the imperfect creation as itself a sign of divine, i.e. perfect, workmanship. The second argument is deployed by *Hume especially effectively against the argument to *design, in his *Dialogues Concerning Natural Religion*: 'Here', says Philo, the sceptic, 'I triumph.'

evil genie (evil demon) *See* METHOD OF DOUBT.

evolution In biology, the genetic transformations of populations through time, resulting from genetic variation and the subsequent impact of the environment on rates of reproductive success. *See also* DARWINISM.

evolutionary ethics In the 19th century, the attempt to base ethical reasoning on the presumed facts about evolution. The movement is particularly associated with *Spencer. The premise is that later elements in an evolutionary path are better than earlier ones; the application of this principle then requires seeing western society, *laissez-faire* capitalism, or some other object of approval, as more evolved than more 'primitive' social forms. Neither the principle nor the applications command much respect. The version of evolutionary ethics called 'social *Darwinism' emphasizes the struggle for natural selection, and draws the conclusion that we should glorify and assist such struggle, usually by enhancing competitive and aggressive relations between people in society, or between societies themselves. More recently the relation between evolution and ethics has been rethought in the light of biological discoveries concerning altruism and kin selection. *See also* EVOLUTIONARY PSYCHOLOGY.

evolutionary psychology The study of the way in which a variety of higher mental functions may be *adaptations, formed in response to selection pressures on human populations through evolutionary time. Candidates for such theorizing include maternal and paternal motivations, capacities for love and friendship, the development of language as a signalling system, cooperative and aggressive tendencies, our emotional repertoires, our moral reactions, including the disposition to detect and punish those who cheat on agreements or who *free-ride on the work of others, our cognitive structures, and many others. Evolutionary psychology goes hand-in-hand with neurophysiological evidence about the underlying circuitry in the brain which subserves the psychological mechanisms it claims to identify. The approach was foreshadowed by *Darwin himself, and William *James, as well as the *sociobiology of E. O. Wilson. *See* JUST SO STORY.

SEE WEB LINKS

- Two pioneers of evolutionary psychology explain its basic principles
- A list of resources on evolutionary psychology and related fields

evolutionism Discredited late 19th- and early 20th-century doctrine associating the changes of *evolution with a progressive view of social change, positive attitudes to competition and war, and justification of inequalities of power. *See also* EVOLUTIONARY ETHICS.

examination paradox *See* PREDICTION PARADOX.

exaptation *See* ADAPTATION.

exchangeability In the subjective or *personalist theory of probability a substitute must be found for the apparently objective or *realist notion of an unknown probability, say of a coin coming up heads. The personalist substitute for the notion, developed by *de Finetti, regards the event as a member of a sequence of tosses, which are in turn thought of as having the property that the probability of any *n*-fold subset of the events being a case of heads depends solely on the number *n*. To regard a sequence in this way is to regard events in it as exchangeable, and provides a personalist substitute for the classical notion of a sequence of independent events sharing a fixed unknown probability.

excluded middle, principle of (excluded middle, law of) The logical law asserting that either *p* or not-*p*. It excludes middle cases such as propositions being half correct or more or less right. The principle directly asserting that each proposition is either true or false is properly called the law of *bivalence.

exclusive/exhaustive It is frequently useful to divide a set into mutually exclusive and jointly exhaustive alternatives, i.e. alternatives such that nothing belongs to more than one, and everything belongs to at least one.

exclusive/inclusive disjunction The disjunction of two propositions, *p* or *q*, is represented in logic by $p \vee q$. This is evaluated as true if both *p* and *q* are true, and is called inclusive disjunction ('vel'). A different notion, exclusive disjunction, is defined true only when exactly one of *p*, *q* is true, and as false if they are both true. It has been contentious whether in natural language 'or' has an exclusive reading, or whether the appearance is the result of *implicature.

ex falso quodlibet Latin, from a false proposition, anything follows. In classical logic it is true that from a contradiction anything follows.

exhaustive *See* EXCLUSIVE/EXHAUSTIVE.

existence For the question of why there is something and not nothing, *see* BEING. The modern treatment of existence in the theory of *quantification is sometimes put by saying that existence is not a predicate. The idea is that the existential quantifier is itself an *operator on a predicate, indicating that the property it expresses has instances. Existence is therefore treated as a second-order property, or property of properties. In this it is like number, for when we say that there are three things of a kind, we do not describe the things (as we would if we said there are red things of the kind), but instead attribute a property to the kind itself. The parallel with numbers is exploited by *Frege in the dictum that affirmation of existence is merely denial of the number nought. A problem for the account is created by sentences like 'This exists', where some particular thing is indicated. Such a sentence seems to express a contingent truth (for this might not have existed), yet no other predicate is involved. 'This exists' is therefore unlike 'Tame tigers exist', where a property is said to have an instance, for the word 'this' does not locate a property, but only an individual. *Possible worlds seem able to differ from each other purely in the presence or absence of individuals, and not merely in the distribution of exemplifications of properties.

existence precedes essence The central slogan of *existentialism, indicating that a person has no predetermined nature or range of choices, but is always free to choose afresh, and thereby reconstitute himself or herself as a different person.

existential generalization The process of inferring from a particular proposition ('Fred is bald') the corresponding *existential quantification ('someone is bald').

existential import The implications of a proposition as to what exists. If a proposition entails the existence of something, then it has existential import. It should be noticed that in the *predicate calculus the universal *quantification $(\forall x)(Fx \rightarrow Gx)$ has no existential import, since it is true when nothing is F.

existential instantiation Rule of classical *first-order logic. Suppose a result B can be proved from a particular proposition 'Fa'. And suppose that 'a' is not mentioned in any of the premises used in the argument, nor in B itself. Then it is as if 'a' is an arbitrary example. In this case the rule allows us to infer B from the weaker premise that $(\exists x)Fx$. Provided that something is F, there is going to be something that could function as a counter, just as 'a' does.

existentialism A loose title for various philosophies that emphasize certain common themes: the individual, the experience of choice, and the absence of rational understanding of the universe with a consequent dread or sense of *absurdity in human life. The combination suggests an emotional tone or mood rather than a set of deductively related theses, and existentialism attained its zenith in Europe following the disenchantments of the Second World War. However, the first significant thinker to stress such themes was *Kierkegaard, whose work is generally regarded as the origin of existentialism. Existentialist writing both reacts against the view that the universe is a closed, coherent, intelligible system, and finds the resulting contingency a cause for lamentation. In the face of an indifferent universe we are thrown back upon our own freedom. Acting *authentically becomes acting in the light of the open space of possibilities that the world allows. Different writers who united in stressing the importance of these themes nevertheless developed very different ethical and metaphysical systems as a consequence. In *Heidegger existentialism turns into scholastic *ontology; in *Sartre into a dramatic exploration of moments of choice and stress; in the theologians *Barth, *Tillich, and *Bultmann it becomes a device for reinventing the relationships between people and God. Existentialism never took firm root outside continental Europe, and many philosophers have voiced mistrust of particular existentialist concerns, for example with *being and non-being, or with the *libertarian flavour of its analysis of *free will.

existential proposition *See* QUANTIFIER.

existential psychology A school of psychology emphasizing the need for understanding patients by means of a grasp of their total orientation towards the world. It is therefore opposed to reductionism, *behaviourism, and scientific methods that objectify the patient in psychology. The principal impact of the approach has been on techniques of psychotherapy.

existential quantifier *See* QUANTIFIER, VARIABLE.

ex nihilo nihil fit Latin, from nothing, nothing is made.

exoteric The opposite of *esoteric: opinions suitable for the uninitiated.

expected utility In *decision theory, the expected utility of an outcome is the utility that is assigned to its occurrence, multiplied by the probability of its occurrence. The central concept was first formulated by Christian Huygens (1629–95).

experience Along with *consciousness, experience is the central focus of the philosophy of mind. Experience is easily thought of as a stream of private events, known only to their possessor, and bearing at best problematic relationships to any other events, such as happenings in an external world or similar streams in other possessors. The stream makes up the conscious life of the possessor. With this picture there is a complete separation of mind and the world, and in spite of great philosophical effort the gap, once opened, proves impossible to bridge: both *idealism and *scepticism are common outcomes. The aim of much recent philosophy, therefore, is to articulate a less problematic conception of experience, making it objectively accessible, so that the facts about how a subject experiences the world are in principle as knowable as the facts about how the same subject digests food. A beginning on this task may be made by observing that experiences have contents: it is the world itself that they represent to us as being one way or another, and how we take the world to be is publicly manifested by our words and behaviour. My own relationship with my experience itself involves memory, recognition, and description, all of which arise from skills that are equally exercised in interpersonal transactions. Recently emphasis has also been placed on the way in which experience should be regarded as a 'construct', or the upshot of the workings of many cognitive sub-systems (although this idea was familiar to *Kant, who thought of experience as itself synthesized by various active operations of the mind). The extent to which these moves undermine the distinction between 'what it is like from the inside' and how things are objectively is fiercely debated. It is also widely recognized that such developments tend to blur the line between experience and theory, making it harder to formulate traditional doctrines such as *empiricism.

e

experiment A controlled manipulation of events, designed to produce observations that confirm or disconfirm one or more rival theories or hypotheses. To experiment is to put questions to nature, and the experimental method is contrasted with the passive acceptance of whatever observations happen along. The method is characteristic of modern natural science. However, a discipline (such as history) may be pursued with greater or less objectivity and success without being able to avail itself of the experimental method. *See also* CONFIRMATION THEORY, DISCONFIRMATION, THOUGHT EXPERIMENT.

experimentum crucis *See* CRUCIAL EXPERIMENT.

explanans/explanandum *See* EXPLANATION.

explanation Since so much of life both inside and outside the study is concerned with finding explanations of things, it would be desirable to have a concept of what counts as a good explanation, and what distinguishes good from bad. Under the influence of *logical positivist approaches to the structure of science, it was felt that the criterion ought to be found in a definite logical relationship between the *explanans* (that which does the explaining) and the *explanandum* (that which is to be explained). This approach culminated in the covering law model of explanation, or the view that an event is explained when it is subsumed under a *law of nature, that is, its occurrence is deducible from the law plus a set of initial conditions. A law would itself be explained by being deduced from a higher-order or covering law, in the way that Kepler's laws of planetary motion are deducible from Newton's laws of motion. The covering law model may be adapted to include explanation by showing that something is probable, given a statistical law. Questions for the covering law model include querying whether laws are necessary to explanation (we explain everyday events without overtly citing laws); querying whether they are sufficient (it may not explain an event just to say that it is an example of the kind of thing that always happens); and querying whether a purely logical relationship is adapted to capturing the requirements we make of explanations. These may include, for instance, that we have a 'feel' for what is happening, or that the explanation proceeds in terms of things that are familiar to us or unsurprising, or that we can give a model of what is going on, and none of these notions is captured in a purely logical approach. Recent work, therefore, has tended to stress the contextual and pragmatic elements in requirements for explanation, so that what counts as a good explanation given one set of concerns may not do so given another.

The argument to the best explanation is the view that once we can select the best of any competing explanations of an event, we are justified in *accepting it, or even believing it. The principle needs qualification, since sometimes it is unwise to ignore the antecedent improbability of a hypothesis which would explain the data better than others: e.g. the best explanation of a coin falling heads 530 times in 1000 tosses might be that it is biased to give a probability of heads of 0·53, but it might be more sensible to suppose that it is fair, or to suspend judgement.

explication Most generally, a synonym for *explanation. More specifically, the explication of a concept is the process of revealing its nature without giving an explicit definition, but for instance by describing its function or otherwise placing it on the intellectual map.

exploitation Originally the term has no moral connotations, referring simply to the use or development of resources. In moral and political philosophy it now applies specifically to the unjust economic and social relationships whereby one class can abuse the labour of others. To characterize a relationship as exploitative thus presupposes a negative moral verdict on its justice.

exportation An *operator is exported from a place within a sentence if it is repositioned so that the whole of the rest of the sentence is within its scope. This may or may not give an equivalent sentence. 'When they come, they frequently dine' is equivalent to 'frequently, when they come they dine', in which 'frequently' has been exported. But 'when they dine, they are amazingly sick' is not equivalent to 'amazingly, when they dine they are sick'. Illicit exportation can easily give rise to *fallacies. *See also* SCOPE.

expression An utterance expresses a thought; a cry expresses grief or pain; a poem may express nostalgia or energy. The simplest view would be that any action that makes public or communicates a state of mind thereby expresses it. However, a mere signal seems not to express what it signals, and a mere statement ('I feel nostalgic about the sixties') does not express nostalgia in the way that a poem does. It seems that expression requires some concept of the action being an adequate or successful rendering of what is expressed. The words or other actions should somehow fit the states they express. The problem is to understand this conception of fit.

In aesthetic theory, a popular view is that a work of art derives its effect by expressing the feelings of its creator. The view that this is their value was forcibly presented by *Croce and *Collingwood and probably strikes many artists as correct. It raises the problem of the existence, and nature, of these feelings before they take shape in words, painting, or whatever other medium is chosen. In *The Principles of Art* (1938), Collingwood insisted that true artistic activity takes place 'in the head', before anything is embodied in the actual medium of the artist. The creation of an artwork is then just a matter of craft, following on the real creative moment. This theory is a manifestation of *Romanticism, in that the artist is now singled out as the person of extraordinary feeling or sensibility, rather than the person of particular skills. The view can be seen as a vindication of expressionism in art, as seen in the use of exaggeration and distortion for emotional effect. But it requires undue confidence in the idea of a determinate (and interesting) inner life with its own properties, existing independently of any actual externalization. If expression is to retain a central place in aesthetic theory, a closer connection between what is expressed and the nature of the work expressing it is needed. Thus a musical movement expresses feeling not just because someone with a feeling hit upon it as a good movement to write, but because the feeling is an appropriate or fitting response to the work. The actual feelings of the artist are then no longer central, and the success of the work does not depend upon its relationship to any such previous episode as the artist feeling sad or happy. The problem for aesthetics remains that of understanding why particular sounds may be sad or funny, or why particular lines or colours in a painting can be energetic or graceful.

expressivism Term used for those theories of ethical discourse that contrast ethical sentences with expressions of belief. Such theories locate the primary function of ethical sentences in the expression of attitudes, emotions, or other practical states, or in the issuing of commands, or the putting of pressure on action (*see* PRESCRIPTIVISM). The older term covering much of the ground was 'emotivism', but this doctrine became linked with naive views about the state of mind expressed, and naive views about the consequences of the theory for notions such as truth and objectivity. *See also* PROJECTIVISM, QUASI-REALISM.

extensionality, axiom of Basic axiom of *set theory. It asserts that sets are identical if and only if they have the same members.

extension/intension The extension of a predicate is the class of objects that it describes: the extension of 'red' is the class of red things. The intension is the principle under which it picks them out, or in other words the condition a thing must satisfy to be truly described by the predicate. Two predicates ('... is a rational animal', '... is a naturally featherless biped') might pick out the same class but they do so by a different condition. If the notions are extended to other items, then the extension of a sentence is its truth-value, and its intension a thought or proposition; and the extension of a singular term is the object referred to by it, if it so refers, and its intension is the concept by means of which the object is picked out. A sentence puts a predicate or other term in an extensional context if any other predicate or term with the same extension can be substituted without it being possible that the truth-value changes: if John is a rational animal, and we substitute the co-extensive 'is a naturally featherless biped', then John is a naturally featherless biped. Other contexts, such as 'Mary believes that John is a rational animal', may not allow the substitution, and are called intensional contexts.

externalism 1. In the philosophy of mind and language, the view that what is thought, or said, or experienced, is essentially dependent on aspects of the world external to the mind of the subject. The view goes beyond holding that such mental states are typically caused by external factors, to insist that they could not have existed as they now do without the subject being embedded in an external world of a certain kind. It is these external relations that make up the *essence or identity of the mental state. Externalism is thus opposed to the *Cartesian separation of the mental from the physical, since that holds that the mental could in principle exist as it does even if there were no external world at all. Various external factors have been advanced as ones on which mental content depends, including the usage of experts, the linguistic norms of the community, and the general causal relationships of the subject. *See also* CONTENT, WIDE AND NARROW; TWIN-EARTH. **2.** In the theory of knowledge, externalism is the view that a person might know something by being suitably situated with respect to it, without that relationship being in any sense within his purview. The person might, for example, be very reliable in some respect without believing that he is. The view allows that you can know without being justified in believing that you know. *See also* RELIABILISM.

external relations *See* RELATIONS, INTERNAL/EXTERNAL.

external world The everyday world of places and things that we perceive, move amongst, and act upon. The word 'external' suggests, misleadingly in the opinion of many philosophers, that this world is separated from the world of the mind, so that our immediate experience is one thing, and the question of the nature of the world of which it is an experience is another thing. This is commonly called a *Cartesian picture of the mind, and has been the target of many epistemologists, especially since the middle of the 20th century. *See also* EXPERIENCE, PERCEPTION.

extrasensory perception *See* PARANORMAL.

extrinsic properties *See* INTRINSIC/EXTRINSIC.

extrinsic value The value something has only in so far as it is conducive to something else; the opposite of intrinsic value.

fa Chinese, law, punishment, custom, discipline, duty. Also specifically the Law taught by the *Buddha.

fact *Wittgenstein wrote that the world was the totality of facts, not of things. But although facts have the nice solid ring about them that opposes them to such things as values or theories, they prove to be slippery items out of which to build anything. Facts seem to be shaped just like sentences: it is a fact that dogs bark and stones sink. It may also be a fact that children have rights or that sun and rain make rainbows. Modern thought has been sympathetic to a *minimalist view of the notion. On this account it is first pointed out that 'it is a fact that *p*' is the same as 'it is true that *p*', and that both reduce to simply: *p*. But if we want to know what makes it the case that *p*, it may be that there is no general answer. One kind of thing (dogs barking) makes it true that dogs bark, another kind of thing (stones sinking) makes it true that stones sink, and so on for any sentence we care to exhibit. This is not a rejection of the category of fact in favour of any kind of *relativism or *scepticism, since it is quite consistent with the view that for many examples of *p* we know whether *p*, there are no two views about *p*, and so on. But it is the denial that these assertions gain anything except perhaps rhetorical force by being couched in terms of facts. An attempt to build a more substantive theory of facts in general needs to address questions such as whether there are negative as well as positive facts, general facts as well as particular ones, facts about values as well as facts about the physical world, *dispositional and categorical facts, and so on. It will also need principles for counting facts: is the fact that I have a sister one fact or two (two people were her parents, and the same two people were my parents). The last well-known systematic philosophy of facts was the *Tractatus Logico-Philosophicus* of Wittgenstein, which depended heavily on a conception of atomic or basic facts, conceived as logically simple, independent structures in a logical space. But Wittgenstein repudiated the metaphysic in his later work. *See also* TRUTH MAKERS.

facticity The question of its facticity is whether a commitment is apt for truth, because purporting to state a fact, as opposed to having some other function. *See* EXPRESSIVISM, PROJECTIVISM, TRUTH-APT.

factive Term to describe verbs that presuppose the truth of an embedded clause: 'I remember that we were there in January'; 'He realizes that the game is up.' *See also* SUCCESS WORD.

fact/value distinction (fact/value gap) The presumed distinction between statements of fact, thought of as value-free, and statements of value. The distinction is often attributed to *Hume, and the separation of fact from value is a platitude of many academic disciplines, and particularly sociology as it was conceived by *Durkheim and *Weber. It also coheres with common sense, in so far as that regards description and evaluation as different activities. Nevertheless the distinction is heavily criticized, most fundamentally on the ground that it fails to appreciate that the perception of anything as a 'fact' may itself involve value-judgements, as may the selection of particular facts as the essential ones. For example, we may say that it is a fact that A owed B money, but that it is a value-judgement that it ought to be paid, yet the entire framework of social arrangements within which there arise such things as money and debt is itself a normative construction, and one evidently endorsed by someone claiming the former fact. In other areas, such as aesthetics, phenomenology suggests that recognizing aspects of things blurs into evaluating them. *See also* THICK TERMS.

faculty psychology The theory that the mind is divided into separate powers or faculties, such as intelligence, memory, perception, etc. The notion that these faculties were associated with distinct spatial locations in the brain gave rise to the pseudo-science of phrenology, in which bumps on the skull could be read as determining psychological characteristics. Although faculty psychology was discredited by the evident interaction of such capacities as perception and memory, a successor is the view, common in *cognitive science, that the tasks the mind and brain perform may usefully be broken down into 'modules', so that we can model the one complex system in terms of the organization of co-operating sub-systems. But the grain is much finer in the modern view: for example, a skill such as facial recognition may be considered as having many components, and certainly not involving just one faculty of 'memory'. The term is sometimes encountered as a derogatory description of the belief in certain distinctions, e.g. between judgement and feeling, or belief and attitude.

faith The conviction of the truth of some doctrine which is the result of a voluntary act of will. According to *fideists who happen to be believers in the same doctrine, this act may be meritorious (and refusal to make it may be a fault or even a *sin); according to others, it may in fact be just as sinful to ride roughshod over the deliverance of reason (itself a divine gift) when that commands us to suspend judgement.

faith, bad/good *See* BAD FAITH.

fallacy Any error of reasoning. Reasoning may fail in many ways, and a great variety of fallacies have been distinguished and named. The main division is into formal fallacies in which something purports to be deductively valid reasoning but is not, and informal fallacies in which some other mistake is made. Such mistakes may include the introduction of irrelevancies, failure to disambiguate terms, vagueness, misplaced precision, and so on. Many fallacies that have been named are here referred to under their names: *see* *ARGUMENTUM AD*...; CIRCLE, VICIOUS, FOUR-TERM FALLACY; GAMBLER'S FALLACY; *IGNORATIO ELENCHI*.

fallibilism The doctrine due to *Peirce, that it is not necessary that beliefs be certain, or grounded on certainty. We may justifiably rest content with beliefs in circumstances in which further evidence, forcing us to revise our opinion, may yet come in. Indeed, since this is always our position, unless we settle for it we shall be driven to *scepticism. The view therefore locates a position between dogmatism and scepticism.

false *See* TRUTH, TRUTH-VALUE.

false consciousness An inability to see things, especially social relations and relations of exploitation, as they really are. The term occurs in late work of *Engels, although the phenomenon is implied in *Feuerbach's account of the religious impulse. The state of false consciousness may be the inevitable result of a way of living, and characterizes the generic and chronic kind of servitude that cannot even perceive its own situation. It may therefore coexist with a kind of illusory contentment. The cure is 'consciousness-raising'. In the later writings of *Marx the concept to some extent supersedes that of *alienation.

false pleasure Either a pleasure based on a delusion, as when you are delighted because you believe you have won the lottery, when actually you have not, or a verdict of disapproval on a particular kind of pleasure, and in particular the pleasures of those who are unaware of higher things: the false pleasures of the corrupt mind or the giddy round. False pleasures are the topic of a long and complex discussion in Plato's dialogue *Philebus*.

falsidical Uncommon opposite of *veridical. A falsidical experience is one that represents things as they are not.

falsifiability The property of a statement or theory that it is capable of being refuted by experience. In the philosophy of science of *Popper falsifiability is the great merit of genuine scientific theory, as opposed to unfalsifiable pseudo-science, notably psychoanalysis and *historical materialism. Popper's idea was that it could be a positive virtue in a scientific theory that it is bold, conjectural, and goes beyond the evidence, but that it had to be capable of facing possible refutation. If each and every way things turn out is compatible with the theory, then it is no longer a scientific theory, but, for instance, an ideology or article of faith. *See also* FALSIFICATION.

falsification The central notion in the philosophy of science of *Popper, although foreshadowed by *Whewell and *Peirce. In his *Logik der Forschung* (1934), Popper argued that the central virtue of science, as opposed to pseudo-science, is not that it puts forward hypotheses that are confirmed by evidence to some high degree, but that its hypotheses are capable of being refuted by evidence. That is, they genuinely face the possibility of test and rejection through not conforming to experience. The scientific method is not, therefore, the mechanical induction of generalizations from accumulated data, but the formation of bold hypotheses that are then subjected to rigorous test: a method of conjectures and refutations. It is no fault in a scientist to put forward an interesting conjecture that is subsequently refuted, but it would be a fault to put forward one which then permits no refutation, or to hold one in the face of refuting evidence.

Popper's idea found an enthusiastic following amongst working scientists, but philosophers of science have detected gaps and oversimplifications in the story. First, by removing *induction and confirmation entirely, Popper seems to give no account of the extent to which it is rational to rely upon scientific theory in practice (for having survived tests so far is no indication of likely truth). Secondly, the actual picture of acceptance and rejection of scientific hypotheses is more complex than Popper suggests: something that one scientist regards as a refutation another might regard as an anomaly, depending on such things as the momentum of the research programme that threw up the hypothesis and the availability of alternative explanations. This blurs the difference between a scientist quite reasonably committed to some general framework of theory, such as Newtonian or relativistic physics, and the Marxists or Freudians whose pseudo-scientific pretensions were one of Popper's targets. *See also* CONFIRMATION THEORY, DEMARCATION PROBLEM, VERISIMILITUDE.

family resemblance The phenomenon stressed in his later work by *Wittgenstein, that the objects denoted by a term may be tied together not by one common property, but by a network of resemblances, like the persons whose faces share features characteristic of a family.

fancy Usually a synonym for imagination. *Coleridge distinguished between fancy, which involves a mere ability to recombine experiences, and imagination, which can invent and create.

Fanon, Frantz (1925–61) French psychologist and theorist of colonialism. Born in French Martinique, Fanon studied medicine and psychiatry in France after the Second World War. His *Peau noire, masques blancs* (1952, trs. as *Black Skin, White Masks*, 1967) analysed the deforming effect of colonialism on both black and white peoples. His best-known work, *Les Damnés de la terre* (1961, trs. as *The Wretched of the Earth*, 1964), legitimizes the *violence necessary to overthrow the established structural violence of colonialism, and had great influence on the emerging black radicalism of the following decades.

al-Farabi, Abu Nasr (Abunaser) (*c*.870–950) The 'second teacher' after *Aristotle of Islamic philosophy. al-Farabi was one of the first philosophers to transmit Aristotelian logic to the Islamic world. He wrote extensively on logic, and expanded Aristotle's description of the intellect. He also exhibits the influence of *Neoplatonism: creation is an emanation, and it is the images of the world-soul or *anima mundi* that become bodies in space. His work *The Virtuous City* is a version of Plato's *Republic*, a description of the ideal civic society in which all the virtues flourish.

Faraday, Michael (1791–1867) English scientist. The son of a blacksmith, Faraday was apprenticed to a bookbinder when he attracted the attention of Sir Humphrey Davy in 1812. His discovery of electro-magnetic 'lines of force' and his view of the atom as merely a centre of force opened up *field theory, and itself owed ancestry to the views of *Kant, and especially *Boscovich.

fascism (Latin, *fasces*, the bundle of rods and axe carried before Roman consuls as insignia of authority) The loose amalgam of aspirations and influences crystallized in the early 20th-century governments of Mussolini in Italy, Hitler in Germany, and General Franco in Spain. Elements include nationalism; hostility to ideals of equality; hatred of minorities, degenerates, and deviants; elitism; hostility towards the ideals of *liberalism, and in particular towards freedom of expression; the cult of the *charismatic leader or **Übermensch*; belief in the destiny of the race; and a love of political symbolism such as uniforms and other emblems of militarism. The whole cocktail is animated by a belief in regeneration through energy and struggle.

fatalism The doctrine that what will be will be, or that human action has no influence on events. 'Either a bullet has my number on it or it does not; if it does, then there is no point taking precautions for it will kill me anyhow; if it does not then there is no point taking precautions for it is not going to kill me; hence either way there is no point taking precautions.' The dilemma ignores the highly likely possibility that whether the bullet has your number on it depends on whether you take precautions. Fatalism is wrongly confused with *determinism, which by itself carries no implications that human action is ineffectual.

Fechner, Gustav Theodor (1801–87) German psychophysicist, and one of the founders of experimental psychology. Fechner studied physiology, but turned to physics which he taught at Leipzig. Philosophically Fechner defended a monism in which the world can be seen in one way physically and in the other mentally (his analogy was with a line that from one point of view traces a convex curve; from another a concave curve). Experimentally he sought to confirm this insight by discovering close quantitative relationships between conscious experience and physiological stimulus, eventually discovering the law that the intensity of a sensation increases as the log of the stimulus ($S = k \log R$) characterizing psychophysical relations. His *Element der Psychophysik* (1860) is often supposed to mark the beginning of experimental psychology.

federalism A political system in which power is vested in an association of constituents, rather than in a central government set over and above them. *The Federalist Papers* were a series of articles written under the pen name of Publius by Alexander Hamilton, James Madison, and John Jay, between 1787 and 1788, in order to gain popular support for the then-proposed Constitution of the United States.

feeling *See* EMOTION, EXPRESSION, PERCEPTION, SENSATION.

felicific calculus The possibility of computing the value of 'units' of happiness, associated with the *utilitarianism of *Bentham. Happiness, or the end of action, is to be measured in terms of units of *pleasure. These are ordered by intensity, duration, and propinquity, although the value of particular pleasures may be discounted by the probable quantity and quality of pleasures or pains to which they are a means. The total is supposed to provide an objective framework with which the comparative value of different courses of action can be measured.

felicity conditions In *speech act theory, the conditions that make an utterance a happy contribution to the exchange. These may include quite sensitive aspects of the dynamics of the conversation, the relationships of the participants, and so on. An action may be infelicitous without being the saying of something false: it may be irrelevant, or ill-mannered, or baffling in its intent. *See also* IMPLICATURE.

feminism The approach to social life, philosophy, and *ethics that commits itself to correcting biases leading to the subordination of women or the disparagement of women's particular experience and of the voices women bring to discussion. Contemporary feminist ethics is sensitive to the *gender bias that may be implicit in philosophical theories (for instance, philosophers' lists of virtues may be typically 'manly' or culturally masculine), and in social structures, legal and political procedures, and the general culture. One controversial claim (influentially made in Carol Gilligan, *In a Different Voice: Psychological Theory and Women's Development*, 1982) is that women approach practical reasoning from a different perspective from that of men. The difference includes emphasis on community, caring, and bonding with particular individuals, in place of abstract impartiality. It is controversial whether or not this is a real difference, and if so whether it arises from innate differences in male and female psychology, or whether the different values reflect the way men and women have been taught to form different aspirations and ideals.

Feminist epistemology has asked whether different ways of knowing, for instance with different criteria of justification, and different emphases on logic and imagination, characterize male and female attempts to understand the world. Such concerns include awareness of the 'masculine' self-image, itself a socially variable and potentially distorting picture of what thought and action should be. A particular target of much feminist epistemology is a *Kantian or *Enlightenment conception of rationality, which is seen as a device for claiming mastery and control, and for refusing to acknowledge differing perspectives and different relations to life and nature. Although extreme claims have been made, such as that logic is a phallic and patriarchal device for coercing other people, it is still unclear how differences between individual capacities, training, and culturally reinforced aspirations, work together in explaining how people acquire knowledge. Again there is a spectrum of concern, from the highly theoretical to the relatively practical. In this latter area particular attention is given to the institutional biases that stand in the way of equal opportunities in science and other academic pursuits, or the ideologies that stand in the way of women seeing themselves as leading contributors to various disciplines. However, to more radical feminists such concerns merely exhibit women wanting for themselves the same power and rights over others that men have claimed, and failing to confront the real problem, which is how to live without such asymmetrical powers and rights. *See also* ESSENTIALISM.

feminist ethics *See* FEMINISM.

Fénelon, François de Salignac de la Mothe (1651–1715) Much admired French theologian and writer. As tutor to the Duke of Burgundy, he wrote *Télémaque* (1699), holding up Ulysses as an example for the young prince. Other writings include a treatise (1687) on female education, and *Explications des maximes des saints* (1697), mystical instructions in faith for which Fénelon was banished. His quietism brought a long quarrel with his former patron Bossuet, which was settled in 1699 when Pope Innocent XII condemned Fénelon. His *Refutation of Malebranche* was a relatively young work; as a philosopher he was influenced by Augustine and Descartes, but is notable for the charm of his writing rather than originality or precision of thought.

feng shui In Chinese thought, a system of laws considered to govern spatial arrangement and orientation in relation to flow of energy (**chi*), and whose favourable and unfavourable effects are taken into account when designing and siting buildings.

Ferguson, Adam (1723–1816) Scottish philosopher of the Enlightenment, and often regarded as a pioneer of sociology. Adam Ferguson was educated at St Andrews and became a chaplain of the Black Watch Highlander regiment (he fought at the battle of Fontenoy in 1745). Gradually losing his faith, Ferguson succeeded David

*Hume in 1757 as librarian to the Faculty of Advocates in Edinburgh. He held successive chairs at the University of Edinburgh, first in Natural Philosophy (1759), then in Moral Philosophy and Pneumatics (1764). In 1767, Ferguson published his most important work, the *Essay on Civil Society*. It was a 'natural' history of the progress of mankind, along the lines that had been pursued by many Enlightenment philosophers, particularly David Hume. However, Hume himself disliked Ferguson's work, regarding it as 'superficial'. Ferguson followed Hume in describing the gradual emergence of civil order by spontaneous processes rather than design, but he had a more pessimistic view of human nature than most Enlightenment thinkers. Ferguson resigned from his chair in 1785 (succeeded by his student, Dugald *Stewart). He published his collected lectures, advocating a Stoic *perfectionism, in 1792.

Feuerbach, Ludwig Andreas (1804–72) German philosopher and anthropologist. Born in Landshut, Bavaria, Feuerbach studied theology and philosophy at Heidelberg and Berlin. He enjoyed only a sporadic teaching career, and lived mainly on income derived from his wife's interest in a pottery factory. His philosophical writings were fired by a perception that *Hegel's system had failed to shake itself free from crippling rationalistic and religious elements. It is therefore itself but a stage in the true emergence of self-consciousness, in a humanistic, scientific, 'philosophy of the future'. Feuerbach's chequered career was the outcome of his conviction that religion is a 'dream of the human mind', or an understandable but distorting projection of our emotional needs: 'Christ is the love of mankind for itself embodied in an image.' This sceptical and anthropological approach to religion is indeed similar in spirit to that of *Hume and *Voltaire, but proved more explosive in the religious and absolutist atmosphere of the mid-19th century. Feuerbach stands for opposition to any philosophical system-building in favour of an empirical study of the way persons respond to the world and to each other. His aphorism, 'man is what he eats', became a useful political slogan for subsequent radicals. Ethically Feuerbach believed that human relations vindicate a close, communitarian spirit in which divisions between 'I' and 'thou' become dissolved. His early writings include many contributions to the *Hallesche Jahrbücher* of which he was joint editor, and which had a decisive influence on the development of secular and political, or left-wing, *Hegelianism. His most important work was *Das Wesen des Christentums* (1846), which was translated by the scholar and novelist George Eliot as *The Essence of Christianity* (1854). Eliot was paid two shillings a page. She herself was more taken with Feuerbach's impassioned descriptions of self-sacrificing, sacred, self-sufficing, and spontaneous love than with his humanism. *Marx's *Theses on Feuerbach* combines an appreciation of Feuerbach's dialectical upstaging of Hegel with recognition that Feuerbach himself falls short of properly resolving self-consciousness, and its religious projections, into fundamental social and economic forces. *Engels said of Feuerbach that the lower half of him was *materialistic, but the upper half an *idealist.

SEE WEB LINKS

- A list of resources on Feuerbach, including bibliographies
- Translations of Feuerbach's writings

Feyerabend, Paul Karl (1924–94) Austrian philosopher of science. Born in Vienna, Feyerabend was educated at the university of Vienna, and became a philosopher of science under the influence of *Popper. During his career he taught at a variety of universities, becoming emeritus professor at Berkeley. He was notorious for his scepticism about the rationality of science. He held that success is achieved by scientists as the consequence of politics, rhetoric, and propaganda, rather than because of their advancement of our objective knowledge of the world. Books included *Against Method* (1975) and *Farewell to Reason* (1987).

Fichte, Johann Gottlieb (1762–1814) German *idealist. Educated in theology then philosophy at Jena, Fichte became known partly because his first book, published anonymously in Königsberg, was mistakenly attributed to *Kant. This was his *Versuch einer Kritik aller Offenbarung* (1792, trs. as the *Critique of All Revelation*), a celebration of the sovereignty of the moral law, on the strength of which he gained a chair at Jena. His combination of rigorous moralism, support for the French revolution, and *Spinozistic downgrading of revealed religion led to the kind of controversy that Fichte seemed to attract: he both unwisely tried to suppress the student fraternities, and by lecturing on Sundays alienated the local clergy. Fichte's belief that God is identical with the moral world order, even if this is in turn the ground of all cognition and the 'only absolutely valid objective reality', seemed little more than atheism, and in 1799 the *Atheismusstreit* or academic row over this issue involved many contemporary German thinkers, and culminated in his effectual dismissal from Jena.

Metaphysically Fichte was the first to strip the transcendental element from Kant, arguing that consciousness is the sole ground for the explanation of experience, and that all consciousness directed towards anything else has consciousness directed towards itself as its origin. This was conjoined with Kant's conception of the moral life as an infinite pursuit of an unattainable goal, so that all existence becomes the insatiable striving of the ego, which posits the external world as an obstacle to its own completion. This dynamic, active *idealism, coupled with the elevation of self-consciousness, laid the groundwork for *Hegel, and can be seen as an early transition from the philosophy of Kant to that of *absolute idealism. Fichte's work is well seen in *Bestimmung des Menschen* (1800, trs. as *The Vocation of Man*, 1848); his *Reden an die Deutsche Nation* (1807–8, trs. as *Addresses to the German Nation*, 1922) is sometimes cited as one of the first expressions of nationalistic totalitarianism.

SEE WEB LINKS

- A list of internet resources on Fichte
- Translations of Fichte's writings

Ficino, Marsilio (1433–99) The main representative of *Platonism and *Neoplatonism in Renaissance Florence, and the founder and head of the *Academy of Florence. In 1484 his complete translation of *Plato's dialogues was published. Ficino's commentaries and translations influenced the interpretation of Plato and *Plotinus until the 19th century, when the extent to which they were in turn influenced by other sources began to be disentangled. His commentary on Plato's *Symposium* is said to be the source of the common phrase 'Platonic love', in the sense of love that does not seek sexual expression, but contents itself with appreciation of the *forms that the beloved instances.

fiction The human propensity for making up stories exposes a strange fact about our minds. Apparently we can become embroiled in the fate of the characters, feel emotions including fear on their behalf or pity or terror, while with one half of our minds we know it is all fictional. It is not only that we do this, but also that we find it important to do it, even when the emotions themselves would normally be unpleasant (*see* TRAGEDY). Apart from raising this problem, fiction gives rise to purely logical and semantic issues. How do we succeed in referring to fictional characters, and is reference the right word when we are representing to ourselves something that does not exist? And what is covered by the idea of truth in fiction, such as the truth that Sherlock Holmes lived in London and not in Paris?

fictionalism *See* VAIHINGER.

fictional names *See* FICTION.

fideism A view that is pessimistic about the role of reason in achieving knowledge of things divine, and that emphasizes instead the merit of acts of *faith.

fides quaerens intellectum Latin, faith seeking understanding.

field A central concept of physical theory. A field is defined by the distribution of a physical quantity, such as temperature, mass density, or potential energy, at different points in space. In the particularly important example of force fields, such as gravitational, electrical, and magnetic fields, the field value at a point is the force which a test particle would experience if it were located at that point. The philosophical problem is whether a force field is to be thought of as purely potential, so the presence of a field merely describes the propensity of masses to move relative to each other, or whether it should be thought of in terms of the physically real modifications of a medium whose properties result in such powers. That is, are force fields purely potential, fully characterized by *dispositional statements or conditionals, or are they categorical or actual? The former option seems to require faith in ungrounded dispositions, or regions of space that differ only in what happens *if* an object is placed there. The law-like shape of these dispositions, apparent for example in the curved lines of force of the magnetic field, may then seem quite inexplicable. To *atomists such as Newton it would represent a return to Aristotelian *entelechies, or quasi-psychological affinities between things, which are responsible for their motions (*see* MOVER, UNMOVED). The latter option requires understanding how forces of attraction and repulsion can be 'grounded' in the properties of the medium.

The basic idea of a field is arguably present in *Leibniz, who was certainly hostile to Newtonian atomism, although his equal hostility to *action at a distance muddies the waters. It is usually credited to *Boscovich and *Kant, both of whom influenced the scientist *Faraday, with whose work the physical notion became established. In his paper 'On the Physical Character of the Lines of Magnetic Force' (1852), Faraday suggests several criteria for assessing the physical reality of lines of force, such as whether they are affected by an intervening material medium, whether they take time to propagate, and how the motion depends on the nature of what is placed at the receiving end. As far as electromagnetic fields go, Faraday himself inclined to the view that the mathematical similarity between heat flow, currents, and electromagnetic lines of force was evidence for the physical reality of the intervening medium.

field theory, quantum The extension of the ideas of *quantum mechanics to deal not with individual particles but with *fields, such as the electromagnetic field.

figure *See* SYLLOGISM.

Filmer, Robert (1588–1653) Filmer is mainly remembered as the target of the *Two Treatises of Government* by *Locke. He was a country gentleman of Kent, whose *Patriarcha* (1630) rests political obligation to the state on its divinely ordained authority, descending to current royalty from the patriarchal sovereignty that Adam was given over his family. In spite of Locke's description of the doctrine as 'glib nonsense', it formed an important object of concern to him.

final cause *See* CAUSES: MATERIAL, FORMAL, EFFICIENT, FINAL.

finitary methods *See* FINITISM.

finite set Intuitively, a *set whose count stops somewhere. Formally, a set whose members can be put into a one-to-one correspondence with the members of the set of all natural numbers less than some given number.

finitism In the philosophy of mathematics, the view that the only legitimate numbers are finite: 'God created the integers, the rest is the work of man' (L. Kronecker). In mathematics the restriction to finitary methods was advocated by David Hilbert. It shares with *constructivism the view that one cannot assert the existence of a mathematical object without indicating how to construct it. It adds the principle that one should never deal with the set of all the objects of an infinite totality. That a theorem holds for all members of such a set simply means that for any particular member of the set one can repeat the argument.

finkish Term due to the contemporary Canadian philosopher C. B. Martin, to describe powers with the uncomfortable habit of failing to operate just as the occasion for their manifestation comes about. Thus intuitively a glass might be fragile, but also be protected by a guardian angel, who steps in and saves it when some accident is about to break it. So no normal manifestation of fragility ever arises. The possibility of finkish properties (or finkish situations) casts doubt on the plausible equation between an object having a *dispositional property, and it being true that if such and such a situation arises, the normal exhibition of that property follows.

first cause argument One of the classic arguments for the existence of God. Every event in the natural world has a preceding cause. But this opens up a regress of causes stretching back forever in time. To stop the regress we must postulate a first cause, and this will be the creative action of God. *Russell supposed that the argument is uniquely bad, in that the conclusion (that there is a first cause) actually contradicts the premise (that every event has a preceding cause). To avoid his complaint a proponent of the argument must distinguish between natural events and unnatural or supernatural events. The former all require causes, but the latter may be their own cause. God is **causa sui*. The difficulty then lies in seeing why the natural world should not be *causa sui*. The argument inherits the problems of the *cosmological argument, of which it is a variant.

first-order language A language in which the *quantifiers contain only variables ranging over individuals and the *functions have as their arguments only individual variables or constants. In a second-order language the variables of the quantifiers may range over functions, properties, relations, and classes of objects, and in yet higher-order languages over properties of properties.

first-order logic The study of inference in *first-order languages.

first philosophy In Aristotle's *Metaphysics*, the study of being, or being in itself. In *Descartes's *Meditations on First Philosophy*, the topics include scepticism, the existence of God, and the nature of the soul. The idea that the methods of philosophy should be continuous with those of science, or that there is no 'privileged' philosophical perspective on other disciplines, is frequently expressed as hostility to first philosophy.

first principles The principles that lie at the basis of an enquiry. The first principles of one phase of enquiry have a nasty habit of being rejected at other stages. *See* *A PRIORI*, AXIOM, DATUM.

Five Ways, the The ways of demonstrating the existence of God formulated by *Aquinas (*Summa Theologiae*, Ia 3: it is important in understanding the significance of these arguments to Aquinas that the entire context stretches from Ia 2 to 11). They are: (1) Motion is only explicable if there exists an unmoved, first mover; (2) the chain of efficient causes demands a first cause; (3) the contingent character of existing things in the world demands a different order of existence, or in other words something that has a necessary existence; (4) the gradations of value in things in the world require the existence of something that is most valuable, or perfect; (5) the orderly character of events points to a final cause, or end to which all things are directed, and the existence of this end demands a being that ordained it. All the arguments are *physico-theological arguments.

The second is a *first cause argument, and the first is the *Aristotelian variety of it (accepted by *Averroës) that singles out the causes of motion as particularly in need of a starting-point (*see* MOVER, UNMOVED). The third is a variety of the *cosmological argument, as it had been formulated by *Avicenna (but rejected by Averroës). The fourth is the *degrees of perfection argument. The fifth is a version of the argument from (or to) *design.

SEE WEB LINKS

- A list of internet resources on the Five Ways
- Translated extracts on the Five Ways from the *Summa Theologiae*

f

flaccid designator Jocular contrast with *rigid designator: a term such as a *definite description that may be satisfied by different things in different *possible worlds.

Fludd, Robert (1574–1637) British alchemist and Rosicrucian. A follower of *Paracelsus, Fludd dabbled in philosophical system-building incorporating arcane knowledge and mystical speculation. His works include *Tractatus Theologo-philosophicus* (1617) and *Philosophia Moysaica* (1638).

flux, doctrine of The view attributed to *Heraclitus that all things flow: everything is in change, nothing abides.

flying arrow paradox *See* ZENO'S PARADOXES.

Fodor, Jerry Alan (1935–) American philosopher of mind. Born in New York city and educated at Columbia and Princeton, Fodor teaches at Rutgers and the City University of New York. He is known for a resolute *realism about the nature of mental functioning. Taking the analogy between thought and computation seriously, Fodor believes that mental representations should be conceived as individual states with their own identities and structures, like formulae transformed by processes of computation or thought. His views are frequently contrasted with those of *holists such as *Davidson, or *instrumentalists about mental ascription, such as *Dennett. In recent years he has become a vocal critic of some of the aspirations of cognitive science. Works include *The Language of Thought* (1975), *The Modularity of Mind* (1983), *Psychosemantics* (1987), *The Elm and the Expert* (1994), *Concepts: Where Cognitive Science Went Wrong* (1998), and *Hume Variations* (2003).

folk psychology Originally a disparaging term, now widely used, for the process of attributing thoughts, beliefs, intentions, and meanings to each other (the 'folk' referred to include such masters of human understanding as Shakespeare and Tolstoy, as well as the rest of us). The term arises from unease that ordinary processes of attribution do not seem 'scientific', and the categories they use fit with difficulty into the categories of physical science (*see* BRENTANO'S THESIS). Often the term invites contrast with a supposed future when there will be a science whose terms will quite eclipse the categories with which we normally describe each other, perhaps by being more comprehensive, less vague, and better matched to a scientific understanding of ourselves. *See also* ELIMINATIVISM, REDUCTIONISM.

follow The essential virtue of a valid argument is that the *conclusion should follow from the premises. This is equivalent to the premises *entailing the conclusion, and usually although not unanimously equated with it being impossible that the premises should be true and the conclusion false. *See* LOGIC, PROOF, STRICT IMPLICATION, VALIDITY.

Fontenelle, Bernard Le Bovier de (1657–1757) French man of letters, polymath, and philosopher. Educated by Jesuits, he settled in Paris, where from 1699 he was permanent secretary of the Academy of Sciences, and as such a considerable influence on the French Enlightenment and the *encyclopedists. The *Entretiens sur la pluralité des mondes* (*Conversations on the Plurality of Worlds*, 1686) was not an anticipation of *possible worlds semantics, but a popular account of the *Copernican world system and the mechanics of *Descartes. Fontenelle represented a cautious but sceptical attitude to the superstitions of myth and religion, and was venerated as their first ancestor by subsequent **philosophes*.

Foot, Philippa (1920–) British moral philosopher. Foot was one of the philosophers responsible for the turn away from emotivism and *prescriptivism among many Oxford philosophers of the 1960s and later. By complicating or denying a fact/value distinction, she found room for a sophisticated kind of *ethical naturalism. This is a version of an *Aristotelian ethic in which the nature of human beings is itself a determinant of their good. Her approach requires firm connections between virtue, rationality, and self-interest, and critics have doubted whether the liaisons are as firm as she may need. Works include numerous papers, the collection *Virtues and Vices* (1978), and her first actual book, *Natural Goodness* (2001).

Fordyce, David (1711–51) Scottish moral philosopher, and professor at Aberdeen. His *Dialogues Concerning Education* (1745–8) were described by an anonymous biographer as 'somewhat tinged by the fopperies of the school of

Shaftesbury, although entirely free from its more injurious notions'. He was best known for his *The Elements of Moral Philosophy* (1754).

foreknowledge The ability to predict events before they occur. Traditionally God's foreknowledge, apparently guaranteed by his omniscience, raises severe problems both about the fixedness of the future, and about whether it can co-exist with our *free will.

forensic Pertaining to or connected with courts of law. Thus forensic medicine is medicine in its relation to law. In the *Essay*, Bk II. 27, *Locke describes 'person' as a forensic term, meaning that the point of describing something as a person, or finding that the same person was present on two different occasions, is essentially the attribution of responsibility. Thus if an octogenarian is found to be the same person as the twenty-year-old prison guard of sixty years ago, then he can be held responsible for the crimes of the latter; otherwise not.

forgery A sharp way of raising some of the problems of *aesthetic theory is to ask why fakes and forgeries, however good, are typically valued much less highly than originals. The difference may seem to be a snobbish and insignificant by-product of the art market, or on the other hand a manifestation of the belief that a work done by a superior artist will, somewhere, have a significance greater than that of an inferior one, however similar it may currently seem to our eyes.

forgiveness To forgive someone is to forswear resentment, anger, or other reactions to their having done something that justifies such responses. The philosophical problem is that this is apparently treating them better than they deserve; but how can it be a requirement, or even be permissible, to treat someone in any other way than as they deserve? The advice of *Augustine that we hate the sin but not the sinner, also suggests an objective or impersonal attitude towards the sinner, as if the character of the agent is only accidentally connected with the hatefulness of his or her actions, and it has been argued, notably by *Strawson, that this objective stance is inconsistent with full recognition of the personhood of others.

forgiveness, paradox of If only people who deserve to be forgiven ought to be forgiven, then forgiveness is either unjustified, in the case of the undeserving, or pointless, since in the case of those who deserve forgiveness, there is nothing to forgive. So justified forgiveness for real transgressions is impossible. Yet it is often asked for, and given, and in some ethical systems it may even be required of us that we forgive transgressors.

form, substantial In Aristotelian thought, the structure or nature that is imposed upon undifferentiated **materia prima* to make the different kinds of substance in the world. *See also* HYLOMORPHISM, MATTER.

formal cause *See* CAUSES: MATERIAL, FORMAL, EFFICIENT, FINAL.

formal implication In a *logical calculus, one proposition A formally implies another B if there is a *proof starting from A as an assumption and ending with B.

formalism, legal *See* LAW, PHILOSOPHY OF.

formalism, logical **1.** Another term for a *logical calculus. **2.** In the philosophy of mathematics, a formalist holds that mathematical statements are to be thought of as uninterpreted strings of symbols. Mathematics has a syntax but no semantics. The formalism is useful only in enabling us to pass from some observations to other empirical conclusions, but it introduces no subject-matter of its own. The position is widely thought to be inadequate to the use of numbers in the empirical procedures of counting and measuring. A modified formalism may hold that some numerical statements (for example, those involving only finite numbers and finite classes of them) are interpretable, whereas the rest of classical mathematics is a kind of *black box, or purely formal machine for taking us from some interpretable statements to others. An example would be the use of imaginary numbers in calculations designed to get us to useful real numbers, but not themselves thought of as corresponding to any physical magnitudes.

formalism in art The doctrine especially associated with the critics Clive Bell and Roger Fry in the early 20th century, that it is the arrangement or structure of its elements rather than their representational content that gives value to a work of art.

formal language *See* FORMAL SYSTEM, LOGICAL CALCULUS.

formally, virtually, and eminently In *scholastic terminology, an effect is contained formally in a cause, when the same nature in the effect is present in the cause: fire causes heat, and the heat is present in the fire. An effect is virtually in a cause when this is not so, as when a pot or statue is caused by an artist. An effect is eminently in a cause when the cause is more perfect than the effect: God eminently contains the perfections of his creation. The distinctions are part of the view that causation is essentially a matter of transferring something, like passing on the baton in a relay race.

formal/material mode of speech A distinction that assumed great importance in the work of *Carnap, particularly in his *Logical Syntax of Language* (1934). In the material mode of speech objects and their relations are the topic; in the formal mode, language itself is mentioned. The distinction thus corresponds to the *use/mention distinction. But for Carnap the background is the 'quasisyntactical sentence', in which features disguised as properties of objects are actually syntactic in character. Thus 'five is a number' is the material mode of what can be put in the formal mode as '"five" is a number-word'. Revealing the statement as basically syntactic in character removes the appearance of a deep logical or metaphysical truth. The cluster of ideas represents Carnap's belief that the logic of science is in fact nothing but the syntax of the language of science. The device of making a sentence the topic, instead of what the sentence purports to refer to, is sometimes referred to as semantic ascent. Correspondingly semantic descent is the move from an assertion about the application of a piece of language to use of that piece of language itself: the shift from '"five" is a number-word' to 'five is a number'. Although many writers see semantic ascent and descent as moves that can be freely used, others worry about the shifts of meaning involved. There is a deal of difference between, for instance, allowing that it is a conventional matter that 'five' is a number-word, and taking it to be a conventional matter that five is a number. *See also* DISQUOTATIONAL THEORY OF TRUTH.

formal system (formal theory) A theory whose sentences are *well-formed formulae of a *logical calculus, and in which *axioms or rules governing particular terms correspond to the principles of the theory being formalized. The theory is said to be couched or framed in the language of a calculus, e.g. first-order *predicate calculus. *Set theory, mathematics, mechanics, and many other sciences may be developed formally, thereby making possible logical analysis of such matters as the independence of various axioms, and the relations between one theory and another.

formation rules The formation rules of a *logical calculus or formal language lay down which sequences of expressions are to count as *well formed. Typically these rules are *recursive in character, and contain three kinds of clauses. There will be rules defining a class of basic or *atomic well-formed formulae; then rules allowing that well-formed formulae may be made out of others by specific operations. Finally there is a closure condition, or rule saying that anything not generated by the first two kinds of rule is disallowed.

form of life Expression used by *Wittgenstein to denote the habitual activities and responses which form the background to any use of language. The emphasis shifts from thinking of language as a given system of signs, to the activities of agents who do things with their language. For example, instead of thinking of arithmetic simply as a device for describing numbers, it should be placed in activities such as counting and measuring. The shift in emphasis can be an encouragement to *pragmatism in place of *representationalism.

forms The theory of forms is probably the most characteristic, and most contested of the doctrines of *Plato. In the background lie the *Pythagorean conception of form as the key to physical nature, but also the sceptical doctrine associated with *Cratylus (said by *Aristotle to have been one of the teachers of Plato) that in the heaving confusion of the perceptible world nothing is fixed, so thought can gain no foothold and nothing can be said. In escaping from this impasse Plato attempts to present a way in which the forms of things are intelligible but abstract shared features. Ordinary things gain their natures by either 'imitating' forms (which then become thought of as transcendent and somehow independent of the sensible world) or 'participating' in them (in which case they are immanent, present in things, and perhaps less mysterious). The train of thought is illustrated with both geometrical and ethical examples. The plate that the potter makes is not itself perfectly round, but perfect roundness is an ideal. It may not be found in the world, but it is something to which things approximate, and it plays a role in rendering intelligible the world in which they do so. Similarly actual human institutions may only approximate to the ideal of justice, but the ideal or form provides an intelligible dimension of description and criticism. Of course, to apply it means having the special knowledge of the geometer, in the case of roundness, or of the thinker who has attained knowledge of what justice consists in, in the case of ethics. Knowledge of the forms thus becomes itself an ideal towards which philosophers strive (*see* LINE, IMAGE OF THE). It is this line of thought that ends up with Plato echoing the *Eleatic distinction between the real world, in this case the world of the forms, accessible only to the intellect, and the deceptive world of unstable perception and mere *doxa* or belief. The world of forms is itself unchanging, as change implies development towards the realization of form. But whereas *Parmenides thinks of the real, eternal world as a kind of physical world, in Plato it becomes entirely non-physical.

The transcendental element in Plato's thought is most visible in the *Symposium*, the *Phaedo*, and the *Republic*. The problem of interpretation is however confused by the question of whether Socrates' voice is also that of Plato (again, according to Aristotle, *Metaphysics* M, xiii. 1078 b, Socrates did not make universals separate, but others, i.e. Plato, did). In the later dialogue *Parmenides*, Plato squarely confronts the problems of thinking of forms either as transcending particular things (*see* THIRD MAN ARGUMENT), or as partaken of by particular things, and therefore divisible. What is needed is an accommodation between the idea that universals are present in particulars, and the idea that they are merely imitated by them. *See also* CONCEPTUALISM, NOMINALISM, UNIVERSALS.

forms of argument Two arguments may be of the same form although their components concern different things. 'All men are mortal, Socrates is a man, so Socrates is mortal' has the same form as 'All dogs are greedy, Sandy is a dog, so Sandy is greedy.' *Logic is the science of isolating these forms, and systematizing the ones that are *valid and the ones that are not.

Forrester's paradox *See* GENTLE MURDER, PARADOX OF.

Foucault, Michel (1926–84) French historian and philosopher. Born in Poitiers, Foucault was educated at the École Normale Supérieure in Paris, taught in Germany, Sweden, and Algiers, and held chairs at Clermont-Ferrand and Vincennes, before being appointed professor of the history of systems of thought at the Collège de France. His work ranged widely across history, philosophy, psychoanalysis, and linguistics, and was extremely influential in raising new questions about the historical character of the categories of social experience. Foucault had a special interest in the use of science and reason as instruments of *power, in domains such as medicine and criminology. His earliest work, *Folie et déraison* (1961, trs. as *Madness and Civilization*, 1965), charted western attitudes to the insane, and had an enormous influence in diagnosing what might seem to be progressive and humane improvements in treatment as one aspect of increasing social and political control. Indeed, his perception of all social relations as fundamentally relationships of power, and usually infused with a generous amount of sadism, has led to it being said that he replaced the distinction between subject and object with that between subject and abject. Foucault's own life sometimes luridly reflected this enthusiasm, contributing to his death as an early victim of AIDS. Subsequent works included *Les Mots et les choses* (1966, trs. as *The Order of Things*, 1970), *L'Archéologie du savoir* (1969, trs. as *The Archaeology of Knowledge*, 1972), *Surveiller et punir* (1975, trs. as *Discipline and Punish*, 1977), and the three-volume *Histoire de la sexualité* (1976–88, trs. as *History of Sexuality*, 1979–88), whose final volumes were completed just before his death.

SEE WEB LINKS

- Foucault explains his philosophical aims and methods
- A list of internet resources on Foucault, including a bibliography

Foucher, Simon (1644–96) French critic of *Cartesianism. Born in Dijon, Foucher was educated at the Sorbonne, and became a canon of the Cathedral of Dijon, although he spent his life in Paris. He was a friend of *Leibniz, whose responses to Foucher's questions provide some of the best statements of his philosophy. Foucher was a sceptic, and one of the principal 17th-century critics of both *Descartes and *Malebranche. His criticism of the former is retailed admiringly by *Bayle in his *Dictionary* article on Pyrrho: 'For if the objects of our senses appear coloured, hot, cold, odoriferous, and yet they are not so, why can they not appear extended and shaped, in rest and in motion, though they are not so?' He was possibly the first philosopher to see that once mind is separated from the world as it is in Cartesian theory, problems of causal interaction and knowledge become insuperable, and he opened the door both to the scepticism of Bayle, and the subjective *idealism of *Berkeley. His principal work was the *Dissertation sur la recherche de la vérité* (1673).

foundationalism The view in *epistemology that knowledge must be regarded as a structure raised upon secure, certain foundations. These are found in some combination of experience and reason, with different schools (*empiricism, *rationalism) emphasizing the role of one over that of the other. Foundationalism was associated with the ancient *Stoics, and in the modern era with *Descartes, who discovered his foundations in the 'clear and distinct' ideas of reason. Its main opponent is coherentism, or the view that a body of propositions may be known without a foundation in certainty, but by their interlocking strength, rather as a crossword puzzle may be known to have been solved correctly even if each answer, taken individually, admits of uncertainty. *See also* COHERENCE THEORY OF TRUTH, NEURATH'S BOAT, PROTOCOL STATEMENTS.

Four Books The definitive texts of *Confucius and *Mencius selected by the scholar *Chu Hsi and that from 1313 until 1905 served as the basis of civil service examinations in China. They comprise the *Analects* of Confucius, the *Book of Mencius*, the *Great Learning*, and the *Doctrine of the Mean*.

four causes, doctrine of the *See* CAUSES: MATERIAL, FORMAL, EFFICIENT, FINAL.

four humours The fluids of the body whose balance is essential to well-being, in the medical theory of *Galen. They are blood, choler (yellow bile), phlegm, and melancholy (black bile).

four noble truths The four great truths of *Buddhism. The first says that all existence is afflicted with suffering. The second truth identifies desire, thirst, or craving as the source of suffering, that binds beings to the cycle of existence (*samsara*). The third truth asserts that through the elimination of craving, suffering can be brought to an end. The fourth truth identifies the *eightfold path as the means to eliminate suffering and escape from *samsara*.

four-term fallacy The fallacy committed when the middle term of a *syllogism has a different sense in each premise (i.e. the syllogism really has four terms instead of the necessary three). For example: 'All men are wolves, all wolves live in the arctic, therefore all men live in the arctic.'

fourth dimension Since the theory of *relativity it has been orthodox to treat time alongside the other three spatial dimensions, as the fourth dimension of a unified *space-time. In the late 19th century, physicists such as Helmholtz popularized work of Riemann that suggested that there might be a fourth spatial dimension, into which things might disappear, only to reappear elsewhere (*see* INCONGRUENT COUNTERPARTS). The idea was taken up by *theosophists and workers on *parapsychology. It is analysed in the 1884 classic *Flatland* by Edwin Abbot, and mentioned in work by H. G. Wells and Oscar Wilde. It reappeared in orthodox physics in the work of Kaluza, who showed in 1919 that when the Riemann tensor metric (*see* RELATIVITY) is rewritten in five dimensions, a unified theory of gravity and electromagnetism can be produced. Currently one favoured number of dimensions is ten. *See also* GEOMETRY.

frame problem A fundamental problem in *artificial intelligence research, first identified by John McCarthy and Pat Hayes ('Some Philosophical Problems from the Standpoint of Artificial Intelligence', *Machine Intelligence*, 1969). A common-sense appreciation of the world includes a great many automatic constraints on belief. For example, if a proposition p is true at one time, and event e occurs, we just know whether e is relevant or not to whether p is true at a later time. We ignore beliefs that are obviously irrelevant to our goals and we keep track of salient changes, despite the *holism of change, or the fact that virtually anything can affect anything else. The frame problem is that of programming 'frame axioms' to reproduce this ability in any remotely realistic device supposed to mimic human intelligence. *See also* NARRATIVE COMPETENCE, TURING TEST.

Frankfurt school The critical *Marxist school emerging in Frankfurt in the 1920s and 1930s, and centred upon the Institute for Social Research, founded in 1923. Its principal philosophical members were Max Horkheimer (director, 1931–58), *Adorno, *Marcuse, and *Benjamin. Its leading later representative is *Habermas. Their approach is sometimes known as *critical theory. Its aim was to provide a version of Marxism uncontaminated by *positivism and *materialism, and giving due role to the influence of the superstructure, or the culture and self-image of people in a historical period, as a factor in social change. The Frankfurt school was faced both with the degeneration of Soviet Marxism into Stalinism, and the failure of communism to inspire the working classes of the west. In response it combined a *Kantian preoccupation with the conditions for the possibility of reason and knowledge, with a *Hegelian emphasis on the historical conditioning of all thought; both these elements led to a sceptical stance towards the prevailing ideologies, or distortions of thought that emerge from, and conceal, actual social inequalities. The Frankfurt school emphasized the interlocking role of aesthetics, psychoanalysis, and popular culture in reinforcing the prevailing western condition of a passive, depersonalized acceptance of the *status quo* ('the system'), with its *commodity fetishism, *fascism, and nationalism. With most individuals at the mercy of such forces, there is no prospect of an inevitable revolution, as classical Marxism predicts, and the role of an enlightened leadership in the struggle for emancipation becomes correspondingly greater. Similarly, since it is the need for a transformation through increased understanding that is stressed, psychoanalysis offers a model for emancipation, since it offers the hope that by becoming aware of hidden aspects of our psychologies we gain the power to overcome them. The school was a major influence on the New Left and other radical movements of the 1960s.

Franklin, Benjamin (1706–90) Although Franklin's distinction rests on his work as a scientist and statesman, his homely moral and political philosophy, particularly as expounded in *Poor Richard's Almanack* (1733–58), has been extremely influential as an expression of a folksy, democratic *virtue ethic.

freedom, positive/negative Narrowly, or negatively, freedom is thought of as the absence of constraint: 'Freedom', said *Hobbes, 'is the silence of the law.' Positively, freedom is a condition of liberation from social and cultural forces that are perceived as impeding full self-realization. To become free is therefore a challenge that is only met by personal transformation, in *Romantic and individualistic thought, or by social transformation, for instance in *Hegel.

freedom of speech *See* FREE SPEECH.

free logic Any logic differing from classical logic in that there is no presumption that the names used actually refer to anything. Thus from Fa it need not follow that $(\exists x)(Fx)$, any more than, in natural language, it follows from the fact that Pegasus is a flying horse that there is such a thing as a flying horse (although an alternative is to say that in the sense in which Pegasus is a flying horse, there are flying horses: i.e. to interpret both statements as implicitly governed by an operator such as 'in the myths it is said that ... ').

free riders Those who are content to partake of the benefits of some cooperative enterprise, without contributing to it. *See also* COLLECTIVE GOODS.

free speech Liberal constitutions accept some principle of protection of free speech, but its scope and rationale are contested. Speech may include various forms of expression: displaying paintings, wearing political slogans, or burning flags, for example. On the other hand, some forms of speech (shouting 'fire' in a crowded theatre; ordering or encouraging a person to use violence on another) seem to deserve no special legal protection. The main positive argument for special protection of free speech is that this protection generates special benefits, either promoting the discovery of truth and error, or serving as a necessary part of educated political decision-making. A negative argument is that the harms caused by speech are somehow less significant than those caused by other actions ('sticks and stones may break my bones, but words will never hurt me'). Or, if harm does ensue, it may be that the hearer bears some responsibility, for instance by being disposed to particular kinds of sensitivity. This, however, is contested. A principled argument for free speech is that silencing someone is a particular trespass against their dignity and against the respect due to a free agent. A pragmatic argument for the principle is that speech is an area in which states are particularly tempted to illiberal intrusion.

free variable A variable not *bound by a quantifier.

free will The problem is to reconcile our everyday consciousness of ourselves as agents, with the best view of what science tells us that we are. *Determinism is one part of the problem. It may be defined as the doctrine that every event has a cause. More precisely, for any event *e*, there will be some antecedent state of nature, *N*, and a law of nature, *L*, such that given *L*, *N* will be followed by *e*. But if this is true of every event, it is true of events such as my doing something or choosing to do something. So my choosing or doing something is fixed by some antecedent state *N* and the laws. Since determinism is universal these in turn are fixed, and so backwards to events for which I am clearly not responsible (events before my birth, for example). So no events can be voluntary or free, where that means that they come about purely because of my willing them when I could have done otherwise. If determinism is true, then there will be antecedent states and laws already determining such events; how then can I truly be said to be their author, or be responsible for them? Reactions to this problem are commonly classified as: (i) Hard determinism. This accepts the conflict and denies that you have real freedom or responsibility. (ii) Soft determinism or compatibilism. Reactions in this family assert that everything you should want from a notion of freedom is quite compatible with determinism. In particular, even if your action is caused, it can often be true of you that you could have done otherwise *if* you had chosen, and this may be enough to render you liable to be held responsible or to be blamed if what you did was unacceptable (the fact that previous events will have caused you to choose as you did is deemed irrelevant on this option). (iii) *Libertarianism. This is the view that, while compatibilism is only an evasion, there is a more substantive, real notion of freedom that can yet be preserved in the face of determinism (or of *indeterminism). In *Kant, while the empirical or phenomenal self is determined and not free, the noumenal or rational self is capable of rational, free action. But since the noumenal self exists outside the categories of space and time, this freedom seems to be of doubtful value. Other libertarian avenues include suggesting that the problem is badly framed, for instance because the definition of determinism breaks down; or postulating a special category of uncaused acts of volition; or suggesting that there are two independent but consistent ways of looking at an agent, the scientific and the humanistic, and it is only through confusing them that the problem seems urgent. None of these avenues has gained general popularity. It is an error to confuse determinism and *fatalism. *See also* DILEMMA OF DETERMINISM.

free will defence Probably the most popular attempt to reconcile the existence of evil with the goodness of God (*see* EVIL, PROBLEM OF; THEODICY). The defence is that evils are entirely due to the bad, free, choices made by human beings (and perhaps other fallen beings, including in some versions fallen angels). It was good of God to create free beings, but bad of them to misuse their freedom. So the good God is not responsible for the evils of the world, and we cannot use the evils of the world as an objection to belief in Him. Although popular, the defence faces many obstacles: it apparently requires a *libertarian (metaphysical) account of *free will; it either ignores the obvious fact that most of the ills that afflict the human world, such as disease, pain, and starvation, are not of our own creation, or it implausibly and arbitrarily assigns them to supernatural bad beings, such as fallen angels; but most fundamentally it needs to discount the logical possibility of God creating free beings who would use their freedom always to choose the good, as some of us manage to do some of the time. It must also reject the possibility of a God who, when free agents he has created choose evil, kindly insulates the rest of us from the would-be evil-doers by isolating them in some kind of playpen.

Frege, Gottlob (1848–1925) German mathematician and philosopher of mathematics. Frege was born in the small town of Wismar in Pomerania, and was sent to the university of Jena when he was twenty-one. He obtained his doctorate at Göttingen, and worked almost the whole of his life in the mathematics department at the university of Jena. His first important work, the *Begriffsschrift* ('Concept Writing', 1879), is also the first example of a formal system in the sense of modern logic. In it Frege undertakes to devise a formal system within which mathematical proofs may be given. It was his discovery of the correct representation of generality, the notion of *quantifier and *variable, that opened the possibility of successfully achieving this aim. With that notation Frege could represent sentences involving multiple generality (such as the form 'for every small number *e* there is a number n such that ... ') on which the validity of much mathematical reasoning depends. The *Begriffsschrift* also contains the elements of the *propositional calculus, including an informal presentation of the notion of a *truth function. It is universally acknowledged to mark the beginning of modern logic. In 1884 Frege published the *Grundlagen der Arithmetik* (trs. as *The Foundations of Arithmetic* by J. L. *Austin, 1959). In this work, Frege brilliantly attacks rival accounts of the status of arithmetic, and then propounds his own approach to the subject, analysing the basic concepts of mathematics in such a form that a reduction of arithmetic to operations that are fundamentally logical in nature becomes a real possibility. The first volume of the *Grundgesetze der Arithmetik* (1893, trs. as *The Basic Laws of Arithmetic*, 1964) formalizes the mathematical approach of the *Grundlagen*, a task that necessitated giving the first formal theory of classes; it was this theory that was later shown inconsistent by *Russell's paradox. Volume 2 of the *Grundgesetze*, concerned mainly with the theory of real numbers, was published in 1903. Frege's own reaction to Russell's paradox, after understandable initial consternation, was to modify one of his own axioms; the result, however, was not eventually tenable, and it was only with Zermelo's work that the modern conception of *set theory was put on a satisfactory footing.

Frege's distinction as a logician is matched by his deep concern with the basic semantic concepts involved in the logical foundations of his work. In a succession of papers he forges the basic concepts and distinctions that have dominated subsequent philosophical investigation of logic and language. The topics of these writings include sense (**Sinn*) and *reference, *concepts, *functions and objects, *identity, *negation, assertion, *truth/falsity, and the nature of thought. Although his relations to the philosophical surroundings of his time are debatable, these concerns and his approach to them stamp Frege as the founding figure of *analytical philosophy. However, his concern to protect a timeless objectivity for thought and its contents has led to accusations of *Platonism, and his own views of the objects of mathematics troubled him until the end of his life. Translations include *Translations from the Philosophical Writings of Gottlob Frege*, edited by P. Geach and M. Black (1960), *The Basic Laws of Arithmetic*, translated and edited by M. Furth (1964), *Conceptual Notation and Related Articles*, edited by T. W. Bynum (1972), and *On the Foundations of Geometry and Formal Theories of Arithmetic*, edited by E.-H. W. Kluge (1971).

Frege–Geach argument An argument against positions such as *expressivism or *prescriptivism in the theory of ethics, or *ascriptivism in the theory of responsibility. Such positions give the meaning of some sentence, such as 'it is wrong to tell lies' or 'Jim is responsible for stealing the apples', in terms of what is done by asserting them. But such sentences, like all others, can occur not only as asserted, but also in less direct contexts such as 'if it is wrong to tell lies, then it is wrong to get your little brother to lie for you', in which no attitude to expressing lies is voiced.

Similarly 'if he is responsible for stealing the apples, he will be caught sooner or later' does not ascribe blame to the subject. We cannot say that meaning shifts in these contexts, because that would make simple inferences involving both kinds of sentence invalid. In his article 'Ascriptivism' in 1960 *Geach argued that this puts a decisive obstacle in front of theories following this strategy. *See also* QUASI-REALISM.

frequency theory of probability The view developed by Richard von Mises (1883–1953), in his *Probability, Statistics, and Truth* (1957; 1st German edn, 1928), that the probability of an event in a situation can be defined in terms of the frequency of occurrence of events of the same kind, in some hypothetical population of repetitions of the same situation. The theory gives the simplest relation between probabilities and the evidence of frequencies on which they are based. However, it needs to define the relevant kind of event, the situation, and the hypothetical population: if the latter is infinite then some notion of a limit must be defined, and probability becomes sensitive to the ordering of outcomes in the series. The theory does not easily apply to single events, such as the probability of Eclipse winning the Derby this year, since no unique 'kind' of event of which this is an instance can apparently be defined. In other words, there is no unique way of specifying what would count as a repetition of the same situation, so that frequencies build up. The other problem facing the theory is that it is not clear that the limit gives what we actually want from judgements of probability: it is itself a non-empirical construction—the target of *Keynes's famous remark that in the long run we are all dead.

Freud, Sigmund (1856–1939) Viennese founder of *psychoanalysis. Freud was born in Freiburg and educated in Vienna. His first work was in biology and clinical neurology; it was after study with Charcot in Paris that he turned his attention to an interest in hypnosis. In Vienna he collaborated with Breuer, who championed a method of having the patient re-live the stressful experiences responsible for his or her neuroses. However, it was Freud who postulated that an active process of repression needed confronting and disarming, and who extended the range of experiences involved to concentrate upon traumatizing experiences remembered or imagined from early childhood. In spite of the influence of psychoanalysis as a framework for psychological and social thought, Freud's handling of some of his most famous cases has attracted increasing scepticism, with it becoming apparent that he himself invented many of the scenes his patients were supposed to have recounted as memory or fantasy. Nevertheless his model for the dynamics of the mind (*see* EGO) has been a potent influence on many philosophers, and of course on the culture in general.

friendship A topic of moral philosophy much discussed by *Plato, *Aristotle, and the *Stoics, but less so in the modern era, until the re-emergence of *contextualist and *feminist approaches to ethics. In friendship an 'openness' of each to the other is found that can be seen as an enlargement of the self. Aristotle writes that 'the excellent person is related to his friend in the same way as he is related to himself, since a friend is another self; and therefore, just as his own being is choiceworthy for him, the friend's being is choiceworthy for him in the same or a similar way.' Friendship therefore opens the door to an escape from *egoism or belief that the rational course of action is always to pursue one's own self-interest, although escaping through the door would require finding what is covered by Aristotle's 'same or similar way'. It is notable that friendship requires sentiments to which *Kant denies moral importance. It is a purely personal matter, requiring *virtue, yet which runs counter to the universalistic requirement of impartial treatment of all, for a friend is someone who is treated differently from others. One problem is to reconcile these apparently conflicting requirements.

fulguration A lightning flash of the mind. To *Leibniz, the *monads are God's fulguration.

function, biological In biology, the function of a feature of an organism is frequently defined as that role it plays which has been responsible for its genetic success and evolution. Thus although the brain weighs down the shoulders, this is not its function, for this is not why entities with brains are successful. A central question will be the unit whose *adaptation is in question: these may be persons, or their *genes, or clusters of genes, or gene pools; it may be said that a person is a gene's way of making another gene, just as a scholar is a library's way of making another library. There are also difficulties in distinguishing fortuitous roles that an adaptation may come to serve from its function proper.

function, logical In logic and mathematics a function, also known as a map or mapping, is a *relation that associates members of one class X with some unique member y of another class Y. The association is written as $y = \mathrm{f}(x)$. The class X is called the domain of the function, and Y its range. Thus 'the father of x' is a function whose domain includes all people, and whose range is the class of male parents. But the relation 'son of x' is not a function, because a person can have more than one son. 'Sine x' is a function from angles onto real numbers; the length of the perimeter of a circle, πx, is a function of its diameter x; and so on. Functions may take sequences $\langle x_1 \dots x_n \rangle$ as their arguments, in which case they may be thought of as associating a unique member of Y with any ordered *n-tuple as argument. Given the equation $y = f(x_1 \dots x_n)$, $x_1 \dots x_n$ are called the independent variables, or arguments of the function, and y the dependent variable or value. Functions may be many-one, meaning that different members of X may take the same member of Y as their value, or one-one, when to each member of X there corresponds a distinct member of Y. A function with domain X and range Y is also called a mapping from X to Y, written $fX \rightarrow Y$. If the function is such that

(i) if $x, y \in X$ and $f(x) = f(y)$ then $x = y$,

then the function is an injection from X to Y. If also

(ii) if $y \in Y$, then $(\exists x)(x \in X \,\&\, y = f(x))$

then the function is a bijection of X onto Y. A bijection is also known as a one-one correspondence. A bijection is both an injection and a surjection where a surjection is any function whose domain is X and whose range is the whole of Y. Since functions are relations a function may be defined as a set of *ordered pairs $\langle x,y \rangle$ where x is a member of X and y of Y.

One of *Frege's logical insights was that a concept is analogous to a function, and a predicate analogous to the expression for a function (a functor). Just as 'the square root of x' takes us from one number to another, so 'x is a philosopher' refers to a function that takes us from persons to truth-values: true for values of x who are philosophers, and false otherwise.

functional explanation An explanation of a phenomenon that cites the functional properties of contributing elements, rather than their physical or mechanical natures. The explanation of a computer's behaviour that cites the software it is running is a functional explanation. *See also* FUNCTION, BIOLOGICAL.

functionalism In the philosophy of mind, functionalism is the modern successor to *behaviourism. Its early advocates were *Putnam and *Sellars, and its guiding principle is that we can define mental states by a triplet of relations: what typically causes them, what effects they have on other mental states, and what effects they have on behaviour. The definition need not take the form of a simple analysis, but if we could write down the totality of axioms, or postulates, or platitudes that govern our theories about what things are apt to cause (for example) a belief state, what effects it would have on a variety of other mental states, and what effects it is likely to have on behaviour, then we would have done all that is needed to make the state a proper theoretical notion. It would be *implicitly defined by these theses. Functionalism is often compared with descriptions of a computer, since according to it mental descriptions correspond to a description of a machine in terms of software, that remains silent about the underlying hardware or 'realization' of the program the machine is running. The principal advantages of functionalism include its fit with the way we know of mental states both of ourselves and others, which is via their effects on behaviour and other mental states. As with behaviourism, critics charge that structurally complex items that do not bear mental states might nevertheless imitate the functions that are cited. According to this criticism functionalism is too generous, and would count too many things as having minds. It is also queried whether functionalism is too parochial, able to see mental similarity only when there is causal similarity, when our actual practices of interpretation enable us to ascribe thoughts and desires to persons whose causal structure may be rather different from our own. It may then seem as though beliefs and desires can be '*variably realized' in causal architectures, just as much as they can be in different neurophysiological states. *See also* HOMUNCULAR FUNCTIONALISM, PHYSICALISM, TURING TEST.

functional kind A class of objects associated through sharing the same function: knives, forks, spoons. Sometimes contrasted with a *natural kind, although especially in biology there is no good reason why natural kinds cannot be functional kinds: thumbs, kidneys, eyelashes.

functor In formal systems, an expression denoting a function.

fundamentum divisionis (Latin, the basis of division) The principle according to which a genus is divided into species. *See* *PER GENUS ET DIFFERENTIAM*.

future *See* A-SERIES, TIME.

future contingents *Contingent propositions concerning what will be the case. *See* NECESSARY/CONTINGENT TRUTHS, SEA-BATTLE.

future generations The ethical problem of thinking about our responsibility to future generations is compounded by the fact that it is we who create those generations, and we can determine, in principle, how many lives there shall be. Questions raised include whether more lives are preferable to fewer lives, if all are worth living, and how to balance the resulting competition between quantity and quality. 'Total' *utilitarianism sums the imagined utility of each life; 'average' utilitarianism looks at the average utility. Each is open to problems. Other questions concerning non-existent persons arise if we ask what kind of duty is violated if we choose to have a child with a predictable disability, now, rather than waiting and generating a normal child a little later. No person seems to be harmed by the former decision (for the disabled child does not exist on the other alternative), yet it seems callous and wrong. *See also* PARFIT.

futurology The activity of predicting the state of the world at some future time, by extrapolating from present trends. Mainly a pseudo-science, given the complexities of social, political, economic, technological, and natural factors. *See* CHAOS.

fuzzy sets/fuzzy logic The variant of *set theory and logic that recognizes degrees of applicability of predicates. Thus although classical logic regards 'this room is hot' as either true or false, it may better represent the way we actually reason (or the way we ought to reason) to say that it is pretty much true, or truer than saying that the room is cold. In fuzzy logic a determinate quantity of merit (represented by 1) is shared between a proposition and its negation: if it becomes pretty much true that the room is hot (e.g. to degree 1 – n) it becomes pretty much false (degree n) that it is not hot. Fuzzy logic has extensive application in *artificial intelligence, and in the design of systems that control real events and which need to be responsive to changes of degree in important features. The first mathematical treatment was the paper 'Fuzzy Sets', in *Information and Control* (1965), by L. A. Zadeh.

Gadadhara Bhattacharya (1604–1709) Indian philosopher. A member of the Navya-Nyaya school of extreme realists, Gadadhara wrote on the philosophy of language and of mind, and an legal theory. His most original work is the *Saktivada* or theory of the expressive power of words, thought to have anticipated many themes of *pragmatism, and western investigations in the *emotive and other practical powers of language.

Gadamer, Hans-Georg (1900–2002) German philosopher. Born in Marburg, Gadamer was a student of *Heidegger's. His first post was at the university of Marburg, followed by chairs at Leipzig, Frankfurt, and Heidelberg. Gadamer is renowned for his work on the theory of interpretation, and for exploring what has come to be known as 'reader response theory'. According to this the meaning of a text is never a function purely of facts about the author and his original public; it is equally a function of the historical situation of the interpreter. The leading metaphor is that of a 'fusion of horizons' created when the historically situated author and the equally historically situated reader manage to create a shared meaning. There is thus room for constant reinterpretation and re-evaluation, as different meanings are projected upon the work concerned. The idea is one fundamental element of *postmodernism. Gadamer's most influential work is *Wahrheit und Methode. Grundzüge einer philosophischen Hermeneutik* (1960, trs. as *Truth and Method*, 1975). Selections from his critical essays are collected in *Philosophical Hermeneutics* (1976).

Gaia *See* PANPSYCHISM.

Galen of Pergamum (AD 129–*c*.210) Famous Greek physician and anatomist, although he also wrote as a philosopher. Galen's influence on medieval thought and medicine was second only to that of *Aristotle, not so much for any philosophical doctrine but rather as an example of excellence in empirical science combined with what was taken to be an ardent religious faith. However, his philosophy has again become the focus of scholarly interest. *See also* FOUR HUMOURS.

Galilean world view The early 17th century saw a change in the European attitude to nature that replaced the Aristotelian conception of nature with the one that, in essence, remains to the present. The name of *Galileo provides a convenient label for the new world view, although virtual contemporaries such as *Descartes are equally implicated. Essential changes include: (i) the mathematization or geometrization of physics. Galileo wrote that 'Philosophy is written in this grand book, the universe, which stands continually open to our gaze. But the book cannot be understood unless one first learns to comprehend the language and read the letters in which it is composed. It is written in the language of mathematics, and its characters are triangles, circles, and other geometric figures'; (ii) replacement of the Aristotelian conception of nature as an organism, like a plant, animated by a **nisus* or force driving it towards a natural goal. In place of this the new image is mechanical: nature becomes a clock or machine; (iii) the replacement of piecemeal Aristotelian explanations with general theories; (iv) the replacement of an Aristotelian confidence in the senses by a view of the world as possibly very different from the way we perceive it as being (*see* COLOUR, PRIMARY/SECONDARY QUALITIES); and (v) a corresponding emphasis on the primary authority of experimental observation, conducted with entirely new standards of accuracy.

Galileo Galilei (1564–1642) Italian scientist. Although Galileo's distinction belongs to the history of physics and astronomy rather than philosophy, his mature philosophy and methodology of science, particularly as derived from the *Dialogue Concerning the Two Chief World Systems* (1632) and the *Dialogues Concerning Two New Sciences* (1638), have been much debated. Galileo unquestionably holds that science based on observation is the true source of knowledge of the physical world, as opposed to traditional authority and philosophical speculation. He also advocates a becoming modesty concerning what we know about nature, in opposition to the dogmatic certainties of much late medieval thought. But within science the relative roles of mathematics, *a priori* reasoning, pure observation, and model-building are not so clear, and Galileo has been seen as an example of Platonistic rationalism as well as of Aristotelian naturalism. Particular doctrines for which he is known in philosophy include the distinction between *primary and secondary qualities, and the relativity of motion. The conception of the world associated with modern science is frequently referred to as the *Galilean world view.

SEE WEB LINKS

- A multimedia introduction to Galileo's life and works
- An archive of articles on Galileo, with a bibliography

gambler's fallacy Also known as the Monte Carlo fallacy. Either (i) the mistake of supposing that results on a system such as a roulette table will continue to display some pattern they have recently been showing (e.g. reds are 'hot'), or (ii) the converse mistake of supposing that an opposite pattern must be becoming due (by 'the law of averages'). In fact a fair gambling system is one on which the probability of some outcome remains exactly the same on each occasion: a roulette wheel has no memory. It should be noticed that if a system is not known to be like this there may be no fallacy. If we are betting on the weather, or a horse, it may be quite reasonable to take a sequence of rainy days, or a sequence of wins, as increasing the chance of another.

gamete A single male or female reproductive cell (sperm or egg cell), capable of joining with a similar single cell of the other sex to form a *zygote. Each gamete contains a single (haploid) *chromosome: the double (diploid) chromosome of the resulting zygote contains the genetic information programming the growth of the new individual.

game theory The mathematical theory of situations in which two or more players have a choice of decisions (strategies); where the outcome depends on all the strategies; and where each player has a set of preferences defined over the outcomes. *See also* CONVENTION, NASH EQUILIBRIUM, PRISONERS' DILEMMA.

SEE WEB LINKS

- An online tutorial on game theory and its applications
- A list of internet resources on game theory

Gandhi, Mohandas Karamchand (1869–1948) Inspirational Indian political and spiritual leader. Originally trained as a lawyer, Gandhi left India for South Africa in 1893. His philosophy of non-violence, celibacy, and absence of personal possessions was informed by wide reading, including such opponents of modernity as Ruskin, Thoreau, and Tolstoy. In 1907 he organized his first *satyagraha* (holding to the truth), a campaign of civil disobedience and non-violent resistance. Returning to India in 1915 he led many such campaigns, both in protest against particular injustices and in order to secure Indian independence from the British Empire. His programme included the revival of cottage industries, especially the production of handwoven cloth; and the abolition of untouchability. He was shot by a Hindu fanatic, while holding a prayer and reconciliation meeting with the aim of stopping the violence between Hindus and Muslims that followed upon Indian independence. The title Mahatma commonly given to him means 'great souled'.

Gangesa (*fl.* *c.*1325) Indian philosopher of the *Nyaya school. Gangesa is the founder of the 'new' school of Nyaya, the Navya-Nyaya. He is notable for extensive realist and *externalist writings in epistemology. The principal work is *Tattvacintamani*, or 'Jewel of Reflection on the Truth (about epistemology)'.

Gassendi, Pierre (1592–1655) French philosopher and mathematician. Born in Provence and educated as a priest, Gassendi taught at Digne and at Aix before being appointed to the chair of mathematics at the Royal College of France in Paris in 1645. His earliest work (*Exercitationes Paradoxicae adversus Aristoteleos*, 1624, trs. as *Exercises against the Aristotelians*, 1972) develops the 'mitigated scepticism' that characterizes much of his philosophical outlook. Gassendi had a deep respect for ancient *scepticism, and his objections to *Descartes's *Meditations* (collected as the fifth set of objections) mount a withering attack on the foundational role of 'clear and distinct ideas' in Descartes's work. These were later expanded into the *Disquisitio Metaphysica* (1644). But along with his scepticism Gassendi reserved a place for genuine scientific knowledge and enquiry, and cultivated an atomism owing much to *Epicurus, and itself much in tune with the emergent materialistic science of the 17th century. Gassendi's three volumes of commentary on *Epicurus were among the works collected in the posthumous *Opera Omnia* of 1658.

SEE WEB LINKS

- An introduction to Gassendi, including his philosophy
- A chronology of Gassendi's life and works

Gauguin problem The problem that although behaving rightly is supposed to override other goals, nevertheless ethical considerations may justifiably be subservient to other artistic, cultural, or scientific aims. *Williams (*Moral Luck*, 1981) uses the painter Gauguin as a symbol of someone behaving rather badly (at least to his family) for the sake of art, and who is justified in the event by the successes he achieved in that sphere. *See also* MORAL LUCK.

Gautama, Aksapada Legendary founder of the *Nyaya ('Logic') school of Indian philosophy. He is known only from the compilation of the *Nyaya-sutra* of around AD 400 in which the fundamental question is that of valid ways of knowing.

Geach, Peter Thomas (1916–) Polemical British Catholic logician and moral philosopher, who was professor at Leeds from 1966 to 1981. Geach's notable work on logical theory included *Reference and Generality: An Examination of some Modern and Medieval Theories* (1962) and *Logic Matters* (1972). He also translated and edited many of the writings of *Frege, while moral and theological concerns are visible in *God and the Soul* (1969). His deployment of points due to Frege against *expressivism have been much debated. *See* FREGE–GEACH ARGUMENT.

Gedankenexperiment German, *thought experiment.

Geist (German, spirit, soul) A quality that animates the mind. The *Zeitgeist* is the spirit of the age (*see* ROMANTICISM). *Geisteswissenschaften* are the human or mental sciences. This term appears in some Hegelian writing, and occurs in the influential translation into German by Schiel of J. S. *Mill's *Logic*, where it corresponds to the moral sciences. It is particularly associated with the later works of *Dilthey.

gender The distinction between sex and gender is attributed to the anthropologist Margaret Mead (*Sex and Temperament in Three Primitive Societies*, 1935). Sex is the biological category, whereas gender is the culturally shaped expression of sexual difference: the masculine way in which men should behave and the feminine way in which women should behave. It is emphasized by de *Beauvoir that in this system woman is the Other: the kind of person whose characteristics are described by contrast with the male *norm. It is a central aim of much *feminist thought to uncover concealed asymmetries of power in differences of gender, and to work for a society in which the polarization of gender is abolished.

genderlect *See* LECT.

gene The 'unit of inheritance' that controls the passing of a hereditary characteristic from parent to offspring, by controlling the structure of proteins or other genetic material. The term was introduced by W. L. Johannsen in 1909 as an abbreviation of 'pangene'. It is interesting as having been consciously intended as a purely functional notion: 'completely free from any hypothesis; it expresses only the evident fact that, in any case, many characteristics of the organism are specified in the gametes by means of special conditions, foundations and determiners'. Genes are now identified with lengths of DNA or RNA. Simplistic forms of biological *determinism suppose that arbitrary characteristics of an organism (e.g. poverty, criminality) are genetically specified.

genealogy A term particularly associated with *Nietzsche, occurring in the title of his book *The Genealogy of Morals*. Genealogy is part historical reconstruction of the way certain concepts have come to have the shape they do, and part a 'rational reconstruction' or story about the function they serve, which may or may not correspond to historical evolution. In the hands of Nietzsche himself, and those influenced by him such as *Foucault, genealogies tend to be subversive and destructive, undermining any attachment to the concepts they consider. But similar stories surrounding the evolution of law or society, conventions, and other institutions may be quite reassuring, highlighting the adaptive functions such developments have served.

generalization A remark made about all things of some kind, or typical things of a kind. In philosophy the term does not retain the pejorative air sometimes associated with it in ordinary contexts. *See* LAWS OF NATURE, QUANTIFIER.

general will (French *volonté générale*) Term used by *Rousseau to denote the will of society as manifested through its political institutions, as opposed to the 'will of all', which is the preference of members on this or that occasion. The distinction applies when a constitution to which all have contracted enacts legislation to which not all consent (*see* DEMOCRACY, PARADOX OF). The citizen is 'forced to be free' by being constrained to follow the general will.

generative grammar The theory of language structures first proposed in *Chomsky's *Syntactic Structures* (1957). Just as physics studies the forms of physically possible processes, so linguistics should study the form of possible human languages. This would define the limits of language by delimiting the kinds of processes that can occur in language from those that cannot. The result would be a universal grammar, from which individual languages would derive as, in effect, different ways of doing the same thing. Variations such as vocabulary and principles governing word order would be revealed as different applications of the same underlying rules. Tacit knowledge of this universal grammar is pre-programmed, an innate biological endowment of normal human infants. The argument with which Chomsky supported the claim for such an endowment is known as the argument from the 'poverty of stimulus': it is argued that language-learning proceeds so fast in response to such a relatively slender body of 'data' that the infant must be credited with an innate propensity to follow the grammar of everybody else. The extent to which this argument treats the infant as a theorist or 'little linguist' has been much debated (*see also* LANGUAGE OF THOUGHT HYPOTHESIS). In Chomsky's original model, language consists of phrase structure rules and transformations. Phrase structure rules represent the grammatically basic constituent parts of the sentence (e.g. a sentence might be a noun phrase + a verb phrase). Transformation rules change relations (as in the active/passive transformation) and determine how complex sentences may be formed from more simple ones. This latter function became taken over by the phrase structure rules in the later work (*Aspects of the Theory of Syntax*, 1965) that introduced what became known as the standard theory. In this, phrase structure rules perform the task of defining the deep structure of a sentence, from which its surface structure is thought of as derived by means of possible repeated transformations. Deep structure bears some affinity to the idea of the logical structure of a sentence, thought of as the representation of the sentence that reveals its inferential properties. The notion did not survive in generative semantics, one of the successors to Chomsky's standard theory, in which transformation rules map semantic representations onto surface structures. The introduction of *semantics is often thought to be a necessary amendment to the purely syntactic and grammatical approach of Chomsky's early theory.

After the standard theory came the extended standard theory, and eventually government-binding theory, both of which maintain an abstract and mathematical approach to the discovery of linguistic principles of the highest generality. Philosophically most interest has centred on the claim that complex grammatical principles might be innate, and on the relationship between syntax and semantics that is presupposed in the idea of a generative grammar. In general, philosophical formalists have been more interested in the possibility of unravelling concealed semantic structure, rather than in the more purely grammatical problems of linguistics.

generosity A virtue interestingly distinct from the Christian virtue of charity, in that while the latter responds to the needs and deficiencies of others, generosity may be simply the exercise of an abundance, an overflow of good will or benevolence. *Aristotle regards it as a correct mean between prodigality and meanness, but others would allow that people can be *too* generous, so that although they are not quite perfectly tuned, they do not thereby forfeit their title to generosity.

genetic fallacy The alleged mistake of arguing that something is to be rejected because of its suspicious origins. More widely, any mistake of inferring something about the nature of some topic from a proposition about its origins. Frequently such reasoning is, actually, quite appropriate, as when one uses the make of an automobile as an indicator of its likely quality. *See also* GENEALOGY.

genome The genome is the entire DNA content of an organism. A large proportion of the genome is made of sequences of DNA that are not *genes, i.e. play no part in determining the *phenotype.

genotype An organism's genetic constitution. *See* PHENOTYPE.

Gentile, Giovanni (1875–1944) Italian philosopher. Born in Sicily, Gentile followed a career in education before becoming professor of history of philosophy at Palermo in 1906. He taught at Pisa, was Minister of Education in Mussolini's government in 1922, and in 1924 became first President of the National Fascist Institute of Culture. His support for both Italian and later German *fascism led to his assassination by Italian communist partisans towards the end of the Second World War. Philosophically he is now identified with the 'theory of the spirit as pure act' (sometimes called actual idealism, or actualism), a form of *idealism with historical antecedents in both *Berkeley and *Kant. Gentile, however, was not content with an unanalysed basis for knowledge in experience or sensation, but conceived of sensation in terms of an act of self-constitution or self-affirmation. This act is at the same time a discovery of the self as participant in a language and in a social world defined through norms and values. The social aspect of Gentile's thought too easily became part of an apologia for the organic state of fascism, but cleansed of this association, for instance in the hands of followers such as *Collingwood, it represents a valuable insistence on the place of language and communication in the constitution of our identity as thinking persons. In Italy, Gentile's actual idealism was influential at least in spirit on both Christian and left-wing thinkers.

gentle murder, paradox of Sometimes known as Forrester's paradox. It proves that if you murder someone, then you only did what you ought to do. For if you murder someone, then you ought to murder them gently. If you ought to murder them gently, then you ought to murder them. So, if you murder someone, then you ought to murder them.

This is one of a number of such paradoxes. One version is that if someone does something, such as committing a crime, then there is an obligation on someone else, such as the police, to know about it, and deduces from that obligation that the original action was itself obligatory.

Gentzen, Gerhard Karl Erich (1909–45) German mathematician, who proved the consistency of classical arithmetic in 1936, relying, however, on *transfinite induction. Gentzen was also responsible for the first *natural deduction approach to formal logic.

genus A class of things that share the same character, but divide into different subclasses or species. The *genus summum* is the most inclusive genus, not itself serving as a species to another yet more general kind. To define *per genus et differentiam* is to cite the genus and the differentiated species to which a thing belongs.

geometry Although various laws concerning lines and angles were known to the Egyptians and the *Pythagoreans, the systematic treatment of geometry by the axiomatic method began with the *Elements* of *Euclid. From a small number of explicit *axioms, postulates, and definitions Euclid deduces *theorems concerning the various figures of geometrical interest. Until the 19th century this work stood as a supreme example of the exercise of reason, which all other intellectual achievements ought to take as a model. With increasing standards of formal rigour it was recognized that Euclid does contain gaps, but fully formalized versions of his geometry have been provided. For example, in the axiomatization of David Hilbert, there are six primitive terms, in that of E. V. Huntington only two: 'sphere' and 'includes'.

In the work of *Kant, Euclidean geometry stands as the supreme example of a synthetic *a priori* construction, representing the way the mind has to think about space, because of the mind's own intrinsic structure. However, only shortly after Kant was writing non-Euclidean geometries were contemplated. They were foreshadowed by the mathematician K. F. Gauss (1777–1855), but the first serious non-Euclidean geometry is usually attributed to the Russian mathematician N. I. Lobachevsky, writing in the 1820s. Euclid's fifth axiom, the axiom of parallels, states that through any point not falling on a straight line, one straight line can be drawn that does not intersect the first. In Lobachevsky's geometry several such lines can exist. Later G. F. B. Riemann (1822–66) realized that the two-dimensional geometry that would be hit upon by persons confined to the surface of a sphere would be different from that of persons living on a plane: for example, π would be smaller, since the diameter of a circle, as drawn on a sphere, is relatively large compared to the circumference. In the figure, BCB, the circumference of the circle, is less than 2πAB, where AB is the radius. Generalizing, Riemann reached the idea of a geometry in which there are no straight lines that do not intersect a given straight line, just as on a sphere all great circles (the shortest distance between two points) intersect.

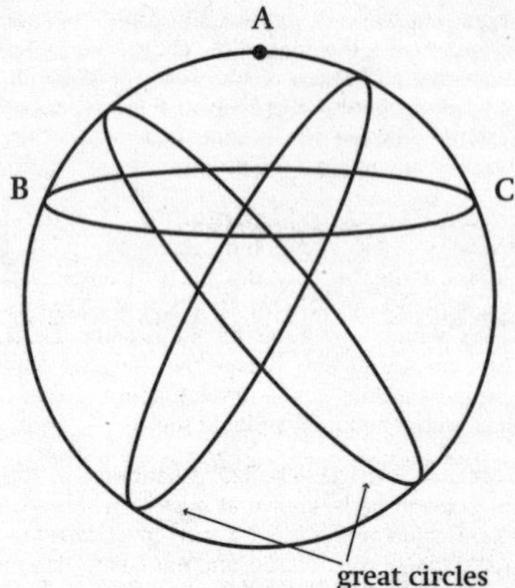

The way then lay open to separating the question of the mathematical nature of a purely formal geometry from the question of its physical application. In 1854 Riemann showed that space of any curvature could be described by a set of numbers known as its metric tensor. For example, ten numbers suffice to describe the point of any four-dimensional manifold. To apply a geometry means finding *coordinative definitions correlating the notions of the geometry, notably those of a straight line and an equal distance, with physical phenomena such as the path of a light ray, or the size of a rod at different times and places. The status of these definitions has been controversial, with some such as *Poincaré seeing them simply as *conventions, and others seeing them as important *empirical truths. With the general rise of *holism in the philosophy of science the question of status has abated a little, it being recognized simply that the coordination plays a fundamental role in physical science. *See also* RELATIVITY THEORY, SPACE-TIME.

Gerard, Alexander (1728–95) Scottish divine. Gerard succeeded *Fordyce as professor in Aberdeen, after the latter drowned in a shipwreck. His one philosophical work was the *Essay on Taste* (1759), the descendant of a prize essay of 1756. *See* SUBLIME.

Gerard of Cremona (1114–87) Italian philosophical translator. Interested in Arabic astronomy, Gerard removed himself to Toledo, where he learned Arabic. He translated the *Almagest* of *Ptolemy, the entire works of *Avicenna, and many of the works of *Aristotle into Latin, opening them up to the scholars of western Europe. He is not known to have authored any original philosophy.

Gerdil, Giancinto Sigismondo (1718–1802) Savoyard theologian, and eventually (1777) cardinal of the church. A disciple of Malebranche, and opponent of *Locke, *Wolff, and *Newton, Gerdil wrote a critique of *Rousseau's *Émile* from an Aristotelian perspective, arguing that spiritual and intellectual development must take place within a morally ordered society.

Gerson, Jean (1363–1429) Chancellor of the university of Paris, known as *doctor christianissimus*. Gerson represented a turn towards a less intellectual and scholastic, and more faith-driven and mystical atmosphere in the church of his time. He is remembered more for attempting to effect a conciliation of the Great Schism in the papacy than for any philosophical achievements. The principal work is an imitation of *Boethius, *De Consolatione Theologiae* (1418; Gerson was in exile in Melk in Austria from 1417 to 1419).

Gersonides (Levi ben Gerson) (1288–1344) The most important Jewish Aristotelian after *Maimonides. His major work, *The Wars of the Lord*, investigates problems that he considers Maimonides not to have resolved, tending to a rather stricter Aristotelianism, and frequently siding with *Averroës against Maimonides. Gersonides was also an astronomer, and an authority on biblical criticism.

Gestalt (German, configuration, pattern, organized whole) The key term of Gestalt psychology was contributed by the Austrian philosopher Christian von Ehrenfels in his paper 'On Gestalt Qualities' (1890), although the movement itself is usually dated from the pioneering paper of Max Wertheimer, 'Experimental Studies on the Perception of Apparent Movement' (1912).

The theory of perception developed in opposition to the classical 'atomistic' model of the *British empiricists and followers such as J. S. *Mill and the German scientist H. L. F. von Helmholtz. On the atomistic view visual patterns arise from a mosaic of independently existing sensations. But phenomena such as the 'figure-ground' switch or the famous *duck-rabbit switch make vivid that to take a scene one way or another goes far beyond having the same blank experience, and then explaining it as the result of one thing or another: the interpretation changes the experience itself. This Gestalt quality is something over and above anything determined in the array of individual sensations. The original Gestalt school of psychology was founded by Max Wertheimer, Kurt Koffka, and Wolfgang Köhler. Although their explanation of Gestalt effects in terms of brain 'fields' has given way, and the attempt to frame laws determining how stimuli will end up being perceived has also withered, the basic idea that higher-level cognitive processes (rememberings, interpretations) are responsible for the nature of experience has flourished. Its philosophical importance has been in undermining the '*myth of the given', since even the straightforward perception of three-dimensional spatial objects proves not to be 'given'.

Gettier examples Since *Plato's *Theaetetus* there has been a tradition of defining knowledge as true belief plus a **logos* or reason. In the most familiar form, knowledge is justified true belief. In 1963 the American philosopher Edmund Gettier provided a range of *counterexamples to this formula. In his cases a belief is true, and the agent is justified in believing it. But the justification does not relate to the truth of the belief in the right way, so that it is relatively accidental, or a matter of luck, that the belief is true. For example, I see what I reasonably and justifiably take to be an event of your receiving a bottle of whisky and on this basis I believe you drink whisky. The truth is that you do drink whisky, but on this occasion you were in fact taking delivery of a medical specimen. In such a case my belief is true and justified, but I do not thereby know that you drink whisky, since this truth is only accidental relative to my evidence. The counterexamples sparked a prolonged debate over the kinds of condition that might be substituted to give a better account of knowledge, or whether all suggestions would meet similar problems. *See also* NO FALSE LEMMAS PRINCIPLE.

Geulincx, Arnold (1624–69) Born in Antwerp, Geulincx studied and taught at Louvain, until in 1658 he was deprived of his chair. Leaving Louvain he settled at Leiden, where he became a Calvinist. He is principally remembered for his *occasionalism, or denial of a causal relationship between mind and body, and for using the image of two synchronous clocks, later made famous by *Leibniz, to illustrate his doctrine (*see* PRE-ESTABLISHED HARMONY). But Geulincx requires the constant intervention of God, whereas for Leibniz the harmony is the outcome of the pre-established nature of the related substances. Geulincx also wrote extensively on ethics.

al-Ghazali Abu Hamid Muhammad (1058–1111) Primarily a theologian, al-Ghazali taught in Baghdad, but in 1095 after a breakdown abandoned academic fields for a life of contemplation. He valued the insight given by mystical comprehension of things above that achieved by logic or reason. His *Incoherence of the Philosophers* is an attack on the Aristotelian doctrines of *al-Farabi and especially *Avicenna. Generally speaking al-Ghazali attacks the range of knowledge claimed by philosophers, particularly through a critique of knowledge of causation, about which he defends *occasionalism. The certainty of his own reasoning opened him to counterattack by *Averroës (*The Incoherence of the Incoherence*). Al-Ghazali is also remembered as the author of the *Revival of the Religious Sciences*, an important influence on Sunni Islam.

g

ghost in the machine Derogatory epithet coined by *Ryle for the nature of the person according to *Cartesian dualism.

Giles of Rome (*c.*1247–1316) Augustinian theologian. Giles studied in Paris, but his works faced condemnation in 1277; he was reinstated and eventually appointed bishop of Bourges in 1295. Whilst active in the schisms of his time, he wrote prolifically on matters such as substance, essence, existence, and other topics of theological interest, although fundamentally in the shadow of *Aquinas.

Gilson, Étienne (1884–1978) French philosopher and historian. Gilson taught the history of medieval philosophy at the Sorbonne (1921–32) and then took the chair of medieval philosophy at the Collège de France. In 1929 he helped found the Pontifical Institute of Medieval Studies at Toronto, Canada. Although primarily a historian of philosophy, he was also one of the leaders of the Roman Catholic neo-Thomist movement. He was elected to the French Academy in 1946. His works include *The Philosophy of St Thomas Aquinas* (1919, trs. 1924); *The Christian Philosophy of Saint Augustine* (1929, trs. 1960); *The Spirit of Mediaeval Philosophy* (2 vols., 1932, trs. 1936); *God and Philosophy* (1941); *Being and Some Philosophers* (1949); and *The Philosopher and Theology* (1960, trs. 1962).

given, the *See* FOUNDATIONALISM, MYTH OF THE GIVEN, PROTOCOL STATEMENTS.

Glanvill, Joseph (1636–80) English philosopher. An Oxford-educated proponent of the Royal Society, Glanvill is principally remembered for *The Vanity of Dogmatizing* (1661; the work contains the story that inspired Matthew Arnold's poem 'The Scholar Gipsy'). Glanvill advances a distinction later associated with *Locke, between an ideal science, in which the causal relations and natures of things could be seen as they are by a God-like intuition, and the best that actual people can do, which is to chart the way things appear to us. Glanvill's account of causation and the scope of science contains striking anticipations of *Hume, but is spoiled by supposing that before the Fall we (like angels) probably could have achieved the intellectual intuition that we cannot now manage; for the tough-minded Hume this ideal is incoherent. Glanvill also wrote *Philosophical Considerations touching Witches and Witchcraft* (1666, reissued as *A Blow at Modern Sadducism*, 1668) which reflects extensive work he conducted on what was later called psychical research. *See also* SADDUCISM.

glossolalia The power, attributed to persons in some religious groups, of 'speaking in tongues'.

gnosis (Greek, knowledge) The root is found in *agnosticism, *gnosticism, diagnosis, prognosis, and gnoseology, an obsolete term for epistemology. In theological writings gnosis is the higher knowledge of spiritual things, often with reference to claims to such knowledge made by gnosticism.

gnosticism A doctrine of various sects combining Christian and pagan elements, that came into prominence around the 2nd century. Central importance attaches to 'gnosis', revealed but secret knowledge of God and of his nature, enabling those who possess it to achieve salvation. Gnosticism takes from pagan thought the concept of a *demiurge or subordinate god, who directly rules the world. The material world is associated, as in *Manichaeanism, with evil, but in some men there is a spiritual element that through knowledge and associated ritual may be rescued from it and attain a higher spiritual state. Christ was never truly embodied, nor died, but was associated in a distant way with that which appeared to the disciples. Gnostic elements are present in *Middle Platonism, and helped to fuel the view that there was a secret *aurea catena* or golden chain of hidden Platonic doctrine stretching from the positive cosmology of Plato to initiates of the time. Gnostic texts of the first four centuries have been discovered in Egypt, and in various forms the belief persisted into the Middle Ages.

gnothi se auton (Greek, know thyself) The inscription found on the temple at Delphi; a profound rebuke to those who think they can gain wisdom without this component.

God *See* RELIGION, PHILOSOPHY OF.

God, arguments against the existence of *See* ATONEMENT; EVIL, PROBLEM OF; HELL.

God, arguments for the existence of *See* COSMOLOGICAL ARGUMENT; DEGREES OF PERFECTION ARGUMENT; DESIGN, ARGUMENT FROM OR TO; FIRST CAUSE ARGUMENT; FIVE WAYS; ONTOLOGICAL ARGUMENT; PASCAL'S WAGER.

God, attributes of *See* DIVINE ATTRIBUTES.

Gödel, Kurt (1906–78) Mathematical logician. Born to German-speaking parents in Czechoslovakia, Gödel studied mathematics at the university of Vienna, where he also came into contact with the Vienna circle (*see* LOGICAL POSITIVISM). His ground-breaking results of 1931 became his *Habilitationsschrift* (postdoctoral thesis) in 1932 (*see* GÖDEL'S THEOREMS). In 1938 Gödel emigrated from Austria to America, and subsequently worked at the Institute for Advanced Studies at Princeton. Gödel's achievements are almost synonymous with those of mathematical logic in the middle years of the 20th century. They included the proof of the completeness of the first-order *predicate calculus, and *Gödel's theorems. His proof that no system can show its own consistency effectively put an end to *Hilbert's programme, although *Gentzen's proof that if transfinite induction is allowed the consistency of arithmetic can be demonstrated, afforded a kind of consolation to Hilbert himself.

From 1943 onwards Gödel devoted himself largely to philosophy, including not only the philosophy of mathematics, but that of general relativity and cosmology. His philosophical views were diametrically opposed to those of the Vienna circle, and tended towards a *Platonism that included abstract religious elements. In the following years Gödel was not free of eccentricities. *Einstein tells the story of how Gödel called the *game theorist Morgenstern on the evening of his citizenship interview in the United States, to explain how he had discovered a logical problem in the Constitution: a non-standard model that showed how a dictatorship could be created consistently with it. After a period of ill-health, he effectively starved himself to death for fear that he was being poisoned. Gödel's extensive writings on the foundations of logic and mathematics are published in *Kurt Gödel: Collected Works*, vol. i, *Publications 1929–1936* (1986), and vol. ii, *Publications 1938–1974* (1990).

Gödel numbering A process whereby a unique number can be associated with any formula of a logical system. This is an essential step in realizing the goal of metamathematics, that the proofs of a system should themselves be treated as mathematical objects. By Gödel numbering claims made within the language about proofs and theorems may be mapped onto arithmetical claims.

Gödel's theorems *Gödel's first incompleteness theorem states that for any consistent logical system *S* able to express arithmetic there must exist sentences that are true in the standard interpretation of *S*, but not provable. Moreover, if *S* is *omega-consistent then there exist sentences such that neither they nor their negations are provable. The second theorem states that no such system can be powerful enough to prove its own consistency.

These results, published in 1931 ('Über formal unentscheidbare Sätze der *Principia Mathematica* und verwandter Systeme I'; trs. as 'On Formally Undecidable Propositions of *Principia Mathematica* and Related Systems I'), determined the limits of purely formal methods in mathematics, and in particular marked the end of *Hilbert's programme. Additional philosophical significance attaches to the way Gödel proved his first result. This was by defining a formula *P* that whilst unprovable can be seen to be true, given the way it is constructed. The implied moral is that truth in some way outruns provability, at least when that is considered formally.

Gödel proceeded by encoding logical formulae as numbers, so that to a statement about provability in the metatheory there corresponded by the mapping a simple statement of elementary mathematics. The formalism of arithmetic thus contains sentences that, considered via the enumeration, express propositions of their own metamathematics. The formula *P* is such a one: it expresses, to one interpreting it via the enumeration, its own unprovability. Gödel's procedure thus is an instance of a *diagonal argument, and it bears a vivid analogy to examples of the *semantic paradoxes. It is thus extremely important that all the methods he used are perfectly rigorous.

Gödel's procedure and his results opened the way to a fully rigorous treatment of the notion of a *computable function, and to our modern understanding of the power and limits of computation, and the possibility or otherwise of programs that test for consistency and completeness.

SEE WEB LINKS

- An introduction to Gödel's theorems
- A sceptical view on the uses of Gödel's theorems, with links to other resources

God of the gaps Derogatory term for the tendency to postulate divine action simply to fill up gaps in scientific knowledge, for example in the detail of evolutionary mechanisms.

Godwin, William (1756–1836) English writer and social reformer. Godwin enjoyed a long but mainly undistinguished career as a writer, but his great decade was the 1790s, when he became famous as a prominent defender of radicalism and *anarchism. His principal work was the *Enquiry Concerning Political Justice* (1793). Godwin was a *utilitarian, who believed that all government, and all apparatus of legal coercion, corrupts and perverts human nature. He was married to Mary *Wollstonecraft and was the father of Mary Shelley, the author of *Frankenstein*.

Goethe, Johann Wolfgang von (1749–1832) German man of letters. As a philosopher the great writer is mainly interesting as an influence on others, particularly *Schiller and *Schelling. Goethe was influenced by *Spinoza's pantheism, *Leibniz's panpsychism, and the moral philosophy of *Kant, but he confessed his own lack of a 'proper organ for philosophy'; something of his lack of rigour can be seen in the remark that 'we are pantheists when we study nature, polytheists when we write poetry, monotheists in our morality'. However his work on *colour, inspired by a temperamental revulsion from *Newton's purely mathematical theory of the spectrum, has been rediscovered and re-evaluated in the light of recent work.

g

Goldbach's conjecture The conjecture made by the German mathematician Christian Goldbach in 1742, that every even number greater than 2 is the sum of two primes. It is not known whether this is true or false.

golden age A myth of the original condition of humanity, first found in the *Works and Days* of Hesiod. It is identified with the time of Kronos, before Zeus began to rule (in Roman mythology, the time of Saturn). Justice and honesty ruled; there was no labour, old age, grief, or distress. The golden age has clear affinities with the myth of the garden of Eden, and provided a potent symbol for *Romanticism.

golden mean *See* MEAN (ETHICAL).

golden rule Any form of the dictum, 'Do unto others as you would have them do unto you.' In some form this is found in almost all religions and ethical systems. *Kant's moral philosophy is centred on the enterprise of making a version of the rule compulsory for rational agents (*see* CATEGORICAL/HYPOTHETICAL IMPERATIVE). The rule is sometimes parodied as, 'Do unto others as you would have them do unto themselves.'

good As an adjectival modifier of a noun it is widely accepted that 'good' is *attributive: a good hammer is so in virtue of different qualities from a good dinner. However, there seems room to say that each gets the verdict because of some relationship to our ends or desires, and one of the traditional tasks of *ethics is to say what that relationship is. A simple subjective proposal is made by *Hobbes: 'whatsoever is the object of any man's appetite or desire; that is it which he for his part calleth *good*' (*Leviathan*, i. 6). More objectively, 'the good' is used to denote the supposed final end at which action must aim: an intrinsically valuable state, classically identified with **eudaimonia*, or some compound of happiness, virtue, freedom from care, and success. The relationship between purely private good and social good is then left to be filled in. The good is often identified in economics with the satisfaction of desire or preference, with comparatively little attention paid, in the liberal tradition, to the objects of these desires, or the states of mind likely to ensue if they are satisfied.

good in itself That which is good without being so as a means to some other good, or only dependently upon some other good. *Kant held that the only thing good in itself was a *good will. *See also* SUMMUM BONUM.

Goodman, Nelson (1906–98) American philosopher. Born in Massachusetts and educated at Harvard, Goodman was an art dealer in Boston from 1929 to 1941, and held positions at Pennsylvania and Brandeis before becoming professor at Harvard in 1968. Goodman is associated with an extreme *nominalism, or mistrust of any appeal to a notion of the similarity between two things, when this is thought of as independent of our linguistic propensities to apply the same term to them. His earliest work, *The Structure of Appearance* (1951), is a development of the reductionist programme of *Carnap's *Aufbau*. In his later writings he has expressed what appears to be a radical *idealism, espousing the view that there are as many different 'versions' or 'worlds' as there are human narrative and artistic creations. Goodman's other main works are *Fact, Fiction, and Forecast* (1954), *Languages of Art* (1969), and *Ways of Worldmaking* (1978). *See also* GOODMAN'S PARADOX.

Goodman's paradox The classical problem of *induction is often phrased in terms of finding some reason to expect that nature is uniform. In *Fact, Fiction, and Forecast* (1954) *Goodman showed that we need in addition some reason for preferring some uniformities to others, for without such a selection the uniformity of nature is vacuous. Thus, suppose that all examined emeralds have been green. Uniformity would lead us to expect that future emeralds will be green as well. But now we define a predicate grue: x is grue if and only if x is examined before time T and is green, or x is examined after T and is blue. Let T refer to some time around the present. Then if newly examined emeralds are like previous ones in respect of being grue, they will be blue. We prefer blueness as a basis of prediction to grueness, but why? Goodman argued that although his new predicate appears to be gerrymandered, and itself involves a reference to a difference, this is just a parochial or language-relative judgement, there being no language-independent standard of similarity to which to appeal. Other philosophers have not been convinced by this degree of linguistic relativism. What remains clear is that the possibility of these 'bent' predicates puts a decisive obstacle in face of purely logical and syntactical approaches to problems of *confirmation.

good will In the usage of *Kant, a good will is the unconditional, intrinsic good, independently of what it 'effects or accomplishes' in the world (*Groundwork of the Metaphysic of Morals*). It is the determination to act in accordance with the law of autonomy or freedom, that is, in accordance with universal moral law and regardless of selfish advantage. *See also* CATEGORICAL/HYPOTHETICAL IMPERATIVE.

Gorgias of Leontini (*c*.485–*c*.380 BC) Primarily a teacher of *rhetoric, Gorgias is generally classed as a *Sophist. He came to Athens in 427 BC as an ambassador from his home town in Sicily, and his distinctive antithetical style had considerable literary influence. Philosophically he had serious interests in the science of the day, and wrote a treatise *On That Which is Not, or Nature* which is known only through summaries. It contained an extension of the *Eleatic arguments against motion and in favour of unity, to prove the impossibility of nature existing at all; it is a matter of scholarly debate whether he believed this result (if, indeed, it is possible to believe it), or whether the treatise was a rhetorical exercise. His *Encomium of Helen* is the first clear treatment of the problem of *free will.

grace Theologians attracted to *predestination (Paul, Augustine, Calvin, Pascal, and many others) tend also to believe that people cannot by their own unaided efforts live good lives, or become deserving of salvation. They have to rely on a free gift of God—the gift of grace. In *Protestantism, according to *Weber, the best sign of having been blessed with grace is an abundance of worldly riches.

Gracián y Morales, Baltasar (1601–58) Spanish baroque moralist, and Jesuit scholar, whose works influenced La Rochefoucauld, and later *Voltaire, *Nietzsche, and *Borgès. *Schopenhauer considered Gracián's *El criterión* (1651–7, trs. into English as *The Critick*, 1781) one of the best books ever written. However, according to his Jesuit superiors Gracian himself was choleric, bilious, and melancholic.

grammar The systematic ways in which sentences of a language may be built. Grammar is typically studied independently of *phonetics and *semantics. Its two branches are syntax, or the way words make sentences, and morphology, which includes the recognition of syntactically significant parts of words. A grammar that aspires to find categories and rules applicable to all (human) languages is a universal grammar. Grammar may be pursued in various ways: a formal grammar aspires to the production of a proof procedure or *algorithm separating the well-formed sentences of a language from other strings of words. The different levels of complexity of such algorithms define the hierarchy of abstract structures for languages described originally by *Chomsky. A descriptive grammar describes actual usages in a language, whereas a prescriptive grammar legislates for correct and incorrect usage. *See also* GENERATIVE GRAMMAR.

grammar, deep and surface *See* GENERATIVE GRAMMAR.

grammatical form The representation of the way in which a sequence of words comes to be a well-formed sentence of a language. In a formal or artificial language grammar is laid down in *formation rules, but the formation rules of natural languages are sufficiently complex to make accurate codification hazardous.

Gramsci, Antonio (1891–1937) Italian communist and social theorist. Born in Sardinia and educated in Turin, Gramsci became one of the most celebrated 20th-century interpreters of *Marx. A principal founder and the first general secretary of the Italian communist party, he was imprisoned from 1926 until his death. His major work is the posthumous *Prison Notebooks*, written between 1929 and 1935, which propounds a humanistic Marxism, stressing the need for a transformed self-consciousness or 'battle of ideas' in society before revolution would occur, and therefore dismissing the historical fatalism and materialism of orthodox Marxism. *See also* HEGEMONY.

gratitude Generally treated as a *duty, but an interesting one in that the duty is not to act but to feel a certain way. Although the concept involves the idea of repayment, gratitude is not simply the just repayment of debt, for the benefactor cannot demand gratitude in the way a creditor can demand repayment. Also we should feel gratitude for things that we cannot in any meaningful sense repay, such as life (or, *Aristotle argues, a training in philosophy). What is required is a feeling of love or honour for the benefactor, and deficiency in this feeling is a failing so severe as to be, in *Hume's words, 'of all crimes that human beings are capable of committing, the most horrid and unnatural'.

greatest happiness principle The view that the morally correct action 'procures the greatest happiness for the greatest numbers' is first formulated by *Hutcheson (1725, second treatise of *An Inquiry into the Original of our Ideas of Beauty and Virtue*, iii. 8). But it is especially associated with *Bentham, and is central to classical *utilitarianism. The principle needs a great deal of interpretation, since as it stands it does not speak of issues of distribution, nor of conflicting claims, nor of course of the ways of locating and comparing happinesses.

great-souled man The lofty character portrayed in Bk iv of the *Nicomachean Ethics* of *Aristotle. The great-souled man is of a distinguished situation, worthy of great things, 'an extreme in respect of the greatness of his claims, but a mean in respect of the rightness of them', perfectly virtuous, good at conferring benefits but ashamed of receiving them, neither humble nor vain. The combination involves proper pride or magnanimity. With his slow step, deep voice, and level utterance, he does not appeal to everybody, but he represents Aristotle's robust sense that the aims people have in life include an admiring reflection of themselves in the eyes of others.

Green, Thomas Hill (1836–82) English *absolute idealist. Green was born in Yorkshire, and educated at Oxford. He was a tutor at Balliol College, and in 1878 became professor of moral philosophy at Oxford. His introduction to his edition of *Hume's works (produced with T. H. Grose) is a major attack on traditional *empiricism, but he is mainly recognized for the *Prolegomena to Ethics* published the year after his death. In this he argues that empiricist 'passions' are inadequate springs of action, which are instead provided by the self-conscious pursuit of a good. This is an early example of a line of criticism of Humean and *emotive theories of ethics that is still current, but in Green the springs of action rapidly become identified with immersion in a larger whole, produced by an absolute mind that itself enshrines goodness, truth, and beauty. The 'school of Green' was an influential element in the philosophical climate of Oxford until after the First World War.

Gregory of Rimini (*c.*1300–58) Augustinian theologian and professor at the Sorbonne, known as *doctor authenticus*, but less flatteringly as *infantium tortor* (tormentor of children), because he held extreme views concerning the fate of children who died unbaptized. Gregory is thought to have been responsible for introducing knowledge of English developments in logic and philosophy to Paris. His best-known writings are commentaries on the Sentences of Peter *Lombard. He tackled the general problem of divine foreknowledge and future contingents and the specific dilemma of predestination and free will.

Grelling's paradox Some words refer to themselves: the word 'short' is short, and the word 'common' is common. Other words do not: the word 'long' is not long, and the word 'banana' is not a banana. Call these latter words 'heterological'. Then the question arises: is the word 'heterological' itself heterological? It is if it is not, and is not if it is. This is one of the family of *semantic paradoxes.

Grice, Herbert Paul (1913–88) English philosopher of language. Educated at Oxford, Grice became a Fellow of St John's College, Oxford, in 1939. In 1967 he emigrated to a chair at Berkeley, retiring in 1980. He introduced the important concept of an *implicature into the philosophy of language, arguing that not everything that is said is direct evidence for the meaning of some term, since many factors may determine the appropriateness of remarks independently of whether they are actually true. The point undermined excessive attention to the niceties of conversation as reliable indicators of meaning, a methodology characteristic of *linguistic philosophy. In a number of elegant papers Grice also introduced an approach to the concept of the meaning of a sentence which identifies it with a complex of intentions with which it is uttered. The psychological is thus used to explain the semantic, and the question of whether this is the correct priority has prompted considerable subsequent discussion. *Studies in the Way of Words* (1989) and *The Conception of Value* (1991) were published posthumously.

Grosseteste, Robert (*c.*1168–1253) English medieval philosopher. Born in Suffolk, Grosseteste gained a reputation in medicine, and after study in Paris became perhaps the first Chancellor of the university of Oxford. He taught the Franciscans in Oxford, and became Bishop of Lincoln in 1235. He represented an *Augustinian tradition, filtered through *Avicenna and *Anselm, in contrast to the prevailing Aristotelian influence in the schools of Paris. Grosseteste had scientific interests; he was particularly concerned with the nature of light, which he thought had to be studied by essentially mathematical methods. In the Platonic tradition, he thought that the nature or form of body is itself light, since it is light alone that diffuses itself instantaneously in every direction, and is therefore capable of filling space. Between 1215 and 1235 he composed various works on the subject including *De Luce* ('On Light'). Grosseteste was one of the first western thinkers to realize that, in the pursuit of science, unaided observation and memory must be supplemented by care in isolating relevant factors. His scientific interests were especially influential on Roger *Bacon. He also wrote on *Aristotle's ethics, and translated works by *Dionysius the Pseudo-Areopagite, and John Damascene.

Grotius, Hugo (1583–1645) Dutch philosopher of law. Grotius is the father of modern international law, and developed many of the building blocks for subsequent attempts to establish an international order. Born in Delft, he lived through the Thirty Years' War, and in 1625 wrote his masterpiece *The Laws of War and Peace* (*De Jure Belli ac Pacis*) after escaping from prison to France. Grotius is a defender of *natural law theory, but law as founded on reason rather than on a divine order: 'natural law is so immutable that it cannot be changed by God himself' (*see* EUTHYPHRO DILEMMA). Grotius converted the actual fact of self-interest and self-preservation into the foundation of morals, a natural right whose service provided the rationale for civil society. In this he was immensely influential on 17th-century political theory, and especially *Hobbes. The foundation of relations between the states are that *pacta sunt servanda* (treaties are to be respected). From this, his *Stoic respect for reason, and his experience as a diplomat, Grotius derived a substantial body of precepts and principles. Like *Descartes, he caught pneumonia at the court of *Kristina Wasa, and died on the way back to Holland.

grue *See* GOODMAN'S PARADOX.

guardians The guardians of the *Republic* of *Plato are a combination of the protectors and governors of the state. Their temperament and education is the subject of the latter parts of a large portion of part ii of the work. They play the role of the military, the civil service, and the government, being bulldogs against the enemies of the state, but wise and gentle to its citizens. To maintain these standards the guardians must live a monastic, military life with no need of money or family (representing the impartiality required of the final repository of political and moral authority). They divide into the philosophical rulers, who represent the virtue of wisdom, and the auxiliaries or executive wing, whose main virtue is holding fast to the requirements laid down by the wise. The just organization of the state is not only a topic in its own right for Plato, but a model for the proper hierarchy of functions within the single individual. To the question 'who shall guard the guardians?' ('quis custodiet ipsos custodes?', raised by Juvenal in the slightly different context of guarding a wife from temptation), Plato's answer is their education and virtue alone do so; the modern world hopes that checks and balances do the same.

guilt/shame Guilt is the uncomfortable feeling of having done wrong, and therefore deserving the anger of others. Shame is the sense of deserving the contempt or disdain of others. Although anthropologists and historians sometimes divide societies as more prone to stress one of these emotions rather than the other, both appear to be found in a large variety of human cultures. The social function of each of them is readily seen: with guilt we are primed to tolerate the anger of others that would otherwise make us angry in return; with shame we internalize the values that lead to admiration or rejection. It is noteworthy that each emotion is only easily characterized in moral terms. This makes them dangerous starting-points for *emotive analyses of ethics, although such an account putting guilt at the centre is given in the American philosopher Allan Gibbard's *Wise Choices, Apt Feelings* (1991).

guru (Sanskrit, teacher) This can include parents, teachers in universities, arts, and crafts, as well as the more familiar spiritual guides. All are owed a full measure of trust and obedience, even when they are not understood.

Gyges *See* RING OF GYGES.

Habermas, Jürgen (1929–) Born in Düsseldorf, Habermas was educated at Bonn and Marburg, before holding posts at the Institute for Social Research, and eventually becoming professor of philosophy at Frankfurt. He is the leading contemporary representative of the *Frankfurt school, and is noted for his sustained attack on the problems of the nature of communication and self-consciousness, and their role in the causation of social action. Habermas distinguishes three cognitive interests common to human beings: the technical interest in knowing and controlling the world around us, the interest in being able to understand each other and join in common activity, and the interest in removing distortions in our understanding of ourselves, the last of which gives rise to the critical sciences. These distinct interests stand in the way of the economic determinism of classical Marxism (*see also* BASE AND SUPERSTRUCTURE). He is also prominent for trying to develop a foundation for ethics in the notion of an ideal speech situation, a 'discourse' oriented version of Kant's principle of the *categorical imperative. His works include *Theorie und Praxis. Sozial-philosophische Studien* (1963, trs. as *Theory and Practice*, 1973), *Theorie des kommunikativen Handelns* (1981, trs. as *The Theory of Communicative Action*, 2 vols., 1984, 1986), and *Der philosophische Diskurs der Moderne* (1985, trs. as *Philosophical Discourse on Modernity*, 1986).

Hacking, Ian (1936–) Canadian philosopher, educated at British Columbia and Trinity College, Cambridge, and now centred in Toronto and Paris where he holds a Chair at the Collège de France. Hacking has written widely on the philosophy of probability and the philosophy of science in general. He has been especially interested in the social background and historical conditions underlying the emergence of particular scientific concepts. Early books included *The Logic of Statistical Inference* (1965) and *Why Does Language Matter to Philosophy?* (1975). *The Emergence of Probability* (1975) and *The Taming of Chance* (1990) are contributions to the philosophy and history of probability. His *Representing and Intervening* (1983) emphasized the role of experiment in the natural sciences, while *Le Plus pur nominalisme* (1993) concerned *Goodman's paradox. The social aspect of medical concepts is discussed in *Rewriting the Soul: Multiple Personality and the Politics of Memory* (1995), *Mad Travelers* (1998), and *The Social Construction of What* (1999).

haecceity Term used by *Duns Scotus for that in virtue of which an individual is the individual that it is: its individuating essence making it this object or person. Haecceitism is the doctrine that there are such individual concepts. In modern discussion the term was revived by the American philosopher of language David Kaplan ('How to Russell a Frege-Church', *Journal of Philosophy*, 1975) in the idiom of *possible worlds: 'the doctrine that holds that it does make sense to ask—without reference to common attributes or behaviour—whether *this* is the same individual in another possible world ... and that a common "thisness" may underlie extreme dissimilarity or distinct thisnesses may underlie great resemblance.' *See* COUNTERPART THEORY.

Haeckel, Ernst Heinrich (1834–1919) German biologist and polymath, and passionate Darwinian. Philosophically Haeckel advocated a 'neutral monism' rejecting free will and theism; also, following the *idealist strand in German thinking, he advocated the fundamental unity of organic and inorganic nature in 'a sort of pantheism'. He is famous for the (incorrect) statement that 'ontogeny recapitulates phylogeny'. Here ontogeny is the the development of the embryo, and phylogeny the evolution of the species; the claim is that the embryo of every species repeats the evolutionary development of that species, which is not true.

Hägerström, Axel Anders (1868–1939) Professor at Uppsala, and one of the founders of the Uppsala school. Hägerström had a resolutely anti-metaphysical stance, and was one of the first philosophers to adopt a non-cognitivist theory of evaluative and normative discourse. His aim was to remove metaphysical and ideological preconceptions from the philosophy of law and his work was influential on Scandinavian legal theory, and subsequent writers such as Alf *Ross. Books included the early *The Principle of Science* (1908), and *Inquiries into the Nature of Law and Morals* (1958).

Halevi, Judah (*c*.1075–1141) Spanish Jewish philosopher and poet. Halevi rejected the Neoplatonism of his milieu for failing to distinguish between the God of the Jews and that of Islam. In his greatest poem, *Kuzari*, he argues for a particular, concrete 'God of history' rather than an abstract 'God of the philosophers'.

hallucination The occurrence of an experience in itself indistinguishable from a perception of something, but without an appropriate external cause. Hallucination is sometimes distinguished from pseudo-hallucination, in which the experience occurs but is not mistaken for the perception of an external object. Both are distinct from illusion, in which there is an external source, but its nature is mistaken (a mirage is thus an illusion, but not a hallucination). The possibility of hallucination is a frequent starting-point for the distinction between appearance and reality. *See also* ILLUSION, ARGUMENT FROM.

halting problem The fundamental *decision problem in the theory of computation. It is the problem of finding whether there is an effective procedure for telling whether a *Turing machine computation ever terminates, for an arbitrary input. The negative solution is that there is no such procedure. So there can be no 'program tester' that, given any program and its input, answers the question of whether the program ever terminates.

Hamann, Johann Georg (1730–88) German theologian and philosopher. Hamann was a pioneer of the anti-rationalistic, anti-Enlightenment spirit represented by the **Sturm und Drang* movement in German culture, and was considerably revered by writers such as *Herder. He emphasized the whole person, attacking the *Enlightenment dissociation of reason from passion, and theory from action. In many respects, however, his discomfort with the secular ideals of the Enlightenment resembles that of the English Samuel *Johnson, and stems not from a 'heaven-storming' Byronic *Romanticism, but from a conservative, religious, and inner-directed 17th-century piety. He lived, like *Kant, in Königsberg, and was known as the Magus of the North. The standard edition of his writings is the *Sämtliche Werke* (1949–57), edited by Joseph Nadler.

hamartia Term used by *Aristotle to denote the error or failure (the 'fatal flaw') that leads the central figure of a tragedy to eventual catastrophe.

Hamilton, William (1788–1856) Scottish philosopher and logician, who from 1836 held the chair of logic and metaphysics at Edinburgh. He held the view that perception gives us a direct or immediate relation with its objects, although one that is in Kantian vein 'conditioned' by the medium and the nature of the knowing subject. Of ultimate or unconditioned reality we can know nothing. Like *Kant, Hamilton applies this result to show our inability to know the nature of space and time. In logic, Hamilton was famous for the doctrine of the 'quantification of the predicate', the subject of acrimonious dispute with *De Morgan. His principal work is the four-volume *Lectures on Metaphysics and Logic* (1859–60). One of J. S. *Mill's major works is the *Examination of Sir William Hamilton's Philosophy* (1865).

happiness All ethical theories accord some importance to human happiness. They differ first in their conception of what that happiness consists in, secondly in views of how an agent's own personal happiness is aligned with, or traded against, the general happiness, and thirdly in whether it is necessary to acknowledge any other end for human action. The simplest doctrine is that happiness is itself quite straightforward, consisting for example in occasions of pleasure; that agents only do seek or ought to seek their own happiness; and that there is no other possible or desirable end of action (*see* HEDONISM). The *Cyrenaics may have held a doctrine along these lines. Complexity arises with more subtle conceptions of the nature of happiness (*see*, for example, EPICUREANISM, FELICIFIC CALCULUS, STOICISM), and more concern for the possibility of incorporating the good of others into one's own ends (*see*, for example, ALTRUISM, FRIENDSHIP, PRISONERS' DILEMMA). Finally, theories of ethics that are not *consequentialist in nature may recognize other ethically important features of action than those arising from the goal of maximizing either personal or social happiness. For the paradox of happiness, *see* HEDONISM, PARADOX OF.

hardware/software The familiar distinction in computer science between the actual engineering and circuitry making up a computer, and the program or set of instructions it then performs. The distinction is frequently employed in the philosophy of mind, where it may be illuminating to think of the psychological description of persons as analogous to a software description, describing the 'program' they are following, without reference to the particular neurophysiological set-up that enables them to function: the hardware, or more jocularly, wetware. The distinction becomes more problematic when a machine's hardware becomes permanently modified in order to run some particular set of commands, as is the case with certain *connectionist systems. *See also* FUNCTIONALISM.

Hare, Richard Mervyn (1919–2002) English moral philosopher, and professor of moral philosophy at Oxford, then at the university of Florida. Hare's first book, *The Language of Morals* (1952), made *prescriptivism a leading theory of the nature of moral judgement. His analyses of the notion of commendation, and of *universalizability in ethics, remain landmarks in the application of philosophy of language to moral theory. In subsequent works (especially *Freedom and Reason*, 1963, and *Moral Thinking: Its Levels, Method, and Point*, 1981) Hare attempted to show that ethical arguments can be underwritten by reason, in that moral concepts obey a logic sufficiently powerful to show some variety of *utilitarianism to be true. Hare's utilitarianism tries to balance the virtues of both direct and indirect or rule-orientated versions of the doctrine. The resulting 'two-level' view has proved controversial, with critics claiming that the agent is left in an unstable position, not knowing whether to deliberate as an 'archangel' capable of utilitarian reasoning, or in a more everyday, intuitive and *agent-centred fashion.

SEE WEB LINKS

- A brief interview with Hare on his career in philosophy

harm A contested concept, whose central cases include bodily injury and injury to one's central and legitimate interests. Harm has some connotations of permanence, so one might hurt oneself temporarily without harming oneself (stubbing one's toe, for example). Given that one of the main accepted reasons for legal restraint is the prevention of harm to others, it remains important to determine the limits of the concept. Disputed cases include the causing of discomfort, insult, nuisance, and offence.

harmony, pre-established *See* LEIBNIZ.

harmony of the spheres A doctrine often traced to *Pythagoras and fusing together mathematics, music, and astronomy. In essence the heavenly bodies, being large objects in motion, must produce music. The perfection of the celestial world requires that this music be harmonious; it is hidden from our ears only because it is always present. The mathematics of harmony was a central discovery of immense significance to the Pythagoreans.

Hart, Herbert Lionel Adolphus (1907–92) English philosopher of law. Hart's first career was as a lawyer; he became fellow and tutor in philosophy at New College, Oxford (1945–52), then professor of jurisprudence at Oxford (1952–68), and principal of Brasenose College (1973–8). He was the most influential legal philosopher of his time, whose masterpiece *The Concept of Law* (1961) set the agenda for a generation of jurisprudence. The work applies techniques from *linguistic philosophy to a sophisticated defence of the view that law consists essentially in a system of rules located in social practices: a version of legal *positivism. Hart also wrote, with A. M. Honoré, *Causation in the Law* (1959), a study of causation in questions of civil and criminal liability. A liberal in his political views, Hart became well known to a wider public through the debate with Lord Devlin over the Wolfenden report on the function of the law in the sphere of sexual behaviour, where his *The Morality of the Criminal Law* (1965) remains a classic defence of the liberal position on the limits of law in moral matters. Other works include *Punishment and Responsibility* (1968), *Essays on Bentham: Jurisprudence and Political Theory* (1982), and *Essays in Jurisprudence and Philosophy* (1983). The definitive biography is by Nicola Lacey (2004).

Hartley, David (1705–57) English physician and philosopher. Hartley is best remembered for being the founder of *associationist psychology. His *Observations of Man: His Frame, his Duty, and his Expectations* (1749) is a *naturalistic attempt to provide an integrated theory of human nature. Hartley believed that the task of education was to bring about an association of private pleasure with the exercise of public benevolence and virtue. In the well-adjusted person there is a 'ladder of pleasures' with those of benevolence towards the top, because of their associations with various other kinds of pleasure. Hartley's thought significantly influenced the later generation of *utilitarians such as James *Mill.

Hartmann, Eduard von (1842–1906) German metaphysician. Hartmann's 19th-century reputation depended centrally upon *The Philosophy of the Unconscious* (1869), a fashionably pessimistic mixture, reconciling the absolute idealism of *Hegel with the primacy of the will in *Schopenhauer, but with a dash of the pantheism of *Schelling thrown in.

Hartmann, Nicolai (1882–1950) German ontologist. Hartmann held posts at Marburg (1922–5), Cologne (1925–31), Berlin (1931–45), and Göttingen (1945–50). His philosophy aims to establish a unified ontological system, not containing God, but with room for absolute values. Works included *Ethik* (1926, trs. in 3 vols., 1932); *Grundzüge einer Metaphysik der Erkenntnis* (1921); *Das Problem des geistigen Seins* (1933); *Möglichkeit und Wirklichkeit* (1938); *Der Aufbau der realen Welt* (1940); *Neue Wege der Ontologie* (1949, trs. as *New Ways of Ontology*, 1952); and *Ästhetik* (1953).

Hartshorne, Charles (1897–2000) American religious philosopher. Hartshorne was a doctoral student at Harvard, and held posts at the University of Chicago, at Emory University, and the University of Texas at Austin. Hartshorne was best-known for his rehabilitation of the *ontological argument for the existence of God, but he wrote widely on systematic metaphysics, defending a kind of panpsychism. Books included *The Philosophy and Psychology of Sensation* (1934), *Beyond Humanism* (1937), *Reality as Social Process* (1953), *Whitehead's Philosophy* (1972), and a volume on birdsong, *Born to Sing* (1973).

hatha-yoga The system of physical and mental training and discipline commonly known as yoga. It is a part of, but not identical with, the *Yoga system of philosophy.

Hayek, Friedrich (1899–1992) Austrian economist and philosopher. Born and educated in Vienna, Hayek taught at London and Chicago before returning to his native country in 1962. In a succession of economic analyses, and in more popular works (such as *The Road to Serfdom*, 1944), he propounded an extreme **laissez-faire* economic individualism, allied with the political belief that anything in the nature of state action or collective action (such as that of trade unions) undermines liberty and paves the way to totalitarianism. Similar analyses were applied to the history of positivism since *Comte, in *The Counter-Revolution of Science: Studies in the Abuse of Reason* (1952). He was a notable influence on the economic and political right wing in Britain and the USA, especially after his views were revivified by the award of the Nobel prize in 1974.

heap, paradox of the *See* SORITES PARADOX.

heaven *See* ETERNITY, HELL, MAKROPOULOS CASE, *SUMMUM BONUM*.

hedonic calculus *See* FELICIFIC CALCULUS.

hedonism The pursuit of one's own *pleasure as an end in itself; in ethics, the view that such a pursuit is the proper aim of all action. Since there are different conceptions of *pleasure there are correspondingly different varieties of hedonism. Unless one's own pleasure can somehow be identified with that of others (*see* FRIENDSHIP) hedonism stands opposed to the disinterested concern for others commonly thought to be an essential element of morality, although there are various ways of trying to align the pursuit of selfish pleasure with some degree of concern for others. Psychological hedonism is the view that either contingently, because of our human nature, or as a matter of conceptual necessity, people only pursue their own pleasure. It is not true, on either construction.

hedonism, paradox of The paradox (Joseph *Butler, Sermon xi, para. 1. 9; *Sidgwick, *The Methods of Ethics*, 7th edn, pp. 136, 403) that agents who consciously attempt to maximize their own pleasures are more likely to fail than those who have concerns for other things and other persons for their own sakes. *See also* PRISONERS' DILEMMA, SELF-DEFEATING.

Hegel, Georg Wilhelm Friedrich (1770–1831) German philosopher. Born at Stuttgart, Hegel studied at Tübingen, where his contemporaries included *Schelling and the poet Hölderlin. After holding positions as a tutor he went to Jena in 1801 as a *Privatdozent* in philosophy, qualified by his thesis *De Orbitis Planetarium* ('On the Orbits of the Planets'; the false view that Hegel thought that he could prove *a priori* that there are seven planets arises from misunderstanding the last chapter of this work). While in Jena he collaborated with Schelling in editing the *Kritisches Journal der Philosophie*, to which he contributed many articles, and wrote his first major work, the *Phänomenologie des Geistes* (1807, trs. as *The Phenomenology of Mind*, 1910; also as *The Phenomenology of Spirit*, 1977). Promoted to a chair in 1805, he then was forced to leave Jena because of the Napoleonic war, became editor of a newspaper, and from 1807 spent eight years as director of the Gymnasium in Nürnberg. While there he published the two volumes of the *Wissenschaft der Logik* (1812–16, trs. as *The Logic of Hegel*, 1874). In 1816 he became professor of philosophy at Heidelberg, where he produced the *Enzyklopädie der philosophischen Wissenschaften im Grundrisse* ('Encyclopaedia of the Philosophical Sciences in Outline'). Two years later he succeeded *Fichte as professor in Berlin and entered into his most famous and influential period. His *Naturrecht und Staatswissenschaft im Grundrisse* and *Grundlinien der Philosophie des Rechts* (trs. as *The Philosophy of Right*, 1896) appeared in 1821, and many lecture notes by pupils were subsequently collected. The standard edition of Hegel's works (Stuttgart, 1927–30) runs to twenty volumes. Hegel attracted great numbers of foreign students to Berlin, and had an unparalleled influence on German philosophy in the 19th century. He was also the central philosophical influence on *Marx and *Engels, and on English philosophy in the *absolute idealist phase, and although his reputation in the Anglo-American world has suffered periods of eclipse, he continues to be a focal point for many thinkers.

The cornerstone of Hegel's system, or world view, is the notion of freedom, conceived not as simple licence to fulfil preferences but as the rare condition of living self-consciously and in a fully rationally organized community or state (this is not, as is charged for example by *Popper, a defence of the totalitarian state or the doctrine that 'might is right', since Hegel requires a rational state to meet very stringent conditions, including the consent of the rational conscience of its members). Surprisingly, history can be seen as progress towards freedom: here Hegel follows the spirit of his own age (*see* ROMANTICISM), voicing a confidence in progress and purpose in the otherwise jumbled kaleidoscope of history, but incidentally providing a dangerously intoxicating model for all social and political movements that pride themselves that they are on the side of the future. For Hegel such a progress is required by a proper theory of knowledge. Hegel admires *scepticism as a movement that respects the freedom of reason, but starting from the Kantian response to scepticism he charts in the *Phenomenology* the development of all possible forms of consciousness, to the point where awareness becomes possible not of mere phenomena, but of reality as it is in itself, identified both with knowledge of the Absolute and with the moment when 'mind' finally knows itself. Although this desirable outcome is left rather vague, the *Phenomenology* contains brilliant analyses of the fragile nature of self-consciousness, and in particular the way it depends upon recognition by others. Thus the emergence of the singular 'mind' as opposed to the normal plurality of many minds is justified by the social nature of self-consciousness. Hegel's understanding that to have value in my own eyes I must achieve value in the eyes of others was arguably the foundation for subsequent social philosophy (*see* ALIENATION, MASTER/SLAVE MORALITY). Apart from his social and political philosophy, one of the most important of Hegel's legacies has been his conception of logic (*see* DIALECTIC, DIALECTICAL MATERIALISM). Hegel's own attitude to logic is complicated by the equation between history on the one hand and thought or spirit on the other, meaning that disharmony or 'contradiction' in the world is an instance of contradiction in thought. Hegel's own attitude to the idea that actual events might embody contradictions, and thus in some sense make contradictions true, has been the topic of much debate.

SEE WEB LINKS

- An illustrated biography of Hegel
- An audio discussion of Hegel by three philosophers

Hegelianism The history of Hegel's influence is complicated by conflicting elements within his own system. Until *Feuerbach's *Thoughts regarding Death and Immortality* (1830), the torch was carried by the 'Old Hegelians' who emphasized the Christian and conservative elements in his writings. After Feuerbach and especially the *Life of Jesus* (1835) of D. F. Strauss, the denial of personal religion became more prominent. In politics the 'New Hegelians', including the young *Marx, found in Hegel's *dialectic the ammunition to assail the bourgeois, religious, monarchical social order, now revealed as only a moment in the forward development of history.

Hegelianism as a self-conscious philosophy was transported to Britain with the publication of *The Secret of Hegel* by J. H. Stirling in 1865 and, transmuted into *absolute idealism, became part of the dominant academic philosophy in Britain until attacked by *Russell and *Moore in Cambridge, and writers such as J. Cook-Wilson and H. H. Prichard at Oxford, at the beginning of the 20th century.

hegemony A term especially associated with *Gramsci, to whom it denotes the concealed domination of all the positions of institutional power and influence by members of just one class. The hegemony of one class could indefinitely postpone revolution; an important revolutionary activity is therefore to infiltrate and weaken the structures that it occupies.

Heidegger, Martin (1889–1976) German existentialist and social critic. Heidegger was probably the most divisive philosopher of the 20th century, being an acknowledged leader and central figure to many ('continental') philosophers, and either a convenient example of meaningless metaphysics, or else an apologist for Nazism, or both, to other ('analytical') thinkers. Heidegger was born in Baden, and educated at Freiburg in the phenomenological tradition of *Husserl. He became *Privatdozent* at Freiburg in 1915, professor at Marburg in 1923, and professor at Freiburg in 1928.

His most important work, *Sein und Zeit* (1927, trs. as *Being and Time*, 1962), clears the space for the quest for Being that informs Heidegger's works. Modern humanity has lost the 'nearness and shelter' of Being; we are no longer at home in the world as primitive man was; truth is no longer revealed; thought is separated from Being and only a favoured few have any hope of recapturing oneness with Being. Many of these themes, and especially belief in the possibility of escaping from metaphysics and returning into an authentic communion with independent nature, were commonplaces of German *Romanticism, but Heidegger reworked them in a way that caught the 20th-century imagination. Although *Aristotle makes the science of Being the apex of enquiry and the proper subject of metaphysics, it is somewhat difficult to say anything about Being as such, so what in effect replaces it is people's own consciousness of their place in the world, or of what the world is for them (their **Dasein*), which then becomes the topic. Freedom, existence in the world, inauthenticity, dread, guilt, and destiny therefore become the major themes. However, before they became the staple topics of *existentialism, they had a more sinister political embodiment: in 1933 Heidegger became Rector of Freiburg, and his notorious *Rektorsrede* or inaugural speech, 'The Role of the University in the New Reich', was a call for Germany to move itself into the primordial realm of the powers of Being, with the Nazi party in the vanguard.

In his later work Heidegger became more inclined to a kind of historical fatalism, and is sometimes seen as an heir to the tradition of *Dilthey. Heidegger's continuing influence is due at least in part to his criticism of modernity and democracy, which he associates with a lack of respect for nature independent of the uses to which human beings put it. However, he has also been hailed (notably by *Rorty) as a proponent of *pragmatism, and even more remarkably many French intellectuals have taken him as a prophet of the political left. When he writes that 'from a metaphysical point of view, Russia and America are the same; the same dreary technological frenzy, the same unrestricted organization of the average man' (*An Introduction to Metaphysics*, 1953), it is easy to forget that his contempt for the mass culture of the industrial age springs from a nationalistic and conservative elitism, rather than from any left-wing or egalitarian agenda.

Heisenberg uncertainty principle The principle of *quantum mechanics that associates the physical properties of particles into pairs, such that both together cannot be measured to within more than a certain degree of accuracy. If A and V form such a pair (called a conjugate pair) then: $\Delta A \Delta V > k$ where k is a constant and ΔA and ΔV are variances in the experimental values for the attributes A and V. The best-known instance of the equation relates the position and momentum of an electron: $\Delta p \Delta x > h$ where h is Planck's constant. This is the Heisenberg uncertainty principle. *See also* BELL'S THEOREM, EINSTEIN–PODOLSKY–ROSEN THOUGHT EXPERIMENT.

SEE WEB LINKS

- An online exhibit on the principle's history, with a bibliography
- An audio discussion of quantum indeterminacy by three philosophers

hell Place or state reserved for unrepentant sinners after death, where they suffer both separation from God, and other traditional punishments. Hell is designed by a benevolent deity, which seems surprising: *Russell believed that no truly good person could ever have invented the doctrine. In the 20th century there has been a growing tendency to personalize the matter. *Sartre held that hell is other people; T. S. Eliot said that hell is oneself. *See also* EVIL, PROBLEM OF.

Helmholtz, Hermann von (1821–94) German scientist and philosopher. Helmholtz graduated from the Medical Institute in Berlin in 1843, and subsequently held appointments at Königsberg, Bonn, Heidelberg, and Berlin. His physicalist leanings led him to disparage 'vital forces', then common in medicine, and to formulate the principle of conservation of energy. Work on hydrodynamics led to fundamental discoveries in topology, and he also studied the physiology of auditory perception. In physics, after an initial defence of the *a priori* status of Euclidean geometry, Helmholtz repudiated his Kantian heritage and followed the lead of *Riemann and Lobachevsky. Helmholtz was the most influential German scientist of the Victorian period, and a leading figure in the conception of science as the search for fundamental laws.

Héloïse (1101–64) French philosopher and writer. Educated at the Benedictine convent of Argenteuil and intellectually renowned from an early age, Héloïse was tutored privately by *Abelard, who seduced her (apparently with some violence) and made her pregnant. Against her will she married Abelard secretly, and returned with the child Astralabe to the home of her uncle, Fulbert, but when Fulbert made the marriage public she was ordered by Abelard to take the veil. Angry at the denial of the marriage, Fulbert had Abelard castrated (sympathy with Abelard's fate tends to disguise the fact that he played a rather shoddy part in the affair). Héloïse became abbess and prioress of the Paraclete house, a nunnery. Her writings include the *Problemata Heloissae*, a set of philosophical questions addressed to Abelard. The letters between her and Abelard purport to have begun after Abelard had written the *Historia Calamitatum Abaelardi*. They were published in 1616 and testify to Héloïse's deep moral learning, as well as her passion for Abelard; although they have sometimes been regarded as forgeries written by Abelard himself the weight of opinion is that they are authentic.

Helvétius, Claude-Adrien (1715–71) One of the moving spirits behind the **Encyclopédie*, Helvétius defended a theory of human motivation founded on sensation: we are pushed to action solely by self-interested love of pleasure and desire to avoid pain. He is principally remembered for *De l'esprit* (1758), which was influential upon *Bentham and subsequent *utilitarian theory.

Hempel, Carl Gustav (1905–97) Philosopher of science. Hempel was born in Orianenberg, Germany, and went to the United States in the 1930s. He taught from 1939 at New York, Yale, Princeton, and Pittsburgh. His work on the nature of explanation and the structure of scientific theory has been the focus of all subsequent investigation into those subjects. Books include *Fundamentals of Concept Formation in Empirical Science* (1952) and *Aspects of Scientific Explanation* (1970).

Hempel's paradox The principle of *induction by enumeration allows a suitable generalization to be confirmed by its instances. Thus observation of black ravens should confirm the generalization that all ravens are black. It is also clear that if evidence confirms a hypothesis, it should confirm any hypothesis logically equivalent to it. Now 'all non-black things are non-ravens' is logically equivalent to 'all ravens are black'. Its instances are things like white shoes. So observation of a white shoe should confirm that all non-black things are non-ravens, and hence that all ravens are black. But intuitively the observation is entirely irrelevant to this hypothesis. The paradox depends upon (i) *Nicod's criterion and (ii) the principle that whatever confirms a hypothesis confirms any logically equivalent hypothesis. Solutions include restricting the kinds of generalization that can be confirmed by their instances, denying the principle that if evidence confirms a hypothesis it confirms any logically equivalent hypothesis, and accepting the conclusion that the observation is, in fact, relevant, although very weakly so. This last solution (Hempel's own) points out that if the numbers of things involved, or the background information, were different we might well allow something that was neither A nor B to confirm that all As are B. Nevertheless the paradox forces further investigation of the rationale behind Nicod's criterion.

henological argument The fourth of the *Five Ways: the *degrees of perfection argument for the existence of God.

henotheism The worship of one God while conceding that other Gods exist. Kathenotheism is the worship of a succession of gods, but only one god at a time: serial henotheism.

Henry of Ghent (*c.*1217–93) Belgian theologian and significant Augustinian thinker. Henry taught theology at Paris, managing a fusion of Aristotelianism, doctrines derived from *Avicenna, and the more Platonic illuminationism of *Augustine. His works include *Summa quaestionum ordinarium.*

Heraclides of Pontus (4th c. BC) A member of Plato's *Academy and pupil of Speusippus, Heraclides was a contemporary of Aristotle and wrote on ethics, astronomy, physics, history, and politics. His extant dialogues show an attractive light style, illustrated by anecdote and myth, an influence on subsequent writers such as *Cicero.

Heraclitus of Ephesus (d. after 480 BC) Both the life and work of Heraclitus are shadowy, and overlain by later legends and reworkings of his views. The one book he is known to have produced is lost, probably from early in antiquity, although he was often quoted and discussed. The guiding idea of his philosophy was that of the *logos* (law or principle) governing all things: this *logos* is capable of being heard or hearkened to by people, it unifies opposites, and it is somehow associated with fire, which is pre-eminent among the four elements that Heraclitus distinguishes: fire, air (breath, the stuff of which souls are composed), earth, and water. Although he is principally remembered for the doctrine of the 'flux' of all things, and the famous statement that you cannot step into the same river twice, for new waters are ever flowing in upon you, Heraclitus was probably more interested in measured, balanced processes. The more extreme implications of the doctrine of flux (e.g. the impossibility of categorizing things truly) do not seem consistent with his general epistemology and view of meaning, and were left to his follower *Cratylus to develop. The primacy of the divine, eternal *logos* and the contrast between the unstable world of appearance and the order behind it exercised tremendous influence on *Plato, and then on the *Stoics.

Herbart, Johann Friedrich (1776–1841) German philosopher and educational theorist. Herbart studied under Fichte, but was influenced by Leibniz and Kant, whom he succeeded in the chair at Königsberg from 1808. He held that change was nothing but changing relationships between independent real simple elements; applied to the philosophy of mind this generated a kind of *associationist psychology. In educational theory this in turn meant that new ideas become assimilated by a process of 'apperception', itself dependent upon the ground laid by preceding experience. His major work in psychology was *Psychologie als Wissenschaft* (1824–5) and his most important philosophical work the *Allgemeine Metaphysik* (1828–9).

Herbert of Cherbury, Edward (*c.*1583–1648) Herbert is remembered as a target of *Locke's attack on innate ideas (*Essay*, Bk i. 3, 15). He held that *notitae communes* or common notions can be seen to be true by unaided and innate reason, granted to us by divine providence. Amongst these are the five that Locke cites for criticism: belief that there is one God, that he must be worshipped, that this is to be done with worship and piety together, that sin requires repentance, and that we will be awarded rewards and penalties in an afterlife (*De Veritate*, 'On Truth', 1624). Herbert's other works include *De*

Causis Errorum ('On the Causes of Errors', 1645) and one of the first attempts at comparative religion in the modern era, the posthumous *De Religione Gentilium* ('On the Religion of the Gentiles', 1663). He was known as the father of *deism.

Herder, Johann Gottfried (1744–1803) German philosopher and historian, and an important influence on German *Romanticism. Herder was originally destined for medicine, but at the university of Königsberg he changed his subject to theology, and made the acquaintance of *Kant and *Hamann. After various travels he took up the post of *Generalsuperintendent* of the clergy at Weimar.

Herder published continuously, his most important works being *Abhandlung über den Ursprung der Sprache* (1772, trs. as *Treatise upon the Origin of Language*, 1827) and *Ideen zur Philosophie der Geschichte der Menschheit* (four parts, 1784–91, trs. as *Outlines of a Philosophy of the History of Man*, 1800). His work, like that of *Vico, is marked by a historical depth that led to dissent from the *Enlightenment assumptions of a uniform, if progressing, human nature, and to a stress on the pervasive influence of history in the shaping of human language and art. Herder also attacked the prevailing *faculty psychology of the time, holding that only nonsense arose from the standard distinctions between reason, will, desire, affection, and so forth. Rather, the person is a single unity (infused by a spirit or vital force, *Kraft*) that reasons, wills, and desires. Herder was also one of the first philosophers to identify the ability to reason with the ability to use language, and to equate thinking with inner speaking.

hereditary property A property is hereditary over a relation R if when x has the property, and Rxy, then y also has the property.

heresy Defined by the medieval church as 'an opinion chosen by human perception, founded on the scriptures, contrary to the teaching of the church, publicly avowed and obstinately defended'. It became a problem only when unorthodox opinion began to weaken the authority of the church itself, when responses included the Albigensian crusade of 1208, and the foundation of the Inquisition in 1231.

heritability Widely misunderstood concept used in debates about nature versus nurture. The heritability of a trait in a population is the proportion of *phenotypic variance (variance in some observable feature, whether of shape or size or behaviour) attributable to genetic variance. It is a measure that itself may vary with the range of genetic backgrounds and range of environments studied. For example, if all environmental factors are identical, any variation will have a genetic explanation, and heritability will approach 100%; but if genetic origin is kept constant and environment varied then heritability of the same trait may decrease towards 0%. It is therefore a mistake to argue from any particular high figure for heritability in some population in some environment, to a 'genetic determinism' or pessimism about the effects of environmental intervention.

hermeneutic circle The problems in the process of interpretation that arise when one element, for instance in a text, can only be understood in terms of the meanings of others or of the whole text, yet understanding these other elements, or the whole text, in turn presupposes understanding of the original element. Each can only be understood in the light of the others. Similarly, we may hold that the past can only be understood in the light of the present, and the present only understood in the light of the past. The phenomenon has preoccupied German thinkers from *Schleiermacher and *Dilthey through to *Heidegger and *Gadamer. In Anglo-American philosophy a similar problem arises from the *holism of meaning, but is not generally felt to pose a fundamental difficulty: as *Wittgenstein said, light dawns gradually over the whole.

hermeneutics The method of interpretation first of texts, and secondly of the whole social, historical, and psychological world. The problems were familiar to *Vico, and raised in connection with biblical criticism by *Schleiermacher. Under the title of **Verstehen* the method of interpretation was contrasted with objective scientific method by *Weber and *Dilthey. Its inevitable subjectivity is the topic of the major writings of *Gadamer.

Hermetic corpus A collection of writings from the first three centuries after Christ, combining magical, religious, and tangentially philosophical fragments. Translated by *Ficino, it had undue influence on Renaissance thought, partly through being misattributed to ancient Egyptian authorship by 'Hermes Trismegistus' supposedly from a time before *Plato. Hermes Trismegistus ('Thrice-Great Hermes') is a fusion of elements of the Greek god Hermes with the Egyptian god Thoth; the Hermetic corpus supposedly comprised the fundamental books of the Egyptian religion, including astrological, cosmological, geographical, medical, and pedagogic books and also hymns and instructions on how to worship. The extant corpus, in Greek, Latin, and Coptic, includes astrological, alchemical, medical, and philosophical works, offering insight into 'popular Platonism' in the Roman world.

hermeticism Adherence to *Hermetic teachings.

Hertz, Heinrich Rudolf (1857–94) German scientist. Hertz gave the first experimental proof of the existence of radio waves in 1887; he also discovered the photoelectric effect. His influence on philosophy came through his axiomatization of Newtonian mechanics which avoids the concept of force and derives Newton's equations from a single axiom.

Herzen, Alexander Ivanovich (1812–70) Russian writer and social philosopher, who lived in exile in Europe from 1847. Herzen was an early fugitive from *Hegelianism, expressing antipathy to all teleological and future-orientated philosophies of society, and, anticipating Dostoevsky, stressing the contingent and muddled human mess that gives them their seductive hold. A revolutionary and ally of *Proudhon and *Bakunin, he published a radical Russian newspaper, *The Bell*, from his base in London. His translated works include *My Past and Thoughts* (1866, trs. 1979) and *From the Other Shore* (1850, trs. 1956).

Hesiod (*c.*700 BC) Early Greek poet. His *Theogony* is about the origins of the gods, while *Works and Days* contains advice on how to live, a sermon inveighing against dishonesty and idleness.

heterodox Unorthodox.

heterological A word that does not apply to itself. Thus 'long' is not a long word; 'antediluvian' is not an antediluvian word. *See* GRELLING'S PARADOX.

heterologicality, paradox of *See* GRELLING'S PARADOX.

heteronomy *See* AUTONOMY/HETERONOMY.

heterophenomenology (Greek, other + *phenomenology) Term introduced in 'Beyond Belief' (1982) by *Dennett, to describe an exploration of consciousness that takes the reports we and others give of what a particular state is like as part of the admissible data. *Introspective reports are not rejected out of hand, as in methodologies influenced by *behaviourism. For producing such a report gives an intentional identification of mental states (that is, shows what we take them to be), and this can be studied regardless of whether such states really exist.

heuristic A process, such as trial and error, for solving a problem for which no *algorithm exists. A heuristic for a problem is a rule or method for approaching a solution.

hierarchy *See* SET.

Hierocles (2nd c. AD) Stoic of the time of Hadrian (AD 117–38). Hierocles wrote *Elements of Ethics* and other ethical works, important for the theory of *oikeiosis* or affiliation, a form of self-perception and self-love. He also uses the image later made famous by the 20th-century moral philosopher Peter Singer, of expanding concentric circles as an analogy to the expansion of the range of proper concern for others.

higher-order logic One in which the *variables of the *quantifiers are permitted to range over properties and functions as well as individuals (*see also* FIRST-ORDER LANGUAGE).

Hilbert's programme In a famous speech in 1900 the mathematician David Hilbert (1862–1943) identified 23 outstanding problems in mathematics. The first was the *continuum hypothesis. The second was the problem of the consistency of mathematics. This evolved into a programme of formalizing mathematical reasoning, with the aim of giving *metamathematical proofs of its consistency. (Clearly there is no hope of providing a relative consistency proof of classical mathematics, by giving a *model in some other domain. Any domain large and complex enough to provide a model would be raising the same doubts.) The programme was effectively ended by *Gödel's theorem of 1931, which showed that any system strong enough to provide a consistency proof of arithmetic would need to make logical and mathematical assumptions at least as strong as arithmetic itself, and hence be just as much prey to hidden inconsistency.

Hinduism The principal religious tradition of India, centred upon the sacred texts of the *Vedas. Philosophically Indian thought is separated into various **darshanas* or schools, exhibiting a rich variety of approaches and interests. Central concepts of Indian thought include **atman*, **brahman*, **karma*, **moksha*, and **samsara*, and the various Indian schools often anticipate the later topics of Western philosophical thought.

Hintikka, Jaakko (1929–) Finnish philosopher who has worked at Helsinki and in various universities in the United States. While Hintikka has written extensively on a variety of the great historical philosophers from Plato to Wittgenstein he is best-known for developments in formal semantics, particularly in its less usual applications, to deontic logic, the logic of question and answer, and intensional and epistemic logic. His leading analytical tool is that of a 'model set' known as a Hintikka set, or set of formulae constituting a consistent but partial description of a *possible world. Works include *Knowledge and Belief* (1962), *Models for Modalities* (1969), *Ludwig Wittgenstein: Half-Truths and One-and-a-Half-Truths*

(1996), *On Gödel* (2000), and numerous edited volumes and collections.

Hipparchia The wife of *Crates the *Cynic, whom she had chosen to marry in spite of the poverty and unconventionality of the life he offered her. She was a source of speculation because, since the Cynics insisted that nothing natural was shameful, she and Crates are reported as having copulated together in public. *Augustine (*City of God*, xiv. 20) thinks that they only pretended to do so, under the concealment of the Cynic's cloak. But he was properly reprimanded for this unwarranted scepticism by *Bayle.

Hippasus of Metapontum (6th c. BC) The member of the school of *Pythagoras credited with having discovered irrational numbers. According to one legend the discovery was made during a voyage, and Hippasus was then either divinely punished by shipwreck, or perhaps thrown into the sea by other Pythagoreans.

Hippias (*c.*485–415 BC) A citizen of *Elis, Hippias was a polymath and teacher, and is represented by *Plato as a leading *Sophist. He was a distinguished mathematician who probably discovered the quadratrix, the first curve other than the circle recognized in Greek mathematics. Philosophically he appears to have stood for an anti-Platonic empiricism, perhaps similar to the later standpoint of *Aristotle, and he is known to have been interested in the antithesis between nature and convention.

Hippocrates (5th c. BC) Greek physician. Hippocrates was a contemporary of *Socrates. Little is known of him except that he was short, travelled much, and probably died at Larissa. The *Corpus Hippocraticum* or body of writing to which his name became attached in fact contains no part that can be reliably attributed to him. His fame as the ideal doctor, and the first to treat the body as a whole organism, rests on *Plato (*Phaedrus* 270 a) and the subsequent escalating attribution of medical wisdom to him. The Hippocratic oath enjoining doctors to heal rather than to harm is possibly of *Pythagorean origin.

historical explanation The central question is whether the form of *explanation in history is typically the same as that of the natural sciences. Principal proponents of the claim that there is no essential difference included the *logical positivists, for whom all legitimate explanation would conform to the pattern they believed to be exhibited in natural science. The opposing view stresses the differences characteristic of historical enquiry. These include the fact that historical events are particular, dated, and unrepeated complexes of human interaction, unlike the repeatable events of science (*see* IDIOGRAPHIC/NOMOTHETIC METHODS). They also depend upon human intention and motivation, although different schools of historians have seen individual human endeavours as more or less important to particular social and political explananda. There is also the residual question of whether explanation by motivation and intention is itself of the same form as scientific explanation (*see* FUNCTIONALISM, SIMULATION, *VERSTEHEN*). The most celebrated proponents of the distinctive nature of historical explanation are *Dilthey and *Collingwood.

historical materialism The classical *Marxist view of history. It is described by *Engels in the introduction to *Socialism: Utopian and Scientific* as seeking 'the ultimate cause and the great moving power of all important historic events in the economic development of society, in the changes in the modes of production and exchange, in the consequent division of society into distinct classes, and in the struggle of these classes against one another'. Historical materialism is described by Marx and Engels as a scientific, empirical hypothesis, but in fact is a framework or guide for historical explanation, and as such measured more by the unifying insights it gives and the success of the research programme it generates. According to historical materialism, changes in the productive forces of a society lead to social conflict, and the specific forms of social organization that emerge reflect the underlying structure of the means of production (*see* BASE AND SUPERSTRUCTURE). One of the main problems in understanding Marxism is to relate historical materialism to *historicism, or the idea that history takes a determined, inevitable shape, with movements and aims that are not in accord with that shape being doomed in advance to failure. In principle historical materialism has no such implication, and Marx himself took care to distance it from any *fatalistic interpretation.

historicism In the work of *Popper (*The Open Society and its Enemies*, 1945, and *The Poverty of Historicism*, 1957), historicism is any belief in the necessity of historical processes, or belief that such processes are governed by laws, and are immune to human choice and agency. Popper influentially attacked this belief as he found it in *Hegel, *Marx, and their followers, both as a mask for a *totalitarian ideology, and as itself unscientific because compatible with any course of events. More loosely, historicism may refer to other positions. One is the general view that historical periods must be understood 'in their own terms', as opposed to the terms of the present, although how we escape the categories of the present is not so clear. Another is the view that to understand a social phenomenon is to be able to trace its genesis and development; there is no understanding a phenomenon such as democracy or liberalism (or even perhaps the language) by considering it as we have it now in abstraction from its history.

history, philosophy of Reflection upon the nature of history, or of historical thinking. The term was used in the 18th century (e.g. by *Voltaire) to mean critical historical thinking, as opposed to the mere collection and repetition of stories about the past. In *Hegel it came to mean universal or world history. The *Enlightenment confidence that the age of superstition and barbarism was being replaced by science, reason, and understanding gave history a progressive moral thread, and under the influence of *Herder and *Kant this idea took further hold, so that philosophy of history came to be the detection of a grand system, the unfolding of the evolution of human nature as witnessed in successive stages (the progress of rationality or of Spirit). This essentially speculative philosophy of history is given an extra Kantian twist in *Fichte, in whom the association of temporal succession with logical implication introduces the idea that concepts themselves are the dynamic engine of historical change. The idea is only readily intelligible within the framework of *absolute idealism, in which the world of nature and that of thought become identified. The work of Herder, Kant, Fichte, and *Schelling is synthesized by *Hegel: history has a plot. This is the moral development of man, equated with freedom within the state; this in turn is the development of self-consciousness of spirit, a process of thought or a logical development in which various necessary moments in the life of the concept are successively achieved and improved upon. Hegel's method is at its most successful when the subject is the history of ideas, and the evolution of thinking may march in step with the logical oppositions and their resolution encountered by various systems of thought.

With *Marx and *Engels there emerges a rather different kind of story, based upon Hegel's progressive structure but delaying the achievement of the goal of history to a future in which the political conditions for freedom come to exist, so that economic and political factors rather than 'reason' are in the engine room. Although large-scale speculative history continued to be written (*Spengler's *The Decline of the West*, 1918, is a notable late example), by the late 19th century large-scale speculation of this kind became supplanted by a more critical concern with the nature of historical understanding, and in particular with a comparison between the methods of natural science and those of the historian. For writers such as Windelband and *Dilthey, it is important to show both that the human sciences such as history are objective and legitimate, but that they are in some way different from the enquiry of the scientist. Since the subject-matter is the past thought and actions of human beings, what is needed is an ability to relive that past thought, knowing the deliberations of past agents as if they were the historian's own. The most influential British writer on this theme was *Collingwood, whose *The Idea of History* (1946) contains an extensive defence of the **Verstehen* approach (*see also* SIMULATION THEORY). The question of the form of historical explanation, and the fact that general laws have either no place or an apparently minor place in the human sciences, are also prominent in thought about the distinctive nature of our historical understanding of ourselves and others.

Hobbes, Thomas (1588–1679) English philosopher, mathematician, and linguist. Hobbes was born of an impoverished clerical family in Malmesbury, Wiltshire. He was fond of the joke that his mother fell into labour with him on hearing the rumour of the Spanish Armada coming, 'so that fear and I were born twins together'. At school he quickly excelled, making a reputation as a linguist and fluent poet and translator. After Oxford he entered the employment of William Cavendish, 3rd Earl of Devonshire, and except for a short interval remained secretary, tutor, and general adviser to the family for the rest of his career. His employment included several 'Grand Tours', during which he met the leading European intellectuals of his time. He and his patron took a particular interest in the devious political affairs of Venice, and from this political literature Hobbes became acquainted with sceptical attitudes towards political morality (*see* MACHIAVELLI), the inadvisability of commitments such as those of religion and patriotism, and the necessity for people to look after their own interests to the exclusion of others. As a spokesman for the royalist Devonshires, Hobbes was caught up in the turmoil preceding the Civil War, and fled to France in 1640, remaining there until 1651. During this period he published the short *Elements of Law*, partly as a kind of brief for his patrons to use on behalf of the sovereign, but also as a general (and most accessible) statement of his philosophy. He was also busy on a major treatise to be known as the *Elements of Philosophy*. Part III of this was published as *De Cive* (*The Citizen*) in 1642. *De Corpore* (*On Matter*) appeared in 1656, and *De Homine* (*Man*) in 1658. *Human Nature* had appeared in 1650, and his most famous work, *Leviathan*, was published in 1651 (the title is a reference to Job 41, in which the terrifying power of the sea monster is described: a metaphor for the absolute power of Hobbes's state).

In its time *Leviathan* shocked Hobbes's friends (who had looked to him for a defence of the English royalty against the Puritan revolution), mainly because of its attack on the Church of England and its endorsement of the freedom of religion from state and ecclesiastical control. This was the very doctrine associated with Cromwell's party. From this time onwards Hobbes became 'the Beast of Malmesbury', a symbol of atheism, *egoism, and heresy, and although his defence of the independence of religious life was indeed congenial to Cromwell, Hobbes lived in serious danger of prosecution after the restoration of Charles II. Hobbes's principal interests in his later years were translations, and he lived out his old age at the Devonshires' home, Hardwick, allegedly remarking that he 'was 91 years finding a hole to go out of this world, and at length found it'.

In his writings on physics Hobbes shared the general *Cartesian outlook of his time, but with several variations. His (early) theory of light was prescient in postulating a pulsating source for light, as opposed to the mechanical connection between the eye and its object postulated by *Descartes. He believed that 'whatsoever accidents and qualities that our sense makes us think there be in the world, they are not there, but are seemings and apparitions only' (*Elements of Law*, i. 2. 10). The real cause of these seemings is external 'motions'. Hobbes had no time for the Cartesian appeal to the deity as the foundation of natural knowledge. His general sympathy with the solipsistic or sceptical predicament led him to the interesting position that words and reasoning (both of which are available to the person whose whole life is a dream) are essentially self-contained; their relationship to the outside world is not what matters to their meaning (*see* CONTENT, WIDE AND NARROW). Hobbes frequently took as his paradigm of science the self-contained axiomatic system of Euclidean geometry, which had always inspired him and in which he dabbled extensively. Part of his dislike of the rising scientific establishment of the time concerned the use of technical language, and Hobbes is one of the earliest British philosophers both to pay attention to and mistrust the enchantment of words: 'words are wise mens' counters, they do but reckon by them: but they are the mony of fooles' (*Leviathan*). His realism about the power of civil society and pessimism about philosophical systems and 'right reason' imply what is currently thought of as modern *pragmatism, or even the *postmodernist doctrine that, in linguistic matters, might is right. He held, for instance, that 'upon the occasion of some strange and deformed birth, it shall not be decided by Aristotle, or the philosophers, whether the same be a Man or no, but by the Laws' (*Elements of Law*, ii. 10. 8), which if true would put many thinkers in fields such as bioethics out of business. His life in political and religious controversy also gave him a sage mistrust of the rhetorical power of empty words.

Hobbes's political and ethical writings set the agenda for much subsequent theorizing. In ethics his mechanical philosophy leads him to identify the judgement that a thing is good with the purely personal pleasure felt upon contemplating it (a suggestion later refined by *Hume). He follows *Grotius in taking the universal desire for self-preservation as giving rise to a fundamental right. Imagining people without a social or civil order, we see the emergence of that order as a device for self-preservation, a way of avoiding the 'war of every man against every man' that constitutes the *state of nature, 'and the life of man nasty, solitary, brutish and short' (*Leviathan*, ch. 13). The remedy is the appointment of a sovereign, and a trade of personal freedom in return for personal safety. The doctrine of the absolute power of the sovereign that this seems to imply caused a good deal of trouble to Hobbes (and his commentators). The other famous crux is how men can contract together (promise) in order to lift themselves from the state of nature into civil society, for Hobbes himself sees clearly that the first person to make a promise and then turn aside from his own interests to keep it 'does but betraye himself his enemy' (ch. 14).

Hobbes remains permanently important, not least because his adoption of a rigorously minimal metaphysics (materialism) and ethics (a kind of egoism), and his impatience with theory that does not confront these underlying truths squarely, make him the enduring model for sceptical and pragmatic philosophies.

SEE WEB LINKS

- An audio discussion of Hobbes's political philosophy by three historians
- A list of internet resources on Hobbes, including bibliographies

Holbach, Paul-Henri Thiry, Baron d' (1723–89) German-born French intellectual. Paul Heinrich Dietrich took the name and French nationality of his maternal uncle, who had made a fortune in Paris. For many years Holbach's salon in Paris was the central meeting-point of many of the thinkers of the French *Enlightenment. His own philosophical stance was one of unswerving atheistic materialism, and he took pains to demonstrate that this is compatible with a life of altruism and virtue. His most important philosophical work was the *Système de la nature* (1770, trs. as *The System of Nature*, 1795).

Hölderlin, Johann Christian Friedrich (1770–1843) German lyric poet. Hölderlin trained as a theologian at the university of Tübingen where he met *Schelling and *Hegel. In his novel *Hyperion* (1797/9), Hölderlin venerated the sacred aspects of nature, and attempted to unite religion and art as 'overseers of reason'. But his interest to philosophy derives not from any theory or doctrine, but from his influence on a variety of thinkers from *Schiller to *Heidegger. He epitomizes the poet as youthful, idealistic, Romantic, blessed with superior knowledge, and above all as someone standing 'bare-headed beneath God's thunderstorms', midway between the gods and man, and so inevitably doomed. He became incurably but harmlessly insane in 1807.

holism Any doctrine emphasizing the priority of a whole over its parts. In the philosophy of language, this becomes the claim that the meaning of an individual word or sentence can only be understood in terms of its relations to an indefinitely larger body of language, such as a whole theory, or even a whole language or form of life. In the philosophy of mind, a mental state similarly may be identified only in terms of its relations with others. Moderate holism may allow that other things besides these relationships also count; extreme holism would hold that the network of relationships is all that we have. A holistic view of science holds that experience only confirms or disconfirms large bodies of doctrine, impinging at the edges, and leaving some leeway over the adjustments that it requires (*see* DUHEM THESIS).

holy spirit In Christian theology the consubstantial third member of the Trinity. Commonly symbolized by a dove or pigeon, its distinct substantial existence has been denied, for example by the 4th-century *Pneumatomachi* (adversaries of the spirit) denounced by St Athanasius.

holy will In the ethics of *Kant, a holy will would be spontaneously inclined to obey the dictates of morality; it would not have to struggle against countervailing desires and inclinations, or the innate human tendency to evil. This moral perfection (unlike a *good will) is not a possible achievement for human beings.

homo economicus Economic man, or the rational agent depicted in economic models. Such an agent has consistent and stable preferences; he is entirely forward-looking, and pursues only his own self-interest. When given options he chooses the alternative with the highest expected utility for himself. It is controversial whether this figure is realistic, and if not, how much that matters to economic theory.

homoeomereity *See* ANAXAGORAS.

homoiousion (Greek, of like substance) Of similar but not identical essence or substance; a subtle compromise between the belief that the members of the Trinity are of one substance (**homoousion*) and the belief that they are of different substances.

homological Word that applies to itself. *See* AUTOLOGICAL, GRELLING'S PARADOX.

homomorphism In *model theory, a structure-preserving mapping from one structure to another.

homonyms Words having the same sound or shape, but different meanings. Heteronymy in grammar is partial homonymy, as when words have the same sound but different spelling (through, threw). This is also a case of homophony, or sameness of sound, but heteronymy also occurs when words have the same spelling but different sounds (good conduct, conduct the band). Homonymy is a central concern of *Aristotle, who recognizes that we speak in several ways of what is good, or what love or honour is (e.g. *Nicomachean Ethics*, 1118b, 1125b). Homonymy also applies to cases of different people sharing a name: it is reported in *Diogenes Laertius that a certain Demetrius of Magnesia wrote a treatise entitled *Of Men of the Same Name*.

***homoousion* (*homousion*)** (Greek, of one substance) Term used by *Augustine to express the identity of the substance of the members of the Trinity; the principal doctrine affirmed in the Athanasian creed, drawn up to confute the *Arian heresy. Not to be confounded with **homoiousion*.

homosexuality Sexual relations between members of the same sex. The question whether homosexual practices are of legal concern raises questions of the proper extent of the law, and of the way a distinction may be drawn between the public and the *private. It has also been a focus for discussing the relation between law and morality, between morality and *nature, and, when it is accepted that homosexuality is not a moral issue, for querying the relation between law and majority preferences and prejudices. *See also* SEX.

homuncular functionalism An intelligent system, or mind, may fruitfully be thought of as the result of a number of subsystems performing more simple tasks in coordination with each other. The subsystems may be envisaged as homunculi, or small, relatively stupid agents. The archetype is a digital computer, where a battery of switches capable of only one response (on or off) can make up a machine that can play chess, write dictionaries, etc.

homunculus A small person. A bad idea in the philosophy of mind is to explain a person's agency, or intelligence, or experience, as if there were a smaller agent, or intelligent thing, or experiencing subject 'inside the head'. But *homuncular functionalism decomposes complex functions into simpler ones, thereby avoiding the obvious regress.

Hooker, Richard (1554–1600) English ecclesiastical writer and political theorist. Hooker's masterpiece is a work in eight books, *Of the Laws of Ecclesiastical Polity*. The first four books were published together in 1593, the fifth was published in 1597, and the rest appeared after his death. Hooker based his defence of the Church of England on the natural law tradition, and lying behind that on Aristotelianism. He was a major influence on John *Locke.

Horkheimer, Max (1895–1973) *See* FRANKFURT SCHOOL.

horns of dilemma *See* DILEMMA (LOGIC).

horseshoe Name formerly given to the sign for the *truth function of *material implication, which in some systems is written $p \supset q$.

hsü (Chinese, vacuous) In *Taoist and *Neo-Confucian thought, absolute peacefulness, purity of mind, freedom from selfish desire. *See also* APATHY, *ATARAXIA*.

Hsün Tzu (*fl.* 298–238 BC) Realistic Chinese Confucian. Unlike *Confucius and *Mencius, Hsün Tzu believed not in natural goodness but in the depravity of humanity, to be relieved only by study of the classics, and an education that channelled the wayward direction of desire, supported desires in the right channel by enabling the student to relish their satisfaction, and ennobled personal character. He opposed all kinds of superstition, and set education in the Chinese empire on its subsequent course.

Huai Nan Tzu Name for a compendium of twenty-one essays on the *Taoist knowledge that a ruler needs. It describes the universe as a harmonious unity, which the ruler must cultivate himself to understand. It is a hard-headed, practical work that stands opposed to the forms and rites of *Confucianism, and opposed as well to the more superstitious developments of Taoism aimed at immortality. As a result its principal author, Liu An, was eventually executed.

hubris The general connotation of the pride that goes before a fall is a later, and partially Christian reinterpretation of the classical concept. In *Aristotle (*Rhetoric* 1378b 23–30) hubris is gratuitous insolence: the deliberate infliction of shame and dishonour on someone else, not by way of revenge, but in the mistaken belief that one thereby shows oneself superior. *Tragedy is not therefore the punishment of hubris, since tragedy concerns unjust suffering, whereas hubris deprives the agent of sympathy from the outset.

humanism Most generally, any philosophy concerned to emphasize human welfare and dignity, and either optimistic about the powers of human reason, or at least insistent that we have no alternative but to use it as best we can. More particularly, the movement distinctive of the Renaissance and allied to the renewed study of Greek and Roman literature: a rediscovery of the unity of human beings and nature, and a renewed celebration of the pleasures of life, all supposed lost in the medieval world. Humanism in this Renaissance sense was quite consistent with religious belief, it being supposed that God had put us here precisely in order to further those things the humanists found important. Later the term tended to become appropriated for anti-religious social and political movements. Finally, in the late 20th century, humanism is sometimes used as a pejorative term by *postmodernist and especially *feminist writers, applied to philosophies such as that of *Sartre, that rely upon the possibility of the autonomous, self-conscious, rational, single self, and that are supposedly insensitive to the inevitable fragmentary, splintered, historically and socially conditioned nature of personality and motivation.

humanity, principle of Principle doing the same work as the principle of *charity, but suggesting that we regulate our procedures of interpretation by maximizing the extent to which we see the subject as humanly reasonable, rather than the extent to which we see the subject as right about things.

human nature A basic topic of ethics, different accounts of which underlie such different conceptions of human life as that of the classical Greeks and of Christianity. A preoccupation of *Enlightenment philosophy was to find a constant human nature beneath superficial differences due to culture and society. The common core would contain sufficient natural sympathy with others, benevolence, perception of self-interest, and capacity for acquiescing in just institutions, to provide a foundation for a purely secular ethics. This hope was dashed by the *Hegelian perception of human beings as only possessing natures that are moulded by their historical and social circumstances. However, it then recurs at a higher level, with the thought that we have natures that make us capable of some political and social arrangements under which we flourish, and incapable of others. *See* ESSENTIALISM, EVOLUTIONARY PSYCHOLOGY, SOCIOBIOLOGY.

Humboldt, Wilhelm von (1767–1835) German polymath and philosopher of language. The elder brother of the explorer Alexander, Wilhelm von Humboldt was born in Potsdam and educated at Frankfurt and Göttingen. He combined the general scholarly interests of his time with a special concern for political philosophy. Until 1819 he was active in public service in Prussia. His collected works (seven volumes, 1841–52) cover a great variety of topics, but his principal philosophical importance lies in the role that he attributed to language, not as the mere external vehicle of thought, but as a repository of the spirit, and something whose 'inner form' itself dictates the kind of thought that can be available for comprehension. *See also* SAPIR–WHORF HYPOTHESIS.

h

Hume, David (1711–76) Scottish philosopher, historian, and essayist. Hume is the most influential thoroughgoing *naturalist in modern philosophy, and a pivotal figure of the *Enlightenment. Born the second son of a minor Scottish landowner, Hume attended Edinburgh university. In 1734 he removed to the little town of La Flèche in Anjou to write and study (it is possible that the presence of the Jesuit College at which *Descartes and *Mersenne had been educated influenced this decision). In 1739 he returned to oversee the printing of the *Treatise of Human Nature*, his first and greatest philosophical work. Hume settled down to a life of literary work, mainly residing in Edinburgh, although he was a rather improbable aide to General James St Clair, a distant relation, for a time between 1746 and 1748. Earlier he had produced the *Essays Moral and Political* (1742). These range from light-hearted exercises in the manner of Joseph Addison to weighty and important treatments of the foundations of ethics, politics, and economics. They were followed by *An Enquiry Concerning Human Understanding* (1748) and *An Enquiry Concerning the Principles of Morals* (1751). These works are usually regarded as attempts to lay out the philosophy of the *Treatise* in a more accessible manner, although particularly the second *Enquiry* contains distinct differences at least of emphasis. In the following decade Hume began publication of the work by which he was best known in his own time, the *History of England* (in six volumes, 1754–62; the work was subsequently extended by Smollett). During this period his reputation slowly grew until he became acknowledged as one of Britain's principal men of letters. In 1763 he was appointed Secretary to the Embassy and later chargé d'affaires in Paris, and during this period enjoyed unprecedented fame and adulation as one of the principal architects of the Enlightenment. He failed, however, to win the hand of the mistress of Louis-François de Bourbon, Prince de Conti, the Comtesse de Boufflers, to whom he formed a deep romantic attachment. Perhaps this was because at this time he began to resemble, in *Diderot's words, 'un gros Bernardin bien nourri' (a fat well-fed Bernardine monk). In 1766 Hume accompanied *Rousseau to England, but the trip ended with paranoid complaints of persecution by Rousseau, against which Hume defended himself with dignity. Out of his 'abundant caution' he delayed the publication of his last sceptical philosophical work, *The Dialogues Concerning Natural Religion*, until after his death, when they were published by his nephew. Adam *Smith wrote of Hume that 'upon the whole, I have always considered him, both in his lifetime and since his death, as approaching as nearly to the idea of a perfectly wise and virtuous man, as perhaps the nature of human frailty will admit.'

The avowed aim of the *Treatise* was to bring the experimental method into the study of the human mind. Hume believed that the success of natural science, culminating in Newtonian mechanics, lay in finding the few simple principles that would enable one to discern order in the apparent chaos of natural systems. Events in nature are in themselves 'loose and separate', and the art of the scientist is to detect the patterns in which they fall. Similarly separate events in the mind, such as the onset of ideas, impressions, and passions, should be seen as natural events, ordered by principles that are open to empirical discovery. The first components of the mind are individual 'perceptions' or impressions and ideas. Ideas for Hume, as for earlier empiricists such as *Berkeley, are faint or less forceful versions of impressions. They are the components of thought, and Hume was the first modern philosopher seriously to explore the difficulty of explaining how, on the basis of this private kaleidoscope, we attain a conception of ourselves as inhabiting a public world of independent objects extended in space and ordered by causal laws. Hume's resolute naturalism rejects any model in which sense experience enables us to reason our way to such a conception; instead it arises purely as the result of 'custom and habit', and reason can neither assist nor oppose the process. Similarly the passions, under which Hume includes any pressure on practical choice, including ethical pressure, are outside the sway of reason but themselves rise and fall in naturally detectable patterns.

Hume was the first modern empiricist to refuse any aid either from *a priori* principles of reasoning, or from any other ideology that ensures a harmony between our perceptions and the world. His genius lay in the rigour with which he reconstructs the scaffolding of everyday thought on this slender basis. Thus the causal connection between events is something of which we have no impression, hence no idea, so a Humean theory of causation instead sees us as projecting onto events our own tendency to infer one from another (*see* PROJECTIVISM). The mind that is the owner of my perceptions is something that itself is never given to me in perception, so a Humean theory of the self regards it as a fiction arising from imagination (*see* BUNDLE THEORY OF THE MIND OR SELF, PERSONAL IDENTITY). A Humean theory of ethics sees moral thought as the expression of sentiments that evolve because we must cooperate in societies if we are to meet our natural needs. Although Hume is often called a sceptic in these and other areas, it is only the power of reason about which he is sceptical, not the propriety of natural processes of belief-formation, against which, in any event, it is futile to argue.

In the *Enquiries*, Hume downplays the original foundations of his philosophy, in favour of a more accessible presentation of the way he would have us think about theoretical belief-formation, and practical reasoning. His scepticism about reason did not leave him lacking any distinction between proper and improper processes of arriving at belief, although his right to such a distinction has been challenged. In section x, on Miracles, in the first *Enquiry*, he gleefully shows that it makes no sense to credit human reports of *miracles: the falsity of such a testimony through 'folly or knavery' would be a natural event, less miraculous and more probable than that which it relates. His sceptical attitude both to revealed and *natural theology culminated in the sustained attack on the argument to *design in the posthumous *Dialogues*.

Hume's Olympian intelligence earned him incalculable influence: almost all anthropological, sociological, and comparative studies find a seed in his work, whilst the attempt to escape his radical *empiricism has motivated philosophers from *Kant to the present day. The standard modern biography was by Ernest Mossner.

SEE WEB LINKS

- A list of internet resources on Hume
- Bibliographies of writings by or on Hume

Hume's fork A term mostly applied to the distinction between 'relations of ideas' and 'matters of fact', a distinction central to Hume's epistemology and one that he wields with great argumentative effect. It is more rarely a name sometimes given to the dilemma that either our actions are determined, in which case we are not responsible for them, or they are the result of random events, in which case we are also not responsible for them. *See also* DILEMMA OF DETERMINISM, FREE WILL, MATTER OF FACT.

Hume's law A name for the contested view that it is impossible to derive an 'ought' from an 'is', or in other words, that there is no logical bridge over the gap between fact and value. Hume's own statement is in the *Treatise of Human Nature*, iii. 1. 1, where he wrote that it seems 'altogether inconceivable that this new relation [ought] can be derived from others, which are entirely different from it'. The 'law' in fact appears as something of an afterthought to other discussion,.

Hume's principle The principle that the number of things with the property F equal the number of things with the property G if and only if there is a *one-to-one correspondence between those that are F and those that are G. The attribution to Hume derives from the discussion in *Treatise*, i. 3. 1: 'When two numbers are so combined as that the one has always an unit answering to every unit of the other we pronounce them equal; and it is for want of such a standard of equality in extension that geometry can scarce be esteemed a perfect and infallible science.' The principle was central to *Frege, and the 'neo-Fregean' approach to the philosophy of mathematics hopes to define the idea of number on the foundation it provides.

humour *See* LAUGHTER.

humours, doctrine of the four *See* FOUR HUMOURS.

Husserl, Edmund Gustav Albert (1859–1938) German mathematician and a principal founder of *phenomenology. Trained at Leipzig and Berlin, Husserl discovered philosophy by attending lectures of *Brentano in Vienna. He subsequently taught at Halle, Göttingen, and Freiburg. From Brentano he inherited the view that the central problem in understanding thought is that of explaining the way in which an intentional direction, or content, can belong to the mental phenomenon that exhibits it. Mental phenomena are founded in sensory data, but whereas for Brentano there is no sharp distinction between 'intuitions' (*Anschauungen*) and concepts (*Begriffe*), Husserl reinstates the Kantian division. The distinctive feature of this way of thinking is that the content is immanent, existing within the mental act, and anything external drops out as secondary or irrelevant to the intrinsic nature of the mental state. In his earliest work, *On the Concept of Number* (1887, recast as the *Philosophie der Arithmetik*, 1891), Husserl applies Brentano's psychology to the problem of our knowledge of arithmetic, attempting to find an acceptable empiricist account of the process of abstraction whereby we apprehend the numerical properties of aggregates. *Frege believed that the mingling of subjective and objective elements in this work of Husserl produced an 'impenetrable fog', but he may have been insufficiently sympathetic to the dominant psychological aim of Husserl's work. The problem of reconciling the subjective or psychological nature of mental life with its objective and logical content preoccupied Husserl from this time onwards. The next fruit of his attack on the problem was the elephantine *Logische Untersuchungen* (3 vols., 1900–13, trs. as *Logical Investigations*, 1970). Husserl eventually abandoned his attempt to keep both a subjective and a naturalistic approach to knowledge together, abandoning the naturalism in favour of a kind of *transcendental idealism. The precise nature of this change is disguised by his penchant for new and impenetrable terminology (*see* NOEMA), but the '*bracketing' of external questions for which he is well-known implies a solipsistic, disembodied *Cartesian ego as its starting-point, with it thought of as inessential that the thinking subject is either embodied or surrounded by others. However, by the time of *Cartesian Meditations* (trs. 1960, first published in French as *Méditations cartésiennes*, 1931), a shift in priorities has begun, with the embodied individual, surrounded by others, rather than the disembodied Cartesian ego now returned to a fundamental position. The extent to which this desirable shift undermines the programme of phenomenology that is closely identified with Husserl's earlier approach remains unclear, but later phenomenologists such as *Merleau-Ponty have worked fruitfully from the later standpoint.

Hutcheson, Francis (1694–1746) Moral and political philosopher. Born in Ulster, Hutcheson was educated at Glasgow as a Presbyterian, but returned to work in Dublin until 1740, when he was elected professor of moral philosophy at Glasgow. His central philosophical concerns lay in ethics and aesthetics. In the *Inquiry into the Origins of our Ideas of Beauty and Virtue* (1725) Hutcheson develops a theory of the '*moral sense' whereby to perceive an action as virtuous is in effect to be pleased by it in a very specific way; the 'amiable or disagreeable' ideas of actions that we form constitute our moral approval or disapproval. The moral sense is an innate endowment and its direction is towards approval of those actions that benefit human beings. Hutcheson is therefore one of the earliest *utilitarians, and indeed was in danger of prosecution by the Presbytery at Glasgow for teaching the 'false and dangerous doctrine that the standard of moral goodness is the promotion of the happiness of others'. The *greatest happiness principle, the watchword of the 19th-century *utilitarians, is first found in his work. In his political theory Hutcheson advocates the sovereignty of the people, and the right of rebellion against political authority that fails to aim at their happiness. He was a major theoretical influence on the American revolution, and a favourite author of both Thomas Jefferson and John Adams, the second President (1796–1800) of the United States. In addition to the *Origins* Hutcheson wrote *A Short Introduction to Moral Philosophy* (1747) and *A System of Moral Philosophy*, in two volumes published posthumously in 1755.

Huxley, Thomas Henry (1825–95) British physiologist and zoologist. One of the most eminent Victorian men of science, famous as 'Darwin's bulldog', Huxley made unsystematic forays into philosophy. His writings included 'The Physical Basis of Life' (1868), 'On the Hypothesis that Animals are Automata' (1874), a monograph on Hume (1879), and the Romanes lecture *Ethics and Evolution* (1893). Huxley is credited with the invention of the term 'agnosticism'.

***hylē* (*hylas*)** (Greek, matter) The stuff of material things, thought of by *Aristotle as needing a *form to make up a thing. *Berkeley names Hylas the spokesman for materialism in the *Three Dialogues*.

hylomorphism The doctrine that every thing is a combination of matter (**materia prima*) and form. The doctrine was asserted by *Aquinas, who possibly erroneously believed it to be Aristotelian, and was developed in increasingly subtle and confident ways in late scholasticism. It served as a convenient target for proponents of the 17th-century revolution in natural science, such as *Boyle and *Locke.

hylozoism The doctrine that all matter is endowed with life.

Hypatia (*c*.370–415) *Neoplatonist philosopher, mathematician, and astronomer, and the author of commentaries on the mathematicians Diophantus and Apollonius. She was educated under Plutarch the younger, and lived in Alexandria as an influential teacher, becoming the head of her father's academy. The source of knowledge of her life is the collection of letters of one of her pupils, Synesius of Cyrene. She was murdered when Cyril, the patriarch of Alexandria, had a Christian mob drag her to a church, where his monks scoriated her with oyster shells; according to the historian Gibbon the event shocked even contemporary Christian opinion. Cyril was later canonized.

hypostasis (Greek, standing under) The underlying subject or *substance that supports attributes; matter without form. This is a concept subject to repeated fatal criticism, and repeated resurrection.

hypostatic union The substantial union of divine and human nature in the one person of Jesus Christ. Belief in this is a formal doctrine of the Christian church. *See also* NESTORIANISM.

hypothesis A proposition put forward as a supposition, rather than asserted. A hypothesis may be put forward for testing or for discussion, possibly as a prelude to acceptance or rejection.

hypothetical A proposition claiming that one thing is so upon the hypothesis of another, i.e. given another, or if another is supposed. The more usual term is a *conditional.

hypothetical imperative *See* CATEGORICAL/HYPOTHETICAL IMPERATIVE.

hypothetico-deductive method The method particularly associated with a philosophy of science that stresses the virtues of *falsification. Most simply, a hypothesis is proposed, and consequences are deduced, which are then tested against experience. If the hypothesis is falsified, then we learn from the attempt, and are in a position to produce a better one. If not, then we can try other tests. One philosophical divide is between radical followers of *Popper, who deny that probability accrues to a theory through its having survived such tests, and others who insist that it must, since otherwise it would be irrational to rely upon hypotheses that have survived until now. *See also* EXPLANATION, VERISIMILITUDE. Other criticisms of the method point out that in practice auxiliary assumptions are always made in working out the experimental consequences of a theory, and that theories acquire credibility in other, indirect ways. *See also* DUHEM THESIS.

Hyppolite, Jean-Gaston (1907–68) French philosopher. Initially attracted to the early, more religious or spiritual writings of Hegel, Hyppolite moved to a more *Marxist position. He was prominent in reviving Hegel for the post-war generation of French philosophers, and was highly influential in French academic philosophy in the 1950s and 1960s, numbering among his students *Foucault, *Deleuze, *Althusser, and *Derrida.

Iamblichus (*c.*AD 245–*c.*325) Probably a student of *Porphyry, Iamblichus did much to further the advance of *Neoplatonism. He incorporated elements of *Pythagoras, extended mathematical ideas in philosophy, incorporated religious ideas from a variety of traditions, and established the direction taken by later Neoplatonist philosophy.

I and thou A notion heralded in *Feuerbach, but especially deployed by the religious thinker *Buber, emphasizing the interpersonal dialogue between God and man. The conception of this dialogue opposes it both to the religious goal of a mystical union with God, and to the idea of any impersonal or objective knowledge of God. To many religious thinkers, such as *Spinoza and *Kant, the idea of such a dialogue would have seemed to be the perversion of religion called theurgy. *See* RELIGION, PHILOSOPHY OF.

Ibn Bajja *See* AVEMPACE.

Ibn Daud, Abraham ben David Hallevi (*c.*1110–80) The first Jewish Aristotelian, Ibn Daud was concerned, as *Aquinas was in the following century, to reconcile philosophy with revealed religion. His principal work is *The Exalted Faith*, written in Arabic but only surviving in Hebrew translation. He espouses a rationalist but unorthodox set of views, that include limiting God's omniscience in order to make room for *free will. He also celebrated the *via negativa*, or belief of *negative theology, that God can only be described in terms of what he is not.

Ibn Gabirol, Solomon (*c.*1021–*c.*1058/70) Also known as Avicebron, the first Spanish Jewish philosopher, and a considerable Hebrew poet, whose mystical ideas play a role in the *Kabbala. Ibn Gabirol stood for a *Neoplatonism which was subsequently one of the targets of *Aquinas. His principal work was the *Fountain* (or *Source*) *of Life*, composed in Arabic but widely known through its 12th-century Latin translation.

Ibn Khaldun, Abd al-Rahman (1336–1406) The Islamic historian is remembered in philosophy principally for a simple version of the cyclical view of history (*see* ETERNAL RECURRENCE). He believed that in a period of about 120 years a people would pass through the cycle of primitivism, nomadic life, and civilization, the last of which would fall as a new cycle commenced. He is regarded as the first (and still the greatest) historian of Arabic logic, possibly the most outstanding figure in the social sciences between Aristotle and Machiavelli.

Ibn Miskawayh, Ahmad ibn Muhammad (*c.*940–1030) Islamic humanist and Neoplatonist. Although he applied Greek philosophy to specifically Islamic issues, he rarely used religion to modify philosophy. He provides rules for moral health based on cultivation of character, and in this respect is allied to *virtue ethics. His best-known work is the *Tahdhib al-akhlaq*, translated as *The Refinement of Character* (1968).

Ibn Rushd *See* AVERROËS.

Ibn Sina *See* AVICENNA.

Ibn Tufayl, Abu Bakr Muhammad (d. 1185) Spanish Arabic philosopher most famous for his *Hayy Ibn Yaqzan* ('The Living Son of the Vigilant'), a charming narrative of the hero Hayy, who is abandoned as a boy on a desert island, and arrives at a complete knowledge of the world and God through his own unaided philosophical efforts; later contact with human civilization leads him to recognize the necessity of religious laws in the imperfect social world. The work was influential through its translation as *Philosophus Autodictatus* ('The Self-Taught Philosopher') in 1671.

I ching Ancient Chinese system of divination. The system contains eight blocks of short or long lines, forming 64 hexagrams, that can be combined to give 11520 situations, deployed in a manner analogical to astrology to make predictions. Also, the name refers to the book explaining the system.

SEE WEB LINKS

- An introduction to the *I ching* (by C. G. Jung)
- A list of internet resources on the *I ching*

icon In its most general sense, a sign or symbol. More specifically, the term is sometimes reserved for a sign that resembles the thing it represents:

images, diagrams, and onomatopoeic words. Iconic features of a message are those that resemble features of what is reported: for example a temporal order of reporting typically mirrors the temporal order of events, as in Caesar's 'Veni, vidi, vici' ('I came, I saw, I conquered').

iconoclasm The odd pair of beliefs shared by *enthusiasts including Cromwell and the Taliban, that while 'false idols' have no supernatural powers they are nevertheless so dangerous that they must be destroyed rather than ignored.

idea (Greek, *eidos*, visible form) A notion stretching all the way from one pole, where it denotes a subjective, internal presence in the mind, somehow thought of as representing something about the world, to the other pole, where it represents an eternal, timeless unchanging form or concept: the concept of the number series or of justice, for example, thought of as independent objects of enquiry and perhaps of knowledge. These two poles are not distinct meanings of the term, although they give rise to many problems of interpretation, but between them they define a space of philosophical problems. On the one hand, ideas are that with which we think, or in *Locke's terms, whatever the mind may be employed about in thinking. Looked at that way they seem to be inherently transient, fleeting, and unstable private presences. On the other hand, ideas provide the way in which objective knowledge can be expressed. They are the essential components of understanding, and any intelligible proposition that is true must be capable of being understood. *Plato's theory of *forms is a celebration of the objective and timeless existence of ideas as concepts, and in his hands ideas are *reified to the point where they make up the only real world, of separate and perfect models of which the empirical world is only a poor cousin. This doctrine, notable in the *Timaeus*, opened the way for the *Neoplatonic notion of ideas as the thoughts of God. The concept gradually lost this other-worldly aspect, until after *Descartes ideas become assimilated to whatever it is that lies in the mind of any thinking being.

Together with a general bias towards the sensory, so that what lies in the mind may be thought of as something like images, and a belief that thinking is well explained as the manipulation of images, this was developed by *Locke, *Berkeley, and *Hume into a full-scale view of the understanding as the domain of images, although they were all aware of anomalies that were later regarded as fatal to this doctrine (*see* ABSTRACTION). The defects in the account were exposed by *Kant, who realized that the understanding needs to be thought of more in terms of rules and organizing principles than of any kind of copy of what is given in experience. Kant also recognized the danger of the opposite extreme (that of *Leibniz) of failing to connect the elements of understanding with those of experience at all (*Critique of Pure Reason*, A270).

It has become more common to think of ideas, or concepts, as dependent upon social and especially linguistic structures, rather than the self-standing creations of an individual mind, but the tension between the objective and the subjective aspect of the matter lingers on, for instance in debates about the possibility of objective knowledge, of *indeterminacy in translation, and of identity between the thoughts people entertain at one time and those that they entertain at another.

ideal evidence, paradox of A paradox in the philosophy of *confirmation. Suppose a hypothesis is assigned a quite low or quite high probability given some body of evidence. Then in principle more evidence might be found confirming that assignment. What is the difference this evidence makes? On the one hand the low or high probability stays the same; on the other hand such evidence seems, intuitively, to make confidence in the hypothesis more irrational, i.e. to lower its probability, if it is already low, or to make confidence in the hypothesis better founded, i.e. to raise its probability, if it is already high. The problem is that *weightier* evidence justifying an existing low or high assignment of probability seems to have something of the effect of evidence in favour of a yet lower or higher probability.

idealism Any doctrine holding that reality is fundamentally mental in nature. The boundaries of such a doctrine are not firmly drawn: for example, the traditional Christian view that God is a sustaining cause, possessing greater reality than his creation, might just be classified as a form of idealism. *Leibniz's doctrine that the simple substances out of which all else is made are themselves perceiving and appetitive beings (*monads), and that space and time are relations among these things, is another early version. Major forms of idealism include subjective idealism, or the position better called *immaterialism and associated with *Berkeley, according to which to exist is to be perceived, *transcendental idealism, and *absolute idealism. Idealism is opposed to the *naturalistic belief that mind is itself to be exhaustively understood as a product of natural processes. The most common modern manifestation of idealism is the view called linguistic idealism, that we 'create' the world we inhabit by employing mind-dependent linguistic and social categories. The difficulty is to give a literal form to this view that does not conflict with the obvious fact that we do not create worlds, but find ourselves in one.

idealization *See* MODEL (SCIENTIFIC).

ideal language *See* CHARACTERISTICA UNIVERSALIS.

ideal limit theory of truth The theory of truth as that which would be agreed upon in the ideal limit of enquiry. This view was suggested by *Peirce in his essay 'How to Make our Ideas Clear' (1868). Its principal merit is to connect together the idea of truth as the goal of enquiry with the idea of the virtues (simplicity, comprehensiveness) that belong to an enquiry. However, it needs some view about what makes these features into virtues without presupposing that they act as midwives to the truth. It also faces the problem that there is no prospect of an empirical determination of whether the ideal limit of enquiry has been reached, and whether in the absence of such a criterion the notion of a limit makes good sense.

ideal market *See* PERFECT COMPETITION.

ideal observer The view that what is morally best is what would be approved of by a benevolent, impartial, and all-knowing observer. The motive behind the view is to combine the idea that the good is that which is approved of or chosen, with acknowledgement that because of imperfections such as failure of sympathy, or partiality to friends and family, or ignorance, we as we are may actually choose and approve of what is bad. The remedy is to idealize the subject whose approval sets the standard. Adam *Smith is often associated with the view, although his own position is actually more complex (*see* IMPARTIAL SPECTATOR).

ideational theory of meaning View according to which the meaning of sayings is a matter of the ideas that they express. *See* IDEA; LANGUAGE, PHILOSOPHY OF; MEANING.

identity All of us agree with Joseph *Butler that everything is what it is and not another thing. The difficulty is to know when we have one thing and not two. A rule for telling this is a principle of *individuation, or a criterion of identity for things of the kind in question. In logic, identity may be introduced as a primitive relational expression, or defined via the *identity of indiscernibles. *See also* PERSONAL IDENTITY.

identity of indiscernibles The principle associated with *Leibniz, that if A and B have exactly the same properties, then they are identical. *See also* INDISCERNIBILITY OF IDENTICALS.

identity theory of mind The theory that mental events are identical with physical events, more commonly called *physicalism. Historically identity philosophy, associated with *Schelling, held that spirit and nature are fundamentally the same, both being aspects of the absolute. More generally any *monism is the doctrine of the identity of what may seem to be many different kinds of thing.

identity theory of predication (identity theory of truth) Theory articulated by *Bradley, according to which there is no division between a true proposition and the fact making it true. The idea is the outcome both of Bradley's belief that only a world-sized whole can really be true (there is strictly no such thing as partial truth), and his *idealist denial of a distinction between the knowing subject and what it is that is known.

ideology Any wide-ranging system of beliefs, ways of thought, and categories that provide the foundation of programmes of political and social action: an ideology is a *conceptual scheme with a practical application.

Derogatorily, another person's ideology may be thought of as spectacles that distort and disguise the real *status quo* (*see* FALSE CONSCIOUSNESS). Promises that political philosophy and morality can be freed from ideology are apt to be vain, since allegedly cleansed and pure programmes depend, for instance, upon particular views of *human nature, what counts as human flourishing, and the conditions under which it is found.

idiographic/nomothetic methods Distinction in method drawn by the historian Wilhelm *Windelband. An idiographic method is concerned with individual matters of fact, as in history, or map-making. A nomothetic method is concerned to formulate general laws. Windelband was concerned to show that the human sciences, or *Geisteswissenschaften*, such as history, had their own methods and discipline, in spite of their dissimilarity from natural science. The extent to which disciplines such as economics are nomothetic or idiographic is debatable: roughly speaking, while map-makers do not draw morals, make predictions, or give explanations of what they map, historians and economists like to do all three.

idiolect *See* LECT.

idols of the mind The four idols distinguished by Francis *Bacon are the idols of the tribe, den, market, and theatre. Idols in this sense are **eidola*, the transient, and therefore to Bacon erroneous, images of things. (i) Idols of the tribe are general tendencies to be deceived, inherent in our nature as human beings. They include uncritical reliance on sense perception, and tendencies to overgeneralize or jump to conclusions and ignore countervailing evidence against our views. (ii) Idols of the den are distortions arising from our particular perspectives (the metaphor is that of Plato's *myth of the cave); the corrective is to remember that whatever our mind 'seizes and dwells upon with peculiar satisfaction is to be held in suspicion'. (iii) Idols of the market-place are errors that come in the course of communication with others: misunderstandings arising through abuses of words. (iv) Idols of the theatre are the errors introduced by theories: the abstract schemata of Aristotelianism, and the introduction of theological notions into science. Bacon here compared philosophical and religious systems to theatrical, and therefore fantastical, representations of the world.

if *See* CONDITIONALS.

iff Common abbreviation for 'if and only if'.

ignoratio elenchi The mistake or fallacy of arguing to a conclusion that does not bear on the issue at hand, and is therefore irrelevant.

illicit major Fallacy committed when a *syllogism has a major term distributed in the conclusion but not in the premise. 'Some mortals are herbivores; no lions are mortal; therefore no lions are herbivores.'

illicit minor Fallacy committed in a *syllogism when the minor term is *distributed in the conclusion but not in the premise in which it occurs. 'Some lions are friendly; no friendly things roar; therefore no lions roar.'

illocutionary act (illocutionary force) Term introduced by J. L. *Austin, in his book *How to Do Things with Words*, for an act done *in* uttering what one does. Thus in saying 'I promise' in suitable circumstances I make a promise; in saying 'Hooray!' I cheer you on, and so forth. The illocutionary act is distinguished from anything effected by the utterance (its perlocutionary force): it makes no difference to the fact that I promised or cheered whether you believe my promise or are heartened at my cheering. Austin alerted philosophers to the possibility that certain terms might be treated illocutionarily. For example, in saying 'I know that *p*' I give you my word that *p*. It may well be that this insight sheds a different light on the traditional problems of defining knowledge, which assume that knowledge is a special state, described by one who says truly that she knows that *p*. *See also* SPEECH ACTS.

Illuminationism Doctrine propounded by the Persian philosopher and mystic Suhrawardi (1154–91) in *The Philosophy of Illumination* (1186). Knowledge, like vision, consists in the unveiled presence of the object of knowledge before the self-aware knower; with suitable training, we can apprehend immaterial beings such as angels and Platonic forms (and God). Light is the most self-aware of entities, 'that which is manifest in itself and manifests others'. Self-subsistent or immaterial lights are identified with intellects or minds; anything that is alive must be an immaterial light (self-aware and aware of other things, like a Leibnizian monad). God, at the top of the tree, is the Light of Lights, an immaterial light not caused by another immaterial light. A popularized form of Suhrawardi's philosophy enjoyed a vogue in India in the shape of a forged Persian scripture, the *Dasatir*, thought by many *Zoroastrian scholars to be the lost secret wisdom of the Zoroastrian sages.

illusion, arguments from Arguments from illusion take as premises either the existence, or the possibility, of illusions, and draw as conclusions either the possibility of total illusion, or *scepticism concerning claims to knowledge. Thus the senses sometimes deceive us, and may do so on any occasion; hence, it is argued, perhaps they always deceive us, or at any rate we should never trust them implicitly. In some forms the arguments are undoubtedly invalid: thus, even if it is true that the senses may deceive us on any occasion, it does not follow that they may deceive us on every occasion. Any coin may be counterfeit, but it cannot follow that all coins together may be counterfeit, since forgeries have to be parasitic upon the real thing. Illusions have always been a starting-point for *epistemology, and motivate the *foundationalist desire for absolutely certain starting-points, free from their possible contamination. *See also* METHOD OF DOUBT.

image The nature, the importance, and even the existence of mental images is a subject of dispute amongst psychologists and philosophers. On the one hand it seems evident that normal people enjoy a moderately rich inner life, in which remembered scenes, tunes, tastes, and smells can be conjured up and new versions created and relished; the state of mind once this is done is somehow like but also quite unlike the state of seeing, hearing, and tasting original things. Images are typically 'faint' or 'blurry', but merely imagining a tiger does not differ from seeing a tiger only in its faintness or blurriness, or it would resemble seeing a tiger in a fog or poor light, which it does not. Furthermore an imagined tiger, unlike any actual tiger, need not have a definite number of stripes or claws. It is not therefore simply an 'inner picture' of a tiger, and visual images are unlike pictures in other ways as well: for instance they cannot withstand scrutiny, and there is a limit to the manipulations one can make while retaining them. The view that images play a fundamental role in thinking was attacked by *Wittgenstein, one of whose arguments was that if they are thought of as inner presences that explain, for instance, capacities for recognition and classification, then we must ask how they themselves are recognized and classified. The shadowy nature of images has led some philosophers to think of them as a useless adjunct to underlying cognitive processes of representation, not themselves part of the machinery. But it is likely that evolution will favour an animal with the capacity to generate an 'off-line' simulation of experiencing various situations, perhaps in order to rehearse successful strategies. Hostility to images also makes it difficult to account for their central role in the creative lives especially of primarily non-linguistic thinkers, such as artists and musicians. *See also* IDEA.

imagination Most directly, the faculty of reviving or especially creating *images in the mind's eye. But more generally, the ability to create and rehearse possible situations, to combine knowledge in unusual ways, or to invent *thought experiments. *Coleridge was the first aesthetic theorist to distinguish the possibility of disciplined, creative use of the imagination, as opposed to the idle play of fancy. Imagination is involved in any flexible rehearsal of different approaches to a problem and is wrongly thought of as opposed to reason. It also bears an interesting relation to the process of deciding whether a projected scenario is genuinely possible. We seem able to imagine ourselves having been Napoleon, and unable to imagine space being spherical, yet further reflection may lead us to think that the first supposition is impossible and the second entirely possible.

imitation game *See* TURING TEST.

immanent Operating from inside a thing or person: not external or *transcendent.

immaterialism The denial of *materialism.

immediate In logic an immediate inference is one made by a single application of a single *rule of inference.

immortality The condition of being exempt from death or destruction, of living forever. Personal immortality entails that after our death (as identified by others) we ourselves shall enjoy experiences, possibly after an interval, and shall live another life, and continue to do so forever. The doctrine may involve only the survival of our '*soul' conceived of as an immaterial thinking substance contingently and temporarily lodged in our present body. Or it may involve resurrection of the body itself. In the Platonic tradition the former is possible. But for *Aristotle the soul is the form of the body, and cannot exist without it as a separate substance could, any more than a grin can exist without the grinning face. The arguments that the soul is immortal include metaphysical arguments (e.g. that it is simple, and hence cannot decompose), moral arguments (e.g. that immortality is a presupposition of morality, providing the arena in which the just triumph and the unjust are punished), and empirical arguments (e.g. that there are cases of living people having experience of spirits of the dead or of ghosts). No argument from these families enjoys much respect among contemporary philosophers. The first kind of argument was attacked by *Hume and especially by *Kant in Bk ii of the Transcendental Dialectic of the *Critique of Pure Reason*. Those of the second, moral, class seem more like wishful thinking than arguments, although Kant himself held a highly nuanced version of them. The third kind are included in the general mistrust of *parapsychology. Special revelation or faith remain the most powerful sources of belief in immortality, and belief that it is incoherent to postulate the separation of mind and body remains the most powerful philosophical response. Less attention has been paid to the question of why immortality appears desirable: *see* MAKROPOULOS CASE.

In the Platonic and *Neoplatonic traditions immortality may be given a 'timeless' twist. Rather than living for ever the goal is to live out of time altogether (*see* ETERNITY); the coherence of this ideal is not, however, at all evident, although frequently testified to by mystics and practitioners of meditation. It should be noticed that whilst the foregoing points apply to personal immortality, the immortality, or at least the continued existence, of some of a person's features may well survive death. One's work, or fame, or notoriety, or genes may well survive in the minds or bodies of others. *See also* LIFE, MEANING OF.

immutability A number of currents lead to divine immutability being seen as an aspect of God's perfection. A perfect being cannot change for the better and would not change for the worse; change is associated with the sublunar world, or the world of shadows, or the material as opposed to the spiritual world. However God's immutability is opposed by those who argue for the power of prayer, or those who argue that ability to change is essential to God's omnipotence.

impartiality A central virtue, associated with justice and fairness. A distribution of benefits and burdens is made impartially if no consideration sways it except those that determine what is due to each individual. Different views of *desert will assess this differently. A difficulty with applying the concept is that in much of life the claims of people to whom one stands in special relations, such as friends and family, oppose strict impartiality, making it seem more a part of public morality than of private virtue.

impartial spectator Central concept in the ethical system of Adam *Smith. The impartial spectator is an imagined 'man within the breast' whose approbation or disapproval makes up our awareness of the nature of our own conduct. Smith is concerned to give an explanation of the voice of conscience, without departing totally from the *sentimentalist and *naturalistic tradition of Scottish moral philosophy. Conscience is not a mysterious or inexplicable force, since 'the jurisdiction of the man within is founded altogether on the desire of praise-worthiness and in the aversion to blame-worthiness' which underlies our 'dread of possessing those qualities, and performing those actions, which we hate and despise in other people' (*Theory of the Moral Sentiments*, iii. 2. 33).

imperative The standard mood of sentences used to issue requests and commands. Questions in the philosophy of language arising from imperatives include estimating whether the need to issue requests and commands might be as basic as the need to communicate information (animal signalling systems may often be interpreted either way), and understanding the relationship between commands and other action-guiding uses of language, such as ethical discourse. The ethical theory of *prescriptivism in fact equates the two functions. A further question is whether there is an imperative logic. 'Hump that bale!' seems to follow from 'Tote that barge and hump that bale!' in something like the way that 'It's raining' follows from 'It's windy and it's raining.' But it is harder to say how to include other forms: does 'Shut the door or shut the window!' follow from 'Shut the window!', for example? The usual way to develop an imperative logic is to work in terms of the possibility of satisfying the one command without satisfying the other, thereby turning it into a variation of ordinary deductive logic.

implication Informally, the implications of a proposition *p* (or set of propositions S) are those propositions which one would accept in the schema 'if *p* then ... ', (or, if each of S, then ...). These will include things accepted only because of common sense, things which are common knowledge or presupposed in some context, or a sense of what regularly happens ('if we go to London we will get caught in the crowds'). *Logic tries to codify what is implied by sets of propositions in the more rigorous sense of what cannot possibly be false if they are each true. *See also* IMPLICATURE.

implicature Term introduced by *Grice for the implications of an utterance that go beyond what is strictly implied by the content of the utterance. Thus, if I am asked what I think of my new colleague and I reply, 'They tell me his spelling is good', then although nothing about his philosophical abilities follows from what I actually say, nevertheless my saying it implies that I hold a low opinion of those abilities. A conversation may largely hinge on implicatures, as when one damns with faint praise. Views about the meanings of terms will often depend on classifying the implications of sayings involving the terms as implicatures or as genuine logical implications of what is said. Implicatures may be divided into two kinds: conversational implicatures of the kind illustrated, and the more subtle category of conventional implicatures. Here a term may have the same content as another, but its use may as a matter of convention carry an implicature. Thus one view of the relation between 'he is poor and honest' and 'he is poor but honest' is that they have the same content (are true in just the same conditions), but that as a matter of the meaning of the term 'but' the second has implicatures (that the combination is surprising or significant) that the first lacks.

implicit definition An implicit definition of a term is given when a number of principles or axioms involving it are laid down, none of which gives an equation identifying it with another term. Thus number may be said to be implicitly defined by *Peano's postulates; force is implicitly defined by the postulates of mechanics; and so on. *See also* RAMSEY SENTENCE.

import, existential *See* EXISTENTIAL IMPORT.

impossibility A proposition is impossible if it could not have been true. For some of the issues, *see* NECESSITY, POSSIBLE WORLDS.

impredicative definition Term coined by *Poincaré for a kind of definition in which a member of a set is defined in a way that presupposes the set taken as a whole. Poincaré believed that paradoxes like those of *Russell and the *barber were due to such definitions, and therefore proposed banning them. But it turns out that classical mathematics requires such definitions at too many points for the ban to be easily observed. *See also* VICIOUS CIRCLE PRINCIPLE.

inalienable Used especially of rights: an inalienable right is one that cannot be abridged or suspended or even (more stringently and often controversially) signed away voluntarily. The right to possession of one's limbs, or the right to life, or the right not to be owned by another are candidates, but not the right to things that make potentially unlimited demands on others, like the right to holidays or freedom from disease or want.

inauthenticity *See* AUTHENTICITY.

inclusive/exclusive disjunction *See* EXCLUSIVE/INCLUSIVE DISJUNCTION.

incoherent In *probability theory a set of probability assignments is incoherent if it lays their possessor open to a *Dutch book; equivalently, it is incoherent if it disobeys the classical axioms of probability theory. *See* REPRESENTATION THEOREM.

incommensurable *See* COMMENSURABLE.

i

incompatibilist Term for one who believes that *free will is incompatible with *determinism.

incompleteness *See* COMPLETENESS.

incomplete symbol Term used by *Russell to describe *definite descriptions and other expressions which have the feature that they cannot be defined in isolation, but only by means of giving an analysis of any entire sentence in which they are embedded.

incompossible Mutually exclusive. Ambrose Bierce's definition and example from *The Devil's Dictionary* cannot be bettered: 'Two things are incompossible when the world of being has scope enough for one of them, but not enough for both—as Walt Whitman's poetry and God's mercy to man.'

incongruent counterparts (incongruous counterparts) Spatial items which relate to each other as mirror-images do, so that although the same shape, they cannot be superimposed so as to occupy exactly the same volume of space. In three dimensions, a right hand cannot occupy exactly the same space as a left hand. On a two-dimensional plane, a letter L cannot be moved to cover the same letter L reversed. It is notable that in three-dimensional space the letter can be flipped over to cover the reversed version. Similarly, if there were a *fourth dimension of space, we could in principle disappear from the three familiar dimensions, flip round, and return with, for instance, our hearts on the right-hand side of our bodies. *Kant (*Metaphysical Foundations of Natural Science*, i. 13) advances incongruent counterparts as a problem for a purely relational theory of space. If we imagine a universe with just one object, say a single hand, it would seem to be determinate whether it is a left hand or a right hand, yet all the spatial relations of its elements will be the same whichever one it is. So a relational theory of space seems unable to account for the difference, and therefore seems to be inadequate.

inconsistent *See* CONSISTENT/INCONSISTENT.

incontinence *See* AKRASIA.

incorrigible A proposition is incorrigible if it cannot be corrected; that is, it is not possible that belief in it should be found to be mistaken. Although many candidates have been proposed, ranging from first-person introspective reports to basic logical axioms, it is widely held that a proposition could achieve the status only by saying nothing. Any proposition with real content would involve bringing a particular situation under some rule of description, and the possibility of mistaken application always arises. In that case the search for incorrigible starting-points in the theory of knowledge is misguided. *See also* EPISTEMOLOGY, FOUNDATIONALISM.

indefinite description A phrase talking about a thing of a sort, or things that satisfy some description with no implication that just one thing does. The sentence 'a man came here this morning' contains the indefinite description 'a man'. *See* DEFINITE DESCRIPTION.

independence In logic the question of whether an *axiom is independent of others is frequently of great importance. It may be investigated in *model theory by finding a model for the set consisting of the other axioms and the negation of the one in question. Important independence results include the independence of the axiom of *choice from the rest of classical set theory, and that of the *continuum hypothesis from the rest of set theory plus the axiom of choice.

indeterminacy of translation The doctrine of *Quine unveiled in ch. 2 of *Word and Object*, that the totality of subjects' behaviour leaves it indeterminate whether one translation of their sayings or another is correct. Since there is nothing more than the totality of behaviour to fix one interpretation as the true one, the very notion of a determinately correct interpretation, or equivalently a single meaning that their sayings have, is undermined. Quine argued for his thesis 'from below' by pointing out that consistently with what we see of someone's linguistic behaviour the individual terms they utter may be given different interpretations, and that these could ramify to infect the whole language (*see* INSCRUTABILITY OF REFERENCE). He also argued 'from above', saying that in the case in which two different theories are each adequate to the whole of experience, the question of which one a subject really holds seems to lapse. At different times more weight was placed on one or other of these arguments, but each has found its critics. Perhaps the most puzzling implication of the view is that in one's own case the meaning of terms becomes indeterminate, so that there is no real truth of the matter whether one uses the word 'cat' to refer to cats or to do something quite different. This seems hard to square with an understanding of oneself as capable of thought at all. Quine believes that you can avoid such a catastrophic conclusion by what he calls 'acquiescing' in one's natural language, but again critics have doubted whether this meets the difficulty. The doctrine of the indeterminacy of translation has, however, been widely influential. It is the focus of many debates about the reality of psychological states, and may be said to represent the analytic tradition's version of the general mistrust of determinate meaning that is characteristic of *postmodernism.

indeterminism The view that some events have no causes. They just happen, and nothing in the previous state of the world explains them. According to *quantum mechanics, quantum events have this character. *See also* DETERMINISM.

indexical An expression whose reference on an occasion is dependent upon the context: either who utters it, or when or where it is uttered, or what object is pointed out at the time of its utterance. The terms *I, you, here, there, now, then, this,* and *that* are indexicals.

indicative The standard mood of sentences intended to make assertions or deliver information; it is contrasted with *imperative, hortative ('would we were free!'), and sometimes conditional moods.

indicative conditionals Sentences such as 'if Alfred comes, there will be a row' or 'if Oswald did not shoot Kennedy, then someone else did'. These are standardly contrasted with *counterfactual conditionals: for example the second of them is true, whereas the corresponding counterfactual 'if Oswald had not shot Kennedy, then someone else would have' is false. But the nature of the contrast, and indeed the right account of the meaning of indicative conditionals, are both highly controversial. In standard *propositional calculus, indicative conditionals are treated as expressing the *truth function of *material implication, although this generates well-known paradoxes.

indicator word (indicator term) Uncommon name for an *indexical expression.

indifference, principle of The principle named (but rejected) by *Keynes, whereby if there is no known reason for asserting one rather than another out of several alternatives, then relative to our knowledge they have an equal probability. Without restriction the principle leads to contradiction. For example, if we know nothing about the nationality of a person, we might argue that the probability is equal that she comes from England or France, and equal that she comes from Scotland or France, and equal that she comes from Britain or France. But from the first two assertions the probability that she belongs to Britain must be at least double the probability that she belongs to France. *See also* BERTRAND'S PARADOX.

indirect proof Term sometimes used for **reductio ad absurdum*.

indirect utilitarianism Indirect versions of *utilitarianism apply in the first place to such things as institutions, systems of rules of conduct, or human characters. These are best if they maximize happiness, but actions are judged only in so far as they are those ordained by the institutions or by the system of rules, or are those that would be performed by the person of optimal character. Indirect versions of the doctrine overcome some of the problem that we are not likely to know, on individual occasions, which action will in fact maximize happiness. Even if we do not know that, we may know of the general impact institutions, rules, and character have on the happiness of those affected by them. Our position becomes like that of a referee in a game, who knows in a general way that the point of the rules is to maximize the participants' pleasure, but whose job is simply to enforce the rules, not to worry about their consequences.

indiscernibility of identicals The principle that if A is identical with B, then every property that A has B has, and vice versa. This is sometimes known as *Leibniz's law. *See also* IDENTITY OF INDISCERNIBLES.

individual The things counted as single for the purpose in hand. What is counted as an individual, therefore, depends on what kind of thing is being counted: an individual book may consist of many words and the individual words consist of many letters. *See also* INDIVIDUATION, PRINCIPLE OF; SORTAL.

individualism The view that the single person is the basic unit of political analysis, with social wholes being merely *logical constructions, or ways of talking about numbers of such individuals and the relations among them. The consequence for the study of social facts is that they must be approached through the actions and intentions of individuals (methodological individualism). The approach has been a principal target of many sociologists, such as *Durkheim. In liberal individualism the individual is the primary possessor of *rights, with the activities of the state confined to the protection of those rights. Individualism is often charged with dissociating the 'free' individual from the matrix of social relations and norms that in fact make agency, freedom, and even self-consciousness possible. It is thus opposed by views holding that individual persons cannot be understood apart from linguistic, moral, legal, and social factors that shape their natures: such views are versions of *holism, and the associated methodology that insists on the social whole as the basis of individual description is methodological holism. *Marx expressed the position in the 6th thesis of the *Theses on Feuerbach*: 'the essence of man is not an abstraction inherent in each particular individual. The real nature of man is the totality of social relations.' Politically, individualism is associated with the right wing (the British Prime Minister Margaret Thatcher famously said that there is no such thing as society, only individuals), while holism at its extreme is apt to be expressed in such doctrines as *collectivism and *totalitarianism.

A similar division exists in the philosophy of *language, over whether the properties of individual words are prior to, or derivative from, the properties of larger linguistic entities such as *sentences or whole collections of beliefs or theories.

individuation, principle of Also known as the criterion of *identity. The principle associated with a kind of thing, telling when we have two of them and when we have one. Thus to count words it is necessary to know whether we suppose that variations of spelling, or meaning, or etymology, give us two different words, and when they allow us to rest with one word (*see also* TYPE–TOKEN AMBIGUITY). We also need to know when two appearances or stages can rightly be regarded as appearances or stages of just one thing of the kind. A principle of individuation for nations would tell whether a nation survives such things as shift of territory, of government, of origin of inhabitants, of language, and so on. A relaxed attitude is that we solve such cases as we go along, depending on the consequences of the different verdicts, and apparently doing without cast-iron principles. This relaxed attitude was opposed by *Quine, at least for languages fit to express proper scientific facts, with the slogan 'no entity without identity' ('Speaking of Objects', 1958).

indubitable That which cannot be doubted. A weaker category than *incorrigible, since we may as a matter of fact be unable to doubt propositions that might turn out to be false through bizarre enough possibilities. To hold that we ought to doubt things that are not incorrigible is to enter on one quite swift road to *scepticism.

induction The term is most widely used for any process of reasoning that takes us from empirical premises to empirical conclusions supported by the premises, but not deductively *entailed by them. Inductive arguments are therefore kinds of *ampliative argument, in which something beyond the content of the premises is inferred as probable or supported by them. Induction is, however, commonly distinguished from arguments to theoretical explanations, which share this ampliative character, by being confined to inference in which the conclusion involves the same properties or relations as the premises. The central example is induction by simple enumeration, where from premises telling that Fa, Fb, Fc..., where a, b, c, are all of some kind G, it is inferred that Gs from outside the sample, such as future Gs, will be F, or perhaps that all Gs are F. If this, that, and the other person deceive them, children may well infer that everyone is a deceiver. Different but similar inferences are those from the past possession of a property by some object to the same object's future possession of the same property, or from the constancy of some law-like pattern in events and states of affairs to its future constancy: all objects we know of attract each other with a force inversely proportional to the square of the distance between them, so perhaps they all do so, and always will do so.

The rational basis of any such inference was challenged by *Hume, who believed that induction presupposed belief in the *uniformity of nature, but that this belief had no defence in reason, and merely reflected a habit or custom of the mind. Hume was not therefore sceptical about the propriety of processes of induction, but sceptical about the role of reason in either explaining it or justifying it. Trying to answer Hume and to show that there is something rationally compelling about the inference is referred to as the problem of induction. It is widely recognized that any rational defence of induction will have to partition well-behaved properties for which the inference is plausible (often called projectible properties) from badly behaved ones for which it is not (*see* GOODMAN'S PARADOX). It is also recognized that actual inductive habits are more complex than those of simple enumeration, and that both common sense and science pay attention to such factors as variations within the sample giving us the evidence, the application of ancillary beliefs about the order of nature, and so on (*see* MILL'S METHODS). Nevertheless, the fundamental problem remains that any experience shows us only events occurring within a very restricted part of the vast spatial and temporal order about which we then come to believe things. *See also* CONFIRMATION, EXPLANATION, FALSIFICATION, VINDICATION.

induction, mathematical *See* MATHEMATICAL INDUCTION.

induction by elimination *See* ELIMINATIVE INDUCTION.

induction by enumeration *See* ENUMERATIVE INDUCTION.

inductive logic *See* CONFIRMATION.

ineffable That which is particular to an experience, and cannot be communicated. It is sometimes thought that the precise feels of particular *qualia of experience are ineffable. The other examples of philosophical interest are the states of mind achieved in mystical *ecstasy, which are often felt to be especially revelatory of the true nature of the world, but also incommunicable. However the notion of an incommunicable content is commonly regarded with grave suspicion, on the grounds that genuine content involves the recognition of something; that this requires the application of rules; but rules must be public and communicable. *See also* PRIVATE LANGUAGE ARGUMENT, RULE-FOLLOWING CONSIDERATIONS.

inequality *See* EQUALITY.

inertial frame A frame of reference for measurements of motion, space, and time. An inertial frame (also called a Newtonian frame or system) is one in which a body subject to no net forces moves in a rectilinear path with constant velocity. In Newtonian physics, distances measured in two such systems will be related by the 'Galilean transformation', $x' = x + \text{vt}$, where x, x' are the two measures, t is the common time, and v is the relative velocity. The Michelson–Morley experiment showed that this was not true for the speed of light, which is a constant for all observers. *See also* CLOCK PARADOX, RELATIVITY.

inevitability *See* FATALISM.

inference The process of moving from (possibly provisional) acceptance of some propositions, to acceptance of others. The goal of *logic and of classical *epistemology is to codify kinds of inference, and to provide principles for separating good from bad inferences. *See also* RULE OF INFERENCE.

inference to the best explanation Concept formulated by Princeton philosopher Gilbert Harman in his paper 'The Inference to the Best Explanation', *Philosophical Review* 74 (1965). Arguably the idea goes back to *Peirce, although Peirce's views are not altogether easy to excavate. The idea is that when we have a best explanation of some phenomenon, we are entitled to repose confidence in it simply on that account. Sometimes thought to be the lynchpin of scientific method, the principle is not easy to formulate and has come under attack, notably since our best current explanation of something may be only the best of a bad lot. There exist cases in which the best explanation is still not all that convincing, so other desiderata than pure explanatory success seem to play a role. *See also* CONSTRUCTIVE EMPIRICISM.

inferential role semantics The view that the role of sentences in inference gives a more important key to their meaning than their 'external' relations to things in the world. The meaning of a sentence becomes its place in a network of inferences that it legitimates. Also known as functional role semantics, procedural semantics, or conceptual role semantics, the view bears some relation to the *coherence theory of truth, and suffers from the same suspicion that it divorces meaning from any clear association with things in the world.

infima species In traditional logic, terms are ordered with respect to generality. In decreasing order we have a series such as: thing, body, organism, animal, horse. The *infima species* is the lowest limit of this process. It may not be obvious why there should be such a limit since the process of subdivision can go on indefinitely. The idea, however, is that after some point further qualifications only add *accidents, not *essential properties or essences, whereas genuine species are marked off by what is essential.

infinitary logic Logic extended to countenance expressions of infinite length. The step is taken to expand the powers of expressions, particularly in the light of results for finitary *first-order logic, such as *Godel's theorems or the *Löwenheim–Skolem theorem.

infinite divisibility *See* BAYLE'S TRILEMMA, INFINITY, ZENO'S PARADOXES.

infinite regress *See* REGRESS.

infinite set (infinite collection, infinite number) *See* DENUMERABLE/NON-DENUMERABLE.

infinitesimal Both the infinitely large and its inverse, the infinitely small, cause headaches. The first philosophical explorations that turned disquiet into something more tangible were *Zeno's paradoxes. The 18th-century development of the calculus led to the consideration of magnitudes changing over 'indefinitely' smaller intervals of time, and the reaction on Zeno's behalf came from *Berkeley, who saw that the infinitesimals resulting ('the vanished ghosts of departed quantities') were treated inconsistently as finite quantities or as nothing, depending on the exigencies of the argument. A rigorous treatment of the notion of a limit was only provided by K. T. W. Weierstrass (1815–97) in the 19th century: it need only refer to finite numbers, and thus removes the place of the infinitesimal from the foundations of mathematics. However, a consistent non-standard analysis has been developed by the mathematician Abraham Robinson (1918–74): in it infinitesimals have the disturbing property that while they are not nothing, no sum of n of them is ever greater than any finite number, so the number sequence that includes them is not *Archimedean.

i

infinity The unlimited; that which goes beyond any fixed bound. Exploration of this notion goes back at least to *Zeno of Elea, and extensive mathematical treatment began with Eudoxus of Cnidus (4th c. BC). The mathematical notion was further developed by *Cantor and K. T. W. Weierstrass (1815–97) in the 19th century. In the philosophy of *space and *time problems arise both with the infinitely small (*see* BAYLE'S TRILEMMA, ZENO'S PARADOXES) and with the infinitely large or boundless nature that each seems, intuitively, to possess. *Kant argued in the *antinomies that consistently regarding space or time as either finite or as infinite was impossible, and this formed a key element in his *idealist theory of them as imposed upon an unknown (*noumenal) nature by our own forms of sense. Philosophically one important division is between thinkers such as Cantor who can countenance actual completed infinities, and those such as *Aristotle or the mathematician Leopold Krönecker (1823–91) who reject any such notion in favour of merely 'potential' infinities.

infinity, axiom of Axiom needed in *Russell's development of set theory to ensure that there are enough sets for the purposes of mathematics. In the theory of *types, if there were only finitely many objects of the lowest type, then there would only be finite sets at any level. To avoid this Russell postulated that there are infinitely many individuals or objects of the lowest type, but the non-logical nature of this assumption was a grave obstacle to his *logicist programme. In *Zermelo–Fraenkel set theory the axiom asserts that there is a set of which the null set is a member, and such that if any set is a member, the *union of it and its *unit set is also a member: $(\exists S)(\varnothing \in S \,\&\, (\forall R)(R \in S) \rightarrow R \cup \{R\} \in S)$.

infirmation Uncommon term for *disconfirmation.

informal fallacy *See* FALLACY.

information theory The theory of measurement of information in which the information content of an event is measured by its statistical improbability.

Ingarden, Roman Witold (1893–1970) Polish phenomenologist and aesthetician. Ingarden studied under Husserl, but rejected the latter's 'transcendental' turn, favouring instead a realism which is nevertheless sensitive to the role of consciousness in generating so much of the world as it is for us. Much of Ingarden's work is in systematic ontology: for example, in his best-known work on literature and art he develops a 'stratified' theory of the different objects involved in physical space and in the intentional stance of the onlooker or reader. Works include *Das literarische Kunstwerk. Eine Untersuchung aus dem Grenzgebiet der Ontologie, Logik und Literaturwissenschaft* (1931, trs. as *The Literary Work of Art*, 1973), *Erlebnis, Kunstwerk und Wert. Vorträge zur Ästhetik 1937–1967* (1969), and *Selected Papers in Aesthetics* (1985).

innate ideas Ideas that are inborn and not the product of experience. The controversy over their existence formed a major element in *Locke's rejection of the philosophy of *Descartes, and Locke was in turn attacked over the issue by *Leibniz. The question was whether the mind is equipped with highly general concepts—God, freedom, immortality, substance—that can be known **a priori* to be applicable to the world, and that could therefore afford us clear and distinct knowledge unlike any that can be certified by experience. It thus formed a pivotal issue between rationalists and their empiricist opponents. The connection between innateness as such and any right to think of these ideas as yielding a distinct kind of knowledge was queried by *Hume, but the need for *a priori* categories of the understanding through which experience is organized was again defended by *Kant. In the 20th century the view that children carry with them an innate universal *grammar, enabling them to pull off the remarkable feat of learning a first language, has been defended by *Chomsky.

inscrutability of reference The doctrine due to *Quine that no empirical evidence relevant to interpreting a speaker's utterances can decide among alternative and incompatible ways of assigning referents to the words used; hence there is no fact that the words have one *reference or another. Although the doctrine is similar to that of the *indeterminacy of translation, they are not identical. First, inscrutability of reference might be compatible with the different interpretations of the speaker all sharing the same truth-value, whereas indeterminacy is often supposed by Quine to require that the different interpretations stand in no kind of equivalence, so that on one interpretation what is said might be true, and on another false. Secondly, translation might be indeterminate even though reference is scrutable, if, for instance, it is a goal of correct translation to fix more than the references of terms. However 'inscrutability' is not quite the right term for Quine's doctrine, since the term implies something real but unknowable, whereas it is Quine's position that terms have no real unique reference. In the late book *Pursuit of Truth* (1990) Quine prefers the title 'indeterminacy of reference'. *See also* INDETERMINACY OF TRANSLATION, PROXY FUNCTION.

instinct (Latin, *instinctus*, impulse or urge) The term implies innately determined behaviour, inflexible to change in circumstance and outside the control of deliberation and reason. The view that animals accomplish even complex tasks by nature and not by reason was common to *Aristotle and the *Stoics, and the inflexibility of their routines was used in defence of this position as early as *Avicenna. A continuity between animal and human reason was proposed by *Hume, and followed by *sensationalists such as the naturalist Erasmus Darwin (1731–1802). The theory of *evolution prompted various views of the emergence of stereotypical behaviour, and the idea that innate determinants of behaviour are fostered by specific environments is a guiding principle of ethology. In this sense it may be instinctive in human beings to be social, and for that matter to reason. *See also* ANIMAL THOUGHT.

institutional facts Contrasted with *brute facts in that they only exist in a society with certain conventions, rules, or norms in place, such as those which determine that we are owed money, or have given a promise, or are playing chess.

institutional theory of art The view championed by George Dickie in 1974, following on work by Arthur *Danto, that art institutions such as museums and galleries, and specific agents working within them, have the power to dictate what is art and what is not. There is no property of being a work of art other than being deemed to be such by authorized members of the art world. Like other *social constructivist views, the theory has some difficulty understanding what the experts go on when they themselves debate whether something should be counted as art.

institutions As well as organizations and corporations, philosophers talk of the institution of money or the institution of promises. The idea is that money, or promises, become possible only when a set of rules or norms or *conventions implemented in society's arrangements generate 'institutional facts', such as having a debt or having made a promise. The emergence of these norms and conventions is seldom due to explicit contract, but more a matter of gradual growth, fuelled by their evident utility.

instrumentalism The view that a scientific theory is to be regarded as an instrument for producing new predictions or new techniques for controlling events, but not as itself capable of literal truth or falsity. The most famous example of this claim is that of Andreas Oseander (or Osiander, 1498–1552), whose Preface to *De Revolutionibus Orbium Coelestium* advocated that *Copernicus's heliocentric theory of the solar system should be accepted as a device for predicting eclipses and tides, but not regarded as true (and therefore potentially in conflict with Church doctrine). Instrumentalism diminishes the difficulty over our right to confidence in scientific theory, since it is easier to suppose that we have a right to adopt a theory as an instrument, than that we have a right to regard it as true. A tempting reaction to deep theoretical stress, such as the apparently incompatible wave–particle duality of *quantum mechanics, is to suggest that each view serves as an instrument within its own proper sphere, and thereby to sidestep the theoretical urge to reconcile them. It is also tempting to take an instrumentalist (sometimes called heuristic) attitude to the use of devices such as sets, numbers, or possible worlds, that seem to facilitate our thinking in important ways, but not to deserve a place in our *ontologies.

A difficult question in the philosophy of mind and language is to tell what distinguishes acceptance in a purely instrumentalist spirit from true belief. Some philosophers of a *pragmatist bent, whilst sympathetic to instrumentalism, will be especially prone to deny that there is a real distinction here, since in such a philosophy all belief is simply acceptance into the system deemed most useful.

instrumental value Value that something has as a means to something else.

insufficient reason, principle of *See* INDIFFERENCE, PRINCIPLE OF.

integrity Most simply a synonym for honesty. But integrity is frequently connected with the more complicated notion of a wholeness or harmony of the self, associated with a proper conception of oneself as someone whose life would lose its unity, or be violated by doing various things. It has been argued, notably by *Williams, that *utilitarianism can make no sense of the range of thoughts this properly engenders, although others have claimed that the aim of living life as a good utilitarian provides its own standards of integrity.

intelligence Most generally, the capacity to deal flexibly and effectively with practical and theoretical problems. Since people's capacities to do this vary with the problem, it may be doubted whether there is a useful level of abstraction at which one thing, intelligence, can be thought of as equally manifested in whatever logical, theoretical, practical, mathematical, linguistic, etc. successes we achieve. Nor is there much confidence left that intelligence tests measure any such general capacity, as opposed to measuring the subject's capacity to take intelligence tests, often of very specific and culturally peculiar kinds. For the question whether humans alone possess intelligence, *see* ANIMAL THOUGHT, INSTINCT.

intelligent design The view that biology exhibits phenomena that cannot be explained by natural selection, and that it is therefore good science to attribute them to a guiding intelligence. The view is itself a mutation of *creationism. Its view of biology has been rejected by nearly all practising biologists, and its view of both biology and science has been rejected by American courts who viewed it, correctly, as an attempt to sneak religion into the science curriculum in schools. The landmark case was Kitzmiller vs. Dover School Board, brought in Pennsylvania in 2005. *See also* DARWINISM; DESIGN, ARGUMENT FROM OR TO.

intension *See* EXTENSION/INTENSION.

intensional logic Any system unlike classical logic in that it admits contexts in which substitution of co-referring proper names, or predicates that have the same extension, or sentences that have the same truth value, need not preserve the truth-value of sentences in which they are embedded.

intensive magnitude The measure of a quality such as hardness where there is no physical process of addition for producing more of the quality by combining given amounts. Such magnitudes contrast with extensive magnitudes (length, volume) where this can be done.

intention To have an intention is to be in a state of mind that is favourably directed towards bringing about (or maintaining, or avoiding) some state of affairs, but which is not a mere desire or wish, since it also sets the subject on a course to bring that state of affairs about. The notion thus inherits all the problems of *intentionality. The specific problems it raises include characterizing the difference between doing something accidentally and doing it intentionally. The suggestion that the difference lies in a preceding act of mind or volition is not very happy, since one may automatically do what is nevertheless intentional, for example putting one's foot forward while walking. Conversely, unless the formation of a volition is intentional, and thus raises the same questions, the presence of a volition might be unintentional or beyond one's control. Intentions are more finely grained than movements: one set of movements may both be answering the question and starting a war, yet the one may be intentional and the other not.

intentional fallacy In aesthetics, the supposed mistake of holding that the author's intentions in making a work form an authoritative basis for interpretation and criticism. It is often remarked (especially in *deconstructionism) that even when we have access to the author's intentions through a direct statement, this statement is only an act of self-interpretation by the author, and for us can only be another text, itself ripe for reinterpretation and criticism.

intentionality The directedness or 'aboutness' of many, if not all, conscious states. The term was used by the *scholastics, but revived in the 19th century by *Brentano. Our beliefs, thoughts, wishes, dreams, and desires are about things. Equally the words we use to express these beliefs and other mental states are about things. The problem of intentionality is that of understanding the relation obtaining between a mental state, or its expression, and the things it is about. A number of peculiarities attend this relation. First, if I am in some relation to a chair, for instance by sitting on it, then both it and I must exist. But while mostly one thinks about things that exist, sometimes (although this way of putting it has its problems) one has beliefs, hopes, and fears about things that do not, as when the child expects Santa Claus, and the adult fears Zeus. Secondly, if I sit on the chair, and the chair is the oldest antique in London, then I sit on the oldest antique in London. But if I plan to avoid the mad axeman, and the mad axeman is in fact my friendly postman, I do not therefore plan to avoid my friendly postman (*see also* EXTENSIONAL/INTENSIONAL, REFERENTIALLY OPAQUE/TRANSPARENT). Intentional relations seem to depend on how the object is specified, or as *Frege put it, on the mode of presentation of the object. This makes them quite unlike the relations whose logic we can understand by means of the *predicate calculus, and this peculiarity has led some philosophers, notably *Quine, to declare them unfit for use in serious science (*see also* ELIMINATIVISM). More widespread is the view that since the concept is indispensable, we must either declare serious science unable to deal with the central feature of the mind, or explain how serious science may include intentionality. One approach is to suggest that while the linguistic forms in which we communicate fears and beliefs have a two-faced aspect, involving both the objects referred to, and the mode of presentation under which they are thought of, we can see the mind as essentially directed onto existent things, and extensionally related to them. Intentionality then becomes a feature of language, rather than a metaphysical or ontological peculiarity of the mental world.

interactionism The view that, as indeed appears to be the case, mind and body interact. The contrary views include *epiphenomenalism, *occasionalism, and *parallelism.

interests Those things that a person needs, or that are conducive to his or her flourishing and success. The central examples of things against someone's interests are the things that *harm or injure them. The concept thus inherits the problems of understanding what makes for success in life (*see* *EUDAIMONIA*). People may not desire, or value, what they need; hence people's real interests may not be revealed by their immediate choices and preferences. Different political views will advocate different approaches to this divergence, particularly according to the degree to which they allow *paternalistic interventions. *See also* CAPABILITIES.

inter finitum et infinitum non est proportio Latin tag: between the finite and the infinite there is no proportion.

internalism/externalism *See* EXTERNALISM.

interpretation (logic) Informally, an interpretation of a logical system assigns meaning or semantic value to the formulae and their elements. More formally, if we consider a language whose non-logical terms include names, function symbols, predicate letters, and sentence letters, then an interpretation of a language specifies the following: (i) a domain, or universe of discourse. This is a non-empty set, and forms the range of any variables that occur in any of the sentences of the language. (ii) For each name in the language, an object from the domain as its reference or denotation. (iii) For each function symbol a *function which assigns a value in the domain to any sequence of arguments in the domain. (iv) For each predicate letter a property or relation, specifying which sequences of objects in the domain satisfy the property or stand in the relation to each other. (v) For each sentence letter, a truth-value. The *logical constants such as expressions for *truth functions and *quantifiers will be assigned their standard meanings, via rules such as truth tables specifying how formulae containing them are to be evaluated. *See also* MODEL THEORY.

intersection An element belongs to the intersection of two sets, A and B, if and only if it belongs to both A and B. The intersection is denoted by $A \cap B$.

intersubjectivity An intersubjective property is one on which the opinion of different subjects does or can coincide. If this is so because the subjects simply happen to share some nature, the property may be thought to fall short of full objectivity. Thus aesthetic tastes may be intersubjective, in the sense that we respond to things similarly, but not objective, if the fact that we do so owes as much to an accidental coincidence of taste as to the nature of the object. *See* PRIMARY/SECONDARY QUALITIES, RELATIVISM, SUBJECTIVISM/OBJECTIVISM.

intervening variables A notion that is an essential part of the deductive structure of a scientific theory, but itself does not refer to a real thing or aspect of things. An intervening variable may have no physical reality, although it organizes thought about things that do.

intolerance *See* TOLERATION.

intrinsic/extrinsic properties The intuitive idea is that the intrinsic properties of a thing are those that make it what it is, regardless of its surroundings or its relation to other things. They are therefore properties it could continue to have even if it did not affect other things as it does, for example by being in a world with different laws of nature. They are even compatible with 'loneliness', or it being the only thing in its universe. The puzzle is to establish what properties these may be, given that all the properties we know about are ones to which we are directly or indirectly receptive, this then being a matter of the dispositions or powers they have, which in turn depend on the laws of nature and perhaps surrounding fields and forces of the world in which they exist.

introspection Looking into one's own mind, to find what one thinks and feels. The idea that this process is rather like that of perception, only turned inwards, is rejected by most current philosophers of mind. Instead of perceiving what one thinks and feels, the process is probably better thought of in terms of wondering what to say, or rehearsing a narrative that could be made public: 'How do I know what I think until I hear what I say?' Introspection was a particular target of *behaviourism in psychology, but the opposition may have been misconceived, since making reports of one's mental life is itself a piece of behaviour, and one that can be studied as objectively as any other. *See* HETEROPHENOMENOLOGY.

intuition Immediate awareness, either of the truth of some proposition, or of an object of apprehension such as a concept. Awareness of the passage of time, or of the ineffable nature of God, have equally been claimed as intuitions. The notion is frequently regarded with suspicion, as simply labelling the place where the philosophical understanding of the source of our knowledge stops. In the philosophy of *Kant intuition (*Anschauung*) has an empirical form, covering the sensible apprehension of things, and as pure intuition it is that which structures sensation into the experience of things in space and time.

i

intuitionism (ethics) The position associated with *Moore, that identifies ethical propositions as objectively true or false, different in content from any empirical or other kind of judgement, and known by a special faculty of 'intuition'. Critics charge that the term explains nothing, but may merely function as a disguise for prejudice or passion.

intuitionism (mathematics) The philosophy of mathematics propounded by *Brouwer, although heralded in the *constructivist views of the mathematicians Leopold Krönecker (1823–91), *Poincaré, and Félix Borel (1871–1956). In reaction against mathematical *Platonism, intuitionism holds that the subject-matter of mathematics is the mental constructions of mathematicians. These are thought of as actual processes that have an existence in time, and in Brouwer's thought connect with the appreciation of time and its division. It was with the development of *intuitionistic logic that intuitionism took the stage as a serious constructivist rival to classical mathematics.

intuitionistic logic The logical system developed initially by A. Heyting (b. 1898) to formalize the reasonings allowed by mathematical *intuitionism. It is designed so that $p \vee \neg p$ is not a theorem, and the *rule of inference from $\neg\neg p$ to p is disallowed (the logic can be obtained from standard *natural deduction treatments of the propositional calculus by dropping this rule, provided there is added a rule that from a contradiction anything follows). It should be noticed that intuitionism does not assert the negation of $p \vee \neg p$. On the contrary, its double negation, $\neg\neg(p \vee \neg p)$, is itself a theorem of intuitionistic logic. A further important property is that from $\neg(\forall x)Fx$ it cannot be shown that $(\exists x)\neg Fx$. This accords with the *constructivist instincts behind intuitionism, since the premise gives us no way of constructing an instance of a thing that is not F. *Gödel showed that intuitionistic logic can be mapped into the *modal logic S4 by various translations of which this is an example. Here v is a propositional variable; A, B are any well-formed formulae of the intuitionistic logic; and Tr(a) is the translation of any formula into S4:

$$\mathrm{Tr}(v) = \Box v$$
$$\mathrm{Tr}(A \vee B) = \mathrm{Tr}A \vee \mathrm{Tr}B$$
$$\mathrm{Tr}(A \,\&\, B) = \mathrm{Tr}A \,\&\, \mathrm{Tr}B$$
$$\mathrm{Tr}(A \rightarrow B) = \mathrm{Tr}A \rightarrow \mathrm{Tr}B$$
$$\mathrm{Tr}\,\neg A = \neg\Diamond\mathrm{Tr}A.$$

This suggests that Heyting was guided by the thought that making a statement is equivalent to stating that the statement is provable or constructible. Denying a statement would be claiming that it is not possible that it should be constructed, or that a contradiction can be derived from the claim that it has been constructed. However, although these equivalences may help classical logicians to understand intuitionism, philosophically intuitionists would not accept that the classical modal logic is fundamental, or that such an explanation in classical terms is appropriate. An interesting property of intuitionistic logic is that no finite *truth tables can be given for the connectives.

intuition pump Derogatory term for a *thought experiment, especially one seeking to support a view by means of an analogy that is superficially compelling but more fundamentally doubtful. For example, one might compare all human action to the mechanical behaviour of insects in order to undermine any notion of freedom, without dwelling on the respects in which human behaviour is flexible and adaptable while that of insects is not.

invalid An argument is invalid when the conclusion does not follow from the premises. *See* ENTAILMENT, VALIDITY.

inventio medii (Latin, the finding of the middle) In traditional logic, a name for a method invented by Petrus Tartaretus around 1480, by which the middle term of a *syllogism can be found. It has sometimes been called the *pons asinorum or bridge of asses of logic.

inverse methods The mathematics of probability enable us to derive some probability judgements from others. For example, if we are given the probability of an event of some kind occurring on some occasion, we can derive the probability that the frequency of the event on a succession of occasions falls within some interval. An inverse method is an attempt to derive probabilities themselves purely from observed frequencies of events. The possibility of inverse methods is the subject of correspondence between Jakob Bernoulli (1654–1705), who was optimistic about such methods, although not in the *Ars Conjectandi*, and *Leibniz (sceptical). The most notorious example of an inverse argument is *Laplace's *rule of succession.

inversion In traditional logic, producing the *obverse of a proposition.

inverted spectrum The apparent possibility of two persons sharing their colour vocabulary and discriminations, although the colours one sees are systematically different from the colours the other sees. Once this possibility is allowed there seems to be no evidence that could bear on whether we do see colours the same way, and many philosophers of mind have found it important to deny that it is a real possibility.

invisible hand *See* SMITH.

Ionian school Those *Presocratics based in Ionia, otherwise known as the Milesians: *Thales, *Anaximander, and *Anaximenes.

iota operator A term that may be attached to a *variable to give an expression denoting the entity satisfying some condition. From the predicate F*x* it forms (ι*x*)F*x*, denoting the unique thing that is F, if there is such a thing.

ipso facto Latin, by that very fact.

Irigaray, Luce (1930–) Belgian feminist theorist, whose work explored the construction of sexual difference in Western philosophy and psychoanalysis. Irigaray was educated at Louvain, and taught in Brussels and Paris. Her early work in linguistics concerned the disruptive effects of mental illness on speech. But since being attached to the École Freudienne of *Lacan she has been especially concerned with the repression of female joy and sexuality, the *jouissance féminine*, and the distortion of its organic nature by male categories. She is notable for associating a different female voice and mode of experience with the different bodily natures of men and women. The female body is seen as the threshold of the female mind with its joyous wisdom and faith: 'beyond the classic opposites of love and hate, liquid and ice lies this perpetually *half-open* threshold, consisting of *lips* that are strangers to dichotomy' ('The Politics of Difference'). Some feminist thinkers regard such pronouncements as savouring of *essentialism. Her writings included *Speculum de l'autre femme* (1974, trs. as *Speculum of the Other Woman*, 1985), *Ce sexe qui n'en est pas un* (1977, trs. as *This Sex which is Not One*, 1985), and *Éthiques de la différence sexuelle* (1984).

irrationalism As a starting point, a view that accords authority to some other faculty than reason. However that might cover *empiricism, since use of the senses is not the same as the use of reason. In a more restricted sense, then, a view which releases the deliverance of some faculty, such as faith, or intuition, from the critical scrutiny of reason. A characteristic stance of *fideism in theology, and *Romanticism in the general culture.

irrational number A real *number that is not rational.

irrealism Coinage from the late 1980s for positions either that believe that traditional *realism versus anti-realism debates are not well formed, or that sympathize with opposition to realism without wanting to commit themselves to *idealism, *relativism, *reductionism, or other anti-realist options. *See also* MINIMALISM.

irreflexive A relation is irreflexive if nothing bears it to itself: ¬(∃*x*)R*xx*. Nothing is larger than itself, so 'is larger than' is an irreflexive relation.

is It is common to distinguish the 'is' of identity (Mount Everest is Chomolungma); the 'is' of predication (Jones is a bore); and the 'is' of existence (there is a life after death). In the treatment of propositions of this complexity in the *predicate calculus there is no symbolism common to these three, and the theory of why a natural language such as English finds a common element is not at all certain. It seems quite possible to present the same information without any such common element: Jones bores; life after death exists.

Ishmael effect The claimed ability of some philosophical theory to escape from the fate to which it condemns all other discourse. The effect was named by the 20th-century Australian philosopher D. C. Stove after Ishmael's epilogue to *Moby Dick*: 'and I only am escaped alone to tell thee'. This is something it must have been impossible for him to do, given the tale he tells. 'It is (absolutely) true that truth is relative'; 'we ought to think that there is no such thing as thought'; and 'the one immorality is to believe in morality' would be examples of doctrines that require the effect. *See also* PERITROPE.

Isocrates (436–338 BC) Greek philosopher and follower of *Socrates. An important source for knowledge of 4th-century Greece, Isocrates was an orator and teacher of rhetoric, and known mainly as a historian, commentator on current affairs, educationalist, and adviser to one and all. He is praised, perhaps ironically, as a rhetorician by Plato at the end of the *Phaedrus*, but his own down-to-earth prescriptions for education, avoiding unnecessary speculative flights, suggest that he was more of a political realist than Plato himself.

isolationism In aesthetics, the view that a work of art should be taken in isolation, understood entirely in its own terms and without reference to external factors such as its place in a tradition, or the social circumstances in which it is set, or the life or intentions of the artist (*see* INTENTIONAL FALLACY). The view is associated with the stress on pure aesthetic form celebrated by the English critics Roger Fry (1866–1934) and Clive Bell (1881–1965). The opposing position is *contextualism.

isomorphic One system is isomorphic with another if there is a *one-to-one representation or mapping of its properties associating them with properties of the other system. To say that there is an isomorphism between two systems is thus to say that they share the same structure. *Measurement is a process of finding an isomorphism between real magnitudes and relations within the series of numbers.

is/ought gap *See* HUME'S LAW.

Jacobi, Friedrich Heinrich (1743–1819) German philosopher and friend of *Hamann, *Herder, *Lessing, and *Goethe. Jacobi was a notable early critic of *Kant, and indeed of the *Enlightenment in general, which he believed led only to atheism and nihilism (a term he originally coined). He held that ordinary empirical or scientific reasoning does no more than collect together empirical fact; it cannot touch the essential nature of things, which is given by revelation or faith. His most significant works are *Über die Lehre der Spinoza* (1785; enlarged edn, 1789) and *David Hume über den Glauben, oder Idealismus und Realismus* (1787). Jacobi also had a celebrated quarrel, the '*Pantheismusstreit*' with Moses *Mendelssohn over the question of *Lessing's adherence to Spinozism.

Jainism One of the three heterodox **darshanas* or branches of Hinduism. Jainism traces its origins to Vardhamana, a successor to 23 previous 'fordmakers', or teachers who enabled the faithful to cross the stream leading to release from the cycle of existence. Its practice demands a monastic life of extreme austerity; for example, one sect is the *Digambara* or 'sky-clad', perhaps identical with the gymnosophists (Greek, naked + wisdom) reported by the companions of Alexander on his conquest of Northern India, who practise nudism. The *Buddha practised Jain asceticism before realizing that it did not in itself contain the key to the radiant release from the cares of the world that he was seeking.

James, William (1842–1910) American psychologist and philosopher. James was born into a wealthy New York family, and surrounded from an early age by a humanitarian, literary, and scholarly family life (his father was a theologian, and his brother the novelist Henry James). James had already spent years in Europe and begun an education as an artist, when he entered Harvard medical school in 1863, and he travelled in Brazil and Europe before he graduated with a medical degree in 1869. There followed years lecturing both on psychology and philosophy. James's first major work was the two-volume *Principles of Psychology* (1890), a work that does justice both to the scientific, laboratory study of experimental psychology, and the importance of a sound phenomenology of experience. James's own emotional needs gave him an abiding interest in problems of religion, freedom, and ethics; the popularity of these themes and his lucid and accessible style made James the most influential American philosopher of the beginning of the 20th century. His Gifford Lectures of 1901–2 were published as *The Varieties of Religious Experience: A Study in Human Nature*; they are widely regarded as the most important work on religion produced in America (although *see* SANTAYANA).

The philosophy of *pragmatism, of which together with *Peirce he is the founding figure, became a rallying-point for opposition to *absolute idealism. Its central tenets are, however, not easy to disentangle in James. He believed that philosophies express large currents of feeling as much as rigorous intellectual theorems, so that exactitude is not a particular virtue, and refuting a philosopher by seizing upon and refuting some statement is like trying to divert a river by planting a stick in it. This goes some way towards excusing his lecturer's fondness for aphorism and overstatement. Formulae such as 'the true is only the expedient in the way of our thinking, just as the right is only the expedient in the way of our behaving' (*Pragmatism: A New Name for some Old Ways of Thinking*, 1907, p. 222) brought instant denunciation, and James wrote many papers (collected in *The Meaning of Truth*, 1909) softening the doctrine and replying to detractors. Part of the trouble is that whilst James is in many respects a humanist and empiricist, he also wanted to preserve a place for religious belief, allowable if it 'works', in spite of the fact that working is here not the survival of verification or integration with the rest of our world view, but the generation of emotional benefits. James's later philosophy also included a 'radical empiricism' in which streams of experience regarded in one way constitute minds, and in another way constitute the objects of the external world (*see also* NEUTRAL MONISM). As well as those mentioned, major works include *The Will to Believe* (1897) and *Essays in Radical Empiricism* (1912).

SEE WEB LINKS

- An audio discussion with James's biographer
- A chronology of James's life and works, with bibliographies and extracts from his writings

James–Lange theory of emotion The theory first published by *James in *Mind* in 1884 and by the Dutch psychologist C. G. Lange (1834–1900) in 1885 that, rather than causing bodily and visceral responses, an *emotion is itself a perception of these specific reactions.

Jansenism Christian sect owing allegiance to the doctrines of the Dutch theologian Cornelius Otto Jansen (1585–1638). The principal tenet is that without the operation of divine grace, obedience to God's commands is impossible. Grace itself is irresistible when offered, so the upshot is a theological determinism. The tragedian Racine was influenced by Jansenism, which was condemned as heretical by Pope Innocent X. It is important in the history of philosophy because of the *Port-Royal logic, and the influence of the Jansenist leader *Arnauld.

Jaspers, Karl (1883–1969) German existentialist theologian. Born in Oldenberg in Germany, Jaspers began his career as a medical student. From 1921 to 1937 he was professor of philosophy at Heidelberg, but was removed by the Nazis, and although reinstated in 1945 he eventually settled in Basel. Jaspers was centrally a psychologist and theologian, concentrating upon the psychological nature of encounters with God, and deriving from *Kierkegaard and *Nietzsche a sense of philosophy not as a rational investigation of the world, but as a private, lived-out struggle.

Although sharing the *existentialist preoccupation with moments of death, guilt, and *angst, Jaspers was somewhat more optimistic about the possibilities for human existence than some of his contemporaries. His numerous works include the three-volume *Philosophie* (1932, trs. as *Philosophy*, 1967–71).

Jefferson, Thomas (1743–1826) The statesman and third President of the United States was also the principal author of the Declaration of Independence. A polymath and widely-read man, his ideal of tolerant and representative government by an educated citizenry was profoundly influenced by *Enlightenment ideas, and especially the *Second Treatise of Government* of John *Locke. This example of the direct and benign influence of a philosopher on a major political figure in a Western democracy has seldom been paralleled since the 18th century, and is utterly remote from the 21st.

jen Etymologically, a Chinese term referring to man in society. In *Confucian thought, *jen* is the principle of common humanity, or the moral qualities such as benevolence that make for humanity.

Jevons, William Stanley (1835–82) British political economist and logician. Jevons was educated at London, and taught at Manchester and London. He wrote various works on logic, and in 1870 exhibited a 'logical piano' or primitive mechanical computer at the Royal Society. He was not an original logician of note, but his work in the philosophy of science, and in particular upon the nature of the *hypothetico-deductive method, still bears revisiting.

Joachim of Fiore (Joachim of Floris) (*c*.1135–1202) Benedictine monk, and commentator on the Book of Revelations. He held a tripartite view of history, and was the inspiration of heretics (the Joachimites) who believed that the year 1260 would usher in the era of the Holy Spirit, replacing the era of Christ. This doctrine was condemned by the Lateran Council of 1215.

John of Salisbury (1115/20–1180) English churchman and diplomat. A student of *Abelard, John was one of the most learned of early medieval writers on moral and political matters. He was secretary to Theobald, archbishop of Canterbury, and to St Thomas à Becket, of whom he wrote a biography. From 1176 to 1180, he was bishop of Chartres. His two main works are the *Polycraticus*, a treatise on the principles of government, and the *Metalogicus*, a defence of logic showing considerable acquaintance with *Aristotle.

Johnson, Alexander Bryan (1786–1867) American philosopher of language. Born in England, Johnson emigrated to America in 1801 and had a successful career as a banker. His philosophical interests centred upon language, whose misunderstanding he regarded as responsible for endless confusion and error. In a manner reminiscent of *Berkeley he distinguished the 'sensible' meaning of terms, tied closely to the experiences to which they refer, from merely 'verbal' meaning. The sensible meaning of a sentence is given by what would now be thought of as the verification conditions or assertibility conditions of a sentence. Johnson's conviction that we erroneously attribute extra significance to sentences is a forerunner of the *logical positivists' polemic on the same point. Johnson's principal work was the *Treatise on Language* (1836). His remark that 'we can no more exemplify with words that there is a limit to their applicability, than a painter can demonstrate with colours, that there are phenomena that colours cannot delineate', is a striking anticipation of *Wittgenstein's more famous distinction between what can be shown and what can be said.

Johnson, Samuel (1696–1772) American philosopher. A symptomatic figure rather than an independently important philosopher, Johnson was born in Connecticut and taught at Yale. He was instrumental in founding the university of Pennsylvania and Columbia university. His career shows a gradual evolution from narrow New England *Calvinism, under the impact of *Locke, *Newton, and above all *Berkeley, with whom Johnson became friendly during the latter's visit to Rhode Island. Johnson became an enthusiastic *immaterialist, and defender of free will, tempering the harsh doctrine of *predestination even to the point of joining the Church of England. *See also* PLENITUDE, PRINCIPLE OF.

Johnson, Samuel (1709–84) The famous English man of letters and author of the *Dictionary of the English Language* is to be distinguished from the American of the same name. It is the English Johnson whose response to *Berkeley was to kick a stone, saying 'I refute him *thus*', thereby revealing a complete misunderstanding of Berkeley's thought. Johnson's analytical capacities in philosophy ('we know our will is free, and there's an end on't') did not match the intensity of his moral and religious wrestlings, while his conviction that the infidel *Hume could not have died in tranquillity is an unattractive instance of someone projecting his own fear of extinction onto others. However, his definition of a lexicographer as a harmless drudge is a consolation to his many followers.

Johnson, William Ernest (1858–1931) Cambridge logician. Born and educated in Cambridge, Johnson's main livelihood was teaching mathematics, until he was made a Fellow of King's College, Cambridge, in 1902. He had considerable personal and intellectual influence on the younger Cambridge generation that included *Broad, *Keynes, and the empiricist and philosopher of probability R. B. Braithwaite. His own major work, *Logic*, was collected in three volumes in the last decade of his life, but has not achieved a large subsequent impact.

judgement At different times philosophers have expressed their concern with the nature of judgement in different terms: the investigation may be called the theory of content, of belief, of propositions, of representation, of sense, etc. depending on which aspect of the matter is taken to predominate. The central problem is that of understanding the capacity of the mind to form, entertain, and affirm judgements, which are not simply strings of words but items intrinsically representing some state of affairs, or way that the world is or may be. The affirmation of a judgement is thus the making of a true or false claim. This capacity has been approached by thinking of the mind as stocked with *ideas, or as capable of apprehending *universals, or as stocked with inner *representations, or by seeing the capacity as essentially linguistic in nature, or as arising from problem-solving behaviour that we share with animals (*see* ANIMAL THOUGHT), but no extensive consensus on the matter exists.

judicial review The system, especially entrenched in the United States, whereby a supreme court or other legal body is empowered to review and possibly to strike down legislation enacted by a democratically elected body, on the grounds that it transgresses against fundamental principles enshrined in a constitution. It is seen by many, especially lawyers, as a bulwark against *majority tyranny, and by politicians who cannot find a way to co-opt it as a legalistic obstacle to democratic process.

Jung, Carl Gustav (1875–1961) Swiss psychoanalyst. Born at Kesswil in Switzerland, Jung took his degree in medicine at Basel and subsequently studied with the Swiss psychiatrist Eugen Bleuler (1857–1939). He met *Freud in 1907, and collaborated with him until 1912. Jung's subsequent work centred upon the process of 'individuation' whereby a person undergoes a developmental journey littered with myth, archetypes, and symbols pointing towards the final destiny, which may be a religious wholeness and integration (*see* COLLECTIVE UNCONSCIOUS). Jung is not a systematic philosophical thinker, but his religious and spiritual vision in general, and his interest in oriental religion in particular, have had their own influence.

jurisprudence *See* LAW, PHILOSOPHY OF.

justice, commutative Term derived from *Aristotle via *Aquinas for the restoration of justice by means of exchange or payment. *See also* JUSTICE, DISTRIBUTIVE.

justice, distributive The problem is to lay down principles specifying the just distribution of benefits and burdens: the outcome in which all receive their due. A common basis is that persons should be treated equally unless reasons for inequality exist; after that the problems include the kind of reasons that justify departing from equality, the role of the state in rectifying inequality, and the link between a distributive system and the maximization of well-being. *See also* DIFFERENCE PRINCIPLE.

justice, retributive (justice, rectificatory) The idea of seeking to balance an injustice by rectifying the situation, or by regaining an equality that the injustice overturned. It is most simply summed up in the principle of revenge 'an eye for an eye, and a tooth for a tooth'. Rectification suggests taking from the offender and giving to the injured party (*see* JUSTICE, COMMUTATIVE), whereas retribution acknowledges that this is sometimes impossible (e.g. if the victim is dead), but embodies the idea that an offence may 'cry out' for punishment, and that the moral order is out of balance until this is administered. Such an idea is clearly difficult to reconcile with forward-looking, *consequentialist moralities, since it makes no reference to the goods achieved by the retribution, but simply sees it as an end in itself. *See also* ERINYES, PUNISHMENT.

justice as fairness *See* DIFFERENCE PRINCIPLE, ORIGINAL POSITION.

justification A central concept both in ethics and epistemology. An action or a belief is justified if it stands up to some kind of critical reflection or scrutiny; a person is then exempt from criticism on account of it. The philosophical question is one of the standards that have to be met and the source of their authority. A surprisingly popular line of thought in epistemology is that 'only a belief can justify another belief' (*Davidson). The implication that neither experience nor the world plays a role in justifying beliefs leads quickly to *coherentism.

j

justification by faith Doctrine derived from Romans 5:1 and especially dear to Protestant Christianity, that the supreme virtue is faith. According to *Luther, 'if this article concerning Christ—the doctrine that we are justified and saved through Him alone and consider all apart from Him damned—is not professed, all resistance and restraint are at an end. Then there is, in fact, neither measure nor limit to any heresy and error.' *See also* ANTINOMIANISM.

Justinian (AD 482–565) Roman emperor from 527 until his death. Justinian's philosophical problems centred on the *monophysite heresy, although his wife, the ex-actress Theodora, was a monophysite and Justinian eventually became one. He is remembered more for the great codification of Roman law, the million-word *Codex Justinianus*, first promulgated in 529.

just so story An explanation of an admittedly speculative nature, tailored to give the results that need explaining, but currently lacking any independent rationale. The term is applied, more or less aggressively, especially to explanations offered in *sociobiology and *evolutionary psychology. It derives from the explanations of how the leopard got its spots, etc., in the *Just So Stories* (1902) of Rudyard Kipling.

just war The doctrine that a state may justly go to war for some restricted reasons, which are centrally those of self-defence, and the rescue of another state from an aggressor. Problems include deciding whether self-defence may be broadened from defence against actual attack to defence against threats, or against perceived threats, and whether it is permissible to make pre-emptive strikes. In addition to theorizing about when it is just to go to war (*jus ad bellum*), just war theory embraces principles about the way war may be conducted (*jus in bello*), generally ruling out gratuitous violence, assassinations, war against civilians, and so on, although grave difficulties confront any distinction between those parts of a population engaging in modern war, and those innocents whose work is irrelevant to it.

SEE WEB LINKS

- Video lectures on just war theory
- A survey of related philosophical, religious, and legal debates

kabbala (kabbalah) (Hebrew, *kabbala*, tradition, that which is handed down) Originally, in the Talmud, the books of the Bible other than the Pentateuch. Gradually after around 1200 the term became applied to the oral tradition supposedly handed down from Moses to the Rabbis of the Mishnah and the Talmud; it accumulated aspects of cosmology, angelology, magic, and *gnosticism, becoming a mystical and *esoteric tradition of interpretation of the books of the Old Testament. A specialist in this study is called a kabbalist. Like astrology, it is a magnet for the weak-minded.

kalam (Arabic, speech) In Islamic philosophy, the processes of systematic theology, or more widely the general tradition of commentary and interpretation of Islamic doctrine, which may include adducing philosophy to support elements of religious doctrine. Sometimes (as with the opposition between *al-Ghazali and *Avicenna) the relationship to philosophical reason could be fairly hostile. *Kalam* played a role in Islam roughly parallel to that which scholastic philosophy played in the development of Christian theology, from around the time of *al-Kindi onwards. The practitioners of *kalam* were known as the *Mutakallimun*. Early *Mutakallimun* included the *Mutazilites* ('those who withdraw themselves') of the 8th century.

Kant, Immanuel (1724–1804) German philosopher and founder of critical philosophy. The son of a saddler, Kant was born and educated in Königsberg (Kaliningrad) in East Prussia. After leaving the university he spent a number of years in private tutoring, but taking his master's degree in 1755, he settled to teach a variety of subjects as *Privatdozent*. Kant's early writings concern physics and astronomy: his *Allgemeine Naturgeschichte und Theorie des Himmels* (1755, trs. as *Universal Natural History and Theory of the Heavens*, 1969) predicted the existence of the planet Uranus, later discovered by Herschel in 1881. In 1770 he was appointed to the chair of logic and metaphysics at Königsberg. It was after this that he entered on his greatest, 'critical' period. His life was orderly to the point of caricature: he never left Königsberg, and never married.

The intellectual landscape in which Kant began his career was largely set by *Leibniz, filtered through *Wolff, who had erected a structured and orderly system out of Leibniz's thought. Wolff believed that the principle of *sufficient reason, and much resulting metaphysics, could be known *a priori*, although the status of this knowledge was already doubted by such men as *Crusius. However, it was generally felt that 'intuition' afforded us knowledge and was guaranteed by God, so all was well. In his pre-critical *Dreams of a Spirit-Seer* (*Träume eines Geistersehers*, 1766), the most hostile to metaphysics of all his works, Kant treats the speculations of Crusius and Wolff as spun out of nothing, like the spiritual imaginings of *Swedenborg. The first step to the critical philosophy was the *Inaugural Dissertation* of 1770 (Latin title: *De Mundi Sensibilis atque Intelligibilis Forma et Principiis*), in which for the first time Kant unveils the view that we can have *a priori* knowledge of space and time only because they are forms imposed by our own minds upon experience (*see* COPERNICAN REVOLUTION). Space is a 'schema, issuing by a constant law from the nature of the mind, for the coordinating of all outer sensa whatever'. The *Dissertation* heralds themes that were worked out for the next ten years: the subjective origin of the schema of space and time, the distinction that it creates between things as they are in themselves and things as they are to us, and the distinction between experience and thought.

The Critique of Pure Reason (*Kritik der reinen Vernunft*, 1781, known as the first *Critique*) extends these themes to cover all the *categories used in thought. Its aim is to 'assure to reason its lawful claims, and dismiss all groundless pretensions, not by despotic decrees, but in accordance with its own eternal and unalterable laws' (Preface to the 1st edition). In answer to its guiding question (how is synthetic **a priori* knowledge possible?), the first part of the work isolates legitimate categories and provides them with a 'transcendental deduction', guaranteeing their objective applicability by showing that without them experience is itself impossible. One of Kant's central moves is to argue that the unity of consciousness itself presupposes orderly experience, tied together in accordance with universal and necessary laws. It is this part of his work that constitutes his attempt to answer the inductive scepticism, and subjectivity about causation, left by *Hume. (Kant's famous remark that it was Hume who awoke him from his dogmatic slumbers was made in the *Prologomena to any Future Metaphysics* in 1783, but in fact the influence of Hume on the first *Critique* is quite slight.) Having established the proper authority and provenance of reason, Kant turns, in the section of the first *Critique* called the Dialectic, to cases where the pretensions of reason get out of hand, producing the dogmatic metaphysics that purports to establish doctrines about the nature of the self, the constitution of an independent order of space and time, and the knowability of God.

The first *Critique* is a preparation for the concern with practical reason that now occupied his attention. Having laid the foundations of a critical philosophy he produced the *Fundamental Principles of the Metaphysic of Morals* (*Grundlegung zur Metaphysik der Sitten*, 1785) and the *Critique of Practical Reason* (*Kritik der praktischen Vernunft*, 1788, known as the second *Critique*). Kant said that 'two things move the mind with ever increasing admiration and awe, the oftener and more steadily we reflect on them: the starry heavens above and the moral law within' (conclusion of the second *Critique*; the identical formula is found in St John Chrysostom and derives from the 19th Psalm). His ethics is based uncompromisingly on the search for a single supreme principle of morality, a principle moreover that has rational authority, leading rather than following the passions, and binding on all rational creatures. Every action springs from some subjective principle, or maxim, and the moral worth of an individual lies entirely in the question of whether the maxim of his or her action is respect for the law, the duty of obeying the *categorical imperative. Kant's own applications of this test forbid lying, suicide, revolution against the extant political order, solitary sex, and selling one's hair for wig-making, but the extent to which his ethics can be disentangled from its Lutheran matrix is controversial. Kant's restriction of moral worth to a specific kind of concern with duty has frequently seemed to downgrade normal human virtues such as benevolence, but commentators try to discern a more humane Kant behind the stern and rigorous ethic of respect for law (*see* APATHY). Other contested components of his ethical system include the association of freedom with capacity for self-control and self-legislation, and the practical need to think in terms of a just God sustaining the moral order.

The third *Critique*, the *Critique of Judgement* (*Kritik der Urteilskraft*, 1790), confronts the difficulty of making aesthetic judgements objective, given that they are not made in accordance with a rule but in response to subjective pleasure. Kant connects our right to demand accord from others in such matters to a *teleology or goal-directed conception of nature, an idea common to the *Romanticism of the time and to which he lent his great authority (*see also* AESTHETICS). Kant's concern with the basis of metaphysics and knowledge had not vanished, for at this time he also produced the *Metaphysical Foundations of Natural Science* (*Metaphysische Anfangsgründe der Naturwissenschaft*, 1786). This work treats the nature of motion, matter, and mass, and espouses a kind of *field theory that was to become influential in 19th-century physics. Later works include *Religion within the Limits of Reason Alone* (*Die Religion innerhalb der Grenzen der bloßen Vernunft*, 1793), which got Kant into trouble with the repressive religious censorship of Frederick William II of Prussia; *Perpetual Peace* (*Zum ewigen Frieden*, 1795); and *Die Metaphysik der Sitten*, 1797 (trs. as *The Metaphysics of Morals*, but often in two different parts, *The Metaphysical Principles of Right* and *The Metaphysical Principles of Virtue*).

In spite of the notorious difficulty of reading Kant, made worse by his penchant for scholastic systematization and obscure terminology, his place as the greatest philosopher of the last three hundred years is well assured. He made the first decisive break with the sensationalist *empiricism that prevailed in the 18th century, but without retreating to an indefensible rationalism. Whilst his confidence in the *a priori* and the structure of his *idealism have been widely rejected, it is not too much to say that all of modern epistemology, metaphysics, and even ethics is implicitly affected by the architecture he created. The standard modern biography is by Manfred Kuehn.

SEE WEB LINKS

- An audio discussion of Kant by two philosophers and a historian
- A list of internet resources on Kantian ethics

karma (Sanskrit, deed) In Hindu and Buddhist philosophy, the universal law of cause and effect, as applied to the deeds of people. A (deliberate) good or bad deed leads a person's destiny in the appropriate direction. The ripening of the deed may take more than one lifetime, tying the agent to the cycle of rebirth, or **samsara*; only deeds free from desire and delusion have no consequences for *karma*.

katalepsis (Greek, seizing, taking possession) In *Stoic thought, basic truths were apprehended by *katalepsis*, in the sense of being intuited or 'given'. The doctrine was the focus of a great deal of *sceptical attack.

katharsis *See* CATHARSIS.

Kelsen, Hans (1881–1973) Austrian jurist and philosopher of law. Kelsen is known for the most rigorous development of a 'positivist' theory of law, i.e. one that rigorously excludes from its analysis any ethical, political, or historical considerations, and finds the essence of the legal order in the 'black letter' or laid-down law. A system of law is based on a *Grundnorm* or ground rule, from which flows the validity of other statements of law in the system. The ground rule might be that some particular dictates or propositions, such as those of the sovereign, are to be obeyed. The *Grundnorm* can only be changed by political revolution. The theory is best known in its development in the *Allgemeine Staatslehre* (1925, trs. and revised as *General Theory of Law and State*, 1945).

Kemp Smith, Norman (1872–1958) Scottish philosopher and translator. Kemp Smith was educated at St Andrews, where he was awarded a doctorate for his *Studies in Cartesian Philosophy* of 1902. He held a post at Princeton from 1906 to 1916, before becoming professor at Edinburgh in 1919. After his *Commentary to Kant's Critique of Pure Reason* (1918), he produced his definitive translation of the same work (1929). Although he also produced philosophy of his own, he is otherwise remembered especially for *The Philosophy of David Hume* (1941), a work which set the standard for all subsequent interpretations of Hume.

Kepler (Keppler), Johannes (1571–1630) The founder of modern astronomy, Kepler was born near Stuttgart. It was as an assistant to the Danish astronomer Tycho Brahe (1546–1601) that he began his astronomical career, and from Tycho he derived his respect for minute and accurate observation. He said that it was the slight discrepancy between the actual position of Mars and its predicted position (eight minutes of arc) that pointed the road to a complete reformation of astronomy. Kepler himself harboured many *Pythagorean, occult, and mystical beliefs, but his laws of planetary motion are the first mathematical, scientific, laws of astronomy of the modern era. They state (i) that the planets travel in elliptical orbits, with one focus of the ellipse being the sun; (ii) that the radius between sun and planet sweeps equal areas in equal times; and (iii) that the squares of the periods of revolution of any two planets are in the same ratio as the cube of their mean distances from the sun.

Keynes, John Maynard (1883–1946) English economist and philosopher. Although primarily known as an economist, Keynes produced one philosophical classic, the *Treatise on Probability* (1921). This develops the theory of probability and *confirmation theory on the basis of an objective, logical relation of degrees of implication amongst propositions. Although subsequent work has not been kind to such a notion, Keynes's working-out of its possibilities remains, together with the work of *Carnap, the main showpiece of confirmation theory. In particular, Keynes realized that in order for induction to increase the probability of generalizations as progressive evidence eliminates potential falsifications, a 'principle of *limited independent variety' must be assumed, giving the necessary structure for probability to increase.

Kierkegaard, Søren Aabye (1813–55) Danish philosopher and theologian, generally acknowledged to be the first *existentialist. Born to scholarly and pietistic parents, Kierkegaard enrolled at the university of Copenhagen, then much under the influence of *Hegel, in 1830. He rebelled against both the system-building of Hegel and the formalities of the surrounding Danish Lutheran church. After a period of mild hedonism he completed his religious studies, but, narrowly avoiding marriage, thereafter lived the life of a scholarly recluse. Kierkegaard utterly rejected the Hegelian system as an attempt to put man in the place of God, ignoring the partial, subjective, and limited standpoint from which all human judgement is made. Hence he is led to emphasize the primacy of the will and of free choice unconstrained by reason or cause: where human action and judgement are involved there is no objectivity, no external rails or authority. True to this creed his works are many-sided and apparently contradictory; some were published under pseudonyms, so that he himself could attack them in later work. His influence expanded in the 20th century, in particular amongst thinkers concerned with problems of religious and ethical choice, and especially amongst existentialists concerned with the same problems. His works include *Enten-eller* (1843, trs. as *Either/Or: A Fragment of Life*, 1944), *Afsluttende Uvidenskabelig Efterskrift* (1846, trs. as *Concluding Unscientific Postscript*, 1941), and *Sygdomen Til Døden* (1849, trs. as *The Sickness unto Death*, 1941).

SEE WEB LINKS

- A biography of Kierkegaard
- A commentary on Kierkegaard's writings, with a bibliography

killing For the distinction between killing and letting die, *see* ACTS/OMISSIONS DOCTRINE; *see also* ABORTION, DEATH, EUTHANASIA, JUST WAR.

Kilvington, Richard (1302/5–1361) Along with Walter Burley and Thomas *Bradwardine, one of the school known as the 'Oxford Calculators', whose principal efforts were devoted to the development of Aristotelian physics. He is remembered philosophically for his *Sophismata*, a collection of philosophical and logical problems.

kind, natural *See* NATURAL KIND.

al-Kindi, Abu Yusuf (d. after AD 866) The earliest important Islamic philosopher, al-Kindi began the process of assimilating *Neoplatonic and Aristotelian thought into the Islamic world. He taught in Baghdad, and was responsible for translations of Aristotle and Plotinus. His own philosophy tended to allow the ascendancy of faith over reason, and he is generally thought to have been eclipsed by later thinkers such as al-*Farabi and *Avicenna.

kinesis Aristotelian term for motion or change, thought of as contrasted with **energeia*.

KK-thesis Term sometimes used for the thesis that if one knows something, one knows that one knows it.

knowledge *See* EPISTEMOLOGY.

knowledge, causal theory of The view that in order to know a proposition it is necessary to be in some kind of causal connection to the fact it relates. The idea works better for some things, such as those we remember, than for others, such as truths of mathematics or universal generalizations.

knowledge by acquaintance and description *See* ACQUAINTANCE AND DESCRIPTION.

knowledge *de re/de dicto* *See* DE RE/DE DICTO.

koan (Japanese, literally an official document or public notice; a final arbiter of truth or falsehood) *Koan* are stories, often in the form of questions and answers, set as problems for meditation in the practice of *Zen Buddhism, although the problems are not for solving by linear or rational processes. The most famous is the problem of the noise made by one hand clapping. The *mu-koan* is the reply *mu* (meaning nothing) given by the master Joshu in answer to the question whether a dog has the nature of Buddha. Another is the interchange: 'What is Buddha?' 'Three pounds of flax.'

Köhler, Wolfgang (1887–1967) One of the founders of the *Gestalt school of psychology, Köhler also wrote *The Place of Value in a World of Facts* (1938), the result of his William James lectures delivered at Harvard in 1934. Köhler attempted to work out a theory of value, including aesthetic value, on the basis of the phenomenally objective Gestalt-quality which he called 'requiredness'. One part of a visual field, for example, may demand completion in some specific way, rather as a melody may require resolution.

König's paradox Also known as the Zermelo-König paradox. There are non-denumerably many real numbers, but only denumerably many of them are finitely definable. Given Zermelo's proof that the reals can be well-ordered, the set of reals that are not finitely definable must have a first member. But this is itself a finite definition of that real. The paradox is similar to those of *Richard and *Berry, although König himself thought it turned into a proof that the reals cannot be well-ordered.

Kotarbinski, Tadeusz (1886–1981) Polish philosopher and logician. A pupil of *Twardowski, Kotarbinski removed to Warsaw where he became professor and helped found the Centre of Logical Research. In the philosophy of language Kotarbinski was a firm *nominalist and *realist, mistrusting all abstraction, and firmly committed to a scientific philosophy. He had wide ethical and humanistic interests, and influence. Works included *Elements of the Theory of Knowledge, Formal Logic, and Methodology of Science* (1929) and *Meditations on Worthy Life* (1966).

Krause, Karl Christian Friedrich (1781–1832) German post-Kantian philosopher, educated at Jena and much influenced by *Fichte and *Schelling. He developed Kant's views in the direction of pantheism and mysticism, giving a result he christened 'panentheism', promising historical progress to a fusion of world and spirit which in some ways anticipated *Hegel.

Kripke, Saul Aaron (1940–) American logician and philosopher. Born in New York and educated at Harvard and Oxford, Kripke made his early reputation as a logical prodigy, especially through work on the completeness of systems of modal logic. The three classic papers are 'A Completeness Theorem in Modal Logic' (1959, *Journal of Symbolic Logic*), 'Semantical Analysis of Modal Logic' (1963, *Zeitschrift für Mathematische Logik und Grundlagen der Mathematik*), and 'Semantical Considerations on Modal Logic' (1963, *Acta Philosophica Fennica*). In *Naming and Necessity* (1980), Kripke gave the classic modern treatment of the topic of reference, both clarifying the distinction between names and *definite descriptions, and opening the door to many subsequent attempts to understand the notion of reference in terms of a causal link between the use of a term and an original episode of attaching a name to a subject. His *Wittgenstein on Rules and Private Language* (1983) also proved seminal, putting the *rule-following considerations at the centre of *Wittgenstein studies, and arguing that the *private language argument is an application of them. Kripke has also written influential work on the theory of truth and the solution of the *semantic paradoxes.

Kripke semantics The standard semantic treatment for modal languages with symbols for necessity and possibility, due to Saul *Kripke. The model is a set of possible worlds and a relation on them, corresponding to the idea of one world being 'accessible' from another. A valuation function then evaluates sentences as true or false at worlds. Using these models, Kripke was able to bring new treatments to issues such as the decidability, independence, and completeness of different systems of modal logic, where different conditions on the accessibility relation correspond to different strengths of system.

Kristeva, Julia (1941–) French *feminist. Born in Bulgaria, Kristeva came to Paris in 1965 and became a leading member of the *Tel Quel* group of activist left-wing theorists. Since 1974 she has worked as professor of linguistics at the university of Paris, and as a practising psychoanalyst. Together with *Irigaray and *Cixous, Kristeva has been the most influential of French feminists whose thought has been shaped by psychoanalysis as well as Marxism, philosophy, and literature. Just as her Bulgarian background inhibited her from embracing Maoism with the enthusiasm of many Parisian intellectuals of the late 1960s, so her experience of psychoanalysis keeps her at some distance from more extreme *postmodernist pronouncements on the death of the subject, and the nonexistence of meaning, love, and other human categories. Her work has centred upon the balance between a 'semiotic', a pre-Oedipal, rhythmic, and sensual order, and the conventional or 'symbolic' system of propositions and representations. Unlike Cixous and Irigaray she does not appeal to biological *determinism (a view of what is inherently or essentially female) in her view of femininity and female writing. When they work as marginal and avant-garde artists, men such as the poet Mallarmé also can channel the irruption of the semiotic into the symbolic order. Her works include *La Révolution de langage poétique* (1974, trs. as *Revolution in Poetic Language*, 1984), and *Histoires d'amour* (1983, trs. as *Love Stories*, 1987).

Kristina Wasa (Queen Kristina of Sweden) (1626–89) The daughter of Gustav II, Kristina inherited the crown of Sweden in 1632. In 1652 she suffered a breakdown, and in 1654 abdicated, the first step in a process that led her to Catholicism, and in later years she lived largely in Rome, although occasionally trying her hand at becoming monarch elsewhere. Her maxims are collected as *Les Sentiments héroïques* and *L'Ouvrage de loisir: les sentiments raisonnables*, addressing mainly ethical issues. But her academic interests were wide and absorbed her time even while she remained a sovereign. She is remembered in philosophy partly as the correspondent of both *Descartes and *Grotius. Each travelled to visit her in Sweden (Grotius in 1644 and Descartes in 1650), and both died of pneumonia as a result. Kristina's life after her abdication caused some scandal. In 1656, still believing in the divine right of monarchs (and ex-monarchs), she had a servant executed.

Kropotkin, Peter (1842–1921) Russian nobleman, and main proponent of anarcho-communism. Kropotkin believed that *Darwin's theory of evolution, properly applied, showed that human beings are social creatures who flourish best in small communities cemented together by mutual aid and voluntary associations (*see* ALTRUISM). The centralized state with its apparatus of coercion represents a backward step, or obstacle to the implementation of this ideal. Kropotkin's works include *Mutual Aid* (1897) and *Fields, Factories, and Workshops* (1901). He lived largely in England, but died in Russia.

Kuhn, Thomas Samuel (1922–96) American philosopher of science. Born in Ohio, Kuhn was educated at Harvard as a physicist before his book *The Structure of Scientific Revolutions* (1962) became one of the most influential modern works of the history and philosophy of science. Like Alexandre Koyré (1892–1964) and the French writers *Bachelard and Jean Cavaillès (1903–44), Kuhn stresses that the history of science is not a smooth progressive accumulation of data and successful theory, but the outcome of ruptures, false starts, and imaginative constraints that themselves reflect many different variables. In his account, science during a normal period works within a framework of assumptions called a *paradigm, but in exceptional and revolutionary periods an old paradigm breaks down and after a period of competition is replaced by a new one. The process is something like a *Gestalt switch, and has seemed to many to have disquieting implications for the rationality and objectivity of science. Kuhn's other books include *The Copernican Revolution* (1957) and *Sources for the History of Quantum Physics* (1967).

Kundalini In Hindu thought, the coiled and dormant 'feminine' energy, or psychic energy contained within us all. It is normally symbolized as a serpent coiled into three-and-a-half circles, with its tail in its mouth, and spiralling around the base of the spine. The awakening of this serpent and the manifestation of its powers is a primary aim of the practice of Kundalini Yoga.

Kyoto school A loose group of 20th-century Japanese philosophers united in bringing key Buddhist concepts together with Western ones. Key figures include *Nishida Kitaro and *Nishitani Keiji.

labour theory of value In economics, the view that the value of a commodity reflects the amount of labour involved in its production. Although espoused as an approximation by *Pufendorf, *Hutcheson, Adam *Smith, and David Ricardo (1772–1823), it is now mainly held by *Marxist economists, since it denies any real productive role to capital.

Labriola, Antonio (1843–1904) Italian Marxist philosopher, and teacher of moral and political philosophy and philosophy of history in Rome. Labriola corresponded extensively with *Engels, and after his death became a staunch upholder of orthodoxy and opponent of revisionist movements in Marxist thought. His letters and essays are an important source for Marxist thought, while his influence extended through pupils such as *Croce and *Sorel.

La Bruyère, Jean de (1645–96) One of the French **moralistes*. His philosophical reputation depends upon his work *Les Caractères* (1688), a long series of illustrations of different varieties of human follies, corruptions, and abuses. He was a particular favourite of David *Hume.

Lacan, Jacques (1901–81) French psychoanalyst and intellectual. Lacan was director of the École Freudienne de Paris from 1963, but his influence rested more on the series of seminars that he gave at the university of Paris from 1953, and which decisively influenced French thought of the time. His endeavour was to reinterpret Freud in the light of the structural approach to linguistics inaugurated by *Saussure. Language becomes a manifestation of the structures present in the unconscious. The central theme is that the growing child must give up the narcissistic stage of absorption in the mother, and becomes aware of loss and difference as it begins to take its place in a network of linguistic and social roles. The repressions involved in this procedure open up a world of insatiable desires. Lacan's work is notoriously obscure, repeating the same shifting nature of dreams and, presumably, the unconscious; like that of *Derrida after him it is also replete with wordplays, puns, and reason-defying leaps. His lectures, in transcript, are collected in the two-volume *Écrits* (1966, 1971, trs. under the same title, 1977).

La Forge, Louis de (1632–66) Prominent follower of *Descartes. His work *Traité de l'esprit de l'homme* (1665) is a development of Descartes's views about mind and body, but he is credited with moving Cartesian thought towards the *occasionalism that surfaces fully in *Malebranche.

laissez-faire (French, leave to do) In economic and social thought, the doctrine of non-interventionism by government in the workings of markets. The doctrine is wrongly attributed to Adam *Smith, who in fact advocated qualified intervention for social action in areas of market failure, for example in order to ensure education of the poor.

Lakatos, Imre (1922–74) Hungarian philosopher of mathematics. Lakatos fled Hungary after the Soviet invasion in 1956, studied at Cambridge, and submitted his doctoral thesis in 1961. In 1960 Lakatos was appointed to the London School of Economics and he taught there for 14 years until his death. He published his most brilliant and influential work, *Proofs and Refutations*, in 1963–4 in four parts in the *British Journal for Philosophy of Science*, but it only appeared as a book posthumously. He rejected the idea of mathematics as a patient accumulation of ever more complex truth, in favour of a dramatic model of proofs and refutations, akin to Karl *Popper's account of the processes of science.

Lamarckism The doctrine that offspring may inherit the acquired characteristics of their parents (that is, the features they acquired during their lives, rather than those with which they were genetically endowed). In fact the view of the French botanist and zoologist Jean-Baptiste de Lamarck (1744–1829) was slightly different. He held that it was a desire for change, or a *besoin*, that caused change in the organism itself, and thence in its offspring. The view is discredited, with evolutionary theory firmly wedded to the mechanism of random genetic variation followed by natural selection.

lambda notation A term such as 'Sine 60°' or 'the father of Hegel' refers to a number or a person. But it includes the term 'Sine ... ' or 'father of ... '. 'Sine *x*' or 'father of *y*' stand for a *function referring respectively to a number or a person for particular values of *x* and *y*. If we wish to refer to the function itself, the notation (λx)(Sine *x*) or (λy) (father of *y*) is adopted. A *logical calculus with rules involving such terms is called the lambda calculus.

Lambert, Johann Heinrich (1728–77) German mathematician and cosmologist. Largely self-taught, Lambert became one of the most distinguished German scientists and mathematicians of the 18th century. Philosophically he attempted to ally rationalism in metaphysics with the mathematical treatment of reasoning and logic, continuing the tradition of *Leibniz. He was much admired by *Kant.

La Mettrie, Julien Offroy de (1709–51) French materialist. La Mettrie's first career was as a doctor, and he served from 1743 to 1745 as surgeon in the army during the War of the Austrian Succession. In 1745 he published *Histoire naturelle de l'âme* ('The Natural History of the Soul'), whose materialistic tendencies caused enough uproar for La Mettrie to retreat to Holland. Unabashed however, in 1748 he produced his most influential work, *L'Homme machine* (trs. as *Man a Machine*, 1749), whose atheism and materialism outraged even the Dutch. Frederick the Great of Prussia invited La Mettrie to Berlin, where he continued to offend pious and *dualistic orthodoxy with *L'Homme plante* (1748), *Le Système d'Epicure* (1750), and *Discours sur le bonheur* (1750). Although his opinions were scandalous, when La Mettrie died prematurely (according to his enemies, because of hedonistic over-indulgence), Frederick composed his eulogy. La Mettrie's materialism is firmly based on the physics, chemistry, anatomy, and physiology of his time. But his forceful advocacy of the dependence of mental function on the state of the central nervous system and brain, and his resolutely scientific approach to the dynamics of motion and motivation, make him the earliest committed example of what is now the dominant *functionalist and *physicalist biomedical approach to the nature of human beings. In ethics La Mettrie saw happiness as the natural aim of each organism (akin to health), and a century before *Nietzsche drew the corollary that the bad conscience, as a prime enemy of happiness, is merely a disease that needs a cure.

La Mothe le Vayer, François de (1588–1672) French sceptic and tutor of Louis XIV. His principal work is *Dialogues faits à l'imitation des anciens* (1630–31) published under the pseudonym Orasius Tubero; they show the influence of Montaigne, advocating a civilized scepticism.

Lamy, Bernard (1640–1715) French teacher and priest. His treatise on rhetoric and the philosophy of language, *Rhétorique ou l'art de parler* (1675, enlarged 1688), became known as the 'Rhétorique de Port-Royal', a counterpoint to the Port-Royal Logic of Arnauld. His work *Entretiens sur les sciences* (1683) influenced Rousseau.

Lange, Friedrich Albert (1828–75) German reformer, sociologist, and *Neo-Kantian philosopher. His most important work was the wide-ranging *Geschichte des Materialismus und Kritik seiner Bedeutung in der Gegenwart* (1866, trs. as *A History of Materialism*, 1877).

language, philosophy of The general attempt to understand the components of a working language, the relationship the understanding speaker has to its elements, and the relationship they bear to the world. The subject therefore embraces the traditional division of *semiotics into *syntax, *semantics, and *pragmatics. The philosophy of language thus mingles with the philosophy of mind, since it needs an account of what it is in our understanding that enables us to use language. It also mingles with the metaphysics of truth and the relationship between sign and object. Much philosophy, especially in the 20th century, has been informed by the belief that philosophy of language is the fundamental basis of all philosophical problems, in that language is the distinctive exercise of mind, and the distinctive way in which we give shape to metaphysical beliefs. Particular topics include the problems of *logical form, and the basis of the division between syntax and semantics, as well as problems of understanding the number and nature of specifically semantic relationships such as *meaning, *reference, *predication, and *quantification. Pragmatics includes the theory of *speech acts, while problems of *rule-following and the *indeterminacy of translation infect philosophies of both pragmatics and semantics. *See also* FORMAL LANGUAGE.

language game The pattern of activities and practices associated with some particular family of linguistic expressions. The notion is associated with the later philosophy of *Wittgenstein, encouraging us to think of the use of language in terms of a rule-governed, self-contained practice, like a game. Such a comparison enables us to avoid simplistic theories of what we accomplish with language. The notion has uneasy associations with a certain kind of *relativism, the link being that games are worth playing for themselves alone, and have no point outside themselves and the satisfactions they give to participants. The worrying implication would seem to be that if, for instance, the religious language game is found to be worthwhile, then that would seem to settle the question of the value, and even the truth, of the remarks made using it. *See also* PRAGMATISM.

language of thought hypothesis The hypothesis, especially associated with *Fodor, that mental processing occurs in a language different from one's ordinary native language, but underlying and explaining our competence with it. The idea is a development of the *Chomskyan notion of an innate universal grammar. It is a way of drawing the analogy between the workings of the brain or mind and those of a standard computer, since computer programs are linguistically complex sets of instructions whose execution explains the surface behaviour of the computer. As an explanation of ordinary language learning and competence the hypothesis has not found universal favour. It apparently only explains ordinary representational powers by invoking innate things of the same sort, and it invites the image of the learning infant translating the language surrounding it back into an innate language whose own powers are a mysterious biological given. *See also* THEORY-THEORY.

langue/parole Distinction due to *Saussure between language as used, *parole*, and language as a system, *langue*. *See* COMPETENCE/PERFORMANCE.

Lao Tzu (*c.*6th c. BC) The legendary founder of *Taoism, whose teachings are encapsulated in *The Treatise on the Way and its Power* (the *Tao Te Ching*). Whereas *Confucianism represents the social development of human potential, Lao Tzu represents unity with the universe, achieved by the simple, uncomplicated life with minimal desires and maximum absorption in nature. The identity and life of Lao Tzu himself are shadowy, and there has been controversy over whether the 6th-century date is correct, or whether he may have lived two to three centuries later, or even whether 'Lao Tzu' is a composite of legendary early sages. He is thought to have been a native of Ch'u in the province of Hunan.

Laplace, Pierre Simon de (1749–1827) The French mathematician is remembered in philosophy partly for his contributions to probability theory, and also for his strict *determinism. He himself proved the mechanical stability of the solar system within Newtonian mechanics, thereby removing the need for any regulation by divine intervention. It is this that occasioned his celebrated remark to Napoleon about God: 'Je n'ai pas besoin de cette hypothèse' ('I have no need of that hypothesis'). His determinism is frequently presented in the figure of a superhuman intelligence, to whom the entire state of nature at a time is known, and who can therefore compute the way it will evolve through subsequent times. Laplace, however, accepted that human beings would have to make do with probabilities. His *Essai philosophique sur les probabilités* (1814, trs. as *A Philosophical Essay on Probabilities*, 1951) is famous not only for its mathematical originality, but for the confidence with which Laplace applies *inverse methods to give probabilities for such things as the rising of the sun or the correctness of a verdict by a jury of a given size. His reliance on both the *rule of succession and on the principle of *indifference have been subsequently criticized.

large numbers, law of *See* BERNOULLI'S THEOREM.

La Rochefoucauld, François, duc de (1613–80) One of the French **moralistes*, author of *Réflexions ou Sentences et maximes morales* (1665, with a more definitive edition of 1678). The *Maximes* are pithy, often epigrammatic, reflections on human nature, typically written from a disillusioned or cynical point of view. One of La Rochefoucauld's favourite categories is that of 'amour propre', whose workings can be detected across large tracts of human life.

Lassalle, Ferdinand (1825–64) German social theorist and one of the principal founders of German social democracy. A flamboyant Hegelian, Lassalle (born Lasal; he Frenchified his name since France was the home of revolution) lived a colourful and hectic life that was ended by a duel. He agitated for the cause of the workers and the ending of capitalism. His works include *Die Philosophie Herakleitos des Dunklen von Ephesos* (1858) and the *System der erworbenen Rechte* (1861).

lateral thinking Popular term for a creative, imaginative approach to problem-solving that changes one's perceptions and conception of a problem, allegedly contrasted with 'linear' or 'logical' thinking. The contrast is misleading, in that *logic does not tell you how to think, but only how to avoid inconsistency. *See also* LAWS OF THOUGHT.

Latitudinarianism The progressive and tolerant approach to religion associated with a group of late 17th-century Church of England notables, including John Tillotson, Archbishop of Canterbury; Edward Stillingfleet, Bishop of Worcester; Simon Patrick, Bishop of Chichester and Ely; Gilbert Burnet, the Reformation historian and Bishop of Salisbury; and Thomas Tenison, Archbishop of Canterbury.

laughter We laugh at things that are laughable, but also laugh exultantly at a success, or bitterly at a failure, or at the unexpected or even the typical. We may even laugh but not at anything—with pure joy, or nervousness, or embarrassment, or merely because we have been physically *tickled. The variety of causes or objects of laughter, and the absence of any obvious explanation of its function, have not deterred theorists. *Hobbes thought that the passion of laughter is a 'sudden glory arising from some sudden conception of some eminency in ourselves' (*Human Nature*, ix. 12). *Hutcheson wrote against the egoism of this account ('Reflections on Laughter', *Dublin Journal*, 1725), locating humour instead in a perception of incongruity, although he offered no real evidence that incongruity is either a necessary or a sufficient condition of something appearing comical. *Bain (*The Emotions and the Will*, 1859) identifies the ludicrous with 'the degradation of some person or interest possessing dignity, in circumstances that excite no other strong emotion'. *Kant (*Critique of Judgement*, 1790) emphasizes the element of the unexpected, identifying laughter as 'an affection arising from a strained expectation being suddenly reduced to nothing'. His view is expanded by *Schopenhauer, who again finds incongruity at the basis of laughter. But as the Hobbes–Bain approach reminds us, it is not only the insult to reason that is funny but often the insult to other people. In his book *Le Rire: essai sur la signification du comique* (1900), perhaps anticipating the comedians Jacques Tati or Charlie Chaplin, *Bergson locates comedy as a defence against automatic, disjointed qualities that trespass against the essential spontaneity of life.

The capacity to take something as an occasion for humour evidently has a social function: it connects with play and with the rehearsal and defusing of potential conflict, but also can give rise to the more aggressive exclusion of persons and groups from consideration, by refusal to take them seriously, or by mockery and ridicule.

law, philosophy of The philosophy of law concerns itself with questions about the nature of law and the concepts that structure the practice of law. Its topics include the definition of law, or, if strict definition proves unfruitful, descriptions or models of law that throw light on difficult and marginal cases, such as international law, primitive law, and immoral or unjust law. Concepts that require understanding include those of a legal right or duty, of legal action and the place of concepts such as intention and responsibility, the nature of legal reasoning and adjudication, and the overwhelming political importance of the rule of law.

Considered strictly in empirical terms, law may appear to be a system of coercion: the salient fact about being under a legal duty to do X is that failure to comply will bring in its wake various penalties. Law seen this way is regarded as a sequence of predictions about what judges will do and what events will ensue upon performance of various kinds of action. In the writing of so-called legal realists, a term such as 'right' becomes one with which we describe to each other the prophecies we make of the behaviour of various officials. A difficulty with realism of this kind is that it offers no satisfactory account of the reasoning processes of those very officials, as they conceive themselves to be guided by a structure of rights and duties (similarly, if saying that a ball is out of court is a prediction of what the tennis umpire will do, the umpire cannot in turn cite the fact of the ball being out of court as the justification of his decision).

In normative terms, law is a system of rules that justifies demands for conformity, and the idea of legal duty is one of being bound by a rule, whether or not it is likely that suffering will follow upon failure to comply. Legal action, such as saying in the right circumstances words like 'I do' or 'I hereby ... ', creates a different kind of normative relationship between persons, such as marriage or contractual agreement, and the existence of such relationships is not, from the normative standpoint, the same thing as the likelihood of various consequences following various actions. In the same way a rule of grammar is not simply a prediction that various forms of words will or will not be understood.

The tradition following *Bentham and John *Austin, known as legal positivism, recognizes a sharp separation between law as it is and law as it ought to be. Bentham criticized his predecessors, especially the 18th-century jurist *Blackstone, for the 'spirit of obsequious quietism' visible in the assumption that actual law represented a God-given structure of rights and duties. In separating law as it is from law as it ought to be, Bentham saw himself as opening the way to *utilitarian criticism of both the content and the ramshackle structure of English law. Legal positivism is sometimes taken to include other elements: the contention associated with Austin that laws are the commands of the sovereign; the contention that the study of legal concepts is to be distinguished from historical enquiries into the origins of laws or sociological enquiry into the effect of laws, or moral criticism of the workings of the law; the contention that law is a frozen, closed system (in German jurisprudence, a *Begriffshimmel* or concept-heaven) with a determinate logical structure, from which verdicts may be derived without reference to wider pragmatic, social, and moral issues; and even the view that moral judgements are themselves *non-cognitive in nature, and for this reason no part of the essence of legal practice.

Opposition to a picture that includes some or all of these elements will typically stress the inseparable connection between a legal system and the wider social and moral circumstances in which it is set. Judicial reasoning, for example, is not and perhaps should not be a self-contained formalistic application of determinate laws in defined ways, but is an exercise of practical reasoning that is, or ought to be, fully open to moral, political, and social claims. The issue of whether these points undermine the positivist distinction between law as it is and law as it ought to be remains open. Questions belonging not strictly to the philosophy of law but to political philosophy include those of the scope of law, the nature and justification of *punishment, and the justification of the legislative and coercive power of the state. These wider concerns include assessing the *Marxist critique of law as an instrument of oppression, necessarily reflecting the ideas and therefore the partisan interests of the ruling political class.

SEE WEB LINKS

- An audio discussion about philosophy and the law
- A list of resources on the philosophy of law, including bibliographies

l

lawlike *See* LAWS OF NATURE.

law of effect The view formulated by the psychologist E. L. Thorndike (1874–1949) that actions that lead immediately to pleasure are remembered and repeated, eventually fossilizing into habits, whereas actions leading to pain are suppressed or avoided. It is notable that the law explains actions in terms of the past, not in terms of expected pleasure or pain. Although it formed a major tenet of the theory that learning is essentially a matter of *conditioning, and hence suffered with the eclipse of *behaviourism, the law is commonly held to encapsulate something essential to the nature of pain and pleasure, which is their function in controlling learning. A version of the law of effect governs neural networks, or artificial parallel distributed processing systems, which are trained by the 'back propagation of error'; *see* CONNECTIONISM.

laws of nature One of the centrally contested concepts in the philosophy of science. The phrase suggests the dictate or fiat of a lawgiver, and for most thinkers, at least until the 18th century, discovering the laws of nature would be discovering how God had ordained that events should unfold. Without that backing the notion may seem to disappear, leaving only a conception of nature as a succession of different events that just happen to show patterns and regularities: 'just one damn thing after another'. To this can be added the view that the human mind, contemplating the regularities in events, selects some as reliable and adopts them as fixed premises for purposes of prediction and action: these we call laws. This is in effect the approach of *Hume. It gives rise to a programme of describing just which regularities are 'lawlike' or fit to be selected for this status. Suggestions include those which are universal or simple, or contain the right kind of vocabulary, or fit with our other beliefs in various ways. *Realists about laws of nature insist that no such approach gives us enough. They demand a more substantial or robust conception of laws as real features of the world: a kind of stabilizing glue or straightjacket, ensuring that natural events not only happen to fall out as we find them, but *must* do so. The problem for realism about laws of nature is to make sense of this necessity. It seems to transcend experience, since the methods of natural science seem adapted to showing us only how things do happen, not how or why they must happen in the ways we find.

laws of thought *Logic is badly described as investigating the laws of thought. Logic seeks to discover how thoughts, in the sense of the combination of propositions held at one time, must be structured, if they are to conform to the demands of consistency. It does not deal with the diachronic processes whereby one thought succeeds another. The laws of thought in this sense are not known and neither is it known that there should be any such laws, not because the mind is a sphere of *chaos, but because mental descriptions may not be apt for embedding in laws. *See* ANOMALOUS MONISM.

lazy sophism Nickname for the line of thought leading to *fatalism, and the consequent paralysis of action.

learning paradox One of the problems to which the doctrine of **anamnesis* is an answer in *Plato's dialogue *Meno*. If we do not understand something, then we cannot set about learning it, since we do not know enough to know how to begin. Teachers also come across the problem in the shape of students who cannot understand why their work deserves lower marks than that of others. The worry is echoed in philosophies of language that see the infant as a 'little linguist', having to translate surrounding language back into a home medium at least equally rich in conceptual resources to the language being learned. *See* LANGUAGE OF THOUGHT.

least upper bound A number is an upper bound of a set S of numbers if every member of the set is less than or equal to it. A number n is the least upper bound of the set if there is no number less than it that is also an upper bound. It is a non-trivial result that every set of real numbers that has an upper bound has a least upper bound.

If we reverse the order, considering 'greater than or equal to' instead of 'less than or equal to', we obtain the mirror notion of a greatest lower bound.

Lebensphilosophie (German, life philosophy, or philosophy of life) A term for the general emphasis on 'life' as an important philosophical vocabulary, especially as that emphasis was found in writers such as *Dilthey in the 19th century. Generally speaking the movement stood for paying philosophical attention to life as it is lived 'from the inside', rather than to bloodless Kantian abstractions or the scientific reductions of *positivism or naturalism. As a movement it heralded the *phenomenology of *Husserl. *See also* VERSTEHEN.

lect A variety of language having some basis within a community. An *acrolect* is a variety associated with prestige (e.g. BBC English); a *basilect* is the reverse; *dialect* is regional variation, and *genderlect* is difference of speech based on the gender of either speaker or hearer. An *idiolect* is a personal dialect. It is regarded as important in the philosophy of mind and language not to think of a public, shared language as simply a number of coincident idiolects, but rather as something prior, from which idiolects are derivative.

left (political) Most generally, any political stance which is for the poor, the oppressed, and the underprivileged, and against the power, property, and privilege selectively conferred by class interests and established economic and social institutions. *See also* ANARCHISM, COLLECTIVISM, MARXISM, RIGHT (POLITICAL), SOCIALISM.

legalism Excessive respect for the letter of the law, and the forms and institutions of law, at the expense of wider moral and social considerations.

legal positivism *See* LAW, PHILOSOPHY OF.

legal realism *See* LAW, PHILOSOPHY OF.

Leibniz, Gottfried Wilhelm (1646–1716) German philosopher, mathematician, and polymath. Leibniz was born in Leipzig, where he attended university from the age of 15, and submitted a thesis for the degree of doctor of law at the age of 20. In 1667 he entered the service of the Elector of Mainz, where he remained until 1672, engaged largely in political writing. He travelled to Paris in 1672, partly to try to persuade Louis XIV to expel the Turks from Egypt (thereby diverting his attention from Germany; the plan did not succeed). He visited England in 1673, and again in 1676, at which time he had completed his discovery of the differential calculus. In this year he travelled to Amsterdam and met *Spinoza, and became librarian to the Duke of Brunswick at Hanover, a post he held until his death. Between 1680 and 1697 he was working on his own system of philosophy. Leibniz was the greatest polymath of modern philosophers, making contributions to mathematics, jurisprudence, and history, as well as philosophy. He corresponded extensively with all the major learned men of the time, and was the founder of the Academy of Berlin.

Leibniz's mature philosophical system is both intricate and strange, resting on a small number of highly general principles. The foundation of his thought is the conviction that to each individual there corresponds a complete notion, knowable only to God, from which is deducible all the properties possessed by the individual at each moment in its history. It is contingent that God actualizes the individual that meets such a concept, but his doing so is explicable by the principle of *sufficient reason, whereby God had to actualize just that possibility in order for this to be the best of all possible worlds (the thesis subsequently lampooned by *Voltaire in *Candide*). This deducibility of each of an individual's properties from its complete concept is due to there being an ontological correlate of the complete concept, or in other words a modification of the substance of an individual corresponding to each truth about it. In turn this connects with Leibniz's belief that relations, including causal relations between separate individuals, are only **phenomena bene fundata*, or constructions that the mind places upon what are at bottom monadic, non-relational facts. However, Leibniz was entirely hostile to 17th-century *atomism, so that eventually the individuals of his mature system are the *monads: non-physical individual unities, each 'windowless', or independent of other things, and each evolving in a way that is entirely dependent upon their intrinsic natures, but each capable of perceptions that in turn 'express' the nature of external reality. It is arguable that at this point Leibniz reverts to an *Aristotelian conception of nature as essentially striving to actualize its potential. Naturally it is not easy in such a system to make room for space (which Leibniz considered to be relational), corporeal substance, matter (which again he thought of as a *phenomenon bene fundatum*), or free will. Along with those of *Descartes and Spinoza, that of Leibniz is the third of the great *rationalist systems of the 17th century, and in many respects the most unusual. Leibniz's major works, none of which contains a finally developed account of his system, are *Discourse of Metaphysics* (1685); *The New System* (1695); *Theodicy* (1710); and *Monadology* (*c.*1713). His correspondence with *Arnauld, Jean Bernoulli, Burcher de Volder, Bartholemew des Bosses, and *Clarke have been published in separate volumes, as have his controversy with

*Bayle, and the *Nouveaux Essais* which contain his reaction to *Locke's *Essay*.

SEE WEB LINKS

- A list of internet resources on Leibniz, including his writings
- Bibliographies of writings by or on Leibniz

Leibniz's law *See* INDISCERNIBILITY OF IDENTICALS.

lemma An intermediate conclusion in a *proof, marking a point en route to a conclusion.

Lenin, Vladimir Ilyich (1870–1924) Revolutionary leader and principal architect of the success of the Bolshevik revolution in Russia in 1917. Philosophically Lenin contributed a number of ideas to *Marxism: these include emphasis on the role of a professional revolutionary vanguard, drawn from the intelligentsia, the moral absolutism whereby everything may be sacrificed to the revolution, and the association of imperialism with *capitalism that partly explained why Russia, which was not a developed capitalist economy, might nevertheless be in the vanguard of the revolution. Influential works by Lenin include *The Development of Capitalism in Russia* (1899), *What is to be Done?* (1902), and *Imperialism, the Highest Stage of Capitalism* (1916). His earlier *Materialism and Empirio-Criticism* (1909) is an attack on what he saw as the subjective idealism of Russian thinkers influenced by *Avenarius and *Mach.

Lesniewski, Stanislaw (1886–1939) Polish logician and philosopher, and, together with *Łukasiewicz and *Kotarbinski, founder of the Warsaw school of logic. Lesniewski combined researches into formal problems such as *Russell's paradox with a profound metaphysical bent, intending to design a logical system which could be a foundation for all knowledge. He is especially remembered as the pioneer of *mereology.

Lessing, Gotthold Ephram (1729–81) German dramatist and critic. Lessing is not remembered for any first-rate philosophy, but he was a major influence on German thinking of his time. His *Laokoön* (1766) espouses the view that whilst classical ideals of noble static harmony serve well for painting, poetry is concerned with action and passion. His conversion towards the end of his life to the philosophy of the then shocking *Spinoza was reported by F. H. *Jacobi in 1785, and precipitated the *Pantheismusstreit*, or row over pantheism, in which *Mendelssohn attempted to defend the dead Lessing from the charge.

Leucippus of Miletus (*fl.* 450–420 BC) Greek *atomist. Little is known of the life of Leucippus, who is yet treated by *Aristotle as the founder of Greek atomism. Two works are attributed to him: *On Mind* and *Great World-System*, but nearly nothing is known of what they contained. It is impossible to distinguish his doctrines from those of Democritus, whose more extensive writings form the basis of what is known of the system he shared with Leucippus. For an outline, *see* ATOMISM, DEMOCRITUS OF ABDERA.

Leviathan *See* HOBBES.

Levinas, Emmanuel (1906–95) French phenomenologist, moral thinker, and Talmudic commentator. Born in Lithuania, Levinas was based in France from 1923, apart from some years residing in Germany and studying with *Husserl and *Heidegger, and other years incarcerated in Germany during the Second World War. His translations and his first book, *Théorie de l'intuition dans la phénoménologie de Husserl* (1930), played a major role in introducing Husserl and Heidegger to French philosophy. His own work explores, as far as, and perhaps beyond, the limits of intelligibility, the problem generated by the Other, whereby we encounter a different being which cannot be grasped by means of representations but only ethically, a fact which therefore shows the necessary limits on understanding and truth. Works include *Totalité et infini: essai sur l'extériorité* (1961) and *Autrement qu'être ou au-delà de l'essence* (1974).

Lévi-Strauss, Claude (1908–) French anthropologist and structuralist. Educated in law, Lévi-Strauss received a doctorate in philosophy at the Sorbonne. He was appointed to a French university mission to Brazil, serving as professor at São Paulo from 1935 to 1938. From there he led several expeditions into the Mato Grosso and the Amazon. Subsequently he taught in the United States before receiving the chair of social anthropology in the Collège de France, from which he retired in 1982. Lévi-Strauss is the most important structuralist anthropologist. He learned from *Saussure the importance of studying the unconscious infrastructure of human phenomena, and of seeing the elements of a system only in terms of their positional significance or relations with other elements. Part of his doctoral thesis made *Les Structures élémentaires de la parenté* (1949, trs. as *The Elementary Structures of Kinship*, 1969), demonstrating the formal similarity between kinship systems and the phonetic systems studied by Saussure. Later works include *La Pensée sauvage* (1966, trs. as *The Savage Mind*, 1968), in which he opposes *Lévy-Bruhl's doctrine of 'primitive mentality', and *Tristes Tropiques* (1955, trs. under the same title, 1961).

Lévy-Bruhl, Lucien (1875–1913) French philosopher and social anthropologist, noted for stressing the need for empirical investigation of the categories and methods of thought of different societies, and for interpreting the results in terms of a 'pre-logical' primitive mentality. His works include *Les Fonctions mentales dans les sociétés inférieures* (1910, trs. as *How Natives Think*, 1926) and *La Mentalité primitive* (1922, trs. as *Primitive Mentality*, 1923).

Lewis, Clarence Irving (1883–1964) American logician and philosopher. After teaching briefly in California, Lewis taught at Harvard from 1920 until his retirement. Although he wrote extensively on most central philosophical topics, he is remembered principally as a critic of the *extensional nature of modern logic, and as the founding father of *modal logic. His two independent proofs showing that from a contradiction anything follows, still constitute the main problem for developing a *relevance logic, using a notion of *entailment stronger than that of *strict implication. His works include *A Survey of Symbolic Logic* (1918) and *Mind and the World Order* (1929).

Lewis, David (1941–2002) American philosopher. Lewis was born in Oberlin, Ohio, and educated at Swarthmore, at Oxford for a year, and at Harvard where he gained his doctorate in 1967. He taught at the university of California, Los Angeles, from 1966 to 1970, after which he taught at Princeton. Lewis contributed to a wide range of issues, and in the second half of the 20th century became the most influential metaphysician working in the analytic tradition. His first book, *Convention: A Philosophical Study* (1969), rehabilitated the notion of *convention, at the time regarded with deep suspicion both by philosophers of language and by political theorists. *Counterfactuals* (1973) introduced the now classic *possible worlds treatment of such statements. Lewis was remarkable for an uncompromising *realism about the possible worlds in terms of which his analyses work, and much modern discussion has centred on ways of having the benefits of his accounts without incurring the metaphysical costs. Such attempts were rebuffed in *The Plurality of Worlds* (1986). Lewis addressed a wide variety of other issues in his *Collected Papers* (3 vols., 1983, 1986, 2000). His book *Parts of Classes* (1991) developed a *mereological approach to set theory.

lexeme A word, in the sense of a dictionary entry. Distinct strings of letters may be forms of the same lexeme ('fills', 'filled', 'filling'); conversely, identical strings of letters ('bank', the institution, 'bank' of the river) may be forms of different lexemes, since they would standardly be thought of as different words, i.e. having very different senses, in dictionaries. However, the lexicographic principles by which to count words as the same or different are not cut and dried.

lexical A lexicon is a dictionary, and lexical is descriptive either of dictionaries or the terms they are about. A lexical *ambiguity is an ambiguity in a term, as opposed to a structural ambiguity that results from there being two different possible structures for a sentence.

li In Chinese thought, *li* originally means a religious sacrifice. By extension: rules of propriety, good form, decorum. *Li* also plays the role of a higher law or natural law, approximating to the Greek **logos*. *See also* CHI.

Liar paradox Paradox allegedly due to *Epimenides. There are a number of paradoxes of the Liar family. The simplest example is the sentence 'This sentence is false', which must be false if it is true, and true if it is false. One suggestion is that the sentence fails to say anything. But sentences that fail to say anything are at least not true. In that case, we consider the sentence 'This sentence is not true', which, if it fails to say anything, is not true, and hence is true (this kind of reasoning is sometimes called the strengthened Liar). Other versions of the Liar introduce pairs of sentences, as in a slogan on the front of a T-shirt saying 'The sentence on the back of this T-shirt is false', and one on the back saying 'The sentence on the front of this T-shirt is true'. It is clear that each sentence individually is well formed, and, were it not for the other, might have said something true. So any attempt to dismiss the paradox by saying that the sentences involved are meaningless will face problems. *See also* SEMANTIC PARADOXES.

liberalism A political ideology centred upon the individual (*see* INDIVIDUALISM), thought of as possessing rights against the government, including rights of due process under the law, equality of respect, freedom of expression and action, and freedom from religious and ideological constraint. Liberalism is attacked from the *left as the ideology of free markets, with no defence against the accumulation of wealth and power in the hands of a few, and as lacking any analysis of the social and political nature of persons. It is attacked from the *right as insufficiently sensitive to the value of settled institutions and customs, or to the need for social structure and constraint in providing the matrix for individual freedoms.

libertarianism (metaphysical) A view that seeks to protect the reality of human *free will by supposing that a free choice is not causally determined but not random either (*see* DILEMMA OF DETERMINISM). What is needed is the conception of a rational, responsible intervention in the ongoing course of events. In some developments a special category of *agent-causation is posited, but its relationship with the neurophysiological workings of the brain and body, or indeed any moderately naturalistic view of ourselves, tends to be very uneasy, and it is frequently derided as the desire to protect the fantasy of an agency situated outside the realm of nature altogether.

libertarianism (political) In politics, libertarians advocate the maximization of individual rights, especially those connected with the operation of a free market, and the minimizing of the role of the state. In the libertarian vision, exercises of state power for positive ends, such as amelioration of social disadvantage through social welfare programmes, constitute infringements of the rights of others ('taxation is forced labour'). The state is confined to a 'nightwatchman' role of maintaining order and providing only those public services that will not arise spontaneously through the free market. The most influential text of modern libertarianism is the American philosopher Robert *Nozick's *Anarchy, State, and Utopia* (1974).

libertins Term used to describe groups of thinkers of *atheist tendencies, from the late 16th to the 17th century in France. Influences included *Cardano, *Bruno, *Campanella, and in France itself *Montaigne. The term could cover the dissipated and hedonistic way of life supposedly indulged in by those who throw off the shackles of religion, or the scholarly and dispassionate interest in the new science shown by philosophers such as *Gassendi and *Mersenne (so-called *libertinage érudite*).

liberty While the protection of the liberties of the subject is one of the main aims (and boasts) of almost all constitutions, there is less consensus about what those liberties include, or when liberty (good) becomes licence (bad). The problem is to define a class of actions that lie outside the proper jurisdiction of law, i.e. those which one has a right to perform (*see* PRIVACY (SOCIAL), RIGHTS). The value of liberty is dependent upon that of rational self-legislation, or *autonomy, in the Kantian tradition, and dependent upon the nature of the social context rather than on individual rights in *collectivist political philosophies.

licentious In contrast with the person suffering from **akrasia*, who feels the conflict yet succumbs to temptation, the licentious person is supposed to feel no conflict at all between low desire and the promptings of a better self or a higher reason. The latter voice is completely silent. It is thus more fun being licentious than being akratic.

Lichtenberg, Georg Cristoph (1742–99) German scientist and philosopher. Lichtenberg was born near Darmstadt, the seventeenth child of a Protestant clergyman. Curvature of the spine affected him from childhood. He attended the university of Göttingen from 1763, and apart from brief travels, including visits to England, he remained there for the rest of his life, teaching mainly mathematics and physics. His philosophical reputation rests on his aphorisms, which he collected in notebooks throughout his adult life. Probably the most famous is his remark on Descartes's **cogito*, seized upon admiringly by later empiricists such as *Mach: 'We should say, "it thinks", just as we say, "it thunders". Even to say *cogito* is too much if we translate it with "I think". To assume the "I", to postulate it, is a practical need.' Lichtenberg held the modern-sounding doctrine that the task of philosophy was not to resolve disputes such as that between *realism and idealism, but to enable us to get beyond them. He also wrote that his entire philosophy was a correction of linguistic usage. *Wittgenstein is known to have admired his work and adopted a similar aphoristic style. Some of his works are collected in *The Lichtenberg Reader* (trs. H. Mautner and H. Hatfield, 1959).

life *See* BIOLOGY, PHILOSOPHY OF; VITALISM.

life, form of Term associated with the later work of *Wittgenstein. A form of life is what two groups need to share if their languages can be mutually comprehensible.

life, meaning of For nearly everyone it is important to think that his or her life has a purpose. But these purposes may be various: the purpose of one person's life may be to achieve one kind of goal, that of another person may be to achieve a very different kind of goal. There need be no one thing that forms the purpose of every life. (Compare: 'everyone has a mother' versus 'there is someone who is the mother of everyone'. *See* QUANTIFIER SHIFT FALLACY.) Similarly, for many people it will be enough if at each moment there is a purpose to what they are doing, without every moment being devoted to the same purpose, and without the overall pattern itself having a purpose. The view that we are put here for a purpose, rather like being in the army, is characteristic of many religious frames of mind. It leads to *bad faith when apparent certainty about what the purpose is blinds people to other possibilities and opportunities.

life, value of Both Stoic and Epicurean philosophies stress that since nobody experiences it, *death is not an evil and not to be feared. The difficulty then is to say why life is a value and should be protected, and why the curtailment of life by wilful murder ranks as such a serious crime. If this question is tackled by talking of features that give life its value, such as enjoyment or wisdom or knowledge, then the embarrassing consequence arises that lives with more of these things must be of more value than lives with less, threatening the doctrine that everybody's life is of equal value. A religious fudge is to claim that every life is of 'infinite' value, but while this may sound good it is not usable in a world of finite resources.

light Although in physics light is well understood as electromagnetic energy of a very specific wavelength (between 390 and 740 nanometers: a nanometer is 10^{-9} metre), the fact that this is just the energy that illuminates the world for us is evidently contingent upon the nature of our senses, and upon the adaptations they have made to the environment. Light can thus come to inherit the problems of secondary qualities (*see* PRIMARY/SECONDARY QUALITIES), and just as the fact that trees are green can seem due to our design as much as to non-human nature, so the fact that it is light or dark may seem disturbingly anthropocentric or subjective. *Descartes put the problem by asking 'could nature not also have established some sign, which would make us have the sensation of light, even if the sign contained nothing in itself which is similar to this sensation?' (*Le Monde*). Light has been associated with the original primal creative principle in many religious and philosophical traditions, including *Zoroastrianism and *Neoplatonism.

limited independent variety, principle of Principle needed in the attempt to develop a logic of *probability, in the *Treatise on Probability* (1921, ch. 22) by *Keynes. It assures us that 'the objects in the field, over which our generalisations extend, do not have an infinite number of independent qualities; that, in other words, their characteristics, however numerous, cohere together in groups of invariable connection, which are finite in number'. The principle is needed if inductive methods, such as *Mill's methods, are to give us trustworthy conclusions; more strictly, we need a finite probability that an object about which we seek to generalize is not infinitely complex in the way it excludes. Keynes was well aware of the apparently metaphysical and unverifiable nature of the principle.

limit number In the theory of ordinal *numbers, a limit ordinal is an ordinal *x* such that there is no greatest ordinal smaller than *x*. The first limit ordinal is w, the ordinal that measures the length of the standard ordering of the natural numbers.

line, image of the Image for the stages of the understanding given in Plato's *Republic*, vi. 509–11, immediately before the famous *myth of the cave. At the bottom is the world of images, known only by **eikasia*. Objects of sense are known by *pistis* or opinion; mathematical and scientific objects by **dianoia* or reasoning; and at the summit the *forms are known by **noēsis*.

linear ordering *See* ORDERING RELATION.

linguistic acts Acts of communication, by speech or by other actions. *See* SPEECH ACTS.

linguistic determinism/relativism *See* SAPIR–WHORF HYPOTHESIS.

linguistic philosophy A not entirely happy name for the philosophical method of taking language, rather than what the language ostensibly concerns, as the primary datum. Rather than studying numbers, or space and time, or the mind, the philosopher distinctively studies the language of mathematics, or physics, or psychology. The ruling thought is that it is only through a correct appreciation of the role and point of this language that we can come to a better conception of what the language is about, and avoid the over-simplifications and distortions we are apt to bring to its subject-matter. We understand a subject by scrutinizing the ideas we hold about it, and our only access to these ideas is by seeing what we say. Put thus broadly almost all philosophical investigation in the 20th century (and much before) has been in one form or another linguistic in its orientation, and the history of philosophy contains constant warnings against the way in which we can be blinded by what *Berkeley calls the 'mist and veil of words'. Philosophers such as *Leibniz, *Locke, Alexander *Johnson, and *Wittgenstein have conceived it as their chief task to penetrate this mist. *See also* FORMAL/MATERIAL MODE OF SPEECH.

More specifically, the title is sometimes given to a possibly excessive concern with the contours of everyday linguistic usage, characteristic of some philosophers at Oxford in the years following the Second World War, and sometimes called Oxford philosophy. Practitioners of the approach included J. L. *Austin and Gilbert *Ryle.

Lipsius, Justus (1547–1606) Latin name of Joost Lips, Flemish humanist and scholar, renowned for his editions of Tacitus (1574) and Seneca (1589–1605). Lipsius sought to revive Stoicism, finding parallels between the classical submission to fate and Christian submission to providence. His own philosophical writings included *De Constantia* (1584), *Manuductio ad Stoicam philosophiam* (1604), and *Physiologia Stoicorum* (1604).

literature, philosophy of The attempt to articulate a general theory of literature, or to explore the relationship between literary presentations of themes and ideas and their more formal embodiment in philosophy. While this exploration has traditionally taken the form of privileging the second-order philosophical reflection over the literary, *postmodernist writings often reverse the priority, pointing out that philosophy itself is one more kind of writing, and not free of discontinuities and preconceptions that affect writing in general. *See also* FICTION.

locality (physics) *See* BELL'S THEOREM.

Locke, John (1632–1704) English philosopher. Locke was born in Wrington, Somerset, and educated at Oxford, where he seemed destined for a career in medicine. In 1666 he met Anthony Ashley-Cooper, later the 1st Earl of Shaftesbury, who became his friend and patron. Locke supervised a major operation to remove a hydatid cyst of the liver from Shaftesbury in 1668; the wits of the time found it very amusing that Shaftesbury's liver needed a silver tap for the rest of his life. From 1675 to 1679 Locke lived in France, where he studied the work of *Descartes and *Gassendi. Shaftesbury, who had been much engaged with parliamentary opposition to the house of Stuart, fled to Holland in 1681, and Locke followed in 1683, returning to England after the accession of William of Orange in 1688. In the course of the next year Locke's major philosophical works, the *Essay Concerning Human Understanding* and the *Two Treatises of Government*, as well as the *Letter on Toleration*, were published, the latter two anonymously. Locke's final years saw *Some Thoughts Concerning Education* (1693) and *The Reasonableness of Christianity* (1695). He was given minor administrative functions by the government, and lived out his life quietly at the house of Damaris, Lady *Masham, in Essex.

Although he is famous as the senior figure of British *empiricism, Locke's philosophy is more complex than this suggests. The *Essay* rejects any place for 'innate ideas' in the foundations of knowledge, and is in that sense anti-*rationalistic. It puts experience, or ideas of sensation and reflection, firmly at the basis of human understanding. However, Locke retains the possibility of knowing that some of our ideas (those of *primary qualities) give us an adequate representation of the world around us. But the power to know things derives from the all-knowing God, and 'we more certainly know that there is a GOD than that there is any thing else without us' (*Essay*, iv. 10). Although Locke is thought of as the first great English philosopher of the scientific revolution, the ally and 'under-labourer' for *Boyle and *Newton, he himself was doubtful whether such natural philosophy could ever aspire to the condition of a science, by which he meant an activity capable of yielding us God-like rational and adequate insight into the real essences of things (*Essay*, iii. 26). The task of a scientific epistemology is to display what we do know, the various sources of knowledge, the proper employment, and above all the limits and doubtful capacities, of our minds. It is through this theme that Locke connected his epistemology with the defence of religious toleration. This radical doctrine, together with his work on property and on the relationship between government and consent, is his enduring legacy to political philosophy.

Locke's great distinction lies in his close attention to the actual phenomena of mental life, but his philosophy is in fact balanced precariously between the radical empiricism of followers such as *Berkeley and *Hume, and the theological world of reliance on reason underpinning the deliverances of the Christian religion that formed the climate in which he lived. His view that religion and morality were as much open to *demonstration and proof as mathematics stamps him as a pre-*Enlightenment figure, even as his insistence on the primacy of ideas opened the way to more radical departures from that climate.

SEE WEB LINKS

- A list of internet resources on Locke
- A bibliography of writings by or on Locke

locutionary act A saying. As introduced by J. L. *Austin, a locutionary act is the basic linguistic action of voicing (or writing or otherwise making public) a meaningful sequence of words. It is by means of locutionary acts that one succeeds in expressing information or doing other things with words. *See also* ILLOCUTIONARY ACT, PERLOCUTIONARY ACT.

logic The general science of inference. Deductive logic, in which a conclusion *follows from a set of premises, is distinguished from inductive logic, which studies the way in which premises may support a conclusion without entailing it. In deductive logic the conclusion cannot be false if the premises are true. The aim of a logic is to make explicit the rules by which inferences may be drawn, rather than to study the actual reasoning processes that people use, which may or may not conform to those rules. In the case of deductive logic, if we ask why we need to obey the rules, the most general form of answer is that if we do not we contradict ourselves—or, strictly speaking, we stand ready to contradict ourselves. (Someone failing to draw a conclusion that follows from a set of premises need not be contradicting him or herself, but only failing to notice something. However, he or she is not defended against adding the contradictory conclusion to his or her set of beliefs.) There is no equally simple answer in the case of inductive logic, which is in general a less robust subject, but the aim will be to find reasoning such that anyone failing to conform to it will have improbable beliefs. *Aristotle is generally recognized as the first great logician, and Aristotelian logic or traditional logic (*see* SYLLOGISM) dominated the subject until the 19th century. It has become increasingly recognized in the 20th century that fine work was done within that tradition, but syllogistic reasoning is now generally regarded as a limited special case of the forms of reasoning that can be represented within the *propositional and *predicate calculus. These form the heart of modern logic. Their central notions, of *quantifiers, *variables, and *functions were the creation of the German mathematician *Frege, who is recognized as the father of modern logic, although his treatment of a logical system as an abstract mathematical structure, or algebra, had been heralded by *Boole (*see* BOOLEAN ALGEBRA). Modern logic is thus called mathematical logic for two reasons: first, the logic itself is an object of mathematical study, but secondly, the forms introduced by Frege provided a language capable of representing all mathematical reasoning. This was something traditional logic had been quite incapable of tackling. The propositional and predicate calculus study ways of combining propositions with the connectives expressing *truth functions, and of combining information about the quantity of times predicates are satisfied. These highly general operations can occur in any discourse, from mathematics to discussion of the football results. More specific logics study particular topics such as time, possibility, and obligation. Thus there exist *deontic logics, *modal logics, logics of tense, and so on. For other notions associated with the study of logic *see* INTERPRETATION, LOGICAL CALCULUS, LOGICAL CONSTANTS, LOGICAL FORM, MODEL THEORY, PROOF THEORY, QUANTIFIER, TRUTH FUNCTION, VARIABLE.

SEE WEB LINKS

- An online logic tutorial, with interactive exercises
- A list of internet resources on the philosophy of logic

logic, traditional *See* LOGIC, SYLLOGISM.

logical atomism The philosophy of the *Tractatus Logico-Philosophicus* (1921) of *Wittgenstein, and the paper 'The Philosophy of Logical Atomism' by *Russell (1918). Both share the belief that there is a process of logical and philosophical analysis of language which ultimately terminates in 'atoms' of meaning. To such atoms correspond elements in states of affairs or facts, so the process reveals the basic metaphysics implied by our language, or, in the case of Wittgenstein, by all possible languages (since the process of analysis reveals what must be the case for picturing, or meaning, to be possible). In Russell the doctrine had a generally *empiricist character, since he conceived of the process as terminating in elements with which we have direct *acquaintance. Optimism about the possibility of revealing hidden and basic logical structure was passed on to *logical positivism, but both Russell and Wittgenstein eventually turned away from the enterprise.

logical calculus Also called a formal language, and a *logistic system. A system in which explicit rules are provided for determining (a) which are the expressions of the system; (b) which sequences of expressions count as well formed (*well-formed formulae, or wffs); (c) which sequences of wffs count as *proofs. A system may contain *axioms, and a wff that terminates a proof will be a *theorem. The two most famous calculi are the *propositional calculus and the *predicate calculus.

logical consequence *See* ENTAILMENT, PROOF.

logical constants The expressions selected to indicate the *logical form of a sentence. A sentence will play a proper role in inference in virtue of a structure that can be exhibited by means of these expressions. The basic logical constants include expressions for the *truth functions &, ∨, →, ↔, and ¬, the *quantifiers (∃) and (∀), and the identity relation =. The parentheses, ( ), which indicate the *scope of functions, may be counted as logical constants. Richer conceptions of logical form will include other constants: *modal logic includes the operators □ and ◊, and tense logic will include operators signifying past, present, and future. *See* APPENDIX: LOGICAL SYMBOLS.

logical construction To show that As are logical constructions out of Bs is to show that facts about As reduce to facts about Bs, or that everything said using the A vocabulary may be said in a more basic or fundamental way referring only to Bs. Thus rights will be logical constructions out of duties if everything said about rights can be said more openly by referring only to duties. *Behaviourism attempts to show that mind is a logical construction out of behaviour, *phenomenalism that matter is a logical construction out of experience. The programmes of translation necessary to making good these claims have not, however, appeared to succeed, and other ways of relating the different vocabularies have gained more general assent: *see* HOLISM, REDUCTIONISM.

logical empiricism *See* LOGICAL POSITIVISM.

logical fiction *Russell called items shown to be *logical constructions out of other items, logical fictions; an example is the way 'the average man' is shown to be a logical fiction when we see how to translate statements made using the term into others that do not even appear to refer to such an entity. The usage is slightly confusing since, unlike fictions, logical constructions really exist. For example, showing that *numbers are logical constructions out of sets is not so much showing that numbers do not exist, as showing what it means to say that they do.

logical form The logical form of a sentence is the structure, shareable with other sentences, responsible for its powers in inferences. That is, its logical form determines the way in which it can be validly deduced from other sentences, and the way other sentences can validly be deduced from sets of premises that include it. Obviously there is something common to the argument 'All men are mortal, Socrates is a man, so Socrates is mortal' and 'All horses bite, Eclipse is a horse, so Eclipse bites'. This common form may be revealed by abstracting away from the different subject-matter, and seeing each argument as of the form 'All Fs are G; a is F; *so* a is G'. The 'symbols' of symbolic logic simply represent such common forms and the methods of combining elements to make up sentences. It is frequently controversial to what extent reduction to simple forms is possible, and how much hidden structure it is fruitful to look for, in order to reveal similar logical forms under the surface diversities of ordinary language.

logical implication *See* ENTAILMENT, LOGIC, PROOF.

logically perfect language One in which the surface form of each sentence correctly exhibits its *logical form: one therefore in which the inferential powers of sentences are represented on the surface.

logically private language *See* PRIVATE LANGUAGE.

logically proper name In *Russell's writings of the period between 1905 and 1918, a logically proper name is a term whose true logical role is to refer to an object. A cluster of considerations led Russell to believe that ordinary names function differently, as *definite descriptions in disguise, and that only items with which we are directly acquainted could strictly be named. These would be items presented in current experience. A logically proper name is a tag for such an item. There are, however, not many kinds of them, since relatively few types of item qualify as elements of immediate experience. They include the self (perhaps), the present time, sense data, and universals. *See also* LOGICAL ATOMISM.

logical paradoxes Paradoxes such as *Russell's paradox, in which there is no use of *semantic terms, are sometimes described as purely logical, in contrast to the *semantic paradoxes.

logical positivism Also known as logical empiricism and scientific empiricism; the ideas and attitude towards philosophy associated with the Vienna Circle. This group was founded by *Schlick and the mathematician Hans Hahn before the First World War, but entered its most famous period after being reconstituted in 1924. In effect the circle ended with Schlick's death in 1936 and the dispersal of Austrian intellectuals at that time. Its members included Gustav *Bergmann, Rudolf *Carnap, Herbert Feigl (1902–88), Otto *Neurath, and Friedrich *Waismann. *Wittgenstein was not a full member of the circle, although closely in touch with its work, maintaining regular meetings with it from 1927 to 1929, and thereafter remaining in contact with Schlick and Waismann. The central interest of the Vienna Circle was the unity of science and the correct delineation of scientific method. The idea was that this would act as a final solvent of the disputes of metaphysicians. The task of constructive philosophy became that of analysing the structure of scientific theory and language. The movement can be seen as a development of older *empiricist and *sensationalist doctrines in the light first of a better understanding of the methodology of empirical science, and secondly of the dramatically increased power of formal logic to permit the definition of abstractions and to describe the structures of permissible inferences. The combination is to some extent foreshadowed in *Russell, whose logic and whose concept of a *logical construction played a significant role in the doctrines of the movement. The most characteristic doctrine of logical positivism was the *verification principle, or denial of literal or cognitive meaning to any statement that is not verifiable: 'the meaning of a statement is its method of verification.' The movement gained publicity in the English-speaking world when *Ayer published *Language, Truth, and Logic* in 1936, and maintained some impetus, especially in the philosophy of science, after Carnap and Feigl emigrated to the United States. From 1930 onwards it took over the journal *Erkenntnis* as the journal of unified science.

Logical positivism retreated under a combination of pressures. First, it shared the traditional problems of radical *empiricism, of satisfactorily describing the basis of knowledge in experience (*see* PROTOCOL STATEMENTS). Secondly, it depended on there being one logic for science, or in other words a *confirmation theory with a unique authority, yet no such structure, and certainly no basis for its authority, ever forthcame. These two problems bedevilled accurate formulation of the verification principle, and gradually persuaded philosophers of science that a more *holistic and less formal relationship existed between theoretical sentences and the observations supporting them. When this relationship was allowed to be indirect, the despised theses of metaphysics began to look capable of climbing back into respectability. Finally, although logical positivism allowed that science contains statements thought of as logically *necessary, its own account of the status of these claims (*conventionalism) proved widely unacceptable, and the status of its claims about the basis of meaning in sensation appeared correspondingly doubtful. However, its influence persists in the widespread mistrust of statements for which there are no *criteria or assertibility conditions: Wittgenstein's slogan that meaning is use has frequently been adopted as a rather less forthright invitation to work within the constraints of the principle of verification.

logical product The logical product of two propositions *p*, *q*, is their *conjunction, *p* & *q*. The logical product of two sets is their *intersection.

logical subject The logical subjects of a sentence are whatever would be referred to by the *referential expressions in a sentence whose surface form truly exhibited its *logical form.

logical sum The logical sum of two propositions *p*, *q*, is their *disjunction, $p \vee q$. The logical sum of two sets is their *union.

logical theory *See* LOGIC.

logical truth A truth that is a theorem of some logic, or that is *valid or true in any *interpretation of the logical system.

logicism The approach to the philosophy of mathematics pioneered by *Frege and *Russell. According to logicism the truths of mathematics are logical truths, deducible by logical laws from basic logical *axioms. The programme of showing this started with Frege's brilliant demonstration that elementary truths of counting (e.g. 'there are four apples here') can be formalized using only the *quantifiers and identity. No irreducible mention of number is demanded. The greatest achievement of logicism was *Principia Mathematica* (1912) by Russell and *Whitehead. The problem for the programme was that the complexity necessary to avoid *paradoxes led to a mapping of mathematics onto *set theory, with its own structures and axioms, rather than to anything recognizable as 'purely' logical.

logistic method The approach to a scientific, mathematical, or other theory that exhibits it as a *formal system, thereby making it possible to treat formally the question of its implications, its compatibility with other theories, and the logical independence of its different axioms.

logocentrism Term used in *postmodernist writing to criticize what is perceived as an excessive faith in the stability of meanings, or excessive concern with distinctions, or with the validity of inferences, or the careful use of reason, or with other traditional aids to sifting truth from falsity, or indeed an excessive faith in the notions of truth and falsity themselves.

logomachy (Greek, *logos*, word, + *machē*, battle) A purely verbal dispute.

logos (Greek, statement, principle, law, reason, proportion) In *Heraclitus, the cosmic principle that gives order and rationality to the world, in a way analogous to that in which human reason orders human action. In *Plato and *Aristotle a similar function is performed by **nous*. In *Stoicism the seminal reason (*logos spermatikos*) is the cosmic source of order; its aspects are fate, providence, and nature. Subordinate *logoi* seem to perform something of the function of Plato's *forms. *Logos* also has another aspect: it is what enables us to apprehend the principles and forms, i.e. it is an aspect of our own reasoning. The view becomes fused with Christian doctrine when *logos* is God's instrument in the development (redemption) of the world. The notion survives in the idea of *laws of nature, if these are conceived of as independent guides of the natural course of events, existing beyond the temporal world that they order.

Lombard, Peter (1095/1100–1160) Italian theologian. Lombard's importance in scholastic thought derives from his four books making up the *Book of Sentences*, composed between 1145 and 1151. These treat of matters such as predestination, God's relationship to creation, free will, and so forth, and were the frequent topic of commentaries by subsequent theologians.

loneliness *See* INTRINSIC/EXTRINSIC PROPERTIES.

Longinus (1st c. AD) Shadowy author of the Greek treatise usually known as *On the Sublime*. This is one of the most important works of literary criticism to come down from the classical world, containing both detailed appreciations of passages from Homer, Euripides, Demosthenes, and others, and general reflections, especially on the element of pathos involved, and the relation between great writing and greatness of mind. The work gained influence in Europe through the French translation of 1674 by Boileau. *See also* SUBLIME.

lottery paradox Suppose a lottery with a large number of tickets. Then it is rational to believe of each particular ticket that it will lose. If it is rational to hold two beliefs separately, then it must be rational to hold their conjunction. But if we conjoin all these beliefs and we know that we have considered each ticket, then this is equivalent to believing that every ticket will lose, which is irrational. The structure is similar to the *preface paradox.

Lotze, Rudolf Hermann (1817–81) German idealist logician and metaphysician. Lotze studied at Leipzig, and in 1844 became professor at Göttingen, where he remained until the last year of his life, when he briefly held the chair at Berlin. His philosophy tempered idealism with *empiricism, and in contrast to the monolithic systems of the time embraces the pluralities of the universe, although finding ultimate intelligibility only in the activities of spirits and their relationship with God (*see* PANPSYCHISM). Lotze's principal works are his *Logik* (1874) and *Metaphysik* (1879); these were translated together by *Bosanquet as *Lotze's System of Philosophy* (1884).

love In Greek thought, *eros* connotes desire, longing, disequilibrium, and is generally sexual in nature. However, in *Plato (especially the *Symposium* and *Phaedrus*), although *eros* may start with a particular person as its object, it soon becomes transferred from the particular person to their *beauty (a characteristic that in principle another person could possess to the same or a greater degree), and finally it gravitates towards immaterial objects such as the *form of beauty itself. The desire for immaterial beauty is a kind of recollection of the vision of forms (such as those of justice, wisdom, and knowledge) that the soul was able to perceive on the 'plains of truth' in its previous life. Bodily beauty induces remembrance of this state, **anamnesis*, and enables the soul to begin to climb the ladder back to spiritual truth. The philosopher, the poet, the lover, and the follower of the muses (or creative artist) are all inspired by the divine power of *eros*, which dictates the passionate pursuit of the truly real, pure intellectual light, through beauty, wisdom, and the arts of the muses. It is not often recorded how persons who believe themselves to be beloved are supposed to react to these fleshless rivals, although *Dante's Beatrice is the principal example of a beloved person both initiating and then conducting a spiritual ascent of this kind. Unfortunately, however, before conducting Dante up to the highest circles of Paradise, she has to be dead. The idea of beauty as the visible trigger of a spiritual ascent was transmitted to the medieval world through *Neoplatonism, and especially the *City of God* of *Augustine.

Philia in Greek thought is more akin to friendship, and includes fondness and desire for the good of another. In *Aristotle, quite stringent conditions are required for reciprocal and recognized *philia*: familiarity, virtue, and equality. **Agapē* is the Christian addition to the forms of affection here recognized, and suggests a less focused, universal benevolence that pays little or no regard to reciprocity. *See also* APATHY, SEX.

Lovejoy, Arthur O. (1873–1962) Influential historian of ideas. Lovejoy was born in Berlin, but after studying in California was hired at Stanford and then in 1910 by Johns Hopkins, where he stayed for the rest of his working life. His method was premised on the concept of a 'unit-idea': a building block of thought traceable across time, assemblages of which make up different philosophies and ideologies. His most famous work was *The Great Chain of Being* (1936). *See also* CHAIN OF BEING; PLENITUDE, PRINCIPLE OF.

Löwenheim–Skolem theorem Theorem stating that any class of well-formed formulae of the *predicate calculus that has a *model, has a model with a *denumerable domain. *See also* SKOLEM PARADOX.

loyalty Of ethical interest because although loyalty to a friend, family, or other group can be a *virtue, it is one that conflicts with the *impartiality necessary to justice or to generalized universal altruism. *See also* FRIENDSHIP, GRATITUDE.

Lucretius (Titus Lucretius Carus) (99/94–55/51 BC) Roman *Epicurean. Very little is known about the life of Lucretius. His only surviving work is the philosophical poem *De Rerum Natura* (*On the Nature of Things*), expounding the *atomistic philosophy of Epicurus. The poem contains six books: (1) introduces the basic atomism of *Democritus, and rejects the rival views of *Empedocles, *Heraclitus, and *Anaxagoras; (2) introduces the distinction between *primary and secondary qualities of things, and introduces the doctrine of the continuous creation and destruction of worlds; (3) explains the composite and perishable nature of the soul, and the folly of fearing death; (4) gives the Epicurean theory of perception and the passions, including a famous denunciation of love; (5) deals with the progress of events in the natural world; and (6) treats of natural oddities and prodigies such as earthquakes and plagues. The poem is deservedly famous for its moral consolation as well as its cosmology, and its rugged literary power is often compared favourably to Virgil.

Lukács, György (1885–1971) Hungarian *Marxist philosopher. Lukács was briefly a minister in the Hungarian government in 1919 and again in 1956, although he spent years in exile in Russia. Lukács saw in Marxism the way to overcome the duality of subject and object inherent in Western thought: the experience of the working class can become both the subject and the object of history, thereby achieving the necessary harmony and totality (the thought here depends on a *Hegelian framework). At this point, too, the blinkers of capitalist ideology, and in particular *commodity fetishism, would be transcended. Lukács wrote extensively on literary theory as well as the interpretation of Marx. His works include *Die Seele und die Formen* (1911, trs. as *The Soul and its Forms*, 1971) and *Geschichte und Klassenbewußtsein* (1923, trs. as *History and Class Consciousness*, 1971).

Łukasiewicz, Jan (1878–1956) Polish mathematician and logician. Łukasiewicz was a central figure of the Lvov–Warsaw school of logic (and the inventor of the *Polish notation for formal logic). He studied mathematics at the university of Lvov but his career included becoming Minister of Education in 1919 and a professor at Warsaw University from 1920 to 1939. During this period between the wars he was also twice rector of Warsaw University. Łukasiewicz published his text *Elements of Mathematical Logic* in Warsaw in 1928 (the English translation appeared in 1963). From 1946 he lived in Dublin.

Lull (Llull), Ramon (*c*.1232–1316) Spanish Franciscan philosopher and crusader. Lull's life was a relentless attempt to convert the heathen Muslims and Jews. To this end he designed his 'Art', published in the *Ars Magna* (*c*.1274) and the *Ars Generalis Ultima* (1308). It is an elaboration of *Neoplatonism, with a rigorous attempt at identifying the categories ('dignities') making up the absolute principles of God. These unfold into triads of agent, patient, and action. Lull shared the belief of both Jewish and Muslim thinkers of his time in secret numerical and geometrical knowledge whereby the elect can understand the nature of the cosmos. The Art of combinations is therefore regarded as a first attempt at a logically perfect language in which proofs of the correctness of Christianity may be framed. His position may have been an influence on *Leibniz's later ambition to develop a **characteristica universalis*. Lull was killed campaigning against infidels in North Africa.

lust One of the traditional *seven deadly sins, and the particular enemy of many of the early Christian fathers, including saints Jerome, Anthony, and *Augustine. Unfortunately the term is apt to stray in meaning, sometimes covering sexual desire in general, but sometimes confined to sexual desire in which the other person is merely used, or seen as a mere object. In Spanish and Italian the sin is called 'lusuria', which has different connotations again. *See* LOVE, SEX.

Luther, Martin (1483–1546) German Augustinian monk and originator of the Reformation in Europe. Luther was professor of biblical theology at Wittenberg when in 1517 he nailed his *Ninety Five Theses* to the door of the university chapel. Luther was much influenced by William of *Ockham, from whom he derived a sceptical view of the edifices of scholasticism, and in particular *Thomism. The leading idea of his theology was the doctrine of *justification by faith or grace alone—a doctrine which irritated the Catholic church by denying any institutional role in defining or delivering (or selling) proper religious status (grace). Similarly Luther had a dim view of the place of reason and philosophy ('the devil's whore') in underpinning proper Christian faith, which comes from God and is revealed not by reason but by revelation. His sermons and hymns are one of the treasures of German literature.

Lyceum The name of the school founded in Athens by *Aristotle, in a grove or gymnasium dedicated to Apollo Lyceus (either derived from *lukeios*, belonging to a wolf; or Lycian, coming from Lycia; or *lukē*, light). Its members were the *Peripatetics.

lying Philosophical discussions embrace the usage according to which a lie is the deliberate utterance of a falsehood, with the intent to deceive or mislead an audience. Saying something false inadvertently, or saying something false knowing that the audience will misunderstand it and interpret it as something which is in fact true, or merely uttering false pleasantries when no question of deception arises, are not therefore cases of lying. The prohibition on lying in any circumstance (even when the mad axeman asks where your children are sleeping) is a notorious part of *Kant's ethics. On the other hand, *consequentialist and *utilitarian theories are frequently charged with failing to explain the peculiar gravity of lying, since some lies have few, if any, bad consequences.

Lyotard, Jean-François (1924–98) French postmodernist. Lyotard held posts at many universities in France and the United States, although his works influenced literary theorists as much as or more than philosophers. Starting life as a *Marxist he eventually rejected all 'totalizing' theories or grand 'metanarratives' such as Marxism itself, or liberal or other *Enlightenment philosophies, in favour of more piecemeal, contingent, local historical understandings. His books translated into English include *Phenomenology* (1954), *The Libidinal Economy* (1974), *The Post-Modern Condition: A Report on Knowledge* (1979), *The Differend: Phrases in Dispute* (1983), *Peregrinations* (1988), *The Inhuman* (1988), and two collections, *Political Writings* (1993) and the *Lyotard Reader* (1989).

Mach, Ernst (1838–1916) Austrian physicist and philosopher. Born in Turas, Mach studied at Vienna, and held chairs in mathematics at Graz, physics at Prague, and then history and theory of inductive science at Vienna. He is widely regarded as the major precursor of *logical positivism. His philosophy is usually interpreted as radically empiricist: the mind knows only its own sensations, and theory is nothing but an instrument for predicting how they will occur. It was as a kind of subjective *idealism that it was attacked by *Lenin, and ironically the belief that the theory of *relativity was inspired by Mach impeded its acceptance in the Soviet Union. But Mach's empiricism is allied with a new insistence on the importance of a logical analysis of the structure of scientific theory. Probably the most important work in which this combination is developed is *Die Mechanik in ihrer Entwicklung historisch-kritisch dargestellt* (1883, trs. as *The Science of Mechanics*, 1893). Mach's principal other treatise was the *Beiträge zur Analyse der Empfindungen* (1906, trs. as *The Analysis of Sensations*, 1914). *Einstein paid him this tribute: 'I can say with certainty that the study of Mach and Hume has been directly and indirectly a great help in my work' (obituary, *Physikalische Zeitschrift*, 1916).

SEE WEB LINKS

- An essay on Mach's philosophy
- A translation of Lenin's critique

Machiavelli, Niccolò (1469–1527) Florentine political philosopher, and a major presence in subsequent political philosophy. His works *Il Principe* (1512/13, first trs. in its entirety as *The Prince*, 1640, although excerpts circulated much earlier) and the *Discorsi* (*c.*1516, trs. as *Discourses*) brought a new realism into the study of politics. Machiavelli's shocking contention was that although the Prince or ruler was supposed to be an embodiment of virtue and honour, yet given the way of the world, the successful ruler is only the one who acts effectively without regard to the conventional morality of actions. By seeing political organizations as organic entities subject to their own laws of development, flourishing and disintegrating in ways that owe nothing to an independent moral order, Machiavelli may also be regarded as the first sociologist.

Mach's principle The physical principle that the inertia of a body in a system is determined by the distribution of mass and energy in the rest of the system.

MacIntyre, Alasdair C. (1929–) Foremost Aristotelian moral and political philosopher. An engaged and foreful critic of *liberalism, MacIntyre has moved the basis of his assault from Marxism to Thomism. His pessimistic vision of contemporary ethics compares us to the survivors of some catastrophe faced with the remnants of sciences that they can no longer understand. They would no longer be able to follow rational scientific reasoning, and neither can we rise to rational ethical thought. As MacIntyre sees it, we have a choice between Aristotelian teleology, with its promise of a determinate view of human life as it should be lived, and a lawless *emotivism, a *Nietzschean chaos of mere assertions of will. But our capacity to articulate the Aristotelian vision properly is crippled by the contemporary world. MacIntyre himself sketches a *communitarian vision of practices that carry their own reward, undertaken in a kind of enclave of Benedictine security. Books include *A Short History of Ethics* (1966); *After Virtue* (1981); *Whose Justice? Which Rationality?* (1988); *Three Rival Versions of Moral Enquiry* (1990); and *Dependent Rational Animals* (1999).

macrocosm and microcosm The macrocosm is the world as a whole, with a microcosm being one small part, often mankind, taken as a model of it. Thus the universe may be regarded as a large living organism (*see* PANPSYCHISM). The idea was central to most Greek thought, and especially that of *Pythagoras, *Plato, and subsequent *Neoplatonism. In *Leibniz the monads are microcosms of the world, since each in itself mirrors the entire universe.

McTaggart, John McTaggart Ellis (1866–1925) British *idealist. Born in London, McTaggart was educated at Trinity College, Cambridge, where he remained for his working life. His philosophy took Hegelian or *absolute idealism as a starting-point, but developed a unique blend of the belief that reality is ultimately spiritual, belief in the immortality of the soul, and belief in a direct relationship of love between souls, but coupled with denial of the existence of material objects, space, and most famously time. McTaggart's proof that the *a-series is necessary to time, yet itself involves contradiction, is currently his best-remembered contribution to metaphysics, and still forms a pivotal issue in the subject. His works include *Studies in the Hegelian Dialectic* (1896) and the two-volume *The Nature of Existence* (1921–7).

Madhva (*c.*1238–*c.*1317) Indian founder of philosophical school Dvaita Vedanta. Madhva espoused a dualist philosophy or pluralist philosophy, holding absolute distinctions between various categories of being (the self, objects, other people, God) in opposition to the *monist tendencies of much Indian thought and especially the *advaita school of *Shankara. He wrote extensive commentaries on preceding philosophical texts.

Madhyamika (Sanskrit, the middle way) A school of Buddhist philosophy. The middle way emphasizes the emptiness (**shunyata*) of things, and the way in which truth lies beyond all dichotomies and oppositions. But it also allows some value to relative or phenomenal knowledge of things. The middle way is in some respects similar to the *Kantian conjunction of the unknowable nature of the *noumenal and the possibility of a science of the phenomenal. The school was founded by *Nagarjuna, and has a long philosophical development.

magic The philosophical questions posed by the practice of magic and witchcraft in many cultures concern the nature of rationality and the nature of interpretation. The simplest interpretation of magical practices is that they are bad science: they represent attempts to control events by means that are in fact inadequate. Only a 'primitive mentality', inferior to Western scientific thought, could overlook the inadequacy (*see* LÉVY-BRUHL). The problem is that if an interpretation of a practice has to posit widespread irrationality it offends against the principle of *humanity, and suggests the need for a less prejudiced and more empathetic understanding. An alternative pioneered by the anthropologist E. E. Evans-Pritchard in *Witchcraft, Oracles, and Magic among the Azande* (1937) highlights the function of belief in magic in sustaining social order, defusing tensions and aggressions, and serving as an outlet for envies and jealousies. Magic, like other religious practice, becomes non-rational rather than irrational, with a symbolic social function. Evans-Pritchard himself believed that the Azande explain events at two different levels, one of which accords with Western norms of reason, and one of which does not; so the question of whether this second level involves irrationality is therefore still open. A fully *relativistic response to this is given by the British philosopher Peter Winch in *The Idea of a Social Science* (1958), in which it is argued that reality itself is a social construction, with Western conceptions of rationality enjoying no privileged status above that of other ways of taking the world to be. New Age beliefs and the rising prevalence of astrology, homeopathy, and alternative medicines of all kinds remind us of the power of magical thinking even in the West.

magnitude *See* MEASUREMENT.

Magus of the North *See* HAMANN.

Mahavira (6th–5th c. BC) A contemporary of Buddha venerated as a founder of the *Jain branch of Hinduism.

maieutic method (Greek, *maieutikos*, one who acts as a midwife) The maieutic method is that of eliciting ideas by questioning; the image is that the ideas are already there in the pregnant subject's mind, but require midwifery to be made manifest.

Maimon, Salomon (1754–1800) Lithuanian Jewish critic of Kant. Well versed in rabbinical literature, Maimon (who took the name out of respect for *Maimonides) lived a prickly and peripatetic life moving between various occupations and various Jewish communities. His works include *Versuch über die Transcendentale Philosophie* (1790), which caused Kant to declare, in a letter to Marcus Herz, that Maimon was the most acute of all his critics and opponents. His most important work was the *Kritische Untersuchungen über den Menschlichen Geist* (1797), an early expression of *idealism that subsequently influenced *Fichte and *Hegel.

Maimonides (Moses ben Maimon) (1135–1204) The greatest Jewish philosopher of the medieval world, Maimonides was born in Cordoba in Spain and educated in rabbinical and biblical studies as well as philosophy and science. With the conquest of Cordoba by the Almohads in 1148 the family fled to North Africa, to Palestine, and finally settled in Egypt. He supported himself as a physician, and became the revered head of the Egyptian Jews. Maimonides wrote extensively and authoritatively on Jewish law, but as a philosopher is remembered primarily for his *Guide for the Perplexed*, first written in Arabic and subsequently translated into Hebrew and Latin. In keeping with the rabbinical doctrine that certain matters are reserved for the select few, Maimonides' work has an enigmatic form, and has been intepreted in various ways. It is a guide for those who believe in the Law but are perplexed by the meaning of various biblical terms. This leads Maimonides to a discussion of the nature of divine attributes. He holds with *Avicenna a distinction between existence and essence, but adds the distinctive doctrine that no positive essence may be attributed to God, who is therefore known only by negation. However, he goes on to establish the existence, unity, and incorporeal nature of God, and proves his existence by standard *physico-theological arguments (he appears to have held that Avicenna's cosmological argument was a physical argument).

Major (Mair), John (1467–1550) Scottish historian and theologian. Mair was born near Edinburgh, and educated at Oxford and Paris, where he rapidly rose to become professor of theology. He became Principal of the university of Glasgow, but from 1523 spent several more years in Paris, before returning to Scotland to become Provost at St Andrews. He commented on the *Sentences* of Peter *Lombard, and was a teacher of John *Knox. His most important work was *A History of Greater Britain*.

major premise *See* SYLLOGISM.

major term *See* SYLLOGISM.

majority tyranny The Achilles heel of modern democracies, whereby once one party has gained power it can systematically ignore or predate upon the interests of the minority. The idea of a constitution, and of *judicial review of law-making in the light of the constitution, is one check on this process.

Makropoulos case A case highlighted by *Williams in *Problems of the Self* (1973). In the story by Karel Capek (1890–1938), made into an opera by Janáček, Elina Makropoulos, alias Emilia Marty, alias Ellian MacGregor, has imbibed an elixir of life. At the time of the play she has been 42 years old for three hundred years, and life has become entirely meaningless. Williams uses the example to suggest that eternal life is not at all desirable, and that we are fortunate in having the opportunity to die. However, Makropoulos is an immortal living an otherwise normal life amongst mortals, and it takes more profound imaginings to recognize that heaven itself would be insupportable. The case was made by Julian Barnes in *History of the World in 10½ Chapters* (1989). *See also* ETERNITY.

Malebranche, Nicolas (1638–1715) French *Cartesian philosopher. Malebranche was born in Paris and educated in philosophy and theology at the Sorbonne. Deeply impressed by the philosophy of *Descartes, he produced in 1674 and 1675 the two volumes of *De la recherche de la vérité* ('On the Search for Truth'). In this work Malebranche expounds and develops many of the views of Descartes, but his own originality is apparent in two main areas. He inherits the Cartesian view that pure sensation has no representative power, and so adds the doctrine that knowledge of objects requires other representative *ideas that are somehow surrogates for external objects. These are archetypes or ideas of objects as they exist in the mind of God, so that 'we see all things in God'. *Berkeley (*Three Dialogues*, ii. 43) takes care to distinguish himself from Malebranche, whose doctrine might sound similar. The point was the subject of acrimonious debate with *Arnauld. The other doctrine for which he is remembered is the denial of causal efficacy to bodies. Like Islamic *occasionalists such as *al-Ghazali, Malebranche reserves causal power to God. On both the denial of empirical causation, and the nature of the soul, there is much in common between his philosophy and that of *Hume, who always refers to him with respect. Malebranche defended his system further in the *Entretiens sur la métaphysique et sur la religion* (1688, trs. as *Dialogues on Metaphysics and Religion*, 1923).

SEE WEB LINKS

- A biography of Malebranche
- A brief tutorial on Malebranche's philosophy

malin génie (French, evil genius or demon) The common French phrase for the 'mauvais génie' introduced in the first of the *Meditations* of *Descartes. *See* METHOD OF DOUBT.

Malthus, Thomas Robert (1766–1834) English social theorist. Although belonging principally to the history of science, Malthus's *Essay on Populations* (1798) was philosophically influential in undermining the *Enlightenment belief in unlimited possibilities of human progress and *perfection. The 'principle of population', or natural tendency of populations to expand geometrically, and therefore faster than resources (which are constrained by available area), seemed to promise instead a grim vista of inevitable epidemic and famine. The principle was, and remains, an uncomfortable argument against attempting to check poverty by providing food and other resources, since such a policy will only renew the same problems in subsequent, larger, generations.

Mandeville, Bernard (*c.*1670–1733) Dutch doctor and moral philosopher. Born in Rotterdam of a distinguished medical family, Mandeville settled in Britain shortly after taking his degree in 1691. He is known for *The Fable of the Bees; or Private Vices, Public Benefits* (the work grew from a poem published in 1705, to its final form in the 6th edition of 1729). Mandeville analyses the way in which private vices, such as vanity, luxury, and desire for fashion and change, give rise to public benefits, such as industry and employment. Vice is the behaviour that alone promotes profitable economic activity. The sardonic or even cynical implications of this work called forth rebuttals from both *Berkeley and *Hutcheson, but the work clearly influenced Adam *Smith, and anticipates the doctrine of conspicuous consumption made famous by *Veblen.

Manichaeanism (Manicheism) The doctrine that the world is not governed by one perfect Being, but by a balance of the forces of good and evil. The doctrine elevates the devil, as the personification of evil, into a position of power comparable to that of God. It derives from *Zoroastrianism and was held by the Manichees, followers of the Persian teacher Manes or Manichaeus. It flourished between the 3rd and 5th centuries AD. St *Augustine adhered to Manichaeanism for several years, before becoming a bitter opponent.

manifest image Term introduced by *Sellars in papers collected in his *Science, Perception, and Reality* (1963), for the common way of thinking of oneself in the world, as a perceiving person and agent, amongst other similar persons inhabiting a single space of coloured, three-dimensional objects. The manifest image contrasts with the scientific image, which deals in the behaviour of conglomerates of the physical particles postulated by scientific theory. What Sellars called the 'perennial philosophy' from *Plato onwards accepts the reality of the elements and features of the manifest image, but it is also a perennial problem to compare and reconcile its claims with that of the scientific image, which is in reality the arbiter 'of what is, that it is, and of what is not that it is not'. Similar contrasts are found throughout philosophy. *See also* COLOUR, ELIMINATIVISM, INTENTIONALITY, PRIMARY/SECONDARY QUALITIES.

manifold In the philosophy of *Kant, the manifold is the unorganized flux presented to the senses, but not experienced, since experience results from the mind structuring the manifold by means of concepts. The nature of the unstructured manifold is unknowable (transcendental).

Mannheim, Karl (1893–1947) German sociologist. Born in Budapest, Mannheim was educated at Heidelberg, before becoming professor of sociology at Frankfurt. In 1933 he left Germany and taught at London until 1946. His major work, *Ideologie und Utopie* (1929, trs. as *Ideology and Utopia*, 1936), was influential in opening up the sociology of knowledge, or the attempt to relate all modes of thought to the economic and cultural forces surrounding their occurrence (*see* BASE AND SUPERSTRUCTURE). His own attempts to explain how objective knowledge is possible despite the matrix of interests that give it its shape have not met general acceptance.

mantra A powerful and pregnant set of syllables, repeated in devotional incantations. The most famous is '*Om Mani Padme Hum*' (Sanskrit, 'Om, jewel of the lotus, hum'), a central mantra of Tibetan *Buddhism.

many questions, fallacy of The lawyers' fallacy of inferring or implying some kind of guilt when a person cannot give a straight yes-or-no answer to a question that in fact does not permit of such an answer. The classic example is 'Have you stopped beating your wife?' to which an innocent person can give no one-word answer. The question conceals two others (Did you ever do so? Do you do so now?) and innocence means answering 'no' to each. Unfortunately, since we normally talk about stopping things that we have once started, simply answering 'no' to the overall question carries a strong *implicature that you used to do so, and go on doing so. So you do not want to say (only) that, nor of course do you want to say 'yes'.

many-sorted logic A logic in which the *variables range over different domains. In classical *predicate calculus a proposition like 'All Fs are G' is represented as saying: take anything; if it is F, it is G. In a many-sorted logic the representation will be: take any F; it is G. This may accord better with natural language, and it matches traditional *syllogistic forms better than the predicate calculus does.

many-valued logic A logic that acknowledges more than the two classical *truth-values of truth and falsity. Intermediate values may be motivated by the demands of *vagueness, of avoiding the logical *paradoxes, and of avoiding the view that future contingent propositions are determinately true or false, this being thought to lead to *fatalism. The original three-valued system in modern logic is due to the Polish logician *Łukasiewicz. *See also* FUZZY LOGIC, SEA-BATTLE.

Maoism Named after the Chinese revolutionary and leader Mao Tse-Tung (or Mao Zedong, 1893–1976), Maoism is the transposition of the theory and practice of *Marxism to apply to the conditions not of the urban proletariat, but of the Chinese peasantry. In some quarters in the West, especially during the late 1960s, it became optimistically regarded as the ultimate egalitarian and communitarian political ideal.

Marburg school A *Neo-Kantian school mainly concerned with the presuppositions of natural science. Its members included Hermann *Cohen, Paul Natorp, and Ernst *Cassirer.

Marcel, Gabriel (1889–1973) French Christian *existentialist. A Catholic convert, Marcel disliked this label, but his meditations upon the central concepts of the Christian life have a characteristic existentialist flavour. His emphasis on the personal nature of 'mystery' as opposed to the external nature of mere problems has had some influence in religious circles. His works include *Être et avoir* (1935, trs. as *Being and Having*, 1949), *The Mystery of Being* (1951), the transcription of his Gifford lectures at Aberdeen, and *The Existentialist Background of Human Dignity* (1963), the transcription of his William James lectures at Harvard.

Marcus, Ruth Barcan (1921–) American logician and philosopher, best-known for her work on systems of modal logic. Marcus gained her PhD at Yale in 1946, and subsequently held posts at Illinois-Chicago and Northwestern before becoming Halleck professor at Yale. Her seminal papers showed how formal languages could consistently combine names and *quantificational structure with modal operators, contrary to the prevailing negative opinion energetically voiced by *Quine. Marcus has also made significant contributions to *deontic logic. A doughty champion of analytic rigour, Marcus has been a formidable opponent of *continental and literary tendencies in Anglo-American philosophy. Her papers are collected in *Modalities: Philosophical Essays* (1993). *See also* BARCAN FORMULA; IDENTITY, NECESSITY OF; MODAL LOGIC.

Marcus Aurelius *See* AURELIUS, MARCUS.

Marcuse, Herbert (1898–1979) Political and social theorist. Marcuse was born in Berlin, and became associated with the *Frankfurt school. His early work was a synthesis of *Marxism, *phenomenology, and *existentialism. In 1934 he fled Nazi Germany to America and began teaching at Columbia university, subsequently holding posts with the Office of Strategic Services and the Office of Intelligence Research. He held posts at Brandeis (1954) and at San Diego (1965). His first work in English, *Reason and Revolution* (1941), is an introduction to Hegel and Marx, while *Eros and Civilization* (1955) ropes Freud into the cause of sketching a non-repressive society. Marcuse's fame rests largely on his elevation to 'Father of the New Left' when his book *One-Dimensional Man* (1964) became a bible of radical student movements of the 1960s. Like other analysts of the Frankfurt school, and theorists such as *Gramsci, Marcuse argued that the workers in modern society were stupefied by the products of their own labour; revolution, therefore, must come from those outside the system, such as students, intellectuals, and minorities.

Maritain, Jacques (1882–1973) French *Thomist philosopher, most influential during his teaching years at the Institut Catholique in Paris, from 1914. Initially a Protestant, Maritain was educated at the Sorbonne. He and his wife converted to Catholicism in 1906, partly under the influence of *Bergson. From 1945 to 1948 Maritain was French ambassador to the Vatican. His work sought to sustain an Aristotelian and Thomistic 'realism' against the subjectivism of philosophy since *Descartes. This involved recognizing multiple ways of knowing, and Maritain is also remembered for his work on non-conceptual knowledge, as occurring in moments of mysticism and of poetic intuition. His many works include *Distinguer pour unir* (1932, trs. as *The Degrees of Knowledge*, 1959) and *Humanisme intégral* (1936, trs. as *True Humanism*, 1938).

markets In property-owning societies there will arise opportunities for exchange. Since property is itself a social institution, society will have a stake in ensuring that the terms of exchange are fair and that limits of exchange and property are set, so that some things, such as the labour of children, should not be traded at market prices. Extreme political and economic *libertarianism denies that anything other than the free operation of markets themselves is needed to solve this and practically all other political problems. Extreme *communism takes the diametrically opposing line that the social evils of exploitation and injustice can only be solved by eliminating private property itself. *See also* IDEAL MARKET, MARXISM.

Marsilius of Padua (Marsiglio) (1275/80–1342) Probably educated at Padua, Marsilius was rector of the university of Paris in 1313. His philosophical fame rests on *Defensor Pacis* ('Defender of the Peace', 1324, trs. under the same title, 1956), a devastating indictment of Papal claims to temporal power. Marsilius defends an Aristotelian theory of the political state as subserving the good life. Law is essentially the coercive power of the state necessary to promote this end. The people therefore form the only legitimate source of political authority. The positivist and republican implications of all this were well before their time; in 1326 Marsilius was forced to flee to the court of Louis of Bavaria and was branded a heretic by Pope John XXII.

Martineau, Harriet (1802–76) Pioneering feminist and social theorist. Born of Huguenot family in Norwich, Martineau earned her own financial independence by journalism and writing books, in particular using fiction to illustrate the new science of political economy. These writings gave her the independence to travel, and she used a visit to America to produce *Society in America* (1837) and *Retrospect of Western Travel* (1838). These empirical studies came at the same time as her foundational treatise on sociological data collection, *How to Observe Morals and Manners* (1838). This book articulated the principles and methods of empirical social research, covering such matters as social class, religion, suicide, national character, domestic relations, and women's status. Having lost her Unitarian religion, in 1851 she translated Comte's *Cours de philosophie positive* into English.

Martineau, James (1805–1900) Unitarian minister and philosopher of religion. The brother of Harriet *Martineau was born in Norwich in 1805. He was ordained in the Unitarian ministry in 1828, and served as a minister in Dublin and Liverpool. In 1841 he was appointed professor of moral philosophy at Manchester New College. While at Manchester he published his first influential book, *Endeavours After the Christian Life* (1843). In 1869 he became principal of the college. He wrote several books on religion and philosophy including *A Study of Spinoza* (1882), *Types of Ethical Theory* (1885), *A Study of Religion* (1888), and the *Seat of Authority in Religion* (1890).

m

Marx, Karl (1818–83) The founder of revolutionary communism. Marx was born in Trier, and studied law at the university of Bonn, then history and philosophy at Berlin. From 1841 he worked on a radical newspaper, the *Rheinische Zeitung*. In 1843 Marx married and moved to Paris, where he met *Engels. His principal work of this time was the text now known as *The Economic and Philosophical Manuscripts of 1844*, which were published in the 1930s. During the period he was distancing himself from the young *Hegelians, and studying the work of the British political economists Adam *Smith, David Ricardo (1772–1823), and James *Mill. In the *Manuscripts* Marx introduces the pivotal concept of *alienation, and takes issue with the tradition of political economy that takes inequality as a natural fact, failing to understand its social creation. The *Theses on Feuerbach* (written 1845) and *The German Ideology* (1846) begin Marx's concern with the different forms of human society, and their evolutionary succession in response to '*contradictions' or irresoluble tensions between the different classes, or productive forces, in society. In 1848 Marx settled in London, where the most famous of his writings, *The Communist Manifesto*, was completed. Marx's theoretical account of human society and its economics found its final monument in *Capital*, whose three volumes appeared in 1867, 1885, and 1893. *See also* BASE AND SUPERSTRUCTURE, DIALECTICAL MATERIALISM, HISTORICAL MATERIALISM, LABOUR THEORY OF VALUE.

SEE WEB LINKS

- An audio discussion of Marxist philosophy by three experts
- An archive of writings by and on Marx

Marxism Theoretically, Marxism is an adherence to at least some of the central ideas of *Marx. These will typically include perceiving the social world in terms of categories of class as defined by relationships to economic and productive processes, belief in the development of society beyond the capitalist phase towards a revolution of the proletariat, in economics the *labour theory of value, and above all rejection of the *exploitation inherent in private control of productive processes. Practically, Marxism is a commitment to the exploited and oppressed classes, and to the revolution that should better their position.

masculinity *See* GENDER.

Masham, Damaris (1658–1708) The daughter of *Cudworth and close friend of *Locke, who lived with her and her husband in the last period of his life, from 1691 to 1704, at their house Oates in Essex. She was an early protagonist of women's education, and corresponded with Leibniz. She wrote *A Discourse Concerning the Love of God* (1696) in reply to the writer John *Norris, and *Occasional Thoughts in Reference to a Christian Life* (1694), the latter an appeal to women to study intelligently the grounds of their religious belief.

masked man fallacy Fallacy allegedly committed by *Descartes, when he supposes that since he can know things about his mind while not knowing them about his body, his mind cannot be identical with his body. This, according to the charge, is like arguing that since I can know who my father is without knowing who the masked man is, the masked man cannot be my father. It is doubtful whether Descartes made such a superficial mistake.

mass noun A noun classifying a type of stuff (e.g. wool, tobacco) rather than a kind of thing (sweater, cigarette); generally contrasted with a *count noun.

master argument The master argument of Diodorus Cronus (*fl.* *c.*3rd c. BC) seems designed to show that nothing is possible which neither is nor will be true. It proceeded by finding an inconsistency between three propositions: everything that is past is necessary, the impossible does not follow from the possible, what neither is nor will be is possible. If these are inconsistent, and the first two are true, then the conclusion follows, but modern modal logic does not sustain the argument. *Berkeley's argument that it is impossible to have an idea of a tree of which nobody is conscious (for your having the idea of it makes it true that someone is conscious of it) is also referred to as his master argument.

master/slave morality A stage in the evolution of moral and political consciousness, described in the *Phenomenology of Spirit* (1807) of *Hegel, and subsequently influential on many theories of freedom and history. On emerging from the *state of nature, there is a 'moment' of consciousness in which one party enslaves the other. The slave, involved in production and activity, is conscious of ends in his or her life, whilst the master retreats to a meaningless state of leisure and consumption. Neither can give the other the recognition and acknowledgement that is required if a person is to have value in his or her own eyes. An initial response to this impasse is a retreat to *Stoicism, and then to the 'unhappy consciousness' of religion. However, the slave at least achieves a self-consciousness through his or her own activity. The inner freedom thus acquired allows an overthrow of the master, and the *dialectical cycle returns until a higher, Kantian, 'moment' is achieved when respect for each other as ends emerges from the process.

material adequacy condition *See* CONVENTION T.

material cause *See* CAUSES: MATERIAL, FORMAL, EFFICIENT, FINAL.

material contradiction There are processes such as fire that consumes itself, or capitalism that arguably brings about its own collapse, that contain the seeds of their own destruction. In *Marxist thought it is found useful to put this by saying that they thereby embody contradictions. Marxism also derives from *Hegel the idea that at any point in the historical process adequate descriptions of reality must embody contradictions, which are there to be overcome.

material implication The *truth function of two propositions *p*, *q*, defined as false if *p* is true and *q* false, but true in the other three cases. It is normally written $p \rightarrow q$. The first logician to distinguish the four ways in which truth-values can be associated with two propositions (TT, TF, FT, FF), and to suggest identifying 'if *p* then *q*' as the proposition true in every case except the second, was probably Philo of Megara, in the 4th century BC. *See also* MATERIAL IMPLICATION, PARADOXES OF.

material implication, paradoxes of The *truth function of material implication gives a proposition $p \rightarrow q$ which is true except in the case in which *p* is true and *q* is false. It also corresponds fairly well to the *conditional form 'If *p* then *q*'. But whenever *p* is false, $p \rightarrow q$ is true, and whenever *q* is true, $p \rightarrow q$ is true. So 'If Paddington Station is in France, London is in England' is true (it has a true consequent) and 'If the moon is made of cheese, it is made of ketchup' is true (it has a false antecedent). The 'paradox' is not a genuine paradox, but puts some pressure on the identification of the conditional form as it is found in natural languages, with material implication.

materialism In philosophy, the view that the world is entirely composed of matter. Philosophers now tend to prefer the term *physicalism, since physics has shown that matter itself resolves into forces and energy, and is just one amongst other physically respectable denizens of the universe. Materialism in this philosophical sense has a history stretching back to Greek *atomism, and emerges in the modern period in *Hobbes's *Leviathan*, and the works of *La Mettrie. It is opposed to mind–body dualism, and bears uneasy relations to realism about *universals and other abstract entities.

In this sense materialism has nothing to do with the excessive desire for goods and wealth, which is a different meaning of the term, although the ambiguity is frequently exploited in polemics against an undifferentiated 'materialism'. *See also* CENTRAL STATE MATERIALISM, DIALECTICAL MATERIALISM, HISTORICAL MATERIALISM.

material mode of speech *See* FORMAL/MATERIAL MODE OF SPEECH.

materia prima (Latin, first or prime matter) The primary matter is the indeterminate common nature, which needs a specific principle or form determining the substance that actually exists at any time. Prime matter is related to specific forms as potential is to actual. Matter without form is indescribable since only its form gives the specific differences whereby we can refer to any substance. The term is deployed in *Aristotelian and *scholastic thought in order to describe change in the physical world. Consider the way one substance (an acorn, a living body) may change into another (an oak tree or earth). There must be something common to the original and the later state, for otherwise the one would not change into the other, but would cease to exist and be replaced by something else entirely. The concept formed a major target for 17th-century proponents of the new scientific or *corpuscularian view, such as *Boyle and *Locke, although perhaps ironically Locke is attacked by *Berkeley for his adherence to a parallel notion of *substance. *See also* HYLOMORPHISM, MATTER.

mathematical induction The principle stating that for all properties, given that a property holds of the number 1, and given that when it holds of one number it holds of its successor, then it holds of all positive numbers. When more numbers are introduced, such as rational or real or transfinite numbers, corresponding principles of induction may be used to prove properties of all of them.

mathematical logic A term for modern formal *logic, particularly those *logical calculi powerful enough to express classical mathematics.

mathematics, philosophy of The philosophy of mathematics attempts to explain both the nature of mathematical facts and entities, and the way in which we have our knowledge of both. Modern philosophy of mathematics began with the foundational studies of *Cantor, *Dedekind, and K. T. W. Weierstrass in the late 19th century. It received its fundamental impulse from the work of *Frege and *Russell on the relations between numbers, sets, and logic. The *logicist programme in the philosophy of mathematics, culminating in Russell and *Whitehead's great *Principia Mathematica* of 1910–13, attempted to reduce mathematics to logic, in the sense of proving that all of mathematics could be represented in a system whose axioms were simply axioms of pure logic. It is generally thought that the programme failed over the need to admit sets as entities subject to their own particular axioms, whose logical status was not at all obvious. At the beginning of the 20th century the place of *set theory in mathematics was well established, but the contradictions of naive set theory, and the sheer scale of the full transfinite hierarchy, divided mathematicians into several camps, reflecting different philosophies of mathematics. Full-scale *realism or *Platonism takes mathematical entities to be real, independent objects of study about which discoveries (and mistakes) can be made. *Constructivism takes it that we ourselves construct what we talk about. *Formalism assimilates mathematics to the purely syntactic process of following proof procedures, without any question being raised about the interpretation of the *theorems proved. The Achilles heel of formalism has always been the application of mathematics in our best descriptions of the world, so realism and constructivism have emerged as the main contrasting ideologies. The division has mathematical consequences. For the realist there is no problem in admitting completed infinite collections, whether or not we have an effective method of specifying their members. For the constructivist this will be inadmissible.

Quite apart from this issue modern debates on the epistemology of mathematics have been infected by the general flight from the category of **a priori* knowledge. Suggestions taking its place include the general *conventionalism associated with *Wittgenstein, the view that *abstract objects such as sets are not so frightening after all, and indeed are in fact perceptible, and the view that the general success of science, of which mathematics is an indispensable part, affords an argument for the truth of mathematics.

matter That which occupies space, possessing size and shape, mass, movability, and solidity (which may be the same as impenetrability). Its nature was historically one of the great subjects of philosophy, now largely pursued through the philosophy of physics. *Plato and *Aristotle passed on a classification of matter into four kinds (earth, air, water, and fire) but also the view (not necessarily held by Aristotle himself) that any such division reflected a different form taken by one prime, undifferentiated matter or **hylē* (*see* MATERIA PRIMA). In Aristotle there is also a fifth kind of matter (*quintessence) found in the celestial world, whose possessors were thereby exempt from change. This physics was replaced from the 17th century onwards by the classical conception first of corpuscles (*see* CORPUSCULARIANISM) and then of modern atoms. In modern physics, the tidy picture of inert massy atoms on the one hand, and forces between them on the other, has entirely given way. The *quantum mechanical description of fundamental particles blurs the distinction between matter and its energy, and between particles and the forces that describe their interaction. Philosophically, however, quantum mechanics leaves considerable unease of its own.

matter of fact In *Hume, objects of knowledge are divided into matters of fact (roughly, empirical things known by means of impressions) and relations of ideas. The contrast, also called *Hume's fork, is a version of the **a priori/a posteriori* distinction, but reflects the 17th- and early 18th-century belief that the *a priori* is established by chains of intuitive comparison of ideas. *See also* DEMONSTRATION, RELATIONS OF IDEAS.

maxim Generally, any simple and memorable rule or guide for living: 'neither a borrower nor a lender be', etc. Tennyson speaks of 'a little hoard of maxims preaching down a daughter's heart' (*Locksley Hall*), and maxims have generally been associated with a 'folksy' or 'copy-book' approach to morality. In the usage of *Kant, each action proceeds according to a maxim or subjective principle in accordance with which it is performed. The first form of the *categorical imperative asserts that one can tell whether an action is right by seeing whether its maxim can consistently be willed to be universal law.

maximin principle A principle of *decision theory, that counsels that at least in some circumstance, the right decision is that which maximizes the minimum outcome: i.e., that which makes the worst outcome as good as can be. The principle is often described as risk-aversive. It is a key component in the influential work *A Theory of Justice* (1971) by *Rawls. *See also* DIFFERENCE PRINCIPLE.

maya (Sanskrit, the veil of illusion) The way in which the world is experienced and which disguises the true unity of reality (*see also* ATMAN, BRAHMAN).

Mead, George Herbert (1863–1931) Influential American pragmatist. Mead was educated at Oberlin College, graduating in 1883. He subsequently studied at Harvard, Leipzig, and Berlin. From 1891 he worked at Michigan, where he became the friend and collaborator of John *Dewey, under whose aegis he moved to Chicago in 1894. His influence was probably most pronounced in social psychology, where he attempted to show the origins of human personality and self-consciousness in processes of 'symbolic interaction', of both gestures and language. Mead never published a book, but his papers were collected in four volumes, *The Philosophy of the Present* (1932), edited by Arthur E. Murphy; *Mind, Self, and Society* (1934), edited by Charles W. Morris; *Movements of Thought in the Nineteenth Century* (1936), edited by Merritt H. Moore; and *The Philosophy of the Act* (1938), Mead's Carus Lectures of 1930, edited by Charles W. Morris.

mean (ethical) In many ethical systems the right path is presented as one that strikes a happy medium. It strays neither one way nor the other, but represents moderation, harmony, balance, and the avoidance of pitfalls on either side. *Aristotle's doctrine of the mean represents all virtues as striking a balance between vices of excess and vices of defect. The man who fears everything is a coward, but the man who fears nothing is rash; the man who indulges every pleasure is self-indulgent, but the man who indulges none is a boor. A similar idea was already present in the *Philebus* of *Plato and is derived from *Pythagoras. The doctrine is prominent in *Confucianism: in the *Analects*, Confucius writes of the harmonious life as one avoiding excesses and deficiencies, and in which wisdom is gleaned from both old and young, low and high. K'ung Chi, the grandson of Confucius, wrote a work entitled the *Chung Yung*, or mean of equilibrium and harmony. The anonymous work *The Doctrine of the Mean* was a basic text for civil service examinations in China from 1313 until 1905. In the *Buddhist *System of the Middle Way* the principle repudiates both exaggerated asceticism and easy-going hedonism. The term 'golden mean' is from the Latin poet Horace, whose *aurea mediocritas* is described in *Odes* 2. 10. 5.

mean (mathematical) That which occupies a middle position. In mathematics an arithmetical mean of n quantities is their sum, divided by the number n. The geometrical mean of n quantities is the nth root of their product. The harmonic mean is the reciprocal of the arithmetical mean of their reciprocals. In statistics the mean value of a distribution of a *random variable x is a weighted mean of its values, where the weight of a value $f(x)$ is the probability of the value. The mode of a distribution is the most common value, and the median is the value such that the probabilities of x being less than or greater than this value are each 0·5 (or as near 0·5 as the distribution permits).

meaning Whatever it is that makes what would otherwise be mere sounds and inscriptions into instruments of communication and understanding. The philosophical problem is to demystify this power, and to relate it to what we know of ourselves and the world. Contributions to this study include the theory of *speech acts and the investigation of communication and the relationship between words and *ideas, and words and the world. For particular problems *see* CONTENT, IDEAS, INDETERMINACY OF TRANSLATION, INSCRUTABILITY OF REFERENCE, LANGUAGE, PREDICATION, REFERENCE, RULE-FOLLOWING, SEMANTICS, TRANSLATION, and the topics referred to under headings associated with LOGIC. The loss of confidence in determinate meaning ('every decoding is another encoding') is an element common both to *postmodernist uncertainties in the theory of criticism, and to the analytic tradition that follows writers such as *Quine.

meaning postulates Term employed by *Carnap as a proposed explanation of *analyticity. The idea is that we can lay down a logical connection (x is a bachelor $\rightarrow$ x is not married) as a postulate governing the two predicates 'bachelor' and 'married'; the analyticity that all bachelors are unmarried is then exhibited as a logical consequence of a convention that we have adopted. The approach was attacked by *Quine and others, both as presupposing that central or obvious truths achieve the status of conventions when there is no reason for them to do so, and as failing as a general account of necessity since it requires a separate account of the status of logic.

means–ends reasoning Working out how to adapt means to ends is one characteristic function of reason. The controversial claim, associated with *Hume and *Weber, is that such instrumental or technical rationality exhausts the place of reason in practical affairs. On such an account, questions of ends are not subject to reason, but are non-rational matters of emotion or desire; reason therefore cannot adjudicate between conflicting ends, but only tell us how to achieve them. To many the equation of reason with instrumental reasoning is a symptom of industrial, technical societies. *See also* DISENCHANTMENT, NATURAL LAW THEORY.

measurement The fundamental concepts of the theory of measurement are that of a quantity being measured, an empirical determination for a lesser, equal, or greater amount of the quantity, and then a rule assigning numerical values to the quantities empirically determined. Different quantities are therefore represented by different numbers. The rule must require procedures for assigning the same numerals to the same things under the same conditions, and it must be non-degenerate, in the sense that the rule allows for the possibility of assigning different numerals to different things, or the same thing under different conditions. The rule then defines a scale from the least value of the quantity to the greatest. Moh's hardness scale is an ordering of minerals from the softest (talc, 1) to the hardest (diamond, 10). Such a scale gives no sense to the idea of one point on the scale (say, orthoclase, 6) being twice as hard as another (calcite, 3), nor to the question of whether the difference between one pair of intervals on the scale is the same as that of another. In the terminology of Brian Ellis, *Basic Concepts of Measurement* (1966), Moh's scale is simply an ordering, or an ordinal scale. Features that can be ordered but no more are sometimes called qualitative, or non-metric. If, in addition, formulae providing for the absolute sameness or difference of intervals on the scale can be interpreted, we have an interval scale; if such intervals can be compared we have an ordinal-interval scale; and if $a = nb$ can be interpreted where (a,b) are numbers on the scale and n is any positive integer, we have a ratio scale. The date scales of the calendar are ordinal-interval scales, whereas ordinary scales of mass, length, and time are ratio scales. Questions for the philosophy of science include the nature and objectivity of measurement, the question of whether the same quantity can be measured by scales which are not simple transformations of one another (as the Celsius and Fahrenheit scales of temperature are), and the nature of the considerations, such as mathematical simplicity, that guide the choice of fundamental scales for measuring physical quantities. In particular disciplines, for instance economics, the question of whether a quantity such as utility or welfare is purely qualitative, or is susceptible of more structured measurement, may assume great importance. Similarly philosophical, scientific, and pragmatic considerations affect finding the correct quantities to measure in order to understand multi-dimensional complexes such as an economy or a society.

mechanism The belief that everything can be explained in ways modelled on 17th-century conceptions of scientific explanation. This took its *paradigm from the quantitative laws governing the interactions of particles, in terms of which the other properties of materials could ultimately be understood (*see* ATOMISM, CORPUSCULARIANISM, GALILEAN WORLD VIEW). Mechanism in biology is the view that animals are to be regarded as material systems, and it is as a result hostile to final *causes or *teleology. Modern *physicalism has a more sophisticated conception both of scientific explanation, and of the possibility of reconciling it with teleological explanation, thought of as founded on a basis of natural selection.

median *See* MEAN (MATHEMATICAL).

medical ethics *See* BIOETHICS.

Megarian school The philosophical school centred on Megara, near Athens, from the late 5th to early 3rd century BC, owing something both to *Socrates and to the *Eleatics. The Megarians were notorious for subtle logic-chopping. The founder of the school was Euclides, and the most distinguished member was Philo of Megara.

Meinong, Alexius von (1853–1920) Austrian psychologist and philosopher. A pupil of *Brentano at the university of Vienna, Meinong taught at Graz from 1882 until his death. He there established a laboratory for experimental psychology, and in the tradition of Brentano his philosophical interests derived very largely from the problems of establishing a satisfactory psychology. Meinong's most famous doctrine derives from the problem of *intentionality, which led him to countenance objects, such as the golden mountain, that are capable of being the object of thought, although they do not actually exist. This doctrine was one of the principal targets of *Russell's theory of *definite descriptions. However, it came as part of a complex and interesting package of concepts in the theory of meaning, and scholars are not united in supposing that Russell was fair to it. Meinong's works include *Über Annahmen* (1907, trs. as *On Assumptions*, 1983) and *Über Möglichkeit und Wahrscheinlichkeit* (1915).

meiosis The process of division of sex cells, resulting in the formation of gametes (eggs or sperm cells). In meiosis the nucleus undergoes two separate divisions, but the chromosomes are duplicated only once. So the four daughter cells each possess only half the chromosomes of the parent cell. When the egg and sperm, each with half a complement of chromosomes, unite, the two halves join together, resulting in a fertilized egg with the full number of chromosomes. This is a principal source of the difference between offspring and parents. During meiosis the original chromosomes may break and rejoin with others lying alongside them; this process (crossing over) is also a source of genetic variation. In philosophical discussion of *abortion, it is sometimes suggested that it is only after the joining up process that we have a single entity with the potential for life, and that this separates the morality of abortion from that of birth control.

meliorism Term, possibly coined by George Eliot, for a position midway between pessimism and optimism: the view that the world can be made better by human effort. In political contexts, the view that the world can be made better by government effort, a rather more controversial doctrine.

Melissus of Samos (*fl.* 441–440 BC) Possibly the least influential of the *Eleatic philosophers, but a fine naval commander, since his fleet defeated the Athenians in 441 BC. He was heavily criticized by *Aristotle (*De Sophisticis Elenchis*, 167 b, and *Physics*, 186 a 6). Melissus held a cosmology comparable to that of *Parmenides. He argued that change is impossible, on the grounds that all change involves something becoming nothing; what exists must therefore be eternal, and spatially infinite, and finally incorporeal. Melissus is principally remembered for turning the argument against non-being into an argument against the void, and in favour of the *plenum, although of course it is populated by incorporeal stuff.

meme A meme is a cultural object like the miniskirt, the computer virus, or the belief in ghosts, that can be replicated or passed on, and which in the processes of transmission evolves and seems to have a life of its own. The term was coined by the zoologist Richard Dawkins in his book *The Selfish Gene* (1976): it has affinities with *gene (the unit of biological selection), memory, and *mimesis or imitation. Dawkins's idea is that processes of evolution can occur given any entities that can be replicated. In the abstract, the process does not require that the entities involved are biologically defined. It is controversial whether the idea assists or obstructs attempts to understand cultural change through time.

memory The power of the mind to think of a past that no longer exists poses both empirical, psychological problems, and more abstract philosophical ones. The scientist wants to know how the brain stores its memories, and whether the mechanism is similar for different types of memory, such as short-term and long-term memories. The philosopher is particularly puzzled by the representative power of memory. That is, if I summon up a memory of some event, how do I know to interpret it as representing the past, rather than being a pure exercise of imagination? Is there a specific 'feeling of pastness'? But if so, might I not then have the feeling, but not know to interpret that as a feeling of pastness? Indeed, is there always a present representation, or might memory be a form of direct acquaintance with the past? This might at least give us a justification of the confidence we place in memory. But is not the sceptical hypothesis proposed by *Russell, that the earth might have sprung into existence five minutes ago, with a population that 'remembers' a wholly unreal past, at least logically possible? But if it is logically possible, the question of how we know that this is not what has happened is set to look intractable.

Mencius (Meng Tzu) (371–289 BC) The greatest *Confucian, Mencius was born in Shantung, and studied under the grandson of Confucius, Tzu Ssu. Like Confucius he travelled extensively, vainly trying to persuade rulers to improve their ways, before retiring to write the seven books that make up *The Book of Mencius*. He added to Confucianism the doctrine of the original goodness of human beings, so that the end of learning is to seek the lost state of virtue. The way of righteousness is opposed to utilitarian considerations of advantage and profit. Politically one consequence is that since goodness is inherent in people, they have the right to partake in government and to revolt against bad government.

Mendelssohn, Moses (1729–86) The most influential German Jewish philosopher of the 18th century. Born in Dessau, Mendelssohn received a rabbinic education. He is mainly remembered for his work on aesthetics, which had some influence on *Kant, although his proof of the immortality of the soul (the soul is simple, therefore indestructible) is one of Kant's most famous targets. Mendelssohn was a friend of *Lessing and in his later years became involved in the *Pantheismusstreit* or pantheism controversy, whose ostensible point was whether *Lessing was a closet Spinozist, but which drew all the central

German philosophers of the time into the muddy waters of teleology and theology.

Meno's puzzle *See* LEARNING PARADOX.

mens rea (Latin, a mind to be accused; a guilty mind) In many systems of law, criminal guilt requires not only that an act was performed (*actus reus*) but also that it was performed with an appropriate mind-set. Having the intention to perform a crime is sufficient, but not necessary, to *mens rea*. Foreseeing a side-effect such as a death could count, even if the death is not intended, and reckless negligence could also constitute *mens rea*.

mental causation An adequate conception of mind and its relationship to matter should explain how it is possible for mental events to interact with the rest of the world, and in particular to themselves have a causal influence on the physical world. It is easy to think that this must be impossible: it takes a physical cause to have a physical effect. Yet everyday experience and theory alike show that it is commonplace. Consciousness could hardly have evolved if it had had no uses. In general, it is a measure of the success of any theory of mind and body that it should enable us to avoid *epiphenomenalism.

m

Mentalese *See* LANGUAGE OF THOUGHT.

mental events The events of feeling, thinking, willing, and so on that make up the conscious life of an individual. The issue of whether mental events are identical with complex physical events, or whether such an identity even makes sense, is central to the *mind–body problem. *See also* ANOMALOUS MONISM, PHYSICALISM, TYPE–TYPE IDENTITY THEORY.

mental illness It is reasonably clear that there can be chronic mental malfunction, when people's capacities to respond to the world, to absorb and remember information, respond with appropriate emotions, and form coherent plans are impaired. What is not so clear is that the mind can be the self-contained locus of an illness, or whether mental malfunction should always be thought of as the by-product of physical or bodily illness or impairment. If the former, then the mind might be cured by mental means, such as conversation with a therapist. If the latter, the only effective responses would be medical or pharmacological. So the issue has practical as well as purely philosophical importance.

mentality The possession of a mind, or the kind of mind possessed.

mental reservation The internal act of adding a qualification to, or exploiting an ambiguity in one's words, or privately vowing that one does not mean what one is saying, like children keeping their fingers crossed in order to nullify a promise they are making. Some *casuists argued, unconvincingly, that the private addition of such a reservation may make permissible what would otherwise seem to be a lie. *Hume made the stout Scottish response that it might do when it came to questions of salvation, but it would not be allowed in affairs of business.

mention (and use) of words *See* USE/MENTION DISTINCTION.

mereological sum The mereological sum of two elements is the whole that consists of both of them, regardless of their spatial or other distance. The notion is not the same as that of the *set whose members are the pair of objects: a mereological sum of two spatial objects is itself a larger spatial object, whereas a set is not.

mereology The logic of the relationship of part to whole. The subject was pioneered by *Lesniewski.

merit A person's merits are his or her admirable qualities. Moral merits usually include such *virtues as benevolence, temperance, justice, mercy, etc. Non-moral merits may include cheerfulness, intelligence, strength, musicality, etc. The basis of the distinction is unclear, especially when lack of moral merit is thought to be a fault, whereas lack of non-moral merit merely argues bad luck. In *Kant, moral merit shrinks to respect for the duty of governing conduct by the *categorical imperative, with everything else a mere handmaiden to this end. At the other end of the scale, in Greek thought, and in *Hume, there is no serious distinction between moral and non-moral merit. *See also* DESERT, MORAL LUCK.

Merleau-Ponty, Maurice (1908–61) French *phenomenologist, who became professor at the Collège de France in 1952. His major work, the *Phénoménologie de la perception* (1945, trs. as *The Phenomenology of Perception*, 1962), anticipates many of the concerns of later analytical philosophy of perception. In particular, Merleau-Ponty emphasizes the way in which our experience does not form a shut-off, private domain, but a way of being-in-the-world; we live our lives in the perceptual milieu of a human world, or *Lebenswelt*, irreducible to pure or private consciousness. Merleau-Ponty's work draws upon empirical psychology as well as the tradition of *Husserl to explore the experiential relationship that we have with the world. His book is particularly notable for its extended and illuminating description of our relationship with our own bodies in perception and action. *See also* BODY.

Mersenne, Marin (1588–1648) A key figure of the French 17th century, Mersenne studied, like *Descartes, at La Flèche, and subsequently taught in Nevers and Paris. Mersenne was a correspondent of all the great mathematicians and scientists of the time, and was described by *Hobbes as 'the pole round which revolved every star in the world of science'. Mersenne's principal philosophical preoccupation was the refutation of Pyrrhonian *scepticism, and the correct acceptance and interpretation of scientific and mathematical knowledge. His attitude to science and mathematics is a forerunner of modern *instrumentalism, for although the Pyrrhonist is right that knowledge of reality is unattainable, science suffices to serve as the guide of our actions. Mersenne's writings include *La Vérité des sciences contre les sceptiques ou pyrrhoniens* ('The Truth of Science against the Sceptics or Pyrrhonians', 1625), and he is the author of the 2nd and 6th sets of Objections to Descartes's *Meditations.* He died in the arms of *Gassendi.

metaethics The second-order activity of investigating the concepts and methods of ethics, rather than directly engaging with practical ('first-order') issues of what to do and how to behave. The distinction is apt to blur, in that different views about the structure of ethics usually have implications for first-order decision making.

metahistory The overarching narrative or 'grand récit' that gives order and meaning to the historical record, especially in the large-scale philosophies of history of writers such as *Hegel, *Marx, or *Spencer.

metalanguage The language in which remarks are made about another language. The language talked of is the object language. The distinction is made by *Tarski, whose reaction to the *semantic paradoxes was that no language could be semantically complete, i.e. capable of saying everything that there is to say. If we take a language capable of saying many things, then nevertheless, on pain of contradiction, it cannot give a *truth definition, defining its own *truth predicate. To discuss truth and falsity in the first or object language, we must ascend a level, to a metalanguage, and so up a hierarchy. The term is abused when any discourse about other sayings (e.g. the discourse of literary criticism) is said to be couched in a metalanguage, since there is here no reason why it should not be in just the same language as the original, and it usually is.

metalogic A theory whose subject-matter is a *logistic system: *see* METAMATHEMATICS.

metamathematics The theory of formal languages powerful enough to serve as the language of mathematics. In a formal metamathematical treatment, the formulae that occur in mathematics: axioms, theorems, and proofs, are treated as themselves mathematical objects, and theorems established about them. Major metamathematical results include *Gödel's theorems and *Church's theorem.

metamerism Two coloured materials are metamers, or form a metameric pair, when they match in colour, but the light they reflect differs in spectral composition. When this is so the surfaces will differ in colour under different incident lighting. The existence of metamerism is a severe difficulty for theories trying to identify *colour of surfaces with the physical nature of reflected light. Interestingly, there is no parallel phenomenon for sound, since sounds composed of different energy levels at different frequencies are heard differently.

metaphilosophy Writing or thinking whose subject is philosophy itself; often large-scale descriptions of the 'death of philosophy' and prophecies of a world in which its place is occupied by poetry, music, or dance. *See also* RORTY.

metaphor The most important figure of speech, in which one subject-matter (sometimes called the tenor) is referred to by a term or sentence (the vehicle) that does not literally describe it: the ship of state, the light of faith, etc. Philosophical problems include deciding how the border between literal and metaphorical meaning is to be drawn (*Nietzsche, for example, thought that literal truth was merely dead or fossilized metaphor), understanding how we interpret metaphors with the speed and certainty which we often manage, and deciding whether metaphors can themselves be vehicles of understanding, or whether they should be regarded only as signposts to literal truths and falsities about the subject-matter.

Particular disputes in philosophy can also centre on the extent to which a phrase is metaphorical, as when philosophers talk about the foundations of knowledge, beliefs in the head, the goodness of God, or abstract objects. In a mixed metaphor, or catachresis, the combination of properties suggested becomes illogical or ridiculous, although even then interpretation need not fail, as when Hamlet contemplates taking up arms against a sea of troubles.

metaphysics According to *Bradley, metaphysics is the finding of bad reasons for what we believe on instinct, although as *Broad remarked, to find these reasons is no less an instinct. Originally a title for those books of *Aristotle that came after the *Physics*, the term is now applied to any enquiry that raises questions about reality that lie beyond or behind those capable of being tackled by the methods of science. Naturally, an immediately contested issue is whether there are any such questions, or whether any text of metaphysics should, in *Hume's words, be 'committed to the flames, for it can contain nothing but sophistry and illusion' (*Enquiry Concerning Human Understanding*, Bk xii, Pt 3). The traditional examples will include questions of *mind and body, *substance and accident, *events, *causation, and the categories of things that exist (*see* ONTOLOGY). The permanent complaint about metaphysics is that in so far as there are real questions in these areas, ordinary scientific method forms the only possible approach to them. Hostility to metaphysics was one of the banners of *logical positivism, and survives in a different way in the scientific *naturalism of writers such as *Quine. Metaphysics, then, tends to become concerned more with the presuppositions of scientific thought, or of thought in general, although here, too, any suggestion that there is one timeless way in which thought has to be conducted meets sharp opposition. A useful distinction was drawn by *Strawson, between descriptive metaphysics, which contents itself with describing the basic framework of concepts with which thought is (perhaps at a time) conducted, as opposed to revisionary metaphysics, which aims for a criticism and revision of some hapless way of thought. Although the possibility of revisionary metaphysics may be doubted, it continues to the present time: *eliminativism in the philosophy of mind and *postmodernist disenchantment with objectivity and truth are conspicuous examples.

metempsychosis The transmigration of the soul, whereby upon death the soul takes up residence in a new body. The doctrine is embedded in the Indian notion of **samsara*, and in the Western tradition is especially associated with *Pythagoras and *Empedocles, and frequently supported by appeals to memories of past lives.

method Since philosophy is largely the activity of reflecting on modes of thought, it is not surprising that its own methods are subject to its scrutiny. While different schools have frequently made claims for the one correct approach to philosophical problems, the march of history has not seen any consensus emerge. The early 20th century was dominated by philosophical attention to the nature of language, issuing in the two schools of *analytical philosophy and *phenomenology. *Logical positivism and later *linguistic philosophy were successors of the former, whilst a more historical approach to the nature of conceptual schemes is one of the legacies of the latter. Currently there is reasonable enthusiasm for a 'naturalism' that sees the activity of philosophy as continuous with that of science, differing mainly in the abstract nature of its problems and subject-matter: *see* NATURALIZED EPISTEMOLOGY. However critics doubt whether there is very much resembling science in the work of thinkers who enjoy this self-image, which can therefore seem more to be a piece of self-deception or science-envy. There is a natural temptation for philosophers to model themselves on the best-accepted paradigms of successful disciplines of the time, be they mathematics, theology, history, linguistics, physics, or neuroscience.

method of doubt Sometimes known as the use of hyperbolic (extreme) doubt, or Cartesian doubt. This is the method of investigating the extent of knowledge and its basis in reason or experience used by *Descartes in the first two *Meditations*. It attempts to put knowledge upon a secure foundation by first inviting us to suspend judgement on any proposition whose truth can be doubted, even as a bare possibility. The standards of acceptance are gradually raised as we are asked to doubt the deliverance of memory, the senses, and even reason, all of which are in principle capable of letting us down. The process is eventually dramatized in the figure of the evil demon, or **malin génie*, whose aim is to deceive us, so that our senses, memories, and reasonings lead us astray. The task then becomes one of finding a demon-proof point of certainty, and Descartes produces this in the famous 'Cogito ergo sum': I think therefore I am. It is on this slender basis that the correct use of our faculties has to be re-established, but it seems as though Descartes has denied himself any materials to use in reconstructing the edifice of knowledge. He has a basis, but no way of building on it without invoking principles that will not be demon-proof, and so will not meet the standards he has apparently set himself. It is possible to interpret him as using 'clear and distinct ideas' to prove the existence of God, whose benevolence then justifies our use of clear and distinct ideas ('God is no deceiver'): this is the notorious Cartesian circle. Descartes's own attitude to this problem is not quite clear: at times he seems more concerned with providing a stable body of knowledge that our natural faculties will endorse, rather than one that meets the more severe standards with which he starts out. For example, in the second set of *Replies* he shrugs off the possibility of 'absolute falsity' of our natural system of belief, in favour of our right to retain 'any conviction so firm that it is quite incapable of being destroyed'. The need to add such natural belief to anything certified by reason is eventually the cornerstone of *Hume's philosophy, and the basis of most 20th-century reactions to the method of doubt. *See also* NATURALIZED EPISTEMOLOGY.

methodological holism *See* INDIVIDUALISM.

methodological individualism *See* INDIVIDUALISM.

methodological solipsism The view that the study of cognitive processes should consider those processes in abstraction from the environment in which the subject is placed. The most powerful motive for this suggestion is the comparison between cognitive processing and the following of a computer program. Any interpretation the elements of a computer program may have in the outside world (such as the fact that the symbol $ means a unit of currency) is irrelevant to the execution of the program. The doctrine may also be motivated by the idea that the psychological states of a person must *supervene upon the states of the brain and on nothing else. Environment indeed affects the state of the brain, but then it is that state alone that creates and fixes the resultant psychology. This line of thought has been severely challenged, notably in the debates over wide and narrow *content.

methodology The general study of method in particular fields of enquiry: science, history, mathematics, psychology, philosophy, ethics. Obviously any field can be approached more or less successfully and more or less intelligently. It is tempting, then, to suppose that there is one right mode of enquiry logically guaranteed to find the truth if any method can. The task of the philosopher of a discipline would then be to reveal the correct method and to unmask counterfeits. Although this belief lay behind much *positivist philosophy of science, few philosophers now subscribe to it. It places too great a confidence in the possibility of a purely **a priori* 'first philosophy', or standpoint beyond that of the working practitioners, from which their best efforts can be measured as good or bad. This standpoint now seems to many philosophers to be a fantasy. The more modest task of methodology is to investigate the methods that are actually adopted at various historical stages of investigation into different areas, with the aim not so much of criticizing but more of systematizing the presuppositions of a particular field at a particular time (*see also* NATURALIZED EPISTEMOLOGY). There is still a role for local methodological disputes within the community of investigators of some phenomenon, with one approach charging that another is unsound or unscientific, but logic and philosophy will not, on the modern view, provide an independent arsenal of weapons for such battles, which indeed often come to seem more like political bids for ascendancy within a discipline.

methods of agreement, concomitant variation, difference *See* MILL'S METHODS.

microcosm *See* MACROCOSM/MICROCOSM.

middle knowledge *See SCIENTIA MEDIA.*

Middle Platonism The last head of the Academy of Athens was Philo of Larissa, who substantially continued the sceptical tradition of *Arcesilaus and *Carneades. Around 88 BC the Academy was disbanded, as philosophers left Athens and fled to Rome before the advance of Mithridates. At this time *Antiochus of Ascalon made a celebrated break with the doctrines of Philo (recorded in Cicero's dialogue, *Lucullus*), instigating a return to the 'Old Academy', or in other words to reliance on a positive science of philosophy, a system owing its inspiration to *Plato. Antiochus himself was extremely close to *Stoicism. New elements, such as an emphasis on the transcendence and immaterial nature of God, an interest in Pythagorean mystical numerology, and the attempt to work out a divine hierarchy of reality, were introduced by Publius Nigidius Figulus (98–45 BC) and Eudorus of Alexandria (*fl. c.*25 BC). These continued with the reconciliation of pagan and Jewish writings by *Philo Judaeus. The times were characterized by a conservative tone, leading philosophers to look to the past and to attempt to prove the essential unity of different philosophical schools, and by a flowering of many forms of occultism and mysticism. Prominent Middle Platonists include *Plutarch, and the overall orientation is shared by many minor figures, of whom the last, *Ammonius Saccus, was the teacher of *Plotinus, with whom a fully-fledged new synthesis, or departure, *Neoplatonism, is born.

middle term *See* SYLLOGISM.

Milesian school (Ionian school) The first *Presocratics were citizens of Miletus, a trading port where Oriental and Egyptian influences could mingle with Greek thought. The upshot was a bold, speculative cosmology, and conviction that rational explanation must start with the identification of the one primary substance, identified by Thales (as in the Babylonian myths) as water. Other Milesian philosophers are *Anaximander and *Anaximenes.

Mill, James (1773–1836) Scottish philosopher, economist, and man of letters. Born in Forfar, Mill was educated at Edinburgh university. Working in London first as a freelance journalist, and subsequently for the East India Company, Mill became friendly with *Bentham and grew to be a leading member of the 'philosophical radicals', the liberal and predominantly utilitarian group that included

John *Austin and the economist David Ricardo (1772–1823). Although most of his writing is an application of utilitarian principles to practical subjects such as education, the liberty of the press, and government, Mill also produced *An Analysis of the Phenomena of the Human Mind* (1829), an elaboration of the *associationist psychology of *Hume and *Hartley. Associationism is an appropriate philosophy of mind to put alongside utilitarianism, since it means that the task of the educator is to bring the student to associate private pleasure with advancement of the public welfare. In spite of Mill's extensive concerns with education, the upbringing of his son J. S. *Mill has generally been regarded as excessively rigorous.

Mill, John Stuart (1806–73) English philosopher and economist, and the most influential liberal thinker of the 19th century. As the son of James *Mill, John Stuart was given an intensive private education, in which he began Greek at the age of 3, and Latin (and six of the Dialogues of Plato) at the age of 8 (Mill himself remarks that the *Theaetetus* might have been a little much for him). As a teenager he was immersed in his father's philosophical and political interests until a nervous breakdown at the age of 20 led to a revaluation, and softening, of his *Benthamite position. Thereafter, influenced by *Saint-Simon and others, Mill maintained a more sophisticated appreciation of the historical forces moulding people's ideas, and a less cynical view of the forces of reaction. From 1831 his friendship with the married Harriet *Taylor was central to Mill's life; in 1849 after the death of her husband they married. In general philosophy, Mill was an *empiricist whose aim was to construct a genuine system of empirical knowledge for use in social and moral affairs as much as in science. To this end he set about rescuing the doctrine from its sceptical, *Humean associations. His major discussion of the foundations of knowledge and inference is the *System of Logic* (1843), whose six books treat of deductive inference in general, mathematical knowledge, induction (*see* MILL'S METHODS), observation, abstraction and classification, fallacies, and finally social, political, and moral sciences. His distinctions, between *connotation and denotation, and between general and *singular terms, influenced the later semantics of *Frege (who, however, roundly rejected his empiricist 'pebble and gingerbread' view of arithmetic); while his work on induction is still the foundation of methodologies of discovering causal laws. As in his later *Examination of Sir William Hamilton's Philosophy* (1865), Mill's project is that which has subsequently been called *naturalized epistemology: the attempt to understand mental operations as the upshot of known laws of psychology working on the data of experience.

In ethics, Mill is best remembered for his *Utilitarianism* (1861 in *Fraser's Magazine*, 1863 as a separate publication), and *On Liberty* (1859). Each is a classic of its kind, although *Utilitarianism* suffers a Victorian strain in its combination of hedonism with distinctions of quality between pleasures, as well as an uneasy blend of act-utilitarian and rule-utilitarian elements (*see* UTILITARIANISM). It was the principal target of all subsequent critics of utilitarianism, and especially the idealists *Green and *Bradley. *On Liberty* is the classic defence of the principle of freedom of thought and discussion, arguing that the 'sole end for which mankind are warranted, individually or collectively, in interfering with the liberty of action of any of their number, is self-protection'. Among his other works, Mill wrote *Principles of Political Economy* (1848), and *The Subjection of Women* (1861, published in 1869).

SEE WEB LINKS

- An audio discussion of Mill by three experts
- Bibliographies of writings by or on Mill

millenarianism Any religious movement that predicts the collapse of the world order as we know it, with its replacement by the millennium, or period of justice, equality, salvation, etc. Millenarian movements are thought to be an extreme example of the use of religion as a 'way out' or reaction to social stress and its resulting **anomie*. They are found within Christianity and Islam, and in the cargo-cults of Melanesia.

millet seed paradox A version of the *sorites paradox, although associated with *Zeno's paradox, as it concerns the creation of a finite quantity from enough cases of 'nothing'. A single millet seed falling makes no noise. And for any number n, $n \times 0 = 0$. But a finite number of millet seeds falling, or in other words a multiplication of these zero noises, is a discernible finite noise.

Mill's methods (Mill's canons) The five inductive principles proposed by J. S. *Mill as those regulating scientific enquiry. They are: (i) The method of agreement. If two cases of a phenomenon share only one feature, that feature is their cause or their effect. (ii) The method of difference. If a case in which a phenomenon occurs, and one in which it does not, differ by only one other feature, that feature is the cause, or a necessary part of the cause, of the phenomenon, or it is its effect. (iii) The joint method of agreement and difference. This combines the previous two. (iv) The method of residues. If we subtract from a phenomenon what is already known to be the effect of some antecedent events, then the remainder is the result of the remaining antecedents. (v) The method of concomitant variation. Phenomena that vary together are linked through some causal relationship. While the methods make good scientific sense they do depend upon a preceding analysis of the relevant factors, and they are not immediately applicable to cases where causation proceeds more 'holistically', or in virtue of a field of interlocking factors.

Mimamsa (Sanskrit, investigation) One of the six orthodox schools (**darshanas*) of Hindu philosophy, and the most concerned to interpret the texts of the *Vedas as a system of ritual. The fundamentalism of Mimamsa includes a reverential, non-conventional view of the nature of the meaning of the Sanskrit language in which the scriptures were written. In this school, as in some modern theology, ritual and worship become ends in themselves, with the actual divine dropping out of sight by comparison. Like the Vedas, Mimamsa conceives of heaven as a positive goal, rather than as the release from the cycles of living, as in other Indian schools.

mimesis (Greek, imitation) A key concept in *Plato's troubled relationship with artistic activity. The artist who produces imitations of things seems to be some kind of deceiver; at best concerned only to represent appearances and not reality itself (*Republic*, Bk x). The artist is therefore a collaborator in **eikasia*: things are already imitations of their *forms, and imitations of imitations take us a long way from knowledge. Plato did not assign the artist a significant role in taking us towards acquaintance with the form of *beauty, or beauty itself.

mind, philosophy of The philosophy of mind seeks to answer such questions as: is mind distinct from matter? Can we define what it is to be conscious, and can we give principled reasons for deciding whether other creatures are conscious, or whether machines might be made so that they are conscious? What are thinking, feeling, experience, remembering? Is it useful to divide the functions of the mind up, separating memory from intelligence, or rationality from sentiment, or do mental functions form an integrated whole? The dominant philosophies of mind in the current Western tradition include varieties of *physicalism and *functionalism. For particular topics *see also* COGNITION, EMOTION, LANGUAGE, MEMORY, MIND–BODY PROBLEM.

mind–body problem For many people understanding the place of mind in nature is the greatest philosophical problem. Mind is often thought to be the last domain that stubbornly resists scientific understanding, and philosophers differ over whether they find that a cause for celebration or scandal. The mind-body problem in the modern era was given its definitive shape by *Descartes, although the *dualism that he espoused is far more widespread and far older, occurring in some form wherever there is a religious or philosophical tradition whereby the soul may have an existence apart from the body. While most modern philosophies of mind would reject the imaginings that lead us to think that this makes sense, there is no consensus over the best way to integrate our understanding of people as bearers of physical properties on the one hand and as subjects of mental lives on the other. *See also* CONSCIOUSNESS, EPIPHENOMENALISM, FUNCTIONALISM, OCCASIONALISM, PERCEPTION, PHYSICALISM.

minimalism A minimal theory of a term or concept rejects the idea that it is a substantial focus for theory. A minimal theory of truth, for example, holds that there is no general problem about what makes sentences or propositions true; a minimal theory of value holds that there is nothing useful to say in general about values and valuing. Minimalist approaches arise when the prospects for a substantial meta-theory about some term seem dim. They are thus consonant with suspicion of '*first philosophy', or the possibility of a standpoint over and above involvement in some aspect of our activities, from which those activities can be surveyed and described. Minimalism is frequently associated with the anti-theoretical aspects of the later work of *Wittgenstein, and has also been charged with being a fig-leaf for philosophical bankruptcy or anorexia. *See also* DISQUOTATIONAL THEORY OF TRUTH, IRREALISM, QUIETISM, REDUNDANCY THEORY OF TRUTH.

minor premise *See* SYLLOGISM.

minor term *See* SYLLOGISM.

miracle (Latin, *miror*, I wonder at) *Augustine propounds a subjective definition of a miracle: it is 'whatever is hard or appears unusual beyond the expectation or comprehension of the observer'. It is only our habits of mind, therefore, that prevent us from seeing the entire cosmos as the miracle that it is, and that it would appear to be to someone who could see for the first time. In the medieval period the idea arises that a miracle is something special, 'contra consuetum cursum naturae' (contrary to the usual course of nature). The rise of the concept of hard, mechanical *laws of nature in the 17th century set the stage for the definitive account of *Hume in his famous essay 'On Miracles' (1750): 'A miracle may be accurately defined, a transgression of a law of nature by a particular volition of the Deity, or by the interposition of some invisible agent.' Hume argues that it can never be reasonable to believe in such an event on the evidence of human testimony, at least when that testimony is being used in support of a system of religion. For a miracle needs to be quite outside the normal run of things, whereas human 'knavery and folly', the kind of thing that leads to false or misunderstood reportage, is a recognized and regular natural occurrence. So the chance of any report being due to knavery or folly is always greater than the chance of it being due to an event that is quite outside the normal run of things. Hence, they provide the better explanation of the testimony. Hume was aware that a consilience of independent and otherwise creditable testimonies might reasonably lead to people supposing that something they would have regarded as miraculous has actually happened, but he thought the condition was never met in religious contexts, where *enthusiasm, piety, and other emotions clouded judgement.

mixture of labour *See* PROPERTY.

mnemic causation (Greek, *mnēmē*, memory) The causal relation existing between an earlier event and a subsequent episode of remembering it. The term was used by *Russell but is not current, because there may be such a relation without the causation being of a special type, for instance if we suppose the *memory to be carried by traces in the brain. The relation between the *content of the memory and the early event is what is so special.

m

modality The modality of a proposition is the way in which it is true or false. The most important division is between propositions true of necessity, and those true as things are: necessary as opposed to contingent propositions. Other qualifiers sometimes called modal include the tense indicators 'It will be the case that *p*' or 'It was the case that *p*', and there are affinities between the *deontic indicators 'it ought to be the case that *p*' or 'it is permissible that *p*', and the logical modalities. *See also* MODAL LOGIC.

modal logic A logic studying the notions of necessity and possibility. Modal logic was of great importance historically, particularly in the light of various doctrines concerning the necessary properties of the deity, but was not a central topic of modern logic in its golden period at the beginning of the 20th century. It was, however, revived by C. I. *Lewis, by adding to a *propositional or *predicate calculus two operators, $\Box$ and $\Diamond$ (sometimes written N and M), meaning necessarily and possibly, respectively. Theses like $p \rightarrow \Diamond p$ and $\Box p \rightarrow p$ will be wanted. Controversial theses include $\Box p \rightarrow \Box\Box p$ (if a proposition is necessary, it is necessarily necessary, characteristic of the system known as S4) and $\Diamond p \rightarrow \Box\Diamond p$ (if a proposition is possible, it is necessarily possible, characteristic of the system known as S5). The classical *model theory for modal logic, due to *Kripke and the Swedish logician Stig Kanger, involves valuing propositions not as true or false *simpliciter*, but as true or false at *possible worlds, with necessity then corresponding to truth in all worlds, and possibility to truth in some world. Various different systems of modal logic result from adjusting the accessibility relation between worlds. *See* KRIPKE SEMANTICS.

modal realism The doctrine advocated by David *Lewis, that different *possible worlds are to be thought of as existing exactly as this one does. Thinking in terms of possibilities is thinking of real worlds where things are different. The view has been charged with making it impossible to see why it is good to save the child from drowning, since there is still a possible world in which she (or her *counterpart) drowned, and from the standpoint of the universe it should make no difference which world is actual. Critics also charge either that the notion fails to fit with a coherent theory of how we know about possible worlds, or with a coherent theory of why we are interested in them, but Lewis denied that any other way of interpreting modal statements is tenable.

mode Term used in *scholastic philosophy for a determination, a focusing of being in the abstract into some specific form. In the modern era the term is made prominent by *Locke (*Essay*, ii. 12). Modes are introduced as one kind of complex idea, and are distinguished into simple modes, which are 'different combinations of the same simple idea' (Locke cites numbers, such as a dozen or a score), and mixed modes, which are 'compounded of simple ideas of several kinds, put together to make one complex one' (Locke cites beauty and theft). Later, fundamental qualities of space, time, and sense are described as simple modes, and mixed modes become 'scattered and independent ideas, put together by the mind': again, the central examples remain the ideas connected with action, and moral and legal categories. The idea is that in these areas we can mix ideas to make definitions according to our purposes, whereas in science finding the right words is a matter of tracking the kinds of substances, with their different essences, that independently exist. In *Berkeley and *Hume there is no distinction between modes and qualities. For *Spinoza there is a fundamental distinction between substance and its modes, and ordinary objects are in fact modes of the one real substance, identified equally as the universe, or God.

model (logic), A model for a set of sentences is an *interpretation under which they are all true. *See also* MODEL THEORY.

model (science) A representation of one system by another, usually more familiar, whose workings are supposed analogous to that of the first. Thus one might model the behaviour of sound waves upon that of waves in water, or the behaviour of a gas upon that of a volume containing moving billiard balls. Whilst nobody doubts that models have a useful *heuristic role in science, there has been intense debate over whether a good explanation of some phenomenon needs a model, or whether an organized structure of laws from which it can be deduced suffices for scientific explanation. The debate was inaugurated by *Duhem in his *The Aim and Structure of Physical Theory* (1906), which attacked the 'shallow' pictorial imaginings of British physicists, contrasting them with the pure deductive structures of proper science. Models often represent simplifications and idealizations (perfect gases, frictionless planes, perfectly elasic collisions) and even while fertile and useful can be approximations to more complex real phenomena.

model theory The use of a *model to test for the consistency of an *axiomatized system is older than modern logic. Descartes's algebraic interpretation of Euclidean geometry provides a way of showing that if the theory of real numbers is consistent, so is the geometry. Similar mappings had been used by mathematicians in the 19th century, for example to show that if Euclidean geometry is consistent, so are various non-Euclidean geometries. Model theory is the general study of this kind of procedure: the study of *interpretations of formal systems. *Proof theory studies relations of deducibility between formulae of a system, but once the notion of an *interpretation is in place we can ask whether a formal system meets certain conditions. In particular, can it lead us from sentences that are true under some interpretation to ones that are false under the same interpretation? And if a sentence is true under all interpretations, is it also a theorem of the system? We can define a notion of validity (a formula is valid if it is true in all interpretations) and semantic consequence (a formula B is a semantic consequence of a set of formulae, written $\{A_1 \ldots A_n\} \models B$, if it is true in all interpretations in which they are true). Then the central questions for a calculus will be whether all and only its theorems are valid, and whether $\{A_1 \ldots A_n\} \models B$ if and only if $\{A_1 \ldots A_n\} \vdash B$. These are the questions of the soundness and completeness of a formal system. For the propositional calculus this turns into the question of whether the proof theory delivers as theorems all and only *tautologies. There are many axiomatizations of the propositional calculus that are consistent and complete. *Gödel proved in 1929 that the first-order *predicate calculus is complete: any formula that is true under every interpretation is a theorem of the calculus.

modernism Generally, any movement or climate of ideas, especially in the arts, literature, or architecture, that supports change, the retirement of the old or traditional, and the forward march of the avant-garde. More specifically, adherence to the ideas and ideals of the *Enlightenment. This is the sense that gives rise to the contrary movement of *postmodernism.

modulo To the modulus. In mathematics, two numbers are said to be congruent modulo n when they differ by some multiple of n. For instance, 40 is congruent to each of 24 and 32 modulo 8. In *Quine's *Word and Object* the modulus of a stimulus is its duration, and two stimuli may be equivalent modulo one duration, but not modulo another. Other uses of the term have been temporarily fashionable in philosophy, and have to be picked up, if possible, from the context.

modus ponens Common shorthand for 'modus ponendo ponens', the rule of inference entitling us to pass from p, and $p \rightarrow q$, to q.

modus tollendo ponens An argument of the form p or q, not-p, so q.

modus tollens Common shorthand for 'modus tollendo tollens', the principle of inference entitling us to pass from not-q, and $p \rightarrow q$, to not-p.

moksha (Sanskrit, liberation) Liberation from the cycle of existence (**samsara*) often identified with a state of knowledge in which the phenomenal world and its concerns are shut out in favour of a mystical identification with the ultimate, changeless ground of all things.

molecularism *See* SENTENCE.

Molina, Luis de (1535–1600) Spanish Jesuit. He is remembered in philosophy for his work *Concordia liberi arbitrii cum gratiae donis* (1588), attempting to reconcile *free will with God's foreknowledge and his divine grace. By knowing what human beings would freely choose to do under any circumstances, God can then arrange the circumstances so their free choice goes one way or the other, without this amounting to an infringement of their freedom. *See* *SCIENTIA MEDIA*.

Molinism *See* *SCIENTIA MEDIA*.

Molyneux's problem William Molyneux, an Irish surgeon, wrote to *Locke: 'Suppose a man born blind, and now adult, and taught by his touch to distinguish between a cube and a sphere

m

of the same metal. Suppose then the cube and the sphere were placed on a table, and the blind man made to see: query, whether by his sight, before he touched them, could he distinguish and tell which was the globe and which the cube?' Molyneux, like Locke and *Berkeley, thought the answer would be that he could not. Empirical research has produced few definitive answers, although there is evidence that in cases where a good retinal image is made suddenly available (for example after corneal grafting) immediate visual perception can take place, of objects with which the subject is familiar through touch. It may, however, take months to learn to see things not previously taught by touch, and objects such as shadows. Philosophically the question bears on the way we are to think of the relation between visual space and tactile space. In other words, the issue affects the way to think of the integration of information provided by the different senses, in the building of perceptual knowledge.

SEE WEB LINKS

- Transcript of a radio discussion about Molyneux's problem
- A list of philosophical articles on Molyneux's problem

m

momentariness The doctrine that everything that exists in time exists only for a moment is a keynote doctrine of *Buddhism. It analyses apparently continuous existence into something like the apparently continuous existence of the image cast by projected movie film: a succession of discrete momentary existences comes to appear as a continuous existence. *See also* ENDURANCE/PERDURANCE, FULGURATION, LEIBNIZ.

monad Concept developed by *Leibniz, in whose philosophy monads are the true unities and hence the only true substances. Monads are extensionless, mental entities, capable of perceptions and appetitive states, but each of them self-sufficient and developing without relation to any other (*see* PRE-ESTABLISHED HARMONY). Their self-sufficiency is often registered by calling them 'windowless' monads. The foundation of the doctrine is that relations must ultimately be explained by the categorical, non-relational nature of things. *See also* CONWAY.

monadic A predicate is monadic if it requires only one singular term to make a sentence: '... is mortal' is monadic. The contrast is with n-adic predicates (relational predicates) that require n places to be filled where n > 1. The monadic predicate calculus is a fragment of the full *predicate calculus restricted to dealing with monadic predicates.

Monadology The title given to one of *Leibniz's works, and the name for any system sharing the basic concept of a *monad.

monism Monism finds one where *dualism finds two. Physicalism is the doctrine that everything that exists is physical, and is a monism contrasted with mind-body dualism; *absolute idealism is the doctrine that the only reality consists in modifications of the Absolute. *Parmenides and *Spinoza each believed that there were philosophical reasons for supposing that there could only be one kind of self-subsistent, real thing. *See also* NEUTRAL MONISM.

monophysite The doctrine that in the person of Jesus Christ there was but one, divine, nature, rather than two natures, divine and human. A point of dispute between the Coptic and Abyssinian churches, which accept the doctrine, and Roman Catholicism, which denies it in favour of the opposing, dyophysite doctrine of two natures.

monotheism Belief in one God. It is not always easy to count gods. *See* POLYTHEISM.

Montague grammar A type of formal language set up by the logician Richard Montague in his seminal 'The Proper Treatment of Quantification in English' (1974). A Montague grammar is based on a *first-order language to which are added powerful logical tools for the construction and evaluation of sentences. The formal language includes: (i) first-order predicate logic, (ii) *modal operators, (iii) tense operators, (iv) *lambda abstraction, (v) operators forming the *intensions and *extensions of predicates. Montague provides a type-theoretic structure, but permits *quantification over every type of expression. This language is called IL (intensional language). He gives IL a model theory, in terms of individuals, truth-values, coordinates of possible worlds and times (indexes), and functions of all these. IL enables us to give an indirect interpretation of any sentence of a natural language: first the sentence is mapped onto a translation in IL, and then the interpretation of this sentence is given. Montague's ideal was a full translation of natural language into the interpreted formal language thus generated.

Montaigne, Michel Eyquem de (1533–92) French essayist. The father-figure of *scepticism in France and modern Europe, Montaigne was born near Bordeaux. He followed a sporadic career in public life before retiring in 1571, although he continued to play a role in politics on behalf of the Protestant Henri de Navarre, and was mayor of Bordeaux in 1581. As befits someone involved in the civil and religious unrest of the time, Montaigne had no very high opinion of the faculties and achievements of mankind. His attitude found ample confirmation in the work of *Sextus Empiricus, whose motto, 'Que sais-je?' ('What do I know?'), Montaigne adopted for himself. His fame rests on his *Essais* (1580, trs. as *Essays*, 1603, and possibly known to Shakespeare), which reveal an engaging, humane, shrewd, and self-conscious philosophical personality. His most famous philosophical essay, the 'Apology for Raimond Sebond', is a masterly compendium of sceptical arguments, and had an immense influence on the following generation of French philosophers (*see* DESCARTES, FOUCHER, GASSENDI, MERSENNE). In the 'Apology' Sebond, an otherwise minor theologian who undertook to show how Catholic belief can be established by the light of reason, is defended by the backhanded device of admitting that his reasons for his beliefs are bad, but showing that they are no worse than other human reason for belief. Montaigne can be interpreted both as a forerunner of *Kant, confining reason to make room for faith, and as an *Enlightenment figure before his time.

SEE WEB LINKS

- Digital facsimiles and a list of internet resources on Montaigne's *Essais*
- Montaigne timeline with a searchable translation of the *Essais*

Monte Carlo fallacy *See* GAMBLERS' FALLACY.

Montesquieu, Charles-Louis de Secondat, baron de (1689–1755) Born in Bordeaux as a member of the aristocracy, Montesquieu acquired an intense admiration of the English revolution of 1688, and the associated ideals, voiced particularly in *Locke, of toleration, freedom, and government by constitution. In his version, however, this means a strengthening of the ancient privileges of the aristocracy against the encroaching power of the French monarchy. Montesquieu's own life, which included marriage apparently for a fortune, social climbing, and a rather unaristocratic avarice, somewhat reflects the self-serving appearance of this doctrine. His masterpiece, *De l'esprit des lois* (1748, trs. as *On the Spirit of the Laws*), introduced a *positivist note into the discussion of the laws of nations, hitherto the provenance of various kinds of theological and rationalistic deductions. Montesquieu relates the system of law of different countries to external accidents, such as those of geography and trade; for this he was hailed by *Durkheim as a founder of modern sociology (although similar connections had been made by Jean Bodin, 1530–96). In religious matters Montesquieu maintained a vague and tolerant *deism, but his alleged deathbed conversion to Catholicism, attested by an opportunistic Irish Jesuit, was widely publicized.

Monty Hall problem A decision problem associated with the American television game show host Monty Hall. Contestants are shown three closed curtains. Behind one is a prize, behind the other two are lemons. They pick a curtain. Monty Hall (who knows where the prize is) then pulls one of the other curtains, revealing a lemon, and contestants are asked if they would like to switch to the remaining closed curtain, or stay with their original choice. There seems to be no particular reason to switch, yet in fact switching doubles the chances of winning: your chance if you stay with your original curtain is what it always was, namely ⅓; the remaining curtain has a probability of containing the prize of ⅔. The problem was the subject of a minor scandal when several distinguished statisticians failed to see how this could be true. In fact it is true because there is now a significant difference between the curtain originally chosen, and the other one on offer, namely that Monty Hall avoided the second. The logic is more easily seen with a greater number of curtains. If there were 100, and you picked one, then by the time Monty Hall has pulled open 98 with lemons behind them, the chance that the remaining one *that he did not pick* conceals the prize is 99%. *See also* THREE PRISONERS, PARADOX OF.

m

mood 1. In the theory of the *syllogism the valid forms with each figure are called the moods of that figure. **2.** In the philosophy of language the mood of a sentence (indicative, imperative, subjunctive, etc.) is a feature whose best representation is problematic. The most common view is that mood indicates the force of an utterance, rather than being a feature affecting its sense, so that 'shut the door!' and 'the door is shut' can be thought of as having a common content, but presenting it in a different way and for a different purpose. *See also* PHRASTIC/NEUSTIC.

Moore, George Edward (1873–1958) British philosopher, educated at Trinity College, Cambridge. He was a lecturer at Cambridge from 1911, professor from 1925 to 1939, and the editor of *Mind* from 1921 to 1947. Moore began philosophy under the influence of *absolute idealism, but in the last years of the 19th century he and *Russell came to break with that tradition, and to espouse various kinds of realism centred upon the possibility of relating minds to independent facts. Moore was one of the founders and most skilled practitioners of *analytical philosophy. He came to wider fame with *Principia Ethica* (1903). In that book he (somewhat unfairly) pins the famous *naturalistic fallacy on preceding moral philosophers, and advocates the view that goodness is a simple, unanalysable quality, fortunately known by intuition. This intuition enables us to see that the good things of life are certain wholes, consisting of pleasures of aesthetics and love and friendship. The doctrine was highly influential, in ways that Moore may have deplored, on the Bloomsbury group. *Principia Ethica* achieved its success partly because of its intense concern to set out problems with unparalleled precision, and thereby get matters exactly right, and it was this moral force in Moore as much as his philosophical intellect that exerted a profound and uplifting influence on those around him, including Russell and *Wittgenstein. His mature works are famous for their defence of common sense. Moore came to believe that whenever a substantial philosophical doctrine was in conflict with common sense it was more likely that the argument had gone astray than that common sense had done so (the argument is reminiscent of *Hume's argument against belief in *miracles). Although Moore was a major influence on Anglo-American philosophy for the first half of the 20th century, there now remains less confidence in the method of analysis with which he is identified. Moore's works include *Ethics* (1912), *Philosophical Studies* (1922), *Some Main Problems of Philosophy* (1953), and the posthumously published *Philosophical Papers* (1959).

Moore's paradox A puzzle arising when someone says '*p* but I do not believe that *p*'. What is said is not contradictory, since (for many instances of *p*) both parts of it could be true. But the person nevertheless violates some presupposition of normal practice, namely that you assert something only if you believe it; by adding that you do not believe what you just said you undo the natural significance of the original act of saying it.

moot To moot a question is to broach it or open it; a question is moot when it is debatable, or still subject to dispute.

moral argument for the existence of God **1.** The argument that our capacity for moral thought requires a divine explanation. The most famous version of the argument is that of *Descartes, who held that our conception of perfection required a perfect archetype or origin. **2.** The argument that without a divine order and purpose in the universe there could be no such thing as moral truth. *Kant thought that the idea of a just lawgiver was a presupposition of moral reasoning. In effect, God is needed for reassurance that the just will flourish and the unjust suffer, without which practical reasoning would be a kind of mockery. The argument has not fared well in the face of *naturalistic explanations of our propensity for good behaviour.

moral dilemmas Situations in which each possible course of action breaches some otherwise binding moral principle. Serious dilemmas make the stuff of many tragedies. The conflict can be described in different ways. One suggestion is that whichever action the subject undertakes, she or he does something wrong, or something she or he ought not to do. Another is that this is not so, for the dilemma means that in the circumstances what she or he did was right, or as right as any alternative. It is important to the phenomenology of these cases that action leaves a residue of guilt and remorse, although again (provided it was not the subject's fault that she or he got into the dilemma) the rationality of these emotions can be contested. Any morality with more than one fundamental principle seems capable of generating dilemmas, but dilemmas exist such as that where a mother must decide which of two children to sacrifice, even although no principles are pitted against each other (only children). If we accept that dilemmas of principle are real and important, this fact can then be used to attack theories such as *utilitarianism, that recognize only one sovereign principle. Alternatively, regretting the existence of dilemmas and the unordered jumble of principles that creates many of them, a theorist may use their occurrence to argue for the desirability of locating and promoting a single sovereign principle.

moralistes Term used primarily of 17th- and 18th-century French authors, including *La Rochefoucauld and *La Bruyère, whose short texts serve to make a moral point, or to encourage self-examination, reflection, and discussion, appropriate to a salon culture. Later *moralistes* include *Diderot, *Voltaire, and *Montesquieu.

morality Although the morality of people and their *ethics amount to the same thing, there is a usage that restricts morality to systems such as that of *Kant, based on notions such as duty, obligation, and principles of conduct, reserving ethics for the more *Aristotelian approach to practical reasoning, based on the notion of a virtue, and generally avoiding the separation of 'moral' considerations from other practical considerations. The scholarly issues are complex, with some writers seeing Kant as more Aristotelian, and Aristotle as more involved with a separate sphere of responsibility and duty, than the simple contrast suggests.

moral law Some theories of ethics see the subject in terms of a number of laws (as in the Ten Commandments). The status of these laws may be that they are the edicts of a divine lawmaker, or that they are truths of reason, knowable **a priori*.

Other approaches to ethics (e.g. *eudaimonism, *situation ethics, *virtue ethics) eschew general principles as much as possible, regarding them as at best rules-of-thumb, frequently disguising the great complexity of practical reasoning. For the *Kantian notion of the moral law, *see* CATEGORICAL IMPERATIVE. *See also* NATURAL LAW THEORY.

moral luck A phenomenon identified and christened by Bernard *Williams and investigated by Thomas *Nagel. In the *Kantian tradition, a person's moral worth depends only on the quality of their will, and is thus independent of external circumstance. But reflection shows that our ordinary estimates of persons may depend greatly on external matters, and even matters of chance. For example, it may be chance whether my driving has an accident as a consequence, yet I will rightly feel worse about myself, and be judged more harshly by others, if it does. It may be luck whether or not I am put in circumstances in which my weaknesses come to the fore, but again, if I am so placed, I will be judged more harshly than if I am not. Equally, the beneficiary of good luck will find his or her character estimated more highly than an equally deserving victim of misfortune. In some cultures (e.g. that of the Icelandic sagas), possession of good luck was a merit or virtue, akin to wisdom or strength. *See also* GAUGUIN PROBLEM.

moral motivation In some moral systems, notably that of Kant, real moral worth comes only with acting rightly *because* it is right. If you do what you should but from some other motive, such as fear or prudence, no moral merit accrues to you. Yet that in turn seems to discount other admirable motivations, such as acting from sheer benevolence or *sympathy. The question is how to balance these opposing ideas, and also how to understand acting from a sense of obligation without duty or rightness beginning to seem a kind of fetish.

moral particularism The view owing its ancestry to *Aristotle, and defended by the contemporary British philosopher Jonathan Dancy, that in deciding the rights and wrongs of action general principles are of little value: the devil lies in the details. It thus stands opposed to ethics relying on highly general and abstract principles, particularly those associated with the *Kantian categorical imperative. The view may go so far as to say that taken on its own, no consideration points in any particular way, but taken to this extreme the view seems to threaten any kind of reasoning about what to do, since that can only proceed by identifying salient features of a situation that weigh on one side or another.

moral philosophy *See* ETHICS.

moral psychology A major topic of philosophical enquiry, especially in *Aristotle, and subsequently since the 17th and 18th centuries, when the 'science of man' began to probe into human motivation and emotion. For writers such as the French **moralistes*, or *Hutcheson, *Hume, *Smith, and *Kant, a prime task was to delineate the variety of human reactions and motivations. Such enquiry would locate our propensity for moral thinking among other faculties, such as perception and reason, and other tendencies, such as empathy, sympathy, or self-interest. The task continues especially in the light of a post-Darwinian understanding of ourselves. *See also* EVOLUTIONARY PSYCHOLOGY, MORAL MOTIVATION.

moral realism *Realism as applied to the judgements of ethics, and to the values, obligations, rights, etc. that are referred to in ethical theory. The leading idea is to see moral truth as grounded in the nature of things rather than in subjective and variable human reactions to things. Like realism in other areas, this is capable of many different formulations. Generally speaking moral realism aspires to protecting the objectivity of ethical judgement (opposing *relativism and *subjectivism); it may assimilate moral truths to those of mathematics, hope that they have some divine sanction (but *see* EUTHYPHRO DILEMMA), or see them as guaranteed by human nature. *See also* ETHICAL NATURALISM, PROJECTIVISM, QUASI-REALISM.

moral rearmament *See* BUCHMANISM.

moral relativism *See* RELATIVISM.

moral scepticism The view that there is no such thing as moral knowledge, either because there is no moral 'world' to know about, or because, even if there is a domain of moral truth, we are not adapted for knowing about it. *See also* RELATIVISM.

moral sense theory The view, particularly associated with *Hutcheson, that we possess a moral sense partially akin to the other senses, that disposes us to the approvals and disapprovals that we feel. The 'sense' in question is certainly to be distinguished from any exercise of rationality, but seems unlike sight or hearing in that its output is an attitude: it is more like a sense of humour or sense of balance. Hutcheson was part of the 'sentimentalist' school, initiated by *Shaftesbury, and opposed to such rationalists as *Price and *Clarke. Although *Hume refers approvingly to the moral sense, he develops his own version of morality as based on the passions without using the concept at all: here he anticipates Adam *Smith, who finds it unnecessary to posit any extra sense. Instead, moralizing is explained by the normal operation of other sentiments, such as sympathy, regulated by various mechanisms.

moral status A concept featuring in discussion of animal welfare and *animal rights, also in debates about *abortion and *euthanasia, as well as in *feminist ethics. In the former debates, the issue will be whether animals or foetuses or terminally ill or comatose patients have the same standing as persons in general. In the feminist debate, the issue is whether insidious social pressures and norms deny women a voice or a full membership of the moral community.

moral virtues *See* MERIT, VIRTUE.

More, Henry (1614–87) English philosopher and theologian, and leading member of the *Cambridge Platonists. More was educated at Christ's College, and remained there after his Fellowship was conferred in 1639. He breathed a spirit of Renaissance Christian Platonism, in which there exists a way of relating the individual to God through moral and mystical ascent. He conceived it his principal aim to combat the rising scientific world view; although initially receptive to the philosophy of *Descartes he eventually opposed it vehemently. He was a major influence on the theological elements in the thought of *Newton.

More, Thomas (1477/8–1535) English lawyer, writer, and saint. More was born and educated at London, and enjoyed a brilliant career at the Bar, giving him the leisure to enjoy literary and political pursuits. He became Lord Chancellor in 1529, but resigned in 1532 and lived for some time in retirement. After Henry VIII's divorce from Catherine in 1534, More's principled refusal to take any oath impugning the authority of the Pope led to his execution a year later. He is remembered philosophically partly as a friend of *Erasmus and a key figure of the Renaissance in England, but also as the author of *Utopia* (1516), a description of the quest for a political ideal that is satisfied by a system of *communism, national education, and free toleration of religion.

morpheme The minimal unit of *grammar. Free forms of morphemes are those that can occur as separate words; bound forms are items such as affixes and suffixes that must be recognized as components of grammatical structure. Morphology studies morphemes, and includes the study of inflectional as well as lexical units.

Moses ben Maimon *See* MAIMONIDES.

motion *See* SPACE-TIME, ZENO'S PARADOXES.

motivation Philosophically, the perennially fascinating problem is what people 'really' want. When people say what they want, or describe the purposes, intentions, emotions, or goals they have, are we to believe them? And what are the empirical tests? Radical strategies of interpretation such as *psychoanalysis or psychological *egoism suppose that we are systematically deceived about our own motivations. But does it make sense to suppose that our own self-interpretations are so generally fallible, or do we have some kind of authority in saying how we are motivated? *See also* MORAL MOTIVATION.

Mo Tzu (Mozi) (5th c. BC) Founder of Mohism, a precursor of *utilitarianism. Mo Tzu dissented from *Confucian emphasis on ritual and on the family, in favour of a more generalized impartial benevolence.

mover, unmoved That which initiates motion, but which is itself unmoved. The first of the *Five Ways of *Aquinas argues for such an entity. It may seem as though this is a version of the *first cause argument, with God seeming like the railway engine that starts the shunting of connected waggons. But in the *Aristotelian and medieval tradition the argument is different. Nature, for the Greeks, is characterized by a **nisus* or tendency to actuate what is potential; change is driven by a kind of striving or direction towards a goal, an ethical action at a distance. The process of change or becoming is intelligible only if the goal acts in the world; it is the initiator of motion because it is the *final cause of it. The idea is that a natural motion, such as that of the iron filings towards the magnet, is analogous to the impulses of agents (thus, we still speak in one breath of the filings being drawn towards the magnet, and the man being drawn to the woman). The single unmoved mover is the one thing that has a self-contained activity (self-consciousness) of its own, and that is not therefore caused to move by the need to actualize any potential. It is in some way identical with the forms that it thinks, and the movements of nature are inspired by the things of nature being drawn towards it. Thus the **primum mobile* or outermost sphere of the heavens best imitates the self-contained nature of God by its perfect, spherical rotation. In this system it is, literally, love that makes the world go round. Unfortunately however the unmoved mover, being entirely wrapped up in itself, cannot act in the world, nor possess any awareness of it, and this aspect of the doctrine was formally condemned in 1277. *See also* NEOPLATONISM.

moving rows paradox (moving blocks paradox) *See* ZENO'S PARADOXES.

Mulla Sadra (Sadr Al-Din Muhammad Al-Shirazi) (1571–1641) Muslim philosopher who still maintains sovereign status as a spiritual leader for the Islamic East. Born in Shiraz, Mulla Sadra developed a unification of *Sufi mystical or *Illuminationist traditions in Islam with Neoplatonic influences: his main precursor was Ibn Arabi (1165–1240). His 'metaphilosophy' is as much a spiritual exercise or route to salvation as a body of doctrine. The principal work is the *Al-Asfar al-arbaa*, translated as *The Four Journeys*.

Müller–Lyer illusion The visual illusion in which outward pointing arrowheads at the end of a line decrease its apparent length, and inward pointing ones increase it, compared to a neutral line of the same length.

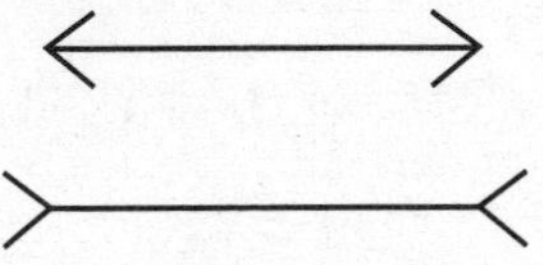

multi-valued logic *See* MANY-VALUED LOGIC.

Murdoch, Iris Jean (1919–99) English philosopher and novelist. Born in Dublin, and educated at Somerville College, Oxford, Murdoch became Fellow of St Anne's College, Oxford, in 1948. She is best known as a novelist, but her philosophical writings begin with *Sartre, Romantic Rationalist* (1953) and include *The Sovereignty of Good* (1970) and *Metaphysics and Morals* (1992). As in many of her novels, she has been centrally concerned philosophically to explore the place of religious thought and morality as *Platonic bulwarks against an apparently fragmented and meaningless world.

music Philosophical questions surrounding music include that of understanding the source of the pleasure music gives, and understanding its expressive, dramatic, and emotional power. Our *aesthetic response to music is more than the passive reception of pleasure, since it involves elements of understanding and anticipation: does this imply that it is appropriate to talk of the meaning of a piece of music, or of a musical language?

music of the spheres *See* HARMONY OF THE SPHERES.

Mu'takallimun *See* *KALAM*.

mutatis mutandis Latin, 'things having been changed that have to be changed'; that is, with the necessary alterations.

Mu'tazilites *See* *KALAM*.

mutually exclusive/jointly exhaustive *See* EXCLUSIVE/EXHAUSTIVE.

mysticism Belief in union with the divine nature by means of ecstatic contemplation, and belief in the power of spiritual access to ultimate reality, or to domains of knowledge closed off to ordinary thought. Also applied derogatorily to theories that assume occult qualities or agencies of which no empirical or rational account can be offered.

myth of Er The final parable in *Plato's *Republic* in which the warrior Er, killed in battle, returns to tell of the nature of the afterlife, and the consequent importance of wisdom and justice to the long-term health of the soul. Disembodied souls are assigned their future lives at the spindle of necessity.

myth of the cave Not properly a myth, but the figure or allegory used by Plato in Bk vii. 514–18 of the *Republic*, to demonstrate the degrees to which our natures may be enlightened, or unenlightened. At the first stage are prisoners, tied so that they can perceive only shadows on the back of the cave. The shadows are cast by artificial objects, and the light is thrown by a fire. Their only reality would be the shadow of these artificial objects. With enlightenment a prisoner might be turned to see first the artificial objects, then the fire, then the real world, and last of all the Sun. Each stage would be difficult and unfamiliar, and at the end the enlightened subject would be unable to communicate his knowledge to the prisoners remaining below. Plato says that the ascent stands for the upward journey of the soul into the region of the intelligible (the *forms), identified with that which is alone truly real. The myth may be read purely as an invitation to think, rather than to rely on the way things appear to us, but it is often used as an open invitation to belief in esoteric and *mystical states of knowing. *See also* *EIKASIA*; LINE, IMAGE OF; NEOPLATONISM.

myth of the given Name adopted by *Sellars for the now widely-rejected view that sense experience gives us peculiar points of certainty, suitable to serve as foundations for the whole of empirical knowledge and science. The idea that *empiricism, particularly in the hands of *Locke and *Hume, confuses moments of physical or causal impact on the senses with the arrival of individual 'sense data' in the mind, was a central criticism of it levelled by the British Idealists, especially *Green and *Joachim. *See* FOUNDATIONALISM, PROTOCOL STATEMENTS, SENSE DATA.

Naess, Arne (1912–) Norwegian philosopher and 'ecophilosopher' or 'ecosopher'. Naess was professor at Oslo from 1939 to 1970, and founder of the 'Oslo school'. His prolific academic work moved from original involvement with the *Vienna circle to an interest in *Pyrrhonian scepticism, and an undogmatic and pluralistic epistemology. He was also influential in injecting an empirical and sociological element into *semantics, requiring evidence of how language is actually used rather than simple models of how logicians think it is used. He was a celebrated outdoorsman (he made the first ascent of 7690-metre Tirich Mir, the highest peak in the Hindu Kush, in 1950) and founder of the 'deep ecology' movement, enjoining an emphasis on the self-realization and development of all things, based on a *holistic view of nature deriving from *Spinoza's pantheism. Books include *Scepticism* (1968) and *Ecology, Community and Lifestyle: Outline of an Ecosophy* (1989).

Nagarjuna (*fl.* 2nd c. AD) One of the principal philosophers of *Buddhism, and founder of the *Madhyamika school. Little is known of his life, although his name derives from *naga*, a serpent, symbol of occult knowledge. Nagarjuna holds that the multiple world of appearances depends upon the existence of oppositions. But oppositions arise from futile and false discriminations. They are relative, and hence unreal. The rejection of all oppositions (the middle way, or *madhyamika*) leaves real truth lying only in emptiness, or in a world characterized entirely negatively. The eight negations are: no elimination, no production, no destruction, no eternity, no unity, no multiplicity, no arriving, no departing. Nagarjuna's teaching resembles that of *monists in the Western tradition, such as *Parmenides and *Bradley.

Nagel, Ernest (1901–85) Philosopher of science. Born in Novemesto, in the former Czechoslovakia, Nagel emigrated to the USA in 1911, and was a teacher at Columbia for more than forty years. His best-remembered work was one of the last major *empiricist and positivist discussions of the nature of scientific explanation, *The Structure of Science* (1961).

Nagel, Thomas (1937–) American moral and political theorist. Born in the former Yugoslavia, Nagel was educated at Cornell, Oxford, and Harvard. He taught at Princeton from 1966 to 1980, and subsequently at New York University. His work is centrally concerned with the nature of moral motivation and the possibility of a rational theory of moral and political commitment, and has been a major stimulus to interest in realistic and *Kantian approaches to these issues. One of the most discussed papers of modern philosophy of mind has been his 'What is it Like to Be a Bat?', arguing that there is an irreducible, subjective aspect of experience that cannot be grasped by the objective methods of natural science, or by philosophies such as *functionalism that confine themselves to those methods. Works include *The Possibility of Altruism* (1970), *Mortal Questions* (1979), *The View from Nowhere* (1986), and *Equality and Partiality* (1991).

naive realism The view that in sense experience we directly perceive the objects of the external world is direct realism. The view is the natural view of people everywhere, and of philosophers when they are off-duty, but it remains naive until is is buttressed by explanations of how experience may change while things do not, how illusion is possible, how colours and sounds can be regarded as properties of things independent of us, and so forth.

naive subjectivism The view in the theory of ethics that when people make a moral judgement about some topic, they are strictly and literally describing their own feelings about the topic. The view has the disadvantage that if the speaker is sincere, then what is said will be true. That is, if when I say that liberalism is good I merely describe my feelings about liberalism, then, so long as I feel that it is good, what I say will be true. This unacceptable conflation of sincerity and truth is avoided by more subtle approaches to moral discourse: *see* EXPRESSIVISM, PROJECTIVISM.

name, logically proper *See* LOGICALLY PROPER NAME.

narrative competence The system of cultural, historical, or other textual knowledge that a reader brings to a text and that makes it possible to understand it. Such knowledge is sometimes thought of as the possession of a script or stereotype. For example, the reader of a novel knows the sort of thing that goes on when one visits a restaurant; hence on being told that the party was seated, she can fill in that they were seated facing a table rather than facing a wall, all at the same table, on chairs rather than on each other, and so on. The *frame problem in artificial intelligence research emphasizes the pervasive need for such knowledge.

Nash equilibrium In *game theory, an outcome or set of strategies, one for each player, is in Nash equilibrium if it yields an outcome such that no player can improve her position by unilaterally withdrawing from it. A game may permit several Nash equilibria. In the *prisoners' dilemma the strategy that each cheat on the other is, unfortunately, a Nash equilibrium, whereas the socially preferable outcome that each cooperates is not. *See also* PARETO PRINCIPLE.

nativism *See* FODOR, LANGUAGE OF THOUGHT.

natural deduction A system of *logic developed notably by Gerhard *Gentzen, solely in terms of rules of inference. In the place of axioms there are only rules, saying what can be derived from any given assumption. However, there will be rules for 'discharging' assumptions, leading to results derivable from anything at all, and these are the theorems of the system. The rule of *conditional proof is one such rule. Such systems are useful for three reasons: (i) they conform better than axiomatic systems to the view that logic is about inference, rather than about a special set of 'logical truths'; (ii) they avoid the arbitrariness of choosing just one set of logical truths as axioms; and (iii) they are often easier to manipulate.

naturalism Most generally, a sympathy with the view that ultimately nothing resists explanation by the methods characteristic of the natural sciences. A naturalist will be opposed, for example, to mind–body *dualism, since it leaves the mental side of things outside the explanatory grasp of biology or physics; opposed to acceptance of numbers or concepts as real but non-physical denizens of the world; and opposed to accepting real moral duties and rights as absolute and self-standing facets of the natural order. The central problem for naturalism is to define what counts as a satisfactory accommodation between the preferred sciences and the elements that on the face of it have no place in them. Alternatives include *instrumentalism, *reductionism, and *eliminativism, as well as a variety of other anti-realist suggestions (*see* REALISM/ANTI-REALISM). The term naturalism is sometimes used for specific versions of these approaches in particular areas: *Moore, for example, defined naturalism in ethics as the doctrine that moral predicates actually express the same thing as predicates from some natural or empirical science. This suggestion is probably untenable, but as other accommodations between ethics and the view of human beings as just parts of nature recommend themselves, these then gain the title of naturalistic approaches to ethics. *See also* NATURE.

naturalistic ethics *See* ETHICAL NATURALISM.

naturalistic fallacy Alleged fallacy, identified by *Moore in *Principia Ethica* (1903), of identifying an ethical concept with a 'natural' concept, or description of the features of things in virtue of which they are supposed good or bad. Thus if one's standard is *utilitarian, to say that some action is good will mean the very same as saying that it creates more happiness than rival actions would. This equation of meaning is almost certainly wrong, but subsequent work has not confirmed that Moore's opponents, particularly J. S. *Mill, made the identification or committed any error of reasoning based on it. *See also* OPEN QUESTION ARGUMENT.

naturalized epistemology Term due to *Quine for the enterprise of studying the actual formation of knowledge by human beings, without aspiring to certify those processes as rational, or proof against *scepticism, or even apt to yield the truth. Naturalized epistemology would therefore blend into the psychology of learning and the study of episodes in the history of science. The scope for 'external' or philosophical reflection of the kind that might result in scepticism or its refutation is markedly diminished. Although the term is modern, distinguished exponents of the approach arguably include *Aristotle, *Hume, J. S. *Mill, and *Piaget, although few philosophers are prepared to give up a critical or normative dimension, privileging some ways of forming belief above others. *See also* EPISTEMOLOGY, METHODOLOGY.

natural kind A believer in natural kinds holds that nature is itself divided into different kinds and species, and that our predicates and classifications must coincide with these divisions: in one familiar metaphor, we must aim to 'carve nature at the joints'. Opponents stress the historical, theoretical, and mutable nature of processes of scientific classification or taxonomy, insisting that we see joints only where we carve.

natural language Any language actually spoken, as opposed to artificial languages, whose syntax and rules are laid down for theoretical purposes.

natural laws *See* LAWS OF NATURE.

natural law theory The view of the status of law and morality especially associated with *Aquinas and the subsequent *scholastic tradition. More widely, any attempt to cement the moral and legal order together with the nature of the cosmos or the nature of human beings, in which sense it is also found in some Protestant writers, and arguably derivative from a Platonic view of ethics, and is implicit in ancient *Stoicism. Law stands above and apart from the activities of human lawmakers; it constitutes an objective set of principles that can be seen true by 'natural light' or reason, and (in religious versions of the theory) that express God's will for creation. Non-religious versions of the theory substitute objective conditions for human flourishing as the source of constraints upon permissible actions and social arrangements. Within the natural law tradition, different views have been held about the relationship between the rule of law and God's will: *Grotius, for instance, sides with the view that the content of natural law is independent of any will, including that of God, whilst *Pufendorf takes the opposite view, thereby facing the problems of one horn of the *Euthyphro dilemma. In modern writers the natural law tradition may either assume a stronger form, in which it is claimed that various facts entail values, or a weaker form, which confines itself to holding that reason by itself is capable of discerning moral requirements. As in the ethics of *Kant, these requirements are supposed binding on all human beings, regardless of their desires. *See also* CATEGORICAL IMPERATIVE, NATURE, SYNDERESIS.

natural numbers *See* NUMBER.

natural rights *See* RIGHTS.

natural selection *See* DARWINISM.

natural theology Doctrines concerning God that are attainable by natural processes of reasoning, as opposed to those that require the assistance of revelation. Atheists and agnostics deny that there are such doctrines, as do Protestant theologians who emphasize the limitations of fallen human faculties, stressing instead the special need for divine grace. *See also* DEISM.

nature An indefinitely mutable term, changing as our scientific conception of the world changes, and often best seen as signifying a contrast with something considered not part of nature. The term applies both to individual species (it is the nature of gold to be dense or of dogs to be friendly), and also to the natural world as a whole. The sense in which it applies to species quickly links up with ethical and aesthetic ideals: a thing ought to realize its nature; what is natural is what it is good for a thing to become; it is natural for humans to be healthy or two-legged, and departure from this is a misfortune or deformity. The association of what is natural with what it is good to become is visible in *Plato, and is the central idea of *Aristotle's philosophy of nature. Unfortunately the pinnacle of nature in this sense is the mature adult male citizen, with the rest of what we would call the natural world, including women, slaves, children, and other species, not quite making it.

Nature in general can, however, function as a foil to any ideal as much as a source of ideals: in this sense fallen nature is contrasted with a supposed celestial realization of the *forms. The *Galilean world view might have been expected to drain nature of its ethical content, but the term seldom loses its normative force, and the belief in universal natural laws provided its own set of ideals. In the 18th century, for example, a painter or writer could be praised as natural, where the qualities expected would include normal ('universal') topics treated with simplicity, economy, regularity, and harmony. Later on, nature becomes an equally potent emblem of irregularity, wildness, and fertile diversity, but also associated with progress and transformation (*see* ABSOLUTE IDEALISM, ROMANTICISM). Contrasts with nature may include (i) that which is deformed or grotesque, or fails to achieve its proper form or function, or just the statistically uncommon or unfamiliar; (ii) the supernatural, or the world of gods and invisible agencies; (iii) the world of rationality and intelligence, conceived of as distinct from the biological and physical order; (iv) that which is manufactured and artificial, or the product of human intervention; (v) related to that, the world of *convention and artifice.

Different conceptions of nature continue to have ethical overtones: for example, the conception of 'nature red in tooth and claw' often provides a justification for aggressive personal and political relations, or the idea that it is women's nature to be one thing or another is taken to be a justification for differential social expectations. Here the term functions as a fig-leaf for a particular set of stereotypes, and is a proper target of much *feminist writing. *See also* DARWINISM, ENVIRONMENTAL ETHICS, LAWS OF NATURE, *NATURPHILOSOPHIE*, SOCIOBIOLOGY.

Naturphilosophie The philosophically orientated approach to natural history that flourished in Germany at the end of the 18th and the first half of the 19th centuries. Its exponents include *Herder, *Goethe, *Schelling, *Hegel, and anatomists such as

Lorenz Oken (1779–1851). The approach absorbed from *Kant (and as a forerunner, *Aristotle) the idea of a progress and *teleology in the development of species and animals, but paid less attention to Kant's attempts to curb the pretensions of human reason. The result was a mixture of botanical and biological observation with unfettered metaphysical theory, largely directed to seeing nature in terms of a hierarchy of orders culminating in mankind. *See also* ABSOLUTE IDEALISM, ROMANTICISM.

SEE WEB LINKS

- A lecture on Schelling's view of *Naturphilosophie*
- An essay on Hegel's and Schelling's philosophy of nature

necessary and sufficient conditions *See* CONDITION, NECESSARY/SUFFICIENT.

necessary/contingent truths A necessary truth is one that could not have been otherwise. It would have been true under all circumstances. A contingent truth is one that is true, but could have been false. A necessary truth is one that must be true; a contingent truth is one that is true as it happens, or as things are, but that did not have to be true. In *Leibniz's phrase, a necessary truth is true in all *possible worlds. If these are all the worlds that accord with the principles of logic, however different they may be otherwise, then the truth is a logically necessary truth. If they cover all the worlds whose metaphysics is possible, then the proposition is metaphysically necessary. If a proposition is only true in all the worlds that are physically possible, then the proposition is true of physical necessity.

A permanent philosophical urge is to diagnose contingency as disguised necessity (Leibniz, *Spinoza), although especially in the 20th century there have been equally powerful movements, especially associated with *Quine, denying that there are substantive necessary truths, instead regarding necessity as disguised contingency. *See also* ANALYTIC/SYNTHETIC, *A PRIORI/A POSTERIORI*, QUINE.

necessary existence A thing exists necessarily if however things had been, it would still have existed. The standard candidates include such abstract entities as numbers, and in religious thought, God. The difficulty lies in understanding how a thing could have this kind of status, and what kind of things could be supposed to have it. The *ontological and *cosmological arguments for God require a being with this peculiar property as their endpoint. *See also* PERSEITY.

necessity A proposition is necessary if it could not have been false. We can contemplate various possibilities describing how things might have been but are not; if in all these possibilities a proposition is true, then it is true in all *possible worlds or true of necessity. *See also* NECESSARY/CONTINGENT TRUTHS, MODALITY, MODAL LOGIC.

The fundamental explanation of the necessity of a proposition is controversial, and some have doubted whether the category is a useful aid to thought (*see* QUINE). A relatively clear class of necessary propositions would be those that are analytic (*see* ANALYTIC/SYNTHETIC) since they seem 'trivially' true. More substantive problems arise with apparently synthetic necessary truths: classical examples include the proposition that every number has a successor, or nothing can appear red and green all over at the same time. The possibility of synthetic **a priori* truth is the basic problem faced by *Kant in the *Critique of Pure Reason*. *Conventionalist theories suggest that we deem certain propositions to be necessary by linguistic convention ('invention is the mother of necessity'). Other theories stress the imaginative block we encounter when we try to imagine the possibility of such propositions being true, although if this block is a contingent aspect of our psychologies, the explanation seems to undermine the idea of necessity rather than to explain it. A category of particular interest is that of propositions which are 'metaphysically necessary', yet not in any sense *a priori*: the proposition that heat in a gas is motion of molecules, or that water is H_2O, for example.

A rather different set of philosophical problems also arises with the idea of the necessary unfolding of events in time; in many philosophies the march of events has been seen as inexorable, or preordained, and this is held to have consequences for how we react to problems of choice, or how we think of what has already happened. *See also* FREE WILL, LAWS OF NATURE. The cluster of considerations focusing on the *cosmological argument seek to show that if anything exists contingently, then something must exist of necessity.

SEE WEB LINKS

- A bibliography of philosophical writings on necessity

needs Something is needed for some end if the end cannot be achieved without it. If living things are thought of as having a set of real or true ends, as in *Aristotelian teleological accounts of human beings, then their real or true needs will be whatever is required for those ends to be achieved. The meeting of needs can then be the foundation of an ethic. The difficulty is to shake the idea loose from its Aristotelian underpinnings. Without those, the idea of a need is apt to dilute into the idea of an interest or a desire. *See also* CAPABILITIES.

negation The negation of a proposition is its denial: classically, that proposition which is true when it is false, and false when it is true. The sign ¬ (for alternatives *see* APPENDIX) expresses a *truth function, defined in the table:

p	$\neg p$
T	F
F	T

A proposition may be controverted in other ways than by asserting its strict negation. For instance 'that's red' is controverted by 'that's green', since both cannot be true together. But both can be false and one is not the direct denial of the other. *See* CONTRARY, SQUARE OF OPPOSITION.

negative freedom *See* FREEDOM, POSITIVE/NEGATIVE.

negative theology The 'via negativa' or negative way is the approach to religion that supposes that we can better say what God is not than say anything about what he is. He is not (for instance) gendered, bearded, besandalled, present in some places or times and not others, or like us in any other specifiable way. The approach of saying 'that's not quite right' after any attempt to describe God does full justice to the unimaginable and incomprehensible nature of God, but it does less well in countering *Wittgenstein's dictum that 'nothing will do as well as something about which nothing can be said'.

Neo-Confucianism The school of Chinese philosophy that developed the thought of *Confucius from the Sung period (960–1279) onwards. It adds to Confucian ethics metaphysical discussion of the nature of such concepts as **chi*, **li*, and **yin* and *yang*, none of these being concepts that are developed in the work of Confucius himself.

Neo-Kantianism A general term for any doctrine in metaphysics or ethics owing its inspiration to *Kant, but more particularly a term for various philosophical trends of this kind prominent in Germany between 1870 and 1920. The slogan 'back to Kant' was pronounced by Kuno Fischer (1824–1907) in 1860, partly as a reaction to the prevailing *naturalism of the time, and ethically in opposition to the *evolutionary ethics beginning to gain ground and to propagate myths of biological *determinism and racial superiority. The general tendency was to separate the humane from the natural sciences (*see* DILTHEY, *VERSTEHEN*), and to reduce emphasis on the *noumenal, so interpreting Kant's thoughts as a more *positivistic blend of empiricism and rationalism. Neo-Kantianism was especially influential in the social thought of *Durkheim and *Weber.

Neoplatonism The fusion of *Plato's philosophy with religious, Pythagorean, and other classical doctrines, originated by *Plotinus in his *Enneads*. Plotinus conceived of the universe as an emanation or effulguration of the One, the omnipresent, transcendental Good derived from Plato's Parmenides. The One gives rise to the realm of **nous* (ideas, intelligence), and that in turn to soul, or souls, some of which sink into bodies (others remain celestial). For further detail, *see* PLOTINUS. *Porphyry added Aristotelian elements. The school of Athens developed Neoplatonism in theological, but anti-Christian, directions, most notably in the work of *Proclus in the 5th century. In Alexandria, however, a blending of Neoplatonic and Christian elements took place, at its most developed in the work of *Boethius. Neoplatonism had a profound influence on medieval and Renaissance philosophy (*see*, for example, DANTE), whilst elements from Plotinus are also present in the tradition of the *kabbala. However, eventually the God of the Neoplatonists is too remote from the world to serve satisfactorily as the God of Judaism, Christianity, or Islam. He or it is like a pool that is the source of a river, but is separated from its lower reaches by all the intervening waterfalls; it is not accessible to prayer nor remotely cognizant of nor concerned with events further down. One of the principal problems of early scholastic philosophy was to define and defend a concept of a God that, while entirely self-sufficient, was not entirely self-absorbed. *See also* MOVER, UNMOVED.

Neo-Pythagoreanism The resurgence of the mystical and numerological interests of *Pythagoras, fused with elements from *Plato and other Greek philosophers, in Mediterranean centres in the 1st century BC. According to *Cicero, the founder of the school was a Roman philosopher, Nigidius Figulus. The way of thought contributed to *Middle Platonism, and the later rise of *Neoplatonism.

Neo-Taoism The form of *Taoism that flourished in China in the 3rd and 4th centuries. A principal concern was the relationship between the personal withdrawal to nature characteristic of Taoism, and the more social and political ethics of *Confucianism.

Neo-Thomism The movement that took its starting-point from the encyclical *Aeterni Patris* issued by Pope Leo XIII in 1879, confirming the place of *Aquinas as the guardian of orthodox Catholic theology. Philosophers working in the tradition include the French scholars Étienne *Gilson and Jacques *Maritain.

Nestorianism The doctrine defended by Nestorius, who occupied the see of Constantinople in

428, that Christ consisted of two separate persons, one divine and one human. It was condemned in favour of the doctrine that he was one person, both divine and human. *See also* HOMOOUSION, MONOPHYSITE.

neural net *See* CONNECTIONISM.

Neurath, Otto (1882–1945) Austrian philosopher and social theorist. Neurath, a polymath and a socialist, was one of the most influential members of the Vienna Circle (*see* LOGICAL POSITIVISM). His papers in the journal *Erkenntnis* (particularly his 'Protokollsätze' of 1932) were important in turning the circle away from the attempt to find the foundations of knowledge in uninterpreted sense experience, and towards a more physicalistic and *holistic epistemology. For Neurath, physicalism was a linguistic doctrine that promised a desirable unification of the languages of the different sciences. Neurath was largely the author of the first manifesto of the Vienna Circle, in 1929. *See also* NEURATH'S BOAT.

Neurath's boat The powerful image conjured up by *Neurath, in his *Anti-Spengler* (1921), whereby the body of knowledge is compared to a boat that must be repaired at sea: 'we are like sailors who on the open sea must reconstruct their ship but are never able to start afresh from the bottom ...'. Any part can be replaced, provided there is enough of the rest on which to stand. The image opposes that according to which knowledge must rest upon foundations, thought of as themselves immune from criticism, and transmitting their immunity to other propositions by a kind of laying-on of hands. *See also* FOUNDATIONALISM, METHOD OF DOUBT.

neurolinguistics The joint study of the areas of the brain that subserve linguistic competence, and of the light they shed upon the structures of that competence.

neuroscience The most general term for the cluster of studies that advance our understanding of the brain and its functions.

SEE WEB LINKS

- A list of internet resources on neuroscience
- An audio discussion about the philosophy of neuroscience

neustic *See* PHRASTIC/NEUSTIC.

neutral monism The doctrine propounded by *James in his essay 'Does Consciousness Exist?' (1904, reprinted in *Essays in Radical Empiricism*, 1912), that nature consists of one kind of primal stuff, in itself neither mental nor physical, but capable of mental and physical aspects or attributes. *Russell espoused the doctrine for a short period.

New Academy Name given to the *Academy of Athens in the 3rd century BC when it became controlled by the sceptics, including *Arcesilaus and *Carneades.

Newcomb's paradox You are faced with two boxes. In one you can see $1000, but you cannot see what is in the other. You may take either box singly, or you may take both. You are told that a Supreme Being has already placed $1 000 000 in the closed box if He has predicted that you would take only the closed box. Otherwise, He has put nothing there. Furthermore this is how it has always turned out: those who have taken the one closed box have found $1 000 000, but those who took both got only $1000. Do you take both boxes, or just the closed box? The argument for taking both is that the Supreme Being has already made his move. Whatever He has done, you get $1000 + the contents of the closed box by choosing both, so this choice dominates any other choice (*see* DOMINANCE). The argument for choosing just the closed box is that the people who make this choice are the people who end up rich.

New England transcendentalism The movement whose leading figure was *Emerson, centred on the 'Transcendental Club' formed in Boston in 1836. It was much influenced by German *idealism and *Romanticism, and tended towards *pantheism, *mysticism, and a general uplifting optimism about the progress of the spirit. Self-reliance and simple, communal living were associated with the doctrine that the soul is in itself a microcosm, reflecting the entire world. *The Dial* was the quarterly journal of the club. Other members of the movement included *Thoreau, W. E. Channing (1817–1901), and Bronson Alcott (1799–1888).

SEE WEB LINKS

- A list of internet resources on New England transcendentalism, including bibliographies

Newman, John Henry (1801–90) English theologian. Together with John Keble and Edward Pusey, Newman was one of the founders of the Oxford movement or Tractarian movement within the Church of England in 1833. This high-church movement foundered with Newman's own conversion to Roman Catholicism in 1845. Philosophically Newman is remembered for his idea of conviction arrived at rationally, but in an informal way, conditional upon pre-existent immersion in a subject matter and its associated practices. The idea is elaborated in terms of an 'illative sense' or internal subjective authority that leads to our sense of the truth of propositions in all 'concrete reasonings' including science, history, and theology. This idea can be seen as anticipating much in later 20th-century epistemology, especially that of *Wittgenstein. The principal work is *Essay in Aid of a Grammar of Assent* (1870).

new realism The reaction at the beginning of the 20th century against the dominant *idealist and *Hegelian metaphysics. In England the reaction is associated especially with *Russell and *Moore. In America philosophers defining themselves as new realists included F. J. Woodbridge (1867–1940) and R. B. Perry (1876–1957). The view tended to dismiss any special status of mind, and to lead towards *behaviourism. *See also* CRITICAL REALISM.

new riddle of induction *See* GOODMAN'S PARADOX.

Newton, Isaac (1642–1727) British mathematician and physicist, and a principal source of the classical scientific view of the world. The man *Hume called 'the greatest and rarest that ever arose for the ornament and instruction of the species' was born in Lincolnshire and educated at Trinity College, Cambridge. His major mathematical discoveries are usually dated to between 1665 and 1666, when he was secluded in Lincolnshire, the university being closed because of the plague. In 1669 he became professor of mathematics. His great work, the *Philosophiae Naturalis Principia Mathematica* ('Mathematical Principles of Natural Philosophy', usually referred to as the *Principia*), was published in 1687. He supervised reform of the currency when in 1696 he was given the post of Warden of the Mint (according to *Voltaire, because the Treasurer, Lord Halifax, was enamoured of his niece).

Throughout his career, Newton engaged in scientific correspondence and controversy. The often-quoted remark, 'If I have seen further it is by standing on the shoulders of Giants,' occurs in a conciliatory letter to Robert Hooke (1635–1703), the secretary of the Royal Society, concerning priorities in making optical discoveries (wittingly or not, Newton was in fact echoing the remark of Bernard of Chartres in 1120: 'we are dwarfs standing on the shoulders of giants'). The dispute with *Leibniz over the invention of the calculus is his best-known quarrel, and certainly the least edifying, with Newton himself appointing the committee of the Royal Society that judged the question of precedence, and then writing the report, the *Commercium Epistolicum*, awarding himself the victory. Although the father of the 'age of reason', Newton was himself interested in alchemy, prophecy, gnostic wisdom, and theology (his manuscripts include some 1300000 words on biblical subjects, as well as *Observations upon the Prophecies of Daniel, and the Apocalypse of St John*, 1733).

The philosophical influence of *Principia* was incalculable, and from *Locke's *Essay* onwards philosophers recognized Newton's work as a new paradigm of scientific method, but without being entirely clear what different parts reason and observation play in the edifice. Although Newton ushered in so much of the scientific world view, in the general scholium at the end of Bk iii of *Principia* he argues that 'it is not to be conceived that mere mechanical causes could give birth to so many regular motions', and hence that his discoveries pointed to the operations of God, 'to discourse of whom from phenomena does certainly belong to natural philosophy'. Newton confesses that he has 'not been able to discover the cause of those properties of gravity from phenomena': *hypotheses non fingo* (I do not make hypotheses). It was left to *Hume to argue that the kind of thing Newton does, namely place the events of nature into law-like orders and patterns, is the only kind of thing that scientific enquiry can ever do. *See also* ACTION AT A DISTANCE, FIELD.

SEE WEB LINKS

- A biography of Newton, with links to other websites
- Electronic archive of Newton's works (ongoing), together with a list of internet resources on Newton

Newton's laws of motion Newton's laws of motion state: (i) every body preserves its state of rest, or uniform motion in a straight line, except in so far as it is compelled to change that state by forces impressed upon it; (ii) the rate of change of linear momentum is proportional to the force applied, and takes place in the straight line in which that force acts; (iii) to every action there is an equal and opposite reaction.

nexus *See* CAUSAL NEXUS.

Nicholas of Autrecourt (*c.*1300–69) French opponent of Aristotelianism. Nicholas queried the basis of *Aristotelian theory of knowledge in sense perception, and also, as *Hume did subsequently, queried the basis of *inductive and causal reasoning. A list of propositions from his writings was condemned in 1346, after which he formally recanted and burned his works.

Nicholas of Cusa (1401–64) German cardinal, and Bishop of Brixen. His major work, *De Docta Ignorantia* ('Of Learned Ignorance', 1440), espouses a 'negative theology', in which a *Neoplatonic conception of the cosmos renders its nature entirely unknowable. He is also associated with the doctrine of the 'concordance of contraries', an attack on the Aristotelian law of non-contradiction which was historically influential. In cosmology he was one of the earliest thinkers to deny the geocentric theory of the universe, and to affirm the unbounded nature of space.

Nicod's criterion A condition governing the confirmation of a general hypothesis by particular pieces of evidence, proposed by the French philosopher Jean Nicod (1893–1924) in his *Foundations of Geometry and Induction* (1930). It requires that an instance of a generalization that all As are B provides a positive, confirming piece of evidence for the generalization; evidence of something that is neither A nor B is irrelevant to it, as is evidence of something that is B but not A. The principle is put under pressure by *Hempel's paradox, which apparently yields circumstances in which something that is neither A nor B may confirm the generalization.

Nicole, Pierre (1625–95) French moralist and theologian. A teacher at *Port-Royal and friend of *Arnauld, with whom he often collaborated, especially on the *Logiques de Port-Royal* (1662). He is remembered as well for the *Essais de morale* (1671), some of which were translated by *Locke.

Nietzsche, Friedrich (1844–1900) Born in Prussia, the son of a Lutheran minister who died insane four years later, Nietzsche spent the years of childhood with his mother, sister, grandmother, and two maiden aunts. In 1858 he entered boarding school, and in spite of poor health went on to study theology and classical philology at the university of Bonn, and then removed to Leipzig, where he became influenced by *Kant, *Schopenhauer, and the composer Richard Wagner. A year in the army in 1868 was cut short by illness, but his intellectual distinction was such that in 1869 he was appointed to the chair in philology at Basel, although at the time he was only 24 years old, and had none of the formal qualifications usually required (Leipzig happily gave him his doctorate without requiring any examination or thesis). Nietzsche's first book, *Die Geburt der Tragödie aus dem Geiste der Musik* (1872, trs. as *The Birth of Tragedy*), introduces the famous distinction between the *Apollonian and the Dionysian spirit in Greek life and thought.

The work is, amongst other things, a challenge to the Buddhist resignation of *Schopenhauer, since creating the Apollonian response to the terrors of Dionysius is something positive, active, and heroic rather than apathetic and passive. Nietzsche's next writings, from 1873 to 1876, are the four 'Untimely Meditations' (*Unzeitgemäße Betrachtungen*); the last of these is especially significant as signalling Nietzsche's break with the composer Richard Wagner, partly because of the latter's nationalism and anti-Semitism, partly because of what Nietzsche saw as the soggy Christianity of the opera *Parsifal*, and partly because Wagner was not appreciative of Nietzsche's own flirtation with the French *Enlightenment. In 1879, Nietzsche resigned from the university because of his chronic ill health, and on a modest pension devoted the rest of his time to writing. *Menschliches, Allzumenschliches* (1878–80, trs. as *Human, All Too Human*) was the first of the aphoristic books, followed by *Vermischte Meinungen und Sprüche* (1879, trs. as *Mixed Opinions and Aphorisms*), and *Der Wanderer und sein Schatten* (1880, trs. as *The Wanderer and His Shadow*). *Morgenröte. Gedanken über die moralischen Vorurteile* (1881, trs. as *The Dawn: Reflections on Moral Prejudices*) and *Die fröhliche Wissenschaft* (1882, trs. as *The Gay Science*) begin the crucial exploration of self-mastery, the relations between reason and power, and the revelation of the unconscious strivings after power that provide the actual energy for the apparent self-denial of the ascetic and the martyr. It was during this period that Nietzsche's failed relationship with Lou Salomé precipitated the emotional crisis from which *Also Sprach Zarathustra* (1883–5, trs. as *Thus Spake Zarathustra*) signals a recovery. This work is frequently regarded as Nietzsche's masterpiece. It was followed by *Jenseits von Gut und Böse* (1887, trs. as *Beyond Good and Evil*), *Zur Genealogie der Moral* (1887, trs. as *The Genealogy of Morals*), and other minor works. In 1889 Nietzsche collapsed on a street in Turin, unable to bear the sight of a horse being flogged, and for the remaining years of his life was clinically insane. It is generally accepted that during the years towards his death (and after it) his sister and guardian or nurse, Elisabeth Förster Nietzsche, played a role in muddying the channels of Nietzsche's influence on German life.

Nietzsche is unchallenged as the most insightful and powerful critic of the moral climate of the 19th century. His exploration of unconscious motivations anticipated *Freud. He is notorious for stressing the 'will to power' that is the basis of human nature, the 'resentment' that comes when it is denied its basis in action, and the corruptions of human nature encouraged by religions, such as Christianity, that feed on such resentment. But the powerful human being who escapes all this, the '**Übermensch*', is not the 'blond beast' of later *fascism; it is a human being who has mastered passion, risen above the senseless flux, and given creative style to his or her character. Nietzsche's free spirits recognize themselves by their joyful attitude to *eternal return. He frequently presents the creative artist rather than the warlord as his best exemplar of the type, but the disquieting fact remains that he seems to leave himself no words to condemn any uncaged beasts of prey who best find their style by exerting repulsive power over others. This problem is not helped by Nietzsche's frequently expressed misogyny, although in such matters the interpretation of his many-layered and ironic writings is not always straightforward. Similarly, such anti-Semitism as has been found in his work is balanced by an equally vehement denunciation of anti-Semitism, and an equal or greater dislike of the German character of his time.

Nietzsche's current influence derives not only from his celebration of the will, but more deeply from his scepticism about the notions of truth and fact. In particular, he anticipated many of the central tenets of *postmodernism: an aesthetic attitude towards the world that sees it as a 'text'; the denial of facts; the denial of essences; the celebration of the plurality of interpretations and of the fragmented self; as well as the downgrading of reason and the politicization of discourse. All awaited rediscovery in the late 20th century. Nietzsche also has the incomparable advantage over his followers of being a wonderful stylist, and his *perspectivism is echoed in the shifting array of literary devices—humour, irony, exaggeration, aphorisms, verse, dialogue, parody—with which he explores human life and history.

SEE WEB LINKS

- A chronology of Nietzsche's life and works
- An audio discussion of Nietzsche by three philosophers

nihil in intellectu nisi prius in sensu (Latin, nothing in the intellect unless first in sense (the senses)) The guiding principle of *empiricism, and accepted in some form by *Aristotle, *Aquinas, *Locke, *Berkeley, and *Hume. *Leibniz, however, added *nisi intellectus ipse* (except the intellect itself), opening the way to the view taken up by *Kant, that the forms of reason form an innate structure conditioning the nature of experience itself.

nihilism A theory promoting the state of believing in nothing, or of having no allegiances and no purposes. The term is incorrectly used to characterize all persons not sharing some particular faith or particular set of absolute values.

nirvana In *Buddhism, the perfect or beatific state, characterized by the extinction of desires and passions, and the transcending of the separate existence of the self.

Nishida Kitaro (1870–1945) Japan's first original modern philosopher and founder of the *Kyoto school. Nishida's own philosophy made use of contemporary Western thinkers such as Bergson and James, joining them with a *Buddhist denial of dualisms and differences, in favour of a pure *monism, organic experience before the dualism between subject and object develops. His best-known work is *An Inquiry into the Good* (1911).

Nishitani Keiji (1900–90) Existentialist Japanese religious thinker. A leading light of the 'second generation' *Kyoto school and pioneer in the field of East–West philosophic dialogue. Nishitani's own preoccupation was the nothingness lying at the base of the self, and the possibility of a religious response to the nihilism this would otherwise engender. His main work was *Religion and Nothingness* (1962).

nisus (Latin, endeavour, impulse, effort) A central element of *Aristotle's theory of nature, rejected in the Renaissance, is that change and movement in nature should be thought of as the operation of a *nisus* or principle somewhat like aspiration, yearning, or desire, driving things to develop into what they are drawn to being. *See* MOVER, UNMOVED; TELEOLOGY.

noble lie The myth proposed in *Plato's *Republic* 414–15 that men are born of the earth, and that into each soul is mixed either some gold appropriate for guardians, silver appropriate for forces of law and order or people to act as auxiliaries to the guardians, or iron for craftsmen and labourers. If we can get people to believe this, they will more happily play their roles in a well-ordered and stable city.

noble savage *See* ROUSSEAU.

noema Term used somewhat confusingly in the work of *Husserl. The *noetic elements of an intentional act (such as seeing or intending) are those that are responsible for giving it its sense; for transforming inert sensory data into something with meaning. *Noemata* are the elements doing this conversion. Husserl's own explanations include 'the house-as-intended' or 'the tree-as-perceived', or even 'the noematic "object in the how"'. Although commentators have suggested various interpretations, there is no agreed reason to think that anything answers to these terms.

noēsis (Greek, intelligence, thought) In *Plato, the highest type of knowledge, beyond even mathematical knowledge. The wisdom obtained only by those who understand the nature or *forms of knowledge, justice, or goodness. *See* LINE, IMAGE OF THE; MYTH OF THE CAVE.

noetic (Greek, intellectual, of the mind) Of or pertaining to the mind or intellect; characterized by intellectual activity. 'Noetic rays' are sometimes cited disparagingly as the mysterious connections between minds and facts, that enable us to refer to them and know about them. *See also* HYLĒ, NOEMA.

no false lemmas principle Principle suggested by the contemporary American philosopher Gilbert Harman in response to *Gettier examples in the theory of knowledge. In such cases a person is justified in believing something true, but does not know it, because the truth is somehow incorrectly connected with their evidence. Harman suggested that the incorrect connection lies in the fact that the person's chain of reasoning passes through a false step. However, it has been argued that similar cases can be constructed in which there is no false step.

nomic Resulting from law. A nomic necessity is a lawlike necessity.

nominal definition A definition, for example of a species of substance or animal, that locates it by sufficient of its properties to distinguish it from other kinds of substance or animal, but without getting at its underlying structure or 'essence'. Thus a definition of water as the colourless liquid good for bathing and drinking is a nominal definition; a definition of it as H_2O is a 'real' definition. The distinction is first made explicit by *Locke, although his own attitude towards the possibility of finding real definitions, specifying the real essences, of things is ambivalent. *See* ESSENTIALISM.

nominalism (Latin, belonging to a name) The view that things denominated by the same term share nothing except that fact: what all chairs have in common is that they are called 'chairs'. The doctrine is usually associated with the thought that everything that exists is a particular individual, and therefore there are no such things as *universals. Our common classifications are merely the *flatus vocis* or breath of the voice. Nominalism was suggested by *Boethius, and is one of the most important elements in the philosophy of *Ockham. It is not, however, easy to state the doctrine in a stable way, since if chairs can share the feature of being called 'chairs', then they ought to be able to share other features as well; the issue ought to be not how many cases of shared features there are, but what it is to share a feature, and whether language plays some fundamental role in creating the phenomenon. Nominalism is an extreme version of the permanently attractive idea that the common features of things are some kind of creation of human responses and ideas. *See also* CONCEPTUALISM.

nomological Lawlike (*see* LAWS OF NATURE). A nomological dangler is a lawlike connection that appears as a brute contingency, not explained by other elements within a scientific theory. The term is associated with the philosopher Herbert Feigl and commonly applied to the philosophy of mind, where for instance the connection between perceived colour and other properties of incident light may seem brute and inexplicable, even if regular or lawlike.

nomothetic Law-giving, legislative. *See* IDIOGRAPHIC/NOMOTHETIC.

non-being Often thought to be a misfortune, but happily one that afflicts *nothing.

non-cognitivism A common but potentially misleading title for *projectivist, *expressivist, *emotive, or *prescriptive theories of ethics. A state of mind is non-cognitive if it involves no cognition or knowledge of any kind. A pure example might be a sensation such as a *tickle, or a mood such as elation. Doctrines such as expressivism deny that ethical commitments represent features in their objects; instead they express attitudes of their possessors. Hence, it is supposed, there is nothing ethical to know, for knowledge aims to track or represent independent truths about things. This justifies labelling such doctrines as non-cognitive. But the question whether such views can tolerate or explain ordinary claims to ethical knowledge should not be prejudged. Someone claiming to know that killing innocents is wrong may be interpreted quite charitably by the expressivist; roughly, they hold the attitude condemning killing innocents, and we and they are confident that no improvement in their natures would undermine this attitude. *See also* QUASI-REALISM.

non-constructive methods In mathematics and the theory of computation, a proof is non-constructive if it enables you to know that some construction exists, but does not enable you to identify it. For example, it might be known that a solution to a problem, or a method for winning at a game, exists, without it being thereby established what the solution or method is. Non-constructive proofs are the particular target of *intuitionist criticisms of classical mathematics and logic.

non-contradiction, principle of (non-contradiction, law of) The law of logic that it is not the case that (p & not-p). *Contradiction is the final logical stopping point: if we can derive a contradiction from a set of premises, then at least one of them is false (*see* REDUCTIO AD ABSURDUM). If we ask what is so bad about contradiction, one answer is that a contradiction cannot be true (classically, if one conjunct p is true, then the other not-p is false, and vice versa, so they cannot be true together; *see also* NEGATION). Another answer is that from a contradiction anything whatsoever can be derived, which is true in classical logical systems. *See* DIALETHEIA; STRICT IMPLICATION, PARADOX OF.

non-Euclidean geometry *See* GEOMETRY.

non-monotonic logic Logic that duplicates the 'defeasible' nature of much informal and everyday reasoning. In such reasoning, a set of premises may entitle one to draw a conclusion, yet the addition of further information force its withdrawal. From the fact that Tweety is a bird it is reasonable to infer that Tweety can fly; but if you add the premise that Tweety is a penguin then the inference is nullified.

non-natural properties Name given by *Moore to properties, notably ethical properties, that are not natural, i.e. not the kind of property mentioned in a scientific and empirical description of the world. The existence of such properties is contested by both *emotivists and other *non-cognitivists, who do not think in terms of there being real moral properties at all. Their existence is also queried by latter-day *naturalists, who seek to identify ethical properties with varieties of natural property. The problem with Moore's separation of natural and non-natural properties is that it seems to leave him with no reasonable way of knowing about the latter type, and although he defended an ethical *intuitionism, the term 'intuition' seems to many philosophers merely to label the difficulty. *See also* FACT/VALUE DISTINCTION.

non sequitur (Latin, it does not follow) An argument in which the conclusion does not *follow from the premises.

no-ownership theory Theory of the self that rejects the model of a single unified owner of many experiences, usually in favour of some version of a *bundle theory. *See also* *ATMAN*, PERSONAL IDENTITY.

norm A norm is a rule for behaviour, or a definite pattern of behaviour, departure from which renders a person liable to some kind of censure. In this sense there are grammatical norms, and norms of etiquette, as well as moral norms. Indeed, almost all aspects of human behaviour will be to some extent norm-governed. The nature of norms, the source of their authority, and the form they should take occupy centre-stage in any theory of ethics, philosophy of language, and of law, and they also play at least a major role in distinguishing the human sciences or *Geisteswissenschaften* from the natural sciences. *See also* RULE-FOLLOWING CONSIDERATIONS.

normal form A *well-formed formula of the *propositional calculus is in conjunctive normal form when it is of the form A & B & ... where each of A, B ... is a formula consisting of a disjunction of atomic propositions or negations of atomic propositions (e.g. $p \vee q \vee \neg r \ldots$). In disjunctive normal form it is a disjunction of conjuncts subject to the same condition.

normative Couched in terms expressive of requirements or standards. A normative epistemology determines how you ought to conduct your cognitive life; a descriptive one only describes how people in fact do so. However, the distinction is not clear-cut in practice: according to the principle of *charity the only way of interpreting what people do in fact think, is by assuming that by and large they think what they ought to think. The philosophy of *social sciences is fraught with problems of distinguishing between fact and value. *See also* DAVIDSON, FACT/VALUE DISTINCTION, WEBER.

Norris, John (1675–1711) English churchman. Norris was a Neoplatonist, and admirer of Henry *More and *Malebranche. In 1690 he wrote *Reflections upon the Conduct of Human Life with reference to the Study of Learning and Knowledge, in a letter to an excellent Lady*, the Lady Masham (*see* MASHAM). Masham replied anonymously with *Occasional Thoughts in Reference to a Virtuous or Christian Life* (1691).

notation, logical *See* APPENDIX.

nothing The non-existence of all things; a concept that can be frightening, fascinating, or dismissed as the product of the logical confusion of treating the term 'nothing' as itself a referring expression instead of a *quantifier. This confusion leads the unwary to think that a sentence such as 'nothing is all around us' talks of a special kind of thing that is all around us, when in fact it merely denies that the predicate 'is all around us' has application. The feelings that lead some philosophers and theologians, notably *Heidegger, to talk of the experience of Nothing, are not properly the experience of nothing, but rather the failure of a hope or expectation that there would be something of some kind at some point. This may arise in quite everyday cases, as when one finds that the article of furniture one expected to see as usual in the corner has disappeared. The difference between *existentialists and *analytical philosophers on the point is that whereas the former are afraid of Nothing, the latter think that there is nothing to be afraid of. A rather different set of concerns arises when actions are specified in terms of doing nothing: saying nothing may be an admission of guilt, and doing nothing in some circumstances may be tantamount to murder (*see* ACTS/OMISSIONS DOCTRINE, TROLLEY PROBLEM).

Other substantive problems arise over conceptualizing empty *space and *time.

noumenon A term especially associated with *Kant, denoting things as they are in themselves, as opposed to things as they are for us, knowable by the senses (*phenomena). The noumenal lies behind the mind-imposed forms of time, space, and causation, and is therefore unknowable. On one view Kant is locked into a 'two-worlds' view, so that the noumenal is rather like *Berkeley's God, in being responsible for the phenomenal world, except that we cannot know anything of its nature. On a different view, the distinction merely reflects Kant's understanding that all knowledge is knowledge from a standpoint, so the noumenal is the fraudulent idea of that which would be apprehended by a being with no point of view. It is unclear how on Kant's own view we can mean anything by the term, but Kant does suppose that we need to postulate a noumenal reality and especially a noumenal self as a condition of human *free will, the phenomenal self being all too determined in its actions.

nous (Greek, mind) Reason, and especially the faculty of intellectual apprehension, as distinct from mere empirical knowledge. In *Plato *nous* is the quality enabling one to apprehend the *forms. *Aristotle distinguished between *nous pathetikos* (passive reason) and the higher *nous*, the immortal aspect of the soul, related to *nous pathetikos* as form is to matter.

Novalis Pseudonym of the German Romantic poet and philosopher Friedrich von Hardenberg (1772–1801). In 1790 he entered the University of Jena, where he met Friedrich von Schiller and Friedrich Schlegel, completing his studies at Wittenberg in 1793. In 1798 Novalis published a series of philosophical fragments. Novalis' only finished collection of poems, *Hymnen an die Nacht* (1800), was dedicated to his first great love, Sophie von Kühn, who died in 1797. Together with *Fichte, Novalis represents German idealism fused with Romanticism. In *Die Christenheit, oder Europa* (pub. 1826) Novalis proclaims 'magical idealism': the limitless power of imagination, generating a 'magical knowledge' that combines all the elements of senses and scientific principles invented by reason.

Nozick, Robert (1938–2002) Harvard philosopher. Nozick's early reputation rested on *Anarchy, State, and Utopia* (1974), an uncompromising rejection of more than minimal state action, and in particular a rebuttal of redistributive taxation, as had been advocated by John *Rawls. The result is a *libertarian heaven of absolute property rights, at any rate for those who possess any property. *Philosophical Explanations* (1981) was a wider-ranging exploration of *epistemology and *metaphysics, most memorable for its defence of a *counterfactual account of knowledge, highlighting the idea of a knowing subject 'tracking' the truth, and notoriously challenging the *deductive closure principle. Later works included *The Examined Life* (1989) and *Invariances: The Structure of the Objective World* (2001).

n-place operation *See* OPERATION.

n-place predicate A predicate thought of as an *open sentence that requires n variables to be either bound or substituted by a referring expression to make a closed sentence. Thus '*x* is the daughter of *y*' is a two-place predicate, that can be turned into a sentence either by substitution of names: Mary is the daughter of Emma; or by a name and a quantification binding one variable: $(\exists x)$ Mary is the daughter of *x*; or by binding both variables: $(\exists x)(\exists y)$ *x* is the daughter of *y*.

nullibism (Latin, no place) The doctrine that spirits have no spatial extension. The term is due to Henry *More.

null set *See* EMPTY SET.

number The natural numbers are 0, 1, 2, 3 ... The integers are ... −3, −2, −1, 0, 1, 2, 3 ... The rationals, as their name implies, measure ratios: any number that can be written as a/b, where a and b are integers, and $b \neq 0$ (in other words, values of *x* that give solutions of an equation $bx - a = 0$ where a and b are integers). The real numbers contain all the rational numbers, but also numbers such as $\sqrt{2}$ or π that are not rational. The reals can be thought of as the points of a line, with the integers equally spaced along the line. Every real number can be expressed as an infinite decimal. There are more reals than rationals (*Cantor's theorem), and a number of rigorous ways of defining the set of reals (*see also* DEDEKIND CUT, DIAGONAL ARGUMENT). Transfinite numbers measure the size of infinite sets. The first transfinite number is aleph-null, written $\aleph_0$, which measures the set of natural numbers. *See also* CONTINUUM HYPOTHESIS. The cardinal numbers measure the size of sets: the cardinality of a set is the number of its elements. The ordinal numbers measure the length of a well-ordering (*see* ORDERING RELATION). The difference is not apparent in finite cases, where an ordering is bigger simply if it has more members, but in transfinite cases the notions come apart. Thus the natural numbers can be ordered in the standard way: 1, 2, 3, 4 .... The length of this ordering is ω. But they can also be ordered in ways that themselves tail off to infinite successions 1, 3, 5 ... ; 2, 4, 6 .... Even although this ordering contains just the same elements, there is no order-preserving one-to-one correspondence between members of the two orderings, and it is of greater length, 2ω.

numbers, law of large *See* BERNOULLI'S THEOREM.

Numenius of Apamea (*fl.* mid-2nd c. AD) Platonist or possibly Pythagorean from Syria. Only fragments of his writings remain, but he appears to have been a radical dualist, interested in connecting Plato to the ancient wisdom of the Brahmins, Magi, and Jews; hence his description of Plato as 'Moses speaking Attic'. He was a considerable influence on *Plotinus and Neoplatonism.

Nussbaum, Martha (1947–) American classical and moral philosopher. Nussbaum was educated at New York University and Harvard, and is the Ernst Freund Distinguished Service Professor of Law and Ethics at the University of Chicago. She has written extensively on moral and political philosophy, often bringing classical learning to bear on her writings, and equally often bringing literary and humane studies to bear on her learning. She stands for a liberalism that pays due attention to issues of diversity and of economic and social injustice. Works include *Aristotle's De Motu Animalium* (1978), *The Fragility of Goodness: Luck and Ethics in Greek Tragedy and Philosophy* (1986), *Love's Knowledge* (1990), *The Therapy of Desire* (1994), *Poetic Justice* (1996), *For Love of Country* (1996), *Cultivating Humanity: A Classical Defense of Reform in Liberal Education* (1997), *Sex and Social Justice* (1998), *Women and Human Development* (2000), and *Upheavals of Thought: The Intelligence of Emotions* (2001). *See also* CAPABILITIES.

Nyaya (Sanskrit, logical analysis) One of the six orthodox Hindu schools (**darshanas*). The Nyaya (or, in its alliance with Hindu metaphysics of nature, the Nyaya–Vaisheshika) school concentrates upon our knowledge of reality. Perception, inference, analogy, and testimony are distinguished as the four ways of knowing things. Nyaya generally tends towards a realist metaphysics, and anticipates many later Western concerns, for instance with the problem of distinguishing true from misleading perceptions, with *induction, and the nature of knowledge via testimony. Nyaya metaphysicians fought running battles with Buddhist philosophers over the doctrine of the reality of the self (*See* UDAYANA). The earliest text of the school is the *Nyaya-sutra* of *Gautama, which was the subject of commentary in the succeeding period. Around 1200 the school of Navya-Nyaya or new logic was formed, mainly through the work of the logician *Gangesa, and the school changed direction from epistemological to more formal concerns.

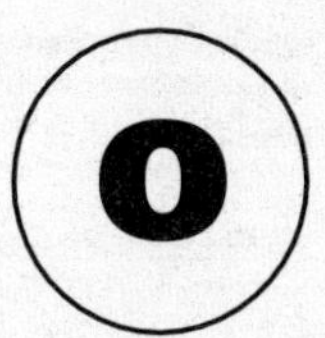

Oakeshott, Michael Joseph (1901–90) English political philosopher. Educated as a Cambridge historian, Oakeshott became interested in McTaggart, and his resulting philosophy blended elements of *idealism with a scepticism derived from *Montaigne and *Hume, the mix in turn infused with the conservatism of *Burke. He became professor of political philosophy at the London School of Economics in 1950. His political philosophy was anti-Utopian and anti-statist. The role of the State is not to introduce grand designs for society, but to preserve the opportunity for the different practices and experiences of living to flourish (a standpoint thought to have been realized by Britain's Thatcher government of the 1980s). Books include *Experience and its Modes* (1933), *Rationalism in Politics and other essays* (1962), *On Human Conduct* (1975), and *On History and other essays* (1982). Oakeshott also co-authored with a friend, Guy Griffith, *A Guide to the Classics—or how to pick the Derby winner* (1936).

objectivism (ethics) *See* ETHICAL OBJECTIVISM.

object language *See* METALANGUAGE.

objectual vs. substitutional quantification *See* SUBSTITUTIONAL QUANTIFICATION.

obligation An action that is required of one. *See* DEONTOLOGICAL ETHICS, DUTY.

obligationes A late medieval form of disputation or logical exercise, in which the aim was to avoid self-contradiction, or to force one's opponent into it.

oblique context *See* REFERENTIALLY OPAQUE/TRANSPARENT, *SINN/BEDEUTUNG*.

obscenity An obscene representation or display, particularly of the human body or of a part of it, represents it in abstraction from human commitments and emotions, but not entirely objectively either (as in medical textbooks); rather the body or part of the body is more or less disgustingly reduced to a vehicle of a single appetite or function (usually sexual, but there may be obscene displays of violence, or eating, or other functioning). By this definition erotic art, in which human passion is central, is never obscene, but *pornography may be.

observation The procedure whereby the senses of touch, sight, smell, sound, or taste generate information about the objects touched, seen, etc. A fundamental concept of *epistemology, observation has nevertheless proved hard to understand. Observations are more than the mere causal impact of external physical stimuli, since such stimuli only give rise to observations in a properly prepared and receptive mind. Nor are they well thought of in terms of atomistic 'impressions' (*see* GESTALT PSYCHOLOGY, MYTH OF THE GIVEN, SENSE DATA). Observation seems to require the use of cognitive powers of classification and memory in tandem with the use of the senses. This is the partnership celebrated in the second half of Kant's famous remark in the *Critique of Pure Reason* that 'thoughts without content are empty, intuitions without concepts are blind' (A51/B75). Making sense of this partnership is the basic problem of *empiricism, and a central problem for any *epistemology.

obverse In traditional logic the obverse of a proposition is one logically equivalent to it, formed by the operation of obversion. For the four basic forms (*see* SYLLOGISM) this transforms (i) 'All As are B' into 'No As are non-B'; (ii) 'No As are B' into 'All As are non-B'; (iii) 'Some As are B' into 'Some As are not non-B'; and (iv) 'Some As are not B' into 'Some As are non-B'.

occasionalism The view that reserves causal efficacy to the action of God. Events in the world merely form occasions on which God acts so as to bring about the events normally accompanying them, and thought of as their effects. Although the position is associated especially with *Malebranche, it is much older; many among the *Mu'takallimun* (*see* KALAM) of 9th-century Islamic philosophy reserved efficient causation to God, and *al-Ghazali transmitted the doctrine to the medieval world, where it is opposed, for example, by *Aquinas. The doctrine also bears affinities with earlier criticisms of empirical causation found in the *Samkhya school of Indian philosophy, and criticisms later famously associated with

*Hume. In the philosophy of mind, the difficulty of seeing how mind and body can interact suggests that we ought instead to think of them as two systems running in parallel. When I stub my toe, this does not cause pain, but there is a harmony between the mental and the physical (perhaps due to God) that ensures that there will be a simultaneous pain; when I form an intention and then act, the same benevolence ensures that my action is appropriate to my intention. The theory has never been wildly popular, and in its application to the mind–body problem many philosophers would say that it was the result of a misconceived *Cartesian dualism.

Ockham, William of (*c*.1285–1349) English theologian and philosopher. The first certain date of Ockham's life is that he was ordained subdeacon in 1306. He joined the Franciscans, and lectured on the *Sentences* of Peter Lombard in Oxford between 1317 and 1319. His progress towards master of theology was halted by one Peter Lutterell, an 'overzealous Thomist', who accused Ockham of heresy before the university and the Pope. In 1328 his relations with the papacy deteriorated further when he defended, on behalf of the Franciscans and against the papacy, the doctrine that Jesus and the disciples owned no property; Ockham was forced to take refuge with Emperor Louis of Bavaria. He may have died of the Black Death, in the course of moves of reconciliation with the papacy.

Ockham is famous as the leader of the nominalists, or those who denied the reality of *universals, or real distinct properties and natures apart from the things possessing them. While Ockham certainly held that everything that exists outside the mind is singular, he also allowed the mind a power of abstractive cognition (e.g. Bk ii of the *Sentences*, q. 15), so his position may be nearer to a form of conceptualism. With the abandonment of *realism about universals goes the epistemology postulating cognitions of intelligible species, and Ockham's own epistemology depends on the intuitive cognition of particular, single things, and subsequent abstraction. Ockham's scrupulous attention to the nature of language and to logic, as well as his doctrine of abstraction, makes him a forerunner of subsequent British empiricism. Ockham's chief works are the *Four Books of the Sentences*, written around 1323, the *Summa of Logic* (before 1329), and the *Quodlibeta septem* (before 1333).

Ockham's razor The celebrated principle of *Ockham that *entia non sunt multiplicanda praeter necessitatem*: entities are not to be multiplied beyond necessity. A watchword for many *reductionist and *nominalistic philosophies.

Oedipus complex The process alleged in *Freudian psychoanalytic theory whereby the normal infant boy sexually desires his mother and is consequently jealous of his father and secretly wishes to kill him. The guilt this not unnaturally causes precipitates the development of the superego, or restraining conscience. Women's conscience needs a mirror-image origin, sometimes called the Electra complex.

Olivi, Peter John (1247/8–98) Bold and controversial French philosopher and theologian. Principally a theologian, notorious for defending the Franciscan emphasis on poverty within the Church, Olivi was also anti-Aristotle, whom he regarded as a materialist. He held his own views on motion, perception, reason, illumination, relations, the will, and Papal infallibility, and was condemned more than once by the Church.

omega The last letter of the Greek alphabet, used in mathematics for the first infinite ordinal, which measures the ordering by magnitude of the set of finite ordinals.

omega-complete, omega-consistent A set of sentences is ω-complete if whenever it deductively yields every instance of a universal generalization, it also yields the generalization itself. It is ω-consistent if when it yields every instance of such a generalization, it does not also yield that there is an instance not satisfying it. The notions are particularly important in connection with systems generalizing over all the natural numbers, and form a key element in the proof of *Godel's theorem.

omissions *See* ACTS/OMISSIONS DOCTRINE.

Om Mani Padme Hum *See* MANTRA.

omnipotence, paradox of **1.** Not a true paradox, but a term for the difficulties surrounding free will in a universe governed by an all-powerful being, who seems therefore to foresee and connive at our wrongdoing, or even to have abetted it. *See* FREE WILL DEFENCE. **2.** The problem whether God, who can do everything, can create a stone so heavy that He cannot lift it. If He cannot, then he is not omnipotent (since even lowly creatures such as we are can create things we cannot lift), but if he can, then he is not omnipotent, since He would bring about something He could not do (lift what he created). The standard resolution allows that God's omnipotence does not extend to doing what is logically impossible, and points out that for Him, unlike us, it is logically impossible that there be such a stone.

omnipresence The capacity of God to be present everywhere at once.

omniscience The property of knowing everything. The traditional philosophical problem is to reconcile the orthodox idea that God knows everything with the absence of *predetermination, or in other words with the idea that whereas the past is fixed the future remains somehow 'open'. To many thinkers it has seemed that if God knows, already, what will happen tomorrow, then human *free will and responsibility must be a mere sham. *See also* SCIENTIA MEDIA.

one over many principle A principle doubtfully attributed to *Plato on the basis of passages in the *Republic* and *Parmenides*. If we count many leaves, then in addition to the leaves we count there is one thing—a leaf—which they all are. This thing is known to us separately before we can recognize or count the individual leaves. The principle poses one version of the problem of *universals. It does not seem easy to reconcile with Plato's general position that he is more sure about the existence of some *forms (e.g. for terms with opposites) than others, since if forms are necessary for any kind of classification, we should be happy with all of them. *See also* THIRD MAN ARGUMENT.

one-place predicate *See* N-PLACE PREDICATE.

one-to-one correspondence Two sets can be put into one-to-one correspondence when to each element of one there corresponds one element of the other, and to each distinct element of the one a different element of the other. Counting is an operation that puts n-membered sets of objects into one-to-one correspondence with the set of the first n natural numbers. When two sets can be put into such a correspondence they are equinumerous.

This definition makes no use of numbers, and opens the way to defining a number in terms of a set of equinumerous sets. It thus lies at the heart of the *logicist programme of *Frege and *Russell. *See also* HUME'S PRINCIPLE.

onomastics The branch of *semantics that studies the etymology of proper names.

ontic Variant for ontological, describing a thesis in *ontology.

ontological argument The celebrated argument for the existence of God first propounded by *Anselm in his *Proslogion*, ch. 2. The argument is notable as being purely **a priori*, and is usually interpreted as an attempt to prove the existence of God without using any contingent premise. Anselm follows *Boethius by defining God as 'something than which nothing greater can be conceived' (*id quo maius cogitare nequit*). God then exists in the understanding, since we understand this concept. But if He only existed in the understanding, something greater could be conceived, for a being that exists in reality is greater than one that exists only in the understanding. But then we can conceive of something greater than that than which nothing greater can be conceived, which is contradictory. Hence, God cannot exist only in the understanding, but exists in reality. In Anselm's own time the argument was criticized by a monk called Gaunilo, who urged that the same pattern of reasoning would prove the existence of a perfect island (for a perfect island existing only in the imagination is obviously not as good as one that really exists). The argument was not accepted by *Aquinas, but was resurrected by *Descartes, who made plain the requirement that existence be thought of as part of the definition or essence of a supremely perfect being. This, in turn, opened the way to criticism by *Hume and especially *Kant, that existence is not a property or predicate on all fours with others, that can be added or subtracted from definitions at will. This criticism has been generally sustained by modern logic (*see* QUANTIFIER, VARIABLE).

The argument has been treated by modern theologians such as *Barth, following *Hegel, not so much as a proof with which to confront the unconverted, but as an exploration of the deep meaning of religious belief. *Collingwood regards the argument as proving not that because our idea of God is that of *id quo maius cogitare nequit*, therefore God exists, but proving that because this is our idea of God, we stand committed to belief in its existence: its existence is a metaphysical posit, or absolute presupposition of certain forms of thought.

In the 20th century, *modal versions of the ontological argument have been propounded by the American philosophers Charles Hartshorne, Norman Malcolm, and Alvin Plantinga. One version is as follows. Let us define something as unsurpassably great if it exists and is perfect in every *possible world. Now let us allow that it is at least possible that an unsurpassably great being exists. This means that there is a possible world in which such a being exists. But if it exists in one world, it exists in all (for the fact that such a being exists in one world entails that it exists and is perfect in every world). So it exists necessarily. The correct response to this argument is to disallow the apparently reasonable concession that it is possible that such a being exists. This concession is much more dangerous than it looks, since in the modal logic involved, from possibly necessarily *p*, we can derive necessarily *p*. A symmetrical proof starting from the assumption that it is possible that such a being not exist would derive that it is impossible that it exists.

ontological commitment Commitment to the existence of something. According to *Quine we are ontologically committed to the values our variables must take in order for the properly *regimented version of our theories to be true. It is also important to maintain a 'taste for desert landscapes', or in other words to conform to *Ockham's razor, and avoiding inflating our ontologies.

ontology Derived from the Greek word for being, but a 17th-century coinage for the branch of *metaphysics that concerns itself with what exists. Apart from the *ontological argument itself there have existed many **a priori* arguments that the world must contain things of one kind or another: simple things, unextended things, eternal substances, necessary beings, and so on. Such arguments often depend upon some version of the principle of *sufficient reason. *Kant is the greatest opponent of the view that unaided reason can tell us in detail what kinds of thing must exist, and therefore do exist. In the 20th century, *Heidegger is often thought of primarily as an ontologist. *Quine's principle of ontological commitment is that to be is to be the value of a *bound variable, a principle not telling us what things exist, but how to determine what things a theory claims to exist. These are the things the variables range over in a properly regimented formal presentation of the theory. Philosophers characteristically charge each other with *reifying things improperly, and in the history of philosophy every kind of thing will at one time or another have been thought to be the fictitious result of an ontological mistake.

opacity and transparency *See* REFERENTIALLY OPAQUE/TRANSPARENT.

open question argument The argument used by *Moore in *Principia Ethica* (1903) to show that you cannot define an evaluative term as equivalent to the features you use as a standard for applying it. Thus, suppose you value all and only things that create happiness, Moore still seeks to show that this is not what the word 'good' means in your mouth. The argument is that even if this is your standard, you will recognize that it makes sense to ask whether all and only things that create happiness are good. This is a substantial or 'open' question, which, according to Moore, it would not be if the two terms had come to mean the same.

open sentence A sentence containing free *variables, i.e. an expression that is not itself interpretable as true or false, but that requires the addition of one or more *quantifiers to become a *closed sentence. 'x loves y' is an open sentence; '$(\exists x)(\forall y)$ x loves y' is a closed sentence, saying that someone loves everyone. An open sentence with n free variables may be thought of as an *n-place predicate.

open society/closed society Contrast made famous in the works of *Popper, particularly *The Open Society and its Enemies* (1945). Open societies are those in which the actions of individuals can be freely assessed and monitored, and subjected to criticism in liberal and democratic debate. They thus change by 'piecemeal social engineering'. In a closed society these proper processes of change are replaced by the inefficient command structures of *totalitarian government.

open texture The term, due to *Waismann, for the fact that however tightly we think we define an expression, there always remains a set of (possibly remote) possibilities under which there would be no right answer to the question of whether it applies. This is its porosity, or open texture. It is not the same as *vagueness, since in actual situations the application of the term may be quite definite. For example, the term 'mother' is not vague, but its open texture is revealed if through technological advance differences open up between the mother that produces the ovum, the mother that carries the foetus to term, and the mother that rears the baby. It will then be fruitless to pursue the question of which is the 'real' mother, since the term is not adapted to giving a decision in the new circumstances.

operation An operation on a set S is a *function associating some number of elements of S with a resulting element. If the resulting element is also always in S, then S is closed under the operation. An n-ary (unary, binary etc.) operation associates n elements of S with the resulting element. A polyadic operation can take sets of different sizes as arguments.

operationalism (operationism) The *reductive and *positivist philosophy of science associated particularly with *Bridgman. According to operationalism, propositions about theoretical entities such as particles are disguised propositions about the experiences resulting from definite scientific operations. Theoretical terms that are not so definable are to be avoided. Operationalism was supported by the overwhelming importance of *Einstein's recognition that we can mean no more by such a notion as absolute simultaneity than we can measure by signals of finite velocity. However, the view is equivalent to the radical empiricism that holds that theoretical entities are *logical constructions from experience. It is now widely supposed that this is untenable, and that it is necessary to maintain some logical gap between theory and evidence.

operator A term that signifies an *operation. An operation is a *function, so operators include expressions like 'square root' or '&'. The *quantifiers are also known as operators, as are expressions like $(\iota x) \ldots$, or $(\mu x) \ldots$, taking us from a predicate F*x* to the only thing that is F, or the least thing that is F, respectively.

opposites *See* POLAR CONCEPTS.

oppression The unjustifiable placing of a burden on someone or some group, by interfering with their powers, interests, or opportunities. Oppression may be deliberate, or an unintended outcome of social arrangements; it may be recognized for what it is, or may go unremarked even by those oppressed. *See also* EXPLOITATION, POWER (SOCIAL).

optimific Productive of the best outcome. According to *consequentialism, the aim of action should be to act optimifically.

optimism and pessimism The term 'optimism' is first used in English in 1759, in reference to the work of *Leibniz. The term 'pessimism' is recorded as first used by *Coleridge in 1795. The best-known and certainly the starkest expression of pessimism is from the Greek dramatist Sophocles: 'Not to be born is best, but having seen the light, the next best is to go whence one came as soon as may be' (*Oedipus at Colonus*). Optimistic philosophies include *Platonism, with the ruling place assigned to the form of the good, *Aristotelianism, with its sense of the harmony of nature and the attainability of ends, *Epicureanism, which denies the evil of death, and *Stoicism, which denies the evil of pain as well. Christianity can come in either flavour: philosophers have mostly been concerned with the optimistic project of reconciling divine excellence with apparent evil. The most famous result of this exercise (*theodicy) was the *panglossian vision of Leibniz, satirized by *Voltaire in *Candide*. However, Christianity also offers a pessimistic version, with the stress falling on *sin, the Fall, the likelihood of predetermined damnation, and the propriety of anguish and guilt. The Eastern religion that is most closely identified with pessimism is *Buddhism, where the *eightfold path is a training in the renunciation of desire and complete withdrawal from the world. This attitude is again expressed by *Schopenhauer, and becomes common in the 20th century. Other elements in a philosophy may be affected by the optimistic or pessimistic temperament, such as susceptibility to *scepticism (pessimistic) or *realism (optimistic). *See also* APATHY, TENDER- AND TOUGH-MINDED.

or p or q, commonly written $p \vee q$, is that proposition that is true unless both p and q are false. It is sometimes called inclusive disjunction, since it is true when both p and q are true. It is distinguished from exclusive disjunction, which is valued as false unless just one of p, q is true. *See also* CONJUNCTION, DISJUNCTION.

order (logic) *See* FIRST-ORDER LANGUAGE.

ordered n-tuple A generalization of the notion of an *ordered pair to sequences of n objects. The ordered n-tuple $<x_1 \ldots x_n>$ can be treated as $<<x_1 \ldots x_{n-1}>, x_n>$, i.e. the ordered pair that has the first n − 1 objects as first member, and the nth object as second.

ordered pair An object associated with a set of two objects considered in a particular order. Thus the ordered pair $<a,b>$ is not identical with the ordered pair $<b,a>$, just as the queue 'a first and b next' is not the queue 'b first and a next'. In set theory, ordered pairs cannot be identified with the set of their members, since $\{a,b\} = \{b,a\}$, which is exactly what we do not want. The task is to find sets with the property that $<a,b> \neq <b,a>$ if $a \neq b$, and with the property that if $<a,b> = <u,v>$ then $a = u$ and $b = v$. One solution is that of Kazimierz Kuratowski (b. 1896), that identifies the ordered pair $<a,b>$ with the set $\{\{a\},\{a,b\}\}$. This is the definition in general use today. *See also* CARTESIAN PRODUCT.

ordering relation A partial ordering on a set is a relation $<$ that is transitive and reflexive and antisymmetric. That is, (i) $x < y \;\&\; y < z \rightarrow x < z$; (ii) $x < x$; (iii) $x < y \;\&\; y < x \rightarrow x = y$. If we add (iv) that at least one of $x < y$, $x = y$, and $y < x$ holds (the relation is connected, or, all elements of the set are comparable), then the ordering is a total ordering (intuitively, the elements can be arranged along a straight line); otherwise it is a partial ordering. A well-ordering is an ordering such that every non-empty subset of the set contains a minimal element, that is, some element m such that there is no $x \neq$ m in the set such that $x <$ m. A well-ordering on a set A is a linear ordering with the property that every non-empty subset of A has a minimal element.

ordinal number *See* NUMBER.

ordinary language The language of everyday use. Ordinary language philosophy was the variety of *linguistic philosophy that paid particular attention to the nuances of everyday usage, believing that philosophical error often arose from neglecting distinctions embedded in that usage.

orexis (Greek, desire, inclination, appetite) An orectic problem or question is one pertaining to these things.

organic Having parts that are interrelated and interdependent in a way analogous to that of the limbs or organs of a living creature. The notion of an organic unity is prominent in G. E. *Moore. If an entity such as a work of art, or the state, or a complex of pleasure and desire, is thought of as an organic unity, the implication is that the whole cannot be exhaustively understood in terms of the parts, since the parts and their functioning have in turn to be identified by their role in sustaining the whole. *See also* HOLISM.

organicism The doctrine that organic structure is merely the result of an inherent property in matter to adapt itself to circumstances. The theory had a brief life opposing both *Darwinism and *vitalism.

organism, philosophy of Title for the philosophy of nature espoused by *Whitehead.

Organon (Greek, instrument) The name traditionally given to the body of *Aristotle's logical works: *Categories, On Interpretation, Prior Analytics, Posterior Analytics, Topics,* and *Sophistical Refutations*. The title reflects the *Peripatetics' view that logic is not a part of philosophy, but a tool of all enquiry. In *Kant an organon is a system of principles whereby knowledge may be established.

O

Origen (*c*.185–*c*.254) Early Christian theologian. Origen produced an elaborate edition of the Old Testament, the *Hexapla*, in which the Hebrew, the Hebrew transliterated into Greek, and four Greek versions are presented side by side. His work *De Principiis* covered a range of topics from the point of view of reconciling the philosophy of Plato with Christianity (it is usually thought that Origen the Platonist and Origen the Christian, sometimes distinguished, were one person). He favoured an allegorical approach to the Bible, and defended the pre-existence of souls, the unity of God the father (and lesser divinity of the Son), and the original creation of all spirits as equal. He also allowed that in the end all might be saved, a view that particularly shocked St Jerome: 'Origen teaches that after many ages and one restoration of all things, Gabriel will be in the same state as the devil, Paul as Caiaphas, and virgins as prostitutes.' His views were condemned in 400, and then again to make sure in 553 at the second council of Constantinople.

original position The position defined for the consideration of justice in *Rawls's *A Theory of Justice* (1971). In Rawls's *contractarian theory, a social structure is just only if it could have been contracted into by hypothetical rational agents who have 'stripped away' particular allegiances and interests, but retain basic human needs and dependencies. The idea dramatizes the impartiality that is implicit in the idea of justice, since in the original position nobody can indulge in special pleading or bias on behalf of one group (the idea is like that of effecting a just distribution of the cake by having one party cut it, and the other party pick which piece they wish). Rawls himself called the conception that of justice-as-fairness. *See also* DIFFERENCE PRINCIPLE, VEIL OF IGNORANCE.

original sin The state of *sin that has captured human beings since the Fall. The idea that we have plenty to be ashamed about simply through being alive is one of the less appealing of ethical doctrines, but is also one of the main components of any variety of Christianity, since without it the doctrine of the *atonement loses its rationale. The precise way in which Adam's guilt was transmitted to us all has, naturally, exercised theologians. For *Augustine, it simply comes as a consequence of sexual reproduction and its accompanying *concupiscence. For *Aquinas, it is not so much sin that is passed on as the loss of a supernatural capacity to govern the lower appetites by means of reason. Original sin is functionally necessary to dramatize the importance of redemption, and the religious practices that facilitate it. *See also* TRADUCIANISM.

Orphism Mystical Greek religious and philosophical cult derived from the myth of Orpheus and the so-called 'Orphic literature'. It involved stories of creation, reincarnation, and punishment after death, and had a large influence on *Pythagoras and *Plato. The mysteries of Eleusis were the initiation into Orphism.

Ortega y Gasset, José (1883–1955) Spanish philosopher and essayist. Ortega y Gasset was born in Madrid, and educated by Jesuits, before studying in Germany. He taught metaphysics in Madrid from 1910 until 1936, when his republican activities compelled him to leave for Argentina, and then Portugal. He left few academic philosophical works, but exerted a great influence on the modernization of Spanish intellectual life through newspaper articles and teaching. In his *Meditaciones del Quijote* (1914, trs. as *Meditations on Quixote*, 1961), he looks for a way between *idealism, which overemphasizes the mind, and *realism, which overemphasizes things, finding it in the priority of life, or in the Hegelian composite of the self-with-things. Each life is one point of view on the universe; truth is therefore plural, for no one view is uniquely true. A life is a drama, chosen in an *existentialist fashion. In spite of his republicanism Ortega y Gasset had little respect for the thinking of the mob, mired in lazy common-sense empiricism. The aristocratic first principles of a *Plato or a *Descartes are to be chosen and embraced for their fertility; only the plebeian *Aristotle would want to found them in sense experience. Works include *La Rebelión de las masas* (1930, trs. as *The Revolt of the Masses*, 1931) and *En torno a Galileo* (1933, trs. as *Man and Crisis*, 1958).

orthodox (Greek, right belief) The term now denotes not so much right or true belief, as belief that is commonly shared.

ostensive definition A definition that proceeds by ostension, or in other words by simply showing what is intended, as one might ostensively define a shade such as magenta, or the taste of a pineapple, by actually exhibiting an example. It relies on the hearer's uptake in understanding which feature is intended, and how broadly the example may be taken. A direct ostension is a showing of the object or feature intended, whilst in deferred ostension one shows one thing in order to direct attention to another, e.g. when showing a photograph to indicate a person, or a thermometer to indicate the temperature.

Other, the Term intended to circumscribe other human beings, and their differences from me (or us). The otherness of other people can be underplayed, leading to charges of privileging the self or selves from whom they are supposed to be not so different, or overplayed, leading unfortunately to just the same charge, as when women are thought of as failed men, Orientals as failed Europeans, etc. *Levinas insisted that the Other can never be an object of consciousness, but must be encountered ethically; *Derrida wondered in turn whether putting the matter in those terms already implies a privileged status for the self or the home point of reference. *See also* OTHER MINDS, PRIVATE LANGUAGE, *VERSTEHEN*.

other minds Since *Descartes it has been common, but arguably misdirected, to think of knowledge of my own mind as particularly certain, and even as the basis of my knowledge of other things. Once this orientation is adopted, other things become relatively problematic. But even if knowledge of other things is somehow protected, the belief that some amongst them have minds like my own is an extra, theoretical, belief whose foundations can quickly seem insecure. The traditional way of arguing for other minds is by *analogy. Critics complain that this involves generalizing from the one case (my own) and rather extravagantly supposing that all things resembling me physically also resemble me mentally. It also presupposes that I can make sense of the very notion of another person's consciousness, whereas within the Cartesian world view there is no explanation of how I could acquire such an idea. More social and public approaches to knowledge see knowledge of my own mind as itself dependent upon knowledge of the world, and indeed upon knowledge of other people's minds, as these are exhibited in their language and behaviour. *See also* PRIVATE LANGUAGE.

other-regarding Having as an object some state of another person. Other-regarding virtues include benevolence and sensitivity; self-regarding virtues include prudence and temperance, which, while they might benefit others, do not have this as their point.

ouden mallon (Greek, nothing more) The watchword or battle-cry of Greek *scepticism, signifying that because of the equal power of opposing arguments we have reached a state of **epochē* or mental equilibrium.

ought The principal term with which we express *obligation and *duty, but also the conclusion of less weighty practical reasoning: 'if we want a drink we ought to find a café.' *See also* CATEGORICAL/HYPOTHETICAL IMPERATIVE, ETHICS.

ousia (Greek, substance, entity, being, essence, nature) The highest of the *categories in *Aristotle; the one which picks out basic unified subjects. *See* BEING, SUBSTANCE, SUBSTRATE.

overdetermination An event is overdetermined if there exist more than one antecedent events, any of which would be a sufficient *condition for the event occurring. Analogously, a conclusion is overdetermined if it can be proved in any of a number of independent ways. The concept is employed by *Freud to describe the possibility of multiple causes and interpretations of dreams.

overman *See* *ÜBERMENSCH*.

Owen, Robert (1771–1858) Welsh social reformer. Owen is best remembered as a campaigner against the abuses of the industrial revolution, and for the model cotton factory he set up in New Lanark. In political philosophy he was an early advocate of communal ownership of the means of production by workers' cooperatives rather than the State. *See* SYNDICALISM.

owl of Minerva A traditional symbol of wisdom, most famously invoked in *Hegel's remark at the end of the Preface to the *Philosophy of Right*: 'when philosophy paints its grey in grey, then has a shape of life grown old. The owl of Minerva spreads its wings only with the coming of the dusk.' Hegel means that the kinds of self-conscious reflection making up philosophy can occur only when a way of life is sufficiently mature to be already passing, but the doctrine neglects the fact that self-consciousness and reflection co-exist with activity. For example, an active social and political movement will co-exist with reflection on the categories within which it frames its position.

Oxford Calculators Modern term for a group of thinkers centred upon Merton College, Oxford, in the mid-14th century, who attempted to bring mathematical technique to bear not only on physics but on scholastic philosophy and theology. They included *Bradwardine and *Kilvington.

Oxford philosophy *See* LINGUISTIC PHILOSOPHY.

O

pain A favourite example of an experience that seems to resist *reduction in terms of behaviour. Although pain obviously has behavioural consequences, being unpleasant, disruptive, and sometimes overwhelming, there is also something more than behaviour, something 'that it is like' to be in pain, and there is all the difference in the world between pain behaviour accompanied by pain and the same behaviour without pain. Theories identifying pain with neural events subserving it have been attacked (e.g. by *Kripke) on the grounds that whilst a genuine metaphysical identity should be necessarily true, the association between pain and any such event would be contingent. *See also* MIND–BODY PROBLEM, QUALIA.

Paine, Thomas (1737–1809) English political theorist and activist. Born in Thetford, Norfolk, Paine emigrated to America in 1774, after meeting *Franklin who encouraged him, in London. His pamphlet *Common Sense* (1776) was the first public call for American independence. The *Rights of Man* (1791–2) was a response to *Burke's *Reflections on the Revolution in France*, in which Paine affirms basically Lockean principles of democracy and liberty against Burke's conservative attack on the revolution. Paine had a brief success in France, but narrowly escaped being guillotined (he credited his escape to divine providence). His last major work, *The Age of Reason* (1794), a defence of the *Enlightenment, contributed to his notoriety as an atheist, although it is more properly *deistic in its political philosophy. He lived in France until 1802, when he returned to America where he died in relative obscurity.

SEE WEB LINKS

- A list of internet resources on Paine
- A brief biography, with texts of Paine's works

Paley, William (1743–1805) English theologian and moral philosopher. Paley is remembered for two contributions to natural theology. The first is the sustained defence of the argument to *design for the existence of God, in his *Natural Theology* (1802). Paley draws extensively on biology and anatomy to convince the reader that natural organisms are like contrivances and machines, and irrefutably the product of intelligent design. The argument had already been intellectually blocked by *Hume's *Dialogues*, and the coming of the theory of *evolution is usually thought to have dissolved its residual appeal. Paley is also remembered for his hugely successful *A View of the Evidences of Christianity* (1794), an attempted rebuttal of Hume's argument that in the sphere of religious *miracles the credibility of witnesses is always lower than the probability of a miracle that they claim to have witnessed.

Panaetius of Rhodes (*c.*185–109 BC) Panaetius was head of the Stoa from 129 BC until his death. He was a companion of the general Scipio Aemilianus and accompanied him to the east. His views were mainly ethical, diluting Stoicism with enough Aristotelianism to make it suitable for the Roman world in which he moved: as well as the Stoical virtues of fortitude and justice we should aim for some of the more magnificent traits appropriate to the *great-souled man. Panaetius also held the modern-sounding view that there are several *personae* or characters that we should each develop, and that different ethical rules go with our different roles. His work was an influence on *Cicero.

panentheism *See* KRAUSE.

panglossian Ludicrously optimistic. Dr Pangloss is the character in *Voltaire's satire *Candide* who embodies *Leibniz's view that this is the best of all possible worlds.

panpsychism Either the view that all parts of matter involve consciousness, or the more holistic view that the whole world 'is but the veil of an infinite realm of mental life' (*Lotze). The world, or nature, produces living creatures, and accordingly ought to be thought of as itself an alive and animated organism, literally describable as possessing reason, emotion, and a 'world-soul'. The view that man is a microcosm, or small version of the cosmos, which can therefore be understood in *anthropomorphic terms, is a staple theme in Greek philosophy. It passed into the medieval period via *Neoplatonism, and became shared by *Leibniz, *Schopenhauer, *Schelling, and many others. Its most intelligible modern version is perhaps the view that for environmental reasons we do well to think as if the world is a complex organism (sometimes rather preciously called Gaia), whose unity is as fragile as that of any living thing. *See also* HYLOZOISM.

pantheism The view that God is in everything, or that God and the universe are one. The most celebrated pantheistic system of modern philosophy is that of *Spinoza, although pantheistic rhetoric flourished in the 19th century, for example in the work of *Emerson.

Pantheismusstreit *See* LESSING, MENDELSSOHN.

Paracelsus (1493/4–1541) Philippus Aureolus Theophrastus Bombastus von Hohenheim was born in Switzerland. He practised as an alchemist and doctor, and left *pantheistic and *hylozoic treatises influenced by the *kabbala, and other *gnostic and occult sources.

paraconsistent logic A logic is paraconsistent if it does not share the classical property that from an inconsistent statement anything at all can be deduced. The motivating idea is that inconsistency can be contained; in everyday thought there is no tendency to let it become a licence to infer anything we wish. In some developments, such as that of the Australian logician Graham Priest, selected inconsistencies such as those generated by the *semantic paradoxes or *Russell's paradox can even be evaluated as true.

paradiastole A rhetorical figure in which a gloss or spin is put on a report, particularly by using an expression which suggests only part of the truth. One philosophical worry about objectivity in practical reasoning is that so much moral and political reasoning consists in exchanging rival paradiastoles.

paradigm In the philosophy of science the notion is associated with *Kuhn's influential book *The Structure of Scientific Revolutions* (1962). Kuhn suggests that certain scientific works, such as *Newton's *Principia* or John Dalton's *New System of Chemical Philosophy* (1808), provide an open-ended resource: a framework of concepts, results, and procedures within which subsequent work is structured. Normal science proceeds within such a framework or paradigm. A paradigm does not impose a rigid or mechanical approach, but can be taken more or less creatively and flexibly. The concept was influential in supplanting the positivist conception of science as an abstract, rationally and logically structured set of propositions. Kuhn's view emphasizes its concrete historical situation in the space of problems and approaches inherited from preceding achievements. A paradigm is only upset in periods of revolutionary science, typically arising in response to an accumulation of anomalies and stresses that cannot be resolved within its framework.

paradigm case argument The argument that since a term, such as 'certain' or 'knowledge' or 'free will', is taught partly with reference to central cases, any *sceptical philosophical position denying that it applies in those cases must involve an abuse of the term. In one famous example, we might point to the smiling bridegroom and say that his choice of his bride is a paradigm example of free choice; hence any philosophies that reject the notion of free choice are surreptitiously changing the meaning of the notion, and are therefore out of court. The argument is widely rejected, on the grounds that even if a term is taught with reference to central cases, it may only be because of a cluster of false beliefs that those cases are singled out in the first place. We may think of the bridegroom as free, but it may be that in so thinking we have a vision of his decision-making processes (not to mention those of his bride) that philosophical reflection discredits. However, investigations of meaning are partly constrained by what we say about central cases, and there may be fields where some restricted form of the paradigm case argument is not entirely worthless.

paradox A paradox arises when a set of apparently incontrovertible premises gives unacceptable or contradictory conclusions. To solve a paradox will involve either showing that there is a hidden flaw in the premises, or that the reasoning is erroneous, or that the apparently unacceptable conclusion can, in fact, be tolerated. Paradoxes are therefore important in philosophy, for until one is solved it shows that there is something about our reasonings and our concepts that we do not understand. Famous families of paradoxes include the *semantic paradoxes and *Zeno's paradoxes. At the beginning of the 20th century, *Russell's paradox and other set-theoretic paradoxes led to the complete overhaul of the foundations of set theory, whilst the *sorites paradox has led to the investigation of the semantics of *vagueness, and *fuzzy logics. Paradoxes are indexed under their other titles: *see* ANALYSIS, PARADOX OF; LOTTERY PARADOX; MOORE'S PARADOX; OMNIPOTENCE, PARADOX OF; PREDICTION PARADOX; ST PETERSBURG PARADOX; TWO-ENVELOPE PARADOX.

parallel distributed processing *See* CONNECTIONISM.

parallelism *See* OCCASIONALISM.

paralogism Generally, any *fallacy or error in reasoning. In *Kant, the four paralogisms of pure reason attempt to show (i) that the soul is a substance; (ii) that it is not an aggregate, but simple; (iii) that it is one and the same subject at different times; and (iv) that it is conscious of the existence of itself only, and of other things only as representations. These are examples of reasoning beyond the bounds of possible experience, and result (especially in *Descartes and the *rationalists) from misinterpreting what is given by 'I think'. That Descartes misunderstood this had been charged before, notably by *Gassendi and *Lichtenberg, but Kant is credited with the definitive treatment.

paranormal Paranormal phenomena are those supposedly due to powers of the mind that go beyond the normal, such as extra-sensory perception, or perception by means independent of the normal use of the senses, *telepathy, *psychokinesis, *precognition or powers of prophecy, and survival of bodily death. Paranormal psychology, also known as psychical research, is the attempt to establish these phenomena scientifically, and then to theorize about their nature. Philosophers who have interested themselves in this area of investigation include *Glanvill, *Sidgwick, *James, and *Broad.

parapsychology The study of allegedly *paranormal phenomena. Also known as psychical research.

paratactic In grammar, a paratactic construction is one in which elements of equal status are linked by pronunciation, or juxtaposition and punctuation. It contrasts with a hypotactic construction, where one element is signalled as subordinate to another. The paratactic theory of indirect speech, proposed by *Davidson, suggests that the construction 'Gorgias said that nothing exists' is to be thought of as equivalent to two utterances: one of 'nothing exists', and another of 'Gorgias samesaid that', where samesaying means that Gorgias said something equivalent, and 'that' picks out the previous utterance. This last feature proves controversial, especially in connection with repeated contexts. Suppose I say truly 'Aristotle said that Gorgias said that nothing exists', then I cannot be presenting Aristotle as saying something about Gorgias's relation to my own utterance of 'nothing exists', occurring at the end of my remark, since that utterance lies beyond Aristotle's ken and he cannot have been commenting on Gorgias's relation to it. Grammatically an analysis in which this problem is met by having the demonstrative pick out an abstract object, such as a proposition or statement, would still be paratactic.

Pareto principle Principle put forward by Italian economist Vilfredo Pareto (1848–1923) in his *Manual of Political Economy* (1906, trs. 1972). Put in terms of preferences, this is the principle that (i) if everyone in a society is indifferent between two alternatives then the society should be indifferent as well, and (ii) if at least one individual prefers *x* to *y*, and everyone else regards *x* as at least as good as *y*, then the society prefers *x* to *y*. When (ii) is satisfied *x* is Pareto-wise better than *y*, or a Pareto improvement over *y*. A choice is described as Pareto optimal if there is no alternative that is Pareto-wise better; that is, there is no alternative that everyone will regard as at least as good, and which at least one person will regard as better. The principle can also be stated in terms of well-being rather than preferences. Whether the Pareto principle delivers a *social welfare function clearly depends on how unanimous the members of the society are. The great advantage of Pareto optimality is that no interpersonal comparisons of utility are needed in the application of the principle; it therefore avoids problems connected with the strength of preferences. The weakness of basing policy on the principle is that it tends to favour the *status quo*, since only one dissent is sufficient to prevent a change from being a Pareto improvement.

Parfit, Derek (1942–) English philosopher. Parfit was born in China, and educated at Balliol College, Oxford. In 1967 he gained a Fellowship at All Souls College, Oxford, and has subsequently worked at Oxford, New York University, and Harvard. Parfit's interest is in those metaphysical questions that have moral and emotional significance. His book *Reasons and Persons* (1984) is a fertile exploration of both moral and metaphysical problems concerned with the nature of the self, arguing, like *Buddhism and *Hume, that its identity through time is an illusion, and discussing the impact of such a metaphysics of the self on problems of rational agency and ethics.

Parmenides of Elea (b. *c.*515 BC) Probably the most important of the *Presocratics. In his poem *On Nature* a goddess instructs him that reality must necessarily be, or must necessarily not be, or must both be and not be, which is impossible. Given the first option, it can be deduced that what is real must be ungenerated, imperishable, indivisible, perfect, and motionless. This, the Parmenidean One, obviously contrasts with the relative and specious appearances of things, which arise only through the opposition of two equally unreal forms, Light and Dark. Parmenides' exact position is controversial; in his poem positions that are apparently accepted are also described as deceptive. His legacy included a profound consciousness of the conflict between reason and experience, and the potentially illusory nature of the latter: if, as *Whitehead said,

Western philosophy is a series of footnotes to *Plato, it might be added that Plato is often a series of comments on Parmenides. Certainly the contrast between the changing perceptible world and the unchanging and eternal intelligible world has exercised philosophy ever since. *Zeno's arguments against the reality of motion are usually interpreted as part of a defence of Parmenides' system, although Zeno himself probably remained unpersuaded either by *monism or pluralism.

parole *See* LANGUE/PAROLE.

paronym Expression used in *Aristotle for terms that do not signify substances directly, but only indirectly, by picking out accidental qualities belonging to the substances. 'Colour' and 'justice' signify qualities, but 'coloured' and 'just' describe things by means of these qualities, and are therefore paronyms, indicating substances derivatively.

parsimony, law of Another name for *Ockham's razor, or more generally for any methodological principle that counsels us to expect nature to use the simplest possible means to any given end.

parsing The process of determining the syntactic or grammatical structure of a sentence. The interesting philosophical point is that for natural languages, this process is extremely difficult to do explicitly. Yet ordinary speakers have no difficulty recognizing grammaticality, nor the way in which words and other features of sentences contribute to their structure. This raises the question of whether it is right to think in terms of tacit or implicit deployment of rules, or whether our ordinary knowledge is better thought of in some other way.

partial ordering *See* ORDERING RELATION.

particularism *See* MORAL PARTICULARISM.

particulars A particular is a single thing, thought of in contrast to qualities or *universals, or in contrast to an aggregate of things. Universals themselves can be regarded as particulars, themselves having higher order properties and relations. However, a universal can be instanced by particular things, whereas a genuine particular cannot.

Pascal, Blaise (1623–62) French mathematician, physicist, and philosopher. A mathematical prodigy, Pascal published his discoveries on the theory of conic sections at the age of 16. He invented the first practicable calculating machine, in 1642, while his experimental and mathematical work on the barometer affords a model of mid-17th-century science and methodology. His celebrated correspondence with Pierre Fermat laid the basis of the modern theory of probability. Pascal's family were associated with the Jansenists of *Port-Royal, where his sister was a nun. After a profound religious experience in 1654, Pascal turned to philosophy and theology. His *Lettres provinciales* are a defence of *Arnauld against his Jesuit opponents, but in spite of his efforts the two Port-Royal convents were closed in 1661. *De l'esprit géométrique* contains Pascal's scientific and methodological philosophy, while the *Pensées* (1670) are an acknowledged classic of devotional literature. Both were published posthumously, and the latter, existing only in fragments, was not given a definitive edition until 1952. Because of his prevailing scepticism, coupled, however, with a deep faith, Pascal has been compared to *Kierkegaard as a leading example of religious conviction based on existential commitment and faith rather than on reason. Like *Berkeley, Pascal had a deep concern for the poor, and founded the first ever public bus service, whose profits he gave to charity.

SEE WEB LINKS

- A brief biography of Pascal, with links to other websites
- Discussion of Pascal's wager, with links to other websites

Pascal's wager The ancient and popular (or vulgar) view that belief in God is the 'best bet', given its classic formulation in the *Pensées* of *Pascal. Suppose that metaphysical argument leaves us knowing nothing about divine matters. Nevertheless, we can ask if it is better for us to believe in God. If God exists then it is clearly better: infinitely better, given the prospect of eternal bliss for believers, and eternal damnation for non-believers. If God does not exist, then we lose nothing, and may even gain in this life by losing 'poisonous pleasures'. So belief is the *dominant strategy. It can win, and cannot lose. The wager is 'infini–rien': infinity to nothing.

Pascal knew that you could not just choose to believe because of this kind of consideration, but thought, perceptively, that beliefs are contagious, and you could deliberately deaden your intelligence by choosing to associate with people who would pass their belief to you. You would thus end up believing, and the argument has shown that this is the most desirable strategy.

Critics of the argument point out that Pascal has not considered enough possibilities. It may be that the kind of Christian God he was interested in does not exist, but that another does who reserves bliss for those strong enough not to believe in a Christian kind of God, and damnation for those superstitious enough to do so. In other words, if we are really metaphysically ignorant, our ignorance extends to the rewards and penalties attached to our actions and states of belief. The other uncomfortable feature of the argument is that unlike most arguments for belief, it proceeds without reference to the likelihood of truth. This feature inspired a particularly spirited counter from W. K. *Clifford (1845–79), in his *Lectures and Essays* (1879). Clifford quotes *Coleridge: 'He who begins by loving Christianity better than Truth, will proceed by loving his own sect or Church better than Christianity, and in the end loving himself better than all.' *See also* PRAGMATISM, WILL TO BELIEVE.

passion In *Aristotelian thought a passion is a general category of being complementary to that of action; a receptive power, or the capacity to be affected by the action of another thing (*Metaphysics*, 1022b). In the more restricted and common usage, passions are the affections of the mind, or the feelings by which the mind is affected and moved. *See* EMOTION.

passive euthanasia *See* EUTHANASIA, ACTIVE/PASSIVE.

past *See* A-SERIES OF TIME, MEMORY.

paternalism Government as by a benign parent. The contentious feature is that the parent has traditionally the right and indeed the duty to overrule the children's preferences in the name of their real or true interests, which they may not be mature enough to perceive. (Paternalism in this sense is not gender-specific: it might equally be called maternalism, since a similar right and duty invests in the mother.) Paternalist forms of patronage (gift giving, charitable involvement, provision of amenities and institutions) have frequently had the function of disguising naked relationships of domination, e.g. between capitalists and their workers, husbands and wives, or colonialists and the colonized. But *see also* ULYSSES.

pathetic fallacy Projecting or displacing human emotions and feelings onto things that do not have them, although they may prompt emotions in us. We are supposed to commit the fallacy by talking of angry weather and sad trees. But the descriptions may be apt with no fallacy being committed, because of *systematic ambiguity.

Patocka, Jan (1907–77) Czech phenomenologist philosopher and reformer. A student of Husserl and Heidegger, Patocka was interested in the relationship between the mode of human consciousness and the surrounding 'life-world'. He collaborated with V. Havel and J. Hájek in the dissident movement Charter 77, and died at the hands of the police. Translated works include *Introduction to Husserl's Phenomenology* (1996), *Heretical Essays in the History of Philosophy* (1996), and *Body, Community, Language, World* (1998).

patriarchy The government of a family, church, or society by the fathers. The term patriarch was originally applied to the fathers of the tribes of Israel, then became an honorific designation of the bishops of the Church, and later the official designation of the heads of the Eastern churches.

patristics The study of the writings of the important teachers, or Fathers, of the Christian Church, living between the 1st and the 9th centuries after Christ. Philosophically the interest is to what extent those writings represent problems and doctrines continuous with those of surrounding Graeco-Roman philosophy.

Paul of Venice (*c.*1369–1429) Italian Augustinian. Paul studied at Oxford in the last decade of the 14th century, and subsequently held important teaching posts at various Italian universities. His *Logica parva* was an influential logic textbook, important for the spread of Oxford ideas in Italy.

Pavlovian conditioning *See* CONDITIONING.

Peano's postulates The postulates isolated by Richard *Dedekind and formulated by the Italian mathematician G. Peano (1858–1932), that define the number series as the series of successors to the number zero. Informally they are: (i) zero is a number; (ii) zero is not the successor of any number; (iii) the successor of any number is a number; (iv) no two numbers have the same successor; and (v) if zero has a property, and if whenever a number has a property its successor has the property, then all numbers have the property. The fifth is the postulate justifying mathematical induction. It ensures that the series is closed, in the sense that nothing but zero and its successors can be numbers.

Any series satisfying such a set of axioms can be conceived as the sequence of natural numbers. Candidates from *set theory include the Zermelo numbers, where the empty set is zero, and the successor of each number is its *unit set, and the von Neumann numbers, where each number is the set of all smaller numbers.

Pearson, Karl (1857–1936) English statistician and polymath. Pearson studied mathematics at Cambridge, but philosophy in Germany and law in London. He taught applied mathematics and statistics at the University of London, but his philosophical interests led to *The Grammar of Science* (1892), an empiricist work reminiscent of Ernst *Mach. He pioneered the mathematical treatment of heredity and invented the phrase 'standard deviation'.

Peirce, Charles Sanders (1839–1914) American philosopher of science and language. Peirce was the son of the distinguished Harvard mathematician Benjamin Peirce, and educated to a mistrust of metaphysical reasoning, compared to the laboratory habit of mind. He graduated from Harvard in 1859, and apart from lecturing at Johns Hopkins University from 1879 to 1884, did almost no teaching. His principal employment was with the U.S. Coast and Geodesic Survey. Peirce completed only one major work in his lifetime (*The Grand Logic*), but wrote many lectures, essays, and reviews, reprinted in his *Collected Papers* (eight volumes, 1931–5). Although he aspired to leaving a complete philosophical system, his absorption in many different aspects of science and philosophy prevented him: he himself described his writings as 'a mere table of contents, so abstract, a very snarl of twine'. Nevertheless he has permanent importance as the founding figure of American *pragmatism, perhaps best expressed in his essay 'How to Make our Ideas Clear' (1878), in which he proposes the famous dictum: 'the opinion which is fated to be ultimately agreed to by all who investigate is what we mean by the truth, and the object represented in this opinion is the real.' Peirce also made pioneering investigations into the logic of relations, and of the *truth functions, and independently discovered the *quantifiers slightly later than *Frege. His work on probability and induction includes versions of the *frequency theory of probability, and the first suggestion of a *vindication of the process of *induction. Surprisingly, perhaps, Peirce's scientific outlook and opposition to rationalism coexists with admiration for *Duns Scotus, and a scholastic approach to problems of reality and ontology. *See also* PRAGMATICISM.

SEE WEB LINKS

- Texts of Peirce's writings (ongoing), with a biography and chronology
- A list of internet resources on Peirce

Peirce's law The *theorem of the *propositional calculus stating that $((p \rightarrow q) \rightarrow p) \rightarrow p$.

Pelagianism Pelagius (*c.*354–*c.*425) was a British cleric, active in Rome from around 380, and later in North Africa and the Middle East. He denied the transmission of *original sin, and denied that baptism is necessary to be freed from it. He held the view that man can take the first steps to his own salvation without the assistance of divine grace, and was one of the principal targets of *Augustine, who had his doctrine imperially condemned in 418. The dispute rumbled on, but the declaration was upheld at the Council of Ephesus in 431.

per accidens (Latin, by accident) In *scholastic thought that which is *per accidens* belongs to a substance more or less fortuitously, and is contrasted with that which is *per se*, or through itself, i.e. that springs from its inner or essential nature. Also in scholastic thought, that which is intended is *per se*, whereas that which comes about as a result of action but without being intended is *per accidens*. *See also* DOUBLE EFFECT, PRINCIPLE OF.

perception A fundamental philosophical topic both for its central place in any theory of knowledge, and its central place in any theory of consciousness. Philosophy in this area is constrained by a number of properties that we believe to hold of perception: (i) It gives us knowledge of the world around us. (ii) We are conscious of that world by being aware of 'sensible qualities': colours, sounds, tastes, smells, felt warmth, and the shapes and positions of objects in the environment. (iii) Such consciousness is effected through highly complex information channels, such as the output of the three different types of colour-sensitive cells in the eye, or the channels in the ear for interpreting pulses of air pressure as frequencies of sound. (iv) There ensues even more complex neurophysiological coding of that information, and eventually higher-order brain functions bring it about that we interpret the information so received. (Much of this complexity has been revealed by the difficulties of writing programs enabling computers to recognize quite simple aspects of the visual scene.) The problem is to avoid thinking of there being a central, ghostly, conscious self, fed information in the same way that a screen is fed information by a remote television camera. Once such a model is in place, experience will seem like a *veil getting between us and the world, and the direct objects of perception will seem to be private items in an inner theatre or *sensorium. The difficulty of avoiding this model is especially acute when we consider the secondary qualities (*see* PRIMARY/SECONDARY QUALITIES) of colour, sound, tactile feelings, and taste, which can easily seem to have a purely private existence inside the perceiver, like sensations of pain. Calling such supposed items names like *sense data or *percepts exacerbates the tendency. But once the model is in place, the first property, that perception gives us knowledge of the world around us, is quickly threatened, for there will now seem little connection between these items in immediate experience and any independent reality. Reactions to this problem include *scepticism and *idealism.

A more hopeful approach is to claim that the complexities of (iii) and (iv) explain how we *can* have direct acquaintance of the world, rather than suggesting that the acquaintance we do have is at best indirect. It is pointed out that perceptions are not like sensations, precisely because they have a content, or outer-directed nature. To have a perception is to be aware of the world as being such and such a way, rather than to enjoy a mere modification of sensation. But such direct realism has to be sustained in the face of the evident personal (neurophysiological and other) factors determining how we perceive. One approach is to ask why it is useful to be conscious of what we perceive, when other aspects of our functioning work with information determining responses without any conscious awareness or intervention. A solution to this problem would offer the hope of making consciousness part of the natural world, rather than a strange optional extra. *See also* MYTH OF THE GIVEN, OBSERVATION.

percepts A term for items of a perceptual field, sharing the dangerous tendencies of *sense-data. *See also* EXPERIENCE, PERCEPTION.

Percival, Tomas (1740–1804) English nonconformist physician, and pioneer of public health. Percival is remembered philosophically since his book *Medical Ethics* (1803) is the first comprehensive treatise on the subject.

perdurance *See* ENDURANCE/PERDURANCE.

perfect competition Economic ideal in which many perfectly informed rational self-interested buyers purchase identified and uniform goods from many producers solely interested in maximizing profit, in a market freely able to expand or shrink. Under these conditions the market price of a good becomes the same as the marginal cost of producing it. Real markets depart from the ideal in some or all respects: it is controversial to what extent this vitiates the use of the idealization.

perfect duty *See* DUTY.

perfectibility The idea of the perfectibility of man emerges in the 18th century, with the relaxation of the theological barriers protecting the property for God alone. In *Enlightenment writers such as *Condorcet and *Godwin, perfectibility becomes a tendency actually capable of being realized in human history. Before *Kant, both *Rousseau and the Scottish thinker Lord Monboddo (1714–99) envisaged perfectibility as the power of self-rule and moral progress. The 19th century represented the high-water mark of belief in perfectibility, under the influence first of *Saint-Simon, then *Kant, *Hegel, *Comte, and *Marx. With the arrival of the theory of *evolution it was possible to see successive economic and cultural history as a progress of increasing fitness, from primitive and undeveloped states to a potential ideal associated with freedom and self-fulfilment. This optimism, frequently allied with unlimited confidence in the bettering of the human condition through the advance of science, has not generally survived the battering of the 20th century. *See also* ABSOLUTE IDEALISM, EVOLUTIONARY ETHICS, POSTMODERNISM, PROGRESS.

perfection A powerful but difficult tradition in philosophy and theology associates reality, perfection, absence of change or eternity, and self-sufficiency. A perfect being would be that which is most real; there is a departure from perfection if anything that could be real is not. Hence a perfect being has no potential that is unrealized, and undergoes no change. Evil is downgraded to mere defect, or absence or lack of something positive: criminality is the failure of some genuine potentiality to be actual, and all such actualization is good. The line of thought is at least as old as *Parmenides and the *Eleatics. It issues in the association of perfection with self-sufficiency, since the real cannot depend upon the less real. The results are visible in the ethics of *Plato and *Aristotle, and are crucial in creating the climate of thought for the *ontological, *cosmological, and *degrees of perfection arguments for the existence of God. *See also* CHAIN OF BEING; PLENITUDE, PRINCIPLE OF.

perfection, principle of The principle associated with *Leibniz and parodied by *Voltaire in *Candide*, that this is the best of all possible worlds. For God to have failed to create the best possible world would imply a fault. *See also* PANGLOSSIAN; PLENITUDE, PRINCIPLE OF.

perfectionism The ethical position that the goal of life is to pursue a perfect ideal of character and conduct. The view is held amongst the *Stoics, but also in Christian writing, since Jesus requires perfection of those who would follow him. A 'counsel of perfection' is the way for attaining the ideal; however, common morality and later Christian writers acknowledged that as well as such counsels we need rules whose application is rather more practical, and obedience to which is more of a duty than self-improvement.

perfect right A concept fitted to that of a perfect *duty, identified by *Grotius and *Pufendorf. The holder of a perfect right can 'require' the subject under the related duty to perform that duty.

performance *See* COMPETENCE/PERFORMANCE.

performative utterances Term introduced by J. L. *Austin in his book *How to Do Things with Words*, for an utterance by the making of which some further act is performed. The central examples are 'I promise ... ' or 'I agree ... ', whose saying constitutes promising or agreeing. Such utterances do not describe antecedent states of having made a promise or agreement, but bring it about that one has promised or agreed. The phenomenon had previously been recognized by *Hobbes.

per genus et differentiam (Latin, through genus and a difference) An Aristotelian pattern of definition that proceeds by citing a genus to which a term belongs, and then the difference that gives its species and so locates it within the genus. The classic example is the definition of humans as rational animals.

Peripatetic school The school founded by *Aristotle in Athens in 336 BC, supposedly named after the peripatos or covered walk in the garden of the Lyceum, where he lectured. Apart from Aristotle its important members were *Theophrastus, Eudemus of Rhodes, and *Strato of Lampsacus.

peritrope The turning of the tables, whereby *Plato (*Theaetetus*, 171 a) opposes the relativism of *Protagoras. Protagoras holds the doctrine that whatever seems true for a person is true for them; hence he must accept that those who believe that the doctrine of Protagoras is false are right: its falsity is true for them. It became a standard form of argument, used by both *Epicurus and *Sextus Empiricus. *See also* ISHMAEL EFFECT.

perlocutionary acts An action performed by speech only if certain effects are generated, as persuading, ridiculing, or frightening someone. Perlocutionary acts thereby contrast with *locutionary and *illocutionary acts, which are performed independently of whether the utterance has its intended effects, or indeed any effects at all.

Perry, Ralph Barton (1876–1957) American philosopher. A teacher at Harvard from 1902, Perry was foremost among the '*new realist' opponents of *idealism in the United States. However he is remembered more for works on value, defining value as whatever is an object of an interest. Works include *General Theory of Value* (1926) and *Realms of Value* (1954).

perseity The condition in which a thing is acting out of its own inner nature. God alone is supposed to be describable as *per se esse*, that is, existing out of his or her own inner necessity. It was a doctrine of *Aquinas that 'quod est per se, semper est prius eo quod est per aliud': that which is *per se* is always prior to that which depends upon something else. The notion forms the background to the *cosmological and *ontological arguments.

per se notum (Latin, known through itself) A phrase used in *scholastic philosophy for that which is self-evident: it is such that to know what it is, i.e. to understand the proposition in question, is to realize that it is true. *See also* ANALYTIC/SYNTHETIC.

person One of the central problems of metaphysics is what it is to be a person. The answer ought to account for central phenomena of personhood; rationality, command of language, self-consciousness, control or agency, and moral worth or title to respect are amongst the salient characteristics that have been thought to distinguish persons from other forms of life. In *Locke, 'person' is a *forensic term, applying for moral reasons ('to agents capable of a law, and happiness and misery', *Essay*, ii. 27). A *dualistic approach regards a person as an amalgam of an essentially separate mind and body, with the resulting problem of reinventing their unity in the living person (*see* MIND–BODY PROBLEM, OCCASIONALISM). Monistic theories, such as that of *Strawson's *Individuals* (1959), work with a primitive concept of a person, as some one thing logically capable of being described in bodily or mental terms. A popular modern analogy is with the compatible software and hardware descriptions of a computer (*see* FUNCTIONALISM).

personal equation The correction necessary to take account of individual differences in response times, especially in astronomy. Some observers will report an event earlier than others, because of an element of anticipation whose effects may vary. By analogy, the term covers any personal factor in making judgements, for which some allowance needs to be made.

personal identity The problem is that of what makes the identity of the single person at a time or through time. To take the latter first, we can each imagine ourselves as having been rather different, or as becoming rather different, as indeed we will in the normal course of life. What makes it the case that I survive a change, that it is still me at the end of it? It does not seem necessary that I should retain the body I now have, since I can imagine my brain transplanted into another body, and I can imagine another person taking over my body, as in multiple personality cases. But I can also imagine my brain changing either in its matter or its function while it goes on being me that is thinking and experiencing, perhaps less well or better than before. My psychology might change, so its continuity seems only contingently connected with my own survival. So, from the inside, there seems nothing tangible making it I myself who survives some sequence of changes. The problem of identity at a time is similar: it seems possible that more than one person (or personality) should share the same body and brain, so what makes up the unity of experience and thought that we each enjoy in normal living? The problems of personal identity were first highlighted in the modern era by *Locke, who recognized that the idea that the sameness of a person might consist in the sameness of underlying mental substance, the solution proposed by *Descartes, was incapable of providing any criterion for use in the ordinary empirical world, for instance in connection with the just attribution of responsibility for past action. Locke's own solution lay in the unity of consciousness, and in particular in the presence of memory of past actions; this account has been criticized as either circular, since memory presupposes identity, or insufficiently consonant with normal practice, since people forget things that they themselves did. The unity of the self failed to survive the scrutiny of *Hume, whose own theory that the unity consisted in a kind of fiction (perhaps like that of a nation or a club, whose existence through time is not an all-or-nothing affair) was one of the few parts of his philosophy with which he declared himself dissatisfied. The organizing principle behind the unity of consciousness was a central element in *Kant's reaction to the sensational *atomism of the empiricists. Contemporary philosophy contains successors of all these attacks on the problem.

personalism The philosophy of probability pioneered by *Ramsey and *de Finetti, and furthered by the American statistician L. J. Savage in his *Foundations of Statistics* (1954). Personalism rejects the view that probabilities are 'out there' waiting to be discovered. It views assignments of probability to events as purely personal expressions of the degree of confidence to be had in the occurrence of an event. Saying that an event is 50% probable is simply an expression or endorsement of a strategy of betting on the event at evens. Betting rates must, however, be coherent in the sense of conforming to the mathematics of probability, since if an agent buys and sells bets without obeying its laws (for example, assigning a high probability both to an event *e*, and to its complement, not-*e*) he can be put in the position of losing whatever the outcome. This constraint is known as that of avoiding a *Dutch book. The convergence of arbitrarily different initial betting rates upon a stable ('objective') probability is due to the pressure of evidence, which forces an agent who seeks coherence through time to conditionalize (*see* CONDITIONAL PROBABILITY), or modify his probability assignments in accordance with some version of *Bayes's theorem. *See also* EXCHANGEABILITY, REPRESENTATION THEOREM.

In an older usage, personalism is the theistic stress on the existence of divine personality, or any philosophy according to which the individual person or thinker is the starting-point of theory.

perspectivism (perspectivalism) The view that all truth is truth from or within a particular perspective. The perspective may be a general human point of view, set by such things as the nature of our sensory apparatus, or it may be thought to be bound by culture, history, language, class, or gender. Since there may be many perspectives, there are also different families of truths. The term is frequently applied to *Nietzsche's philosophy. *See also* RELATIVISM, SCEPTICISM.

persuasive definition Term introduced by C. L. Stevenson (1908–79) for a definition that employs a word with a favourable or unfavourable tone, and then proposes that we bestow the attitude on just some particular quality. A proposal to define justice, or democracy, or science, or intelligence in such-and-such a way may appear to be a neutral, analytic proposal, whilst in fact being an invitation to privilege some particular arrangements or qualities. *See also* DEFINIST FALLACY, EULOGISTIC/DYSLOGISTIC, PARADIASTOLE.

pessimism *See* OPTIMISM AND PESSIMISM.

Peter Lombard *See* LOMBARD.

Peter of Spain (*c.*1205–77) A composite caused by conflating two different people. The first wrote about medicine and became Pope John XXI in 1276. The second, a Spanish Dominican, wrote a *Tractatus* which was a popular and influential textbook of Aristotelian logic in the later Middle Ages.

petitio principii Latin, *begging the question.

Petrarch (Francesco Petrarca) (1304–74) The Italian poet and humanist was a major opponent of *scholasticism, indicting it on various counts: it elevated arid disputation; it failed to develop a harmonious community of enquiry and learning; it treated dialectic as an end in itself and not as merely a means. Worst of all it failed to instil proper love of learning in its students, as was done by the great examples of antiquity, particularly the 'three torches', Cicero, Seneca, and Horace. Important moral writings include *On His Own Ignorance* and *On Remedies for Fortune, Fair and Foul.*

Phaedrus (*c.*140–70 BC) *Epicurean who influenced *Cicero. Not the character in the Socratic circle after whom Plato's great dialogue is named, but the head of the Epicurean school in Rome where Cicero heard him lecture some time before 88.

Pharisees Shadowy Judaic political or religious grouping, in the late Hellenistic and early Roman period. They are presented in the New Testament as zealous for the letter but not the spirit of the law, hypocritical, and enemies of Christianity.

phatic *See* SPEECH ACT.

phenomena bene fundata (Latin, well-founded phenomena) The phrase is especially associated with *Leibniz. Any created *monad's perceptions or *phenomena* will be more or less confused. But some correspond to composite substances, or monads connected by a substantial chain. These are the *phenomena bene fundata* that give rise to what we call information about an external world. Perceptions of ordinary objects or even rainbows fall into this class, as opposed to dreams and hallucinations.

phenomenalism The philosophy of perception that elaborates the idea that, in the words of J. S. *Mill, 'objects are the permanent possibilities of sensation'. To inhabit a world of independent, external objects is, on this view, to be the subject of actual and possible orderly experiences. Espoused by *Russell, the view issued in a programme of translating talk about physical objects and their locations into talk about possible experiences (*see* LOGICAL CONSTRUCTION). The attempt is widely supposed to have failed, and the priority the approach gives to experience has been much criticized. It is more common in contemporary philosophy to see experience as itself a construct from the actual way of the world, rather than the other way round.

phenomenology A term that emerged in the 18th century, in the writings of Johann Heinrich Lambert (1728–77) and *Kant, to denote the description of consciousness and experience in abstraction from consideration of its intentional content (*see* INTENTIONALITY). In *Hegel, phenomenology is instead the historical enquiry into the evolution of self-consciousness, developing from elementary sense experience to fully rational, free, thought processes capable of yielding knowledge. The term in the 20th century is associated with the work and school of *Husserl. Following *Brentano, Husserl realized that intentionality was the distinctive mark of consciousness, and saw in it a concept capable of overcoming traditional mind–body *dualism. The study of consciousness, therefore, maintains two sides: a conscious experience can be regarded as an element in a stream of consciousness, but also as a representative of one aspect or 'profile' of an object. In spite of Husserl's rejection of dualism, his belief that there is a subject-matter remaining after **epochē* or bracketing of the content of experience associates him with the priority accorded to elementary experiences in the parallel doctrine of *phenomenalism, and phenomenology has partly suffered from the eclipse of that approach to problems of experience and reality. However, later phenomenologists such as *Merleau-Ponty do full justice to the world-involving nature of experience. In a different usage, the phenomenology of a subject (such as religion) is the study of what it means to pursue a particular form of life, regardless of whether anything that is said in following it out is true or false.

phenomenon Something that is shown, or revealed, or manifest in experience. In *Kantian metaphysics the phenomena are objects and events as they appear in our experience, as opposed to objects and events as they are in themselves (*noumena). It is central to Kant's thought that the former are shaped by the nature of our cognitive faculties: it is because of us that things appear extended in space and time and causally connected. More generally, the phenomenal aspects of things are the aspects that show themselves, rather than the theoretical aspects that are inferred or posited in order to account for them. To 'save the phenomena' is to theorize in a way that does justice to the phenomenal aspects of a subject-matter: philosophers frequently charge each other with giving over-simple theories of things, that ride roughshod over one or another aspect of the phenomena. *See also* PHENOMENOLOGY.

phenotype The gross physical and physiological features of an organism produced by the interaction of its genes and the environment. Contrasted with the genotype, which is an organism's genetic constitution: this may include recessive genes, or those that are not expressed and have no effect on the phenotype. *See also* HERITABILITY.

Philip the Chancellor (1160/70–1236) French churchman. Philip became chancellor of Notre Dame in 1217, a post largely concerned with the teaching work of the associated school. His philosophical significance is due to *Summa de bono*, a study of the goods of nature, creation, grace, virtue, and gifts of God. One major impact was through the theory of those properties that transcend Aristotle's categories—the transcendentals; other discussions to attract attention included psychology of action, freedom of the will, and time and eternity. Those influenced by his work included *Albert the Great.

Philodemus of Gadara (*c.*110–*c.*40 BC) A slightly worldly philosopher, who enjoyed the patronage of the Pisones, a rich Roman family. He taught an Epicurean philosophy, and wrote elegant homosexual love poetry. He is important philosophically for his aesthetics, which contained an early version of the doctrine of art for art's sake. The villa in which he housed his library is that which was reconstructed as the J. Paul Getty museum at Malibu, and his papyri are an important ongoing source for Hellenistic thought.

Philo Judaeus (*c.*20 BC–*c.* AD 50) Hellenistic philosopher. Philo was a member of a prominent Jewish family of Alexandria, and inaugurated the Islamic, Jewish, and subsequent Christian traditions of reconciling scripture with the teaching of the classical Greek philosophers. In particular, he believed that the early books of the Old Testament, properly interpreted, were allegories which wrapped essential philosophical truths in their tales of gross human happenings. His guiding principle was that Moses was a great *Middle Platonist philosopher.

Philolaus of Croton (*c.*470–390 BC) A shadowy figure, principally known from some disputed fragments and mention by *Plato and *Aristotle. He is regarded as an important transmitter of *Pythagorean cosmology and mathematics to mainland Greece. He is mentioned in Plato's *Phaedo* as arguing that suicide is not permissible, and a primary source for Aristotle's account of Pythagoreanism. His cosmology also influenced Plato's *Philebus*; and he was the first Greek thinker to make the earth a planet.

Philo(n) the Dialectician (late 4th–early 3rd c. BC) The dialecticians were an offshoot of the *Megarian school. Philo studied under *Diodorus Cronus, and was an early defender of a truth-functional account of the conditional.

Philo of Alexandria *See* PHILO JUDAEUS.

Philo of Larissa (160–*c.*80 BC) The last undisputed head of the *Academy of Athens. Philo studied under a pupil of *Carneades, before succeeding Clitomachus as head of the Academy in 110/109 BC. Around 88 BC he left Athens for Rome, effectively ending the Academy. He maintained the sceptical doctrines of Carneades, modified by the admission of *to pithanon*, or those things that deserve some kind of confidence as a basis of action (*see* SCEPTICISM). His claim that this scepticism represented the true legacy of *Plato prompted the break from the Academy by *Antiochus that gave rise to *Middle Platonism. Philo's most distinguished pupil and disciple was *Cicero.

Philoponus, John (*c.*AD 490–*c.*570) Christian *Neoplatonist and influential physicist. He held heretical ideas about the beginning of the world, about which he wrote tracts criticizing both *Aristotle and *Proclus. His anti-Aristotelian theory of impetus influenced subsequent science down to *Galileo. He also held that the three parts of the Trinity are three separate Gods (tritheism).

philosopher king According to *Plato (*Republic*, Bk v) the only character capable of ruling a just society must be one with a passion for truth, and who has achieved the greatest wisdom or knowledge of the Good: the philosopher. *See also* GUARDIANS.

philosophes French 18th-century philosophers of the *Enlightenment: *Rousseau, *Condillac, *Voltaire, and the other Encyclopedists. *See* ENCYCLOPÉDIE.

philosophia perennis (Latin, the perennial philosophy) According to Aldous Huxley 'the phrase was coined by Leibniz; but the thing—the *metaphysic* that recognizes a divine Reality substantial to the world of things and lives and minds; the *psychology* that finds in the soul something similar to, or even identical with, divine Reality; the *ethic* that places man's final end in the knowledge of the immanent and transcendent Ground of all being—the thing is immemorial and universal'. In fact the phrase is older than Leibniz, being the title of a book published in 1540. Huxley used the notion to promote the idea of a universal, deep, and revealing *mystical experience.

philosophical anthropology In *Kant and in general, the attempt to delineate a universal human nature, nevertheless plastic enough to take on the different shape it appears to have in different cultures and at different times. More specifically, work with this theme attempting to incorporate *phenomenology. *See also* EVOLUTIONARY PSYCHOLOGY.

philosophical radicals The liberal group who, following *Bentham, were influential in the philosophical and political life of Britain in the first half of the 19th century. They included James *Mill, the economist David Ricardo (1772–1823), and later J. S. *Mill.

philosophy (Greek, love of knowledge or wisdom) The study of the most general and abstract features of the world and categories with which we think: mind, matter, reason, proof, truth, etc. In philosophy, the concepts with which we approach the world themselves become the topic of enquiry. A philosophy of a discipline such as history, physics, or law seeks not so much to solve historical, physical, or legal questions, as to study the concepts that structure such thinking, and to lay bare their foundations and presuppositions. In this sense philosophy is what happens when a practice becomes self-conscious. The borderline between such 'second-order' reflection, and ways of practising the first-order discipline itself, is not always clear: philosophical problems may be tamed by the advance of a discipline, and the conduct of a discipline may be swayed by philosophical reflection (*see also* OWL OF MINERVA). At different times there has been more or less optimism about the possibility of a pure or 'first' philosophy, taking an **a priori* standpoint from which other intellectual practices can be impartially assessed and subjected to logical evaluation and correction (*see* METHODOLOGY). The contemporary spirit of the subject is hostile to any such possibility, and prefers to see philosophical reflection as continuous with the best practice of any field of intellectual enquiry. For the philosophy of various disciplines, *see* the titles of those disciplines.

phonetics The study of the characteristics of human sounds, especially those used in speech. Although phonetics is probably the least interesting branch of linguistics to a philosopher, the discovery that individual significant sounds are not physically definable, but exist in context and in contrast with others, was a major impetus to *structuralism in many areas. The phoneme is the minimal unit in the sound system of a language.

phonocentrism The belief, attacked in *deconstruction, that speech is a more fundamental linguistic activity than writing. This belief was supposed by *Derrida to imply the view that the presence of the speaker constitutes a kind of guarantee of meaning, by contrast with the absent author of writing; whereas the truth is that meaning is never guaranteed, so Derrida concludes that in fact writing is prior to speaking. The paradoxical nature of this consequence suggests that the implications Derrida finds are somewhat fantastical: one can accept the biological or historical priority of speech without having a simplistic view of its interpretation.

phoronomy Term used by *Kant in the *Metaphysical Foundations of Natural Science* (1786) for the study of the motions of bodies, without regard to forces or the nature of the bodies themselves: kinematics.

phrastic/neustic In the analysis of *Hare's *The Language of Morals* (1952), the phrastic is the aspect of a sentence that is common to different moods: between 'the door is shut', 'shut the door', 'is the door shut?', and 'would that the door were shut!' we can isolate the common content of 'the door being shut', to which are added the various neustics or mood indicators giving the indicative assertion, the imperative, and so on.

phronēsis (Greek, intelligence, prudence) Practical wisdom, or knowledge of the proper ends of life, distinguished by *Aristotle from theoretical knowledge and mere means–end reasoning, or craft, and itself a necessary and sufficient condition of virtue.

physicalism The view that the real world is nothing more than the physical world. The doctrine may, but need not, include the view that everything that can truly be said can be said in the language of physics. Physicalism is opposed to *ontologies including abstract objects, such as possibilities, universals, or numbers, and to mental events and states, in so far as any of these are thought of as independent of physical things, events, and states. Whilst the doctrine is widely adopted, the precise way of dealing with such difficult customers is not agreed. Nor is it entirely clear how capacious a physical ontology can allow itself to be, for while physics does not talk in terms of many everyday objects and events, such as chairs, tables, money, or colours, it ought to be consistent with a physicalist ideology to allow that such things exist. Some philosophers believe that the vagueness of what counts as physical, and the vagueness of what counts as incorporating such things into a physical ontology, make the doctrine vacuous. Others believe that it forms a substantive metaphysical position. One common way of framing the doctrine is in terms of *supervenience. Whilst it is allowed that there are legitimate descriptions of things that do not talk of them in physical terms, it is claimed that any such truths about them supervene upon the basic physical facts. However, supervenience has its own problems.

physico-theological argument Term used by *Kant to denote any argument that starts from some facts about the world, and attempts to derive the existence of a deity. The *cosmological argument, argument from (or to) *design, and the *first cause argument are the best known arguments of this kind. *See also* FIVE WAYS.

physics, philosophy of *Aristotle distinguishes seven meanings of the Greek word *physis*, settling on it as the essence of things that have a source of movement within themselves. The world, for Aristotle, is a world of self-moving or self-developing things, and *physis* is the principle of growth and change. The view makes it easy to conceive of things as having a **nisus* or principle within them whereby they are drawn to actualize a potential, or to become what it is in their nature to be (*see* MOVER, UNMOVED). This conception of *physis* enables Aristotle to effect some sort of bridge between *physis* and *nomos*, or the world of what is and the world of what ought to be.

However, it was this *teleological conception of nature that was supplanted by the Renaissance, and by the scientific revolution of the 17th century (*see* GALILEAN WORLD VIEW). With the emergence of physics as a distinct discipline, philosophical reflection turned towards attempts to interpret the results of the science, and its presuppositions and methodology. In this field, there are questions of the nature of experiment, the distinction between observation and theory, the justification of *induction and its methods, the nature of *explanation, and the role played by *falsifiability in science. Increasingly interest has turned from highly abstract models of the logical structure of physical science to a more historical and empirical concern with the dynamics of theoretical change and the nature of research programmes. Another prominent problem is to understand whether physical description is but one kind of description amongst others that we might give of the world, and to assess what peculiar authority it does, or does not, possess.

Although the nature of *space and *time, and of physical magnitudes such as force and mass, have always prompted philosophical reflection (*see*, for example, ACTION AT A DISTANCE, ZENO'S PARADOXES), the onset of *relativity theory and *quantum mechanics provide a yet richer field for foundational conceptual questions. The peculiar nature of time, and the apparent asymmetry of time and space, become extremely puzzling if the underlying reality is best thought of in terms of a unified field of space-time. Problems brought out by the *Einstein–Podolsky–Rosen thought experiment, or the example of *Schrödinger's cat, invite us to ask whether the world quantum mechanics reveals is merely strange, or so unintelligible that it is preferable to treat the theory purely in an *instrumentalist spirit (*see also* COPENHAGEN INTERPRETATION).

SEE WEB LINKS

- An introduction to the history and philosophy of physics
- A list of online resources on the history of physics

physis *See* PHYSICS.

Piaget, Jean (1896–1980) Swiss psychologist and pioneer of learning theory. Although Piaget's fame belongs to experimental psychology and to the science of cognitive development, he himself conceived his work as providing a synthesis of biology, *epistemology, and logic. He worked in terms of a dynamic model of learning, or dialectical progression (*see* HEGEL) in which perceptual inputs are modified by existing structures of knowledge ('assimilation') and these in turn are modified to 'accommodate' the inputs (*see also* REFLECTIVE EQUILIBRIUM). His empirical methods with young children have proved controversial, the question being whether what he regarded as levels of development were more the artefact of children not properly understanding questions they were being set. However, his status as a pioneer of *naturalized epistemology is assured. Influential books included *The Language and Thought of the Child* (1923, trs. 1926), *The Child's Conception of the World* (1926, trs. 1929), and *The Child's Conception of Physical Reality* (1926, trs. 1960).

Pico della Mirandola, Giovanni (1463–94) Renaissance philosopher and scholar. After studying Arabic and Jewish sources, Pico undertook to defend 900 theses in public disputation in Rome. Unhappily, 7 were condemned as unorthodox, and 6 declared doubtful. When Pico tried to defend them, Pope Innocent VIII roundly condemned all 900. Pico fled to France, but eventually settled in Florence under the protection of the Medici. He was an important influence on Renaissance thought both through his defences of the dignity and liberty of human beings, and through the example of his use of philosophical thought from many different sources and traditions. *See* ACADEMY OF FLORENCE.

picture theory of meaning The view expressed in the *Tractatus Logico-Philosophicus* of *Wittgenstein, that a sentence must share a pictorial form with whatever state of affairs it reports. Wittgenstein was impressed by the way a model, for instance of a traffic accident, could be used to illustrate the actual events, and the picture theory takes the relationship of model to situation as the fundamental semantic relationship. It requires that elements of the model correspond to elements of the situation, and that the structure of the model is shared with that of the situation.

pietism A devotional movement in the Lutheran church; also any attitude to religion stressing piety and *faith rather than evidence and reason. *See also* FIDEISM.

Plato (*c*.429–347 BC) Plato was born in Athens of an aristocratic family. He recounts in the *Seventh Letter*, which, if genuine, is part of his autobiography, that the spectacle of the politics of his day brought him to the conclusion that only philosophers could be fit to rule. After the death of *Socrates in 399, he travelled extensively. During this period he made his first trip to Sicily, with whose internal politics he became much entangled; sceptics about the authenticity of the *Seventh Letter* suppose it to be a forgery designed to support the opposition party of Dion against the tyrant Dionysius II. He visited Sicily at least three times in all and may have been richly subsidized by Dionysius. On return from Sicily he began formal teaching at what became the *Academy. Details of Plato's life are surprisingly sparse, partly because of the Athenian convention against naming contemporaries in literary works; *Aristotle, for example, although a student at the Academy for some twenty years, gives us no information about Plato's life. As a result the dating of his works has to be established on internal evidence, and is subject to scholarly dispute.

Plato's fame rests on his Dialogues, which are all preserved. They are usually divided into three periods, early, middle, and late. Early dialogues include *Hippias Minor, Laches, Charmides, Ion, Protagoras, Euthyphro, Apology, Crito, Gorgias, Meno, Cratylus,* and the doubtful *Hippias Major, Lysis, Menexenus,* and *Euthydemus*; middle dialogues include *Phaedo, Philebus, Symposium, Republic, Theaetetus*; and to the late period belong *Critias, Parmenides, Phaedrus, Sophist, Statesman, Timaeus,* and *Laws*. The early dialogues establish the figure of *Socrates, portrayed as endlessly questioning, ruthlessly shattering the false claims to knowledge of his contemporaries. The aim of the elenctic method (*see* ELENCHUS) is allegedly to clear the ground for establishing a just appreciation of virtue, but more is done negatively than positively. When Socrates asks 'What is *x*?' (virtue, justice, friendship, etc.), he is shown as brushing aside mere examples of *x* in favour of pursuit of the essence or *form of *x*, or that which makes things *x*. In the middle dialogues, concern switches to the philosophical underpinnings of this notion of a form, possibly in response to pressure on Plato to justify the dialectical method as more than a sceptical game. The middle dialogues are not in dialogue form, and do not exhibit the Socratic method. The change may have been connected with Plato's belief that the young should not be exposed to such drastic solvents (the teaching method of the Academy prohibited students younger than thirty years old from such exercises).

It is the middle dialogues that defend the doctrines commonly thought of as *Platonism, and the positive doctrines are certainly uncompromising. A pivotal concept is that of the *forms. These are independent, real, divine, invisible, and changeless; they share features of the things of which they are the form, but also cause them (so they are not simply common properties, or *universals). Unique amongst them is the form of the good, the quasi-divine goal of mystical apprehension that could be achieved, if at all, only at the end of the philosophical pilgrimage.

Apprehension of the forms is knowledge (**noēsis*) whereas belief about the changing everyday world is at best opinion (*doxa*). Knowledge is recollection of the acquaintance we had with the forms before our immortal souls became imprisoned in our bodies (*see* ANAMNESIS, BEAUTY). The *Republic* develops the celebrated comparison between justice and order in the soul, and that in the state; the famous *myth of the cave introduces the doctrine that only those who apprehend the form of the good are fit to rule.

The *Parmenides* and *Theaetetus* are late middle or early late dialogues, and the former contains sufficiently devastating criticism of the doctrine of forms to throw Plato's later views into doubt. The latter is a brilliant investigation of the concept of knowledge that ushers in the classical and still widely accepted account of knowledge as true belief plus a **logos*, or certification by reason. In the late works, especially the last and longest dialogue, the *Laws*, Plato returns to the character of the ideal republic in a more sober manner, with civic piety and religion taking much of the burden of education away from philosophy. The *Timaeus* is especially interesting as a scientific treatise, whose cosmology echoed on in the *Neoplatonism of the Christian era. Plato is generally regarded as the inventor of philosophical argument as we know it, and many would claim that the depth and range of his thought have never been surpassed.

SEE WEB LINKS

- A collection of online resources on Plato, including a biography (by W. K. C. Guthrie)
- Articles on Plato's life and works

platonic love *See* FICINO.

Platonism Generally, any view supposed to owe its classical origin to the dialogues of Plato. In modern philosophy the view taken especially from the middle dialogues of *Plato that abstract objects, such as those of mathematics, or concepts such as the concept of number or justice, are real, independent, timeless, and objective entities. Numbers stand to mathematical enquiry rather as countries do to geographical enquiry, and concepts stand in a similar relation to enquiries such as philosophy or law that delve into their nature. *See also* FORMS.

pleasure A surprisingly complex concept, although central to any account of human and animal motivation. Perhaps the simplest theory of pleasure treats it as being on the same dimension as pain: a bodily sensation, but of a positive kind, where pain is of a negative kind. This, however, fails to account for cases where we take pleasure in an activity or from receiving a piece of news, when nothing like a pleasurable taste or other sensation is apparent. As *Aristotle pointed out, we cannot say that the pleasure we take in an activity is a kind of sensation that could in principle have been obtained by some other activity: rather, the pleasure forms a complement of the activity 'as bloom in the case of youth' (*Nicomachean Ethics*,

x. 4). Furthermore, it seems contingent whether any sensation is pleasurable or otherwise, depending upon other desires and concerns. Pleasure seems more to be a quality of consciousness, intimately connected to contentment or happiness, rather than another element within conscious experience. Pleasure has often been proposed as the end of all action, either because this is what actually motivates us, or because there is a concealed contradiction in the idea of action that is not so motivated (*see* HEDONISM). The ideal of much economic and social philosophy would be to measure pleasures, with the object of constructing a *felicific calculus for use in social choice theory. But pleasure proves remarkably resistant to such a treatment. Whilst we can make crude comparative judgements (this year's holiday gave us more pleasure than last year's, when it rained), the subject seems inherently resistant to quantitative treatments. Questions such as whether one gets more pleasure from art or music, leisure or work, seem to become rapidly meaningless. *See also* EPICUREANISM, HEDONISM, MEASUREMENT, UTILITY.

pleasure principle Term associated with *Freud for the way we are motivated by pleasure. The extent of the sovereignty of pleasure is controversial. *See* HEDONISM.

Plekhanov, Georgy Valentinovich (1856–1918) The founding father of Russian *Marxism. Plekhanov was exiled from Russia for revolutionary activity in 1880. Shortly thereafter he founded the Emancipation of Labour, a Marxist association and forerunner of the Russian Social Democratic Workers' Party, which eventually split into the Mensheviks and the Bolsheviks. He believed that Russia had to pass through genuine capitalistic development, in order for the conditions and tools to be built to enable a Socialist revolution to occur. After the revolution of 1905 this precipitated a split with Lenin and the gradual dismissal of Plekhanov's views: Lenin saw him as a compromising defeatist, while he compared Lenin to Robespierre. Although a dialectical materialist (he coined the phrase), Plekhanov maintained vestiges of *Kantianism, particularly in his moral thought. Works included *On the Development of the Monist View of History* (1895).

plenitude, principle of Name given by *Lovejoy to a principle he detected in much Greek and medieval thought, that the existence and abundance of creation must be as great as the possibility of existence, commensurate therefore with an infinite and inexhaustible source. For if such a source could have reason to make any possibility actual, which we know it to have since there is an actual world, then it would have reason to actualize every possibility consistent with its nature. The non-existence of anything that could have existed would argue a niggardliness, or 'envy', in the creative principle that could have brought it about. The principle infused many versions of the view that there is a great *chain of being, stretching from the lowest invisible worm to the highest seraph (for it also ensures that there are creatures intermediate between us and God); it also infuses the optimistic view, found as late as the 18th and 19th centuries, that the soul will, or at least could, rise through a perpetual progress of degrees of *perfection (an idea effectively criticized by the American Samuel *Johnson as giving rise to a version of *Zeno's paradox). *See also* DANTE, NEOPLATONISM.

plenum The conception of space as entirely filled with matter.

pleonotetic logic Also known as pluralitive logic. The logic of the plurality *quantifiers, such as most, few, many, and almost all. These terms cannot be defined in classical *first order or quantificational logic, and obey interestingly different rules of inference.

Plotinus (*c.*AD 205–70) The founder of *Neoplatonism. Plotinus was born in Egypt. After study with the Alexandrian teacher *Ammonius Saccas, he travelled in pursuit of wisdom to Persia, but eventually fled to Antioch and Rome in 244. Under the protection of the emperor Gallienus, Plotinus started a school of philosophy; shortly after the death of Gallienus he died of leprosy, possibly in some kind of political exile.

Plotinus' works of note are the *Enneads*, written between 253 and 270, and collected by his pupil *Porphyry (they are called 'Enneads' from the Greek *ennea*, nine, because each of the six books contains nine sections). Following the largely discredited *Second Letter* attributed to *Plato, Plotinus divides the realm of intelligible things into three: the One, Intelligence or **nous*, and the Soul. The One is the absolutely transcendental, unknowable object of worship and desire. The world of intelligence is that of ideas or concepts, but conceived as ideas in the mind of the One, although also conceived as the realm of number. Finally, below intelligence there is the soul, incorporeal, substantial, and immortal, and capable of transmigration (*see* METEMPSYCHOSIS). (Below even souls are the denizens of nature, but these may be so negative as not to properly partake of existence at all.) Some but not all souls are sunk into terrestrial bodies, which is bad. But the world as a whole is also a living organism, or an example of the one Soul. Perhaps the most characteristic doctrine of Plotinus is that the One 'emanates' or overflows, like light from the sun, to create the realm of Intelligence, and that in turn emanates into the world of the soul, although it remains obscure whether this emanation is a joyful procreative act of the higher creative principle, or a kind of betrayal and polluting fall of the lower. In any event, it is in contemplation of the higher, creative principle that the lower receives its form or impress. But it is also as reflections of the one cosmic Soul that individual souls exist, and their aim must be to direct their contemplation back up the hierarchy, eventually to obtain light and vitality by contemplative absorption in the One. *See also* NEOPLATONISM.

pluralism The general tolerance of different kinds of thing, or more particularly of different and perhaps *incommensurable descriptions of the world, none of which is deemed to be more fundamental than any of the others. Pluralism is often attributed to the later *Wittgenstein, with his emphasis on different *language games and forms of life. It is also a cardinal doctrine of *poststructuralist literary theory, where it frequently consorts with relativism and general suspicion of a notion of 'the truth'. Sometimes this is the relatively innocuous doctrine that there is no way of stating the unique truth or the only truth about some subject-matter; at other times it may be the more sinister doctrine that no view is true, or that all views are equally true.

pluralitive logic *See* PLEONOTETIC LOGIC.

plurality of causes The doctrine, originally propounded by J. S. *Mill, that the same phenomenon may have many different causes. In one sense this is obviously true: the same type of event (e.g. a death) may be caused by different illnesses, accidents, etc. It does not follow that a particular example or token of the type (the death of Henry VIII, for example) has many causes, although it may be fruitful to think in terms of many contributory factors, rather than just one event or state that counts as the cause.

Plutarch (*c.*AD 50–*c.*120) Greek-born writer and Middle Platonist. Plutarch was born in Chaeronea in Boeotia, studied at Athens, and went to Rome, returning to spend the last decades of his life as a priest at Delphi. His most famous work, the *Lives*, is intended to illustrate the workings of virtue and vice in the careers of great men, and had considerable influence on Shakespeare and other Renaissance writers. His philosophical writings exhibit the pious transcendentalism of *Middle Platonism. Opinions of Plutarch's capacities as a philosopher differ. He departs from orthodox Platonism by acknowledging a positive force of evil in the world (*see* MANICHAEANISM, ZOROASTRIANISM), but also anticipates *Plotinus in his concern to find a unified and simple supreme principle at the pinnacle of the hierarchy of reality.

pneuma (Greek, breath) In Greek and particularly in *Stoic thought, the spirit, force, or creative fire that infuses the bodies of human beings.

pneumatology (pneumatics) Term used by *d'Alembert in the *Discours préliminaire de l'encyclopédie* for the study of spirits and souls, including those of God and angels.

poiēsis (Greek, production) In Plato and Aristotle this is contrasted with *praxis*, doing or practical activity. It only requires skill whereas practical activity requires virtue. The idea is that in production, the ends are set, whereas good practice requires knowing which activities and ends are worth pursuing.

Poincaré, Jules Henri (1854–1912) French mathematician and philosopher. Poincaré's main philosophical interest lay in the formal and logical character of theories in the physical sciences. He is especially remembered for the discussion of the scientific status of geometry, in *La Science et l'hypothèse* (1902, trs. as *Science and Hypothesis*, 1905). The axioms of geometry are not analytic, nor do they state fundamental empirical properties of space. Rather, they are *conventions governing the description of space, whose adoption is governed by their utility in furthering the purpose of description. Poincaré's conventionalism about geometry proceeded, however, against the background of a general *realism about the objects of scientific enquiry, and he always insisted that there could be good reason for adopting one set of conventions rather than another. In his late *Dernières pensées* (1912, trs. as *Mathematics and Science: Last Essays*, 1963), Poincaré attacks the *logicist programme of *Frege and *Russell, denying that mathematics can be reduced to logic, and arguing that further intuition is always needed to derive the properties of numbers.

SEE WEB LINKS

- A biography of Poincaré
- An audio discussion of Poincaré's work by three experts

polar concepts Concepts that gain their identity partly through their contrast with one another: seems/is, light/dark, physical/mental, individual/social, masculine/feminine, **yin/yang*, are possible examples. Philosophical problems arise if it is asked whether one of the pair is fundamental: which is the doughnut, and which is merely the hole defined by the doughnut. For instance, ethical implications arise when people write as if masculinity is central, and femininity 'The Other'.

polis (Greek, city) The *polis* emerged from archaic Greece as a self-governing, small community governed by a sense of separate identity, with its own rule of law. The *polis* evolved so that family and religious life and a person's sense of identity and worth all became subordinate to the role of a free citizen and the needs of the *polis*. By Hellenic times stratification of the classes eroded the communitarian ideal, and the *Cynics and *Epicureans could proclaim the independence of men from the *polis*. The nature of the 'ideal' city preoccupied Greek political thought, especially in *Plato (*The Republic*) and Aristotle (*Politics*).

Polish logic *See* POLISH NOTATION.

Polish notation Logical notation devised by the Polish logician Jan Łukasiewicz which dispenses with the need for parentheses indicating the *scope of each logical connective. The propositional functors are N for ¬ (negation); K for & (conjunction); C for → (implication); and E for ↔ (equivalence). Each precedes the symbols to which it applies, and since there is a definite number of these, no scope ambiguity can arise. Thus C*Kpqr* reads (p & q) → r. The different p & (q → r) would be K*p*C*qr*. The quantifiers are ΠxFx and Σ*x*Fx. Although intellectually elegant, Polish notation is hard to read without practice, and is not widely used.

politics, philosophy of Reflection on the nature of human community and government, and relations between the collective and the individual. Topics include the legitimacy of government in its different forms, the foundations of law, the powers and boundaries of state interference with individuals (which includes such things as the nature of property), the relations of states between themselves, and the rights and duties associated with membership of a political unity. For different topics *see* ANARCHISM; COMMUNISM; LIBERALISM; *POLIS*; LAW, PHILOSOPHY OF; SOCIALISM.

polyadic In one usage a term for a *function or *predicate that takes more than one argument. Sometimes a function or predicate is polyadic if it is a function that can take a varying number of arguments, or a relational predicate that can relate a varying number of things. 'a, b ... n are brothers' can be true for varying numbers of people; and similarly 'the eldest of a, b ... n'.

polysemy The association of one word with a number of meanings. If these meanings are quite distinct the words are *homonyms, but frequently there is a range of *analogical uses (plain prose, plain sailing) suggesting that it is wrong simply to distinguish distinct senses.

polysyllogism A chain of *syllogisms, in which the conclusion of one is one of the premises of the next.

polytheism The belief in, or worship of, many gods. It is not easy to count gods, and so not always obvious whether an apparently polytheistic religion, such as Hinduism, is really so, or whether the different apparent objects of worship are to be thought of as manifestations of the one God. Polytheistic cultures tend to be more relaxed about adding compatible gods, or in other words their deities are less jealous than those of monotheistic religions. Hence the historian *Gibbon's observation about the many religions of ancient Rome, 'which were regarded by the people as equally true, by the philosophers as equally false, and by the magistrate as equally useful'.

Pomponazzi, Pietro (1462–1525) Italian Aristotelian. Originally qualified in medicine, Pomponazzi taught philosophy in Padua and then Bologna, where in 1516 he published the *Tractatus de immortalitate animae*, a denial of immortality following on a materialist interpretation of Aristotle. The book was burned publicly in Venice and condemned at Rome. This did not prevent him from publishing in 1520 *De naturaliu effectuum causis sive de incantantionibus liber*, attacking magic, miracles, and superstition, in favour, however, of non-miraculous astrological powers. This and subsequent writings which awaited posthumous publication admirably defended the autonomy of philosophical and scientific research, and played a role in undermining the fragile rapport between Aristotelian natural science and revealed theology.

pons asinorum (Latin) The bridge of asses. Traditionally it is hard to get asses to cross a bridge. In mathematics, the term is applied to the problem from the first book of Euclid that if two sides of a triangle are equal then the angles opposite those sides are also equal. Syllogistic logic had its own pons asinorum: the **inventio medii*.

Popper, Karl Raimund (1902–1994) Philosopher of science. Born and educated in Vienna, Popper shared with the *logical positivists an interest in the foundations and the methodology of the natural sciences. After a period in New Zealand he moved to the London School of Economics where he became professor of logic and scientific method in 1949. Popper came to fame with his first book, *Logik der Forschung* (1935, trs. as *The Logic of Scientific Discovery*, 1959). In it he overturns the traditional attempts to found scientific method in the support that experience gives to suitably formed generalizations and theories. Stressing the difficulty the problem of *induction puts in front of any such method, Popper substitutes an epistemology that starts with the bold, imaginative formation of hypotheses. These face the tribunal of experience, which has the power to falsify them, but not to confirm them (*see* FALSIFIABILITY, FALSIFICATION). A hypothesis that survives the ordeal of attempted refutation can be provisionally accepted as 'corroborated', but never assigned a probability.

The approach was extremely popular amongst working scientists, who recognized the value it puts upon imaginative theorizing and patient refutation, and who responded gladly to the liberating thought that it was not a sin but a mark of virtue to put forward a theory that is subsequently refuted. Philosophers have been more cautious, pointing out that something like induction seems to be involved when we rely upon well-corroborated theories. Nobody flies in an aeroplane purely because it is a bold, imaginative conjecture that it will stay in the air. However, many thinkers accept in essence his solution to the problem of demarcating proper science from its imitators, namely that the former results in genuinely falsifiable theories whereas the latter do not. Although falsification is more complex than Popper initially allowed, the idea encapsulates many people's objections to such ideologies as *psychoanalysis and *Marxism.

Popper's social and historical writings include the influential *The Open Society and Its Enemies* (1945) and *The Poverty of Historicism* (1957), attacking the view that there are fundamental laws of history that render its progress inevitable. In the first work Popper attacks this belief, which he associates with the illiberal totalitarianism that he finds in *Plato, *Hegel, and *Marx, although it is unclear that his readings of these thinkers do justice to the stringent ethical conditions they place upon the rational political systems that they explore. Popper associates political virtue, like scientific virtue, with the possibility of free enquiry subject to constraints that minimize the chance of accepting bad systems.

SEE WEB LINKS

- An audio discussion of Popper by three philosophers
- An internet forum on Popper's work

population Most ethical thinking supposes a fixed population, and considers such things as the distribution of resources amongst them. If population is itself made a matter of decision, then further problems arise. Do numbers matter by themselves, with it being a better world if more people live lives of some positive happiness? Or does only the average level of welfare matter? If a mother conceives in a way that she knows is likely to bring about the existence of a handicapped child, when she could have acted differently and avoided the risk, why has she done wrong? Nobody would have been better off had she acted otherwise, for the only child that does exist would not have existed. These and other questions are subtly explored in *Parfit's *Reasons and Persons* (1984). *See also* MALTHUS.

pornography The definition is controversial: roughly an *obscene representation or display, especially of human sexuality, produced to provide an occasion for fantasy. The condition that the representation should be obscene distinguishes pornography in principle from erotic art. The legal problems arise because although some human fantasies may be innocent and pleasurable, others are pleasurable to some without being innocent, and ministering to them involves representing different sections of the community (especially women and children) in degrading and humiliating lights, as victims of violence, etc. When this is so there is an argument for censorship, from the right of such groups to equal concern and respect. This argument is distinct from a general moralistic distaste for the material in question, and distinct from the contested *consequentialist argument that the existence of such material helps to promote violence. The extent to which other values are infringed by such censorship is controversial.

Porphyry (*c.*AD 232–305) Syrian polymath, and disciple and editor of *Plotinus. Porphyry also wrote commentaries upon *Plato and *Aristotle. His most influential work was the *Isagoge* or *Introduction* to Aristotle's *Categories*, which was responsible for the classic formulation of the problem of *universals, as it preoccupied *Boethius and subsequent medieval philosophy. At the beginning of the *Isagoge* Porphyry asks: 'Do genera and species subsist in themselves, or do they exist only in the mind? If they subsist in themselves, are they corporeal or incorporeal? If they are incorporeal, do they exist in separation from sensible substances or in conjunction with them?' The tree of Porphyry is the method of classification by dichotomy: **per genus et differentiam*. Porphyry's distinction is as a transmitter of other people's work. Even his major editor and commentator, J. Bidez, in his *Vie de Porphyre* (1913), confesses that in the entire extant work of Porphyry there 'is not a thought or an image which one can confidently affirm to be his own'.

Port-Royal The Cistercian foundation which was the home of the *Jansenist sect in France. In 1662 Antoine *Arnauld and Pierre *Nicole (1625–95), possibly with the help of *Pascal, published *La Logique, ou l'art de penser*, often called *The Port-Royal Logic*, which they revised many times between then and 1685, and which eventually became a standard textbook for logic and critical thinking. It shows an impatience with traditional Aristotelian or scholastic logic, and sympathizes with modern movements of thought, in particular the methodology of 'clear and distinct' ideas of *Descartes, and his geometric and rationalistic approach to the investigation of nature. As Jansenists, the members of Port-Royal believed in predestination, and the utter impossibility of words, prayers, or deeds altering one's preordained fate of going to heaven or hell. Perhaps unsurprisingly the historian and critic C.-A. Sainte-Beuve (1804–69) lost his faith while writing the history of the monastery.

Posidonius of Apamea (*c.*135–51 BC) A *Stoic philosopher and polymath, and a major influence on *Cicero (who attended his school in Rhodes), Strabo, *Seneca, and Pompey. What is known of Posidonius' philosophical views contains little that is specific to him, but he had a universalistic and imperialistic conception of history, the shaping of which combines political and religious duty. He was himself active in politics, and intellectually equally important as a naturalist, mathematician, cosmologist, biologist, and historian. He regarded the special sciences as tools of true philosophy, which would synthesize and axiomatize their results. He also discovered a lunar theory of the tides that was not superseded until *Newton, and explored the sphericity of the earth, even describing lines of latitude.

posit Something put forward as a useful assumption or starting-point, but not necessarily regarded as known to be true.

positive freedom *See* FREEDOM, POSITIVE/NEGATIVE.

positive law/positive theology Branch of these subjects treating of particular texts and matters of fact and history, rather than general principles and ideas.

positivism The philosophy of *Comte, holding that the highest or only form of knowledge is the description of sensory phenomena. Comte held that there were three stages of human belief: the theological, the metaphysical, and finally the positive, so-called because it confined itself to what is positively given, avoiding all speculation. Comte's position is a version of traditional *empiricism, without the tendencies to *idealism or *scepticism that the position attracts. In his own writings the belief is associated with optimism about the scope of science and the benefits of a truly scientific sociology. In the 19th century, positivism also became associated with evolutionary theory, and any resolutely *naturalistic treatment of human affairs. Its descendants include the philosophy of *Mach, and *logical positivism. For legal positivism *see* LAW, PHILOSOPHY OF.

possibility *See* NECESSITY.

possible worlds The central notion in the semantic or *model theoretic exploration of *modal logic. A possible world is here considered to be a complete state of affairs, or one in which every proposition under consideration has a definite truth-value. A proposition p is necessary ($\Box p$) if it is true at all possible worlds, possible ($\Diamond p$) if it is true at some, and impossible if it is true at none. Various relations can be defined over possible worlds. For example, to model questions arising over the iteration of modal operators, such as whether $\Box p$ implies $\Box\Box p$, *Kripke defined an accessibility relation over worlds, enabling him to transform this question into the issue of whether, if a proposition is true at all worlds accessible from this, then it is true at all worlds accessible from all worlds accessible from this. To give a theory of *counterfactuals, David *Lewis used a similarity relationship, so a counterfactual conditional 'If p had been true, q would have been' can be regarded as true if it is true at all of the most similar worlds to ours in which p is true.

Although the utility of possible worlds models in exploring modal logic is beyond doubt, the philosophical propriety of the notion has been intensively debated, with the same kinds of position emerging as in the philosophy of *mathematics: *Platonism, alleging their reality (*see* MODAL REALISM), forms of *constructivism, alleging that we create them, and *formalism, regarding the notation as a useful tool for logic but nothing more.

Post, Emil Leon (1897–1954) Polish-born American mathematician and logician. Post introduced the *truth-table method for defining and checking validity in propositional logic. His unpublished researches into problems of *completeness and *decidability interestingly anticipated the 1930s results of Gödel, Church, and Turing.

post hoc ergo propter hoc (Latin, after this, so because of this) The *fallacy of arguing that because one event happened after another, it happened because of it.

postmodernism In the culture generally, postmodernism is associated with a playful acceptance of surfaces and superficial style, self-conscious quotation and parody (although these are also found in modernist literature, such as that of James Joyce), and a celebration of the ironic, the transient, and the glitzy. It is usually seen as a reaction against a naive and earnest confidence in progress, and against confidence in objective or scientific truth. In philosophy, therefore, it implies a mistrust of the *grands récits* of modernity: the large-scale justifications of Western society and confidence in its progress visible in *Kant, *Hegel, or *Marx, or arising from *utopian visions of perfection achieved through evolution, social improvement, education, or the deployment of science. In its *poststructuralist aspects it includes a denial of any fixed meaning, or any correspondence between language and the world, or any fixed reality or truth or fact to be the object of enquiry.

The tendency was anticipated, and perhaps most brilliantly expressed, by *Nietzsche, whose *perspectivism is seen as a philosophical technique for dissolving the presumption that there can be objective knowledge. Objectivity is revealed as a disguise for power or authority in the academy, and often as the last fortress of white male privilege. Logical or rational thought is revealed as the imposition of suspect dichotomies on the flux of events. Postmodernists differ over the consequences of such discoveries, sharing the *sceptic's old problem of how to think and act in the light of the doctrine. While the dismantling of objectivity seems to some to be the way towards a liberating political radicalism, to others it allows such unliberating views as the denial that there was (objectively) such an event as the Second World War or the Holocaust, and to others such as *Rorty (*Contingency, Irony and Solidarity*, 1989), it licenses the retreat to an aesthetic, ironic, detached, and playful attitude to one's own beliefs and to the march of events. This retreat has been criticized as socially irresponsible (and in its upshot, highly conservative). The postmodernist frame of mind, charted, for example, in *The Postmodern Condition* (1984) by Jean-François *Lyotard, may seem to depend on a cavalier dismissal of the success of science in generating human improvement, an exaggeration of the admitted fallibility of any attempt to gain knowledge in the humane disciplines, and an ignoring of the quite ordinary truth that while human history and law admit of no one final description, they certainly admit of more or less accurate ones, just as a landscape permits of no one unique map, yet there can be more or less accurate maps.

SEE WEB LINKS

- An audio discussion of postmodernism by three philosophers
- A list of internet resources on postmodern thinkers

poststructuralism The variety of *postmodernism defined by its reaction against *structuralism in France, and associated with writers such as *Derrida, *Foucault, and *Kristeva. Whilst deriving from *Saussure the view that words mean what they do through their relations with each other rather than through their relationship to an extra-linguistic reality, poststructuralism adds an interest in their origins in relationships of power, or in the unconscious. However, it does not share the structuralist view that the unconscious, or the forms of society, will themselves obey structural laws, waiting to be discovered. Rather, it echoes *Nietzsche's hostility to the reduction of human phenomena to lawlike generalizations, associating such views with the philosophical underpinnings of determinist systems such as *Marxism, and instead celebrating the formless, or the subjective and spontaneous. Leaning heavily on the psychoanalytic dissolution of the self, it provides one manifestation of the sceptical stance of *postmodernism, in particular by refusing any concepts of objectivity, reality, and truth.

postulate A *posit or *axiom.

potentiality The adjective 'potential' sets a logical trap. A potential x is not a kind of x, but at best a thing of a different kind that is capable of becoming an x (so, for example, the destruction of a potential x is not the same as the destruction of an actual x). In Aristotelian terms, potential is a power to change into different states. In biology the nature of this power remained a central question until the discovery of 'instructions' for development in the shape of the DNA molecule. The difference between potentiality and actuality is also one of the puzzling questions raised by *quantum mechanics, according to which a particle such as an electron or photon is completely described by a set of potentialities with different probabilities of being realized, until the moment of measurement, when just one of them is recognized as actual. *See* SCHRÖDINGER'S CAT.

pour-soi *See* BEING IN-ITSELF/FOR-ITSELF.

poverty of the stimulus In general, the psychological fact that our reactions to the stimuli provided by experience outrun and go beyond anything that is neutrally 'given' by the stimulus. In particular, in the polemic of *Chomsky against *empiricist and *behaviourist theories of language learning, the argument that the enormous linguistic repertoire the human language learner acquires cannot be explained in terms of the meagre input of cues bringing it about.

power (metaphysical) A capacity or ability to bring about an effect or undergo a modification. Water has the power to dissolve salt; salt has the capacity to dissolve in water. The metaphysical problem lies in relating powers to other ('categorical') properties, the properties which are *intrinsic to a substance and which do not require it being put in relation to other objects in order to be manifested. Powers seem to depend on more than intrinsic structure, but also on the laws of nature or other natural features of the universe surrounding the bearer of the powers. All claims about powers and their grounds are controversial. *See also* FINKISH.

power (social) The power of an individual or institution is the ability to achieve something, whether by right or by control or influence. Power is the ability to mobilize economic, social, or political forces in order to achieve a result. It can be measured by the probability of that result being achieved in the face of various kinds of obstacle or opposition. It is not essential to this definition that the result be consciously intended by the powerful agent: power may be exercised unknowingly, although of course it is frequently deliberate. However, in the views of some theorists, notably *Foucault, all social relations are systems of power: fundamental power is not exercised by individuals, but is a dispersed, impersonal aspect of society, and in particular is manifested in the modes of surveillance, regulation, or discipline that adapt human beings to the surrounding social structure. The power of society is not limited to its ability to prevent people doing things, but it includes control of the self-definition and preferred way of living of its members. A principal concern of political theory is to determine when the exercise of power is legitimate; this is often posed as the problem of distinguishing *authority from power. *See also* EXPLOITATION, OPPRESSION.

power set The power set of a set S is the set of all subsets of S. *See also* CANTOR'S THEOREM.

practical reason Most generally, any reasoning aiming at a conclusion concerning what to do. More specifically, *Aristotle's attempt to analyse this process in terms of the *practical syllogism. *See also* *PHRONĒSIS*.

practical syllogism *Aristotle appears to have thought that practical reasoning could be represented in the shape of a syllogism, although the passages are fragmentary and not altogether consistent. In one version, the first premise would give a kind of action or outcome a desirability characteristic; the second would identify an instance, and the conclusion would either be an action or a close, practical relation to an action, such as the formation of an intention to act. 'All foods that contain vitamin C are healthy; this orange contains vitamin C, so let me eat it!' might be a sample. Others proceed by giving a goal and a means to obtain it: 'I need a covering, a cloak is a covering, so let me have a cloak!' However it is clearly not a valid general form of reasoning, for there is no logical fault in acknowledging the premises but having no inclination to eat the orange or obtain the cloak. The idea that the conclusion of an argument is something like an action is not readily intelligible, especially as actions are concerned with particulars, and the conclusions of syllogisms have no application to particulars.

praedicabilia (Latin, what can be predicated) The things that can be said about an object. In *Aristotle they come in four families: definition, *genus, **proprium*, and *accident. In *scholastic thought they come in five: genus, species, *differentia, proprium*, and accident.

praedicamenta The ten *categories, distinguished by *Aristotle.

pragmatic contradiction An inconsistency arising because of an *implicature, or one of the normal implications of saying something, rather than because of the content of what is said. '*p* but I do not believe that *p*' is the standard example (*see* MOORE'S PARADOX). Varieties of the *peritrope hope to catch *relativists in some kind of pragmatic contradiction.

pragmaticism Unsuccessful title adopted by *Peirce for *pragmatism, in the hope of distinguishing his version from the views of *James and other contemporaries. Peirce was concerned that he, and not James, was propounding the maxim he expressed as follows: 'consider what effects that might *conceivably* have practical bearings you *conceive* the objects of your *conception* to have. Then, your *conception* of those effects is the whole of your *conception* of the object' (first paragraph of 'Issues of Pragmaticism', 1905).

pragmatics The part of the theory of signs, or *semiotics, that concerns the relationship between speakers and their signs. The study of the principles governing appropriate conversational moves is called general pragmatics; applied pragmatics treats of special kinds of linguistic interaction, such as interviews and speech-making. A pragmatic treatment of a feature of the use of a language would explain the feature in terms of general principles governing appropriate utterance, rather than in terms of a semantic rule. For example, the difference between 'she had a baby and got married' and 'she got married and had a baby' would be treated semantically if it were put down to the meaning of the term 'and', but pragmatically if it were put down to a general regularity that people relate events in the order in which they suppose them to have happened. *See also* IMPLICATURE.

pragmatic theory of truth The view especially associated with *James, that the truth of a statement can be defined in terms of the *utility of accepting it. Put so baldly the view is open to objection, since there are things that are false that it may be useful to accept, and conversely there are things that are true that it may be damaging to accept. However, there are deep connections between the idea that a representative system is accurate, and the likely success of the projects and purposes formed by its possessor. The evolution of a system of representation, either perceptual or linguistic, seems bound to connect success with evolutionary adaptation, or with utility in the widest sense. The *Wittgensteinian doctrine that meaning is *use shares the pragmatic emphasis on technique and practice as the matrix within which meaning is possible. *See also* PRAGMATISM.

pragmatism The philosophy of meaning and truth especially associated with *Peirce and *James. Pragmatism is given various formulations by both writers, but the core is the belief that the meaning of a doctrine is the same as the practical effects of adopting it. Peirce interpreted a theoretical sentence as a confused form of thought whose meaning is only that of a corresponding practical maxim (telling us what to do in some circumstance). In James the position issues in a theory of truth, notoriously allowing that beliefs, including for example belief in God, are true if the belief 'works satisfactorily in the widest sense of the word'. On James's view almost any belief might be respectable, and even true, provided it works (but working is not a simple matter for James). The apparently subjectivist consequences of this were wildly assailed by *Russell, *Moore, and others in the early years of the 20th century. This led to a division within pragmatism between those such as *Dewey, whose humanistic conception of practice remains inspired by science, and the more *idealistic route taken especially by the English writer F. C. S. Schiller (1864–1937), embracing the doctrine that our cognitive efforts and human needs actually transform the reality that we seek to describe. James often writes as if he sympathizes with this development. For instance, in *The Meaning of Truth* (1909), p. 189, he considers the hypothesis that other people have no minds (dramatized in the sexist idea of an 'automatic sweetheart' or female zombie) and remarks that the hypothesis would not work because it would not satisfy our (i.e. men's) egoistic cravings for the recognition and admiration of others. The implication that this is what makes it true that other persons (females) have minds is the disturbing part.

Peirce's own approach to truth is that it is what (suitable) processes of enquiry would tend to accept if pursued to an ideal limit. Modern pragmatists such as *Rorty and in some writings *Putnam have usually tried to dispense with an account of truth (*see* MINIMALISM), and concentrate, as perhaps James should have done, upon the nature of belief and its relations with human attitude, emotion, and need. The driving motivation of pragmatism is the idea that belief in the truth on the one hand must have a close connection with success in action on the other. One way of cementing the connection is found in the idea that natural selection must have adapted us to be cognitive creatures because beliefs have effects: they work. Pragmatism can be found in *Kant's doctrine of the primacy of practical over pure reason, and continues to play an influential role in the theory of meaning and of truth. *See also* INSTRUMENTALISM; LOGICAL POSITIVISM; PASCAL'S WAGER; SCIENCE, PHILOSOPHY OF; WILL TO BELIEVE.

SEE WEB LINKS

- An audio discussion of pragmatism by three American philosophers
- A bibliography on pragmatism, with links for individual thinkers

praise and blame Praise is the public expression of approval and admiration; it acts as a reinforcement of the qualities or actions that are praised, perhaps encouraging their repetition, or their display as a model for others to follow. The opposite of praise may be simply disappointment or regret. Blame implies that the agent could have done better or ought to feel *guilt or shame. It therefore raises issues of *free will and responsibility.

pramana (Sanskrit, measure) A standard of reasoning, or criterion of truth. The sources or bases of knowledge may be distinguished as perception, inference, testimony, analogy, implication in a wider sense than inference, and the interesting category of 'negative perception', whereby our senses give us a penumbra of knowledge of what is not present in the sensible world, as well as what is. Different schools of Indian thought accept or reject different ones of these methods. All methods are accepted by *Mimamsa; only perception, inference, and testimony by *Yoga; only perception and inference by *Buddhism and *Vaisheshika; and only perception by *Carvaka.

praxeology The name given to a Scandinavian movement which hoped to develop a science of efficient action; also a philosophy akin to pragmatism, seeing the idea of action as prior to ideas of representation and truth.

praxis A term in use since *Aristotle, to whom praxis is one of the three basic activities of human beings (the others being *theoria* or theory, and **poiēsis*, or skilful manufacture). Praxis in Aristotle includes voluntary or goal-directed action, although it sometimes also includes the condition that the action is itself part of the end, an action done for its own sake. In *Kant, praxis is the application of a theory to cases encountered in experience, but is also ethically significant thought, or practical reason, that is, reasoning about what there should be as opposed to what there is. Kant's placing of the practical above the theoretical influenced the subsequent thought of

*Fichte, *Schelling, and *Hegel. But it is in *Marx that the concept becomes central to the new philosophical ideal of transforming the world through revolutionary activity. The subordination of theory to practice is connected with the inability of reason to solve contradictions, which are instead removed by the dialectical progress of history. Praxis is also connected with genuinely free, self-conscious, authentic activity as opposed to the *alienated labour demanded under capitalism. *See also* FALSE CONSCIOUSNESS.

prayer Any kind of communication believed to be addressed to a deity.

precognition The *paranormal ability to foresee events before they happen, and before there is normal evidence that they are going to happen. Whilst few philosophers believe that this power exists, the question of whether it is even possible that it should exist raises deep questions about time, causation, and the fixity or otherwise of the future.

predestination The doctrine that some people are born already selected for salvation or damnation, which they cannot avoid even by good deeds in this life. For *Augustine it is a divine mystery that God in His perfect justice makes the apparently gratuitous selection of the elect, while *Calvinism is the form of Christian belief that celebrates the parallel thought that He has made a similar selection of the damned: 'others he did appoint for eternal condemnation, according to the counsel of his most free, most just, and holy will' (*The Westminster Confession*, 1648).

predetermination The idea that events are fixed in advance; that the apparent open nature of the future, contrasted with the fixed nature of the past, is in fact illusory. The view may arise from reflection upon *determinism; from the theological belief that God foresees the future, which is therefore in some sense already a fact; or from the view that persons with psychic powers can do this; or from sheer logic (*see* SEA-BATTLE); or from the belief that time is fundamentally illusory (*see* A-SERIES OF TIME). *See also* PREDESTINATION.

predicables *See PRAEDICABILIA.*

predicate A predicate is any expression that is capable of connecting with one or more *singular terms to make a sentence. A predicate expresses a condition that the entities referred to may satisfy, in which case the resulting sentence will be true. For this reason a predicate may be thought of as a *function from things to sentences or even to truth-values. Although modern logic makes a sharp distinction between predicates and terms that stand for things, traditional logic did not. In the theory of the *syllogism the subject and predicate terms are thought of as grammatically interchangeable, as 'All A is B, all B is C, so all A is C', where the term B is a predicate on its first occurrence, but thought of as a subject on the next. The modern treatment denies that such a form is subject-predicate at all, but sees it as a *quantification, involving two predicates: $(\forall x)Ax \rightarrow Bx$. The letters A, B ..., or more usually F, G ..., are predicate letters, standing where predicates would stand in sentences when we are considering the *logical form of arguments.

predicate calculus The *logical calculus in which the expressions include *predicate letters, *variables, *quantifiers, names, and *operation letters, as well as the expressions for *truth functions and the *propositional variables of the *propositional calculus. The predicate calculus is the heart of modern logic, having proved capable of formalizing the central reasoning processes of modern mathematics and science. In a first-order predicate calculus the variables range over objects; in a higher-order calculus they may range over predicates and functions themselves. The first-order predicate calculus with identity includes '=' as a primitive (undefined) expression: in a higher-order calculus it may be defined by the law that $x = y$ iff $(\forall F)(Fx \leftrightarrow Fy)$.

predication To predicate something of a subject or subjects is to describe it or them as having some property or as standing in some relation. A temptation is to think of a predicate as itself the name of a property or *universal, in which case a sentence seems to be no more than a string of names, a list rather than the expression of a proposition. *See also* CONCEPT AND OBJECT, THIRD MAN ARGUMENT, UNIVERSALS.

predicative *See* IMPREDICATIVE DEFINITION.

predictability *See* CHAOS, DETERMINISM, GOODMAN'S PARADOX, INDUCTION.

prediction paradox The teacher and the class know that the last day of term is Friday. A week before, the teacher tells the class that before the end of term there will be an unexpected examination: the pupils will not know, the evening before, that the examination will occur on the following day. It seems plain that the teacher can set such an examination. But the bright pupil argues as follows. The examination cannot be on the final Friday. For then we would know, on the Thursday evening, that it had to be on that day. So the teacher's effective period, within which the examination must be set, ends on the Thursday. But then we know, on the Wednesday evening, that (since Friday is already excluded) it must be on Thursday. This contradicts the condition again. So the teacher cannot wait until Thursday.

p

By similar reasoning we can show that there is no day on which the examination can be set.

pre-established harmony Doctrine advanced by *Leibniz to explain the fact that the world of experience is not chaotic, although each *monad develops without relation to any other, purely in virtue of its own internal nature. The solution was that just as two clocks can tick in time with each other without interaction and without perpetual interference maintaining a connection between them, but purely because each is properly constructed, so a creating God can from the beginning ensure the harmony of each monad's development with that of the others. The doctrine was criticized by *Foucher as a version of *occasionalism.

preexistence Existence of the individual soul prior to its current embodiment. The doctrine that this actually occurs is found in *Plato, and is a tenet of *Hindu philosophy. Contemporary philosophers are more likely to diagnose it as dependent on an untenable conception of the self.

preface paradox A writer says many things, $p_1 \dots p_n$, in the course of a book. In the preface she reasonably says that she knows the book contains mistakes, and is sorry for them. But given that she knows that $p_1 \dots p_n$ is the set of things she asserted, she now seems to have contradicted herself, by assenting to each of $p_1 \dots p_n$ and to the proposition that at least one of them is false. This is like asserting that Fred is tall and Jill is tall; Fred and Jill are the only people in the room; someone in the room is not tall. The structure is similar to the paradox of the *lottery.

preference-utilitarianism Form of *utilitarianism which abandons the attempt to measure utility in terms of the extent or duration or causes of happiness, and measures instead the satisfaction of desires or preferences. There are questions about which preferences should count, and whether intensity of desire is an independent factor.

premise (premiss) A premise of an *argument is one of the propositions from which together the conclusion is derived. A suppressed premise is one that is in fact necessary for the conclusion to follow, but is not explicitly stated.

prenex normal form A *well-formed formula of the *predicate calculus is in prenex normal form if all the *quantifiers stand at the front, and any other logical constant stands within the scope of all the quantifiers.

prescriptive definition *See* PERSUASIVE DEFINITION.

prescriptivism The approach to moral theory especially associated with *Hare, that assimilates moral commitment to the giving or accepting of a command. Difference of moral opinion is then modelled upon the giving of conflicting commands, and inconsistency in moral thought is assimilated to the giving of commands not all of which can possibly be obeyed. In Hare's development, ethical judgements differ from simple prescriptions by the commitment to universality that they embody: thus whilst I may command you to smoke and someone else not to smoke, if I go into the ethical mode and say that you ought not to smoke, I am committed to supposing that anybody else in a relevantly similar position ought not to smoke. Hare's later development of this idea moves him towards *utilitarianism as the critical level of moral thinking, disguised in everyday life by the more ordinary and less systematic commitments we tend to make. Critics have concentrated upon various differences between ethical commitment and command, including the problem that, whilst accepting a command seems tantamount to setting oneself to obey it, accepting an ethical verdict is, unfortunately, consistent with refusing to be bound by it. The belief that utilitarianism is somehow implicit in the logic of moral concepts has also been vigorously contested. *See also* AGENT-CENTRED MORALITY, *AKRASIA*, INTEGRITY, VIRTUE ETHICS.

presence, metaphysics of Term originally used by *Heidegger to characterize the central mistake of Western metaphysics. In his vision, metaphysics from Plato to Nietzsche postulates a self-knowing and self-propelling autonomous agent, for whom nature exists only in so far as it is present, which means useful. This metaphysical view renders authentic respect for nature impossible, and leads to the enslaved consumer societies of the age of technology. *Poststructuralist critics and literary theorists appropriate the term for the view that there is a privileged fixed point at which the meanings of terms are anchored. This could lie in the intentions of the utterer or writer, or in some other semantic anchorage, such as the presence of a non-linguistic idea or the presence of an ostended thing. The favoured contrasting view is that there is nothing but text, or in other words that any attempt to fix meaning issues only in the production of more text, itself liable to a plurality of interpretations. The view bears affinities to the doctrine of the *indeterminacy of radical translation, and to the Wittgensteinian discussion of the *rule-following considerations. *See also* READER RESPONSE THEORY.

presentism, pastism Presentism is the view that only the present is real. Pastism is the view that the present and past are real, but not the future. The difficulty for presentism is to explain why some statements about the past and future are true, and others not, if there is no corresponding aspect of reality or *truthmaker for them.

Presocratics Although the term ought to refer to any Greek philosopher from *c.* 600 BC to *c.*400 BC, the last year of Socrates' life, it is customarily reserved mainly for those thinkers who attempted systematic cosmologies and were centrally concerned with the nature of physical reality. It thus excludes the *Sophists. The pre-eminent schools with just those concerns were the *Milesian or Ionian school, the *Eleatics, the *Pythagoreans and the post-Eleatic *atomists, as well as *Empedocles and *Heraclitus. Presocratic concerns were as much scientific as purely philosophical: the nature of physical substances, the number of ultimate kinds of thing, the existence of the void, the nature of temporal change (*see* ZENO'S PARADOXES), and of course the nature of the cosmos. They included the first atomists (*Leucippus and *Democritus) and probably the first thinker (*Anaxagoras) to explain correctly the cause of lunar and solar eclipses.

SEE WEB LINKS

- Introductory essays on the major Presocratics
- A bibliography on the Presocratics, with links for individual thinkers

presupposition Informally, any suppressed premise or background framework of thought necessary to make an argument valid, or a position tenable. More formally, a presupposition has been defined as a proposition whose truth is necessary for either the truth or the falsity of another statement. Thus if *p* presupposes *q*, *q* must be true for p to be either true or false. In the theory of knowledge of *Collingwood, any propositions capable of truth or falsity stand on a bed of 'absolute presuppositions' which are not properly capable of truth or falsity, since a system of thought will contain no way of approaching such a question (a similar idea was later voiced by *Wittgenstein in his work *On Certainty*).

It was influentially suggested by *Strawson, in opposition to *Russell's theory of *definite descriptions, that 'There exists a King of France' is a presupposition of 'The King of France is bald', the latter being neither true nor false, if there is no King of France. It is, however, a little unclear whether the idea is that no statement at all is made in such a case, or whether a statement is made, but fails of being either true or false. The former option preserves classical logic, since we can still say that every statement is either true or false, but the latter does not, since in classical logic the law of *bivalence holds, and ensures that nothing at all is presupposed for any proposition to be true or false. The introduction of presupposition therefore means that either a third truth value is found, 'intermediate' between truth and falsity, or that classical logic is preserved, but it is impossible to tell whether a particular sentence expresses a proposition that is a candidate for truth and falsity, without knowing more than the formation rules of the language. Each suggestion carries costs, and there is some consensus that at least where definite descriptions are involved, examples like the one given are equally well handled by regarding the overall sentence as false when the existence claim fails, and explaining the data that Strawson relied upon as the effects of *implicature.

pretending Although on the face of it the difference between pretending that something is so, and actually supposing that it is so, is clear enough, it can come under pressure. Philosophies such as fictionalism (*see* VAIHINGER) or *constructive empiricism, *quasi-realism, and *instrumentalism, counsel that we think of some commitments as useful tools rather than as strict representations of how things are. But taking them in that spirit comes close to believing them, just as pretending to be a window-cleaner, convincingly enough, comes close to cleaning windows.

Price, Richard (1723–91) Welsh dissenting minister, moral philosopher, and actuary. Price's *A Review of the Principal Questions in Morals* (1758) is a late defence of rationalism in moral philosophy, against the moral sense theory of *Hutcheson and the attempt to found morals on the passions in *Hume. Price argues that moral opinion is more like understanding the nature of things than merely responding to them, and attempts to connect morality with an appreciation of the eternal and immutable nature of actions. In the same work Price also attempts a response to Hume's scepticism about *miracles. Although his work is not regarded as in the first rank, Price had considerable influence on the political and philosophical culture of his time: he was a friend of Benjamin *Franklin, wrote an important pamphlet defending the American movement for independence, and was attacked by *Burke for a similar defence of the French revolution. He also wrote on actuarial matters, and on the need for provision to extinguish the national debt.

Prichard, Harold Arthur (1871–1947) English philosopher and White's professor at Oxford from 1928 to 1937. Prichard played something of the role that *Moore did in Cambridge, defending a common-sense realism against the then popular *idealism and defending *intuitionism in ethics against *utilitarianism and *naturalism.

Knowledge and Perception (1950) is a collection of his epistemological writings.

Priestley, Joseph (1733–1804) English scientist and champion of the *Enlightenment. Although remembered chiefly for his part in the discovery of oxygen, Priestley wrote more extensively on religious, philosophical, and educational themes. A nonconformist and eventually a unitarian, he advocated ideals of education and liberalism, based on an *associationist psychology and an optimistic belief in the perfectibility of man. His attacks on orthodox religion, and particularly the doctrine of the Trinity, led to general horror, and in 1791, after a dissenting celebration of the French Revolution, his house, laboratory, and library were burned by a rampaging patriotic mob. Priestley eventually emigrated to America, where he was befriended by Thomas Jefferson, and founded the first Unitarian church in that country.

prima facie (right, obligation) (Latin, on first appearance) In the usage of David *Ross, genuine obligations that may yet have to contend with others, and sometimes yield to them. An obligation to keep an appointment may yield to an obligation to take care of some emergency, in which case it was *prima facie* right to keep the appointment, but not right all things considered. Ross's coinage is perhaps unfortunate, in suggesting a merely *epistemological worry, as if on second appearance, or further thought, the obligation turned out to be illusory; whereas he himself believed that both conflicting obligations are real, even when one must give way to the other. A more modern usage prefers the title '*pro tanto* obligation': an obligation inasmuch as there is this or that aspect of the situation, but again suspending the all-in verdict. In either event the difficulty for a *deontological ethic is to explain how obligations are ranked, without bringing in overarching considerations of *utility.

primary/secondary qualities The division is especially associated with the 17th-century rise of modern science, with its recognition that the fundamental explanatory properties of things are not the qualities that perception most immediately concerns. These latter are the secondary qualities, or immediate sensory qualities, including *colour, taste, smell, felt warmth or texture, and sound. The primary properties are less tied to the deliverance of one particular sense, and include the size, shape, and motion of objects. In *Boyle and *Locke the primary qualities are scientifically tractable, objective qualities essential to anything material: the minimal list is size, shape, and mobility, i.e. the state of being at rest or moving. Locke sometimes adds number, solidity, texture (where this is thought of as the structure of a substance, or way in which it is constituted out of atoms). The secondary qualities are the powers to excite particular sensory modifications in observers. Locke himself thought in terms of identifying these powers with the textures of objects that, according to *corpuscularian science of the time, were the basis of an object's causal capacities. The ideas of secondary qualities are sharply different from these powers, and afford us no accurate impression of them. For *Descartes, this is the basis for rejecting any attempt to think of knowledge of external objects as provided by the senses. But in Locke our ideas of primary qualities do afford us an accurate notion of what shape, size, and mobility are. In English-speaking philosophy the first major discontent with the division was voiced by *Berkeley, who probably took the basis of his attack from *Bayle, who in turn cites *Foucher. Modern thought continues to wrestle with the difficulties of thinking of colour, taste, smell, warmth, and sound as real or objective properties of things independent of us.

prime matter An Aristotelian term for matter prior to its receiving form, sometimes identified with pure extension.

prime mover *See* MOVER, UNMOVED.

primum mobile (Latin, first in movement) In Aristotelian cosmology the first or outermost sphere of the heavens. The perfect, spherical rotation of this sphere is directly activated by love of God; the motion is as like the life of God as movement can be. *See* MOVER, UNMOVED.

principium individuationis Latin, principle of *individuation.

principle of charity *See* CHARITY, PRINCIPLE OF.

principle of contradiction or noncontradiction *See* CONTRADICTION.

principle of double effect *See* DOUBLE EFFECT, PRINCIPLE OF.

principle of excluded middle *See* EXCLUDED MIDDLE, PRINCIPLE OF.

principle of indifference *See* INDIFFERENCE, PRINCIPLE OF.

principle of individuation *See* INDIVIDUATION, PRINCIPLE OF.

principle of insufficient reason *See* INDIFFERENCE, PRINCIPLE OF.

principle of plenitude *See* PLENITUDE, PRINCIPLE OF.

principle of sufficient reason *See* SUFFICIENT REASON, PRINCIPLE OF.

principle of utility *See* UTILITARIANISM.

principle of verifiability *See* VERIFICATION PRINCIPLE.

prior probability The probability assigned to a hypothesis or event before a piece of evidence emerges. In *Bayesian reasoning, the probability after a piece of evidence (the posterior probability) is a function of the prior probability, and the extent to which the evidence fits the hypothesis, but inversely proportional to the prior probability of the evidence—in other words, evidence that might be expected to have arisen on many different hypotheses does not confirm any one of them particularly well. The terminology is criticized by *de Finetti, who prefers to talk of initial and final probabilities.

prisoners' dilemma The classic problem in *game theory. Two prisoners jointly charged with a crime are held apart, and each is given the option of confessing, or not confessing. If each confesses, the prosecutor convicts them both, and they will serve six years each. If neither confesses, he will find a lesser charge, and each will serve two years. If A confesses and B does not, A is released and B serves an aggravated ten years. If B confesses and A does not, B is released, and A serves an aggravated ten years. The matrix is shown in the figure:

	Confess A	Stay Quiet A
Confess	6	10
B	6	0
Stay Quiet	0	2
B	10	2

The surprising truth about the game is that *whatever the other prisoner does* a prisoner does better by confessing (if A confesses, B does better for himself by confessing, and if A does not confess, B does better for himself by confessing; and conversely for A if B confesses or does not confess). Confessing *dominates not confessing. Yet the social result in which each of A and B follows this reasoning is the worst of all (12 person-prison years) and together they would have done much better by sitting tight (4 person-prison years). Many political situations (e.g. whether to vote when there is a cost to doing so, whether to refrain from wage bargaining, whether to be a good citizen and turn off one's hose during a water shortage) can be modelled as prisoners' dilemmas. The structure shows that it is not always the case that the social good is furthered efficiently by each person doing what is in his or her own best interests: as well as an 'invisible hand' whereby unbridled self-interest elevates everybody's position, there can be an invisible boot whereby it diminishes it (*see* SMITH).

An iterated prisoners' dilemma is a sequence of such situations, of either finite or infinite length. In an interesting study (*The Evolution of Cooperation*, 1984) Robert Axelrod showed that an efficient policy in such a situation is 'tit for tat': you start off cooperating (not confessing) until faced with a play on which the opponent 'rats', and then you rat (confess) once in retaliation, but then, if the opponent mends his ways, you go back to not confessing until the same thing happens again. As well as being an efficient strategy 'tit for tat' has some intuitive moral justification. However, the strategy is sensitive to the ratio of rewards and penalties that are in play, and cannot be said to be the single best strategy for all circumstances. *See also* ASSURANCE GAME; CHICKEN; COMMONS, TRAGEDY OF THE.

SEE WEB LINKS

- An online tutorial on the prisoners' dilemma
- Simulations of the prisoners' dilemma

privacy (mind) One of the more obvious, yet baffling, features of the mind is that I alone am privy to my experiences and thoughts. I have them, whereas you must go through some process of interpreting my utterances and actions in order to know, or guess, what they are. Philosophers of mind have either celebrated this privacy or sought to downplay its importance. To downplay it one might argue that what I know about myself, and you do not, may be simply a question of what words I am about to use or what actions I feel like performing. But in that case there is then no deep metaphysical gulf between what I know about myself and what you know, for it is merely a matter of my reports more quickly and accurately registering the state of my own system. There is no special knowledge displayed on a special inner screen, but only the natural upshot of self-monitoring functions of the brain.

privacy (social) In moral and political theory, private conduct is that which it is no business of the public, and particularly the public institution of law, to notice. Similarly, private information about a person would be that to which there can be no right of public access. The right to privacy is deeply connected with a person's self-respect, with invasions of privacy being connected with shame and indignity. *Liberal political theory makes essential use of this category in assessing the permissible sphere of the law. The private is the sphere of family, home, personal taste, and affection; the public is the domain of other relations, including institutional and contractual relations, and those recognized in law. However, it is controversial whether an action such as consuming various kinds of *pornography, even within one's own home, is properly regarded as private. The distinction between public and private is attacked by some *feminist theorists, who believe that the sphere of the private acts as a fig-leaf for areas of unrestricted male domination of children and women. But dismantling the distinction altogether has too many associations with *fascist and *totalitarian ideology to commend itself widely.

private language In the *Philosophical Investigations*, §258, *Wittgenstein invites us to consider a diarist recording the occurrences of a particular kind of sensation, which he proposes to call by some name. Wittgenstein argues that in so far as the sensation is thought of as purely private, disconnected from behaviour and symptoms of its occurrence, the procedure is a pantomime, since the subject cannot give himself a determinate understanding of what he is doing. There is no distinction between being right, in recording an ostensible recurrence, and seeming to be right. The argument is part of an attack on the *Cartesian way of thinking of the mind as an inner theatre, whose show is known in a privileged and unique way by its possessor.

One way of thinking of Wittgenstein's strategy is by seeing it as suggesting that just as other persons and their minds become a problem for the Cartesian, so should our own past minds. 'Always get rid of the idea of a private object in this way: assume that it constantly changes, but that you do not notice the change because your memory constantly deceives you' (*Philosophical Investigations*, Pt II, xi). The vacuous nature of this hypothesis shows that it is illusory to suppose that there is something to be right or wrong about. Although the argument has been immensely influential and widely accepted, commentators have disagreed on whether it has a *verificationist premise, and if so whether this decreases its force. There has also existed uncertainty over whether it leads to a *behaviourist view of the mind. *See also* FUNCTIONALISM, INVERTED SPECTRUM, QUALIA.

private/public distinction *See* PRIVACY (SOCIAL).

privileged access The special way that we each have of knowing our own thoughts, intentions, and sensations. Many philosophers of a *behaviourist and *functionalist tendency have found it important to deny that there is such a special way, arguing instead that I know of my own mind in much the way that I know of yours (e.g. by seeing what I say when asked). Others, however, point out that the behaviour of reporting the result of introspection is a particular and legitimate kind of behaviour that deserves notice in any account of human psychology. *See also* HETEROPHENOMENOLOGY, PRIVACY (MIND).

pro-attitude Any of a variety of attitudes in favour of something: approval, admiration, liking, preference, esteem.

probabilism The doctrine that in some area of science, or ethics, we may settle for hypotheses with reasonable degrees of probability, without being able to obtain knowledge. Probabilism is flanked by the more dogmatic view that we can achieve certainty, on the one side, and the more sceptical view that we cannot even assign probabilities, on the other side. *See also* CONFIRMATION, FALSIFICATION, METHODOLOGY.

probability, philosophy of The mathematics of probability is well understood. Probability is a non-negative, additive set function whose maximum value is unity. What is harder to understand is the application of the formal notion to the actual world. One point of application is statistical: when kinds of event or trials (such as the tossing of a coin) can be described, and the frequency of occurrence of particular outcomes (such as the coin falling heads) is measurable, then we can begin to think of the probability of that kind of outcome in that kind of trial. One account of probability is therefore the *frequency theory, associated with *Venn and Richard von Mises (1883–1953), that identifies the probability of an event with such a frequency of occurrence. A second point of application is the description of a hypothesis as probable when the evidence bears a favoured relationship to it. If this relation is conceived of as purely logical in nature, as in the work of *Keynes and *Carnap, probability statements are not empirical measures of frequencies, but represent something like 'partial entailments' or measures of possibilities left open by the evidence and by the hypothesis. Formal *confirmation theories and *range theories of probability are developments of this idea. The third point of application is in the use probability judgements have in regulating the confidence with which we hold various expectations. The approach sometimes called subjectivism or personalism, but more commonly known as *Bayesianism, associated with *de Finetti and *Ramsey, sees probability judgements as expressions of a subject's degree of confidence in an event or kind of event, and attempts to describe constraints on the way we should have degrees of confidence in different judgements that explain those judgements having the mathematical form of judgements of probability (*see* DUTCH BOOK, EXCHANGEABILITY, REPRESENTATION THEOREM). For Bayesians, probability or chance is not an objective or real factor in the world, but rather a reflection of our own states of mind. However, those states of mind need to be governed by empirical frequencies, so this is not an invitation to licentious thinking.

problematic In the writings of *Althusser, the ideological structure or framework within which particular problems are set up. The problematic may involve an interlocking set of *presuppositions, or a closed space that disguises the correct options and allows only prejudged solutions.

problem of evil *See* EVIL, PROBLEM OF.

problem of induction *See* INDUCTION.

problem of other minds *See* OTHER MINDS.

procedural justice The element of justice concerned with the application of laws, rather than with the content of the laws themselves. If an unjust law is applied, then procedural justice may obtain although the outcome is unjust. Similarly, an irregular procedure might be procedurally unjust, but give the right result on an occasion.

procedural semantics An approach to *semantics that views understanding in terms of a set of procedures for deciding whether terms apply to things, or procedures for deciding the truth-values of propositions. The idea is allied to a *verificationist approach to meaning, and also to the general view that meaning should be connected with practice.

process A sequence of events. In the process philosophy of *Whitehead, the fundamental fact of cosmology is the unfolding of processes, not conceived in terms of modifications of underlying substances, but united by networks of relations, and selected in advance by God. A process theory of mind sees its unity not in terms of underlying substance (*see* PERSONAL IDENTITY) but as the relatively permanent form or pattern displayed by continuously changing processes, just as a wave maintains its form although it is constituted by different volumes of water at different times. Process theology, again stemming from Whitehead and Charles *Hartshorne, develops a concept of God as involved in unfolding processes in a way that brings him into contact with the ordinary human mess without actually being responsible for it.

process–product ambiguity Ambiguity that affects some important philosophical notions, such as observation, explanation, or perception, which can either refer to the process or activity of observing, explaining, or perceiving, or can refer to the product of that process. Philosophies that *reify perceptions, for example, may be charged with falling victims to the ambiguity.

Proclus (*c.*410–85) The last major classical (Greek) philosopher. Proclus was a pupil of Plutarch of Athens. He was a systematic *Neoplatonist, whose *Elements of Theology*, *Platonic Theology*, and various commentaries influenced subsequent Christian philosophers such as *Dionysius the Pseudo-Areopagite and *Eriugena.

Prodicus (*fl.* late 5th c. BC) A Sophist from the island of Ceos, mentioned by *Plato and Xenophon. He is supposed to have offered a natural explanation of Greek theological belief, thus qualifying as an exceptionally early *atheist.

progress The belief that later times are improvements over earlier times. This may be in limited respects, such as in the extent of scientific knowledge or the moral capacities of human beings. Or the improvement may be more global, as in the world view of *Hegel who sees history as the progressive embodiment of rational principles. The 18th century (*Voltaire, *Condorcet, *Kant) saw the greatest flowering of belief in progress, with belief that a benevolent providence had secured for us *perfectibility on earth, through increasing deployment of knowledge and reason. In the 19th century belief in progress continued to flourish, with *Comte and *Marx equally enamoured of it. The theory of evolution through natural selection added (spurious) support to the idea in the work of social evolutionists such as *Spencer. The progressive nature of scientific enquiry is probably the most impressive example of progress that we have, although even this is doubted by philosophies of a sceptical and relativistic bent, that see in science only a history of revolutions. *See also* PERFECTIBILITY.

prohairetic logic The logic of preference and desire. A formalization of the properties of the preference relation.

projectibility A property of predicates, measuring the degree to which past instances can be taken to be guides to future ones. The fact that all the cows I have observed have been four-legged may be a reasonable basis from which to predict that future cows will be four-legged. This means that four-leggedness is a projectible predicate. The fact that they have all been living in the late 20th or early 21st century is not a reasonable basis for predicting that future cows will be. *See also* ENTRENCHMENT, GOODMAN'S PARADOX.

projectivism It is a commonplace that beauty lies in the eye of the beholder, but all the same we usefully talk of the beauty of things and people as if they are identifiable real properties which they possess. Projectivism denotes any view which sees us as similarly projecting upon the world what are in fact modifications of our own minds. The term is often associated with the view of sensations and particularly *secondary qualities found in writers such as *Hobbes (*De Corpore*, 1655) and *Condillac (*Traité des sensations*, 1754). According to this view, sensations are displaced from their rightful place in the mind when we think of the world as coloured or noisy. Other examples of the idea involve things other than sensations, and do not involve literal displacement. One is that all contingency is a projection of our ignorance (*Spinoza); another is that the causal order of events is a projection of our own mental confidences in the way they follow from one another (*Hume). But the most common application of the idea is in ethics and aesthetics, where many writers have held that talk of the value or beauty of things is a projection of the attitudes we take towards them and the pleasure we take in them.

It is natural to associate projectivism with the idea that we make some kind of mistake in talking and thinking as if the world contained the various features we describe it as having, when in reality it does not. But the view that we make no mistake, but simply adopt efficient linguistic expression for necessary ways of thinking, is also held. *See also* ERROR THEORY, EXPRESSIVISM, QUASI-REALISM.

prolepsis *See* EPICURUS.

proletariat *See* BOURGEOISIE/PROLETARIAT.

promise Giving one's word that one will do something creates a reason for action in the future. But when the time comes, by keeping the promise one seems to act because one has done something in the past, rather than for the sake of promoting some goal in the future. Promising therefore excites philosophical theory in two ways. There is first the question of the obligation to obey a promise: how can this exist, given its backwards-looking nature, and what are its stringency and limits? Secondly, there is a peculiarity about the origin of promise-making, in that it can easily seem that in a society with no such institution, it would never arise. This would be because it is essential to promising that at a later date you may have to turn aside from your own interests in order to keep the promise, and an individual who does this is relatively disadvantaged compared to one who does not. The problem is seen clearly by *Hobbes. It is dramatized in the situation of the *prisoners' dilemma, where making a promise to the other prisoner that you will not cheat would seem to be an empty charade, for no words alter the penalties and rewards. The social solution is that by institutionalizing promising, cooperative strategies can develop that further the common good, in spite of their potential for conflict with individual interest. *See also* CONVENTION, SOCIAL CONTRACT.

proof Informally, a procedure that brings conviction. More formally, a deductively *valid argument starting from true premises, that yields the conclusion. Most formally, in *proof theory, a proof is a sequence of formulae of which each member is either an *axiom or is derived from a set of preceding members by application of a *rule of inference, and which terminates with the proposition proved. The final member of such a sequence is a *theorem. In 17th- and 18th-century usage 'proof' has the same implications of a chain of intuitive ideas as *demonstration.

proof theory The study of the relations of deducibility among sentences in a *logical calculus. Deducibility is defined purely syntactically, that is, without reference to the intended *interpretation of the calculus. The subject was founded by the mathematician David Hilbert (1862–1943) in the hope that strictly finitary methods would provide a way of proving the consistency of classical mathematics, but the ambition was torpedoed by *Gödel's second incompleteness theorem. *See also* MODEL THEORY.

propaganda The active manipulation of opinion by means that include distortion or concealment of the truth. It is useful to distinguish agitation propaganda, that seeks to change attitudes, from integration propaganda, that seeks to reinforce already existing attitudes. The borderline between education and indoctrination, or objective statement and political speech, can be hard to define both in practice and theory.

propensity *See* DISPOSITION.

proper names *See* LOGICALLY PROPER NAME, REFERENCE.

proper subset A subset of a set S to which some element or elements of S do not belong.

property (logic and metaphysics) Properties are attributes or characteristics, universals that may belong to one or many things at the same time. Properties have *extensions, that is, a class of things to which they belong, which may be empty.

But different properties (having a heart, having a liver) may characterize the same extensions. Much metaphysics circles around whether two apparently different properties can properly be regarded as one. Other parts tackle the question of the difference between the essential and the accidental properties of things. The problem of *universals is an attempt to understand or even to abolish the distinction between particular things and their properties.

property (social life) To have something as property is to have the right to use it. Use may here include exclusion of other people, consumption, transfer, loan, alteration, destruction, etc., so it can come in various degrees. There is no reason for all such uses to be protected by law as one indivisible whole (for instance, a property right in land need not include the right to exclude the public or destroy the land; ownership of a building may not even include the right to alter it at will; my right to use my arm may not go with a right to sell it to someone else). The foundation of individual property rights is a principal topic of political theory. Suggestions include that of *Locke, that we have a natural right in that with which we have 'mixed our labour'; the *consequentialist argument that without such rights things would be worse all round; and the *Hegelian view that only in a framework of property rights is individual freedom possible. Again, there are differences depending upon what kind of property is in question: private possession of the means of production of goods may be treated quite differently from private rights to consumption of goods (*see* PROUDHON). The abolition of private property is one of the aims of the *Communist Manifesto* (*see* MARX).

proposition That which is proposed or stated; the content of a declarative sentence, capable of truth and falsity. To grasp a proposition is to understand what is said, supposed, suggested, and so on. The same proposition is expressed by any two sentences, from the same or different languages, that are synonymous, or correctly intertranslatable (where translation is judged without regard to tone, rhythm, and other *implicatures). The doctrine of the *indeterminacy of radical translation casts doubt on the objectivity of this test, and some philosophers, notably *Quine, have concluded that no respectable criteria of identity for propositions can be given. For some philosophers, propositions are the primary bearers of truth and falsity, with sentences only true and false derivatively, in virtue of expressing true and false propositions, but for others propositions are the doubtful shadows of what is empirically given, which are utterances in specific contexts. *See also* PROPOSITIONAL ATTITUDE.

propositional attitude If a person X thinks that *p*, desires that *p*, believes that *p*, is angry at *p*, and so on, then he or she is described as having a propositional attitude to *p*. The term suggests that these aspects of mental life are well thought of in terms of a relation to a *proposition, and this is not universally agreed. It suggests that knowing what someone believes, etc. is a matter of identifying an abstract object of their thought, rather than understanding his or her orientation towards more worldly objects.

propositional calculus The *logical calculus whose expressions are letters representing sentences or propositions, and constants representing operations on those propositions, to produce others of higher complexity. The operations include *conjunction, *disjunction, *material implication, and *negation (although these need not be primitive: *see* SHEFFER'S STROKE). Propositional logic was partially anticipated by the *Stoics but reached maturity only with the work of *Frege, *Russell, and *Wittgenstein. *See also* LOGIC, TAUTOLOGY, TRUTH FUNCTION.

propositional function The concept introduced by *Frege of a *function taking a number of names as arguments, and delivering one proposition as the value. The idea is that '*x* loves *y*' is a propositional function, which yields the proposition 'John loves Mary' for those two arguments (in that order). A propositional function is therefore roughly equivalent to a property or relation. In *Principia Mathematica*, *Russell and *Whitehead take propositional functions to be the fundamental functions, since the theory of descriptions could be taken as showing that other expressions denoting functions are incomplete symbols.

proprium In *Aristotle, any property belonging to all and only things of a certain kind, but not part of their essence. Being the only creature that wears clothes is a *proprium* of human beings.

prosentential theory of truth Theory promoted by contemporary philosopher Dorothy Grover and others, according to which 'that is true' or 'S is true' stands in for a sentence, in a way parallel to that in which a pronoun stands in for a noun phrase or name. The truth predicate therefore does not say something about a sentence, but enables us to avoid repeating it.

prosody The study of the way variations of intonation—pitch, loudness, tempo, and rhythm—affect the significance of utterances.

Protagoras of Abdera (*c.*490–420 BC) The most successful of the *Sophists, whose independent importance is attested by *Plato, *Aristotle, and *Sextus Empiricus. He taught virtue (*aretē*) in Athens, was a friend of Pericles, and was employed to draw up the code of laws for the Athenian colony at Thurii. He is famous for the assertion that 'man is the measure of all things': a *relativistic slogan whose precise meaning is debatable, for unless it leads to subjective *idealism, as in *Berkeley, it seems to leave the one object possessing contradictory properties, if one person takes it one way and another takes it in a contradictory way (*see* PERITROPE, but *see also* PERSPECTIVISM). It seems clear that while Protagoras believed that each person's sense perceptions are true (for their owner), he also believed that moral and political doctrines, to which his relativism might seem especially well-adapted, are capable of improvement and can be taught. It is quite possible that Protagoras established in Athens the dialectical method, later made famous through Plato's Socratic dialogues.

pro tanto *See* *PRIMA FACIE*.

protasis An older term for the antecedent of a *conditional.

Protestant work ethic The set of values associated by *Weber with the rise of modern capitalism and industrial society. The ethic is that we fulfil our duty to God by diligence, hard work, and restrained expenditure, with the resulting accumulation of goods acting as a reassuring sign (although not a cause, since the outcome is predestined) of eventual salvation. This combination of attitudes has an *elective affinity with the discipline required for industrial production.

protocol statements (German *Protokollsätze*) The basic statements in the *logical positivist analysis of knowledge, thought of as reporting the unvarnished and pre-theoretical deliverance of experience: what it is like here, now, for me. The central controversy concerned whether it was legitimate to couch them in terms of public objects and their qualities or whether a less theoretically committing, purely phenomenal content could be found. The former option makes it hard to regard them as truly basic, whereas the latter option makes it difficult to see how they can be incorporated into objective science. The controversy is often thought to have been closed in favour of a public version by the *private language argument. Difficulties at this point led the logical positivists to abandon the notion of an epistemological foundation altogether, and to flirt with the *coherence theory of truth. It is widely accepted that trying to make the connection between thought and experience through basic sentences depends on an untenable '*myth of the given'. *See also* FOUNDATIONALISM.

prototype theory The view that human categories typically arise and are embedded in the mind not by means of definition, or the finding of necessary and sufficient conditions, but by a space occupied by one or two central examples (prototypes) and then a penumbra of decreasingly typical examples. Games, for instance, may include poker or football as central examples, and progressively dissimilar activities stretching out to politics or philosophy.

protrepticus An exhortation or advertisement encouraging people to study philosophy. One is mentioned in Plato's dialogue *Euthydemus* (278e–282d), and Aristotle addressed one, now lost, to Themiston, the King of Cyprus.

Proudhon, Pierre-Joseph (1809–65) French founding figure of *anarchism. Proudhon came to fame with *Qu'est-ce que la propriété?* (1840, trs. as *What is Property?*, 1876). The celebrated definition of *property as theft in fact misrepresents the central concern of the work, which is not the abolition of private property but the need for each person to control the means of production that they use. Proudhon saw both unrestricted property rights and *communism as devices for controlling people and destroying equality. The right way out relies on a network of free contracts answering the interests of each participant, and rendering coercive government unnecessary. Proudhon's liberal or libertarian socialism was the central counterpoise to the authoritarian version of *Marxism. He played a role in the revolution of 1848, and was imprisoned for attacks on Louis Napoleon in his newspaper, *Le Représentant du peuple* ('The Representative of the People'). Other works include *Les Confessions d'un révolutionnaire* (1849, trs. as *Confessions of a Revolutionary*, 1876).

Providence The operation of God in the universe; the unfolding of the divine plan. The concept is affirmed by the *Stoics, and all three monotheistic religions. A common corollary is that it is somehow wrong to interfere with the workings of providence, particularly by 'playing God' in matters of life and death. In his essay on suicide, *Hume elegantly demolishes this inference, pointing out that if it is impious to hasten one's own end, it is equally impious to build a ship or a house.

proximate/remote cause *See* CAUSAL CHAIN.

proxy function A *function mapping objects of one domain onto objects of another. For instance, the device of Gödel numbering associates each formula of a system with a particular number. One radical way of defending the thesis of the *inscrutability of reference is to argue that no evidence can determine whether a person is referring to an object, or to its image under a proxy function; instead of referring to a formula, a person might be interpreted equally well as referring to its Gödel number. If the sun is out, then one proxy function would be the relation 'shadow of', mapping a person onto his shadow; the inscrutability claim would be that we cannot tell whether an utterance such as 'that person is tall' means that the person is tall, or that the person's shadow is long.

prudence Concern for one's own future well-being. Prudence requires being able to conceive and empathize with one's own future concerns, and so has been advanced as a half-way house between pure selfishness of the present moment and the altruistic concern for the well-being of others.

Pseudo-Dionysius *See* DIONYSIUS THE PSEUDO-AREOPAGITE.

pseudo-statement Category wielded by the *logical positivists, whereby a statement purporting to make a factual claim is revealed as immune to confirmation or disconfirmation by experience. Hence, by the *verification principle, it is unmasked as lacking cognitive meaning.

psyche (Greek, spirit) Mind, spirit, animating principle.

psychical research *See* PARAPSYCHOLOGY.

psychoanalysis The method of therapy for psychological disorders pioneered by *Freud. The method relies on an interpretation of what a patient says while 'freely associating' or reporting what comes to mind in connection with topics suggested by the therapist. The interpretation proceeds according to the scheme favoured by the analyst, and reveals ideas dominating the unconscious, but previously inadmissible to the conscious mind of the subject. When these are confronted, improvement can be expected. The widespread practice of psychoanalysis is not matched by established data on such rates of improvement.

Philosophically, the unconscious mind postulated by psychoanalysis is controversial, since it requires thinking in terms of a partitioned mind and applying a mental vocabulary (intentions, desires, repression) to a part to which we have no conscious access. The problem is whether this merely uses a harmless spatial metaphor of the mind, or whether it involves a philosophical misunderstanding of mental ascription. Other philosophical reservations about psychoanalysis concern the apparently arbitrary and unfalsifiable nature of the interpretative schemes employed.

Works such as Adolf Grünbaum's *Foundations of Psychoanalysis* (1984) effectively challenge the scientific basis of psychoanalytic interpretations, while there is accumulating evidence that therapists, including Freud himself, are responsible for many of the reports of repressed memories or fantasies that patients are induced to make, or described as having made. However, such schemes have been used to explain otherwise puzzling aspects of all parts of human life, but especially dreams, rituals, myths, and literature, and some philosophers, especially in France, have seen psychoanalysis as a key to all the theory of human nature. *See also* JUNG.

psychokinesis The *paranormal ability to move things other than one's body without physical contact.

psycholinguistics *See* CHOMSKY, COGNITIVE SCIENCE.

psychological egoism *See* EGOISM.

psychological hedonism *See* HEDONISM.

psychologism In the philosophy of logic, psychologism is the view that logic is based upon the laws of thought, where these are descriptions of the actual processes whereby human beings think. Logic becomes not so much a normative discipline, giving laws of truth to which thought ought to conform, but a construction based on patterns to which our thoughts do conform. The term was first used by J. E. Erdmann in 1878, but did not come into general use until the end of the 19th century. Its exact definition is complicated by the various views of psychology prevalent at that period. Psychologism is a natural ally of *naturalism, with its general suspicion of any realm of propositions standing in timeless logical relationships. The great opponent of psychologism was *Frege, whose conception of the subject did, however, give rise to worries about an apparent *Platonism. The approach has gained popularity again with the rediscovery of *naturalized epistemology, and with the attempts of *Wittgenstein in his later work to find a way of basing logic and mathematics on the natural history of human beings.

psychophysical laws Laws connecting psychological or mental states with physical states. The existence of such laws was influentially denied by *Davidson, who argued that descriptions of mental events are intrinsically unsuited to occurrence in genuine laws (*see* ANOMALOUS

MONISM). The idea is that mental ascriptions answer to a wide variety of contextual and other factors that render them unfit for precise correlation with any physical descriptions, either of behaviour or of underlying neurophysiology. Davidson, along with many other philosophers of mind, nevertheless accepts the *supervenience of the mental on the physical, and the question of whether one can have supervenience without lawlike connection has been the topic of vigorous debate.

psychophysical parallelism *See* OCCASIONALISM.

Ptolemaic system Although *Ptolemy's astronomy was a magnificent mathematical structure, observationally adequate as late as the 16th century, and not markedly more complex than its Copernican rival, its basis was a series of disconnected, *ad hoc hypotheses; hence it has become a symbol for any theory that shares the same disadvantage.

Ptolemy (*fl.* AD 146–70) Alexandrian astronomer, mathematician, and geographer. His masterpiece is known by its Arabic title of the *Almagest*, a complete treatment of astronomical knowledge in thirteen books. This work dominated astronomical theory in Byzantium, the Islamic world, and medieval Europe. Ptolemy acknowledges debts to Apollonius and Hipparchus of Rhodes, and his writing is an important source for the history of astronomy. Ptolemy also wrote extensively on geography, where he was probably the first to use systematic coordinates of latitude and longitude, and his work was not superseded until the 16th century. Similarly in musical theory his treatise on *Harmonics* is a detailed synthesis of *Pythagorean mathematics and empirical musical observation.

public choice The study of collective decision-making. *See* ARROW'S THEOREM, SOCIAL WELFARE FUNCTION, VOTING PARADOX

Pufendorf, Samuel von (1632–94) German *natural law theorist and historian. Pufendorf was educated at Leipzig and Jena, and was appointed professor of natural law at Lund, in Sweden. His great work was the *De Jure Naturae et Gentium* (1672, trs. as *Of the Law of Nature and Nations*, 1710). Influenced by *Descartes, *Hobbes, and the scientific revolution of the 17th century, Pufendorf's ambition was to introduce a newly scientific 'mathematical' treatment of ethics and law, free from the tainted Aristotelian underpinnings of *scholasticism. Like that of his contemporary *Locke, his conception of natural law includes rational and religious principles, making it only a partial forerunner of more resolutely empiricist and political treatments in the *Enlightenment.

SEE WEB LINKS

- A list of internet resources on Pufendorf
- Translations of Pufendorf's writings

punishment The deliberate infliction of harm upon somebody, or the withdrawal of some good from them, by an authority, in response to their being supposed to have committed some offence. Sometimes punishment may be inflicted upon an animal, or ritualistically upon an inanimate thing. The philosophical problem with punishment is that since it involves the infliction of some kind of harm, or deprivation of some kind of good, it transgresses normal ethical boundaries, and therefore requires specific ethical justification. The major elements in such a justification have been felt to be: (i) retribution: if a person has inflicted some harm on another, then justice requires retribution (*see also* JUSTICE, RETRIBUTIVE); (ii) reparation: if a person has harmed another, then he owes a duty of reparation to the victim, which his punishment provides; (iii) reformation: the harm inflicted teaches the criminal to behave better in the future; (iv) deterrence: knowledge of the penalties deters potential offenders; (v) prevention: an offender who is deprived of opportunity (e.g. by being imprisoned) cannot repeat the offence. Features (iii) and (iv) are often conjoined with (v), in an indirect *utilitarian approach, in which it is argued that a society with an institution of punishment in place will enjoy better conditions of life than any without it. A thought more popular among judges than philosophers is that punishment simply expresses society's revulsion at some kind of behaviour, and needs no other defence. The difficulty is that judges are often revolted by too many things, such as long hair, youth, and poverty.

pure **1.** In the terminology of *Kant, something is pure in so far as it is unmixed with elements derived from experience. Knowledge is usually made up of what we receive through impressions and what our faculty of knowledge supplies from itself; knowledge is absolutely pure if it is attainable completely **a priori*. Pure reason is reason unmixed with anything empirical or practical: that concerned with the forms rather than the substance of knowledge. A pure concept or *notion* is opposed to an empirical concept, as having its origin in the understanding alone, and not in experience. Pure concepts include those of time and space, that have application in experience. But there are also pure notions that transcend the possibility of experience: God, *free will, and *immortality. **2.** In *set theory, a pure set is one in the Zermelo hierarchy, constructed entirely from the *null set, and sets of sets (*see* ZERMELO–FRAENKEL SET THEORY).

purusa (Sanskrit, mankind) Particularly Cosmic Man, or the creative source. The occupational divisions of Vedic society, and eventually the Indian caste system, correspond to the four parts of the sacrificed body of the *purusa.* The sacrificed God or *demiurge is an essential instrument of creation in many mythologies.

putative A putative F is something on trial for qualification as an F. The qualification is thus an *alienans. A putative proof is an attempted proof, and may not be a proof.

Putnam, Hilary (1926–) American philosopher. Born in Chicago, Putnam was educated at the university of Pennsylvania and the University of California, Los Angeles. He taught at Northwestern, Princeton, and MIT before joining Harvard in 1965. Putnam is widely regarded as one of the most important philosophers of the generation after *Quine, although unlike Quine he does not stand for a monolithic system or body of doctrine, and in his later writings has shown himself gloriously unafraid of changing his mind. Putnam's early work centred upon the philosophy of science, but in the latter part of his career his interests in the human sciences have become more prominent. His *Reason, Truth, and History* (1981) marked a departure from scientific realism in favour of a subtle position that he calls internal realism, initially related to an *ideal limit theory of truth, and apparently maintaining affinities with verificationism, but in subsequent work more closely aligned with *minimalism. Putnam's concern in the later period has largely been to deny any serious asymmetry between truth and knowledge as it is obtained in natural science, and as it is obtained in morals and even theology. Books include *Philosophy of Logic* (1971), *Many Faces of Realism* (1987), *Representation and Reality* (1988), *Renewing Philosophy* (1992), *Pragmatism* (1995), *The Threefold Cord* (1999), and *Collapse of the Fact/Value Dichotomy* (2002); collections of papers include *Mathematics, Matter, and Method* (1975), *Mind, Language, and Reality* (1975), and *Realism and Reason* (1983).

Pyrrho of Elis (*c.*365–275 BC) The founder of Greek *scepticism. Pyrrho was originally a painter, but followed *Anaxarchus to Persia as part of the train of Alexander the Great. There tradition has it that he was influenced by the gymnosophists (perhaps the *Jaina) or magi (*Zoroastrians); at any rate he returned to live a highly respected but poor life in his native city of *Elis, with his sister, a midwife. He left no writings. It is clear that his way of life involved recognizing the vain pursuits and childish folly of humanity, but after that there are two divergent traditions. According to the one, repeated in *Diogenes Laertius and followed by *Hume, Pyrrhonism involved a superhuman refusal to accept the testimony of the senses, to the extent that Pyrrho needed constant protection from falling over precipices, refused to recognize Anaxarchus when the latter was stuck in a bog, etc. The other, more likely, tradition, accepted for instance by *Montaigne, connects him with the mainstream of ancient scepticism, in resting content with the phenomena or appearance of things, with the morals and manners of the society one is in, and with avoiding all unnecessary speculation. It seems likely that Pyrrho himself was not a dialectician, and did not develop the later sceptical armoury used by the *Academy against the *Stoics. But he is credited with the fundamental sceptical rhythm of *isosthenia*, or the balancing of opposite opinions; **epochē*, or suspension of opinion; **aphasia*, or silence; and the goal of **ataraxia*, or tranquillity.

Pythagoras (b. *c.*570 BC) Pythagoras was the son of Mnesarchus of Samos, and emigrated *c.*531 BC to Croton in southern Italy. Here he founded a religious society, but was forced into exile and died at Metapontum. Membership of the society entailed self-discipline, silence, and the observance of various taboos, especially against eating flesh and beans. Pythagoras taught the doctrine of *metempsychosis, or the cycle of reincarnation, and was supposed able to remember former existences. The soul, which has its own divinity and may have existed as an animal or plant, can, however, gain release by a religious dedication to study, after which it may rejoin the universal world-soul. Pythagoras is usually, but doubtfully, credited with having discovered the basis of acoustics, the numerical ratios underlying the musical scale, thereby initiating the arithmetical interpretation of nature. This tremendous success inspired the view that the whole of the cosmos should be explicable in terms of *harmonia* or number. The view represents a magnificent break from the *Milesian attempt to ground physics on a conception of a prime matter, or undifferentiated basis shared by all things, and concentrates instead on form, meaning that physical natures receive an intelligible grounding in different geometric structures. The view is vulgarized in the doctrine usually attributed to Pythagoras that all things are numbers. However, the association of abstract qualities with numbers reached remarkable heights, with occult attachments, for instance between justice and the number four, and mystical significances, especially of the number ten. Cosmologically Pythagoras explained the origin of the universe in mathematical terms, as the imposition of limit on the limitless by a kind of injection of a unit. Followers of Pythagoras included *Philolaus, the earliest cosmologist known to have understood that the earth is a moving planet. It is also likely that the Pythagoreans discovered the irrationality of the square root of two: *see* HIPPASUS OF METAPONTUM. *See also* HARMONY OF THE SPHERES.

Qi *See* CHI.

qua (Latin, insofar as, in the capacity of) Commonly needed in philosophy to distinguish the powers or operation of one thing under one aspect as opposed to those under another.

quadrivium The four liberal studies following the basic *trivium in the medieval university syllabus. They comprise arithmetic, music, geometry, and astronomy.

quaestio (Latin, question) One of the forms of writing and debate in *scholastic philosophy. In the *quaestio disputata* a thesis is proposed, then arguments for and against, then the question is resolved and the arguments against the thesis answered.

qualia The felt or phenomenal qualities associated with experiences, such as the feeling of a pain, or the hearing of a sound, or the viewing of a colour. To know what it is like to have an experience is to know its qualia. The idea that we first of all know qualia, and only indirectly and by their means know the properties of external things, is attacked in *Wittgenstein's *private language argument, but qualia are often felt to be the major stumbling-block in front of scientific philosophies of mind, such as *functionalism and *physicalism. Defenders of those philosophies point out that if qualia are something over and above the physical and functional facts about an organism, they take on a character that makes them unknowable, not just from one creature to another, but even within one consciousness, at least once they have vanished into the past. *Eliminativists ('qualia-phobes') believe that the ways of thinking that make qualia seem both so important and so elusive are wholly erroneous. *See also* PRIVACY, PRIVILEGED ACCESS.

qualitative identity Two things are qualitatively identical if they share all their properties, and numerically identical if they are not two, but one. According to the *identity of indiscernibles, no two distinct things literally share all their properties, although they may share a great many, such as qualities of form and constitution.

qualities *See* PROPERTIES.

qualities, primary/secondary *See* PRIMARY/SECONDARY QUALITIES.

quality of life *See* HAPPINESS.

quantification theory The logical theory of inferences involving *quantifiers, more commonly referred to as the *predicate calculus.

quantifier Informally, a quantifier is an expression that reports a quantity of times that a predicate is satisfied in some class of things (i.e. in a 'domain'). Thus, thinking about a class of children and their diets, one might report that some eat cake, or that all eat cake, or that not all eat cake, or that none eat cake. 'Some' and 'all' are represented in modern logic by the quantifiers. The important point is that the treatment fends off thinking of 'something', 'nothing', and their kin as kinds of names. In classical logic the two interdefinable quantifiers are the existential quantifier $(\exists x) \ldots x$, read as saying that something is …, and the universal quantifier $(\forall x) \ldots x$, read as saying that all things are…. Existential propositions, claiming that things of some kind exist, are represented by the existential quantifier. Less common quantifiers include the plurality quantifiers 'many…' and 'few…', and there are definable mathematical quantifiers such as 'more than half…', 'exactly one…'.

More formally, a quantifier will bind a *variable, turning an *open sentence with n distinct free variables into one with $n - 1$ (an individual letter counts as one variable, although it may recur several times in a formula). When no variables remain free we have a closed sentence, i.e. one that can be evaluated as true or false within a domain. For example, from the open sentence $Fx \& Gx$ we can form $(\exists x)(Fx \& Gx)$, meaning that something is both F and G. The one variable x is bound on each occurrence.

quantifier shift fallacy A fallacy of reversing the order of two *quantifiers. The common form is that of moving from a statement of the form 'every x has a related y' to one of the form 'there is some y related to every x'. An easily detected instance would be inferring from 'everyone has a mother' to 'there is someone who is everyone's mother'. More subtle instances would be trading on the two different meanings that can be given to statements like 'there is some proposition presupposed in every investigation'. Does this mean that for all investigations there is some possibly different presupposition, or that there is some unique common presupposition? Similarly 'there is something that is the meaning of all our activities', which smooths the fallacious transition from 'each activity has a meaning', which is probably true, to 'there is a Purpose common to all of them', which is probably false. The fallacy is obvious in quantification theory, where it is represented as moving from $(\forall x)(\exists y)(Rxy)$ to $(\exists y)(\forall x)(Rxy)$.

quantity of propositions In traditional logic and grammar, the division between universal propositions (all A's are B; no A's are B) and particular propositions (some A's are B, some A's are not B).

quantum logic Logical system that differs from classical logic in ways that reflect the inferential relations between propositions in *quantum theory. The *models of such logics differ in various ways from classical *Boolean algebras. Such a logic was first propounded by G. Birkhoff and John von Neumann, in 1936. A typical, but not universal, feature of quantum logics is failure of the distributive law that from A & (B ∨ C) can be inferred (A & B) ∨ (A & C). It was argued by *Putnam that this failure reflects the strange behaviour of quantum particles in two-slit experiments (*see* QUANTUM MECHANICS).

quantum mechanics Quantum theory, introduced by Max Planck (1858–1947) in 1900, was the first serious scientific departure from Newtonian mechanics. It involved supposing that certain physical quantities can only assume discrete values. In the following two decades it was applied successfully to different physical problems by *Einstein and the Danish physicist Niels Bohr (1885–1962). It was superseded by quantum mechanics in the years following 1924, when the French physicist Louis de Broglie (1892–1987) introduced the idea that a particle may also be regarded as a wave. The Schrödinger wave equation relates the energy of a system to a wave function: the square of the amplitude of the wave is proportional to the probability of a particle being found in a specified position. The wave function expresses the lack of possibility of defining both the position and momentum of a particle (*see* HEISENBERG UNCERTAINTY PRINCIPLE). The allowed wave functions, or 'eigenfunctions', have 'eigen-values' that describe stationary states of the system.

Part of the difficulty with the notions involved is that a system may be in an indeterminate state at a time, characterized only by the probability of some result for an observation, but then 'become' determinate ('the collapse of the wave packet') when an observation is made (*see also* EINSTEIN–PODOLSKY–ROSEN THOUGHT EXPERIMENT, SCHRÖDINGER'S CAT). It is as if there is nothing but a potential for observation or a probability wave before observation is made, but when an observation is made the wave becomes a particle. The wave–particle duality seems to block any way of conceiving of physical reality in quantum terms. In the famous two-slit experiment, an electron is fired at a screen with two slits (like a tennis ball thrown at a wall with two doors in it). If one puts detectors at each slit, every electron passing the screen is observed to go through exactly one slit. But when the detectors are taken away, the electron acts like a wave process going through both slits, and interfering with itself. A particle such as an electron is usually thought of as always having an exact position, but its wave nature ensures that the amplitude of its waves is not absolutely zero anywhere (there is therefore a finite probability of it 'tunnelling' from one position to emerge at another).

The unquestionable success of quantum mechanics has generated a large philosophical debate about its ultimate intelligibility and its metaphysical implications. The wave–particle duality is already a departure from ordinary ways of conceiving of things in space, and its difficulty is compounded by the probabilistic nature of the fundamental states of a system as they are conceived in quantum mechanics. Philosophical options for interpreting quantum mechanics have included variations of the belief that it is at best an incomplete description of a better-behaved classical underlying reality (Einstein), the *Copenhagen interpretation according to which there are no objective unobserved events in the micro-world (Niels *Bohr and W. K. Heisenberg, 1901–76), an 'acausal' view of the collapse of the wave packet (J. von Neumann, 1903–57), and a 'many worlds' interpretation in which time forks perpetually towards innumerable futures, so that different states of the same system exist in different parallel universes (H. Everett).

In recent years the proliferation of subatomic particles (there are 36 kinds of quark alone, in six flavours and three colours) has prompted physicists to look in various directions for unification. One avenue of approach is superstring theory, in which the four-dimensional world is thought of as the upshot of the collapse of a ten-dimensional world, with the four primary physical forces (gravity, electromagnetism, and the strong and weak nuclear forces) becoming seen as the result of the fracture of one primary force. While the scientific acceptability of such theories is a matter for physics, their ultimate intelligibility plainly requires some philosophical reflection. *See also* BELL'S THEOREM.

quasi-memory Term due to the American philosopher Sydney Shoemaker for what remains of remembering an event if we delete the implication that what is remembered actually happened. Quasi-remembering would thus be the state held in common by one who remembers an event, and by one who is in the same current psychological state, although the event they purport to remember never happened. It is contentious whether it is legitimate to isolate such a concept, and to what extent it is parasitical upon the ordinary notion of remembering.

quasi-realism Term coined by the English philosopher Simon Blackburn (1944–) to identify a position holding that an *expressivist or *projectivist account of ethics can explain and make legitimate sense of the *realist-sounding discourse within which we promote and debate moral views. This is in opposition to writers who think that if projectivism is correct then our ordinary ways of thinking in terms of a moral truth, or of knowledge, or the independence of ethical facts from our subjective sentiments, must all be in *error, reflecting a mistaken realist metaphysics. The quasi-realist seeks to earn our right to talk in these terms on the slender, projective basis. The possibility of quasi-realism complicates the methodology of *realist/anti-realist debates in many areas.

question, begging the *See* BEGGING THE QUESTION.

quiddity (Latin, *quidditas*, whatness) The real *essence or nature of a thing; that which makes it the kind of thing that it is (sometimes opposed to *haecceity which makes it the particular individual that it is). The what-ness of things is thus a *universal, in the sense that many different particulars may share the same essential properties. Quidditative knowledge would be knowledge of the real essence or nature of something; according to dominant theological tradition we cannot have quidditative knowledge of God, but at best know things about Him or Her, in a *topic-neutral way. *See also* ABSTRACTION, UNIVERSALS.

quietism In theology, a doctrine condemning all human effort and involvement with the world, in favour of passive devotional contemplation. In philosophy, the doctrine associated with *Wittgenstein that there is no standpoint from which to achieve the traditional philosophical goal of a theory about some concept or another (e.g. truth, experience). *See* MINIMALISM.

Quine, Willard van Orman (1908–2000) The most influential American philosopher of the latter half of the 20th century, Quine was born in Akron, Ohio, of partly Dutch and partly Manx descent. After Oberlin College he did graduate work at Harvard, gaining his doctorate in 1932 for work developing and refining the system of logic of Russell and Whitehead's *Principia Mathematica*. A fellowship and a year abroad brought Quine into contact with the Vienna Circle (*see* LOGICAL POSITIVISM), with *Carnap in Prague, and with *Tarski in Warsaw. Returning to Harvard, Quine eventually became faculty instructor in 1936 and associate professor in 1941. After a wartime period in naval intelligence, Quine became full professor at Harvard in 1948, punctuating the rest of his career with extensive foreign lecturing and travel.

Quine's early work was on mathematical logic, and issued in *A System of Logistic* (1934), *Mathematical Logic* (1940), and *Methods of Logic* (1950). It was with the collection of papers *From a Logical Point of View* (1953) that his philosophical importance became widely recognized. His celebrated attack on the *analytic/synthetic distinction heralded a major shift away from the views of language descended from logical positivism, and a new appreciation of the difficulty of providing a sound empirical basis for theses concerning *convention, *meaning, and *synonymy. Quine's work dominated concern with these problems.

His reputation was cemented by *Word and Object* (1960), in which the *indeterminacy of radical translation first takes centre stage. In this and many subsequent writings Quine took a bleak view of the nature of the language with which we ascribe thoughts and beliefs to ourselves and others. These 'intentional idioms' resist smooth incorporation into the scientific world view, and Quine responded with scepticism towards them, not quite endorsing *eliminativism, but regarding them as second-rate idioms, unsuitable for describing strict and literal facts. For similar reasons he has consistently expressed suspicion of the logical and philosophical propriety of appeal to logical possibilities and *possible worlds. The languages that are properly behaved and suitable for literal and true description of the world are those of mathematics and science. The entities to which our best theories refer must be taken with full seriousness in our ontologies: although an empiricist, Quine thus supposed that the abstract objects of set theory are required by science, and therefore exist. In the theory of knowledge Quine is associated with a *holistic view of verification (*see also* DUHEM THESIS), conceiving of a body of knowledge in terms of a web touching experience at the periphery, but with each point connected by a network of relations to other points. Quine was also known for the view that epistemology should be naturalized, or conducted in a scientific spirit, with the object of investigation being the relationship, in human beings, between the inputs of experience and the outputs of belief. Although Quine's approaches to the major problems of philosophy have been attacked as betraying undue *scientism and sometimes *behaviourism, the clarity of his vision and the scope of his writing made him the major focus of Anglo-American work of the second half of the 20th century in logic, semantics, and epistemology. As well as the works cited, his writings include *The Ways of Paradox and Other Essays* (1966), *Ontological Relativity and Other Essays* (1969), *Philosophy of Logic* (1970), *The Roots of Reference* (1974), and *The Time of My Life: An Autobiography* (1985).

Quine–Duhem thesis *See* DUHEM THESIS.

quintessence (Latin, the fifth essence) In *Aristotle, the fifth element, distinct from earth, fire, air, and water, exempt from change and decay, and found only in celestial bodies.

Quintilian, Marcus Fabius (*c.*AD 35–*c.*90) Roman rhetorician. Much influenced by *Cicero, Quintilian taught rhetoric and oratory in Rome for twenty years, numbering among his pupils the younger Pliny. In retirement he wrote his masterpiece, *Institutio Oratoria*, a massive treatise covering everything needed in oratory: address, memory, style, material, ancient models, discernment, and learning. His dictum 'do not write so that you can be understood, but so that you cannot be misunderstood' may represent an impossible ideal (*see* READER RESPONSE THEORY) but is too often ignored by philosophers.

quotation The primary device indicating that words are being mentioned rather than used. *See* USE/MENTION DISTINCTION.

q

racecourse paradox *See* ZENO'S PARADOXES.

racism The inability or refusal to recognize the rights, needs, dignity, or value of people of particular races or geographical origins. More widely, the devaluation of various traits of character or intelligence as 'typical' of particular peoples. The category of race may itself be challenged, as implying an inference from trivial superficial differences of appearance to allegedly significant underlying differences of nature; increasingly evolutionary evidence suggests that the dispersal of one original people into different geographical locations is a relatively recent and genetically insignificant matter.

Radhakrishnan, Sarvepalli (1888–1975) Indian philosopher and statesman. Born in Southern India, Radhakrishnan held chairs of philosophy at various universities, before becoming professor of Eastern religions and ethics at Oxford, and eventually President of India. His philosophical work is an interpretation and defence of a modernized Hinduism, based on the *Vedas, and drawing especially on the school of *Shankara. However, Radhakrishnan managed to preserve the concept of a personal god, frequently abandoned in Indian theology, as well as the concept of a single personal self. His works are remembered more for their eclecticism and plea for toleration in religious matters than for their philosophical originality. They include the two-volume *Indian Philosophy* (1923–7), and *Eastern Traditions and Western Thought* (1939).

radical interpretation The process of interpreting a foreign language without reliance on existing linguistic knowledge or help from bilinguals. The term is sometimes used as if it applied to any process of coming to understand a foreign language, but this is a mistake, since coming to understand does not entail interpretation back into a previously understood medium. *See also* INDETERMINACY OF TRANSLATION.

radical translation The same process as *radical interpretation, but the term even more notably implies that the process is entirely to be thought of in terms of translation; whereas in principle a language can come to be understood, even as a second language, without being translated back into another. *See also* INDETERMINACY OF TRANSLATION.

Ramakrishna movement Bengali movement founded in 1886 by Sri Ramakrishna Paramahansa and continued by Swami *Vivekananda, offering an interpretation of *Hinduism allied to Christian ideals of compassion, service, and voluntary work in the world, as opposed to renunciation and fatalism. It thus runs schools, colleges, hostels, hospices, and development programmes.

ramified theory of types *See* TYPES, THEORY OF.

Ramsey, Frank Plumpton (1903–30) Cambridge mathematician and philosopher. Ramsey made important contributions to mathematical logic, probability theory, the philosophy of science (*see* RAMSEY SENTENCE), and economics. He showed how the distinction between the semantic paradoxes, such as that of the *Liar, and *Russell's paradox made unnecessary the ramified *type theory of *Principia Mathematica*, and the resulting axiom of reducibility. Much of Ramsey's work was directed at saving classical mathematics from *intuitionism, or what he called the 'Bolshevik menace of Brouwer and Weyl'. In the theory of probability he was the first to show how a *personalist theory could be developed, based on precise behavioural notions of preference and expectation. In the philosophy of language, Ramsey was one of the first thinkers to accept a *redundancy theory of truth, which he combined with radical views of the function of many kinds of proposition. Neither generalizations, nor causal propositions, nor those treating probability or ethics describe facts, but each has a different specific function in our intellectual economy. Ramsey was one of the earliest commentators on the early work of *Wittgenstein, and his continuing friendship with the latter led to Wittgenstein's return to Cambridge and to philosophy in 1929.

Ramsey sentence The sentence generated by taking all the sentences affirmed in a scientific theory that use some term (e.g. 'quark'), replacing the term by a variable, and existentially quantifying into the result. Instead of saying that quarks have such-and-such properties, the Ramsey sentence says that there is something that has those properties. If the process is repeated for all of a group of the theoretical terms, the sentence gives the '*topic-neutral' structure of the theory, but removes any implication that we know what the terms so treated denote. It leaves open the possibility of identifying the theoretical item with whatever it is that best fits the description provided. However it was pointed out by the Cambridge mathematician M.H.A. Newman that if the process is carried out for all except the logical bones of a theory, then, by the *Löwenheim–Skolem theorem, the result will be interpretable in any domain of sufficient cardinality, and the content of the theory may reasonably be felt to have been lost.

Ramsey test The test suggested by F. P. *Ramsey for assessing the acceptability or assertibility or degree of truth of a conditional A→C. It says that you should: (a) take the set of probabilities of propositions that characterizes your current system of beliefs, and add to that the probability of 1 (certainty) of A; (b) adjust in whatever way is needed, and in the most natural and conservative manner consilient with this change; (c) see whether what results includes a high probability of C.

Ramus, Petrus (Pierre de la Ramée) (1515–72) Teacher and professor of philosophy and eloquence at the Collège Royal. His first works included *Aristotelicae animadversiones* and were anti-Aristotelian. The *Dialectique* (1555) is the first substantial philosophical work in French. He converted to Protestantism in about 1560 and was brutally murdered in the St Bartholemew's Day Massacre of 1572.

Rand, Ayn (1905–82) Russian-born novelist whose extreme and simplistic views give her a following on the political right. Her philosophy of 'objectivism' is in fact simple *egoism, a doctrine widely thought untenable (*see* BUTLER, JOSEPH; PRISONERS' DILEMMA). Politically she could see nothing but good in unfettered capitalism.

randomness Informally, an event such as a roulette wheel showing a particular number happens at random if there is no way of telling in advance when it is going to occur. This might be construed metaphysically, meaning that there is no fact of the matter in existence at an earlier time that determines its occurrence. Or it might be construed simply as a limit on our knowledge, with no implications of *determinism (*see also* CHAOS). The mathematical sign of randomness in an event would be that in an infinite sequence of trials, there is no effective method of selecting just those on which the event occurs, i.e. no *recursive function determining the members of the sequence corresponding to the event. *See also* COLLECTIVE, EXCHANGEABILITY.

random variable Intuitively, a variable, such as height, that can take various values in a population, and such that some values have some probability of occurrence, and others a different probability (for example, there might be a probability of one in ten that a person is 5′ 8″ tall, but only one in one hundred that he or she is 6′ 8″ tall). In probability theory a random variable is a *variable X that can take any one of a finite or countably infinite range of values, each with a probability. The distribution of a random variable is the set of pairs (x_i, Prob X = x_i), giving the probability associated with each value in the range. In the example, (5′ 8″, 0.1) would be one member of the distribution of the random variable of height in a population, if 10% of the population is that tall.

range *See* FUNCTION.

range theory of probability The range theory of probability holds that the probability of a proposition, relative to some evidence, is a proportion of the range of possibilities under which the proposition is true, compared to the total range of possibilities left open by the evidence. The theory was originally due to *Laplace, and has guided *confirmation theory, for example in the work of *Carnap. The difficulty with the theory lies in identifying sets of possibilities so that they admit of measurement. Laplace appealed to the principle of *indifference, supposing that possibilities have an equal probability unless there is reason for distinguishing them. However, unrestricted appeal to this principle introduces inconsistency (*see* BERTRAND'S PARADOX). Treating possibilities as equally probable may be regarded as depending upon metaphysical choices, or logical choices, as in the view of *Keynes, or on semantic choices, as in the work of Carnap. In any event it is hard to find an objective source for the authority of such a choice, and this is one of the principal difficulties in front of formalizing the theory of confirmation.

ratiocination An explicit process of *reasoning.

rational Positive term used to commend beliefs, actions, processes as appropriate. In the case of beliefs this means likely to be true, or at least likely to be true from within the subject's perspective. Cognitive processes are rational insofar as they are reliable, and actions rational at least insofar as they provide likely means to an agent's ends. Further constraints on rational action, such as the ends themselves being rational, are of less certain meaning. *See also* RATIONALITY.

rational choice theory *See* DECISION THEORY.

rationalism Any philosophy magnifying the role played by unaided reason, in the acquisition and justification of knowledge. The preference for reason over sense experience as a source of knowledge began with the *Eleatics, and played a central role in *Platonism. Its most significant modern development was in the 17th-century belief that the paradigm of knowledge was the non-sensory intellectual intuition that God would have into the workings of all things, and that human beings taste in their acquaintance with mathematics. The Continental rationalists, notably *Descartes, *Leibniz, and *Spinoza, are frequently contrasted with the British empiricists (*Locke, *Berkeley, and *Hume), but such oppositions usually oversimplify a more complex picture. For example, it is worth noticing the extent to which Descartes approves of empirical enquiry, and the extent to which Locke shares the rationalist vision of real knowledge as a kind of intellectual intuition. In spite of the authority of *Kant, the subsequent history of philosophy has tended to minimize or even to deny the possibility of **a priori* knowledge, so rationalism depending on this category has also declined. However the idea that the mind comes with pre-formed categories that determine the structure of our language and ways of thought has survived in the work of linguists influenced by *Chomsky. The term rationalism is also used more broadly for any anti-clerical, anti-authoritarian *humanism, but it is unfortunate that it is empiricists such as Hume who are in this other sense rationalists.

rationality Pieces of behaviour, beliefs, arguments, policies, and other exercises of the human mind may all be described as rational. To accept something as rational is to accept it as making sense, as appropriate, or required, or in accordance with some acknowledged goal, such as aiming at truth or aiming at the good. Although it is frequently thought that it is the ability to reason that sets human beings apart from other animals, there is less consensus over the nature of this ability: whether it requires language, for example (*see also* ANIMAL THOUGHT). Some philosophers (*Plato, *Aristotle) have found the exercise of reason to be a large part of the highest good for human beings. Others (*Kant, *Hegel) find it to be the one way in which persons act freely, contrasting acting rationally with acting because of uncontrolled passions.

Some, such as *Hume, limit the scope of rationality severely, allowing it to characterize mathematical and logical reasoning, but not to underlie normal empirical processes of belief-formation, nor to play an important role in practical reasoning or ethical or aesthetic deliberation. Hume's notorious statement in the *Treatise* that 'reason is the slave of the passions, and can aspire to no other office than to serve and obey them' is a deliberate reversal of the Platonic picture of reason (the charioteer) dominating the rather unruly passions (the horses).

rationalization The process of interpreting an agent's actions and sayings in order to see them as *rational. It has been influentially argued by *Collingwood and *Davidson that this is an inevitable part of any historical method; equally, however, it is unclear where it tips over into simply reading the present back into the past. *See also* WHIG VIEW OF HISTORY.

rational number *See* NUMBER.

rational reconstruction The process of recasting a theory in some favoured idiom, either imposing a preferred *logic or a preferred *ontology, or both. *See also* REDUCTIONISM, REDUCTION SENTENCE.

ravens, paradox of *See* HEMPEL'S PARADOX.

Rawls, John (1921–2002) American moral and political philosopher. Born in Baltimore, Rawls was educated at Princeton. After teaching at Princeton, Cornell, and MIT, he joined Harvard in 1962. His major work, *A Theory of Justice* (1971), injected new life into the study of political thought in Anglo-American philosophy, and has been a landmark for all subsequent discussion. In it Rawls considered the basic institutions of a society that could be chosen by rational people under conditions that ensure impartiality. These conditions are dramatized as an original position, characterized so that it is as if the participants are contracting into a basic social structure from behind a *veil of ignorance, leaving them unable to deploy selfish considerations, or ones favouring particular kinds of person. Rawls argued that both a basic framework of liberties and a concern for the least well-off would characterize any society which it would be rational to choose. For further details *see* DIFFERENCE PRINCIPLE, ORIGINAL POSITION.

In later work Rawls both extended and modified his work. In response to criticisms he downplayed the Kantian framework of *Theory*, tending to see the construction more in terms of a political solution to the problem of maintaining a democratic society containing groups with disparate conceptions of the good. Later works include *Political Liberalism* (1993); *Collected Papers* (2000: this includes the essays also published under the title *The Law of Peoples*, 1999); and *Essays in the History of Philosophy* (2001).

SEE WEB LINKS

- An introduction to Rawls's philosophy (by Martha Nussbaum)
- A video lecture comparing Rawls's and Plato's views about justice

al-Razi, Abu Bakr (d. 925) Distinguished physician and philosopher; mostly famous as object of rebuttal since he held that the prophets have no advantage over philosophers, and their apparent revelation is generally worthless.

al-Razi, Fakhr Al-Din (1149–1209) Celebrated Islamic theologian, controversialist, and polymath.

reader response theory A view of literary interpretation associated with the American critic Stanley Fish. It holds that meaning does not reside in the text, but in the mind of the reader. The text functions only as a canvas onto which the reader projects whatever his or her reactions may be. The text is a cause of different thoughts, but does not provide a reason for one interpretation rather than another. The theory chimes in with much in *postmodernism, but threatens to make a mockery of the fact that there is such a thing as learning to read, also that a sign such as 'sharp bend' does not only cause some people to expect a sharp bend, but gives them good reason to do so. *See also* INDETERMINACY OF TRANSLATION.

real The term is most straightforwardly used when qualifying another adjective: a real *x* may be contrasted with a fake *x*, a failed *x*, a near *x*, and so on. To treat something as real, without qualification, is to suppose it to be part of the actual world. To *reify something is to suppose that we are committed by some doctrine to treating it as a thing. The central error in thinking of reality and existence is to think of the unreal as a separate domain of things, perhaps unfairly deprived of the benefits of existence. *See also* BEING, EXISTENCE, NOTHING, QUANTIFIER, REALISM/ANTI-REALISM.

real definition A definition thought of as getting at what the object defined really is, as opposed to a *nominal definition, that merely indicates enough properties to locate it: 'gold is the element with atomic number 79 (or atomic weight 196.967)' might be a real definition, as opposed to 'gold is the yellow, shiny, heavy, valuable stuff of which a lot is kept in Fort Knox'. The distinction is associated with *Locke. *See also* ESSENCE.

real essence *See* ESSENCE.

realism/anti-realism The standard opposition between those who affirm, and those who deny, the real existence of some kind of thing, or some kind of fact or state of affairs. Almost any area of discourse may be the focus of this dispute: the external world, the past and future, other minds, mathematical objects, possibilities, universals, and moral or aesthetic properties are examples. A realist about a subject-matter S may hold (i) that the kinds of thing described by S exist; (ii) that their existence is independent of us, or not an artefact of our minds, or our language or conceptual scheme; (iii) that the statements we make in S are not *reducible to other kinds of statement, revealing them to be about some different subject-matter; (iv) that the statements we make in S have *truth conditions, being straightforward descriptions of aspects of the world and made true or false by facts in the world; (v) that we are able to attain truths about S, and that it is appropriate fully to believe things we claim in S. Different oppositions focus on one or another of these claims. *Eliminativists think the S discourse should be rejected. Sceptics either deny (i) or deny our right to affirm it. *Idealists and *conceptualists deny (ii), *reductionists deny (iii), while *instrumentalists and *projectivists deny (iv). *Constructive empiricists deny (v). Other combinations are possible, and in many areas there is little consensus on the exact way a realist/anti-realist dispute should be constructed. One reaction is that realism attempts to 'look over its own shoulder', i.e. that it believes that as well as making or refraining from making statements in S, we can fruitfully mount a philosophical gloss on what we are doing as we make such statements, and philosophers of a *verificationist tendency have been suspicious of the possibility of this kind of metaphysical theorizing: if they are right, the debate vanishes, and that it does so is the claim of *minimalism. The issue of the method by which a genuine realism can be distinguished is therefore critical.

One influential suggestion, associated with *Dummett, is borrowed from the *intuitionistic critique of classical mathematics, and suggests that the unrestricted use of the principle of *bivalence is the trademark of realism. However, this has to overcome counterexamples both ways: although *Aquinas was a moral realist, he held that moral reality was not sufficiently structured to make true or false every moral claim, while *Kant believed that we could use the law of bivalence happily in mathematics precisely because it was only our own construction. Realism can itself be subdivided: Kant, for example, combines empirical realism (within the phenomenal world the realist says the right things—surrounding objects really exist and are independent of us and our mental states) with transcendental idealism (the phenomenal world as a whole reflects the structure imposed on it by the activity of our minds as they render it intelligible to us). In modern philosophy the orthodox opposition to realism has been from philosophers such as *Goodman impressed by the extent to which we perceive the world through conceptual and linguistic lenses of our own making.

reality That which there is. The question of how much of it there is forms the dispute between *realists and anti-realists. Does it include: numbers, possibilities, the future, the past, other minds, colours, tastes, the external world, mind as well as matter, or matter as well as experience?

real number *See* NUMBER.

reason *See* RATIONALITY.

reason, principle of insufficient *See* INDIFFERENCE, PRINCIPLE OF.

reasoning Any process of drawing a conclusion from a set of premises may be called a process of reasoning. If the conclusion concerns what to do, the process is called practical reasoning, otherwise pure or theoretical reasoning. Evidently such processes may be good or bad: if they are good, the premises support or even *entail the conclusion drawn; if they are bad, the premises offer no support to the conclusion. Formal *logic studies the cases in which conclusions are validly drawn from premises. But little human reasoning is overtly of the forms logicians identify. Partly, we are concerned to draw conclusions that 'go beyond' our premises, in the way that conclusions of logically valid arguments do not (*see* ABDUCTION, INDUCTION). Partly, it has to be remembered that reasoning is a dynamic process, and that what to a logician looks like a static contradiction may be the sensible replacement of one set of assumptions with others as the process develops. Furthermore, as we reason we make use of an indefinite lore or common-sense set of presumptions about what is likely or not (*see* FRAME PROBLEM, NARRATIVE COMPETENCE). A task of an automated reasoning project is to mimic this casual use of knowledge of the way of the world in computer programs.

reasons/causes When we act for a reason, is the reason a cause of our action? Is explaining an action by means of giving the reason for which it is done, a kind of causal explanation? The view that it is not will cite the existence of a logical relation between an action and its reason: it will say that an action would not be the action it is if it did not get its identity from its place in an intentional plan of the agent (it would just be a piece of behaviour, not explicable by reasons at all). Reasons and actions are not the 'loose and separate' events between which causal relations hold. The contrary view, espoused by *Davidson in his influential paper 'Actions, Reasons, and Causes' (1963), claims that the existence of a reason is a mental event, and unless this event is causally linked to the acting we could not say that it is the reason for which the action is performed; actions may be performed for one reason rather than another, and the reason that explains them is the one that was causally efficacious in prompting the action.

reciprocity The practice of making an appropriate return for a benefit or harm received from another. Reciprocal altruism is the system whereby a benefit received is returned with a benefit; under a wide range of conditions, groups practising it will flourish better than those practising unbridled self-interest. Reciprocity was a moral imperative in the Homeric world, essential to the creation of binding relationships between otherwise independent warriors. However that code allowed quite indiscriminate orgies of retaliation in face of an insult or provocation (similarly the God of the Old Testament). With the emergence of the **polis* individual reciprocities became less important than action on behalf of the city, which also reserved to itself the business of appropriate retaliation. *See also* RETRIBUTIVE JUSTICE, TIT FOR TAT.

recognition Recognition by others, or by the law or by the State, is a clear ground of well-being, and its absence one of the most damaging of privations. In Hegel it underlies self-consciousness itself, since we only understand ourselves for who we are by incorporating our understandings of how we are regarded by others.

recollection, argument from *See* *ANAMNESIS*.

recurrence, eternal *See* ETERNAL RETURN.

recursive A procedure that is applied once, and then applied to the result of that application, and so on. A recursive definition (definition by induction) defines the result of some operation for 0, and then the result for any number $n + 1$ in terms of the result for n; thus the operation becomes defined for all numbers (the notion may be extended to describe the same process on any well-ordered set). For example, if n' denotes the successor of n, then multiplication may be defined: $a \times 0 = 0$; $a \times b' = (a \times b) + a$.

A function in mathematics is primitive recursive if it is definable by recursion and substitution from a number of basic functions. These are commonly the successor function, the zero function (the function whose value is zero for every argument), the projection functions (that extract the ith member of any ordered n-tuple), and constant functions (that return the same number as value for any arguments).

A function is general recursive (or recursive) if it can be defined by means of primitive recursive functions and the minimization or μ operator. This defines a resulting function, h, out of a given function f according to the schema:

$$h(x_1 \ldots x_n) = \text{the least } y \text{ for which } f(x_1 \ldots x_n, y) = 0$$

and is undefined if there is no such *y*.

A set is recursively enumerable if there is a recursive function that enumerates its members, i.e. if they can be ordered as f(0), f(1), f(2) ... where f is a general recursive function. If both a set and its complement can be ordered, then the set is general recursive, or recursive. The importance of the notion is that it corresponds with being decidable, or effectively computable. Suppose, for example, that the theorems of some system form a recursive set, then we can find whether a candidate formula is a theorem by enumerating both the theorems and the nontheorems; we can be sure that in a finite time the formula will turn up on one list or another, and this procedure decides the matter. According to *Church's theorem the set of theorems of the predicate calculus cannot be represented as a recursive set, so by *Church's thesis the calculus is undecidable.

redefinition, high/low Term introduced by the 20th-century American philosopher Paul Edwards for the manoeuvre of redefining a term more or less tightly, so that an apparently false statement is made true if interpreted in the new way. A high redefinition tightens the criterion of application: 'No, he wasn't drunk—to be drunk you have to be really comatose, after all.' A low redefinition relaxes it: 'You were drunk—a single sherry impairs one's faculties.' Edwards believed that philosophical disputes, e.g. over whether some process of forming belief counts as reasonable, were bedevilled by unwitting shifts of definition of the key terms.

reducibility, axiom of Axiom introduced by *Russell and *Whitehead in *Principia Mathematica.* In that system propositional functions are sorted into levels, as part of the ramified theory of *types. The axiom says that for any function at any level there exists a formally equivalent function at the first level. The axiom is needed to allow the construction of elementary mathematics, in particular to certify the principle of mathematical induction. Its effect, as *Ramsey pointed out, was largely to nullify the point of introducing different orders of functions.

reductio ad absurdum (Latin, reduction to absurdity) The process of reasoning that derives a *contradiction from some set of assumptions, and concludes that the set as a whole is untenable, so that at least one of them is to be rejected. Formally, if $\{A_1 \ldots A_n\} \vdash (B \,\&\, \neg B)$, then $\{A_1 \ldots A_{n-1}\} \vdash \neg A_n$.

reductionism (reductivism) A reductionist holds that the facts or entities apparently needed to make true the statements of some area of discourse are dispensable in favour of some other facts or entities. Reductionism is one solution to the problem of the relationship between different sciences. Thus one might advocate reducing biology to chemistry, supposing that no distinctive biological facts exist, or chemistry to physics, supposing that no distinctive chemical facts exist (*see also* UNITY OF SCIENCE). Reductionist positions in philosophy include the belief that mental descriptions are made true purely by facts about behaviour (*behaviourism), that statements about the external world are made true by facts about the structure of experience (*phenomenalism), that statements about moral issues are really statements about natural facts (*naturalism), and many others. Reductionism is properly speaking not a form of *scepticism (for the claims in the reduced area may be true and known to be true: indeed, one purpose of the reduction will typically be to show how this is so). Nor is it necessarily a form of anti-realism (*see* REALISM/ANTI-REALISM), although it is often classified that way. Reductionist claims were popular in the earlier years of *analytic philosophy, and were pursued by such writers as *Russell and *Carnap in the form of programmes of translating the theses from the target science or discourse into theses from the domain to which it was to be reduced. Subsequent recognition of the *holism of meaning, and the apparent failure of these reductionist programmes, switched attention to other ways of obtaining the benefits of reduction without incurring the costs of providing the promised translations. *See* SUPERVENIENCE.

reduction sentence A device proposed by *Carnap for dealing with sentences of a scientific theory whose logical form is not easily given in the terms of the *predicate calculus. '*x* is soluble in water' cannot be defined as '*x* is placed in water → *x* dissolves', since the → of the predicate calculus is *material implication, and the consequence would be that all things not placed in water are soluble. Carnap's solution was to define 'soluble' only within the scope of being placed in water: if something is placed in water, then it is soluble if and only if it dissolves: $((\forall x)(x \text{ is placed in water} \rightarrow (x \text{ is soluble} \leftrightarrow x \text{ dissolves})))$. The reduction sentence does not define solubility for other things.

redundancy theory of truth The theory also known as minimalism, or the deflationary view of truth, fathered by *Frege and *Ramsey. The essential claim is that the predicate '... is true' does not have a sense, i.e. expresses no substantive or profound or explanatory concept that ought to be the topic of philosophical enquiry. The approach admits of different versions, but centres on the points (i) that 'it is true that *p*' says no more nor less than '*p*' (hence, redundancy); (ii) that in less direct contexts, such as 'everything he said was true', or 'all logical consequences of true propositions are true', the predicate functions as a device enabling us to generalize rather than as an adjective or predicate describing the things he said, or the kinds of proposition that follow from true propositions. For example, the second may translate as '$(\forall p, q)(p \,\&\, p \rightarrow q \rightarrow q)$' where there is no use of a notion of truth.

There are technical problems in interpreting all uses of the notion of truth in such ways, but they are not generally felt to be insurmountable. The approach needs to explain away apparently substantive uses of the notion, such as 'science aims at the truth' or 'truth is a norm governing discourse'. Indeed, *postmodernist writing frequently advocates that we must abandon such norms, along with a discredited 'objective' conception of truth. But perhaps we can have the norms even when objectivity is problematic, since they can be framed without mention of truth: science wants it to be so that whenever science holds that *p*, then *p*. Discourse is to be regulated by the principle that it is wrong to assert *p*, when not-*p*. *See also* DISQUOTATIONAL THEORY OF TRUTH.

reference The basic case of reference is the relation between a name and the person or object which it names. The philosophical problems include trying to elucidate that relation, to understand whether other semantic relations, such as that between a predicate and the property it expresses, or that between a description and what it describes, or that between myself and the word 'I', are examples of the same relation or of very different ones. A great deal of modern work on this was stimulated by *Kripke's *Naming and Necessity* (1970). It would also be desirable to know whether we can refer to such things as abstract objects and how to conduct the debate about such an issue. A popular approach, following *Frege, is to argue that the fundamental unit of analysis should be the whole sentence. The reference of a term becomes a derivative notion: it is whatever it is that defines the term's contribution to the *truth condition of the whole sentence. There need be nothing further to say about it, given that we have a way of understanding the attribution of meanings or truth conditions to sentences. Other approaches search for a more substantive, possibly causal or psychologically or socially constituted, relationship between words and things. *See also* DEFINITE DESCRIPTION, DENOTATION, LOGICALLY PROPER NAME.

referent That which is referred to by an expression. *See* REFERENCE.

referentially opaque/transparent A distinction between the contexts into which referring expressions can be put. A context is referentially transparent if any two terms referring to the same thing can be substituted in it **salva veritate*, i.e. without altering the truth or falsity of what is said. A context is referentially opaque when this is not so. Thus, if the number of the planets is nine, then 'the number of the planets is odd' has the same truth-value as 'nine is odd'; whereas 'necessarily the number of planets is odd' or '*x* knows that the number of planets is odd' need not have the same truth-value as 'necessarily nine is odd' or '*x* knows that nine is odd'. So while '... is odd' provides a transparent context, 'necessarily ... is odd' and '*x* knows that ... is odd' do not. *See also* EXTENSION/INTENSION.

reflective equilibrium A state in which all one's thoughts about a topic fit together; in which there are no loose ends or recalcitrant elements that do not cohere with an overall position. The term is associated with *Goodman, and gained currency from the work of *Rawls, who suggested that the proper method of ethics should be one of trying to achieve reflective equilibrium, testing theories against judgements about particular cases, but also testing judgements about particular cases against theories, until equilibrium is achieved. *See also* COHERENCE THEORY OF TRUTH, NEURATH'S BOAT.

reflexive A *relation is reflexive in a domain if everything in the domain bears it to itself: $(\forall x) Rxx$. Identity and relations couched in terms of identity are reflexive: everyone is the same height, weight, etc. as him or herself.

refute To disprove. This is a *success word; to attempt to disprove something is to argue against it or to reject it, repudiate it, or rebut it, but not yet to refute it.

regimentation A theory is said to be properly regimented when it is presented in the form recognized by some favoured logic, usually *first-order predicate calculus. When this is so the inferential routes between sentences of the theory are especially transparent, and the commitments of the theory laid bare.

regress A strategy gives rise to a vicious regress if whatever problem it was designed to solve remains as much in need of the same treatment after its use as before. Thus a definition is (usually) viciously regressive if the term to be defined recurs in the definition. The definition 'x is good' = 'x is something we think is good' faces the question of what the word 'good' is doing on the right-hand side of the equation: what are we said to think about x? Reapplication gives 'x is good' = 'x is something we think is something we think is ... ' and the procedure continues forever, yielding an infinite regress. A benign regress is a regress which involves no such failure. 'It is true that p' = 'it is true that it is true that ... that p' without any worrisome change of content of what is said. There is frequently room for dispute about whether regresses are benign or vicious, since the issue will hinge on whether it is necessary to reapply the procedure. The *cosmological argument is an attempt to find a stopping point for what is otherwise seen as being an infinite regress. *See also* CIRCLE, VICIOUS.

regulative principles (regulative rules) *See* CONSTITUTIVE/REGULATIVE.

Reichenbach, Hans (1891–1953) Philosopher of science and probability theorist. Born in Hamburg, Reichenbach worked in Berlin until 1933, when he left Germany first for Istanbul, and thence to the United States. Although not a member of the Vienna circle he sympathized with the empiricist ideals of *logical positivism, but substituting relationships of probability between different strata of scientific theories, in place of the positivist ideal of *reduction. Influential works included *Philosophie der Raum-Zeit-Lehre* (1928, trs. as *The Philosophy of Space and Time*, 1958) and *Experience and Prediction* (1938).

Reid, Thomas (1710–96) Scottish philosopher of common sense. Reid was born near Aberdeen and educated at Marischal College. After a period as a Presbyterian minister, he was appointed in 1751 to King's College, Aberdeen. In 1764 he took the chair of moral philosophy at the university of Glasgow. Reid's three important books are the *Enquiry into the Human Mind on the Principles of Common Sense* (1764), *Essays on the Intellectual Powers of Man* (1785), and *Essays on the Active Powers of Man* (1788). Reid was the first serious philosopher to attack the *British empiricist reliance on '*ideas' as satisfactory units on which to found a theory of knowledge and meaning. He regarded *Berkeley, and especially *Hume, as presenting a **reductio ad absurdum* of the approach to knowledge by the way of ideas. In his own approach, sensations of primary qualities of objects speak to us like words, affording us 'natural signs' of the qualities of things. The mind passes naturally over a word to consider what it signifies, and in like manner it passes over its own experience to consider directly the qualities they signify. This is so for 'original perceptions' of primary qualities; perceptions of secondary qualities have to be acquired. Reid's insight here has been recaptured in the 20th century in various kinds of direct *realism. It enables him to defend the basic conceptual scheme of common sense against what he saw as the corrosive *scepticism of Hume. For Reid, as for *Moore later, the basic principles of common sense cannot be avoided or abandoned, although if we raise the question of their truth we can only appeal to divine harmony (he may not have been so far from Hume here as he supposed). Reid's influence persisted in the Scottish school of common-sense philosophy, and his phenomenological insights continue to attract modern attention.

SEE WEB LINKS

- A list of internet resources on Reid
- A searchable archive of Reid material held at the University of Aberdeen

reification To reify is to treat as a thing. To describe philosophers as reifying is usually to charge that they are misled by verbal form into thinking simply because some noun has a use, there must be something to which it refers. Thus *Platonists are charged with reifying numbers or *universals, and people are supposed to have improperly reified great varieties of things, including sets, infinite collections, finite things, sensations, physical objects, the future, the past, the possible, or the will of the people. The charge is itself not entirely transparent, and the fault these philosophies commit may more helpfully be put as treating things of one type as if they were things of another. *See also* ONTOLOGY, REALISM/ANTI-REALISM.

reincarnation *See* METEMPSYCHOSIS.

Reinhold, Karl Leonhard (1758–1823) Austrian philosopher who worked in Germany. Reinhold was professor at Jena from 1787 to 1794, and subsequently at Kiel. After a period as a follower of Kant, he veered towards the idealism of *Fichte and of *Jacobi, eventually rejecting their *idealism in favour of a kind of *realism associated with C. G. Bardili. His influence lay largely in his attempt to systematize Kantian idealism, in his clear and widely-read expositions of Kant. His *Letters on the Kantian Philosophy* appeared originally in the *Deutsche Mercur* for 1786–7. Subsequent work concerned the basis of representation.

relation Philosophically relations are interesting because of the historic prejudice, given its most forceful expression by *Leibniz, that they are somehow 'unreal' compared to the intrinsic, *monadic properties of things. A way of putting the idea is that if all the monadic properties of the objects of a domain are fixed, then the relational properties are fixed as well (relations *supervene on monadic properties). But in modern logic and science there is no justification for this claim.

The central notions in the logical treatment of relations are as follows. The domain of a relation is the set of things that bear the relation to something. The range is the set of things that have something bear the relation to them. The field of a relation is the set of things that belong either to its domain, or to its range. A binary relation relates one element from its domain to one of its range: R*xy*. Relations may be defined over greater numbers of things: for example, we can define R*xyz* to be the relation holding between three numbers when $x+y=z$, and so up to relations defined over n-tuples of any size. For formal and mathematical purposes a relation may be identified with the class of *ordered pairs (or in general *ordered n-tuples) that satisfy it. So 'father of' becomes the set of all pairs *x,y*, such that *x* is the father of *y*, 'is greater than' becomes the set of all pairs *x,y*, such that *x* is greater than *y*, and so on. The main properties to be noticed in the theory of relations are indexed under their own headings: *see* ANTISYMMETRIC, ASYMMETRIC, EQUIVALENCE RELATION, IRREFLEXIVE, ORDERING RELATION, REFLEXIVE, SYMMETRIC, TRANSITIVE.

relations, internal/external The doctrine that all relations are internal was a cardinal thesis of *absolute idealism, and a central point of attack by *Moore and *Russell. It is a kind of *essentialism, stating that if two things stand in some relationship, then they could not be what they are did they not do so. If, for instance, I am wearing a hat now, then when we imagine a possible situation that we would be apt to describe as my not wearing the hat now, we would strictly not be imagining me and the hat, but only some different individuals (*see also* COUNTERPART). Moore ('External and Internal Relations', *Proceedings of the Aristotelian Society*, 1919–20) believed the doctrine to depend upon the simple fallacy of inferring from 'necessarily, if I am wearing a hat then I am wearing a hat' that 'if I am wearing a hat I am necessarily wearing a hat'. It is, however, clear that a more complex combination of thoughts underlay the idealist doctrine, including the *holistic doctrine that the properties of individuals are in some sense secondary to the properties of the whole universe in which they exist, together with an epistemological mistrust of separating what is known from the knowing mind. The combination gave some motive for holding that everything gains its identity simply as an aspect of one indivisible, *Parmenidean whole. The rejection of this, in favour of a more *atomistic conception of the world as a loose plurality of individuals, allowed external relations, these being relations which individuals could have or not depending upon contingent circumstance.

relations of ideas Term used by *Hume in the first *Enquiry* for **a priori* knowledge: 'All the objects of human reason or enquiry may naturally be divided into two kinds, to wit, *Relations of Ideas*, and *Matters of Fact*' (*Enquiry Concerning Human Understanding*, iv). The term reflects the belief that anything that can be known *a priori* must be internal to the mind, and hence transparent to us. *See also* DEMONSTRATION, HUME'S FORK, MATTER OF FACT.

relative identity The view advocated by the 20th-century English philosopher Peter *Geach according to which the identity statement '$a = b$' needs interpreting as '*a* is the same F as *b*' where F is a kind-term or *sortal. The clearest motivation for this view would be if different choices of sortal produce different identity statements with different truth-values. Thus if *a* denotes a statue at an early time, and *b* a statue at a later time, it may be that *a* is the same mass of clay as *b*, but not the same statue. However, it may also be that the choice of sortal is prejudged in the meaning of the names *a* and *b*, in which case no such discrepancy can arise, although sortals are still playing an important role in evaluating identity statements.

relativism The permanently tempting doctrine that, in some areas at least, truth itself is relative to the standpoint of the judging subject ('beauty lies in the eye of the beholder'). The first classical statement is the doctrine of the Sophist *Protagoras that 'man is the measure of all things'. Relativism may be a global doctrine about all knowledge, or a local doctrine about some area (aesthetics, ethics, or judgements of secondary qualities, for example). The aspects of the subjects supposed to determine what truth is 'for them' may include historical, cultural, social, linguistic, or psychological background, or brute sensory constitution. Relativism is one attempt to take these contingencies into account in formulating the relationship between the believer and the truth believed. It may be regarded as an attempt to avoid the *scepticism that almost inevitably follows when an absolute conception of truth is combined with recognizing our differently rooted, variable, contingent ways of making judgements.

Relativism is frequently rejected on the grounds that it is essential to the idea of belief or judgement that there are standards that it must meet, independently of anyone's propensity to accept it. Inability to make sense of such standards eventually paralyses all thought. Sophisticated relativists such as *James (who described *pragmatism as a form of relativism) reply that assessments of truth and falsity may be made in a disciplined way within a framework, even if the framework is itself contingent, and that the 'circumpressure of experience' is all we need and can have as a 'guarantee against licentious thinking' (*The Meaning of Truth*, 1909). The central problem of relativism is one of giving it a coherent formulation, making the doctrine more than the platitude that differently situated people may judge differently, and less than the falsehood that contradictory views may each be true. Much *postmodernist thought may be regarded as a somewhat abandoned celebration of relativism. *See also* PERSPECTIVISM.

relativity theory The assumptions on which *Einstein's special theory of relativity (1905) depends are (i) all *inertial frameworks are equivalent for the description of all physical phenomena, and (ii) the speed of light in empty space is constant for every observer, regardless of the motion of the observer or the light source. (Although the second assumption may seem plausible in the light of the Michelson–Morley experiment of 1887, which failed to find any difference in the speed of light when measured in the direction of the earth's rotation or when measured perpendicular to it, it seems likely that Einstein was not influenced by the experiment, and may not even have known the result.) As a consequence of the second postulate, no matter how fast she travels, an observer can never overtake a ray of light, and see it as stationary beside her. However near her speed approaches to that of light, light still retreats at its classical speed. The consequences are that space, time, and mass become relative to the observer. Measurements made of quantities in an inertial system moving relative to one's own reveal slower clocks, contracted lengths, and heavier masses, with the effect increasing as the relative speed of the systems approaches the speed of light. Events deemed simultaneous as measured within one such system will not be simultaneous as measured from the other: time and space thus lose their separate identity, and become parts of a single *space-time. The special theory also has the famous consequence ($E = mc^2$) of the equivalence of energy and mass.

Einstein's general theory of relativity (1916) treats of non-inertial systems, i.e. those accelerating relative to each other. The leading idea is that the laws of motion in an accelerating frame are equivalent to those in a gravitational field. The theory treats gravity not as a Newtonian force acting in an unknown way across distance, but as a metrical property of a space-time continuum that is curved in the vicinity of matter. Gravity can be thought of as a field described by the metric tensor (*see* GEOMETRY) at every point. The classic analogy is with a rock sitting on a bed. If a ball-bearing is thrown across the bed, it is deflected towards the rock not by a mysterious force, but by the deformation of the space, i.e. the depression in the sheet around the rock. Interestingly, the general theory lends some credit to a version of the Newtonian *absolute theory of space, in the sense that space itself is regarded as a thing with metrical properties of its own (*see also* CLOCK PARADOX). The search for a unified field theory is the attempt to show that just as gravity is explicable as a consequence of the nature of space-time, so are the other three fundamental physical forces: the strong and the weak nuclear forces, and the electromagnetic force (*see also* PHYSICS, PHILOSOPHY OF). The theory of relativity is the most radical challenge to the 'common-sense' view of space and time as fundamentally distinct from each other, with time as an absolute linear flow in which events are fixed in objective relationships.

relevance logics Logics that explore the properties of relations of implication stronger than *strict implication. It was shown by C. I. *Lewis that with the classical notion of *entailment anything whatever follows from a contradiction, and a tautology follows from any arbitrary proposition. Logicians regarding these consequences as unacceptable have sought to define relations of entailment stronger (more restrictive) than strict implication, to preserve the distinction between good and bad ways of arguing even in the presence of contradictions and tautologies.

reliabilism The view in *epistemology that follows the suggestion that a subject may know a proposition p if (i) p is true; (ii) the subject believes p; and (iii) the belief that p is the result of some reliable process of belief formation. The third clause is an alternative to the traditional requirement that the subject be justified in believing that p, since a subject may in fact be following a reliable method without being justified in supposing that she is, and vice versa. For this reason, reliabilism is sometimes called an externalist approach to knowledge: the relations that matter to knowing something may be outside the subject's own awareness. As the suggestion stands, it is open to counterexamples: a belief may be the result of some generally reliable process which was in fact malfunctioning on this occasion, and we would be reluctant to attribute knowledge to the subject if this were so, although the definition would be satisfied (*see also* GETTIER EXAMPLES). Reliabilism pursues appropriate modifications to avoid the problem without giving up the general approach.

religion, philosophy of The attempt to understand the concepts involved in religious belief: *existence, *necessity, fate, creation, *sin, *justice, mercy, redemption, God. Until the 20th century the history of Western philosophy is closely intertwined with attempts to make sense of aspects of pagan, Jewish, or Christian religion, whilst in other traditions, such as *Hinduism, *Buddhism, or *Taoism, there is even less distinction between religious and philosophical enquiry. The classic problem of conceiving of an appropriate object of religious belief is that of understanding whether any term can be predicated of it: does it make sense to talk of it creating things, willing events, knowing things, or being good, or caring, or being one thing or many? The *via negativa* or *negative theology claims that God can only be known by denying ordinary terms any application to it (or them); another influential suggestion is that ordinary terms only apply metaphorically, and that there is no hope of cashing the metaphors. Once a description of a Supreme Being is hit upon, there remains the problem of providing any reason for supposing that anything answering to the description exists. The medieval period was the high-water mark for purported proofs of the existence of God, such as the *Five Ways of *Aquinas, or the *ontological argument of *Anselm. Such proofs have fallen out of general favour since the 18th century, although they still sway many people and some philosophers.

Generally speaking, even religious philosophers (or perhaps they especially) have been wary of popular manifestations of religion. *Kant, himself a friend of religious faith, nevertheless distinguishes various perversions: theosophy (using transcendental conceptions that confuse reason), demonology (indulging an anthropomorphic mode of representing the Supreme Being), theurgy (a fanatical delusion that a feeling can be communicated to us from such a being, or that we can exert an influence on it), and idolatry, or a superstitious delusion that one can make oneself acceptable to the Supreme Being by other means than that of having the moral law at heart (*Critique of Judgement*, ii. 28). The warm touchy-feely tendencies held in contempt by Kant have, however, been increasingly important in modern theology (*see*, for example, BUBER, TILLICH).

Since *Feuerbach there has been a growing tendency for philosophy of religion either to concentrate upon the social and anthropological dimensions of religious belief (*see also* LANGUAGE GAME, MAGIC), or to treat it as a manifestation of various explicable psychological urges. Another reaction is to retreat into a celebration of purely subjective *existential commitment (*see also* KIERKEGAARD). But the *ontological argument continues to attract attention, and modern anti-*foundationalist trends in *epistemology are not entirely hostile to cognitive claims based on *religious experience.

religious experience Any experience carrying as its content the presence of something divine or transcendent. Religious believers may report such experiences as those of being in the presence of God, or Christ, or as being able to comprehend a timeless and eternal divine order to the universe. Much *epistemology has been hostile to these claims, arguing that any such content must be read into an experience rather than read off from it, and that such experiences are simply being interpreted according to the subject's wishful thinking. Reports of religious experience would be the subject of sociological or psychological analysis, rather than having any independent cognitive worth. In contemporary philosophy there is something of a fight back on behalf of religious experience, with some philosophers arguing that all experience is theory-laden, in which case the report of a religious content to experience might be as justified as a report of any other kind, in spite of the supernatural nature of the claim being made. Philosophers hostile to this defence point out that the theory which comes with religious experience seems untestable, and since it is highly variable across cultures, devoid of any except doubtful emotional significance.

religious language A central topic in modern philosophy of *religion. Religious sayings may appear to be mere superstition if they are taken as strict and literal representations of a supposed supernatural world. It is tempting therefore to interpret them differently, in terms of poetry, *metaphor, analogy, *fiction, expressions of attitude, or simply as parts of ritual. Such reinterpretations appeal to intellectuals of a religious bent, but they have an element of 'government house' attitudes about them, since they seem to imply that the theologians know what ordinary people are doing, or ought to be doing, better than they themselves do. *See also* NEGATIVE THEOLOGY.

remainder *See* DILEMMA.

remembering *See* MEMORY.

remote cause An event preceding another in a *causal chain, but separated from it by other events.

Renouvier, Charles (1815–1903) French Neo-Kantian. A student of *Comte, Renouvier modified Kant in order to remove the 'thing in itself', elide the difference between theoretical and practical reason, and emphasize the categories of personality and freedom. He rejected dogmatism in religion and politics, as inconsistent with respect for the individual person. His attitude was influential on *James, and through him on American pragmatism. Books included *Essais de critique générale* (1854–64) and *La Science de la morale* (1869).

replacement, axiom of The axiom added to Zermelo's *set theory by A. A. Fraenkel (1891–1965), to produce the classical set theory known as ZF. Put in terms of second-order logic, the axiom states that any *function whose domain is a set has a range which is also a set. That is, if the arguments of a function form a set, so do the values of the function. This formulation is second-order because it quantifies over functions; in first-order logic the axiom needs to be stated as an axiom schema. *See also* ZERMELO–FRAENKEL SET THEORY.

representation, political Ideally a representative works in a parliament as an authorized voice for the interests of his or her constituents. In modern democracies this whittles down to being a voice for those of the constituents who voted the right way, or still better, contribute to the right campaign.

representationalism (representationism) Generally the doctrine that the mind (or sometimes the brain) works on representations of the things and features of things that we perceive or think about. In the philosophy of perception the view is especially associated with *Malebranche and *Locke, who, holding that the mind is the container for ideas, held that 'of our real ideas, some are adequate, and some are inadequate. Those I call adequate, which perfectly represent those archetypes which the mind supposes them taken from; which it intends them to stand for, and to which it refers them' (Locke, *Essay*, ii. 31). The problems in this account were mercilessly exposed by *Arnauld and *Foucher, writing against Malebranche, and by *Berkeley, writing against Locke. The fundamental problem is that the mind is 'supposing' its ideas to represent something else, but it has no access to this something else except by forming another idea. The difficulty is to understand how the mind ever escapes from the world of representations, or, in other words, how representations manage to acquire genuine content, pointing beyond themselves. In more recent philosophy, the analogy between the mind and a computer has suggested that the mind or brain manipulates symbols, thought of as like the instructions in a machine program, and that those symbols are representations of aspects of the world. The Berkeleyan difficulty then recurs. The programmed computer behaves the same way without knowing whether the sign '$' refers to a unit of currency or anything else. The elements of a machine program are identified purely syntactically, so the actual operations of the system go on without any reference to any interpretation of them (*see* SYNTAX). Hence, according to critics, there is no way, on this model, for seeing the mind as concerned with the representational properties of the symbols. The point is sometimes put by saying that the mind, on this theory, becomes a syntactic engine rather than a semantic engine. Representation is also attacked, at least as a central concept in understanding the mind, by *pragmatists who emphasize instead the activities surrounding a use of language, rather than what they see as a mysterious link between mind and world. *See also* FORM OF LIFE.

representation theorem The proof given by *de Finetti that from the requirement that someone's degrees of confidence in propositions be coherent, in the sense of avoiding the possibility of a *Dutch book, it can be derived that their beliefs correspond to the classical measures of the probability calculus.

representative theory of perception The view that perception is to be thought of in terms of the presence of mental states (or sometimes brain states), that represent the features of the world that is perceived. The view is alluring, but faces the problem that if these states are the only ones to which we can have direct access, then we cannot compare them with the features of the world they supposedly represent. It would be like comparing a portrait with a sitter, but without being given any access to the sitter except via the portrait. The representative theory of perception is generally attributed to *Locke, who thought our ideas represent the primary qualities of bodies, and the charge that the theory leads to scepticism about the external world was pressed by *Berkeley. The philosophy of perception is centrally concerned with the difficulties over the idea of a representative mental state. *See also* IDEALISM, PRIMARY/SECONDARY QUALITIES, REALISM, REPRESENTATIONALISM.

republicanism An ideal of government that emphasizes the role of the active, participating citizen in government, often looking back to the role of the citizen in ancient Rome or Athens. Institutionally it aims at checks and balances to prevent the emergence of faction and *majority tyranny, but also at the town-hall politics whereby decision-making has a bottom-up rather than a top-down structure.

res cogitans (Latin, a thinking thing) The famous answer given by *Descartes to the question 'what am I?' as it occurred after the *method of doubt left him with only the proposition 'I think, therefore I am.' It is contrasted with *res extensa* or extended material things.

res extensa *See* RES COGITANS.

residues, method of *See* MILL'S METHODS.

respect for persons A key concept in *Kantian moral philosophy. Respect is due to every rational being, and so must be distinguished from liking, or admiration, or even esteem. It is best understood through what it forbids, which is treating a person as a mere means to an end of one's own: ignoring their personhood or their humanity. *See also* RIGHTS.

responsibility Socially, people's responsibilities are those things for which they are accountable; failure to discharge a responsibility renders one liable to some censure or penalty. A job, or profession, or social role will be partly defined in terms of the responsibilities it involves. The extent of responsibility not just for oneself but for others is a central topic for political and ethical theory ('Am I my brother's keeper?'). Understanding the nature of our causal responsibility for our own thoughts, natures, and actions is the main problem in any theory of action. *See* FREE WILL.

resurrection The return to life of a person after his or her bodily death, either with his or her original body, or with a new one. The concept raises severe problems of *personal identity. *See also* METEMPSYCHOSIS.

retributive justice *See* JUSTICE, RETRIBUTIVE.

retrocausation *See* BACKWARD CAUSATION.

retrodiction The hypothesis that some event happened in the past, as opposed to the prediction that an event will happen in the future. A successful retrodiction could confirm a theory as much as a successful prediction.

revealed theology Theology concerned with doctrines that are not known or understood by unaided reason, but that can be known or understood through the special dispensation of a divine revelation, e.g. through the incarnation, or the transmission of biblical knowledge.

revelation In theology, God's act of revealing himself to people, or to some privileged subset of people. It includes general revelation (e.g. 'the heavens declare the glory of God') and special revelation, such as particular *miracles shown to particular audiences. *See also* ENTHUSIASM.

revenge The desire for revenge is often thought of as 'primitive' but less negative verdicts are also possible. *Evolutionary psychology tends to be more hospitable to the notion, seeing it as an emotional underpinning of strategies like *tit for tat, themselves flexible and adapted to a wide variety of social interactions. *See also* ERINYES, JUSTICE.

revolution Any major social and political transformation, sufficient to replace old institutions and social relations, and to initiate new relations of power and authority. Revolutions may or may not be violent, progressive, the result of class conflict, initiated by revolutionary agents, or inevitable. *See also* BAKUNIN, LENIN, MARX. For scientific revolutions *see* GALILEAN WORLD VIEW, KUHN, PARADIGM.

rhetic *See* SPEECH ACT.

rhetoric The art of using language so as to persuade or influence others. Although rhetoric is apparently opposed to the philosophical ideal of the exact pursuit of truth, their reconciliation has sometimes seemed desirable, most notably to *Cicero. If one thinks of philosophy as a matter of argument rather than doctrine, as the academic *sceptics did, then rhetoric is good practice in argument. The cultivation of this art was an important study in medieval universities, and began to regain ground with the belief, widely shared in the late 20th century, that all discourse and argument contains a political and persuasive core. *See also* POSTMODERNISM.

SEE WEB LINKS

- An audio discussion of rhetoric by three experts
- A list of internet resources on rhetoric, including bibliographies and texts

Richard Rufus (Richard of Cornwall) (d. *c.*1260) English Aristotelian and Franciscan. Richard's were among the first medieval commentaries on Aristotle. He also wrote on Peter *Lombard's *Sentences*, and was one of the most influential figures in late 13th-century philosophy, logic, and theology. In many respects his doctrines anticipate those of *Duns Scotus.

Richard's paradox A set of numbers, S, may be defined as follows. Write in alphabetical order all permutations of pairs of letters of the alphabet, followed by all triples, and so on (counting a space and punctuation marks as letters). Cross out all combinations that do not refer to a number. S is the sequence whose members are U_1, the first number referred to by such a permutation, U_2, the second, and so on. That is, S contains all the numbers definable by finitely many words. Then consider the following sentence: 'Let p be the digit in the nth place of the nth number in S, and form a number having p + 1 in its nth place if p is not 8 or 9, and 0 otherwise.' Then this phrase refers to a number, N, that cannot be in the sequence S, since it differs from any member of this sequence somewhere. It differs from the nth member of S in the nth place. Yet the sentence in quotation marks is one of the permutations that occurs in the original list defining the members of S: N was defined by finitely many words, and so must be in the sequence S. The paradox is a member of the *Liar family of *semantic paradoxes. The argument generating the paradox is a *diagonal argument.

Ricoeur, Paul (1913–2005) French existentialist, theologian, philosopher, and literary critic. Born in Valence, Ricoeur was educated in the *existentialist and *phenomenological traditions. Captured in the Second World War, he became familiar with the work of *Husserl, *Heidegger, and Jaspers. In 1948 Ricoeur became professor at Strasbourg, and from 1957 was professor at the university of Paris X, Nanterre, and his travels included a post at the university of Chicago. In the French tradition Ricoeur's work is wide-ranging and difficult, but includes a welcome stress on the humility necessary to the pursuit of truth. His works include the series under the general title *Philosophie de la volonté* ('Philosophy of the Will'): vol. i, *Le Volontaire et l'involontaire* (1950, trs. as *Freedom and Nature: the Voluntary and the Involuntary*, 1966); vol. ii, *Finitude et culpabilité* ('Finitude and Blame'), part I, *L'Homme faillible* (trs. as *Fallible Man*, 1965), and part II, *La Symbolique du mal* (trs. as *The Symbolism of Evil*, 1967).

right (political) The branch of political opinion that is for the freedom of the individual in economic matters, and therefore protects the distributions of property and divisions of class that such freedoms generate. The right may frequently be authoritarian, regarding strong law and order as necessary to protect the divisions it favours, or it may extend the protection of liberty to the point of *anarchism. *See also* CONSERVATISM, FASCISM, INDIVIDUALISM, LEFT (POLITICAL), LIBERALISM.

right action Finding what is the right thing to do terminates moral and ethical discussion of what to do. It does not always terminate practical discussion, if, for example, expediency, practicality, cost, etc. are introduced as non-moral factors with an independent voice. The question of whether an analysis of *practical reason should concentrate on what is right, or instead on what is good signals the division between *deontological and *teleological approaches to ethics.

rights Legal rights exist in virtue of *positive law; moral rights are sufficiently independent of it to give a platform from which legal arrangements may be criticized. The basis for analysis is usually a fourfold distinction due to Wesley Hohfeld (1879–1918). A person A has a *claim-right* to *x*, and against person B, if B has a duty to refrain from interfering with A having or doing *x*, or even has a duty to assist A in obtaining *x*. A has a *privilege* (or *liberty-right*) to *x*, and against B, if B has no claim-right that A not do or obtain *x*. A has a *power-right* to *x* with regard to B, if A may render B *liable* to some status connected with *x* (a policeman obtains a power-right to enter my home, when he gets a warrant). A has an *immunity-right* to *x* against B, if A is free from B's power-right with regard to *x*. Questions arising include the relations between these families, and the nature of the ground in virtue of which any of these rights obtain.

Rights are frequently held to 'trump' other practical considerations, which requires seeing them as not themselves simply grounded in the interests of the right-holder, but perhaps existing in virtue of more central considerations of the duties we owe to each other. For *Kant, the fundamental moral right is to be treated as an end in oneself, and reason alone justifies and grounds this right. The basic lists that have been drawn up of human rights to be respected by any legitimate constitution are surprisingly similar, suggesting a common conception of the conditions necessary for societies that accord human beings their full dignity or *respect. This common core may be thought of as 'natural rights', although the term only makes good sense in a metaphysical or theological context in which *nature is conceived of as capable of creating moral imperatives. *Bentham is notorious for having opposed this, claiming that '*natural rights* is simple nonsense: natural and imprescriptible rights, rhetorical nonsense —nonsense upon stilts' (*Anarchical Fallacies*, Art. ii). Nature, according to Bentham, provides a background against which we may wish that there were such things as rights, but they do not exist until law creates them. However, the term remains firmly at the centre of moral, political, and legal thought, particularly since rights are more attractive possessions than duties.

SEE WEB LINKS

- A list of internet resources on human rights law, with links to related sites
- An archive of human rights documents and materials

rigid designator A rigid designator is one that denotes the same thing in all possible worlds, or in all possible worlds in which that thing exists. The term was introduced by *Kripke, to label the fact that if we specify a possibility using a singular term we intend the singular terms to have the same reference in the imagined, or possible, situation as they have in the actual world. For *definite descriptions this is not necessarily so: in 'had Hume been English, the town he died in would not have been Edinburgh', both 'Hume' and 'Edinburgh' refer to what they always do: the philosopher Hume and the town Edinburgh. But we cannot suppose that the phrase 'the town he died in' is referring to the town he actually died in, namely Edinburgh. The sentence is not trying to say that had Hume been English, Edinburgh would not have been Edinburgh. Kripke used the point in his influential criticism of the theory that names function as disguised definite descriptions. Complexity arises in handling cases where we wish to evaluate a sentence in a world in which the normal reference would not have existed, such as 'had his mother died young, Hume would not have existed'. Here we cannot intend the term to have the same reference as usual in the imagined possible situation, since in *that* situation there would be no Hume to refer to, yet intuitively we are still talking about Hume. The other classic modern discussion is David Kaplan, 'Demonstratives', Pt III, in *Themes from Kaplan* (1989).

ring of Gyges Thought experiment introduced by the character Glaucon, in *Plato's *Republic*, Bk II, 359d. The ring rendered its wearer Gyges, a shepherd, invisible, enabling him to commit crimes with impunity. Gyges used the cloak of invisibility to seduce the King's wife and then with her help usurp the kingdom. Glaucon uses the story to make vivid the thought that only fear of penalties deters people from behaving unjustly.

Romanticism The movement that swept European and thence American culture between about 1775 and 1830, although heralded by preceding elements in the 18th century (antiquarianism, novels of sensibility, the taste for the *sublime and the picturesque, and above all *Rousseau's elevation of nature and sentiment above civilization and intellect). Romanticism was partly a reaction against the stiff rationality of the *Enlightenment and its official, static, neo-classical art, in favour of the spontaneous, the unfettered, the subjective, the imaginative and emotional, and the inspirational and heroic. In philosophy, the Romantics took from *Kant both the emphasis on *free will and the doctrine that reality is ultimately spiritual, with nature itself a mirror of the human soul. In *Schelling, nature becomes a creative spirit whose aspiration is ever fuller and more complete self-realization. Knowledge of the nature of this spirit (the Absolute) cannot be acquired by rational and analytic means, but only by emotional and intuitive absorption within the process. The spontaneous innocence of the child (and of humanity in its childhood) is corrupted with the onset of intellectual separation from nature, but the individual, and equally human history, can overcome this separation by a spiral process of regaining the lost unity, albeit cleansed and improved by the journey. Romantic art is thus essentially one of movement, figured in quests, journeys, and pilgrimages whose aim is to return to a lost home or haven. *Coleridge and de *Staël were the main vehicle for the transmission of German philosophical Romanticism to England. Although a movement of more general cultural importance, Romanticism drew on the same intellectual and emotional resources as German *idealism, as it culminates in the philosophy of *Hegel and of *absolute idealism. In the 20th century it survived in nostalgic nationalism and intemperate criticisms of modernity, found most notably in *Heidegger. The problem is that once human beings believe they have suffered a Fall, or a separation from the true grounds of life, they quickly start looking for victims within or without the society, to blame for it.

SEE WEB LINKS

- An audio lecture by Isaiah Berlin on 'The Roots of Romanticism'
- A list of internet resources on Romanticism, including a bibliography

Rorarius, Hieronymus (1485–1556) Papal nuncio to the court of Ferdinand of Hungary. He is remembered entirely because the entry under his name in *Bayle's *Dictionnaire historique et critique* contains Bayle's seminal discussion of the philosophy of *Leibniz. The official pretext is that Rorarius had maintained that beasts make better use of reason than men do (*see also* ANIMAL THOUGHT). This leads Bayle to an extended discussion of the nature of the soul, and eventually of *pre-established harmony.

Rorty, Richard McKay (1931–2007) American philosopher and critic. Educated at Chicago and Yale, Rorty taught at Wellesley College and Princeton, and was professor of humanities at the university of Virginia from 1982 until moving to Stanford as professor of comparative literature in 1998. He was widely known as an analytic philosopher who turned against what he regarded as the traditional categories of concern in that tradition—truth, knowledge, objectivity, and representation—and substituted a free-wheeling *postmodernist version of *pragmatism, linked with writers such as *Heidegger and *Gadamer, in which these topics are banished. Having risen above such concerns the liberal intellectual maintains an ironic and detached attitude even to his or her fundamental convictions; intellectual life becomes less a matter of hard work in laboratories and archives, and more a kind of dilettante conversation in the *après*-truth coffee house. Critics also found unsettling the political *quietism or *conservatism this suggests, but Rorty deployed arguments he derived from *Sellars and *Davidson, in order to pull down the intellectual scaffolding supporting notions such as truth. Influential books include *Philosophy and the Mirror of Nature* (1979) and *Contingency, Irony and Solidarity* (1989). Collections of papers include *Objectivity, Relativism and Truth* (1991), *Essays on Heidegger and Others* (1991), *Truth and Progress* (1998), and *Philosophy and Social Hope* (2000).

SEE WEB LINKS

- A list of on- and offline resources on Rorty, including bibliographies and texts

Roscelin de Compiègne (*c*.1050–*c*.1125) Shadowy French philosopher, known mainly through attacks by his opponents, who included *Abelard and *Anselm. He appears to have been an early *nominalist, and held doubtful views about the Trinity.

Rosicrucianism The writings of Jean Valentin Andreae (1589–1674) relating the stories of one Christian Rosenkreuz and his dabblings in alchemy, astrology, and the *kabbala were not meant to be taken seriously. But secret societies devoted to the occult found them a useful stimulus to their imaginations. Philosophers and scientists who may have had Rosicrucian connections include Francis *Bacon, *Leibniz, and *Newton.

Rosmini-Serbati, Antonio (1797–1855) Reactionary Italian philosopher and theologian, ordained in 1821. He endeavoured to synthesize philosophy and faith, contrary to prevailing *empiricism and *positivism, and with the purpose of elevating church power above that of the state. His principal work, *Nuovo saggio sull'origine dell idee* ('New Essays on the Origin of Ideas') of 1830, was only a small part of his output, which included work on politics, morality, psychology, and logic.

Ross, Alf (1899–1979) Danish philosopher of law, and professor of criminal law at Copenhagen. Ross was a follower of *Kelsen, who added to the basic positivist standpoint a *non-cognitivist view of normative discourse. A statement about what the law should be, or what rights and duties people have, functioned as a prescription or practical expression; statements about what the law is were predictions about what courts will do (*see* LAW, PHILOSOPHY OF). His principal translated works included *On Law and Justice* (1958) and *Directives and Norms* (1968).

Ross, William David (1877–1971) British classical scholar and moral philosopher. Educated in Edinburgh and Oxford, Ross taught in Oxford, where he edited the Oxford translations of Aristotle from 1908 to 1931. His own work included *The Right and the Good* (1930) and *Foundations of Ethics* (1939), defending a version of the *intuitionism of G. E. *Moore. The upshot was a stern ethics opposed to *consequentialism, in which **prima facie* rights and duties jostle one another for priority.

Rousseau, Jean-Jacques (1712–78) Born in Geneva of a learned mother, who died within a week, and an artisan father, Rousseau was brought up to cherish the civic ideal of the ancient Roman republic. His father being exiled for an ill-judged duel, Rousseau was brought up with a cousin until the time came for him to be apprenticed to an engraver. Finding this intolerable he left Geneva, and in Turin was received into the Catholic church. In Savoy he belonged to the household of the slightly disreputable Baroness de Warens, but it was after becoming tutor to the family of the Abbé de Mably that Rousseau became acquainted with philosophers of the French Enlightenment, including Mably's brother *Condillac. In Paris he made friends with *Diderot; a year in Venice saw him dismissed from the service of the Ambassador, the comte de Montaigu, for generally insufferable behaviour. Back in Paris he became secretary to an opulent tax-farmer named Dupin, and began passing an agreeable literary life in the magnificent château of Chenonceaux, where he wrote various contributions to the **Encyclopédie*.

In 1749 Rousseau's prize essay for the Dijon academy, the *Discours sur les sciences et les arts* (pub. 1751, trs. as the *Discourses on the Sciences and the Arts*, 1751, and known as the First Discourse), publicized his sudden realization that arts and sciences contributed neither to the virtue nor the happiness of human beings, but instead brought ruin and corruption. The implicit *Romanticism of this vision was again manifested in his prolonged controversy with the composer Rameau over the true nature of music. Whereas for Rameau music was academic, cerebral, Cartesian, and conservative in its order and its sophistication, for Rousseau it was melodic, flexible, inspired by emotion, and democratic. In 1753 Rousseau again entered the Dijon competition, this time unsuccessfully, with the *Discours sur l'origine et les fondements de l'inégalité parmi les hommes* (pub. 1755, trs. as *A Discourse upon the Origin and Foundation of the Inequality Among Mankind*, 1762, and usually known as the Second Discourse). This essay argued that the ills of the human condition derive from society, and that in the state of nature life is free and independent, healthy, happy, and innocent. People are endowed by nature with the sentiment of pity (stifled as the power of reason develops, separating people from nature and from each other). The less idyllic vision of the state of nature familiar from philosophers such as *Hobbes is quite inadequate: they 'speak of savage man and they depict civilized man'. It is only with the (somewhat unaccountable) move from this pastoral idyll towards society that human beings leave the world of the 'noble savage' and step towards unhappiness and vice. Once a social condition is induced, and the fall from nature has taken place, then for the reasons Hobbes gives a system of law must emerge, although at this stage in his thought Rousseau has no illusions about its justice or objectivity: it is a fraud imposed by the rich on the poor. Similarly, whereas in nature sex is simple, love is an artificial device by which females manipulate men, in order to gain the shelter and protection that their dependent and domesticated state leads them to require.

However, some kind of redeeming political organization is possible, and Rousseau's pessimism is moderated by his commendation of the city of Geneva as a 'democracy welltempered' (he revisited it after finishing the essay, and was predictably disillusioned). In *Du contrat social* (1762, trs. as *The Social Contract*, 1764), Rousseau returns to the defence of democratic, republican ideals modelled upon ancient Sparta, and centred upon the idea of freedom as active participation in politics and legislation. Just as a single person is free in so far as he or she prescribes for himself or herself the rules of his or her life, so a civil society is a single organic unity with a single will: the *volonté générale* or general will. The *Social Contract* is sensitive to the different conditions of different societies, and the different legal, political, and social arrangements that these might require. It inaugurated a new era of anthropological and comparative studies of human societies, reacting against the static, classical, assumption of human uniformity more characteristic of the Enlightenment. Back in the country in 1756 Rousseau began his novel *La Nouvelle Héloïse*, and fell in love with his neighbour, Sophie d'Houdetot. By now reconverted to *Calvinism, Rousseau also defended the ban on the theatre that existed in Geneva, in his *Letter to M. d'Alembert on the Theatre*. Since he himself wrote operas and plays, this seemed surprising. Rousseau subscribes to versions of the argument to *design, and even to the unmoved mover in *The Profession of Faith of a Savoyard Priest*, a rebuttal of the deism or atheism of *Voltaire and the materialism of the *philosophes* of the *Enlightenment (*see* MOVER, UNMOVED). However, in accordance with his philosophy of nature, true religious faith is more an affair of the heart than the head. Nature and innocence are usually corrupted by education, and in *Émile, ou de l'éducation* (1762, trs. as *Émile, or Education*, 1764) Rousseau propounds a better system, concentrating on the senses and bodily health at the expense of the intellect, discouraging books, and enjoying 'the sleep of reason'. *Émile* was promptly banned. Rousseau fled to Neuchâtel in Switzerland (Geneva having also banned *Émile* and *The Social Contract*), where the local pastor inflamed the population against him. His later years were spent in doubtful mental health, travelling in various places including England, where a brief sojourn ended with a paranoid quarrel with *Hume. But these years produced *Les Confessions* (1782–9, trs. as *Confessions*, 1783–90), an autobiography that broke new ground in facing the petty and shameful elements of a human life.

Rousseau's immense influence arises from his being the first true philosopher of *Romanticism. In him many themes that came to dominate intellectual life of the next one hundred years are first found: the lost unity of humankind and nature; the elevation of feeling and innocence and the downgrading of the intellect; a dynamic conception of human history and its different stages; a faith in teleology and in the possibility of recapturing a vanished freedom.

SEE WEB LINKS

- A list of on- and offline resources on Rousseau, including bibliographies
- Translations of Rousseau's writings

Royce, Josiah (1855–1916) The leading American *absolute idealist. Royce studied under *Lotze in Germany, and taught at Harvard from 1892. He was a friend of *James, and probably represents much of what James was rejecting in his *pragmatism. Royce's works include *Religious Aspects of Philosophy* (1885) and *The World and the Individual* (1901).

rule-following considerations The considerations discussed by *Wittgenstein in the *Philosophical Investigations*, §147–202, concerning our conception of what it is for our use of a piece of language to be governed by an understanding of it, or a meaning or rule of use. Different interpretations of these passages exist, but it is generally agreed that Wittgenstein is opposing a conception of ourselves as grasping a 'superlative fact': a set of logical rails that dictate how we should use a term in any of an indefinite number of cases that we have not yet encountered. The deflationary account that he appears to substitute is that there are not both the use of the term and in addition such a rule or principle (or *form, or *universal, or *idea): there is only the use. One influential interpretation is that of *Kripke, which sees Wittgenstein as engaged in a sceptical dialogue, whereby the facts we can offer continually

r

fail to play the role of rules we are following, so that eventually the judgement that we are following one rule or another seems to answer to no facts at all, or to have no truth conditions. It is doubtful whether Wittgenstein would have accepted this description of his conclusion, but the upshot may be a similar re-evaluation of what it is to apply a concept, or think or make a judgement at all.

rule of inference In his famous article 'What the tortoise said to Achilles' in the journal *Mind* in 1895, Lewis Carroll raised the Zeno-like problem of how a proof ever gets started. Suppose I have as premises (1) p and (2) $p \rightarrow q$. Can I infer q? Only, it seems, if I am sure of (3) $(p \,\&\, p \rightarrow q) \rightarrow q$. Can I then infer q? Only, it seems, if I am sure that (4) $(p \,\&\, p \rightarrow q \,\&\, (p \,\&\, p \rightarrow q) \rightarrow q) \rightarrow q$. For each new axiom (N) I need a further axiom (N + 1) telling me that the set so far implies q, and the regress never stops. The usual solution is to treat a system as containing not only axioms, but also rules of inference, allowing movement from the axioms. The rule *modus ponens allows us to pass from the first two premises to q. Carroll's puzzle shows that it is essential to distinguish two theoretical categories, although there may be choice about which theses to put in which category.

rule of law *See* LAW, PHILOSOPHY OF.

rule of succession Principle used by *Laplace in his *Essai philosophique sur les probabilités* (1814), and named by *Venn, for determining a probability of the repetition of an event from its frequency of occurrence in some kind of trial. It is an 'inverse method', i.e. one that gives an allegedly formal or mathematical rule for deriving probabilities from experienced frequencies. It states that if an event has occurred m times and failed n times under given conditions, then the probability of its occurrence when those conditions are next fulfilled is m + 1/m + n + 2. Laplace uses the principle to prove that given the experience of the human race, the probability of the sun rising tomorrow is 1826214 to 1. Unhappily the same reasoning suggests that the chance of it rising every day for the next 4000 years is not more than ⅔. Some form of the principle was accepted by *De Morgan, *Lotze, and the statistician Karl *Pearson; it was rejected by *Boole, *Venn, *Bertrand (1822–1900), and *Keynes.

rule/principle Distinction found in the philosophy of law, between the rules of law as they are found in the settled body of law, and the more general principles that may be supposed to have shaped the way judgements have been given. These principles may have a wider ethical or political source. A controversial claim elaborated by *Dworkin is that they form an integral part of law itself.

rule utilitarianism *See* INDIRECT UTILITARIANISM.

Russell, Bertrand Arthur William (1872–1970) English philosopher. Russell was born into the liberal and aristocratic family descended from the Prime Minister, John Russell, and educated first at home, and then from 1890 at Trinity College, Cambridge, where he read mathematics. From an early age, and especially after meeting the mathematician G. Peano (1848–1932) in 1900, his interests were devoted to the foundations of mathematics. *The Principles of Mathematics* was published in 1902, a year after the discovery of *Russell's paradox. After a period spent wrestling with the problem, Russell propounded the theory of *definite descriptions and the theory of *types, which were central elements in his own solution. From 1907 to 1910 he worked in collaboration with *Whitehead for ten to twelve hours a day for eight months of the year on *Principia Mathematica*, published in three volumes, 1910–13. During this period he also laid the foundations of his life as a radical, active, liberal intellectual, beginning by standing as a suffragist candidate for Parliament. During the First World War he was imprisoned for six months for publishing the statement that American soldiers would be employed as strike-breakers in Britain, 'an occupation to which they were accustomed when in their own country'.

After the war, Russell visited Russia and lived for a period in China. During the 1920s his principal philosophical works included *The Analysis of Mind* (1921) and *The Analysis of Matter* (1927), although he also published a large number of popular and semi-popular works on social and moral issues. He opened and ran a school, but from 1938 to 1944 taught at a number of American universities, including Chicago and the university of California at Los Angeles. He was however denied employment by the City College of New York, on the grounds that he was morally unsuitable. In a famous ensuing law-suit his works were described as 'lecherous, libidinous, lustful, venerous, erotomaniac, aphrodisiac, irreverent, narrowminded, untruthful, and bereft of moral fiber'. During the Second World War he wrote the *History of Western Philosophy* (1945). *Human Knowledge's Scope and Limits* (1948) is Russell's last important philosophical book, but by this time he was a world-famous symbol of philosophy and its radical potential. He was awarded the Nobel Prize for literature in 1950, and as the unmistakable patriarch of the liberal academic world spent the rest of his life actively campaigning for nuclear disarmament.

Russell's philosophy is generally felt to have reached its peak in the first two decades of the

20th century. The seminal work on the foundations of mathematics is accompanied by lucid work on truth and its basis in experience; the theory of definite descriptions provided the logical background to an epistemology based on the distinction between knowledge by *acquaintance and knowledge by description, although the restricted role that Russell allows to acquaintance is generally thought to be problematic. By the time of *Our Knowledge of the External World* (1914), Russell was convinced that scientific philosophy required analysing many objects of belief as '*logical constructions' or 'logical fictions', and the programme of analysis that this inaugurated dominated the subsequent philosophy of *logical atomism, and then the work of *Carnap and the *logical positivists. In *The Analysis of Mind*, the mind itself is treated, in a fashion reminiscent of *Hume, as no more than the collection of neutral perceptions or sense data that make up the flux of conscious experience, and that looked at another way also make up the external world (*neutral monism). In his early period Russell is content with extending his realism to *universals, but *An Inquiry into Meaning and Truth* (1940) represents a more empiricist approach to the problem.

In his general philosophical approach Russell was not only a realist, but also, perhaps in continued opposition to the monolithic nature of *absolute idealism, a pluralist and foundationalist, intent upon bringing the resources of modern logic to a basic empiricism. He had little sympathy with any movement away from those ideas, as, for instance, it developed from the later work of *Wittgenstein. Russell was a gifted raconteur, and as well as his many philosophical works wrote an entertaining three-volume *Autobiography* (1967–9).

SEE WEB LINKS

- An archive of audio and video recordings of Russell
- Bibliographies of writings by or on Russell

Russell's paradox The most famous of the paradoxes in the foundations of *set theory, discovered by *Russell in 1901. Some classes have themselves as members: the class of all abstract objects, for example, is an abstract object. Others do not: the class of donkeys is not itself a donkey. Now consider the class of all classes that are not members of themselves. Is this class a member of itself? If it is, then it is not, and if it is not, then it is.

The paradox is structurally similar to easier examples, such as the paradox of the *barber. But it is not so easy to say why there is no such class as the one Russell defines. It seems that there must be some restriction on the kinds of definition that are allowed to define classes, and the difficulty is that of finding a well-motivated principle behind any such restriction. The paradox also bears a resemblance to others such as the *liar paradox, but since *Ramsey insisted on the distinction it has been usual to distinguish Russell's paradox, and others in the same family, from the *semantic paradoxes of which the liar is a member. *See also* IMPREDICATIVE DEFINITIONS; TYPES, THEORY OF.

Ryle, Gilbert (1900–76) English philosopher and classicist. Ryle was born in Brighton and, educated at Oxford, and, after teaching from 1924 to 1945 at Christ Church, became professor at Oxford. His earliest interests were in the phenomenological tradition of *Husserl and *Heidegger. But from the 1930s onwards he absorbed the influence of the later work of *Wittgenstein, becoming a fierce advocate of the kind of attention to language demanded by Wittgenstein and J. L. Austin. His *Concept of Mind* (1949) is a sustained attack on the *Cartesian philosophy of mind, or dogma of the 'ghost in the machine'. The behaviourism it substitutes is a little too brisk, but Ryle did a great deal to lay the groundwork for later developments such as *functionalism. The brio and verve of his work are unusual in analytical philosophy, and come out further in *Dilemmas* (1953) and *Plato's Progress* (1966).

Saadia ben Joseph (Saadia Gaon) (882–942) The father of medieval Jewish philosophy, Saadia was born in Egypt and educated there and in Palestine. In 928 he was appointed head of the rabbinical academy of Sura, near Baghdad, but, much involved in the sectarian disputes of the time, he was exiled for a while before finally being reinstated. His principal philosophical work is the *Book of Doctrines and Beliefs*, modelled on the work of Islamic theologians but based upon Jewish rather than Islamic scripture. Saadia defends human knowledge against the attacks of scepticism, and attempts to prove the creation of the world. His division of the commandments of the *Torah* into those that are rational and those that are traditional or revealed was later rejected by *Maimonides.

al Sabziwari, Al-Hajj Mula Hadi (1797/8–1873) Influential Iranian theologian and teacher. A follower and interpreter of *Mulla Sadra, his principal work is the *Ghurar al-fara'id* (*The Blazes of the Gems*), a poem in which he gives a systematic and complete presentation of the philosophy of this school, together with the *Sharh al-manzuma*, his own commentary on this poem.

saccade (Old French, the flicks of a sail) The normal darting movements and brief fixations of the eye. The fact that the eye is normally in constant movement helps to undermine the idea that it serves as a lens producing an internal image for our inspection.

sacrifice *Rationalizations of classical sacrificial practices include supposing that they dramatize the violence of killing and the associated guilt, or that they purge the killing of guilt by seeing it as part of legitimate ritual. *Do ut des* (Latin, I give so that you give) is the natural attempt to establish relations of *reciprocity with divine powers, echoed in Christianity in God's sacrifice of his own son (*see* ATONEMENT).

sacrificium intellectus (Latin, sacrifice of the intellect) The more or less enthusiastic subordination of reason to faith, often thought to be a duty in religious cultures.

Sadducism (Sadduceeism) The Sadducees were a Jewish sect of the time of Christ, who denied the resurrection of the body and the existence of spirits. In the 17th century the term was used by the orthodox of those who denied the existence of ghosts, witches, etc., and who were therefore on the dangerous road to atheism. *See also* GLANVILL.

Sade, Donatien Alphonse, marquis de (1740–1814) French pornographer and madman. His nihilism as much as his obsession with the psychopathology of unbridled violent lust has given him a remarkable symbolic role in the thought of writers such as *Foucault, the French theorist Gilles Deleuze (1925–95), and others concerned with sexual desire and its relationship to political *power. *See also* WICKEDNESS.

Sadra, Mulla *See* MULLA SADRA.

St Petersburg paradox Paradox in the theory of probability published by Daniel Bernoulli in 1730 in the *Commentarii* of the St Petersburg academy. Someone offers you the following opportunity: he will toss a fair coin. If it comes up heads on the first toss he will pay you one dollar; if heads does not appear until the second throw, two dollars, and so on, doubling your winnings each time heads fails to appear on another toss. The game continues until heads is first thrown, when it stops. What is a fair amount for you to pay for this opportunity? The incredible reply is: an infinite amount. For your expectation of gain is given by the series $\frac{1}{2} + (2 \times \frac{1}{4}) + (4 \times \frac{1}{8}) + \ldots$, which has an infinite sum. This little offer is apparently worth more to you than all the wealth in the world. Yet nobody in their right mind would pay much at all for it. The paradox has been taken to show the incoherence of allowing infinite utilities into decision theory. Once they are allowed, then it is worth staking any finite sum on any indefinitely small chance of an infinite payoff. If it is specified that the St Petersburg game has to stop when, for example, the payoff reaches the size of the national debt, then the calculation of what you should pay to enter the game remains quite reasonable: if the national debt is, say 2n dollars, you should pay $1/2n$ dollars and no more to enter the game.

Saint-Simon, Claude-Henri de Rouvroy (1760–1825) French social philosopher and founding father of socialism. After considerable political activity during the French revolution, Saint-Simon founded the journal *L'Industrie*. His experience in the revolution led him to perceive that the general optimism of the *Enlightenment needed a deeper understanding of the historical and social conditions of society if durable change for the better was to be produced. Saint-Simon was the first to see that it was the economically based conflict of classes that led to the ruin of the feudal system of government, and of the ecclesiastical world view. His particular target was the class of useless bureaucrats, idlers and wastrels whom he contrasted unfavourably with the men of industry in whose hands the future would and should lie. Saint-Simon was a seminal influence on *Comte (who was his secretary) and above all on *Marx.

sakti In Hindu thought, consciousness as power, the supreme energy, the female counterpart of Siva as pure consciousness allied to *Kundalini.

salva veritate (Latin, saving the truth) Two expressions are intersubstitutable *salva veritate* if the result of substituting one for the other always preserves the truth-value of any sentence in which they are used. If the language is sufficiently strong to express fine distinctions, then this will be a criterion of sameness of meaning. But if the language has only the kinds of context treated in the *predicate calculus, we can only conclude that the two expressions have the same *extension.

samadhi (Sanskrit, concentration) The higher or transcendent state of consciousness attainable by suitable spiritual disciplines, such as *Yoga.

Samkhya (Sankhya) One of the six Hindu 'orthodox' philosophies (**darshanas*), Samkhya is also the oldest, being attributed to the sage Kapila (*c*.7th c. BC). Its metaphysics is based upon a subtle analysis of *causation, whereby effects are seen as pre-existent in their causes (both this doctrine, *satkaryavada*, and its denial, *asatkaryavada*, are criticized by the *Vedanta school, as well as by *Buddhism, in favour of a *Parmenidean rejection of change altogether). Samkhya criticizes the concept of causation as a regular succession of events, or indeed as any relation between distinct events or states of affairs, promoting instead a concept of the unfolding of the cosmos as a unified single process, in which each state is already pregnant with those that are to come. It recognizes two realities, the *purusha* whose essence is consciousness, and *praktri*, the eternal, unconscious, unchanging principle that is the cause of the world. The real self is separate from the body, but suffering is caused by lack of discrimination between the real self and the non-self. This failure can be overcome by a long training in *Yoga and meditation upon the eternal and transcendental nature of the true self.

samsara In *Hindu and *Buddhist philosophy, the 'bondage of life, death, and rebirth': the cycle of birth and rebirth dictated by **karma*. Release comes only with the attainment of true knowledge, requiring austere discipline. *See also* EIGHTFOLD PATH, FOUR NOBLE TRUTHS.

Sanai, Hakim (*c*.1046–1141) Author of the *Hadiqa* or Walled Garden of Truth: the first mystical epic of *Sufism.

Sanches, Francisco (1551–1623) Portuguese-born philosopher and distant cousin of *Montaigne, educated at Montpellier and subsequently professor at Toulouse. In his most important work, *Quod nihil scitur* ('That Nothing is Known', 1581), he presented a sceptical critique not only of prevailing Aristotelian and Platonic philosophies, but of mathematics and science in general, about which he held a kind of *instrumentalism or *constructive empiricism.

Sankara *See* SHANKARA.

Santayana, George (1863–1952) Man of letters and philosopher. Santayana was born in Madrid but, his mother having emigrated to the USA, was educated as a student of *James's at Harvard. James described his doctoral dissertation on *Lotze as the 'perfection of rottenness' (Santayana in turn described James's *Varieties of Religious Experience* as 'slumming'); in spite of this Santayana taught at Harvard until 1912, when he retired to Europe. In early works such as *The Sense of Beauty* (1896) and the five-volume *The Life of Reason* (1905–6) he followed a naturalistic, psychological method, but later (in the four-volume *Realms of Being*, 1927–40) he developed an idiosyncratic combination of *Platonism and *materialism. He is remembered as much for his works of literature and criticism as for his contributions to philosophy.

Sapir–Whorf hypothesis Also known as the thesis of linguistic determinism, the view named after the linguists Edward Sapir (1884–1939) and Benjamin Lee Whorf (1897–1941), that the language people speak determines the way they perceive the world. As such, the view has a long history of adherents, including Aristotle (*Rhetoric*, Bk iii). It is a central theme in *Vico (*The New Science*) and a doctrine of von *Humboldt's. Whilst many philosophers accept that perception is 'theory-laden', and that the theories we can bring to bear are constrained by the concepts we have available, it is more difficult to read off just which concepts are available from the surface phenomena of language. Whilst Sapir himself thought of linguistic determinism in a relatively *a priori* way, his pupil Whorf collected evidence of linguistic and conceptual divergence from many Native American languages. Categories that may be very different include those of time, causation, and the self. It should be noted that some superficial examples of diversity that are frequently cited are in fact spurious. It is not true, for example, that the Eskimo-Aleut languages have a vast number of words for different varieties of snow.

Sartre, Jean-Paul (1905–80) French philosopher, novelist, and dominant French intellectual of his time. Sartre was born in Paris and educated at the École Normale Supérieure. From 1933 he studied in Germany with *Husserl and *Heidegger. His first novel, *La Nausée*, was published in 1938 (trs. as *Nausea*, 1949). *L'Imaginaire* (1940, trs. as *The Psychology of the Imagination*, 1948) is a contribution to phenomenal psychology. Briefly captured by the Germans, Sartre spent the war years in Paris, where *L'Être et le néant*, his major purely philosophical work, was published in 1943 (trs. as *Being and Nothingness*, 1956). The lecture *L'Existentialisme est un humanisme* (1946, trs. as *Existentialism is a Humanism*, 1947) consolidated Sartre's position as France's leading *existentialist philosopher. Sartre was centrally interested in politics, becoming in his time a symbol of all that was vigorous, and complex, in French left-wing thought. Although a *Marxist, he had strained relations with the communist party. Together with de *Beauvoir and *Merleau-Ponty he founded the journal *Les Temps modernes* in which political and ideological questions were aired, and in 1951 he attempted to found his own political party.

Sartre's philosophy is concerned entirely with the nature of human life, and the structures of consciousness. As a result it gains expression in his novels and plays as well as in more orthodox academic treatises. Its immediate ancestor is the phenomenological tradition of his teachers, and Sartre can most simply be seen as concerned to rebut the charge of idealism as it is laid at the door of *phenomenology. The agent is not a spectator of the world, but, like everything in the world, constituted by acts of intentionality and consciousness. The self thus constituted is historically situated, but as an agent whose own mode of locating itself in the world makes for responsibility and emotion. Responsibility is, however, a burden that we frequently cannot bear, and *bad faith arises when we deny our own authorship of our actions, seeing them instead as forced responses to situations not of our own making. Sartre thus locates the essential nature of human existence in the capacity for choice, although choice, being equally incompatible with determinism and with the existence of a *Kantian moral law, implies a synthesis of consciousness (being for-itself) and the objective (*being in-itself) that is forever unstable. The unstable and constantly disintegrating nature of *free will generates anguish. Sartre's 'ontological' works, including *L'Être et le néant*, attempt to work out the implications of his views for the nature of consciousness and judgement. For Sartre our capacity to make negative judgements is one of the fundamental puzzles of consciousness. Like Heidegger he took the 'ontological' approach of relating this to the nature of non-being, a move that decisively differentiates him from the Anglo-American tradition of modern logic (*see* BEING, NOTHING, QUANTIFIER, VARIABLE). Sartre's work on other minds illustrates by contrast a strength of the psychological approach, as he explores in detail such experiences as being in the gaze of another person, and connects them with the choices that then result. Sartre's work is notoriously difficult, but emotionally there is no question that he spoke powerfully to the sombre post-war years, when questions of responsibility and its denial held centre-stage in the political life of France.

SEE WEB LINKS

- An audio discussion with Sartre's biographer
- A list of internet resources on Sartre, including his writings

sarvastivada The *Buddhist doctrine that everything exists: that which was, that which is, and that which is yet to come.

satisfaction A set of sentences is satisfiable in a domain if it can be given an *interpretation in the domain in which it is true. *See* MODEL THEORY.

satisfiable *See* SATISFACTION.

satisfice A solution to a problem is a satisficing solution if it works, but there is no particular reason to think it either the best solution, or the one that maximizes expected *utility. Satisficing strategies put up with what does the job, without expending effort on searching for possibly better solutions.

Saussure, Ferdinand de (1857–1913) Swiss linguist generally considered the father of structural linguistics, and of *structuralism in its wider application. Saussure locates the study of linguistics in the synchronic relationships of **langue* rather than *parole*: the structural and common aspects of language responsible for its use as a medium of communication. Signs, which for

Saussure are combinations of signifier and signified (something like a concept or element of thought, rather than a thing that is represented), are the product of 'systems of differences': a sign has the value that it does in virtue of its place in a network of other possible choices. In his famous phrase, 'there are only differences'. A word has its place in a sentence or other stretch of discourse (its 'syntagmatic' relations) but also its 'associative' relations with other words of its family (the terms that might be listed as partial substitutes in a thesaurus, for example). Saussure's work puts in its own vocabulary many of the distinctions of analytical semantic theory: *see* COMPETENCE/PERFORMANCE, HOLISM, *SINN/BEDEUTUNG*. His lectures were collected and published in 1916 as the *Cours de linguistique générale* (trs. as *Course in General Linguistics*, 1959).

Scandinavian realism *See* HÄGERSTRÖM; ROSS, ALF.

scepticism (Greek, *skepsis*, enquiry or questioning) Although Greek scepticism centred on the value of enquiry and questioning, scepticism is now the denial that knowledge or even rational belief is possible, either about some specific subject-matter (e.g. ethics) or in any area whatsoever. Classically, scepticism springs from the observation that the best methods in some area seem to fall short of giving us contact with the truth (e.g. there is a gulf between appearance and reality), and it frequently cites the conflicting judgements that our methods deliver, with the result that questions of truth become undecidable. In classical thought the various examples of this conflict were systematized in the ten tropes of *Aenesidemus. The scepticism of *Pyrrho and the new *Academy was a system of argument and indeed ethics opposed to dogmatism, and particularly to the philosophical system-building of the *Stoics. As it has come down to us, particularly in the writings of *Sextus Empiricus, its method was typically to cite reasons for finding an issue undecidable (sceptics devoted particular energy to undermining the Stoic conception of some truths as delivered by direct apprehension or **katalepsis*). As a result the sceptic counsels *epochē* or the suspension of belief, and then goes on to celebrate a way of life whose object was **ataraxia*, or the tranquillity resulting from such suspension of belief. The process is frequently mocked, for instance in the stories recounted by *Diogenes Laertius that Pyrrho had to be restrained from sublimely walking over precipices, leaving stuck people in bogs, and so on, since his method denied him confidence that there existed the precipice or the bog (the legends may have arisen from a misunderstanding of *Aristotle, *Metaphysics* G, iv. 1008 b, where Aristotle argues that since sceptics don't do such things, they actually accept the doctrines they pretend to reject). In fact ancient sceptics allowed confidence in 'phenomena', reserving their scepticism for more theoretical confidences, but quite how much fell under the heading of phenomena is not always clear.

Sceptical tendencies emerged in the 14th-century writings of Nicholas of Autrecourt (*fl.* 1340). His criticisms of any certainty beyond the immediate deliverance of the senses and basic logic, and in particular of any knowledge of either intellectual or material substances, anticipate the later scepticism of *Bayle and *Hume. The latter distinguishes between Pyrrhonistic or excessive scepticism, which he regarded as unliveable, and the more mitigated scepticism which accepts everyday or common-sense beliefs (albeit not as the delivery of reason, but as due more to custom and habit), but is duly wary of the power of reason to give us much more. Mitigated scepticism is thus closer to the attitude fostered by ancient sceptics from Pyrrho through to Sextus Empiricus. Although the phrase 'Cartesian scepticism' is sometimes used, *Descartes himself was not a sceptic, but in the *method of doubt uses a sceptical scenario in order to begin the process of finding a secure mark of knowledge. Descartes himself trusts a category of 'clear and distinct' ideas, not far removed from the *phantasia kataleptikē* of the Stoics.

Scepticism should not be confused with *relativism, which is a doctrine about the nature of truth, and may be motivated by trying to avoid scepticism. Nor is it identical with *eliminativism, which counsels abandoning an area of thought altogether, not because we cannot know the truth, but because there are no truths capable of being framed in the terms we use.

Scheler, Max Ferdinand (1874–1928) German phenomenologist and social theorist. Scheler was born in Munich and studied in Jena, returning to Jena to study the phenomenology of *Husserl in 1907. In 1913 he wrote his *Formalism in Ethics and Non-Formal Ethics of Values*, criticizing Kantian ethics for excessive formalism, and comparing moral perception to perception of *secondary qualities. His philosophy developed in terms of the phenomenology of perception of non-Platonic essences, held together by a hierarchical, Kantian architecture. Among others he impressed *Heidegger and *Ortega y Gasset, and his second wife, Märit Furtwängler, was the sister of the conductor. Other translated works include *Man's Place in Nature* (trs. Meyerhoff, 1961).

Schelling, Friedrich Wilhelm Joseph von (1775–1854) The principal philosopher of German *Romanticism. Schelling was born in

Leonberg, and educated at Tübingen, where he was a contemporary of *Hegel and the poet *Hölderlin. Schelling became professor at Jena in 1798, and for some years collaborated with *Fichte. In 1803 he married Caroline, the divorced wife of August Schlegel, to whose daughter (who died, possibly because of Schelling's attempts at medicine) he had previously been informally engaged. In keeping with the spirit of Romanticism Schelling's early work, particularly the *System des transzendentalen Idealismus* (1800), stresses force, self-consciousness, the unfolding dynamic spirit inherent in all things, and the moral striving after unattainable ideals. It is in the emphasis on art and aesthetics that Schelling is at his most impassioned: it is in art alone that abstraction is put aside, nature and history reconciled, and full self-consciousness attained. The 'philosophy of identity', expressed in *Vorlesungen über die Methode des akademischen Studiums* (1803), holds the absolute identity of nature and intelligence, knower and known, and is an important bridge between *Kant and Fichte on the one hand, and Hegel on the other. After Caroline died in 1809, Schelling produced no more books, but turned his attention more to mythology and religion. In the final phase of his life he voiced a mystical, personal, and sombre philosophy recognized as anticipating similar notes in *existentialism.

schema (pl. schemata) In many *logical calculi, axioms and rules are presented as forms or schemata, with the provision that any of an infinite number of substitution instances are axioms. For example, the rule of inference *modus ponens may be presented as A; A → B, so B, where A and B can be substituted by any well-formed formula of the calculus. Statements that are intuitively framed by talking of all functions, all properties, etc., such as Peano's fifth postulate, or the set-theoretic axioms of *separation and *replacement, are represented by axiom schemata in first-order logic.

S

Schiller, Ferdinand Canning Scott (1864–1937) Schiller studied at Oxford and was professor there from 1897 to 1926, when he emigrated to the University of Southern California. His motto was the doctrine that man is the measure of all things, from *Protagoras. He was the most notable exponent of *pragmatism in Britain, bearing strong affinities to William *James, and in everything in opposition to the absolute idealism of *Bradley and his Oxford followers. Works included *Riddles of the Sphinx* (1891), *Humanism* (1912), *Problems of Belief* (1924), *Logic for Use* (1929), and *Our Human Truths* (1939).

Schiller, Johann Cristoph Friedrich (1759–1805) The German poet and man of letters is remembered philosophically principally for his influential insistence on the importance of aesthetics. Whereas *Kant identified freedom with the exercise of reason, for Schiller the aesthetic impulse is a fundamental element of human nature, whose proper expression and development is itself the point at which the phenomenal and noumenal worlds of Kant fuse, and hence the supreme exercise of human freedom (aesthetics is also connected with play, or activity as an end in itself). Schiller shared the *idealism of the contemporary German school (*see* FICHTE, SCHELLING) and played an important role in joining the literary movement of *Romanticism to contemporary philosophical themes. He develops his view of aesthetics into a general account of epistemology that stresses the different character and temperament people bring to their interpretations of the world. In particular, the naive or classic artist is subordinate to the material; the sentimental or romantic artist dominates it. Schiller's most important philosophical works are *Briefe über die ästhetische Erziehung des Menschen* (1794–5, trs. as *Letters on the Aesthetic Education of Mankind*, 1844) and *Über naive und sentimentalische Dichtung* (1795, trs. as *On Naïve and Sentimental Poetry*, 1861).

Schlegel, Friedrich von (1772–1829) German Romantic aesthetician, friend of *Schleiermacher, *Schelling, and *Novalis. Educated in law at Göttingen and Leipzig, he subsequently devoted himself to literature, being in 1798 one of the founders of the *Athenaeum*, a principal organ of Romantic and classically oriented circles at Jena. His later study of Sanskrit and of Indian civilization contributed to his outstanding work, *Über die Sprache und Weisheit der Indier* ('On the Language and Wisdom of India', 1808), after which he entered the service of Prince Metternich and the Austrian court, veering from his youthful radicalism to a kind of Catholic mysticism. Books include *The Philosophy of History* (trs. 1835), *The Philosophy of Life and the Philosophy of Language* (trs. 1847), and *The History of Literature* (trs. 1859).

Schleiermacher, Friedrich Daniel Ernst (1768–1834) German *absolute idealist and theologian. Schleiermacher was born in Breslau, and educated at the university of Halle. He worked mainly in Berlin, and his philosophy represents many of the early themes of absolute idealism. In theology he is notable for associating religion not with the attempt to achieve knowledge of the transcendental, which, following *Kant, he regarded as impossible, but with emotions such as the pious feeling of absolute dependency. His early work *Über die Religion. Reden an die Gebildeten unter ihren Verächtern* (1799, trs. as *On Religion: Speeches to its Cultured Despisers*, 1894) was an instant success in the repressive climate of the Prussia of his time (*see also* KANT). It was followed by other monumental contributions to theology, although his translations of *Plato's Dialogues into German also became a landmark of 19th-century scholarship. Schleiermacher is generally credited with being the first German philosopher to reflect seriously on questions of *hermeneutics, and influenced successors in this tradition such as *Weber and *Dilthey.

Schlick, Friedrich Albert Moritz (1882–1936) German philosopher and leading light of the Vienna circle (*see* LOGICAL POSITIVISM). Born in Berlin, Schlick originally studied physics, eventually under Max Planck. Alongside physics he wrote essays on ethics and aesthetics. In 1922 he became professor of the inductive sciences in Vienna, and formed the association with Hahn, Feigl, Neurath, and others that became known as the Vienna circle. His own distinctive contributions include his *General Theory of Knowledge* written between 1918 and 1925, containing amongst much else his case against synthetic *a priori* knowledge. Schlick was instrumental in luring *Wittgenstein back to philosophy, although the latter's relation to the circle remained wary. Schlick was shot by a deranged student on the steps of the university of Vienna; the case became a catalyst for anti-Semitic feeling in the city (although Schlick was not in fact Jewish) and the student was later released, becoming a member of the Nazi party.

Schmitt, Carl (1888–1985) German political theorist. Schmitt was influential as a conservative or reactionary critic of liberalism, and enthusiast for conflict and antagonism as perennial conditions of politics. A sympathizer with the Nazis, he escaped trial at Nuremberg but was forbidden from teaching thereafter. Before his death he became influential in neo-conservative circles associated with Leo *Strauss. Books included *Die geistesgeschichtliche Lage des heutigen Parlamentarismus* (trs. as *The Crisis of Parliamentary Democracy*, 1985) and *Politische Romantik* (trs. as *Political Romanticism*, 1986).

scholasticism The philosophy taught in the church schools and theological training-grounds in the medieval period. Scholasticism was the dominant philosophical approach in Europe from perhaps the 11th until the 16th century, or the time of *Abelard to that of *Suárez. It combined religious doctrine, study of the Church fathers, and philosophical and logical work based particularly on *Aristotle and his commentators, and to some extent on themes from *Plato. Prominent scholastics included *Aquinas, *Buridan, *Duns Scotus, and *Ockham.

Schopenhauer, Arthur (1788–1860) German philosopher. Born in Danzig of a rich, anglophile, and cosmopolitan family, Schopenhauer was educated in both France and Britain, and was fluent in European and classical languages. Initially intended for a career in business, Schopenhauer could only enter university after the death of his father. He joined the university of Göttingen in 1809 to study medicine but transferred his affections to philosophy, and in 1811 studied for a time in Berlin, where he conceived a profound dislike of *Fichte and *Schleiermacher. He received his doctorate for the work that became *Über die vierfache Wurzel des Satzes vom zureichenden Grunde* (1813, trs. as the *Fourfold Root of the Principle of Sufficient Reason*, 1888). The roots are causality or becoming, knowing, being, and acting. It is said that his mother, with whom his relations were dreadful, commented that a book entitled *The Fourfold Root* was presumably intended for apothecaries. His major work, *Die Welt als Wille und Vorstellung* (1818, trs. as *The World as Will and Idea*, 1886), was not an initial success, but gained him an assistant's position in Berlin. Here Schopenhauer famously lectured at the same times as *Hegel, whom he regarded as a sophist and charlatan, but who was then at the height of his fame. Failing to dislodge Hegel, Schopenhauer ceased lecturing and finally retired to private life in 1831. He lived in Frankfurt and published various works, but only became widely known with his two volumes of aphorisms, *Parerga und Paralipomena* (roughly: comments and omissions) of 1851. In spite of his famous pessimism, Schopenhauer himself lived a moderately selfish and not altogether reclusive life, and seems to have indulged his share of the passions: he dined well at the Englischer Hof, had affairs, was reputed a brilliant and witty conversationalist, and read *The Times* of London every day. He was of a highly nervous and volatile disposition, and had to pay a quarterly allowance to an elderly seamstress whom he permanently injured by throwing her downstairs (and on whose death certificate, which released him from the obligation, he wrote the remark 'obit anus, abit onus': the old woman is dead, the burden departs). He finally achieved considerable fame in the last decade of his life.

Schopenhauer took from *Kant the distinction between the phenomenal and the noumenal, but unlike the majority of Kant's followers he clung on to the 'thing in itself', and, following one strand in Kant, identified it with will. The will thus stands outside space and time, and all reason and knowledge is subject to it. Only in aesthetic contemplation do we escape it. Schopenhauer notoriously allies this doctrine with an extreme pessimism, for conforming to the dictates of the will leads to nothing but illusion and suffering. Admiring the *Upanishads and *Buddhist philosophy of resignation, Schopenhauer extols a kind of extinction as the ultimate goal of the good life; indeed it is not entirely clear why literal suicide is not the best way out. Thus *Nietzsche (*Ecce Homo*, 'Beyond Good and Evil', Sec. 2) says that (along with Plato and Christianity) he requires no refutation: the properly active Dionysian figure can just scent the decomposition.

Although Schopenhauer's attitude to the world has influenced many writers, his glamorization of despair has usually seemed somewhat forced. However, his understanding of the ways in which the mind is subservient to the life of the organism, and the way in which drives and desires become suppressed and distorted, marks a major anticipation of *psychoanalytic doctrine and perhaps of *evolutionary psychology. He was one of the few philosophers whom *Wittgenstein read and admired.

SEE WEB LINKS

- A list of internet resources on Schopenhauer, including bibliographies
- An audio discussion between a philosopher and a psychiatrist on Schopenhauer's pessimism

Schrödinger's cat Celebrated animal introduced by the Austrian physicist Erwin Schrödinger (1887–1961) in 1935, in a *thought experiment showing the strange nature of the world of *quantum mechanics. The cat is thought of as locked in a box with a capsule of cyanide, which will break if a Geiger counter triggers. This will happen if an atom in a radioactive substance in the box decays, and there is a chance of 50% of such an event within an hour. Otherwise the cat is alive. The problem is that the system is in an indeterminate state. The wave function of the entire system is a 'superposition' of states, fully described by the probabilities of events occurring when it is eventually measured, and therefore 'contains equal parts of the living and dead cat'. When we look and see we will find either an alive cat or a dead cat, but if it is only as we look that the wave packet collapses, quantum mechanics forces us to say that before we looked it was not true that the cat was dead and also not true that it was alive. The thought experiment makes vivid the difficulty of conceiving of quantum indeterminacies when these are translated to the familiar world of everyday objects.

science, philosophy of The investigation of questions that arise from reflection upon science and scientific practice. Such questions include: what distinguishes the methods of science? Is there a clear demarcation between sciences and other disciplines, and where do we place such enquiries as history, economics, or sociology? Are scientific theories probable, or more in the nature of provisional conjectures? Can they be verified, or *falsified? What distinguishes good from bad *explanation? Might there be one unified science, embracing all the special sciences? For much of the 20th century these questions were pursued in a highly abstract and logical framework, it being supposed that a general logic of scientific discovery or justification might be found. However, many now take interest in a more historical, contextual, and sometimes sociological approach, in which the methods and successes of a science at a particular time are regarded less in terms of universal logical principles and procedures, and more in terms of the then available methods and *paradigms, as well as the social context.

In addition to general questions of *methodology, there are specific problems within particular sciences, giving rise to specialist philosophies of such subjects as *biology, *mathematics, and *physics.

scientia media (Latin, middle knowledge) The special way God has of knowing the truth about future events, which is supposed to reconcile his present knowledge of them with the possibility that they depend upon real, open choices. The key idea is that there is a simultaneous act of God's giving grace and the individual freely accepting it, rather than a prior donation of grace that determines the individual's acceptance. The concept was elaborated in the *Concordia* of Luis de *Molina and was the cause of fierce controversy with the followers of *Aquinas, who objected that the efficacy of divine grace cannot depend upon us. *See also* OMNISCIENCE.

scientific method *See* METHODOLOGY.

scientific realism *See* REALISM.

scientism Pejorative term for the belief that the methods of natural science, or the categories and things recognized in natural science, form the only proper elements in any philosophical or other enquiry. The classic statement of scientism is the physicist E. Rutherford's saying 'there is physics and there is stamp-collecting'. Philosophers wary of scientism believe that it distorts or denies the special methods of psychology and interpretation (*see* VERSTEHEN), or tries to impose a crass *reductionism where it is neither plausible nor necessary.

scope Intuitively the scope of an *operator is the part of an expression over which it holds its effect. The scope of '+' in '$(3 + 5) \times 7$' would be the sum in the brackets, whereas the scope of '$\times$' is the whole expression. In a formal system the scope of an operator is the smallest well-formed formula in which it occurs. A scope ambiguity arises when there is insufficient indication of the scope of an operator, meaning that an expression can be evaluated in two quite different ways; for example $(3+5\times 7)$ might refer to 56 or to 38.

In a *logical calculus, formation rules prevent scope ambiguities, which are common in natural language. In 'The Master of Balliol College used to be a priest' the ambiguity can be represented as one of the respective scope of the description and the tense operator: it used to be so that the Master of Balliol College was a priest (e.g. in the 14th century) versus: take the Master of Balliol College, it used to be so that he was a priest. *See also* *DE RE/DE DICTO*.

Scotism The system of *scholastic philosophy due to *Duns Scotus.

sea-battle (seafight) The example with which *Aristotle introduces problems of inevitability and necessity in Bk ix of *De Interpretatione*. It is necessary that either there will be a sea-battle tomorrow, or there will not. Whichever happens, it is now true that it is going to happen, and it has always been true that it is going to happen. So its happening is inevitable, a fact that has existed for all time. It seems as though pure logic implies some kind of *predetermination or *fatalism. One possible response is to grade future contingent propositions like this as neither true nor false (*see* MANY-VALUED LOGIC). But a less drastic measure is to distinguish between 'it is now true that a sea-battle will happen' and 'the sea-battle's happening is already fixed', and one test of a theory of *truth will be whether it manages to make such a distinction. The problem is sometimes known as the problem of future contingents.

secondary qualities *See* PRIMARY/SECONDARY QUALITIES.

second-order logic *See* FIRST-ORDER LANGUAGE.

secundum quid (Latin, according to which) Shorthand for **a dicto simpliciter ad dictum secundum quid*.

self The elusive 'I' that shows an alarming tendency to disappear when we try to introspect it. *See* BUNDLE THEORY OF THE MIND OR SELF, CARTESIAN DUALISM, PERSONAL IDENTITY.

self-caused *See* *CAUSA SUI*.

self-contradiction A case of one person assenting to a *contradiction, or to premises from which one can be derived.

self-control The quality of mind with which we resist what we suppose to be temptations to which we should not succumb. *See also* *AKRASIA*.

self-deception The motivated misapprehension of the facts of the case. This may include actively believing what is not true, and refusing to acknowledge a truth, in circumstances where without the motivation the truth would be obvious. The philosophical problem, sometimes called the paradox of self-deception, is that normal deception requires one agent who knows the truth, and who conceals it from another agent. So within a single agent the state appears to be impossible, since the agent must know the truth to begin a process of deceiving him or herself about it. One solution is to postulate one part of the mind that knows the truth, and that sets about deceiving another part of the mind that does not. However, it is not clear that it is useful to employ the spatial analogy of minds with parts, nor to suppose that the 'sub-systems' responsible for the state are usefully thought of as themselves independent 'agents' that not only know things but have plans and projects and can set about doing things. There is nothing problematic about desires influencing beliefs, and some people are better than others at believing what they wish to be true. The problem only arises if achieving this state is thought of as a plan that the agent follows. But even then the project of coming to believe what one knows to be false is coherent, provided that process is spread over time, and the means adopted involve losing the knowledge during the process. *See also* PASCAL'S WAGER.

self-defeating In practical reasoning a strategy is self-defeating when following it interferes with achieving the goals it sets out to further. Thus the strategy of maximizing personal pleasure may be self-defeating if by following it one decreases one's chance of obtaining personal pleasure. Various plausible mechanisms make this quite likely (*see* HEDONISM, PARADOX OF). *Utilitarianism is sometimes thought to be self-defeating, in that a society of persons reasoning in a utilitarian way might do worse than one in which other forms of practical reasoning are used.

S

self-evident Not a very useful philosophical term, since what is evident by itself to one person may not be so to another. *See also* *A PRIORI/A POSTERIORI*, MYTH OF THE GIVEN.

self-fulfilling A self-fulfilling prophecy is one that brings about the events it foretells, as when the chairman of the national bank predicts that the currency will devalue. *See also* SEX AND SEXUAL DESIRE.

self-intimating Supposed property of mental events and states, whereby to enter into the state implies knowing that one is in the state. Being in pain or thinking about a bath may seem to entail knowing that one is in pain, or that one is thinking about a bath.

selfish gene The title of the book published in 1976 by the English biologist Richard Dawkins, propounding the view that 'we are survival machines—robot vehicles blindly programmed to preserve the selfish molecules known as genes'. *See also* FUNCTION, BIOLOGICAL; GENE.

self-realization The goal of some kinds of *Romanticism, of some religious practices, and of most of the self-help industry. The myth is that of the 'mute inglorious Milton', that most people have a hidden self, that but for unfortunate external obstacles would blossom without limits.

self-reference, paradoxes of *See* SEMANTIC PARADOXES.

self-refuting A self-refuting utterance is one which is shown to be false in the very fact of its being made, as when someone says: 'I am not now speaking!'; 'There are no words on this page'; or, more controversially, 'I am asleep', or 'Words have no meaning.'

self-regarding *See* OTHER-REGARDING.

self-respect The capacity to bear one's own self-scrutiny. The phrase is *Hume's, but self-respect is a central concern for ethical theorists working in the *Kantian tradition. Self-respect is a good, and is therefore to be distinguished from such neighbours as *vanity. It is a platform from which to criticize institutions that undermine it or interrupt its full expression, by making it impossible for some members of a community fully to respect themselves. It is associated in the Kantian tradition with possessing equal *rights with others, and with the capacity to see one's actions and patterns of life as consistent with one's own values.

Sellars, Wilfrid (1912–89) The son of the philosopher Roy Wood Sellars (1880–1973), Sellars was educated at Michigan, and after time at Buffalo and Oxford completed his doctorate at Harvard. He taught at Iowa, Minnesota, and Yale, but established himself from 1963 at Pittsburgh. His early work represented a blend of *analytic philosophy with *logical positivism, and together with others he founded the journal *Philosophical Studies* to act as a platform for this approach, and edited influential works bringing such methods before the American profession (*Readings in Philosophical Analysis*, 1949, and *Readings in Ethical Theory*, 1952). Sellars's own work revolved around the difficulties of combining the scientific image of people and their world, with the *manifest image, or natural conception of ourselves as acquainted with intentions, meanings, colours, and other definitive aspects of the human world. His reputation was established by his most influential paper, 'Empiricism and the Philosophy of Mind' (1956), which was possibly the central text introducing *functionalism in the philosophy of mind (*see also* USE (OF WORDS)). In this and many other papers Sellars explored the nature of thought and experience, defending the view of thought as a kind of inner speech, and above all attacking the *myth of the given in all its forms. For Sellars all intentional events live in the 'space of reasons'; that is, even apparently blank experience is a theoretical concept, or a kind of reflection of our thoughts about the world and the authority we allow each other over various kinds of report. It follows that no such experience can play the role demanded by *foundationalism in the theory of knowledge. Collections of papers include *Science, Perception, and Reality* (1963), *Philosophical Perspectives* (1967), and *Essays in Philosophy and its History* (1974).

semantic ascent *See* MATERIAL/FORMAL MODE.

semantic engine *See* REPRESENTATIONALISM.

semantic holism The view that the fundamental unit of significance is neither an individual word, nor a single sentence, but a whole theory or set of thoughts. The idea is that you could not, for example, just believe one thing about an object, for to understand the very idea of an object involves having memories, expectations, views about its powers and dispositions, and so on, eventually involving other things and a whole world view.

semantic paradoxes Following *Ramsey and the Italian mathematician G. Peano (1858–1932) it has been customary to distinguish logical paradoxes that depend upon a notion of reference or truth (semantic notions), such as those of the *Liar family, *Berry, *Richards, etc., from the purely logical paradoxes in which no such notions are involved, such as *Russell's paradox, or those of *Cantor and *Burali-Forti. Paradoxes of the first type seem to depend upon an element of self-reference, in which a sentence talks about itself, or in which a phrase refers to something defined by a set of phrases of which it is itself one. It is easy to feel that this element is responsible for the contradictions, although self-reference itself is often benign (for instance, the sentence 'All English sentences should have a verb' includes itself happily in the domain of sentences it is talking about), so the difficulty lies in forming a condition that excludes only pathological self-reference. Paradoxes of the second kind then need a different treatment. Whilst the distinction is convenient, in allowing *set theory to proceed by circumventing the latter paradoxes by technical means, even when there is no solution to the semantic paradoxes, it may be a way of ignoring the similarities between the two families. There is still the possibility that while there is no agreed solution to the semantic paradoxes, our understanding of Russell's paradox may be imperfect as well.

semantics One of the three branches into which *semiotics is usually divided: the study of the meaning of words, and the relation of signs to the objects to which the signs are applicable. In formal studies, a semantics is provided for a *formal language when an *interpretation or *model is specified. However, a natural language comes ready interpreted, and the semantic problem is not that of specification but of understanding the relationship between terms of various categories (names, descriptions, predicates, adverbs ...) and their meanings. An influential proposal is that this relationship is best understood by attempting to provide a *truth definition for the language, which will involve giving a full description of the systematic effect terms and structure of different kinds have on the *truth conditions of sentences containing them. *See also* INFERENTIAL ROLE SEMANTICS, POSSIBLE WORLD SEMANTICS, REFERENCE, TRUTH.

semantic theory of truth The view that if a language is provided with a *truth definition, this is a sufficient characterization of its concept of truth; there is no further philosophical chapter to write about truth itself or truth as shared across different languages. The view is similar to the *disquotational theory; *see also* REDUNDANCY THEORY OF TRUTH.

semiology *See* SEMIOTICS.

semiotics The general study of symbolic systems, including language. The subject is traditionally divided into three areas: *syntax, or the abstract study of the signs and their interrelations; *semantics, or the study of the relation between the signs and those objects to which they apply; and *pragmatics, or the relationship between users and the system (C. W. Morris, *Foundations of the Theory of Signs*, 1938). The tradition of semiotics that follows *Saussure is sometimes referred to as semiology. Confusingly, in the work of *Kristeva, the term is appropriated for the non-rational effluxes of the infantile part of the self.

sempiternity *See* ETERNITY.

Sen, Amartya (1933–) Nobel prize-winning economist and social theorist. Educated at Presidency College, Calcutta, and then at Trinity College, Cambridge, Sen used the time of a junior research fellowship to study philosophy, leaving to become professor of economics at Delhi from 1963 to 1971. He subsequently taught at the London School of Economics, Oxford, Harvard, and many other universities in the United States, before becoming Master of Trinity College from 1998 to 2003. His work on social choice was directed towards enriching the basis on which a social choice function could be defended, in order to circumvent the negative results of *Arrow. This work culminated in the *capabilities approach to the measurement of social goods or value. Work on more practical problems of measurement and famine also followed, including his study of the 1974 Bangladesh famine that concluded that the root cause of famine was political rather than agricultural. Books include *Collective Choice and Social Welfare* (1970), *Poverty and Famines* (1981), *Choice, Welfare and Measurement* (1982), *Resources, Values and Development* (1984), *Commodities and Capabilities* (1985), and *Inequality Reexamined* (1992).

Seneca, Lucius Annaeus (after 4 BC–AD 65) Roman statesman and a trenchant expositor of *Stoicism. His principal ethical writings are the *Epistolae Morales* ('Moral Letters'), an early literary exploitation of the letter form. He enjoyed a hectic career, which included banishment to Corsica for adultery with Julia Livilla, the niece of the Emperor Claudius; his forced suicide provided an influential model of Stoicism in action.

Sengzhao (AD 384?–414) Early Chinese interpreter of Buddhism. Allegedly overcome with pleasure on first reading the *Vimalakirtinirdesha Sutra*, he eventually wrote various essays exalting wordless insight, knowledge without conceptualization and dichotomization, above more mundane kinds of cognitive activity. His work the *Zhaolun* was seminal in introducing *Madhyamika Buddhism to China.

sensa Those things that are sensed; *sense data.

sensation Sensations are things like *tickles, itches, pains, felt cold and heat, etc. The occurrence of a sensation is the most fundamental modification of *consciousness, and shares all the problems of that concept. It is usually thought of as a primitive inner event distinguished only by its raw feel to the possessor. Sensations are distinguished from thoughts and perceptions, which carry a *content with them, although the relation between the bare occurrences that make up sensations and these cognitive states is intensely debated. The *private language argument of *Wittgenstein is one attempt to overthrow the idea that our knowledge of our own sensations is private, infallible, and a foundation of all the rest of our knowledge. *See also* PERCEPTION, QUALIA.

sensationalism (sensationism) The view associated with *Mach that sensations and their patterns form the only data and the only *ontology that we can comprehend. The view is an extreme version of the *empiricist emphasis on the priority of experience or 'perceptions'. It shares the ambitions, and problems, of *phenomenalism.

sense and reference *See* *SINN/BEDEUTUNG*.

sense data Literally, that which is given by the senses. But in response to the question of what exactly is so given, sense data theories posit private showings in the *consciousness of the subject. In the case of vision this would be a kind of inner picture show which itself only indirectly represents aspects of the external world (*see* REPRESENTATIONALISM). The view has been widely rejected as implying that we really only see extremely thin coloured pictures interposed between our mind's eye and reality. Modern approaches to *perception tend to reject any conception of the eye as a camera or lens, simply responsible for producing private images, and stress the active life of the subject in the world as the determinant of experience (for an early version of this approach, *see* CONDILLAC).

sensibilia Those things that are sensed; the immediate objects of sense perception. For direct realists these include ordinary public objects amongst which we move, but for indirect realists and *sense data theorists, they are private items, with biographies no longer than the moments of their perception.

sensibility A way of feeling. A person's aesthetic or ethical sensibility is described by telling what kinds of situation generate different kinds of aesthetic or ethical response. The cult of sensibility in the mid-18th century celebrated a response to life charged with high emotion, as in the novelist Samuel Richardson, and the philosophers *Rousseau and *Goethe. *See also* ROMANTICISM.

S

sensible knave The character introduced by *Hume (*Enquiry Concerning the Principles of Morals*, Sec. 9, Pt 2), who observes the general rules of justice and honesty, but who takes advantage of exceptions that he can make when doing so benefits him. Many approaches to ethics require that there is something irrational about this behaviour and set out to show that it is akin to self-contradiction; Hume himself sensibly regards the character as simply odious.

sensible world The world as it is for us: the world of colours, tastes, and sounds as well as of objects with geometrical and mechanical relations. *See* MANIFEST IMAGE, PRIMARY/SECONDARY QUALITIES.

sensorium The place within the brain at which sensation happens: the 'inner theatre' of the mind, according to a *Cartesian conception. The term is found in *Boethius, but becomes common in the 17th century, and is especially associated with *Newton, who held that the world was God's sensorium.

sensus communis Not common sense in its ordinary meaning, but in *Aristotle (*De Anima*, II, 1–2) and following him *Aquinas and others, a central cognitive function that integrates and monitors the delivery of the other distinct senses, as when a shape is both seen and felt.

sentence Most generally, the unit of communication: the smallest entity whose production constitutes a message, such as an assertion, a command, or a question. Given such factors as variations of *phonetics or spelling, recognition of two *speech acts as the production of the same sentence is already a matter of interpretation, but one that is usually automatic to speakers of the same native language. Grammatically a sentence is the unit whose structure is subserved by other recognized features of a language. The priority of the sentence in much *analytic philosophy is summed up in *Frege's dictum that it is only in the context of a sentence that words have meaning. The least controversial interpretation of the slogan is that for a word to mean anything is simply for it to contribute systematically to the meaning of whole sentences in which it is embedded. A word is not a thing with its own 'projection' onto parts of the world; instead, the presence of a word (or more accurately, a *morpheme) is a feature of a sentence, one which plays a role in determining its meaning, and whose variation systematically determines the meaning of related sentences. A more radical extension of the same line suggests that it is only in the context of a whole theory, or world view, or language, that a single sentence means anything. In the terminology of *Dummett, according priority to words is semantic 'atomism', to sentences, 'molecularism', and to anything larger, 'holism'. *See also* DUHEM THESIS.

sentential connective *See* SENTENTIAL OPERATOR.

sentential function A predicate may be thought of as a *function from a single term to a sentence, and hence can be called a sentential function. Also, the *truth-functional connectives are occasionally thought of as functions from sentences to sentences, although they are better thought of as functions from sets of *truth-values to other truth-values, since this is how they are evaluated in *interpretations of the *propositional calculus. *See also* PROPOSITIONAL FUNCTION.

sentential operator Any *operator that takes a sentence as its argument, usually to deliver another sentence.

sentimentalism **1.** The position in moral theory especially associated with *Shaftesbury, *Hutcheson, and *Hume, that sees ethics as founded upon human sentiments, such as sympathy. It was especially defined in opposition to the view that ethics is the deliverance of reason or revelation. **2.** The emotionally extravagant and shallow indulgence of feelings.

separation, axiom of Also known as the *Aussonderungsaxiom.* The unrestricted principle of *comprehension leads to contradiction in *set theory. The axiom of separation, due to Zermelo, restored consistency by allowing a set of objects to exist when it is the subset of a previous set, and its members meet a condition: $(\exists y)(\forall x)((x \in y)$ iff $(x \in z \,\&\, Fx))$. That is, a set y of objects exists when it is separated out from a previously given set z, as the subset whose members meet a condition F.

sequence *See* ORDERED N-TUPLE.

sequents, calculus of *See* NATURAL DEDUCTION.

set Intuitively a set is a collection of entities, called its members or elements, itself considered as a single object. The fundamental principle of the theory of sets is the principle of *extensionality: sets are identical if and only if they have the same members. The union of two sets is the set $A \cup B$ that has as members all the things that are members of A or B (or both). The intersection $A \cap B$ is the set of things that are members of both. Sets are disjoint when they have no common members. The complement of a set B within a set A, $A - B$, is the set of elements that are in A but not in B. A set A is a subset of a set B when all the things that belong to A belong to B. This makes A itself a subset of A; a subset of A not itself identical with A is a proper subset of A. To obtain the set-theoretic hierarchy, we start with a list of elements (things that are not themselves sets; in case this sounds mathematically impure, we can start simply with $\emptyset$, the null set). At the bottom level we have the set of all these elements. At the next level we add all sets of elements; at each level we have everything from the previous level, plus all sets of them. We then take the infinite union of all these sets, and continue 'forever'. In fact, if we start with the null set at the lowest level, each ascending level becomes the *power set of the set that constitutes the previous level.

set-theoretic paradoxes *See* BURALI-FORTI'S PARADOX, CANTOR'S PARADOX, RUSSELL'S PARADOX.

set theory The modern theory of sets was largely inspired by *Cantor, whose proof that the set of real numbers could not be put into a *one-to-one correspondence with the set of natural numbers opened the door to the set-theoretic hierarchy, and to the study of transfinite numbers. The first proper axiomatization of the theory was that of Ernst Zermelo (1871–1953) in 1908. The axiomatization followed intense controversy over the nature of the set-theoretic hierarchy, the legitimacy of the axiom of *choice, and the right approach to the paradoxes lying at the centre of naive views about sets, of which the best known is *Russell's paradox. Classical set theory uses the axiomatization of Zermelo, augmented by the axiom of *replacement due to A. Fraenkel (1891–1965). It has been shown that this is equivalent to a natural 'iterative' conception, whereby starting with the *empty set or null set, and forming only sets of sets, the entire set-theoretic hierarchy can be generated. Philosophically set theory is central because sets are the purest mathematical objects, and it is known that the rest of mathematics can be formulated within set theory (so that numbers, relations, and functions all become particular sets). Particular topics within set theory are indexed under their own headings.

Seven Deadly Sins Pride, covetousness, envy, gluttony, anger, **accidie* (sloth), and lust. These are 'leading' sins, or ones that direct and lead other vices. *Aquinas attributes the list to Gregory the Great. A peculiarity of the list is that although a sin is usually thought of as an action, the list names dispositions or sentiments rather than actions. Another peculiarity is that thoroughly nasty traits such as cruelty, malevolence, hypocrisy, or ingratitude are left out. A third is that some of the sins are arguably connected with virtue: for example, proper pride is allied to the self-esteem that derives from doing something well, and a central motivation to virtue; proper anger is allied to the indignation that immoral actions warrant; and lust is nature's way of ensuring procreation.

Seven Sages of Greece. Various lists are given by *Diogenes Laertius, *Plato, *Plutarch, and *Clement. The candidates include statesmen and lawgivers as well as philosophers. Plato's list (*Protagoras,* 343) is Bias, Chilon, Cleobulus, Myson, Pittacus, Solon, and *Thales.

sex and sexual desire The difficulties the Western tradition has had with sexual desire are spectacularly voiced by *Kant: 'Taken by itself [sexual love] is a degradation of human nature; for as soon as a person becomes an object of appetite for another, all motives of moral relationship cease to function, because as an object of appetite for another a person becomes a thing and can be treated and used as such by every one' (*Lectures on Ethics*). Kant seems to be describing a gang rape rather than sexual love, but he thought the only, fragile, escape from the fate of being 'cast aside as one casts away a lemon that has been sucked dry' was a contractual relationship based on marriage, although he himself did not try it (nor, probably, sex). In *Plato, sexual desire is a good, although only the first step on a ladder of perfection (*see* BEAUTY, DANTE, LOVE). The movements of thought whereby Plato's view degenerated to the *Calvinism of Kant include increasing disgust with merely material as opposed to spiritual existence, and the Pauline and *Augustinian conviction that *original sin is somehow associated with sexual desire (*see* CONCUPISCENCE). But older classical and Judaic traditions also associated sexuality and especially female sexuality and menstruation with uncleanliness and pollution. Women came off worst in other ways also, since, as in too many modern cultures, rape was thought to dishonour the victim.

A more optimistic view of the matter than Kant's was voiced by *Hobbes: 'The appetite which men call *lust*... is a sensual pleasure, but not only that; there is in it also a delight of the mind: for it consisteth of two appetites together, to please, and to be pleased; and the delight men take in delighting, is not sensual, but a pleasure or joy of the mind consisting in the imagination of the power they have so much to please' (*Human Nature*, ix. 10). In this area, prophecies are apt to be *self-fulfilling: it is predictable that if we side with Kant our sexual relationships will be a lot worse than if we understand Hobbes. The power of the tradition of *sin is still visible in the ratio of writings that pay serious attention to Kant's view, as opposed to ones that start with Plato, or Hobbes. *See also* OBSCENITY, PORNOGRAPHY.

sexism The inability or refusal to recognize the rights, needs, dignity, or value of people of one sex or *gender. More widely, the devaluation of various traits of character or intelligence as 'typical' of one or other gender. *See also* FEMINISM.

Sextus Empiricus (*fl.* c.AD 200) Doctor of medicine, and author of the most distinguished works of ancient *scepticism that have survived. Sextus was a Greek who may have spent time in Rome and Alexandria, but little is known about his life, including where he was born and died. His works are divided into the *Outlines of Pyrrhonism* and *Adversos Mathematicos* (against the professors, or dogmatists). These works provide the main codification of Greek scepticism. Sextus defends a *Pyrrhonian position whereby even the dialectic undermining the 'trickster reason' is eventually itself to be regarded quizzically: in his famous metaphor, it acts like a purgative, expelling itself along with the diseases it cures. His scepticism is confined to the *adela* or theoretical world beyond experience; central to his philosophy is the distinction between 'indicative' signs, which are signs taken improperly, as pointing to things lying beyond experience, and 'commemorative' or recollective signs, which are signs taken as symptoms of yet other signs, which are legitimate. The distinction anticipates the *British empiricists' difficulties in understanding how ideas can ever represent anything except by functioning as indicators of more ideas to come. Sextus' writings include many central themes of these successors, including a distinction between *primary and secondary qualities, and a view of *causation similar to Hume's. The aim of scepticism is to show how in life we must take appearances as they come, and the virtue of the sceptic is the imperturbability (*ataraxia*) with which he confronts the fact that this is all we can do. *See also* AENESIDEMUS, CARNEADES, PYRRHO.

Shaftesbury, 3rd Earl of (Anthony Ashley Cooper) (1671–1713) British moral philosopher. His grandfather was the patron of *Locke, and upon being made Shaftesbury's guardian (the father being incapable: a 'shapeless lump', according to the poet Dryden), he had Locke direct much of his grandson's education. Shaftesbury suffered from poor health, which encouraged him to exchange a political life for a literary one, and died in Naples escaping from the rigours of the English climate. His *Characteristics of Men, Manners, Opinions, and Times* (1711) collect together his elegant and stylized writings. His main philosophical remnant is the 'Inquiry Concerning Virtue' (collected in the *Characteristics* but completed in 1699), which contains the first occurrence of the phrase 'moral sense', later exploited by *Hutcheson. He was attacked as a *deist by contemporary Christian apologists, including *Berkeley. In his own time his reputation was variable: he was much admired by the Scottish thinker Lord Monboddo (1714–99), and by *Diderot, but viewed as a high-flown declaimer by *Mandeville. However, *Leibniz said that he found almost all his own *Theodicy* in the *Characteristics*, but more agreeably turned.

shame *See* GUILT/SHAME.

Shankara (*c.*788–820) Indian philosopher. Born in Kerala, Shankara is acknowledged as the leader of the *Hindu revival after the *Buddhist period, and a founder of religious orders on the Buddhist model. He led a peripatetic life and wrote a number of treatises, particularly a commentary on the 4th-century *Brahma-sutra* ('power aphorisms'), and one on the *Vedas. Philosophically he was a founder of the doctrine of **advaita*, or non-dualism, having affinities with both Buddhism and *idealism.

Shao Yong (1011/12–77) Chinese Neo-Confucian. Like *Pythagoras he believed that numerical patterns contained the key to the working of the universe. His work on hexagrams attracted the attention of *Leibniz.

Sheffer's stroke Both *Peirce in 1880 and the American logician H. M. Sheffer in 1913 realized that the *truth functions of elementary logic could all be defined from a single function. Defining p / q to mean not both p and q, p / p is equivalent to not-p, $(p / q)/ (p / q)$ means $p \vee q$, and so on. The sign for this truth function is Sheffer's stroke: p / q is true only when p is false or q is false. A functionally complete system can also be built from a single sign for the function that is true when p is false and q is false.

Shelley, Percy Bysshe (1792–1822) The English poet is also an important figure in the history of British radicalism and *atheism. Eton succeeded in instilling in him a strong hatred of tyranny and authority, while his *The Necessity of Atheism* (1811), written together with Thomas Jefferson Hogg, resulted in his being expelled from University College, Oxford. Shelley's poetry is a poetry of ideas: *Queen Mab: A Philosophical Poem* (1813) extols the philosophy of William *Godwin, including republicanism, vegetarianism, atheism, and free love. He also shared the German Romantic idealist vision of a spirit of the age moving humanity and history with it.

Shepherd, Mary (1777–1847) Scottish philosopher. The daughter of the third Earl of Rosebery and largely self-taught, Shepherd was a friend of Charles *Babbage. She published two major philosophical works: *An Essay upon the Relation of Cause and Effect* (1824) and *Essays on the Perception of an External Universe, and Other Subjects* (1827). The first is an attack on *Hume on causation, apparently occasioned by an Edinburgh uproar over whether John Leslie could be a suitable candidate for a chair in mathematics, given that he adhered to Hume's views of causation, and was therefore likely to be an infidel and atheist. She was much admired by *Whewell, who is supposed to have used her treatise as a textbook; Sir Charles Lyell, the geologist, called her an 'unanswerable logician'.

Sherwood, William (1200/10–1266/71) Seminal English logician. Sherwood's works included *Introductiones in Logicam, Syncategoremata,* and *De Insolubilia,* and there are others of more doubtful authorship. He is one of the authors of the 'terminist' logic that concentrates more upon the properties of terms than of whole sentences, especially distinguishing *categorematic from *syncategorematic terms.

Shinto (Chinese, *shin tao*, the way of the Gods) Traditional Japanese religion, an amorphous mix of nature worship, fertility cults, divination techniques, hero worship, and shamanism. Shinto can be traced back to around 500 BC but has no formal bible. Like *Confucianism it emphasizes tradition and the family as the means for preserving tradition. The main celebrations relate to birth and marriage. It also emphasizes love of nature, physical cleanliness, and 'Matsuri': the worship and honour given to the ancestral spirits and gods or 'Kami'.

ship of Theseus An example deriving from a story in Plutarch, and often used to illustrate problems with the identity of composite objects. Theseus has a ship, and in the way of things parts need constant replacement. There comes a point at which none of the original components remain. Is it the same ship? Thomas *Hobbes (*De Corpore*, 2, 11, 7) asks whether if someone went around picking up the discarded parts and constructed a ship with them, which would be the better candidate for being the original ship?

shunyata (Sanskrit, emptiness, void) Central philosophical concept in *Hinduism and *Buddhism, denoting the lack of substance or independent reality of the elements of the phenomenal world. The experience of this emptiness is a necessary part of religious and philosophical enlightenment.

Sidgwick, Henry (1838–1900) English philosopher. Sidgwick was a quintessentially late Victorian Cambridge figure. He was Fellow of Trinity College from 1859 to 1869, when he resigned because religious doubts meant that he could no longer subscribe to the Thirty-nine Articles, and professor of moral philosophy from 1883 to 1900. Sidgwick was a champion of women's education and he and his wife Eleanor Balfour were principal founders of Newnham College, of which she became Principal in 1892. Sidgwick was also a mainstay of the Society for Psychical Research. His most important work is the monumental *Methods of Ethics* (1874). The methods are first, those of intuitive common sense, taking perfection as its goal and relying on a variety of self-evident moral principles; secondly, the method of calculating self-interest; and thirdly, that of general utilitarianism. The work is generally regarded as a classic statement of the different kinds of ethical argument. In particular, Sidgwick anticipated *Moore in his denial that ethical terms are capable of definition. However, at the end of the day, he found himself unable to reconcile the demands of self-interest and those of ethics (*see* SENSIBLE KNAVE), so the relationship between ethical demands and others remains uneasy.

SEE WEB LINKS

- A brief biography and list of internet resources on Sidgwick
- A complete bibliography of Sidgwick's writings

Siger of Brabant (*c.*1240–1284) The acknowledged leader of those who interpreted *Aristotle through the eyes of *Averroës, in 13th-century Paris. *Dante puts him in the circle of wise men in Paradise, and has his praises sung by *Aquinas, which puzzles commentators, since the Averroists were amongst Aquinas's opponents. Siger shows himself well aware of the non-Aristotelian nature of Aquinas's notion of existence. His principal treatise was *On the Necessity and Contingency of Causes*, condemned in 1277 as denying freedom of the will.

sign/symbol A distinction drawn by *Peirce. A sign of a thing or state of affairs is any symptom or trace or portent of it that can be used to infer that it is present. We can make signs, so that for instance a picture on a can is a sign of its contents. Peirce described symbols as such artificial signs. But this is a mistake, for symbols are not typically used to infer the presence of what they symbolize, but to represent them in their absence, or to express intentions or to conjure up thoughts and emotions centred upon them. The theory of this difference lies at the heart of the philosophy of language.

al-Sijistani, Abu Sulaiyman Muhammad (*c.*932–*c.*1000) Islamic *Neoplatonist, centred in Baghdad. The key to understanding is the entire separation of the stable, unchanging higher world and the changing lower world. The intellect and the soul are universal and indivisible, with our souls only a part of it. God is sufficiently removed from mundane creation not to be describable or knowable at all, even negatively. To any proposition stating that God is not (e.g. caring) one must add the double negative that he is not not caring either. On the other hand, something akin to agency on the part of God creates the world.

Simmel, Georg (1858–1918) German writer and together with *Weber one of the principal founders of sociology as a distinct discipline. A cosmopolitan, Simmel studied at Berlin, where he continued to teach, unpaid, for many years (he had a considerable private fortune), only achieving an academic post as professor in Strasbourg as late as 1914. Erratically brilliant, he was described by Ortega y Gasset as an academic squirrel, and wrote about a wide variety of philosophical, sociological, cultural, and historical matters. Books included *Social Differentiation* (1890), *The Philosophy of Money* (1900), *Sociology: Investigations on the Forms of Sociation* (1908), as well as works on Rembrandt and Goethe.

simple/complex ideas *See* COMPLEX IDEAS.

simple enumeration *See* ENUMERATIVE INDUCTION.

simplicity One of the virtues of a good theory, although it may not be clear why, given that there seems to be no *a priori* reason to expect it to be a reliable guide to truth. *See* EXPLANATION; SCIENCE, PHILOSOPHY OF.

Simplicius (6th c. AD) Neoplatonist commentator on Aristotle. Simplicius was a member of the *Academy of Athens at the point at which it was finally closed by Justinian in 529. He was taught by *Ammonius, and wrote extensive commentaries on Aristotle's *De caelo*, *Physics*, and *Categories*. He defended the eternity of the world, in particular sparring with the Christian John *Philoponus.

Simpson's paradox Not a proper *paradox, but a surprising possibility in the application of statistics, in which something true of each subset of a population need not be true of the population as a whole. For example, in each separate faculty of a university the rejection rate of men might be higher than that for women, yet overall the rejection rate of women might be higher than that for men. This is surprising, but it can occur where women apply in higher numbers to those faculties that have higher pressure of numbers and therefore maintain higher rejection rates overall.

simulation The view that our understanding of others is not gained by the tacit use of a 'theory', enabling us to infer what thoughts or intentions explain their actions, but by reliving the situation 'in their shoes' or from their point of view, and thereby understanding what they experienced and thought, and therefore expressed. Understanding others is achieved when we can ourselves deliberate as they did, and hear their words as if they are our own. The suggestion is a modern development of the **Verstehen* tradition associated with *Dilthey, *Weber, and *Collingwood. *See also* THEORY-THEORY.

sin A moral category going beyond that of simple wrongdoing by its implications of evil, disobedience, depravity, stain, and *wickedness. Sin therefore requires atonement, penitence, and self-abasement, not to mention punishment. The abjection and lack of self-respect implied in the cluster of ideas serve to emphasize the importance of redemption. They are therefore an important buttress to the power of those who claim to know how to provide it. The concept is only at home in a religious tradition built around the possibility of God's disgust, and is not found pure and simple in classical thought, where offences were equally liable to divine vengeance whether voluntary or not. *See also* HELL, ORIGINAL SIN, PREDESTINATION, SEVEN DEADLY SINS.

singularity In cosmology, a point at which ordinary calculations break down because certain physical quantities become infinite: for example, the 'event' at the beginning of the big bang, at which in some theories the density of matter and the curvature of space-time is infinite.

singular term *See* TERM.

Sinn/Bedeutung (German, sense/reference or meaning) In his famous paper 'Über Sinn und Bedeutung' ('On Sense and Reference', 1892), *Frege contrasted the sense (*Sinn*) of an expression with its reference (*Bedeutung*). Two expressions might have the same reference, but present it in different ways, and this mode of presentation is the sense of the expression. Thus 'George Eliot' and 'Mary Anne Evans' refer to the same person, but it might come as a surprise to someone to learn that the person he knows as one is the person he knows as the other. This, according to Frege, is because the terms are associated with different modes of presentation of the one person. It is the sense of expressions that determines the thought expressed by a sentence in which they occur, whilst reference determines its truth or falsity. However, there are sentences in which the mode of presentation or sense itself becomes part of the topic, in which case truth-value can shift through substitution of terms that nevertheless have the same reference. Such contexts are called oblique, or indirect, or intensional (*see* EXTENSION/INTENSION). Two conditions on the notion of sense are that if two expressions share the same sense it should not be possible to fail to realize that they share the same reference; also senses are to be public and objective, as thoughts are for Frege. It has proven hard to identify a conception of sense that satisfies both these conditions. The use of a two-part semantic theory of this kind was attacked by *Russell in his paper 'On Denoting' (1905), but theories of meaning are commonly based upon some version of the distinction.

Sins, Seven Deadly *See* SEVEN DEADLY SINS.

Sittlichkeit (German, morality, ethical life) In *Hegel, a way of being in the world: an involvement in the ethical and political life of the time.

situation ethics The view that ethical judgement applies to whole situations, rather as aesthetic judgement is formed in response to total works of art. Any attempt to abstract features in virtue of which situations merit a judgement, and then to argue about new cases in the light of those features, is potentially misleading; for a feature may contribute to the value of one situation, but be irrelevant in another, just as a particular splash of colour might be just what one picture needs, but be inappropriate in another. The principal difficulty in front of this view is that ethics is not just a matter of responding to existing situations, but is essentially a practical subject, in which future options have to be ranked in the light of different features. *See also* CONTEXTUALISM.

situation semantics An approach to *semantics that diverges from the orthodox *Fregean tradition in assigning states of affairs to sentences as that to which they refer. The approach needs to avoid the argument known as the *slingshot, whereby semanticists following Frege seek to prove that the reference of all true sentences is the same—the truth-value True.

Skinner, Burrhus Frederick (1904–90) American psychologist, who gained his doctorate at Harvard and returned there to work in 1948. In his time one of the most influential of world psychologists, Skinner championed an uncompromising *behaviourism. The mind is an unnecessary construct; science concerns itself with inputs and outputs: learning takes place because 'behavior is followed by a consequence, and the nature of the consequence modifies the organism's tendency to repeat the behavior in the future.' It is usually felt that this view of human learning was entirely destroyed by Noam *Chomsky in his 1959 review of Skinner's book *Verbal Behaviour*, while philosophically the rise of *functionalism and *cognitive science in general has superseded Skinner's behaviourism.

Skolem–Löwenheim theorem *See* LÖWENHEIM–SKOLEM THEOREM.

Skolem normal form A formula is in Skolem normal form if it is in *prenex normal form, and all the existential quantifiers come first. There is an effective procedure producing, for any formula, one in Skolem normal form that is valid if and only if the original is valid.

Skolem paradox Leopold Löwenheim (1878–1948) in 1915 and Thoralf Skolem (1887–1963) in 1920 showed that any *denumerable set of sentences that has a *model has a denumerably infinite model. The theory of real numbers can be axiomatized as a theory with a denumerable set of sentences. Yet in that theory it is provable that the set of reals is larger than denumerably infinite, so ordinary or 'standard' models need more than denumerably infinite numbers of elements. Skolem thus showed that the theory admits of 'non-standard' models, or ones which are not isomorphic with the intended interpretation (*see* CANTOR'S THEOREM). The paradox is often regarded as relatively superficial, since the interpretation assigned to the sentences of the theory when they are given a denumerable model is not their 'intuitive' interpretation, according to which they imply the non-denumerable nature of the set of reals. But this raises the question of what fixes the intuitive interpretation. If the intuitive interpretation is fixed by conditions that can be expressed in a denumerable number of sentences, those may be added to the original list, and we have a theory still subject to the same result.

slave morality *See* MASTER/SLAVE MORALITY.

slingshot The argument sometimes known as the Frege–Church argument that if a context is such that co-referring singular *terms (names or descriptions) can be substituted for each other **salva veritate*, then sentences with the same truth-value can also be so substituted. This justifies semantic theory in holding that the reference of a sentence is its truth-value rather than anything more 'fine-grained' such as a situation or state of affairs. The argument works by manufacturing a definite description from a sentence, and substituting a co-referring definite description with another sentence of the same truth-value in it. Suppose two propositions p, q with the same truth-value. Then from 'p' we derive '(the number x such that $2x = 6$ & p) = 3'; substituting for the referring term in parentheses we have '(the number x such that $2x = 6$ & q) = 3' from which we derive q. The attribution to *Frege, based on some remarks in 'On Sense and Reference', is doubtful. The slingshot has been endorsed by many logicians, although a defence against it is provided if definite descriptions are treated not as themselves being referring expressions or names, but in accordance with *Russell's theory of *definite descriptions.

slippery slope One is standing on a slippery slope when arguments one has accepted against a position appear to apply equally to one's own position, forcing one, perhaps little by little, into a conclusion one has no desire to accept. Much argument against compromise positions in politics and ethics attempts to portray them as in an unstable position between an extreme they have rejected, and another extreme to which they do not wish to be committed.

Smart, J. J. C. (1920–) Cambridge-born Australian philosopher. Smart emigrated from England to Australia in 1950, and subsequently held appointments at a number of universities, including the Australian National University. In general philosophy, Smart has been influential in Australia and internationally as a leading scientific *realist and *materialist, whilst in ethics his staunch defence of *utilitarianism has provided landmarks both for defenders and assailants. He was also an early defender of a *block universe view of time. His books include *Philosophy and Scientific Realism* (1963), *Utilitarianism: For and Against* (with Bernard *Williams, 1973), and *Essays Metaphysical and Moral* (1987).

Smith, Adam (1723–90) Scottish philosopher and economist. Although best remembered as an economist, Smith was a polymath, and an eminent social theorist and moral philosopher. Born in Kirkcaldy, he was educated at Glasgow university and Balliol College, Oxford. He resided in Edinburgh, and became friends with *Hume and his circle, from 1748 until 1751, in which year he was appointed professor of logic at the university of Glasgow. In the following year he changed to the chair of moral philosophy. On publication of *The Theory of Moral Sentiments* (1759), he received patronage from the Duke of Buccleuch, enabling him to resign his chair, and subsequently devote himself to scholarship. *An Inquiry into the Nature and Causes of the Wealth of Nations* was published in 1776. Smith's moral philosophy differs from that of *Hutcheson and Hume in its emphasis on *Stoic virtues, and in particular that of self-command. Smith's man of perfect virtue 'joins, to the most perfect command of his own original and selfish feelings, the most exquisite sensibility both to the original and sympathetic feelings of others' (*The Theory of Moral Sentiments*, ii. 3. 34). His system hinges on the operation of sympathy, arising from an intellectual or moral appreciation of the situation of one who is aroused, and provoking a fellow-feeling or analogous sensation in the attentive spectator. The '*impartial spectator' is introduced as an explanation of the working of conscience: it is an internalization of the gaze of others, whereby I imagine what I should feel were I to have an unprejudiced and undistorted view of my own actions. The impartial spectator functions as a 'tribunal within the breast' whose authority derives from the censure of the world, but which nevertheless has the power to overturn the judgements of others (iii. 2. 31).

The 'invisible hand' for which Smith is famous first appears as a phrase in an essay he wrote on the history of astronomy. It recurs in *The Theory of Moral Sentiments* at iv. 1. 11. In spite of their insatiable greed and rapacity, the rich are unable actually to consume much more than anyone else, and so are led by the invisible hand to make 'nearly the same distribution of the necessaries of life, which would have been made, had the earth been divided into equal portions among all its inhabitants'. In *The Wealth of Nations* the emphasis is less on equal distribution and more on the promotion of the common good that arises from the pursuit of self-interest (*see also* MANDEVILLE). In economics, Smith gives the pioneering analysis of the structure of a functioning economy, and the first discussion of the benefits of the 'division of labour'. His general optimism about the economic results of free markets has given his name a lustre in *libertarian political circles that he might not have entirely welcomed, given his low opinion of the motives that lead to economic activity (*see* VANITY). In fact, in Pt v of the book he allows for the provision of public services out of general taxation where market mechanisms fail, and argues that the state has a vital role in providing educational services for the poor, both to ward off the 'mental mutilation' consequent upon industrial working conditions, and to enable them to become better workers and citizens.

SEE WEB LINKS

- A list of internet resources on Smith
- An archive of Smith's writings

social action Actions in which the interaction with other people is of primary importance, as in situations studied in *game theory. Also actions in which the agent is a plurality, a 'we' rather than an 'I'. It is tempting to reduce this latter category to an aggregate of individual actions, but this kind of *reduction or decomposition is not in general available. Social *holists emphasize the reality of the collective agent; others try to dampen it down.

social choice theory The theory of ways to conjure a *social welfare function, or rational choice for a collective as a whole out of the preferences or 'utilities' of its individual members. The theory is bedevilled by results such as *Arrow's theorem, or versions of the *voting paradox. *See also* COORDINATION PROBLEM, GAME THEORY, NASH EQUILIBRIUM, PRISONERS' DILEMMA.

social constructivism The view that some aspect of the world is an artefact of social practices, including language and institutionalized ways of categorizing the world. In his book *The Social Construction of What?* Ian *Hacking reports that books can be found entitled something like 'the social construction of X' for examples beginning with every letter of the alphabet except X itself, from 'anarchy' to 'Zulu nationalism'. A phrase like 'the social construction of heroism' refers to the way in which common perceptions, myths, images, and fantasies go to make up what people understand by the idea. When the aspect of the world in question is not itself obviously social, but taken to include objects of scientific interest like quarks or geological epochs or diseases, the idea of their social construction is apt to be resisted as introducing *idealism, although there is no reason why a concept should not have a social history and carry a good deal of ideological baggage, while the thing it refers to does not.

social contract A basis for legitimate legal and political power in the idea of a contract. Contracts are things that create obligations, hence if we can view society as organized 'as if' a contract had been formed between the citizen and the sovereign power, this will ground the nature of the obligations of each to the other. This form of theory is prominent in *Hobbes. In *Locke and *Rousseau the idea becomes one of a contract between citizens, as a result of which power is vested in government, rather than that of a contract between citizen and sovereign. This aspect is also reproduced in later contractarian writers such as *Rawls. Social contract theory needs to explain whether the contract is thought of as having actually taken place, or as implied by social conformity, or as merely hypothetical, with the idea being that a legitimate body politic is one that a suitably placed agent could rationally have contracted into. *Hume's essay 'Of the Original Contract' is a devastating critique of some uses of the notion, primarily on the grounds that both the obligation we owe to contracts, and that which we owe to civil society, are constructions which themselves stand in need of some other fundamental basis. *See also* CONTRACTARIANISM, GENERAL WILL, ORIGINAL POSITION, STATE OF NATURE.

SEE WEB LINKS

- An introduction to the social contract, with links to related issues
- Hume's critique in 'Of the Original Contract'

social Darwinism *See* EVOLUTIONARY ETHICS.

socialism Political system in which the (major) means of production are not in private or institutional hands, but under social control. Typically this is seen as one aspect of a more general concern for people's equal rights to various benefits (health, education), and of a concern to limit the inequalities of wealth and power produced by the unrestricted operations of market forces. Socialism avoids the totalitarian implications of *communism, and works within liberal democratic constitutions.

social laws *See* SOCIAL SCIENCE.

social philosophy The attempt to understand and to chart the basic categories with which to think about the social aspects of human life. Topics given separate discussions include: anarchism; authority; class (social); exploitation; holism;

individualism; law, philosophy of; liberalism; Marxism; power (social); property; rights.

social science, philosophy of The philosophy of social science is more heavily intertwined with actual social science than in the case of other subjects such as physics or mathematics, since its question is centrally whether there can be such a thing as social science. The idea of a 'science of man', devoted to uncovering scientific laws determining the basic dynamics of human interactions, was a cherished ideal of the *Enlightenment and reached its heyday with the *positivism of writers such as *Comte, and the *historical materialism of *Marx and his followers. Sceptics point out that what happens in society is determined by people's own ideas of what should happen, and like fashions those ideas change in unpredictable ways as self-consciousness changes. They also point out that this self-consciousness is susceptible to change by any number of external events; unlike the solar system of celestial mechanics a society is not at all a closed system evolving in accordance with a purely internal dynamic, but constantly responsive to shocks from outside.

social welfare function A social welfare function is a *function from the ordering of a set of preferences or votes of individuals in a society, to an ordering of the preference or vote of the society as a whole. It takes us from the ways the individuals separately rank alternatives, to the way the society does. The difficulties in the way of providing such a function are shown by the *voter's paradox and *Arrow's theorem.

society A group of persons unified by a distinctive and systematic set of normative relations, whereby actions of one are perceived as meriting characteristic responses by others. To be part of the same society is to be subject to these *norms of interaction.

Socinianism Religious movement founded by the Italian Laelius Socinius (1525–62) and his nephew Faustus Socinius (1539–1603). It stood for the use of reason in theological matters and the downsizing of dogma, denying central orthodox Christian tenets such as the Trinity, the divinity of Christ, original sin, and predestination. It took root in Poland, but in the 17th and 18th centuries the word was widely used in polemical writings as a pejorative term for *Latitudinarians and *deists.

sociobiology The academic discipline best known through the work of Edward O. Wilson who coined the term in his *Sociobiology: the New Synthesis* (1975). The approach to human behaviour is based on the premise that all social behaviour has a biological basis, and seeks to understand that basis in terms of genetic encoding for features that are then selected for through evolutionary history. The philosophical problem is essentially one of methodology: of finding criteria for identifying features that can usefully be explained in this way, and of finding criteria for assessing various genetic stories that might provide useful explanations.

Among the features that are proposed for this kind of explanation are such things as male dominance, male promiscuity versus female fidelity, propensities to sympathy and other emotions, and the limited *altruism characteristic of human beings. The strategy has proved unnecessarily controversial, with proponents accused of ignoring the influence of environmental and social factors in moulding people's characteristics (e.g. at the limit of silliness, by postulating a 'gene for poverty'). However there is no need for the approach to commit such errors, since the feature explained sociobiologically may be indexed to environment: for instance it may be a propensity to develop some feature in some social or other environment (or even a propensity to develop propensities ...). The main problem is to separate genuine explanation from speculative *just so stories which may or may not identify real selective mechanisms. *See also* BIOLOGY, PHILOSOPHY OF; EVOLUTIONARY PSYCHOLOGY.

sociology *See* SOCIAL SCIENCE, PHILOSOPHY OF.

sociology of knowledge The study of the social factors surrounding the emergence of entire systems of belief, or the modifications of such systems by means of changes of theory, experiments, and the acceptance of different *paradigms of explanation. The things to explain will include the shifts in popularity of lines of enquiry, and the mechanisms aiding the rise of some theories at the expense of others. The factors cited may include the social situation and ambitions of particular enquirers. The study blends with the more general history of ideas. It becomes more controversial than it need be, if it is assumed that such explanations are necessarily sceptical and relativistic, and compete with the explanation of scientific progress in terms of the ongoing discovery of truth.

Socrates (469–399 BC) The engaging and infuriating figure of the early dialogues of *Plato, Socrates represented the turning point in Greek philosophy, at which the self-critical reflection on the nature of our concepts and our reasoning emerged as a major concern, alongside cosmological speculation and enquiry. The historical Socrates cannot easily be distinguished from the Platonic character, as there are few other sources for Socrates's life and doctrines (*Xenophon is one). He served as a soldier in the Peloponnesian War, and was married to Xanthippe, with whom he had three male children. He was of strong build and great endurance, and completely indifferent to wealth and luxury.

His subordination of all other concerns to a life spent enquiring after wisdom is the most commanding example, seldom approached, of the proper way of living for a philosopher. He remains the model of a great teacher, but it is uncertain whether he had anything in the nature of a formal school. His friendship with some of the aristocratic party in Athens is often supposed to explain why he was eventually brought to trial, on charges of introducing strange gods and corrupting the youth. Plato's *Crito* and *Phaedo* record the inspirational manner in which he refused to break the laws of Athens and escape during the thirty days between his trial and execution, and they celebrate the fortitude with which he met his death. Whilst his skill at the dialectical, questioning method is unquestioned, his positive contributions and doctrines are matters of some debate, and opinions vary between ascribing to him many of the positive doctrines of Plato, and denying that he had any doctrines at all of his own, apart from his attachment to rigorous dialectical method as the instrument for separating truth from error. All the Greek schools of philosophy conceived of themselves as owing much to Socrates, except for the *Epicureans who disliked him intensely, calling him 'the Athenian buffoon'.

Socratic fallacy *See* SOCRATIC PARADOX.

Socratic irony Socrates's irritating tendency to praise his hearers while undermining them, or to disparage his own superior abilities while manifesting them.

Socratic method The method of teaching in which the master imparts no information, but asks a sequence of questions, through answering which the pupil eventually comes to the desired knowledge. Socratic irony is the pose of ignorance on the part of the master, who may in fact know more about the matter than he lets on. *See also* *ELENCHUS*, MAIEUTIC METHOD.

Socratic paradox Rather than a strict *paradox, the term refers to either of two surprising and unacceptable conclusions drawn from the Socratic dialogues of *Plato: (i) the startling consequence of Socrates's association of knowledge and virtue, according to which nobody ever does wrong knowingly; (ii) the view that nobody knows what they mean when they use a term unless they can provide an explicit definition of it. Although this last is sometimes called the Socratic fallacy, this can be regarded as being uncharitable to Socrates, whose concern was not simply with meaning, but more with notions like justice or reason, for which our inability to provide principles may well reflect ignorance and muddle. On the first issue, *see AKRASIA*.

soft determinism *See* FREE WILL.

software Term used for the instructions or programs executed by a computer, as opposed to the physical hardware that enables the machine to follow them. The comparison of a psychological description of a person to a software description of a machine is exploited in *functionalism.

solipsism The belief that only oneself and one's experience exists. Solipsism is the extreme consequence of believing that knowledge must be founded on inner, personal states of experience, and then failing to find a bridge whereby they can inform us of anything beyond themselves. Solipsism of the present moment extends its *scepticism even to one's own past states, so that all that is left is me, now. *Russell reports meeting someone who claimed that she was a solipsist, and was surprised that more people were not so as well.

solo numero (Latin, only in number) *Leibniz denied that two things could differ *solo numero*: for any two distinct things, there must be a property that one has and the other does not. *See* IDENTITY OF INDISCERNIBLES.

some *See* QUANTIFIER.

Sophia, Electress of Hanover (1630–1714) Daughter of Frederick V and Elizabeth Stuart (daughter of James I of England), Sophia was the mother of George I of England. Her sister was *Elizabeth of Bohemia and she was a distinguished scholar in her own right. She is known in philosophy as a close friend and patron of *Leibniz, whose main employment was at the Hanover court.

sophismata In medieval logic, sentences illustrating logical and semantic puzzles, particularly associated with *scope ambiguities.

Sophists Although the term originally applied to generally wise men, it was applied by *Plato to various teachers of whom he disapproved, including *Protagoras, *Gorgias, Thrasymachus, and Hippias of Elis. Plato generally treats them as charlatans who talked purely for victory and took money for teaching the technique. In fact their general stance seems to have been not unlike that of *Socrates, with a reasonably sceptical attitude to speculative cosmologies, such as those of the *Eleatics, and a reasonable insistence on going to the foundations of morality and epistemology. It seems likely that Plato's attitude betrayed an aristocratic disdain for the democratic tendencies implicit in teaching and spreading rhetorical power to a wider class of citizens, and fear of a democratic government in which the people are swayed by nothing but rhetoric, or spin.

sophrosynē (Greek, self-control, temperance, soundness of mind) One of the cardinal virtues, consisting in a harmonious state of rational control of one's desires. In *Aristotle the temperate person is one who can abstain or indulge appetites to the right degree without a severe effort of will; the person who needs the effort of will is not temperate, and needs to be continent (*see* AKOLASIA, AKRASIA).

Sorel, Georges (1847–1922) French engineer, philosopher, and social theorist. Sorel is principally remembered for *Réflexions sur la violence* (1908, trs. as *Reflections on Violence*, 1914). Sorel argues that one cannot deplore violence in the hands of opponents of the state (itself no stranger to the violence of war and legal coercion) without understanding the situation and the aims of those who use it. Perhaps the most scandalous part of the doctrine was Sorel's recognition that violence might equally be used against those who, appearing to sympathize with a movement, in fact lure it into collaboration with the system that it aims to overthrow. Sorel also perceived the central role of myth and image in creating a dramatic focus for political emotions: myths are the product of vigorous and living social forces, which may transform societies in ways that are necessary to create their own truth. Although Sorel was a theorist of the *left, his contempt for democratic liberalism was most closely echoed by the violent and myth-governed *fascist regimes of the 20th century.

Sorge (German, care, sorrow) A concept made much of by *Heidegger, who sees it as inevitable when we become aware of our mortality, and of the contingency of our own existence.

S

sorites paradox (Greek, *soros*, a heap) One grain of sand is not a heap. And for any number n, if n grains of sand are not a heap, then the addition of just one more grain does not make them a heap. But in that case you can never get a heap, for each grain you add leaves you just as much without a heap as before. The paradox is serious because it raises a tension between classical logical and mathematical reasoning, and the 'vague' predicates of natural language. Solutions include approaches based on denying the second, inductive premise, on introducing 'degrees of truth', and on modifying classical logic into *fuzzy logic. But it is generally recognized that no solution is free of problems.

sortal Term used by *Locke (*Essay*, iii. 3) and resurrected by *Strawson (*Individuals*, p. 168) for a noun or 'predicable' such as 'man', 'woman', 'tiger', that provides a principle for individuating and counting examples of things of a type. 'Butter' and 'thing' are not sortals because there is no principle for counting butter (as opposed to pats of butter, etc.) or things (you cannot tell when you have one thing or two). 'Red' is not a sortal but an adjective. *See also* COUNT NOUN.

Soto, Domingo de (1494–1560) Spanish Dominican, and teacher at Salamanca. He is remembered in the history of philosophy not only as a key figure in the *Thomist revival of Spanish philosophy (and therefore of the Counter-Reformation) in the 16th century, but also as an early theorist of law. His principal work was *De justitia et jure* (1556).

soul The immaterial 'I' that possesses conscious experience, controls passion, desire, and action, and maintains a perfect identity from birth (or before) to death (or after). Modern philosophy of mind has frequently been concerned with dismantling the cluster of views that make it plausible to think in terms of such a thing. *See* BUNDLE THEORY OF THE MIND OR SELF, PARALOGISM, PERSONAL IDENTITY.

sound The immediate object of auditory perception, although the way we hear sounds is affected by such factors as their context or our own musical experience and understanding. Sounds share the problems of secondary qualities: does a tree falling alone in the forest make any sound? *See* PRIMARY/SECONDARY QUALITIES.

soundness Of an argument, the property of being valid and having all true premises. Logical systems are sound if every theorem is valid, that is, true in all *interpretations.

sovereignty Final authority, that is itself subject to no further authority. Philosophical questions include asking whether such an authority is necessary in an orderly political state, or whether systems of 'checks and balances' can provide stable government with no one body claiming absolute sovereignty.

space The classical questions include: is space real, or is it some kind of mental construct, or artefact of our ways of perceiving and thinking? Is it 'substantival' or purely 'relational'? According to substantivalism, space is an objective thing comprised of points or regions at which, or in which, things are located. Opposed to this is relationalism, according to which the only thing that is real about space are the spatial (and temporal) relations between physical objects. Substantivalism was advocated by *Clarke, speaking for *Newton, and relationalism by *Leibniz, in their famous correspondence, and the debate continues today. There is also an issue whether the measures of space and time are objective, or whether an element of *convention enters into them.

space-time The structure specified by treating space and time together as a four-dimensional manifold. Points in space-time are called events. In the theory of *relativity, each event in space-time is associated with a past light cone (the set of past events that could possibly have influenced it) and a future light cone (the set of future events that it could possibly influence), where the possibility in question is limited by the speed of light. Regions outside each light cone of an event are the 'elsewhere'. *D'Alembert may have been the first to suggest that time is regarded as a fourth dimension in his article 'Dimension' for the **Encyclopédie*, but he could not foresee the main physical point of the concept, which is that in relativity theory space and time can be traded, like mass and energy; what is invariant in relating two events is not their spatial distance, nor their temporal distance, but only their distance in space-time.

spatiotemporal continuity The property of well-behaved objects in space and time, that they do not 'jump', or in other words if a body exists at one time and a later time, then it exists throughout the interval, and if it is in one place at a time and a different place at a later time, then it traced a path through space from the one place to another. This behaviour may not belong to objects in the *quantum world, and there are questions of whether it is essential or only accidental for ordinary bodies, and especially for persons, where science fiction scenarios often transgress it.

species Any class of individuals sharing common properties and denoted by one common noun. In biology, the class below a genus, comprising organisms capable of interbreeding. The biological name, e.g. *homo sapiens*, consists of the name of the wider genus (*homo*) plus a distinguishing qualification (*sapiens*). *See* PER GENUS ET DIFFERENTIAM. The 'reality' of species is one aspect of the problem of *universals: *see also* NATURAL KINDS.

speciesism By analogy with *racism or *sexism, the improper stance of refusing respect to the lives, dignity, rights, or needs of animals of other than the human species.

specious present Term due to E. R. Clay and promoted by *James, to describe the view that although the present is itself 'punctiform' or a mere point between past and future, nevertheless in experience some earlier events are still present to us when we perceive later events. Only thus, it was thought, could the experience of hearing a melody as a melody, or seeing movement as real movement, be understood; for unless the past notes or the past position is still somehow present in the mind, the perception would not be of the sequence as a melody or the object as moving. The doctrine was quickly criticized on the ground that what it predicts is not the experience of hearing a melody, but a compacted block of sound in which all the earlier and the later notes are squeezed together, and similarly we would perceive movement as an object with a tail of its previous positions, like a comet.

speckled hen example An example used to cause problems for theories analysing perception in terms of *sense data. If perception is thought of as producing an internal mental 'picture' of the external world, then an internal image of a speckled hen should contain a definite number or configuration of speckles, just as a photograph would. But, according to the argument, experience involves no such precision.

speculative philosophy Term used by *Broad for attempts to synthesize an overall picture of reality as a whole, and of the place of mankind within it. Broad had in mind large-scale philosophies of the kind found in *Hegel or *Bradley, or many religious pictures of the cosmos. He believed that a major question prompting speculative philosophy was whether 'discursive form of cognition by means of general concepts can ever be completely adequate to the concrete Reality which it seeks to describe'. The antithesis to speculative philosophy was critical philosophy.

speech acts Acts performed when words are uttered. In his *How to Do Things with Words* (1962), J. L. *Austin classified these acts as follows: there is the *phonetic* act, of making noises, the *phatic* act of making a grammatical sentence, and the *rhetic* act of saying something meaningful. These together make up the *locutionary* act. There is then what is done *in* saying something, such as threatening or praying or promising: this is the *illocutionary* act. Finally, sayings may produce effects on hearers, such as frightening them: these are *perlocutionary* acts. Austin believed that careful attention to such distinctions would illuminate or eliminate many problems of philosophy, but whilst his classification has proven useful in some circumstances, it has not had this revolutionary effect. An earlier and lucid recognition of the different illocutionary functions of language is *Hobbes, *Human Nature*, xiii. 6.

Spencer, Herbert (1820–1903) English philosopher of evolution. Spencer was born in Derby of radical Wesleyan parents, and suffered a sporadic education, leaving him largely self-taught. His early individualism is recorded in the story that, having been sent to school with an uncle in Somerset at the age of 13, he ran away, returning to Derby in three days, by walking 48 miles the first day, 47 the second, and about 20 the third, with little food and no sleep. He became involved in radical politics, and from 1848 worked in London on the journal the *Economist*, becoming known in literary circles, and narrowly failing to become a suitor of the novelist George Eliot. His health growing precarious, he lived on small legacies and then on the considerable proceeds of his writings. His first major work was the book *Social Statics* (1851), which advocates an extreme political *libertarianism. *The Principles of Psychology* was published in 1855, and his very influential *Education*, advocating natural development of intelligence, the creation of pleasurable interest, and the importance of science in the curriculum, appeared in 1861. In 1857 he began to plan a vast system of philosophy, which, after Darwin's publication of the *Origin of Species* in 1859, turned into a scheme for a synthesis of the whole of scientific knowledge based upon the principles of evolution. His *First Principles* (1862) was followed over the succeeding years by volumes on the principles of biology, psychology (recasting the earlier work of the same title), sociology, and ethics. Although he attracted a large public following and attained the stature of a sage, his speculative work has not lasted well, and in his own time there were dissident voices. T. H. Huxley said that Spencer's definition of a tragedy was a deduction killed by a fact; *Carlyle called him a perfect vacuum, and *James wondered why half of England wanted to bury him in Westminster Abbey, and talked of the 'hurdy-gurdy monotony of him ... his whole system wooden, as if knocked together out of cracked hemlock boards' (*Pragmatism*, p. 39).

S

Spengler, Oswald (1880–1936) German historian and philosopher of history. Spengler was educated at various universities, and gained his doctorate with a thesis on *Heraclitus. His fame depends entirely on *Der Untergang des Abendlandes* (1918, trs. as *The Decline of the West*, 1932), whose oracular pessimism captured the mood of Germany after the First World War. Spengler saw history not as a linear progression, but as the flowering of a number (either nine or ten) of self-contained cultures, each with a characteristic spiritual tone, or conception of the space within which they are to act. The work was important in making a decisive break with the Hegelian concept of history as a process governed by reason. Instead Spengler's metaphors are biological: cultures go through a self-contained process of growing, going through their seasons, and perishing. There are no historically intelligible laws to this process. His speculations have been extensively criticized as insensitive to the interactions of cultures and to the thoughts and intentions of agents involved in the process.

Speusippus (*c*.407–339 BC) *Plato's nephew and successor as head of the *Academy from 347 to 339. Under Speusippus the Academy took the turn towards abstract mathematical studies, and the virtual equation of philosophy and mathematics, that probably led to the withdrawal of *Aristotle.

Spinoza, Benedictus de (1632–77) Dutch Jewish rationalist. Baruch or Benedict de Spinoza was born in Amsterdam into a distinguished Jewish family, exiled from Spain and living in the relative religious freedom of the Netherlands. He attended the Jewish school, and became learned in the work of Jewish and Arabic theologians; one of his teachers was the Rabbi Manasseh ben Israel, a distinguished liberal figure of the time. However, contact with dissident Christian movements, and with the scientific and philosophical thought of *Descartes, led Spinoza to distance himself from orthodox life, and in 1656 he was deemed a heretic, cast out of the synagogue, and cursed with the comprehensive 'anathema where with Joshua anathematized Jericho', of which one clause alone calls for him to be cursed with all the curses of the firmament.

For a short time Spinoza was exiled from Amsterdam, but he returned and began a life supporting himself by grinding lenses and teaching. During this period he wrote the *Short Treatise on God, Man, and his Well Being* (written in Latin but surviving in Dutch, trs. 1883). In 1660 he moved to the country, and began composing the *Renati Descartes Principiorum Philosophiae* (1663, trs. as *The Principles of Descartes' Philosophy*, 1905), a geometrically structured exposition of the philosophical system of Descartes. This was published in 1663. Now living at Voorburg, Spinoza became acquainted with Jan de Witt, the principal focus of opposition to the House of Orange. This led in 1670 to the *Tractatus Theologico-Politicus* (trs. as *Political Treatise*, 1883), a work whose advocacy of tolerance and peace caused it to be condemned by the Reformed Church in 1673, and banned the following year. At this time Spinoza moved to The Hague, where he lived with great frugality on a small pension, working on the *Ethics* and a grammar of Hebrew. In 1672 Spinoza undertook a small diplomatic mission to the invading French army, but on his return was under some suspicion as a spy, and narrowly escaped being killed by the mob, as de Witt had been before him. By now a recognized figure, he refused offers of various posts, and lived out his remaining years in the same frugal state, writing and corresponding. He abandoned his original intention of publishing the *Ethics*, believing that it would simply generate controversy and rancour. Spinoza's final publication was the *Tractatus de Intellectus Emendatione*, published in the year of his death (trs. as *Treatise on the Improvement of the Intellect*, 1883). He died of phthisis, possibly brought on by his trade as a lens-grinder. There remain numerous testimonies to his simplicity, virtue, charm, and courage.

The central themes of the *Ethics* are developed in the four parts of the book. These concern first God, then the nature and origin of the mind, the origin and nature of the emotions, and human servitude and the strength of the emotions. The stage is set by acceptance of a basic rationalist presumption, that the nature of the world is transparent to the intellect, so that relations of dependence amongst ideas reflect (or are perhaps identical with) relations of dependence amongst events and states in nature. Substance being conceived as that which is self-dependent, there follows the *ontological argument for the existence of God as the one necessary being, but not distinct from the world (for there is only one substance: any other substance would owe its existence to God, and therefore not be self-dependent). Rather God is immanent in the world, and individual things are themselves modes or modifications of God: the one reality is 'God or nature', **deus sive natura*. This God is naturally rather removed from the God of simple religious faith, and while Spinoza's crystalline remark that 'whoever loves God cannot strive that God should love him in return' has subsequently spoken to many thinkers, in his own time the accusation of atheism constantly hung over him.

Spinoza's *monism extends to mind and matter: each is a different characteristic, or way of rationally appreciating the essence of the same one eternal reality. Like Descartes, Spinoza believed that it is the intellect rather than the senses that discloses the essential nature of things. A complete and adequate idea of God shows that he has two attributes: he can be conceived under the heading of extension, or under that of thought. In other words God, or reality, can be conceived in these two incommensurable ways, and each discloses an attribute or part of his essence (a problem in interpreting Spinoza is that God is supposed to have infinitely many attributes, although only these two are found). Understanding aims to increase our knowledge of God (or the universe) by discovering the way in which it makes up a closed system, self-sufficient and completely unified, in which everything that happens is necessary, and nothing could be otherwise than it is.

Against this metaphysical background Spinoza clearly faces trouble making sense of the nature of the single self, and human activity, and these form the subject of the latter two books of the *Ethics*. For Spinoza, thinking is a consciousness of the body. The same mode is conceived under the attribute of extension and under that of thought, so that body and mind are not related causally, but as parallel expressions of the one reality. In this God-intoxicated system (as it was called by the German Romantic poet Friedrich Hardenberg), error and evil need explanation, and in each case Spinoza identifies them with privation. Error is the lack of adequate ideas, and evils are merely absences or privations, that 'express no essence'. (This approach to the problem of evil later received especial critical attention from *Hume.) The senses provide only modifications of our body but no knowledge, and most of our notions are only confused and lacking the marks of final adequacy. These are found in Spinoza's version of Descartes's clear and distinct ideas: conceptions of the formal essence of God that are inextricably joined to their own proof. Like the theorems of mathematics, they cannot be understood without being seen to be true.

In such a rigid and deterministic world there may seem to be no room for human *free will. But Spinoza finds its place by abstracting from the dimension of time. Freedom becomes the capacity to see the world under the heading of eternity, and without bondage to emotions and desires. These themselves are the result of ignorance of the causes whereby we are determined. Activity and agency are the result of adequate cognition. In other words, it stops being true that I am controlled by things, and starts being true that I control them, in so far as in my thoughts the course of events is displayed as it then turns out. (The equation of freedom with this unity of reason and reality played a major role in the subsequent philosophy of *Kant.) To advance towards this adequacy, emotions must be understood, and the aim of Spinoza's subtle attempt to provide a 'geometry of the emotions' is to show that most of what drives us is unknown to us, but that when we understand our motivations we gain control over them and emend or improve them (this idea has been hailed as the fundamental truth on which *psychoanalysis depends). In the end, true religion, true science, and true philosophy are identical, and each consists in the intellectual love of God.

In his political writings Spinoza draws out the implications of his system for the theory of government. It is the business of the state not to attempt to put limits on the exercise of reason, but to provide the conditions in which it may flourish: what is necessary is a constitutional democracy providing a forum for reason and freedom of opinion within a framework of law.

Spinoza's method and system went largely unappreciated during the subsequent ascendancy of *empiricist and *Enlightenment ideals, and the decline of the ontological argument at the hands of Hume and Kant. He was rediscovered by the German idealists, and indeed *absolute idealism is well seen as simply adding an element of time, or a capacity for dynamic self-realization, to the attributes of Spinoza's one God, whose essence is equally that of the spatially extended world, and that of reason itself.

SEE WEB LINKS

- An audio debate about Spinoza by three experts
- A list of internet resources on Spinoza, including his writings

spirit (Latin, *spiritus*, breath, life, soul, mind) When we describe things in terms of spirited responses, mean-spirited behaviour, a spirited waltz, and so on, we are characterizing them purely as lively or animated. It is a short, but perhaps philosophically fatal, step to thinking of the spirit as that which animates them: the principle or immaterial source from which the animation flows. One's own spirit becomes a soul or mind or Ego; while the principle from which all natural events emanate becomes the animating principle of the cosmos, or world-spirit. The notion of a **Geist* is that of a spirit that breathes through things, and in *Hegel the highest level of spirit, distinguished from the individual spirit and the social or political spirit, is the absolute spirit to whose realization world history is directed. *See also* ABSOLUTE IDEALISM.

spiritualism In contemporary usage not a version of the doctrine that *spirit is the ultimate substance of the world (*see* ABSOLUTE IDEALISM), but the superstitious belief that the spirits of the dead communicate with the living, usually through the agency of a medium.

split-brain phenomena The functioning of actual patients who have had the two hemispheres of the brain severed is well documented. The procedure is one of cutting the corpus callosum or 'thick-skinned body', a procedure known as cerebral commisurotomy. It was formerly used as a way of controlling various disorders including epilepsy, and has been one of the main techniques for studying the localization of function within the brain, showing for example the dominance of the left hemisphere in linguistic behaviour. Such studies also provide data on the many different layers of functioning (and many different ways it can go wrong) underlying the familiar unities of conscious experience.

Philosophical attention to these matters is apt to simplify, legitimately or not, in order to consider the possibility of two persons cohabiting in one body, or that of one person, whose functions are subserved by each of the different hemispheres, being relocated in two different bodies. The relationship between these *thought experiments and the actual facts is not close, for although the operation results in separate awareness in the right and left halves of the visual and auditory fields, away from experimental conditions subjects need to unify their experience, and except in cases of severe dysfunction do so as much as the rest of us do.

spontaneity/indifference The contrast is used by *Locke and then *Hume in their discussions of *free will. Liberty of spontaneity is the freedom to do something if we so choose, and is contrasted with forcible restraint or inability. It is to be distinguished from the liberty of indifference, a doubtful concept implying the absence of causation or necessity, hopefully coupled with responsibility. *See* LIBERTARIANISM (METAPHYSICAL).

square of opposition In traditional logic the square of opposition summarizes the logical relationships between the four forms of subject-predicate proposition known as A, E, I, O: All X are Y; no X are Y; some X are Y; some X are not Y.

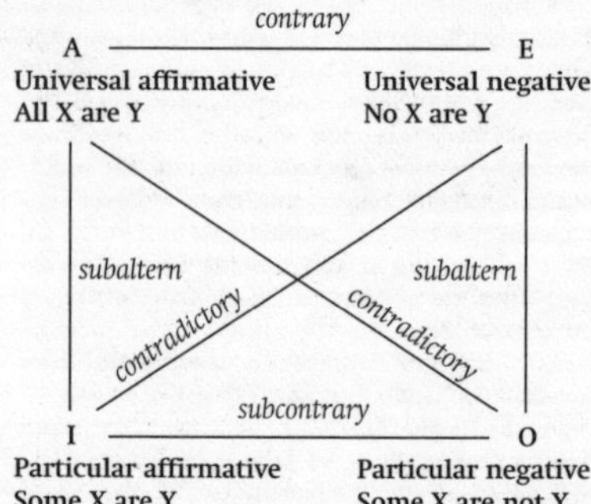

In the diagram, contradictories are propositions that cannot both be true and cannot both be false. Contraries cannot both be true, but can both be false. A proposition is subaltern to another if it is implied by it, but does not imply it. Subcontraries can both be true, but cannot both be false. The relations as indicated depend upon reading existential import into, for example, 'All X are Y'. In modern quantification theory the generalization carries no implication that there are any things that are X, and indeed, is bound to be true when there are none (*see* VACUOUS).

stadium paradox *See* ZENO'S PARADOXES.

Staël, Anne-Louise-Germaine Necker, Mme de (1766–1817) French writer. Mme de

Staël was the daughter of the financier Jacques Necker, and became one of the great *salonistes*, whose political, philosophical, and literary career was closely entwined with *Romanticism. She was exiled after her father's downfall in the French revolution, and again in 1804 by Napoleon, returning to Paris in 1814. Her principal philosophical work was *De l'influence des passions sur le bonheur des individuels et des nations* (1796, trs. as *A Treatise on the Influence of the Passions on the Happiness of Individuals and of Nations*, 1798), in which she develops the theme of the inseparable connection between thought and feeling. Her *De l'Allemagne* ('On Germany', 1813, published in London) was an important instrument for introducing German Romanticism to the French and the English.

stag hunt *See* ASSURANCE GAME.

Stagirite, the A description sometimes used to denote *Aristotle, who was born in Stagirus.

standard model An intended or natural *model of a theory. A non-standard model of a mathematical theory is one which is not isomorphic with the intended or natural model (*see* SKOLEM PARADOX).

statement That which is stated, as a judgement is something that is judged, and a proposition that which is proposed. However, all three terms have been used to indicate the *content of an utterance or written sentence. The distinction between a sentence or utterance and its content introduces a central problem of the theory of meaning. On the one hand, there is such a distinction, for one can identify a sentence without knowing what it means, any given sentence could have had a different content, and different sentences can share the same content (*see* TRANSLATION). On the other hand, to identify what is said is, it seems, no more than to find one's own words in which to say it: the mind has no 'pure' contact with disembodied thoughts, freed from their linguistic expression.

state of nature The state of human beings outside civil society, invoked by philosophers such as *Hobbes, *Locke, and *Rousseau, in order to clarify what is explained by nature as opposed to what is explained by convention, and what is justified in each way. For *Hobbes the state of nature is a war of all against all, and the life of man 'solitary, poor, nasty, brutish and short'. Society is justified as the remedy to this appalling state (*see also* SOCIAL CONTRACT). Others such as Rousseau have been more optimistic, up to the vision of noble anarchy with family-like relations performing all the role of social bonding that modern societies supplement with legal coercion. The whole notion is rejected as an analytic tool by *Hegel and *Marx, since it is society itself that has created the nature of human beings, and their capacity for rational action. *Sociobiology confirms that we naturally inherit a network of adaptations for life in society.

statistical explanation *See* PROBABILITY, PHILOSOPHY OF.

Steiner, Rudolf (1861–1925) German anthroposophist. Steiner's doctoral dissertation from Vienna concerned the philosophy of *Fichte; he also studied Goethe intensively. He eventually evolved a speculative and oracular metaphysic, anthroposophy, akin to *theosophy, and postulating different levels of psychical and astral powers. His educational influence was more benign, stressing harmonious and natural development, and Steiner or 'Waldorf' schools based on his teachings exist in many countries.

Stephen, Leslie (1832–1904) English man of letters and first editor of the *Dictionary of National Biography*. Stephen's main philosophical work was his *Science of Ethics* (1882), an evolutionary ethics, but he also wrote extensively in the history of ideas, including *History of English Thought in the Eighteenth Century* (1876) and *English Utilitarianism* (1900). He was the father of Virginia Woolf, who portrayed him as Mr Ramsey in *To the Lighthouse*.

stereotype In some approaches to *semantics it is supposed that general terms work by an initial connection with a stereotype (sometimes a prototype) or typical example of a class, from which other examples may differ in various ways and to varying degrees before finally losing the classification. In ethical and political contexts, stereotyping is the assumption that some features supposedly true of central examples of the class apply to all its members.

Stevenson, Charles Leslie (1908–79) American moral philosopher. Stevenson taught at Yale, and from 1946 to 1977 at the University of Michigan. His principal work was *Ethics and Language* (1944), a more careful and rigorous development of a *non-cognitive or *emotive theory of ethics than any before and many since. He coined the phrase *persuasive definition.

Stewart, Dugald (1753–1828) Scottish common sense philosopher. Stewart succeeded Adam *Ferguson as professor of moral philosophy in Edinburgh in 1785, having previously held a professorship of mathematics. He continued the tradition of *Reid and Adam *Smith but was more important as an immensely influential teacher, not only in Scotland but in France and America. Works included *Elements of the Philosophy of the Human Mind* (three volumes, 1792, 1814, and

1827) and *Philosophy of the Active and Moral Powers of Man* (1828).

sthenic (Greek, *sthenos*, strength) Adjective applied by Dr John Brown in the mid-18th century to diseases distinguished by excessive nervous energy, and applied by *Kant to vigorous or exciting emotions.

Stillingfleet, Edward (1635–99) English Churchman. A Fellow of St John's College, Cambridge, Stillingfleet became Archdeacon of London in 1677, Dean of St Pauls in 1678, and Bishop of Worcester in 1689. He feared that his own attempts to see reason in Church of England doctrine were undermined by *Locke's new 'way of ideas'. In 1697 he wrote *The Bishop of Worcester's Answer to Mr. Locke's Letter*, in which he criticized John Locke for undermining the Trinity. Locke rebutted his criticisms, but changes made in the later editions of the *Essay* may reflect Stillingfleet's impact.

stipendium peccati mors est Latin, the wages of sin is death.

stipulative definition A definition stipulating how a term is to be used, rather than answering to some previous rule or pattern of usage.

Stirner, Max (1806–56) German firebrand. Originally Johann Kasper Schmidt, Stirner is remembered philosophically for *Der Einziger und sein Eigenthum* (1845, trs. as *The Ego and His Own*, 1907). This was an attack on left Hegelians, particularly Feuerbach, and on the persistence of outright fictions in the theory of the state. It championed not so much psychological *egoism, as an ethic of self-mastery, autonomy, and freedom from the domination of society and other people. Engels and *Marx devoted a great deal of *The German Ideology* to combating it. In recent years Stirner's idiosyncratic writing has been heralded as anticipating both postmodern literary style, and doctrinally the worry that notions like rationality and objectivity are disguises for an inheritance of oppression and domination by semi-religious categories.

S

stoa (Greek, porch) Especially the *stoa poikile* or painted porch in which the Stoics (*see* STOICISM) originally taught.

stochastic process A process characterized by the values taken by a set of *random variables whose values change with time. Standard examples include the length of a queue, where there is a probability of someone leaving or entering in a given interval of time, but the actual events of people leaving and entering are randomly distributed; or the size of a population, or the quantity of water in a reservoir.

Stoicism A unified logical, physical, and moral philosophy, taking its name from the *stoa poikile* or painted porch in Athens where Stoic doctrine was taught. The first recognized Stoic was *Zeno of Citium, who founded the school *c.*300 BC. Other early Stoics were *Cleanthes of Assos and *Chrysippus of Soli. The middle stoa, whose members included *Panaetius of Rhodes and Posidonius of Apamea (*c.*135–*c.*51 BC), was responsible for introducing Stoicism to the Roman world, where it had a lasting effect. The late stoa was Roman, and its most distinguished members included *Epictetus and *Seneca. As a professed system Stoicism fought running battles, especially with the sceptical philosophers of the *Academy.

Stoic epistemology was based on the *phantasia kataleptikē* or apprehensive perception. A perception has to fill certain conditions in order to be veridical, and these conditions (clarity, common consent, probability, system) were variously attacked by sceptical opponents. The cosmology of the Stoics was firmly deterministic and orderly, as the eternal course of things passes through returning creative cycles (*see* ETERNAL RETURN), in accordance with the creative principle or **logos spermatikos*. Stoic proofs of the existence of God centred on versions of the argument to *design (hence the name Cleanthes in Hume's *Dialogues concerning Natural Religion*).

The capstone of Stoic philosophy was an ethic of the consolations of identification with the impartial, inevitable, moral order of the universe. It is an ethic of self-sufficient, benevolent calm, with the virtuous peace of the wise man rendering him indifferent to poverty, pain, and death, so resembling the spiritual peace of God. This fortitude and indifference can sound sublime, but also sound like stark insensibility. As Adam *Smith objects, 'By Nature the events which immediately affect that little department in which we ourselves have some little management and direction ... are the events which interest us the most, and which chiefly excite our desires and aversions, our hopes and fears, our joys and sorrows' (*Theory of the Moral Sentiments*, vii. 2. 1). By being above all that, the Stoic is also less than human, and the pursuit of Stoical indifference becomes a celebration of *apathy (*see also* AGENT-CENTRED MORALITY). However, the generally individualistic cast of Greek ethics is tempered in Stoicism by the need to recognize the creative spark in each individual, giving the Stoic a duty to promote a political and civil order that mirrors the order of the created cosmos.

SEE WEB LINKS

- An audio discussion of Stoicism by three American philosophers
- A list of internet resources on Stoicism, including classic works

Stratonician presumption The presumption voiced by *Strato of Lampsacus that the burden of proof lies not on the atheist, but on those who want to maintain the existence of a deity with some particular cluster of attributes.

Strato of Lampsacus (d. 269 BC) Head of the *Peripatetic school after *Theophrastus. He held a limited theory of the void as a kind of porosity in space. He also argued against the universal teleology of the *Stoics, although it is not known to what extent he rejected Aristotelian teleological thinking in biology.

Strauss, David Friedrich (1808–74) German theologian and historian. His *Das Leben Jesu kritisch bearbeitet* of 1835–6 (trs. as *The Life of Jesus Critically Examined* by George Eliot, 1846) created an enormous storm by viewing the historicity of the New Testament through new and sceptical historical spectacles. Strauss himself preserved a mythological interpretation of the value of Christianity, seeing it in Hegelian mode as a phase in the existence of humanity rather than part of the biography of God, but in later years he became a more forthright atheist.

Strauss, Leo (1899–1973) German *émigré* historian of ideas and political theorist. Strauss was professor of political science in the university of Chicago from 1949 to 1968. An élitist and critic of political egalitarianism, Strauss lamented the morally impoverished political theory of the modern world, from *Machiavelli through Hobbes to modern liberalism, all of which he contrasted unfavourably with the morally rich writings of Plato and Aristotle. He interpreted these as advancing an '*esoteric' philosophy, hidden between the lines and concealed from all except initiates, which meant primarily himself and his students. Strauss's own experience was shaped by the collapse of the Weimar Republic, and he saw the modern liberal state as prey to *relativism, *nihilism, and a flabby inability to defend itself and its ideals. His influence has been much greater in political science, where the right of the government to deceive and ignore the masses is a staple of illiberal conservative doctrine, than in philosophy or classical studies. His students included a galaxy of American 'neo-conservatives', as well as writers such as Allan Bloom whose *The Closing of the American Mind* brought Straussianism into the American mainstream. His own books include *Persecution and the Art of Writing* (1952) and *Natural Right and History* (1953).

straw man To argue against a straw man is to interpret someone's position in an unfairly weak way, and so argue against a position that nobody holds, or is likely to hold.

Strawson, Peter Frederick (1919–2006) English philosopher. Born in London and educated at St John's College, Oxford, Strawson taught at University College, Oxford, from 1948, and became professor of metaphysics in 1968. His early work concerned logic and language, very much in the spirit of the general tradition of *ordinary language philosophy of the time. To this period belongs his celebrated attack on *Russell's theory of *definite descriptions (*see* PRESUPPOSITION). In 1959, his *Individuals* marked a return to wider metaphysical concerns. His reputation was consolidated by *The Bounds of Sense* (1966), which is a magnificent tour of the metaphysics of *Kant, and numerous papers on epistemology, freedom, naturalism, and scepticism. In general Strawson stood for a defence of the *manifest image, or common way of regarding the world. Even on issues such as that of *free will he was sceptical of the power of either scientific theory or philosophical argument to motivate changes to the common conceptual scheme.

stream of consciousness In the *Principles of Psychology*, i. 9. 239, *James wrote: 'Consciousness ... does not appear to itself chopped up in bits ... a "river" or "stream" are the metaphors by which it is most naturally described.'

strict implication In the *modal logic of C. I. Lewis, if it is not possible that *p* and not-*q*, then *p* is said to strictly imply *q*. *See also* STRICT IMPLICATION, PARADOX OF.

strict implication, paradox of It follows from the definition of *strict implication that a necessary proposition is strictly implied by any proposition, and that an impossible proposition strictly implies any proposition. If strict implication corresponds to '*q* follows from *p*', then this means that a necessary proposition follows from anything at all, and anything at all follows from an impossible proposition. This is a problem if we wish to distinguish between valid and invalid arguments with necessary conclusions or impossible premises. *See also* RELEVANCE LOGIC.

structuralism A general intellectual movement whose headquarters have been in France, and whose heyday was in the 1960s. The common feature of structuralist positions is the belief that phenomena of human life are not intelligible except through their interrelations. These relations constitute a structure, and behind local variations in the surface phenomena there are constant laws of abstract structure. Thus superficially diverse sets of myth, or works of art, or practices of marriage might be revealed as sharing the same pattern. Structuralism owes its origin to the work of *Saussure in linguistics, and one form of the doctrine holds that all sign systems are linguistic in nature. One of the early successes of structuralist investigation in linguistics was the discovery that phonetic units (phonemes) gain their identity through a network of relationships (opposition, difference) between sounds rather than through the brute physical nature of a given sound. Structuralism in linguistics embraced not only phonetics but semantics, and describes the approach of the Prague school, and the dominant American school of linguistics (E. Sapir, L. Bloomfield) for the first half of the 20th century. Although *Chomsky's approach to linguistics is in this broad sense structuralist, his opposition to the Bloomfield school lay in their concentration on surface structure at the expense of deep structure (*see* GENERATIVE GRAMMAR).

In anthropology, the leading structuralist was *Lévi-Strauss, whose *Les Structures élémentaires de la parenté* (1949) seeks to show how a wide variety of kinship and institutional arrangements can be referred back to basic structures of communication, thought of as fundamental patterns of the working of the mind, and from which the surface variety is generated. Other structuralist approaches to their respective subjects are found in the psychoanalytic theories of *Lacan and the Marxism of *Althusser. *See also* POST-STRUCTURALISM.

structure, deep and surface *See* GENERATIVE GRAMMAR.

Sturm und Drang (German, storm and stress) The first *Romantic reaction in Germany against the classical calm of the *Enlightenment. The movement, whose leaders included *Herder, *Goethe, and *Schiller, emphasized the values of genius, emotional turmoil, and creative enthusiasm. The movement took its name from a play by Maximilian Klinger.

Suárez, Francisco (1548–1617) Major Jesuit *scholastic philosopher and theologian. Born in Granada, Suárez became a Jesuit in 1564. His principal work is the *Disputationes Metaphysicae* ('Metaphysical Disputations', 1597), although his writings occupy 28 volumes in the Paris edition of 1856. He is frequently ranked next to *Aquinas as the greatest scholastic thinker, and is the principal exponent of the doctrinal thought of the Jesuits; his writings were extensively studied by the great philosophers of the 17th century and his work on divine, natural, and human law influenced *Grotius. His last words were 'I would never have thought it was so sweet to die.'

subaltern *See* SYLLOGISM.

subconscious *See* PSYCHOANALYSIS, UNCONSCIOUS.

subcontraries *See* SYLLOGISM.

subject *See* EGO, SELF.

subjective idealism *See* IDEALISM.

subjective probability *See* PERSONALISM; PROBABILITY, PHILOSOPHY OF.

subjectivism/objectivism One of the leading polarities about which much *epistemology, and especially the theory of ethics, tends to revolve. The view that some commitments are subjective goes back at least to the *Sophists, and the way in which opinion varies with subjective constitution, situation, perspective, etc., is a constant theme in Greek *scepticism (*see* AENESIDEMUS, PYRRHO, SEXTUS EMPIRICUS). The misfit between the subjective source of judgements in an area, and their objective appearance, or the way they make apparently independent claims capable of being apprehended correctly or incorrectly, is the driving force behind *error theories and *eliminativism. Attempts to reconcile the two aspects include moderate *anthropocentrism, and certain kinds of *projectivism. *See also* REALISM/ANTI-REALISM.

subject/object Most Western philosophers have been content with a dualism between, on the one hand, the subject of experience, and on the other hand, the world, the objects of experience. However, this dualism contains a trap, since it can easily seem impossible to give any coherent account of the relation between the two. This has been a permanent motivation towards either *idealism, which brings objects back into the mind of the subject, or some kind of *materialism which sees the subject as little more than one object among others. Other options include *neutral monism.

sublimation The repression of a 'lower' feeling and substitution of a 'higher' one, as when *sexual desire is substituted by *Platonic love.

sublime A concept deeply embedded in 18th-century *aesthetics, but deriving from the 1st century rhetorical treatise *On the Sublime* by Longinus. The sublime is great, fearful, noble, calculated to arouse sentiments of pride and majesty, as well as awe and sometimes terror. According to Alexander *Gerard, writing in 1759, 'When a large object is presented, the mind expands itself to the extent of that object, and is filled with one grand sensation, which totally possessing it, composes it into a solemn sedateness and strikes it with deep silent wonder and admiration: it finds such a difficulty in spreading itself to the dimensions of its object, as enlivens and invigorates its frame: and having overcome the opposition which this occasions, it sometimes imagines itself present in every part of the scene which it contemplates; and from the sense of this immensity, feels a noble pride, and entertains a lofty conception of its own capacity.' In *Kant's aesthetic theory the sublime 'raises the soul above the height of vulgar commonplace'. We experience the vast spectacles of nature as 'absolutely great' and of irresistible might and power. This perception is fearful, but by conquering this fear, and by regarding as small 'those things of which we are wont to be solicitous', we quicken our sense of moral freedom. So we turn the experience of frailty and impotence into one of our true, inward moral freedom as the mind triumphs over nature, and it is this triumph of reason that is truly sublime. Kant thus paradoxically places our sense of the sublime in an awareness of ourselves as transcending nature, rather than in an awareness of ourselves as a frail and insignificant part of it. Most mountaineers and sailors disagree. *See also* ENVIRONMENTAL ETHICS.

subsistence Existence, but of a rather shadowy kind, apt for *universals, fictional characters, and other insubstantial entities. The term is associated with *Meinong, but the idea that varieties of existence can be distinguished has been a favourite target of modern logicians. *See also* DEFINITE DESCRIPTION.

sub specie aeternitatis (Latin, under the heading of eternity) The term is associated with *Spinoza.

substance (Latin, *sub*, under, *stare*, stand: that which stands under) Many concerns and disputes cluster around the ideas associated with this term. The substance of a thing may be: (i) its essence, or that which makes it what it is. This will ensure that the substance of a thing is that which remains through change in its properties. In *Aristotle (*Metaphysics* Z, vii) this essence becomes more than just the matter, but a unity of matter and form. (ii) That which can exist by itself, or does not need a subject for existence, in the way that properties need objects; hence (iii) that which bears properties. A substance is then the subject of predication, that about which things are said as opposed to the things said about it. Substance in the last two senses stands opposed to modifications such as quantity, quality, relations, etc. It is hard to keep this set of ideas distinct from the doubtful notion of a *substratum, something distinct from any of its properties, and hence incapable of characterization. The notion of substance tends to disappear in empiricist thought in favour of the sensible qualities of things, with the notion of that in which they inhere giving way to an empirical notion of their regular concurrence. But this in turn is problematic, since it only makes sense to talk of the concurrence of *instances* of qualities, not of qualities themselves. So the problem of what it is for a quality to be instanced remains.

Metaphysics inspired by modern science tends to reject the concept of substance in favour of concepts such as that of a *field or a *process, each of which may seem to provide a better example of a fundamental physical category.

substitutional quantification A sentence containing a *quantifier is usually interpreted by assigning values to the variable it contains. Values are thought of as 'objects'; hence this is termed objectual quantification. By contrast, the quantifier is interpreted substitutionally if expressions are substituted for the variable, and the result evaluated according to whether any of the substitutions produce a true sentence. Substitutional quantifiers are frequently written Σ and Π. (Σx)(logicians are x) would be evaluated as true, with the quantifier interpreted susbstitutionally, if there is a sentence 'logicians are ... ' which is true.

substitutivity *salva veritate* (Latin, substitution saving truth) *See* EXTENSION/INTENSION, REFERENTIALLY OPAQUE/TRANSPARENT.

substrate (substratum) The dark side of *substance. The thing that bears properties, as opposed to the properties themselves, but conceived as an indescribable 'something we know not what', since any characterization of it merely mentions one of the properties with which it has to be contrasted. *Berkeley charges *Locke, perhaps unfairly, with requiring that this idea be intelligible when, according to Berkeley, it is not.

success word A word whose application entails the truth of an embedded clause, or the achievement of some result. 'I remember, know, realize, perceive that p' all imply the truth of p. Many words describing our knowledge of things presuppose success or achievement. We can only know what is true, remember what happened, or perceive what is there. Other words have to be found for illusions of knowing, remembering, or perceiving, suggesting that success is a kind of default state. The point is sometimes used to query the intelligibility of Cartesian doubt (*see* METHOD OF DOUBT). *See also* FACTIVE.

sufficient condition *See* CONDITION, NECESSARY/SUFFICIENT.

sufficient reason, principle of Principle usually associated with *Leibniz, for whom it had a fundamental status, although found in earlier medieval thought, particularly that of *Abelard. It is sometimes described as the principle that nothing can be so without there being a reason why it is so. But the reason has to be of a particularly potent kind: eventually it has to ground contingent facts in necessities, and in particular in the reason an omnipotent and perfect being would have for actualizing one possibility rather than another. Among the consequences of the principle is Leibniz's relational doctrine of space, since if space were an infinite box there could be no reason for the world to be at one point in it rather than another, and God placing it at any one point would violate the principle. In Abelard, as in Leibniz, the principle eventually forces the recognition that the actual world is the best of all possible worlds, since anything else would be inconsistent with the creative power that actualizes possibilities.

Sufism From around 800 the term *Sufi* (from the Persian for coarse wool, denoting the kind of garment worn) was applied to Islamic mystics who adopted ascetic practices as a means of achieving union with God. The philosophers al-*Ghazali and al-*Farabi practised Sufism and contributed to its mystical doctrines. *See also* ILLUMINATIONISM.

SEE WEB LINKS

- An outline of the history and practice of Sufism
- An annotated bibliography on Sufism

Suhrawardi *See* ILLUMINATIONISM.

suicide Intentional self-killing. Wide definitions would include martyrdom and self-sacrifice; narrower definitions would be motivated by the thought that these cases are frequently noble and heroic, whereas suicide is a common object of moral prohibition. This prohibition was shaky in the early Christian tradition, and uncommon in other cultures, where suicide in various circumstances may be institutionally embedded. The ban was fortified in the Middle Ages and it became a bone of contention between *Enlightenment thinkers, notably *Hume, and conservatives such as *Kant. Suicide became fashionable in the *Romantic era, but diagnosed as the result of either psychological illness (*Freud) or the pressures of social conditions (*Durkheim) by the 20th century. An awakening perception of the intolerable ways the medical profession manages death, especially in the United States, has led to death-with-dignity movements, assisted by sympathetic physicians and self-help groups. *See also* ACTS/OMISSIONS DOCTRINE, EUTHANASIA.

sui generis Latin, of its own kind.

summum bonum (Latin, the maximum good) That which is an *end in itself. The nature of this state preoccupied both ancient and Christian writers (*see* AGATHON), although *Hobbes probably had the last word: 'But for an *utmost* end, in which the ancient philosophers have placed *felicity*, and disputed much concerning the way thereto, there is no such thing in this world, nor way to it, more than to Utopia: for while we live, we have desires, and desire presupposeth a further end.'

sum set The set of all members of members of a set: in other words, the union of all the elements of a set.

sum set, axiom of The axiom of *Zermelo–Fraenkel set theory providing that for each set S the collection $\{x:(\exists y)(y \in S \,\&\, x \in y)\}$, the *union of S, is a set.

Sun Tsu *See* SUNZI.

sunyata (Sanskrit, emptiness) Buddhist concept denying the existence of lonely properties, in other words those intrinsic properties of a thing that could survive it having no relations with other things, or being the only thing in its universe. *See* INTRINSIC/EXTRINSIC PROPERTIES.

Sunzi Much-admired Chinese text on The Art of Warfare, ascribed to Sun Wu, a contemporary of *Confucius. He is supposed to have demonstrated its principles on a bevy of the emperor's concubines, who quickly became a disciplined body after he beheaded a couple of them for giggling.

supererogatory Deeds that are not 'required' but which go beyond the call of duty, as, for example, acts of exceptional goodness and heroism. The category is interesting, in that many ethical theories fail to recognize it: e.g. for a direct *utilitarian, either an action maximizes happiness, in which case it ought to be done, or it does not, in which case it ought not to be done. Protestant theology also rejected the category, since in Catholic theology the moral surplus arising from acts of sainthood was the property of the Church, and hence could be bought and sold.

superman *See* ÜBERMENSCH.

supervaluation An approach to the problems of *vagueness. Suppose a vague predicate has things to which it definitely applies (things in its positive extension), things to which it definitely does not (in its negative extension), and a penumbra. Then we imagine a plurality of interpretations or precisifications, each of which has no penumbra, but behaves classically. However, each may put the division between the positive and negative extensions in different places. Then the assignment of truth-value for all such interpretations is a supervaluation. Anything true in all precisifications is supertrue; anything false is superfalse. A nice property is that classical laws such as $(p \vee -p)$ are supertrue—true in all interpretations, in spite of their variation in placing the boundaries.

supervenience Term introduced by *Hare to describe the way that ethical properties relate to other, psychological and natural properties of things. Properties of one kind, F, supervene upon those of another kind, G, when things are F in virtue of being G. Thus a person cannot just be good, but must be good in virtue of possessing other properties, such as courage or kindness. The supervening property relates to the underlying qualities in at least this way: if one thing possesses the underlying properties and is F, then any other thing with the same underlying properties must share the resultant property F. Sometimes a distinction is made between weak supervenience, where this is held only of other actual things, and strong supervenience, where it applies to all possible things.

The notion is exploited in many areas: for example, biological properties plausibly supervene upon chemical ones; mental properties upon physical ones; *dispositional properties and powers upon categorical ones, and so on. One promise the notion holds out is that by its means we can understand the relation of such different layers of description without attempting a *reduction of the one area to the other. The value of this promise depends on how well we understand the supervenience relation itself. If it is a dangling, inexplicable, metaphysical fact that the Fs relate in this way to the Gs, then supervenience inherits rather than solves the problems of understanding the various areas. *See also* VARIABLE REALIZATION.

suppositio Medieval term for the subject of a proposition, or that for which the general term in subject position stands. It was medieval doctrine that the general terms in a *syllogism stand for things, and are grammatically interchangeable, linked together in a subject-predicate or categorical proposition by the *copula. This raises the question of what they each stand for, and what relation has to hold between the things they stand for in order for a sentence to say something true. If it is also supposed that for a sentence to be true the terms must stand for the same thing, then the matter becomes extremely complex, and the doctrine of *suppositio* eventually embraced distinctions such as formal, material, simple, personal, determinate *suppositio* and others.

sure thing principle A principle used in *game theory and *decision theory, also called the 'strong independence assumption'. It states that if outcome x and outcome x' are indifferent in themselves, then for any outcome y, a probability mix of x and y must be indifferent to a probability mix of x' and y. Denying the principle is a possible response to the *Allais paradox.

surface structure *See* GENERATIVE GRAMMAR.

surjection *See* FUNCTION (LOGICAL).

survival and immortality *See* IMMORTALITY.

sutra (Sanskrit, thread or precept) A single verse or aphorism of Hindu or Buddhist teaching.

Swedenborg, Emanuel (1688–1772) Swedish natural philosopher, theologian, and mystic. Swedenborg was born into a prominent ecclesiastical family, and educated at Uppsala. While working in the Board of Mines between 1716 and 1747 he made various scientific discoveries, and is regarded as one of the founders of crystallography. However, becoming convinced that he had direct contact with the spiritual world, he resigned and set about teaching and creating a new church or fraternity of those who followed his doctrines. His philosophy is a compound of *panpsychism, *pantheism, and *theosophy.

syllogism A syllogism (properly, a categorical syllogism) is the inference of one proposition from two premises. An example is: all horses have tails; all things with tails are four-legged; so all horses are four-legged. Each premise has one term in common with the conclusion, and one term in common with the other premise. The term that does not occur in the conclusion is called the middle term. The major premise of the syllogism is the premise containing the predicate of the conclusion (the major term), and the minor premise contains its subject (the minor term). So the first premise of the example is the minor premise, the second the major premise, and 'having a tail' is the middle term. The four kinds of proposition distinguished in syllogistic reasoning are universal affirmatives (all men are mortal), called A propositions, particular affirmatives (some men are sick), called I propositions, universal negatives (no men are trustworthy), called E propositions, and particular negatives (some men are not lawyers), called O propositions. This enables syllogisms to be classified according to the form of the premises and the conclusions (*see also* SQUARE OF OPPOSITION). The other classification is by figure, or way in which the middle term is placed in the premises. The conclusion is always of subject-predicate (S–P) form, and the middle term is M. The four figures are illustrated in the diagram:

Figure 1	Figure 2	Figure 3	Figure 4
M–P	P–M	M–P	P–M
S–M	S–M	M–S	M–S
S–P	S–P	S–P	S–P

The example given was a syllogism of the first figure. Mnemonics, in the form of names with the vowels indicating the A, E, I, O, forms, help students to remember the valid forms, called moods of the syllogism. Valid syllogisms of the first figure are Barbara (AAA), Celarent (EAE), Darii (AII), and Ferio (EIO); of the second, Cesare, Camestres, Festino, and Baroco; of the third, Darapti, Disamis, Datisi, Felapton, Bocardo, and Ferison; and of the fourth, Bramantip, Camenes, Dimaris, Fesapo, and Fresison.

Rules exist for converting one form to another, and every valid syllogism may be converted to a syllogism of the first figure. Another set of rules concerns the distribution of terms. Roughly, a term is distributed if it covers all of its class. A test is whether the proposition containing the term must remain true if the term is qualified, or replaced with a term applying to only a subset of the class of things to which the original applies. Thus 'all men are mortal' distributes the term 'man' because it implies that all blind men are mortal; 'not every animal is useful' does not distribute 'animal' because it does not imply that not every farmyard animal is useful. In a universal affirmative (A form) the subject is distributed but the predicate is not; in a universal negative (E form) both are distributed; in a particular affirmative (I form) neither is distributed, and in a particular negative (O form) the subject is not distributed but the predicate is. A syllogism cannot be valid unless the middle term is distributed at least once, and any term distributed in the conclusion must be distributed in its premise.

Although the theory of the syllogism dominated logic until the 19th century, it remained a piecemeal affair, able to deal with only a relatively small number of valid forms of argument. There have subsequently been rearguard actions attempting to extend the power of syllogistic reasoning, but in general it has been eclipsed by the modern theory of *quantification (*see also* PREDICATE CALCULUS), which gives greater expressive power for less complexity.

S

symbolic logic General term, not currently much used, for the study of formal *logic. Generally, the study of *logical form requires using particular schematic letters and variables ('symbols') to stand where terms of a particular category might occur in sentences.

symmetric A *relation is symmetric when if R*xy*, then R*yx*. For example, if a person *x* has the same parents as *y*, then *y* has the same parents as *x*.

sympathy The ability to share in another person's feelings and concerns, with the accompanying delight in their joys and grief at their sorrows. Sympathy is supposed by *Hume to be the basis of a more impartial concern for human well-being, and is a central plank in the ethical theory of Adam *Smith.

symptom An empirically detectable feature of a situation which is a reliable sign of some further truth. It is sometimes contrasted with a *criterion, as having only a contingent connection with the further fact of which it is a sign.

synaesthesia Confusion between the senses, as when musical notes are experienced as coloured.

syncategorematic Traditionally, a categorematic term is any term that stands alone, as a meaningful constituent of a proposition, while syncategorematic terms need others to make a meaningful unit. A more precise definition can be given for a formal language, where the distinction corresponds roughly to those expressions that are assigned objects, functions, and relations in the interpretation of a formula, and those that are not. For instance, the parentheses in '$(3+4)\times 2$' are not interpreted as referring to anything when this expression is evaluated, although they play a role in determining how it is evaluated. But modern logic assigns an interpretation to terms like 'and' and 'not' which are traditionally syncategorematic. The distinction loses some of its bite in post-*Fregean theories of meaning, which tend to make the *sentence into the smallest meaningful piece of language, with all word-meaning described in terms of contribution to sentence-meaning.

syncretism A movement aimed at establishing a harmony between apparently opposing positions in philosophy or theology.

synderesis (synteresis) The supposed natural or innate ability of the mind to know the first principles of ethics and moral reasoning. Although traced to *Aristotle, the phrase came to the modern era through St Jerome, whose *scintilla conscientiae* (gleam of conscience) was a popular concept in early scholasticism. But it is mainly associated with *Aquinas, as an infallible, natural, simple, and immediate grasp of first moral principles. *Conscience, by contrast, is more concerned with particular instances of right and wrong, and can be in error.

syndicalism (French, *syndicat*, trade union) The movement that seeks to transfer control of the means of production to associations of workers, rather than to the state. In 19th-century France the movement had connections with *anarchism (making anarcho-syndicalism), since each movement shared a distrust both of private ownership of the means of production, and of the centralizing power of the state. *See also* OWEN, PROUDHON.

synonym Two words are synonyms when they mean the same. Similarly two phrases or sentences are synonymous when they mean the same. The usual criterion is that meaning is preserved when they are substituted one for the other. Two terms may be cognitively synonymous although associated with a different *tone, and the choice of one synonym or another may have *implicatures, but these will not be due to a difference of what is actually said. However, the notorious difficulties for translators of finding synonyms across different languages testify to the delicate problem of quite how much is built into the meaning of terms. Philosophically, synonymy was crucial to the methodology of the *analytic tradition, whose goal of laying out the structure of our concepts is only realistic if we know whether what is displayed is in fact the structure of the original, and not some reconstruction or differing concept altogether. Knowing this will require judging whether the analysans or analysing expression is indeed synonymous with the analysandum or expression to be analysed. Although difficulties with the relationship had always been recognized, it was *Quine who first made an effective attack on the notion of synonymy, in his widely influential article 'Two Dogmas of Empiricism' (1951). Quine complained that the ideal of synonymy demands a sharp division between what we put down to linguistic convention, and what we put down to generally held truths about the world, but that in practice this division cannot be sustained. The question of whether we have 'changed the meaning' of a term when we come to believe something new about its subject matter is generally speaking unanswerable and unprofitable. The extent of Quine's critique is, however, problematic. It seems essential to any understanding of language, and especially any belief that logic applies to language, that terms mean the same on one occurrence as they do on another, so at least in some cases a notion of synonymy must be applicable. A compromise would be that a notion of synonymy is applicable when in our actual practices of interpretation we refuse to contemplate the possibility of meaning shift; however, when such possibilities genuinely arise, the way we settle the matter may be subject to a high degree of indeterminacy. *See also* INDETERMINACY OF TRANSLATION.

syntactic engine *See* REPRESENTATIONALISM.

syntax The syntax of a language is its grammar, or the way its expressions may be put together to form sentences. A syntactic study is one that is not concerned with sentence-meaning, but with the purely formal aspects of word combination in a language. In studying formal languages (*see* LOGICAL CALCULUS) the notion of a *well-formed formula is purely syntactic, as is that of *proof, since each is defined without regard to the interpretation the sentences of the language are intended to have. *See also* MODEL THEORY. It is a doctrine of *Chomskyan linguistics that the syntax of a natural language is so complex, yet picked up by the learning infant so quickly, that we have to postulate an innate universal grammar, or disposition to select only certain forms as grammatical out of the theoretical possibilities.

synthesis The process reconciling a thesis and an antithesis, or the outcome of such a procedure: *see* DIALECTICAL MATERIALISM.

synthetic *See* ANALYTIC/SYNTHETIC.

systematic ambiguity **1.** The phenomenon noticed by *Aristotle whereby terms may apply in different, yet associated, ways, to different categories of thing: a place may be cheerful, and so may a person. **2.** In the theory of *types *Russell had to postulate a systematic ambiguity linking the different meanings that expressions would have when used at different levels in the hierarchy, since it is clear that something is the same about the use, say, of the identity predicate when linking objects at one level, and at another.

system of logic A system of logic is any attempt to codify the rules whereby valid inferences may be made. The preferred term is a *logical calculus or formal language, in which precise meaning is given to the idea of codification.

systems theory Not properly a single theory, but any approach to a complex structure that abstracts away from the particular physical, chemical, or biological nature of its components and simply considers the structure they together implement, in terms of the functional role of individual parts and their contribution to the functioning of the whole.

tabula rasa (Latin, blank tablet or slate) The term used by *scholastics, e.g. *Aquinas (*Summa*, Ia 79. 2), to indicate the state of a mind on which no sensation has been impressed. It is frequently used to describe the similar contention of *Locke that there are no *innate ideas. *See also* *NIHIL IN INTELLECTU NISI PRIUS IN SENSU.*

tacit (knowledge, consent, communication) A state of a person or a relation between people that is not expressed, or one of which the subjects may even be unaware, but which can be inferred from their other capacities and activities. An agent able to construe an indefinite number of sentences of a language may be said to have tacit knowledge of the grammar of the language. Someone who voluntarily remains within the jurisdiction of a state is said by *Locke to have tacitly consented to its laws. Tacit communication is the unexpressed recognition of the position of others that leads to strategies for common activity (*see* CONVENTION). The notion reflects the fact that people often behave 'as if' they have the described knowledge, or have made the consent or communication in question. But attributing further psychological reality to the concept is problematic: for example, *Hume criticized Locke's political application of the notion on the grounds that the subject typically has nowhere else to which it is possible to go, and so is not so much behaving as if consenting to the authority of the state, but is behaving as if having to make the best of a possibly bad job.

Tagore, Rabindranath (1861–1941) Indian philosopher and poet. Tagore was born in Calcutta and studied in London, and became one of the best-known international figures of the intellectual world in the first decades of the 20th century. He won the Nobel Prize for literature in 1913 and was knighted in 1915. His philosophical works have religious and ethical themes, and their tendency is to try to unite and synthesize the best in apparently opposing positions, and especially in the traditions of the East and the West. Probably his best-known book in the West is *The Religion of Man*, delivered as the Hibbert lectures in Oxford and published in 1931.

tantra (Sanskrit, weft, continuous text) A sacred text in Tibetan and other forms of *Buddhism. Many tantras concern the balance between Shiva and Shakti, the male and female principles, and form the basis for various practices of meditation.

tao (Chinese, the way) The source and principle of the cosmic order; the constant flow of the life force (**chi*) in unceasing change. As a cosmic principle the *tao* bears some similarity to **logos*, although it is also elusive, deep, and obscure and cannot be expressed in words. The *tao* of humanity and that of the universe are one, and in this lies the key to a completely satisfying and harmonious human existence. The 'easy way' of *Taoism is one of being in tune with nature and the universe. In *Confucianism the *tao* is the way of the moral law, or the path by which a fully moral existence is achieved.

Taoism The philosophy founded by *Lao-Tzu, and expressed in the book sometimes called by the same name, and also known as the *Tao Te Ching* ('Classic of the Way'), a combination of mysticism, philosophical reflection, and poetry. Unlike *Confucianism, Taoism stresses the unity of humanity and the universe. It is the loss of that unity that is responsible for desire, competition, and the unsuccessful attempts to regulate the resulting strife by means of ethics and moral law (*see also* ROUSSEAU). Lao-Tzu considered that 'When *tao* is lost only then does the doctrine of virtue arise'. As a practical philosophy Taoism is therefore based on the suppression of desire in favour of natural simplicity and tranquillity.

SEE WEB LINKS

- An archive of philosophical and religious articles on Taoism
- An account of the history and practice of Taoism, with bibliography and links to relevant websites

tarot A set of 22 pictorial playing cards, used in the ancient card game of tarot or tarok, but also popular for fortune-telling.

Tarski, Alfred (1901–83) Born Alfred Teitelbaum to a Jewish family, and educated in Warsaw, Tarski studied first biology and then mathematics. In logic he studied with *Kotarbinski, *Łukasiewicz, and *Lesniewski, publishing a succession of papers from 1923 onwards. He changed his name at the time of receiving his doctorate in 1924. He met *Gödel and the leaders of the *Vienna Circle, including Carnap in 1930, and went to the USA in 1939, narrowly escaping internment and probable death at the hands of the Nazis. He conducted research briefly at Harvard, and then moved to the university of California at Berkeley in 1942. Together with Abraham Robinson (1918–74) he created the mathematical theory of *models, and his programme at Berkeley and indefatigable energy were responsible for spreading mathematical logic and model theory worldwide. He worked on decidable and undecidable axiomatic systems, and in the course of his mathematical career he published over 300 papers and books, on topics ranging from set theory to geometry and algebra. Tarski's logical work is well seen in *A Decision Method for Elementary Algebra and Geometry* (1948), and for philosophers he is best represented in the collection *Logic, Semantics, and Metamathematics* (1956). There is a definitive biography (2004) by Solomon and Anita Burdman Feferman.

tarwater Substance allied to turpentine, recommended by *Berkeley in his *Siris* (1744) as a widely beneficial medicine, especially for 'seafaring persons, ladies, and men of studious and sedentary lives'. Berkeley's concerns as a bishop included doing what he could for the ailments of the poor in his diocese.

taste The sense of taste is generally given less philosophical attention than those of touch, sight, and hearing, since it seems itself to give us merely sensation and little by way of knowledge of the world. Judgements of taste are aesthetic judgements. They voice the reactions the subject supposes appropriate to some object of aesthetic contemplation: that it is beautiful, elegant, harmonious, sublime, etc., or insipid, sentimental, over-dramatic, meaningless, etc. The problem of the objectivity or otherwise of such judgements, the way in which they can be cultivated, and their connection to such things as moral approbation was the side of *aesthetics that was most developed in the 18th century, from *Hutcheson's *Inquiry into the Origins of our Ideas of Beauty and Virtue* (1725), through *Hume's essay 'Of the Standard of Taste' (1757), to *Kant's *Critique of Judgement* (1790).

tautology Technically, a formula of the *propositional calculus that is true whatever the truth-value assigned to its constituent propositional variables. (A tautology is thus valid, or true in all *interpretations.) In more informal contexts a tautology is often thought of as a proposition that 'says nothing', or merely repeats a definition.

Taylor, Charles (1931–) Canadian philosopher. Taylor was educated at McGill University and Oxford, where he gained his PhD in 1961, and where he has also taught. A wide-ranging philosopher, Taylor has written extensively on ethics, politics, and the social sciences. His most influential book is *Sources of the Self* (1989), a criticism of Enlightenment views of the self which stand in the way of our understanding our experience as moral agents. Like *MacIntyre, Taylor draws on Aristotelian and *communitarian themes to rectify the deficiencies of modernism. Other works include *Hegel* (1975) and *The Ethics of Authenticity* (1991).

Taylor, Harriet (1807–58) Married to a businessman, John Taylor, at the age of 18, Harriet nevertheless became the guiding muse of John Stuart *Mill after they met in 1830. Mill eventually married her in 1851, two years after John Taylor died. Mill was adamant that many of his works were their joint production, and Taylor was the principal author of 'The Enfranchisement of Women', which appeared in the *Westminster Review* in 1851. After Harriet died her daughter Helen took over her role, becoming an active campaigner for women's emancipation.

te (Chinese, virtue, power) In *Taoism *te* is the virtue or individual principle inherent in a thing, the inner spring connecting it with the universe.

technē (Greek, skill or art) The knowledge of how to do things and make things.

Teilhard de Chardin, Pierre (1881–1955) French Jesuit, palaeontologist, and philosopher of nature. His principal work, *Le Phénomène humain* (completed 1946, published 1955, trs. as *The Phenomenon of Man*, 1959), espouses a synthesis of science and religion, seeing the universe as a system evolving from stage to stage towards higher forms of consciousness, aimed at an eventual unity with God. The vision has philosophical roots in *Bergson. Although influential in its time, its claims to rational respectability were exploded by the biologist Peter Medawar in a famous review in *Mind*, 1961.

telekinesis The movement of objects by supposedly *paranormal means.

teleo-functionalism The variety of *functionalism that augments it with reference to *teleology, usually thought of as analysed by means of reference to natural selection. The leading idea is that we can think of mental states not only in terms of their actual causal relationships, but also in terms of what part in an overall causal structure they are 'supposed' to play, where the 'supposed' is given by the adaptive purpose they serve.

teleological argument *See* DESIGN, ARGUMENT FROM OR TO.

teleology (Greek, *telos*, end) The study of the ends or purposes of things. The idea that there is such a thing as the end or purpose of life is prominent in the Aristotelian view of *nature (and ethics), and then in the Christian tradition. The association with moral thought is visible in the idea that correct human living is in accordance with natural law, or in the idea that human nature can only fulfil its purpose through the exercise of virtue. The theory of evolution through natural selection allows speculation about the function for which particular things are adapted, and so permits assertions about the purpose an *adaptation serves, without any commitment to the idea of a designer who put it there for a purpose, and without the unscientific belief that the future utility of a feature somehow brings about its existence by a kind of *backwards causation. Teleology free of these implications is sometimes called teleonomy. The teleology of a feature may have metaphysical implications: thus one might (controversially) suggest that our spatial vision is for success at coping with a spatial world, whereas colour vision may not be for success at coping with a coloured world, but adapted to the skilful tracking of surfaces through changes of light, and this would be a way of defending a *primary/secondary quality distinction. *See also* FUNCTION (BIOLOGICAL).

telepathy The supposed ability to transmit thoughts directly to the mind of another, or to receive thoughts directly from the mind of another, without any normal causal interaction.

teleportation (teletransportation) Fictional mode of change of place in which a person 'dematerializes' at one place, and emerges at another. The *thought experiment of imagining such cases has a place in the philosophy of *personal identity, since if we concede that teleportation involves no contradiction, then we seem to think of our identity as potentially distinct from bodily continuity.

Telesio, Bernardino (1509–88) Italian philosopher and naturalist. Telesio studied in Padua but resided in southern Italy. The first two volumes of his major work, *De rerum natura juxta propria principia*, appeared in 1565; the work was completed in nine volumes in 1586. Telesio criticized Aristotelian science for its vacuous abstractions such as form, activity, potential, arguing instead for an empirical and mechanical approach to nature. Although highly controversial, and indeed condemned by the church, Telesio's work influenced subsequent empiricists including Francis *Bacon and Thomas *Hobbes.

telos (Greek, end, or purpose) *See* *ARETĒ*, NATURE, TELEOLOGY.

Tel Quel (French, as it is) The influential French literary review *Tel Quel* had a profound impact on literary and cultural debate in the 1960s and 1970s. From its beginning in 1960 to its closure in 1982, it published essays by major poststructuralist figures from Roland *Barthes to Michel *Foucault and Julia *Kristeva.

temporal stage *See* TIME-SLICE.

tender and tough-minded Distinction drawn by *James, who found it illuminating to classify philosophers into one of these two camps (*Pragmatism*, Ch. 1). The tender-minded are: rationalistic (going by 'principles'), intellectualistic, idealistic, optimistic, religious, free-willist, monistic, and dogmatical. The tough-minded are: empiricist (going by 'facts'), sensationalistic, materialistic, pessimistic, irreligious, fatalistic, pluralistic, and sceptical. Like *Nietzsche, James believed that even intellectual and rational constructions, such as philosophical systems purport to be, are expressions of individual temperament.

tense logic Logic first explored by the Oxford philosopher Arthur Prior, obtained by adding two propositional operators 'P' (in the past ...) and 'F' (in the future ...) to classical propositional and first-order logic.

term A singular term is any expression that *refers to an object. Singular terms include names, *indexicals, and *definite descriptions, and in the *interpretation of *logical calculi, bound *variables are treated like singular terms, by being assigned objects in the evaluation of sentences containing them. General terms are those things that, added to singular terms, make sentences: *predicates. In the traditional theory of the *syllogism no such distinction is made, but terms include all the common nouns occurring in the forms of sentence of which the theory treats.

terminus ad quem (Latin, terminus to which) The end point or finishing point of a process. The *terminus a quo* is the starting point.

terrorism The intentional use of violence, particularly in order to sow widespread fear, for political ends. *See* SOREL.

tertiary qualities Qualities or powers a thing has in virtue of its secondary qualities, just as they exist in virtue of its primary qualities: the flower is attractive to the butterfly because of its colour, or the wine expensive because of its taste. *See* PRIMARY/SECONDARY QUALITIES.

tertium non datur (Latin, there is no third thing) A way of saying that two alternatives exhaust the field, as in the logical law $p \vee -p$.

Tertullian, Quintus Septimus Florens (AD *c.*160–*c.*240) Roman Christian polemicist. Born in Carthage, Tertullian converted to Christianity around 196, after which he wrote a string of fierce essays defending Christianity, attacking Platonism and Hellenizing tendencies, and expounding an ethic of martyrdom. Heresy comes from trusting philosophy rather than faith. Tertullian joined a rigorous sect, the Montanists, but seems to have left to promote a sterner asceticism than theirs.

Tertullian's dictum or paradox *See CREDO QUIA ABSURDUM EST.*

testability The capacity of a theory to yield predictions that can be tested, thereby either refuting the theory, or, more controversially, confirming it. *See* FALSIFIABILITY.

testimony The testimony of others is fundamental to the way we gain knowledge about the world. One way of analysing this is to see testimony as just an ordinary empirical sign of what is testified, reliable in general even if far from infallible. However, critics point out that it is impossible for the individual to check what he or she is told enough of the time to generate a statistic of this reliability, so testimony needs to have a default title to credit built into it. The issue is made pointed by *Hume's essay on the incredible nature of testimony to the occurrence of *miracles.

texture The principal explanatory concept in the *corpuscularian natural science of *Boyle, and thence *Locke. Bodies are conglomerates of corpuscles, but the particular way the corpuscles are linked makes the texture of a body, and explains its powers in the rationally satisfying way that the shape of a lock and a key explain the power of the key to fit the lock.

Thales of Miletus (*fl.* 585 BC) One of the Seven Sages of ancient Greece and judged by *Aristotle to be the founder of physical science; that is, he was the first Greek to search for the ultimate substance of things, which he identified with water. A polymath, he is supposed to have predicted the solar eclipse of 28 May 585 BC and to have introduced the study of geometry to Greece. He apparently believed in some kind of *hylozoism and *panpsychism, but claims made in late antiquity about his doctrines and discoveries are regarded as unreliable.

Theaetetus (*c.*414–*c.*369 BC) Theaetetus was a friend of Plato's and a mathematician, who gave his name to one of the greatest of Plato's *Dialogues*. He is supposed to have contributed to the theory of irrationals of *Euclid, Bk x, and to the solid geometry of Bk xiii.

theism Belief in the existence of God. Theism is also a morbid condition brought on by excessive tea-drinking, but this is a different sense of the word, or an instance of *homonymy. *See also* ATHEISM, DEISM, MONOTHEISM, POLYTHEISM, and different topics within the philosophy of *religion.

thema (pl. themata) *Stoic term for the principles enabling one to derive one valid argument form from another, as opposed to schemata, which enable one to derive statements from other statements.

Themistius (AD *c.*317–88) Greek rhetorician and educator. Themistius resided in Constantinople and enjoyed the patronage of a succession of emperors. His paraphrases of various works of *Aristotle were influential in the Middle Ages, and embody material from lost commentaries.

theodicy The part of theology concerned with defending the goodness and omnipotence of God in the face of the suffering and evil of the world. *See* EVIL, PROBLEM OF; FREE WILL DEFENCE.

theological virtues Faith, hope, and charity or love. In Christian writing these are the qualities of mind necessary to strive for salvation. *See also* CARDINAL VIRTUES.

theology *See* RELIGION, PHILOSOPHY OF.

Theophrastus (*c.*370–*c.*288 BC) A pupil and collaborator of *Aristotle's, and his successor as the head of the *Peripatetics. Although he was an influential teacher and an energetic writer, few of his works have survived. His philosophy differed from that of Aristotle mainly in an empiricist direction, and in scepticism concerning the extravagances of Aristotle's teleological approach to nature, but mainly he pursued Aristotelian science and systematization. His treatise *On the Opinions of the Physical Philosophers* was the major source of later knowledge of the *Presocratics.

theorem Something proved in a logical system or *logical calculus. Formally: the last line of a *proof.

theory In science, a way of looking at a field that is intended to have explanatory and predictive implications. The task for the philosophy of science has often been posed in terms of demarcating good or scientific theories from bad, unscientific ones (*see* FALSIFIABILITY, POPPER). In the heyday of *logical positivism, highly formal approaches to theories treated them in terms of axiomatic systems, whose theoretical terms were tightly tied to an observational vocabulary supposed to give a foundation in empirical meaning. A less formal and more contextualized approach, heralded in the work of Thomas *Kuhn, stressed the open-endedness of scientific activity, the heuristic value of analogies and models, and the elasticity and the *holism of meaning, all of which suggested that an excessively formal approach distorted the subject.

theory-laden A statement is theory-laden if its terms only make sense in the light of a set of theoretical principles. The judgement that an electron has been emitted, for example, would be more heavily theory-laden than the judgement that there was a white flash on the screen. However, it is widely believed that all statements are theory-laden, and none has the status attributed by the *logical positivists to basic or *protocol statements, of giving a theoretically innocent report of unvarnished experience. *See also* MYTH OF THE GIVEN.

theory of descriptions *See* DEFINITE DESCRIPTION.

theory of types *See* TYPES, THEORY OF.

theory-theory The view that everyday attributions of intentions, beliefs, and meanings to other persons proceed via tacit use of a theory that enables one to construct these interpretations as explanations of their doings. The view is commonly held along with *functionalism, according to which psychological states are theoretical entities, identified by the network of their causes and effects. The theory-theory has different implications, depending upon which feature of theories is being stressed. Theories may be thought of as capable of formalization, as yielding predictions and explanations, as achieved by a process of theorizing, as answering to empirical evidence that is in principle describable without them, as liable to be overturned by newer and better theories, and so on. The main problem with seeing our understanding of others as the outcome of a piece of theorizing is the non-existence of a medium in which this theory can be couched, as the child learns simultaneously the minds of others and the meanings of terms in its native language. *See also* LANGUAGE OF THOUGHT HYPOTHESIS, SIMULATION.

theosophy (Greek, God + wisdom) Generally restricted to systems, such as that of *Swedenborg, of a pantheistic and mystical nature, and in particular that associated with Madame Blavatsky (1831–91), which includes the transmigration of souls, the brotherhood of man, the denial of a personal God and personal immortality, and belief in the *fourth dimension.

thermodynamics, laws of The three laws were put in a memorable form by the English scientist and novelist C. P. Snow: (i) you cannot win (matter and energy are conserved); (ii) you cannot break even (cannot return to the same entropy state, since disorder always increases); (iii) you cannot get out of the game (absolute zero is unobtainable).

Theseus, ship of *See* SHIP OF THESEUS.

thesis *See* DIALECTICAL MATERIALISM.

theurgy *See* RELIGION, PHILOSOPHY OF.

thick terms Term coined by *Williams for those expressions in ethics that carry a descriptive as well as an evaluative component. Common examples include derogatory racial and sexist epithets, but terms denoting the *virtues are also often argued to carry both kinds of meaning. The notion is often associated with the view that such terms are learned as a unity, so that the two components cannot be factored out separately, and this puts pressure on the *fact/value distinction.

thing in itself For the *Kantian use, *see* NOUMENON. *See also* BEING IN-ITSELF/FOR-ITSELF.

thinking It is common to suppose that people are characterized by their rationality, and the most evident display of our rationality is our capacity to think. This is the rehearsal in the mind of what to say, or what to do. Not all thinking is verbal, since chess players, composers, and painters all think, and there is no *a priori* reason that their deliberations should take any more verbal a form than their actions. It is permanently tempting to conceive of this activity in terms of the presence in the mind of elements of some language, or other medium that represents aspects of the world (*see* IDEAS, LANGUAGE OF THOUGHT HYPOTHESIS). But the model has been attacked, notably by *Wittgenstein, as insufficient, since no such presence could carry a guarantee that the right use would be made of it. And such an inner presence seems unnecessary, since an intelligent outcome might arise in principle without it. *See also* ANIMAL THOUGHT.

third man argument The argument advanced in *Plato's dialogue *Parmenides* against the doctrine of *forms. Suppose we start with the collection of large things. Now suppose that there is some form that they all share: the form of largeness. We now have a new collection, namely all the original things plus the form of largeness. So there must be a further form uniting all the members of this collection, and this launches us on an infinite regress. *Aristotle uses the example of men, and the argument gains its title from him.

Thomasius, Christian (1655–1728) Early figure in the German Enlightenment. Thomasius taught in Leipzig and Halle, where he helped to found the university in 1694. He was an opponent of Aristotelianism, Lutheranism, the divine right of Kings, and Roman Law, instead promoting a non-theological, natural foundation for ethics following in the spirit of *Grotius and *Pufendorf. Although he was one of the earliest to lecture in German, his principal work was the *Fundamenta Juris Naturae et Gentium* (1705).

Thomism The philosophy of *Aquinas, and its development particularly in the Catholic tradition. *See also* NEO-THOMISM.

Thoreau, Henry David (1817–62) American writer and poet. Born in Concord, Massachusetts, Thoreau was a friend of *Emerson's and similarly imbued with the ideas of *New England transcendentalism. In Thoreau's case it harmonized with a natural asceticism and high-mindedness. In spite of its pervasive contempt for what he called 'the mass of mankind', his most famous work, *Walden* (1854), is a continuing inspiration for back-to-nature movements. Thoreau suffered a day's imprisonment for refusing to pay a poll tax, on the grounds that part of the tax went to the Mexican war promoting the expansion of Southern slavery. His record of this experience, the essay 'Civil Disobedience' (1849), became a model for later advocates of passive resistance, notably Mahatma *Gandhi.

thought experiment In a thought experiment, instead of bringing about a course of events, as in a normal experiment, we are invited to imagine one. We may then be able to 'see' that some result follows, or that some description is appropriate, or our inability to describe the situation may itself have some consequences. Thought experiments played a major role in the development of physics: for example, *Galileo probably never dropped two balls of unequal weight from the leaning tower of Pisa, in order to refute the Aristotelian view that a heavy body falls faster than a lighter one. He merely asked us to imagine a heavy body made into the shape of a dumb-bell, and the connecting rod gradually made thinner, until it is finally severed. The thing is one heavy body until the last moment, and then two light ones, but it is incredible that this final snip alters the velocity dramatically. Other famous examples include the *Einstein–Podolsky–Rosen thought experiment. In the philosophy of *personal identity, our apparent capacity to imagine ourselves surviving drastic changes of body, brain, and mind is a permanent source of difficulty (*see* SPLIT-BRAIN PHENOMENA, TELEPORTATION). There is no general consensus on the legitimate place of thought experiments, either to substitute for real experiment, or as a reliable device for discerning possibilities. Thought experiments one dislikes are sometimes called intuition pumps.

Thrasymachus (*fl. c.*430–400 BC) Athenian rhetorician and Sophist. He is remembered philosophically for his role in Book I of *Plato's *Republic* where he defends the thesis that justice is whatever is in the interest of the stronger: might is right.

three prisoners, paradox of There are three prisoners, Archie, Bertha, and you, in the unfortunate situation of knowing that two of you will be executed in the morning. In the night you ask the guard if he can give you the name of one of the others who will be executed. 'OK,' he replies, 'Archie will.' Looked at one way this is good news: it is now either Archie and Bertha, or Archie and you, so your chances have diminished from ⅔ to ½. But looked at another way it is not significant news at all: you already knew that the guard could truly name one of the others, and it does not affect your chances whether he names Archie or Bertha. The problem bears some relation to the *Monty Hall problem: it would certainly be worthwhile swapping places with Bertha after this event, suggesting that Bertha's chances have diminished, but your chances have, unfortunately, remained at ⅔.

tickles Tickles are frequently cited as a pure example of sensation, entirely identified by the *qualia they provide, and lacking any *content or burden of information about the world. However the matter is more complex than that, as is evident from the fact that one cannot tickle oneself. The psychologist Havelock Ellis (1859–1939) thought of the reaction as a defence against premature sexual advances, but this does not explain why the soles of the feet are ticklish. One account of the emotional essence of being tickled is 'the swift interaction of moments of nascent fear with a joyous recognition of harmlessness.' *Aristotle refers mysteriously to 'those who do not get tickled themselves if they tickle someone else first' (*Nicomachean Ethics*, 1150 b 22). *See also* LAUGHTER.

Tillich, Paul (1886–1965) German Lutheran theologian. Tillich fled to the USA in 1933, and taught theology at the Union Theological Seminary, Harvard, and Chicago. His *Systematic Theology* in three volumes (1951–63) attempts a 'method of correlation' whereby Christian revelation answers contemporary cultural questions. It is *existentialist in tone, but infused with Jungian psychology and neo-scholastic metaphysics.

timarchy A government of worthy and competent men, not aristocrats, chosen by some kind of public acclamation.

time The nature of time has been one of the major problems of philosophy since antiquity. Is time well thought of as flowing? If so, does it flow from future to past with us stuck like boats in the middle of the river, or does it flow from past to future, bearing us with it? And might it flow faster or slower? These questions seem hard (or absurd) enough to encourage us to reject the metaphor of time's flow. But if we do not think of time as flowing, how do we conceive of its passage? What distinguishes the present from the past and future, or is there no objective distinction (*see* A-SERIES, PRESENTISM)? What gives time its direction—what accounts for the asymmetry between past and future? Can we make sense of timeless existence, or can we only make sense of existence in time? Is time infinitely divisible, or might it have a granular structure, with there being a smallest quantum or chunk of time? Many of these problems are first posed in *Aristotle's *Physics*, in the form of paradoxes or problems about the very existence of time. One problem is that time cannot exist, for none of its parts exist (the present instant, having no duration, cannot count as a part of time). Again, if we ask when the present instant ceases to exist, every answer involves a contradiction: not at the present, for while it exists it exists; not at the next moment, for in the continuum there is no next moment (any more than there is such a thing as the next fraction to any given fraction); not at any subsequent moment, for then it is already gone. But we cannot think of the present instant as continuously existing, for then things that happened ten thousand years ago would be simultaneous with things that have happened today. Aristotle's puzzles, and *Zeno's paradoxes of time and space, encouraged atomistic solutions, in which the structure of time is made granular. Partisans of atomism included Diodorus Cronus (*fl. c.*300 BC) and *Epicurus, but they were opposed by the *Stoics; the countervailing arguments on each side were marshalled by *Sextus Empiricus as grist to the sceptical mill. A fundamentally idealist solution, allowing different times to exist in the sense of being simultaneous objects of contemplation, is propounded by *Augustine, in the *Confessions*, Bk 11, and is visible in *Leibniz, *Berkeley, *Kant, and *Bergson. Other perplexing problems include the question of whether time may have a beginning, and whether there can be eventless time. *See also* RELATIVITY THEORY, SPACE-TIME.

time-lag argument Argument used by *Russell (e.g. *Human Knowledge: its Scope and Limits*, 1948, p. 172), and other 20th-century writers, to refute naive realism in the philosophy of perception. When we see the sun, our perceptual state is the result of how the sun was eight minutes ago. The sun might not even exist now; yet we would still be seeing exactly what we are seeing. So what we are seeing cannot be identical with the sun.

time's arrow Unlike space, time as we apprehend it has a direction. There is an asymmetry between the past (fixed) and the future (yet to exist). Time's arrow is whatever gives time this direction. Five aspects of the direction are: (i) that according to the second law of *thermodynamics, disorder (*entropy) increases from past to future; (ii) the universe is expanding in time; (iii) causal efficacy works in only one direction in time, since future events cannot influence past events (*see* BACKWARD CAUSATION); (iv) we remember past events whilst we cannot remember later ones; and (v) we can alter the future in a sense in which we cannot alter the past. A complete understanding of time would enable us to relate these five aspects of time's arrow, and to know whether they are true of necessity or only as a consequence of other contingencies. *See* A-SERIES, TIME.

time-slice Modern physical thinking takes the view that time should be regarded as essentially uniform with space. It is one dimension in uniform space-time. Hence many writers have advocated looking at an ordinary, enduring object as a four-dimensional space-time worm. The segments of this worm are the successive stages or time-slices that together make it up, in the way that successive events make up a process, or successive acts make up a play. *See also* ENDURANCE/PERDURANCE.

time travel This staple of science fiction is sometimes argued to harbour a contradiction. If the time traveller goes back to an earlier time, then he can alter things so that he never comes into existence, in which case he will not be there to begin his time travel. It can be replied that this just shows that he doesn't alter things in that way, but then the question remains whether he can introduce any difference whatsoever into the past world without similar contradiction arising. However, Kurt *Gödel produced models of space-time consistent with general relativity, that allow travel into the past, and modern physics can be interpreted so as to countenance the notion. One interpretation, however, is that of the physical unreality of time altogether. *See also* BLOCK UNIVERSE.

Timon of Phlius (*c*.320–230 BC) A sceptical follower of *Pyrrho, principally known for the acerbic and satirical style of his *Silloi* or lampoons against the 'dogmatic' philosophers. To the idea that although the senses and reason are each untrustworthy, possibly they can work together to give knowledge, his response was the pithy 'birds of a feather flock together'.

Tindal, Matthew (1657–1733) English deist. His *Christianity as Old as the Creation, or the Gospel a Republication of the Religion of Nature* (1730) is often described as the textbook of *deism. He argued from the injustice of a special revelation to one people at one place and time, to a 'primitive' Christianity, free of specific dogma and available to all by the light of natural reason.

tit for tat A game-theoretic strategy brought to the attention of philosophers by Robert Axelrod, in his *The Evolution of Cooperation* (1984). The question is how to perform to maximize gain in an interaction that consists of an extended sequence of *prisoners' dilemmas. The program that won the first competition amongst strategies for solving this problem was one that (a) always co-operated unless (b) on the immediately preceding round, its opponent had defected, in which case it defected. The strategy was both *nice*, in that it never initiated a cycle of defecting, and also *forgiving*, in that it punished defection only once. The success of the strategy seemed to give some justification for partially retributive social rules, and might explain the common moral tendency to favour them. However, further work has shown that tit for tat is only the optimum strategy in certain specific circumstances.

token-reflexive Term used by *Reichenbach for *indexical expressions, i.e. those whose interpretation demands knowing the speaker, or place, or time, or context of utterance. The idea is that these indexes can in turn be referred to by means of the token or utterance itself: 'I am cold' becomes 'the utterer of this token is cold'; 'it is cold here' becomes 'it is cold where this is said', and so on.

token–token identity *See* TYPE–TYPE IDENTITY.

Toland, John (1670–1722) Irish religious controversialist. Usually classified as a *deist, and called a freethinker by Bishop *Berkeley, Toland actually pursued a kind of *pantheism, arguing for an intelligible and reasonable theology, free from specific dogma and revelation. Influenced by John *Locke, among others, his *Christianity not Mysterious: A Treatise Shewing, That there is nothing in the Gospel Contrary to Reason, Nor Above It: And that no Christian Doctrine can be properly cal'd A Mystery* (1696) argued for toleration in religious matters, and was burned in Dublin.

toleration Refraining from acting against that which is disapproved of, or politically opposed, or alien. Toleration in religious matters is one of the central planks of the modern democratic state: *Locke's *Letter on Toleration* (1689) is the basic authority, although Locke himself exempted Roman Catholics from the umbrella of protection, on the grounds that their primary allegiance would be to the Church and not to the government. The central philosophical problem is understanding how a principle of toleration can coincide with genuine moral and religious conviction.

Tolstoy, Count Leo (1828–1910) Tolstoy's early life was the unremarkable round of a landed Russian gentleman, although during it he produced his masterpieces *War and Peace* (1862–9) and *Anna Karenina* (1873–6). Around 1876 he underwent a Christian conversion, and from then onwards proclaimed an ascetic, self-denying, and largely anarchistic gospel of renunciation and love, which influenced subsequent thinkers such as *Gandhi. Works expounding this theme include *A Short Exposition of the Gospels* (1881), *What I Believe In* (1882), *What Then Must We Do?* (1886), and *The Law of Love and the Law of Violence* (1908).

tone An aspect of the overall meaning of an utterance separated out by *Frege (as the *Beleuchtung* of an utterance). An utterance may be made in a way that is especially apt to affect the feelings of an audience: it may be disquieting, or exciting, or sad, or arousing. Two utterances may thus share their *content but differ in tone, if their affective impact is different. Separating the tone from the strict content, for example of a poem, is not straightforward.

tonk Logical connective invented by the logician Arthur Prior as a 'runabout inference ticket'. Its rules are two: first, from P you may infer P tonk Q, and second from P tonk Q you may infer Q. Put together these imply that from P you may infer Q, which is incoherent. The example puts pressure on philosophies which think that the laws of logic are no more than conventions governing the stipulated behaviour of defined connectives.

topic-neutral Term originally used by *Ryle to refer to terms that occur in sentences about any kind of subject-matter. The *logical constants are the clearest example. In the subsequent work of *Smart, expressions that refer to things are topic-neutral if they leave open the substantive question of the kind of thing to which they are referring. 'The person who killed her' is not topic-neutral since it must be satisfied by a person, but 'whoever or whatever caused the sound' is, since what is referred to might be the wind, or a person, or anything else. *See also* QUIDDITY, RAMSEY SENTENCE.

totalitarianism The principle of government according to which all institutional and private arrangements are subject to control by the state. There are thus no autonomous associations, nor is there any principled or legally recognized private/public distinction. *See* PRIVACY (SOCIAL).

toxin puzzle Puzzle in the philosophy of action, originally proposed by Greg Kavka (1947–94). An omniscient or at least totally reliable benefactor offers you a million dollars if on Monday you can form the intention to drink a mild but unpleasant toxin on Wednesday. The intention is sufficient for getting the reward; on Tuesday the money will be in your bank, and there will be no other reason to drink the poison on Wednesday, and you know that this will be so. Can you form the winning intention? The puzzle puts pressure on the idea that 'forming an intention' can be treated as an independent action.

trademark argument Term sometimes used for the argument found in *Descartes, that our idea of perfection is related to its perfect origin (God), just as a stamp or trademark is left in an article of workmanship by its maker.

tradition Traditionalists believe that inherited conventions, social forms, modes of government, or social institutions have evolved over time as effective adaptations to the needs of people, and therefore have a default authority. Enthusiasm for reform for its own sake, or for 'rational' schemes thought up by managers and theorists, is therefore entirely misplaced. Major exponents of this theme include *Burke and *Hayek.

traducianism The theory that the soul of a child is transmitted to it (along with *original sin) by its parents. The doctrine avoids the problem that if God creates every soul afresh, He would do well to make them free of sin. *See* CREATIONISM.

tragedy The genre of drama in which the principal action is an unfolding catastrophe. According to *Aristotle the audience then feels pity and fear, and this has a *cathartic effect with value of its own. In his essay 'On Tragedy', David *Hume pondered the fact that were the events of a tragedy to unfold in real life they would be most unpleasant to us, yet we derive pleasure from their dramatic representation. His solution is not that we do not 'really' feel the pity and terror, thinking that after all it is only a fiction, but that we do, yet at the same time admire the form of the presentation, and this admiration accounts for our pleasure.

tragedy of the commons *See* COMMONS, TRAGEDY OF THE.

transcendental A topic or question is transcendental if its resolution is not purely a matter of logic or mathematics, and also lies beyond the scope both of sense experience and of the proper use of theory answerable to sense experience. Transcendental questions include religious questions, but may also include those raised by metaphysical problems, such as *scepticism and *physicalism. Philosophical attitudes to such questions range from fascination to outright denial of their existence (*see* LOGICAL POSITIVISM).

transcendental analytic In *Kant's *Critique of Pure Reason*, the section that deals with the principles of the understanding, and that attempts to prove the application of the *categories to phenomena.

transcendental argument In *Kant, one that proves a conclusion by showing that unless it were true, experience itself would be impossible.

transcendental idealism Term used by *Kant to characterize one element of his philosophy. Kant attempts to combine empirical *realism, preserving the ordinary independence and reality of objects of the world, with transcendental *idealism, which allows that in some sense the objects have their ordinary properties (their causal powers, and their spatial and temporal position) only because our minds are so structured that these are the categories we impose upon the manifold of experience.

transcendentalism *See* NEW ENGLAND TRANSCENDENTALISM.

transcendental number *See* ALGEBRAIC NUMBER.

transcendental signified Derogatory term used in some *poststructuralist writing to denote an external, objective, language-independent point that fixes reference or meaning. These points, it is alleged, cannot play any role in the interpretation of texts: their introduction only provides yet more text. Thus, for example, if an author's intentions, or a legislator's intentions, are invoked in order to interpret a text or a statute, we face the problem that their intentions could only be known, even to themselves, in the guise of more sayings. There is no stepping outside the domain of texts: every decoding is another encoding. The term is not very well adapted to its purpose, since it suggests the belief that everything except words is *transcendental, whereas in fact ordinary things are no less identifiable empirically than words themselves.

transfinite induction The proof schema corresponding to ordinary *mathematical induction taken into the transfinite, i.e. defined over orderings that may be larger than the standard ordering of the set of all natural numbers. *Gentzen showed that if this operation is allowed (involving a relaxation of the finitary methods of theories subject to *Gödel's incompleteness theorem for arithmetic), we may prove the consistency and completeness of arithmetic. But the Gödel results then apply to the mathematics of the transfinite. *See also* FINITISM.

transformation rules In logic, a rule entitling one to transform an expression of one form into that of another. The transformation of $\neg(p \,\&\, q)$ into $\neg p \vee \neg q$ is an example of *De Morgan's laws.

transitive A *relation is transitive if whenever Rxy and Ryz then Rxz. For example, if x is taller than y, and y is taller than z, then x is taller than z.

translation The provision of an expression in one language meaning the same as that of another. In so far as different languages reflect different cultural and social histories, because of the *holism of meaning, and because of the different associations and *tone of different words, translation may be an ideal which can only be approached but never fully achieved. The thesis of the *indeterminacy of radical translation goes beyond this by holding that radically different translations may be equally correct, thereby denying determinacy of meaning to the original expression. *See also* SAPIR–WHORF HYPOTHESIS.

transmigration of souls *See* METEMPSYCHOSIS.

transparent *See* REFERENTIALLY OPAQUE/TRANSPARENT.

transposition Term sometimes used in logic for the *transformation usually known as contraposition, whereby from $(p \rightarrow q)$ we can derive $(\neg q \rightarrow \neg p)$.

transubstantiation In Christian doctrine, the conversion of the substance of bread and wine into the substance of the body of Christ, whilst its appearance remains unaltered. The distinction between *substance and *accident that this entails formed one of the main stimuli to *scholastic metaphysical thought.

transvaluation of values The term used by *Nietzsche for the process of surmounting the reigning decadent and corrupt ethical principles.

transworld depravity An agent is transworld depraved if in any possible world in which he is created, he freely performs at least one morally reprehensible action. The notion was introduced by Alvin Plantinga in *The Nature of Necessity* (1974), as part of an attempt to reconcile God's goodness with human depravity.

tree of Porphyry *See* PORPHYRY.

Trinitarianism The doctrine of the Christian church that each of three persons (the father, the son, and the holy ghost) is God, and yet that there are not three Gods (tritheism) but one. The doctrine teeters on the brink of contradiction, or perhaps beyond it, and has occasioned much reflection on notions such as substance, identity, and person. It is denied by Unitarians, who regard Jesus purely as a human person.

trivium The lower division of the seven liberal arts in medieval universities, consisting of grammar, rhetoric, and logic. The remaining four were the *quadrivium.

trolley problem Problem in ethics posed by the English philosopher Philippa Foot in her 'The Problem of Abortion and the Doctrine of the Double Effect' (*Oxford Review*, 1967). A runaway train or trolley comes to a branch in the track. One person is working on one branch, and five on the other, and the trolley will kill anyone working on the branch it enters. Clearly, to most thinkers, the driver should steer for the less populated branch. But now suppose that, left to itself, it will go to the branch with five people on it, and you as a bystander can interfere, altering the points so that it veers towards the other. Is it right, or obligatory, or even permissible for you to do this, thereby apparently involving yourself in responsibility for the death of the one person? After all, whom have you wronged if you leave it to go its own way? The situation is structurally similar to others in which *utilitarian reasoning seems to lead to one course of action, but a person's *integrity or principles may oppose it. *See also* ACTS/OMISSIONS DOCTRINE; DOUBLE EFFECT, PRINCIPLE OF.

trope 1. In classical philosophy a particular kind of argument, as the ten tropes of *Aenesidemus. **2.** In a usage following work of D. C. Williams (1899–1983), a trope is the instantiation of a *universal at a place and time, an 'abstract particular', such as 'the blue of this cup', that some regard as fundamental to ontology.

Trotter, Catherine *See* COCKBURN.

trust The attitude of expecting good performance from another party, whether in terms of loyalty, goodwill, truth, or promises. The importance of trust as a kind of invisible glue that binds society together is most visible when it is lost. Trust involves an element of risk, and *epistemologists can have trouble categorizing it as rational, since it works best in advance, for example to motivate performance on occasions when defection may be to the advantage of the person trusted. Economically trust is precious, enabling parties to bypass the costly precautions and safeguards needed in transactions with parties whom one does not trust. Trustworthiness is a virtue, subsuming varieties such as truthfulness and fidelity. It is a general ambition of democratic politicians to be trusted whether or not they are trustworthy.

truth apt A sentence is truth apt if there is some context in which it could be uttered (with its present meaning) and express a true or false proposition. Sentences that are not apt for truth include questions and commands, and, more controversially, paradoxical sentences of the form of the *Liar ('this sentence is false'); or sentences ('you will not smoke') whose apparent function is to make an assertion, but which may instead be regarded as expressing prescriptions or attitudes, rather than being in the business of aiming at truth or falsehood. *See* EXPRESSIVISM, PRESCRIPTIVISM.

truth conditions The truth condition of a statement is the condition the world must meet if the statement is to be true. To know this condition is equivalent to knowing the meaning of the statement. Although this sounds as if it gives a solid anchorage for meaning, some of the security disappears when it turns out that the truth condition can only be defined by repeating the very same statement: the truth condition of 'snow is white' is that snow is white; the truth condition of 'Britain would have capitulated had Hitler invaded' is that Britain would have capitulated had Hitler invaded. It is disputed whether this element of running-on-the-spot disqualifies truth conditions from playing the central role in a substantive theory of meaning. Truth-conditional theories of meaning are sometimes opposed by the view that to know the meaning of a statement is to be able to use it in a network of inferences. *See* INFERENTIAL SEMANTICS.

truth definition A definition of the predicate '... is true' for a language that satisfies *convention T, the material adequacy condition laid down by *Tarski. The definition of truth provided by Tarski's methods is a *recursive definition, enabling us to say for each sentence what it is that its truth consists in, but giving no verbal definition of truth itself. The recursive definition of the truth predicate of a language is always provided in a *metalanguage; Tarski is thus committed to a hierarchy of languages, each with its associated, but different, truth predicate. Whilst this enables the approach to avoid the contradictions of the *Liar family, it conflicts with the ideal that a language should be able to say everything that there is to say, and other approaches have become increasingly important.

truth/falsity The two classical truth-values that a statement, proposition, or sentence can take. It is supposed in classical (two-valued) logic that each statement has one of these values, and none has both. A statement is then false if and only if it is not true. The basis of this scheme is that to each statement there corresponds a determinate truth condition, or way the world must be for it to be true; if this condition obtains the statement is true, and otherwise false. Statements may indeed be felicitous or infelicitous in other dimensions (polite, misleading, apposite, witty, etc.), but truth is the central normative notion governing assertion. Considerations of *vagueness may introduce greys into this black-and-white scheme. For the issue of whether falsity is the only way of failing to be true, *see* PRESUPPOSITION. For theories of truth *see* COHERENCE, CORRESPONDENCE, DISQUOTATIONAL, IDEAL LIMIT, IDENTITY, REDUNDANCY, SEMANTIC THEORIES OF TRUTH.

truthfulness The virtue of telling the truth. This can be elevated into the most stringent duty, as in the philosophy of *Kant, where it extends to the duty to tell the mad axeman where your children are sleeping, if there is no way of ducking the question. A less demanding morality might balance the duty against other obligations, or recognize only a duty to tell the truth to those who have a right to the truth.

truth function A truth function of a number of propositions or sentences is a *function of them that has a definite *truth-value, dependent only on the truth-values of the constituents. Thus (p & q) is a combination whose truth-value is true when p is true and q is true, and false otherwise. $\neg p$ is a truth-function of p, false when p is true and true when p is false. The way in which the value of the whole is determined by the combinations of values of constituents is presented in a truth table.

p	q	$p \& q$	$p \vee q$	$p \rightarrow q$	$p \leftrightarrow q$
T	T	T	T	T	T
T	F	F	T	F	F
F	T	F	T	T	F
F	F	F	F	T	T

t

The *propositional calculus is the standard treatment of truth-functional combinations. Its constants, &, ∨, ¬, →, and ↔, are all truth-functors, i.e. expressions standing for truth functions.

truthmaker principle Term brought into currency by the Australian philosopher David *Armstrong. The idea is that propositions cannot be 'barely' true. There must be something making them true: a fact, or substantial complex or state of affairs. The principle motivates substantial metaphysical and *ontological searches for the ultimate nature of such complexes. It also gives rise to certain problems: for instance, what is the truthmaker for 'unicorns do not exist'?

truth predicate The predicate 'is true' thought of as applicable to the sentences of a language. *See* TRUTH DEFINITION.

truth table *See* TRUTH FUNCTION.

truth theory A theory providing the *truth definition for a language.

truth-value In classical logic a proposition may be true or false. If the former, it is said to take the truth-value true, and if the latter the truth-value false. The idea behind the term is the analogy between assigning a propositional variable one or other of these values, as is done in providing an *interpretation for a formula of the *propositional calculus, and assigning an object as the value of any other variable. Logics with intermediate values are called *many-valued logics.

T-sentence The sentence giving the *truth condition of a sentence of an object language, the language under semantic investigation. It is itself framed in a 'metalanguage', which is usually in principle distinguished from the object language in order to avoid problems of inconsistency. T-sentences were the lynchpin of *Tarski's seminal investigation into how to give a theory of truth for a formal language. A T-sentence takes the form of a biconditional: 'S' is true in L if and only if *p*. Here 'S' names a sentence of the object language L, and *p* is substituted by a sentence in the metalanguage which translates it. Such a sentence is *extensional, in the sense that it will be true provided the sentence S has the same truth-value as the proposition *p*. But conditions may be placed on the way the T-sentence is derived in a formal semantic theory, that do something to ensure that the biconditional in fact gives a satisfactory account of the meaning of S.

Tung Chung-shu (*c*.179–*c*.104 BC) Chinese scholar and influential theorist of government. Tung Chung-shu is credited with rescuing Confucian thought from the 'burning of the books' which had occurred during the brief rule of the Ch'in Dynasty. He synthesized Confucian thought and the Yin-Yang school of cosmic metaphysics, interpreting them as practical means of understanding the will of Heaven and the operations of Nature under its guidance. Later in life he composed the *Ch'unch'iu fan-lu* (*Luxuriant Dew of the Spring and Autumn Annals*), a philosophical commentary on the Chinese classics. He persuaded the emperor Wu to adopt Confucian rather than Legalist philosophy as the official basis of Han government.

Turing machine A mathematical device used by the English mathematician Alan Turing (1912–54) to make precise the notion of an *algorithm, or an effective computation. A Turing machine is a computer with a potentially infinite linear tape in both directions, divided into discrete squares that are scanned one at a time. Symbols in the squares are from a finite alphabet. The instructions for the machine are sets of ordered quintuples: $<q_i, s_i, s_k, M, q_j>$ · q_i is the state the machine is in at the first moment, s_i is the symbol it reads on the square, s_k a symbol with which it replaces it, M is the instruction to move one square right or left or remain where it is, and q_j the state at the next moment. A function f(*x*) is Turing computable if, when some representation of the argument *x* is put on the tape, the machine halts on a representation of the value f(*x*). The class of Turing computable functions is identical with the class of general *recursive functions (*see also* CHURCH'S THESIS).

SEE WEB LINKS

- An introduction by Turing's biographer

Turing test The test suggested by Alan Turing (1912–54), in his paper 'Computing Machinery and Intelligence' (*Mind*, 1950), for judging whether a machine is making an adequate simulation of the human mind. The test is also known as the imitation game. A person and the machine communicate with an interrogator who is kept apart. The interrogator may ask questions with the intent of distinguishing the human from the machine. The machine passes the test or wins the game if after an interval of time the interrogator cannot distinguish the machine from the human. Turing was optimistic that within a few years computing machinery that could win the game would be developed. But in the upshot difficulties such as the *frame problem suggest that it is much harder than he expected to program a device to give a passable imitation of common-sense reasoning capacities and ordinary human skills.

SEE WEB LINKS

- A list of internet resources on the Turing test

t

Turnbull, George (1698–1748) Scottish moral philosopher and art historian, and teacher of Thomas *Reid. His works included the two-volume *The Principles of Moral Philosophy: An Enquiry into the Wise and Good Government of the Moral World* (1740) and *A Treatise on Ancient Painting* (1740).

Twardowski, Kazimierz (1866–1938) Pupil of *Brentano, and founder of the Lvov–Warsaw school of philosophy and logic. Twardowski studied in Vienna, and was appointed professor at Lvov in 1895. His charismatic teaching helped to inspire a generation of students, including *Kotarbinski, *Łukasiewicz, and *Lesniewski. The philosophy of the Lvov–Warsaw school was that 'vera philosophiae methodus nulla alia nisi scientiae naturalis est', a motto taken from Brentano (the method of true philosophy is nothing other than that of natural science); later this meant an extraordinarily fruitful alliance with formal logic, which culminated in the work of *Tarski.

twin-earth Twin-earth *thought experiments date back to Hilary *Putnam's *The Meaning of Meaning* (1975). They are conducted by imagining a possible world like this in many or all phenomenal respects, but unlike it in some other way. One then compares one's own situation with that of the twin or *Doppelgänger*. The point of the story is to determine whether your twin or *Doppelgänger* shares one or another psychological state with you, it being argued that if he does not, this shows that the state is essentially 'world involving', i.e. its identity depends on more than the phenomenal circumstances. For example, you may think of Homer, if he existed, and we can imagine a twin on twin-earth who has the same exposure to the same stories, and who contemplates the same word 'Homer', but who is not thereby thinking of Homer, since Homer is not a denizen of the twin's world. *See also* CONTENT, WIDE AND NARROW.

twins paradox *See* CLOCK PARADOX.

two-clock paradox *See* CLOCK PARADOX.

two-envelope paradox I am presented with two envelopes A and B, and told that one contains twice as much money as the other. I choose envelope A, and am offered the options of either keeping it or switching to B. What should I do? I reason: (1) For any amount $x, if I knew that A contained x, then the odds are even that B contains either $2x or $x/2, hence the expected amount in B would be $5x/4. So (2) for all x, if I knew that A contained $x, I would have an expected gain in switching to B. So (3) I should switch to B. But this seems clearly wrong, as my information about A and B is symmetrical—once I have B, by the same reasoning I should switch back to A. It is known that if there is a finite upper bound on x the reasoning is faulty, since (1) and (2) will not together be true. Things become trickier if this restriction is dropped.

two-place predicate *See* N-PLACE PREDICATE.

two-way interactionism The view that physical events cause mental events, and vice versa.

tychism (Greek, *tychē*, luck or chance) The view associated with *Peirce that chance is a real force in the universe; more recently, the view that chance mutations are the basis of evolutionary adaptation.

types, theory of *Russell's own reaction to his paradox of the class of all classes that are not members of themselves (*see* RUSSELL'S PARADOX) was to suggest that the definition is ill-formed because it involves the illegitimate notion of 'all classes'. If the entities of a theory are classified in a hierarchy, with individuals at the lowest level, sets of individuals at the next, sets of sets further up again, and if prohibitions are introduced against sets containing members of different types, then the paradox cannot be formulated.

When Russell published his solution he was also influenced by *Poincaré's constructivist response to the contradictions of *set theory. This suggested that in any application of the axiom of *comprehension, $(\exists y)((\forall x)(x \in y \leftrightarrow Fx))$, the variable x should not range over entities including the set y. If it does, the definition becomes *impredicative, and offends against the *vicious circle principle. To prohibit this, Russell sorted predicates into orders, again with restrictions on well-formedness. The result is called the ramified theory of types. Unfortunately it proved impossible to construct classical mathematics within the ramified theory, and Russell was forced to introduce the axiom of *reducibility, whose effect is to collapse the hierarchy of predicates.

Although the non-ramified or simple theory of types has attracted much subsequent work, all type theory suffers from a problem of unintuitive duplication. Thus for Russell there exists not one but an infinite number of the number 2, since there are sets of all sets having two members at each level in the hierarchy. Expressions needed at each type level, such as '=', are supposedly systematically ambiguous, and in some developments there are an infinite number of identity symbols.

The relative consistency of type theory has been proved within *Zermelo–Fraenkel set theory, thereby also showing that the latter is stronger than the former. Few logicians now believe that there is any reason to build type restrictions into the formal systems within which set-theoretic and mathematical reasoning is best represented.

type–token ambiguity How many words occur in the works of Shakespeare? The question may be asking how many types of word, or in other words how large Shakespeare's vocabulary is, in which case the answer will be several tens of thousands, or it may be asking how many tokens of those types, or words as they would be counted by a printer, in which case the answer will be many more. A car manufacturer may produce half a dozen cars in a year (types, here equivalent to models) but many thousand cars (instances, tokens). Types may themselves be subject to different criteria of *individuation: lexicographers need controversial principles in order to know when to count one word type or two.

type–type identity A form of *identity theory of mind in which it is supposed that mental events can be identified with physical events in such a way that to any kind of the one there will correspond a kind of the other. *Davidson is credited with realizing that there is no *a priori* reason for expecting this to be true, but it may still be so that each mental event is identical with some physical event. The *variable realization of the mental by the physical appears to make this a real possibility, although the issue is delicate, since there are different ways of drawing up the types or kinds of event in question. An identity theory that disclaims type–type correlations is a token–token identity theory. *See also* TYPE–TOKEN AMBIGUITY.

tzu jan (Chinese, naturally, spontaneously) A Taoist term for spontaneous and therefore natural or Heavenly inclinations, favourably contrasted with self-conscious and rationally designed ones.

Übermensch The 'superman' or 'overman' of *Nietzsche's ethical vision. The *Übermensch* transcends the boundaries of classes, creeds, and nationalities; he overcomes human nature itself, and maintains a lordly superiority to the normal shackles and conventions of social life. Although Nietzsche connects the character with Aristotelian virtue, the vision is essentially *Romantic when Aristotle's is not. The idea of a transfiguring freedom finds more pessimistic echoes in the *existentialist doctrine that existence precedes essence. *See also* WILL TO POWER.

Udayana (11th c.) One of the most important philosophers of the *Nyaya-Vaisheshika school. Udayana's masterpiece was the *Atmatattvaryiveka* ('On the Discrimination of the Reality of the Self'), a rebuttal of the Buddhist doctrine of *anatman* (*See* ATMAN), and a synoptic account of the relationship between the controversies over the reality of the self and other philosophical doctrinal differences between Nyaya and Buddhist schools.

ugliness A topic less discussed in *aesthetics than *beauty, but deserving attention. First, it has ethical and political implications, since being surrounded by ugliness is evidently an injury or harm and one that might deserve ethical and political remedy. Secondly, it is important that there can exist aesthetic 'disvalue', or in other words that the kinds of contemplation characteristic of taking an aesthetic attitude to some object are not purely their own reward, but are sometimes preludes to disgust or disenchantment.

Ulysses (sirens) In *Odyssey* 12, 39. 200, Homer relates how Ulysses has himself tied to the mast in order that he may hear the sirens' song, yet not follow all other sailors who, having done so, are driven to follow the sound, shipwreck, and perish. The myth shows that it may be advantageous not to be free, and so is a focus for debates over *paternalism, and the relation between higher and lower inclinations, or reason and desire (for a spectacular example, *see* DEMOCRITUS). Although sirens are popularly depicted as floppy Victorian nymphs it should be remembered that in early representations of the legend they are more formidable, sometimes depicted as birds with women's heads, or even male and bearded, with claws like vultures. They are representatives of alienating, god-like powers whose force we should know but against which we must be forearmed.

Unamuno, Miguel de (1864–1936) Spanish poet and man of letters, and professor of Greek at Salamanca from 1891. Influenced by *James and *Kierkegaard he developed an existentialist Christian theology, premised on a tragic view of life and mortality. His views are largely developed in fiction and drama; his most significant philosophical text is *The Tragic Sense of Life* (1913).

uncertainty principle *See* HEISENBERG UNCERTAINTY PRINCIPLE.

unconscious The idea that the brain is constantly processing information of which we remain unaware is widely attested in the brain and behavioural sciences (*see* BLINDSIGHT). It is also widely agreed that people may have beliefs and desires that they cannot represent to themselves without processes of assistance. The methodological problem that such processes face is to distinguish between uncovering genuine unconscious beliefs and desires, and gratuitously reading them into a subject's behaviour. More detailed theories of the form such assistance should take, and of the lurid content unconscious beliefs and desires are often supposed to possess, are controversial. *See* FREUD, PSYCHOANALYSIS.

underdetermination (of theory) The underdetermination of theory by data is the view that there will always be more than one theory consistent with any body of empirical data. A stronger version claims that this would be so even if the data were to include all possible empirical data. If these theses are purely logical in form, they do no more than claim that the data will not entail that just one theory is the true one, which will be so provided that the content of the theory is more than a mere consequence of the data. A yet stronger version (methodological underdetermination) claims that even all possible data plus the best canons of scientific explanation (simplicity, good inductive sense) will not yield one theory as the unique best choice. The thesis in this form is frequently cited in support of *relativistic and social constructivist theories of science. It requires confidence in the distinction between *theory and evidence, in our ability to understand what it would be for a theory really to be adequate to all empirical data, and finally in our ability to distinguish genuinely different theories from notational variants of the same one theory.

understanding To have a word, or a picture, or any other object in one's mind seems to be one thing, but to understand it is quite another. A major target of the later work of *Wittgenstein is the suggestion that this understanding is achieved by a further presence, so that words might be understood if they are accompanied by ideas, for example; Wittgenstein insists that the extra presence merely raises the same kind of problem again. The better suggestion is that understanding is to be thought of as possession of a technique, or skill, and this is the point of the slogan that 'meaning is use'. The idea is congenial to *pragmatism and hostile to ineffable and incommunicable understandings. *See also* MEANING, PRIVATE LANGUAGE, *VERSTEHEN*.

undistributed middle, fallacy of the If an argument has the form of a *syllogism, but the middle term is not *distributed, it will not be valid: all people are mammals, some mammals are cats, therefore?

unexpected examination paradox *See* PREDICTION PARADOX.

uniformity of nature The principle that the future will resemble the past, in that when sufficiently similar situations recur, similar effects follow. The principle seems to be presupposed in some form both by the reliance we put upon scientific prediction and by the certainties of everyday life. Its exact formulation and justification is the problem of *induction. *See also* GOODMAN'S PARADOX, HUME.

union The union of two sets is the set of things that are members of either. Formally, $x \in S \cup R$ iff $x \in S \vee x \in R$. However, the union of a single set, $\cup A$, is the union of all its subsets, that is $x \in \cup A$ iff $(\exists S)(S \in A \; \& \; x \in S)$. This connects with the first notion via the fact that $\cup\{S, R\} = S \cup R$.

unit set The unit set of x is the set whose sole member is x. The unit set is to be distinguished from its member: for example, the unit set of the set of days of the week has one member, but that member is itself a set that has seven members.

unity of science The doctrine that the special sciences—biology, chemistry, geology, economics, psychology—can eventually be reduced to one overarching science, usually thought of as physics. The reduction will be accomplished by providing an 'image' of the special science in the universal science, so that the laws of the special science turn out to be special cases of the universal way things are. The ideal was a central part of *logical positivist thinking about science, and still influences many philosophers of a *physicalist bent.

universal, concrete The view prominent in *Hegel that ideas or concepts can be seen as historical forces, having actual effects in the real world. It is not entirely clear what level of *realism this suggests. Hegel writes that 'This concrete had manifold forms; social instincts in the practical sphere, laws of nature in the theoretical' (*Lectures on the Philosophy of History*), suggesting something like a physical reality to the universal; a less demanding doctrine would simply stress the operation of ideas like that of equality, or those of reason and freedom, on the minds of people and hence on actions and historical developments.

universal generalization A proposition generalizing over all things of a kind. In first-order logic, one with a *universal quantifier having the rest of the formula within its scope.

universal grammar *See* GENERATIVE GRAMMAR.

universal instantiation The inference from a proposition stating that all things are thus and so to an instance, stating that some particular is thus and so. In classical formal logic, it is also known as universal quantifier elimination

universalism in ethics In one sense, the idea that moral demands apply to everyone, no matter what their local cultural or historical traditions may be. Thus liberalism may assume a budget of human rights that apply worldwide, insisting, for instance, that women have a right to education or to political representation, regardless of their actual oppression in particular traditions. In a different sense, the idea that ethics can be formulated in terms of universal principles, rather than learned as a swirl of potentially conflicting pressures on policy and action. In this sense it is the opposite of *particularism.

universalizability The feature of moral judgements that whilst a moral judgement may concern a particular subject in a particular situation, it must *supervene upon general features of the situation, that can in principle occur in other cases. Someone making a judgement thus incurs an obligation to treat those other cases alike. The principle is purely formal, since its application will depend upon a selection of what it is that makes other cases alike: this may be a highly abstract feature ('telling a lie') or a highly specific concurrence of circumstances (*see* PARTICULARISM, SITUATION ETHICS). Although there is widespread agreement that the idea points to one essential feature of moral thought, there is less certainty about its definition, the source of its authority, and its significance in constraining possible moral positions. *Hume sees adoption of the general or common point of view as a necessary feature of evaluation; Adam *Smith thinks its authority derives from our dislike of being unable to justify ourselves to others; *Kant sees it as a requirement of reason. *Hare was the most resolute recent champion of the substantive ethical significance of universalizability. *See also* CATEGORICAL IMPERATIVE, IDEAL OBSERVER.

universal language *See* *CHARACTERISTICA UNIVERSALIS*.

universal proposition A proposition asserting something of all things meeting some condition. *See* QUANTIFIER.

universal quantifier *See* QUANTIFIER, VARIABLE.

universals A universal is a property or relation that can be instanced, or instantiated, by a number of different particular things: each yellow thing provides an instance of the property of yellowness, and each square thing the property of being square. The things covered by a universal are thus similar in some respect. The general questions asked about universals include: are they discovered or invented? How are we to think of something that has itself no spatial position, yet is instanced at many places and times? What is the relation of instantiation? Can sharing the same property be analysed in terms of resemblance? How does the mind perceive the general property as well as the particular instance of it? Approaches to universals include *Platonism, or the position that universals exist independently of things (*ante rem*); the Aristotelian belief that universals exist in things (*in re*) but not independently of them; *conceptualism, or the view that they are reflections of the propensity of the mind to group things together (*post rem*, or abstracted from things); *nominalism, or the view that the universal is the breath of the voice (*flatus vocis*), i.e. that to share a universal is simply to be describable by the same word; and finally a general suspicion that the whole issue is the result of a misleading *reification, trapping us into thinking of two categories of thing (the particular and the universals it instances) instead of just particulars. However, a theory of universals is vital in many areas: for example, one's attitude to knowledge and science will depend upon whether natural kinds are thought of as invented or discovered, and the problem of *induction is made even less tractable if the similarities we project are thought of as having only a conventional or nominalistic status. The problem of universals was a major topic of controversy in medieval philosophy: *see* BOETHIUS, OCKHAM, PORPHYRY. *See also* FORMS.

universe of discourse The things across which the *quantifiers of a formal theory may range: as it might be, the points on a line, or sets, or physical objects, or whatever else we are treating. The universe of discourse may, but also may not, form a set: for instance, the universe of discourse of set theory includes any set, but there is no set of all sets.

univocal Having one meaning; unambiguous.

unmoved mover *See* MOVER, UNMOVED.

Upanishads (Sanskrit, the act of sitting down by something) The collection of philosophical verses that conclude the *Vedas and make up the main original philosophical commentary on Hindu scriptures.

SEE WEB LINKS

- An introduction to the Upanishads and their interpretation
- An annotated translation of the Upanishads

use (of words) The slogan that 'meaning is use' is associated with the later philosophy of *Wittgenstein. It has affinities with the claims of *pragmatism, that the meaning of a sign consists in the set of practices following upon 'acceptance of the symbol'. The difficulty is to characterize use in a sufficiently general way: no advantage over traditional ideas is gained if it is said, for instance, that the use of a predicate is to refer to a universal, or the use of a sentence is to express an associated proposition. A useful framework due to *Sellars divides use into three parts: there are 'entry rules', describing the kinds of situation justifying application of a term, 'exit rules', describing the practical consequences of accepting the application of the term, and transformation rules taking us to other linguistic applications that themselves bear definite relations to the term.

use/mention distinction The distinction between using a word, such as 'cat', to talk about cats, and mentioning the word, as one would if pointing out that 'cat' has three letters. The distinction becomes important when the possibility of mistaking use and mention arises, and philosophers often like to believe that those who do not share their views have made such a confusion. A belief shared by many *logical positivists was that what appear to be perhaps fundamental or especially profound remarks about things (five is a number; necessarily matter is extended) are in fact reflections of conventions governing terminology ('five' refers to a number; 'matter' refers to whatever fills extended regions of space). *See also* FORMAL/MATERIAL MODE OF SPEECH.

utilitarianism The ethical theory advanced by *Bentham, both James and J. S. *Mill, *Sidgwick, and many others, that answers all questions of what to do, what to admire, or how to live, in terms of maximizing *utility or happiness. As well as an ethical theory, utilitarianism is, in effect, the view of life presupposed in most modern political and economic planning, when it is supposed that happiness is measured in economic terms. In J. S. Mill's statement of the doctrine, 'actions are right in proportion as they tend to promote happiness, wrong as they tend to produce the reverse of happiness'. The view is a form of *consequentialism, in which the relevant consequences are identified in terms of amounts of happiness. Different conceptions of happiness separated Mill's version ('better a Socrates dissatisfied than a pig satisfied'), which recognized qualitative differences between different kinds of pleasure, from Bentham's forthright attempt to reduce all questions of happiness to presence of pleasure or pain ('other things being equal, pushpin is as good as poetry'). Bentham's version aims to render the basic concepts of ethics susceptible of comparison and measurement (*see* FELICIFIC CALCULUS, HEDONISM), but this goal will not be met in Mill's system. Critics of this aspect of the doctrine also query whether there is a conception of human happiness that stands sufficiently apart from general conceptions of behaving and acting well, to act as an independent target of action (*see* *EUDAIMONIA*, VIRTUE ETHICS).

The doctrine that applies utilitarianism to actions directly, so that an individual action is right if it increases happiness more than any alternative, is known as direct or *act utilitarianism; the contrast is with *indirect utilitarianism.

SEE WEB LINKS

- A list of internet resources on utilitarianism, including links to topical websites
- A list of internet resources on utilitarianism, including video presentations and classic writings

utility The basic unit of desirability in much *decision theory, *game theory, and economics. The difficulty is being sure that it refers to anything sufficiently definite to work with. This requires, for instance, that at least some comparison of utility across different times and different people is possible. Stronger assumptions may require that utilities can be ordered in various scales, or summed and manipulated arithmetically (*see* FELICIFIC CALCULUS; MEASUREMENT, PHILOSOPHY OF). This may seem to involve a wild idealization, since although we might judge that this year's holiday was better than last year's, we are not apt to think it makes sense to say it was twice as good, or that it generated half as many units of utility as (say) a lifetime's consumption of chocolate. Cautious work instead uses orderings of preferences: an outcome A has greater utility than outcome B (for subject x) if and only if x prefers A to B. Preferences are in turn revealed in actual or idealized choices, thus allowing the concept some behavioural and scientific respectability. Again, however, most traditions of ethical thought recognize more valuable and worthwhile goals to life than simply satisfying an arbitrary sequence of preferences.

utility calculus *See* FELICIFIC CALCULUS.

utopia (Greek, no place) A utopia is an ideal place or state of life. The term derives from the *Utopia* of Thomas *More (1516). Visions of ideal communities and ways of living have naturally informed many political platforms, although the conceptions of *human nature that they imply are usually highly simplistic. Hence utopianism, or the recommending and criticizing of political action in the light of supposed ideal systems or utopias. *Dystopias tend to be more vividly imagined, just as hell is easier to conceive than heaven.

vacuous A generalization, 'all F things are G things', is represented in formal logic by the quantification $(\forall x)(Fx \rightarrow Gx)$. This has the property that when there are no things that are F, it is true (it means the same as 'there are no F things that are not G', which is obviously true when there are no F things at all). In such a case the generalization is said to be vacuously true. A contrasting view of such generalizations is taken in traditional logic: *see* SQUARE OF OPPOSITION.

vagueness Many sentences are relatively vague; others relatively precise. A term that is perfectly precise would generate no borderline cases, and although this is often presented as a theoretical ideal it is extremely unclear that any learnable, speakable language could begin to meet it. For even basic observations ('this is red') admit of borderline cases (in the oranges and purples), and even when care is taken to make terms as precise as possible, unforeseen contingencies, new kinds of discovery, and things with new combinations of properties may always provide hard cases whose classification is left unclear. The best *semantic treatment of vagueness is unsettled: issues include the correct way to resolve the *sorites paradox, and the question of whether classical logic should be modified to countenance degrees of truth, corresponding to degrees of vagueness. *see also* SUPERVALUATION.

vague objects It is usually indefinite where the mountain ends and the plain begins. Is the mountain then a vague object, or are all objects themselves precise, with vagueness an artefact of the way we pick them out?

Vaihinger, Hans (1852–1933) German philosopher. Vaihinger was educated in theology at Tübingen, and became professor at Halle. He is remembered for his 'fictionalism' or philosophy of 'as if'. Influenced by *Kant's view that the mind sets itself problems that it cannot solve, and by the pessimism of *Schopenhauer, Vaihinger denied that there is any prospect of achieving truth in many areas. Instead, thought proceeds by the use of fictions, or ideas known to be false. Ideas such as those of God, immortality, freedom, the social contract, or the virgin birth can be 'beautiful, suggestive and useful' although we know they have no application to reality. Theories are useful because they enable us to cope with what would otherwise be the unmanageable complexity of things. The doctrine bears some affinity to *pragmatism, but differs in that Vaihinger thinks that our useful theories are nevertheless really false. Vaihinger's most influential work was *Die Philosophie des Als Ob* (1911, trs. as *The Philosophy of 'As If'*, 1924).

Vaisheshika (Sanskrit, *visesa*, difference) One of the six orthodox schools of Indian philosophy. Vaisheshika is concerned with the things that there are, or the *categories of being. Vaisheshika is a kind of *atomism, holding that the basis of physical reality is a plurality of infinitesimal atoms. The Indian school was well aware of the problem of understanding how the combination of *infinitesimals produces a finite quantity of stuff (*see* BAYLE'S TRILEMMA). Vaisheshika is philosophically allied to the *Nyaya school, supplementing its analysis of knowledge with a philosophy of the nature of the things that are known.

validity In its primary meaning it is arguments that are valid or invalid, according to whether the conclusion *follows from the premises. Premises and conclusions themselves are not valid or invalid, but true or false. In *model theory a formula is called valid, when it is true in all *interpretations.

Valla, Lorenzo (1407–57) Italian Renaissance humanist. Valla first exposed as a fraud the Donation of Constantine, the document purporting to express the gift of the western empire to Pope Sylvester by the Emperor Constantine, and thereby incidentally proving the sovereignty of the Pope over secular governments. One of his influential treatises was *De Voluptate* ('On Pleasure', 1431), playing off the systems of the *Stoics, the *Epicureans, and Christian ethics. *De Libero Arbitrio* ('On Free Choice', 1435–9) takes issue with *Boethius's treatment of *free will, arguing that God's foreknowledge is compatible with human free will, but that his power is not. Valla was also an acute early critic of the multiplicity of scholastic *categories and distinctions, and one of the first writers to see that *existence is not a kind of predicate.

valuation (logic) *See* INTERPRETATION (LOGIC).

value To acknowledge some feature of things as a value is to take it into account in decision making, or in other words to be inclined to advance it as a consideration in influencing choice and guiding oneself and others. Those who see values as 'subjective' think of this in terms of a personal stance, occupied as a kind of choice, and immune to rational argument (although often, and curiously, deserving some kind of reverence and respect). Those who think of values as objective suppose that for some reason—requirements of rationality, human nature, God, or other authority—choice can be guided and corrected from some independent standpoint. *See also* EUTHYPHRO DILEMMA, PROJECTIVISM, RELATIVISM, SUBJECTIVISM.

value-free A central concern in the methodology of the social sciences is the extent to which it is possible or desirable for them to be 'value-free'. The claim that they ought to be value-free (German, *wertfrei*) is associated with *Weber: the question is whether insightful or useful descriptions of social phenomena can be given in terms that do not express the values of the author. If this cannot be done, it raises questions of the objectivity of the social sciences, and their dissimilarity from other sciences. The issue connects with the possibility of scientific or value-free interpretation. If interpretation is governed by a principle of rationality or *charity, then values may infuse the entire enterprise of understanding and interpreting social behaviour of any kind.

value of a function *See* FUNCTION.

Vanini, Giulio Cesare (*c.*1584–1619) Italian philosopher. Vanini studied law at Naples and theology at Padua. He travelled in Germany and England in 1612, after which he abandoned his Catholicism. He published *Amphiteatrum aeternae providentiae* ('The Theatre of Eternal Providence') in 1615, and in 1616 *De admirandis naturae reginae deaeque mortalium arcanis* ('On the Secrets of Nature, Queen and Goddess of Mortal Beings'). He was much influenced by Averroës and Pietro Pomponazzi, rejecting revealed religion and divine creation, and advocating a conception of divinity as totally immanent in nature. His works were declared heretical and he was burned at the stake by the Inquisition.

vanity Having an excessively high opinion of one's own attainments and qualities, or excessive desire for the praise of others, regardless of whether it is deserved. *Aquinas makes no clear distinction between vanity and pride, but associates both with the desire for distinction and importance. According to Adam *Smith, vanity is 'always founded upon the belief of our being the object of attention and approbation'. Both Aquinas and Smith regard vanity as the principal motive to the pursuit of wealth and distinction (*Summa Theologiae*, IaIIae 84; *The Theory of Moral Sentiments*, i. 3. 2). *See also* MANDEVILLE, VEBLEN.

variable (logic) A fundamental notion of modern logic. Intuitively, suppose we have a class of objects about which we might be interested (a domain), and we start with a simple sentence 'Jane is hungry'. We then strike out mention of Jane, leaving a gap that we mark with the letter x: 'x is hungry'. This represents something short of a sentence (it is called an *open sentence, or predicate). We can 'point' the letter x at members of the domain in turn, giving successive sentences like the one with which we started. In such a process the letter x is said to function as a variable taking as values each member of the domain successively. We might conclude the procedure with information like this: somewhere in this process one of the sentences is true, or everywhere such a sentence is true. Such information does not tell us who is hungry, but tells us the quantity of times the predicate is satisfied. The information that somewhere the predicate F applies to the value is represented as $(\exists x)Fx$; the information that it always applies as $(\forall x)Fx$. The expressions $(\exists \ldots)$ and $(\forall \ldots)$ are the existential and universal *quantifiers. The power of the idea only becomes apparent when we consider multiple quantifications. If we start with a relational sentence 'Fred loves Jane' and strike out both names, marking the spaces with different variables, we obtain 'x loves y'. We can now build very different kinds of information: everyone loves someone: $(\forall x)(\exists y)x$ loves y; someone loves everyone: $(\exists x)(\forall y)x$ loves y, and so on. The study of these forms and the relations between them is quantification theory. The basic calculus that formalizes their logic is the *predicate calculus.

variable realization Descriptions of a thing at one level can be true in virtue of some underlying properties, in the way that the description of a computer as running such-and-such a program is true in virtue of the configurations of its circuitry. It may then be true that other configurations at the lower level could have had the same result, and where this is so it is said that the higher-level properties can be variably realized by the lower-level ones. In the philosophy of mind, it is plausible to think that a person's psychological states could be realized by a variety of different configurations at the neural level. The point is sometimes used to argue the superiority of *functionalism over mind–brain *identity theories.

Vasubandhu (AD 4th or 5th c.) Indian philosopher, eventually of the *Yogacara school of Buddhism. He taught a kind of idealism, arguing from *illusion that mental images are the sole reality known to us.

vat, brain in a *See* BRAIN IN A VAT.

Vatsyayana (5th c.) Seminal early member of the *Nyaya school, and the first to write a commentary on the *Nyayasutra*. Vatsyayana's commentary laid the foundations of the realism and the concentration on logic characteristic of that school.

Vattimo, Gianni (1936–) Italian follower of *Gadamer and *Heidegger. Vattimo studied at Turin and Heidelberg, and taught aesthetics at the university of Turin, also pursuing a career as an administrator and parliamentarian. Comprehensively rejecting the idea of correspondence between language and the world, he espouses an experimental and non-foundational freedom of flow of interpretation and conversation. Vattimo frequently collaborated with *Derrida. Translated works include *The End of Modernity: Nihilism and Hermeneutics in Postmodern Culture* (1988) and *Beyond Interpretation: The Meaning of Hermeneutics for Philosophy* (1997).

Vauvenarges, Luc de Clapiers de (1715–47) French soldier and writer. Vauvenarges resigned from the army in ill-health in 1744, disappointed in his quest for glory. Before his death he published *Introduction à la connaissance de l'esprit humain suivie de réflexions et maximes* ('Introduction to Knowledge of the Human Spirit, followed by Reflections and Maxims', 1746), a work greatly admired by *Voltaire and others. It turns its back on the pessimism both of Christian writers and of *La Rochefoucauld, championing instead man's Stoicism, his capacity to attain glory, and the human passions.

Veblen, Thorstein (1857–1929) American economist and sociologist. He is remembered in political and moral philosophy for the doctrine of conspicuous consumption, expressed in *The Theory of the Leisure Class* (1899). He identifies the fundamental need to display financial well-being in what would otherwise seem wasteful display, in order to manifest status and stability, and to distinguish oneself from those slightly less well-off. Veblen argues that the principle is a human universal that explains a large variety of social phenomena. For example, we appreciate a well-trimmed lawn because it is a sign of surplus labour and wealth, or employ a butler because having an able-bodied man doing next to nothing is more meritorious than having someone who could not do much else. *See also* MANDEVILLE, SMITH, VANITY.

Veda (Sanskrit, knowledge, sacred lore) The Vedas are the scriptures derived from the Vedic period (*c.*1500–700 BC) following the migration of Aryan people into the Indus valley. The four chief collections are the *Rig-Veda*, or book of prayers and hymns, the *Yajur-Veda*, or book of sacrificial formulae, the *Sama-Veda*, or book of chants, and the *Athar-Veda*, a book of magical spells and philosophical speculation. The most famous text is the *Rig-Veda* (verses of wisdom). The philosophical component of the Vedas is mainly contained in the concluding sections or explanations, known as the *Upanishads.

Vedanta The school of Hindu philosophy most concerned to protect the literal truth of the *Upanishads, and therefore most critical of the dualistic and realistic tendencies in other Indian philosophical schools. The purest monism (**advaita* or non-duality) recognizes only **brahman* (identified with **atman*, as the Upanishads require), and is especially associated with the philosopher *Shankara.

SEE WEB LINKS

- An introduction to the origins of the Vedanta
- An overview of the Vedanta with links to other sites

vegetarianism The theory and practice of refusing to eat the meat of dead animals; sometimes taken to include refusing to use (*exploit) other remains of animals, e.g. by wearing leather. More radical stances include that of vegans, who refuse to use the produce of live animals, such as eggs and milk. Since it is hard to make divisions within the natural order, *slippery slopes lead in one direction to the accusation from vegetarians that meat-eaters have no reason for avoiding cannibalism, and in the other direction to the accusation from meat-eaters that vegetarians ought really to respect the lives of cabbages.

veil of appearance (veil of perception) Pejorative term for any model of perception according to which *sense data become the direct objects of experience. Visual sense data then seem to make a thin, coloured film getting between us and the world.

veil of ignorance In the work of *Rawls, the metaphorical description of the barrier against using special concerns in order to assess principles of justice. The veil of ignorance defines the *original position. It is as if the parties have to contract into basic social structures, defining for example the liberties that their society will allow, and the economic structure it will recognize, but not knowing which role in the society they themselves will be allocated. Only if a social system can rationally be chosen or contracted into from this position, does it satisfy the constraints on justice. *See also* DIFFERENCE PRINCIPLE.

Venn, John (1834–1923) English logician and probability theorist. Born in Hull, Venn was educated at Gonville and Caius College, Cambridge, where he became a Fellow in 1857, and President in 1903. His work *The Logic of Chance* (1867) is an early exploration of the frequency theory of *probability. His *Symbolic Logic* (1881) was hugely influential as the first successful formulation of the algebraic approach to logic pioneered by the mathematician *Boole.

Venn diagram A kind of diagram invented by *Venn in 1881, for representing and assessing the validity of elementary inferences either of a *syllogistic form, or from the *Boolean algebra of classes (Venn was attempting to illustrate Boole's own methods). In a Venn diagram for the syllogism there are three circles, corresponding to S, M, and P. Shaded areas indicate which combinations are empty, and a cross indicates which ones have members, while a cross on a border between two classes represents that at least one class has a member. For example, to illustrate the syllogism 'Some S is M, all M is P, so some S is P', the first premise is represented by (i). Here the cross hovers between the area of P and the area outside P. However, the second premise adds the shading of (ii), since any M region outside P is empty.

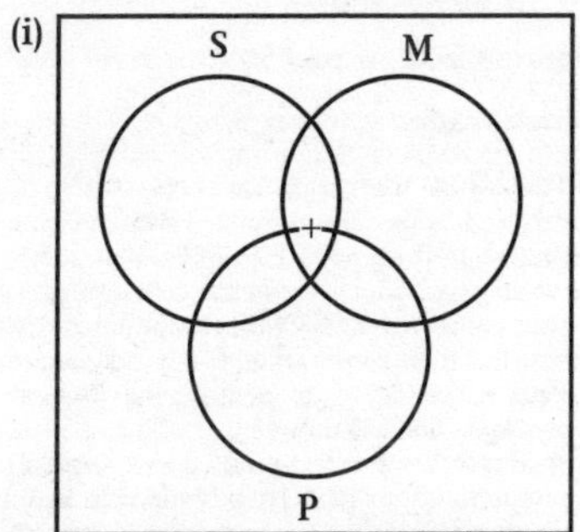

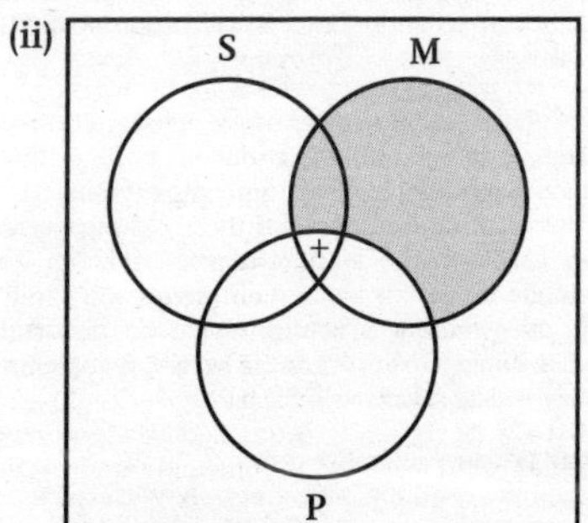

Hence, the cross cannot be there, and is driven into the P area. This shows that some S is indeed P; hence the syllogism is valid. Venn generalized the method. For statements in the algebra of classes involving four terms, ellipses can be drawn, but the method becomes cumbersome. Strips and charts of various kinds were invented in the late 19th and early 20th centuries to give graphical representations of such problems.

verbal definition A definition of some word or words in terms of others, as opposed to *ostensive definition, which proceeds by indicating an example. The term is sometimes used of *nominal definitions.

veridical Truthful. A veridical perception is one that represents things as they are, contrasted with an illusory or even delusory one that does not.

verification principle (verifiability principle) The principle central to *logical positivism, according to which the meaning of a statement is its method of verification. Sentences apparently expressing propositions that admit of no verification (such as those of metaphysics and theology) are in consequence meaningless, or at least fail to put forward theses with cognitive meaning, capable of truth or falsity. The principle requires confidence that we know what a verification consists in, and tended to coexist with a fairly simple conception of each thought as answerable to individual experiences. To avoid undue simplification the principle moved from requiring a strong or conclusive verification as the condition of meaning, to admitting indirect and inconclusive methods of verification. However, more complex and *holistic conceptions of language and its relation to the world suggest a more flexible set of possible relations, with sentences that are individually not verifiable nevertheless having a use in an overall network of beliefs or theory that itself answers to experience.

verisimilitude The extent to which a hypothesis approaches the truth. The first attempt to define this notion, due to *Popper, identifies this with the extent to which a theory captures the whole truth: a theory T will have more verisimilitude than a rival T' just in case T implies more truths and fewer falsities than T'. But the formal development of the notion has proved extremely tricky, especially as the verisimilitude of theories is apt to vary with variations in the language in which they are couched.

Verstehen (German, understanding) A term especially associated with *Dilthey and *Weber, to denote the understanding we have of human activities. In the *Verstehen* tradition these are understood from within, by means that are opposed to knowing something by objective observation, or by placing it in a network of scientific regularities (*see* THEORY-THEORY). The exact difference is controversial: one approach is that understanding a human expression is a matter of knowing what in oneself would gain expression that way, and 'reliving' by a process of empathy the mental life of the person to be understood. But other less subjective suggestions are also found. The question of whether there is a method distinct from that of science to be used in human contexts, and so whether *Verstehen* is necessarily the method of the social as opposed to the natural sciences, is still open. *See also* SIMULATION THEORY.

via negativa *See* NEGATIVE THEOLOGY.

vice The classic discussion is Book 7 of *Aristotle's *Nicomachaean Ethics*, in which he distinguishes incontinence from intemperance. Incontinent people are impetuous, or weak. They know what they should do, but succumb to temptation, being carried away by their passions. Intemperate people on the other hand do wrong deliberately. They have an incorrect notion of the proper ends of human action. They are less prone to remorse, and less curable, than incontinent ones. *See also* VIRTUE.

vicious circle principle Principle proposed by *Poincaré and *Russell in order to solve the logical and semantic paradoxes. It would ban any collection (set) containing members that can only be defined by means of the collection taken as a whole. It is effectively a ban on *impredicative definitions.

vicious regress *See* REGRESS.

Vico, Giambattista (1668–1744) Italian philosopher of history. Vico was born in Naples, and educated by the Jesuits. From 1699 he held the chair of rhetoric at the university of Naples. Vico's principal work was the *Scienza Nova* (1725, recast in new editions in 1730 and 1744, trs. as *The New Science of Giambattista Vico*, 1949). This work was largely unread in the 18th century, until it was picked up by the theorists of German *Romanticism, who responded to many of its original themes. Vico distanced himself from the prevailing Cartesianism of his time in two important ways. First, he denied that *Descartes had correctly located the sources of certainty and knowledge. These are not found via 'clear and distinct ideas' but in our own activities and actions: one of Vico's mottos was *verum factum* ('the true and the made are identical'). Thus mathematics, for example, admits of certainty only because it is a human construction. Secondly, Vico believed that Cartesians overplayed the role of physical and mathematical science, and neglected the possibility of social and historical knowledge. Vico showed an entirely original appreciation of the delicacy with which a historian must confront this task of understanding past modes of thought. This understanding must take as its data all the languages, myths, and traditions that are handed down, interpreted not in terms of a fixed idea of a universal human nature, but by an imaginative capacity for re-entering the modes of consciousness that they represent. Vico is thus a father-figure for many subsequent writers in the **Verstehen* tradition, such as *Dilthey and *Collingwood.

A further prescient doctrine of Vico's was that human history goes through connected and coherent stages, resulting in a pattern of *corsi e ricorsi*, growth and decay. At a given moment the life of a society will manifest a typical unity of which all its social aspects, including its literature, language, law, art, politics, and philosophy, are expressions, but such periods successively pass through the various stages, until the cycle starts again. As we look back on such an evolution we can see that institutions served quite other functions than those for which they were ostensibly designed. This view subsequently formed the foundation of the work of *Hegel and *Marx, although Vico, himself a Catholic, saw in the whole cycle the guiding operations of providence.

Vienna Circle *See* LOGICAL POSITIVISM.

Vijnanavada *See* YOGACARA.

vindication The pragmatic approach to the problem of *induction associated with *Reichenbach and Herbert Feigl (1902–88), that tries to show not that inductively based conclusions will be true, nor even that they will probably be true, but instead that there can be no other better strategy for predicting the future, or generalizing from evidence: induction will do well if anything at all will. An analogy is being stranded on a desert island with the opportunity to float off a bottle with a note requesting rescue: it may not be knowable how probable it is that this action will be successful, but it may be known that it will be successful if anything is, and hence the strategy is rational.

violence Action that injures or destroys that to which it is applied. Structural violence is that which is inherent in a situation whose intentional or unintentional result is injury and destruction, and to which the authors of the situation are indifferent. In this sense coal-mines, or family life, may conceal structural violence. The main social thinker to recommend or glorify violence as a political means was *Sorel.

vipassana Meditative practice in *Buddhism, aimed at obtaining a true metaphysical picture of reality, which means dissolving the stable categories of substance and self in favour of the evanescent time-slices or bundles of sensation that give rise to them.

virtue A virtue is a trait of character that is to be admired: one rendering its possessor better, either morally, or intellectually, or in the conduct of specific affairs. Both *Plato and *Aristotle devote much time to the unity of the virtues, or the way in which possession of one in the right way requires possession of the others; another central concern is the way in which possession of virtue, which might seem to stand in the way of self-interest, in fact makes possible the achievement of self-interest properly understood, or **eudaimonia*. But different conceptions of moral virtue and its relation to other virtue characterize Platonic, Aristotelian, *Stoic, Christian, *Enlightenment, *Romantic, and 20th-century ethical writing. These divisions reflect central preoccupations of their time and needs of the cultures in which they gain predominance: the humility, charity, patience, and chastity of Christianity would have been unintelligible as ethical virtues to classical Greeks, whereas the 'magnanimity' of the *great-souled man of Aristotle is hard for us to read as an unqualified good. Syntheses of Christian and Greek conceptions are attempted by many, including *Aquinas, but a resolute return to an Aristotelian conception has been impossible since the emergence of generalized benevolence as a leading virtue. For *Hume a virtue is a trait of character with the power of producing love or esteem of others, or pride in oneself, by being 'useful or agreeable' to its possessors and those affected by them. In *Kant, virtue is purely a trait that can act as a handmaiden to the doing of duty, having no independent ethical value, and in *utilitarianism, virtues are traits of character that further pursuit of the general happiness.

virtue epistemology An approach to *epistemology modelled upon virtue ethics. The idea is to approach the notion of justification through investigating the qualities of mind that lead to the 'right' or virtuous attitude to a belief, which may be conviction, moderate confidence, or more or less firm disbelief. These virtues will be analogous to other moral virtues, such as patience, diligence, integrity, generosity. The difficulty for virtue epistemology is to distinguish its approach from one that simply collects epistemic virtues together as those qualities of mind making for reliability.

virtue ethics The theory of ethics that takes the notion of virtue as primary, rather than a view either of the 'good', for the sake of which we act, or of duty, law, or reason thought of as providing rules of action. Virtue ethics is typically modelled on the work of *Aristotle (especially the *Nicomachean Ethics*), although other virtues than those that he recognized may be introduced. At a superficial level virtue ethics may establish more or less peaceful relationships with the ethics of *Hume, *Kant, the *Thomist and the *utilitarian traditions. But the basic theoretical difference remains that for these thinkers virtues are derivative, prized for ends they serve or duties they enable us to perform. So, for Hume for example, virtues are qualities of mind useful or agreeable to their possessor or others around him. For virtue ethics the direction of explanation must be reversed, with virtue providing the concept with which to elucidate happiness, usefulness, duty, and practical reason. This actually makes Aristotle, for whom the concept of **eudaimonia* is fundamental, only an impure predecessor of virtue ethics. The main problem for the approach is to account for how the virtuous agent thinks, as courses of action are contemplated, without admitting that it will be in terms of duties, or consequences, which thereby regain a certain priority.

vision *See* PERCEPTION.

vitalism The doctrine that there is some feature of living bodies that prevents their nature being entirely explained in physical or chemical terms. This feature may be the presence of a further 'thing' (such as a soul), but it may also be simply the emergence of special relations or principles of organization arising from the complexity of the biological organism. The former kind of doctrine envisages Life as a kind of fiery fluid (animal electricity, life force), that needs pouring into an inanimate body in order for it to become alive. *Aristotle (*De Anima* and *De Generatione*) is the principal source of a more sophisticated vitalism, holding that the life of an animal consists in its *psyche*, which provides a principle of explanation determining the morphological development of the organism, by a principle of teleological or *final causation. In the 19th century the two great exponents of vitalism were *Bergson and the biologist Hans Driesch (1867–1941).

Vitalism has been eclipsed by the advance in molecular genetics, and consequent understanding of the development of organisms in terms drawn from normal science, so the consensus amongst philosophers and biologists is that it offers no explanatory principles that the life sciences need. However, there do remain problems in understanding how different levels of description and explanation of one thing, such as those of psychology and those of biology, or those of biology and those of chemistry, relate to each other. *See also* SUPERVENIENCE.

Vitoria, Francisco de (*c.*1486–1546) Dominican professor of theology at Salamanca. Vitoria studied in Paris and gained his chair in 1526. His writings cover a variety of topics, but he is remembered mainly for discussions of the nature of political society, authority, and ownership, with particular reference to the newly-discovered Spanish domains in South America. He has been honoured by Dutch scholars as an influential predecessor of *Grotius, and hence a founder of international law.

Vives, Juan Luis (1493–1540) Spanish humanist and scholar. Owing to the perturbed state of Europe, Vives lived in many places, including Paris and Oxford, although often based at Bruges, where his Stoic teaching and hostility to Aristotle were largely tolerated. He edited Augustine's *City of God*, and wrote widely on educational matters, producing among other things a highly popular teaching manual for Latin. *De anima et vita* ('Of the Soul and Life', 1538) is an early empirical study of the emotions.

void The notion of empty space (like that of eventless time) proved repugnant to *Parmenides and the *Stoics, and much later, but for similar reasons, to *Descartes. One reason for disliking the idea may be based on confusion about the allegedly paradoxical existence of *nothing (for nothing is precisely what there is in empty space); others find it contrary to the *plenitude of God that he should allow there to be nothing where he could have put something. Other problems arise from trying to conceive of the passage of force and information through a vacuum. In modern *quantum mechanics, space is not empty, but seething with latent or virtual particles, ready to spring into being if various physical events occur. *See also* ACTION AT A DISTANCE, FIELD.

volition A mental act of willing or trying, whose presence is sometimes supposed to make the difference between intentional or voluntary action and mere behaviour. The theory that there are such acts is problematic, and the idea that they make the required difference is a case of explaining a phenomenon by citing another that raises exactly the same problem, since the intentional or voluntary nature of the act of volition now needs explanation. *See* REGRESS.

volonté générale, volonté de tous (French, general will, will of all) *See* GENERAL WILL.

V

Voltaire (1694–1778) French man of letters and philosopher. Voltaire was born François-Marie Arouet, into a wealthy Parisian family, and educated at the Jesuit school of Louis-le-Grand. His satirical writing led to exiles in Holland (1713) and England (1726–9; it was said that he went to England a poet and returned a philosopher). He returned to France, and published the *Lettres philosophiques* (1734, trs. as *Philosophical Letters on the English Nation*), whose admiration for the liberal spirit of England made it necessary for him to retire to the country to avoid arrest. For the next fifteen years he lived mainly in the country of Lorraine in the company of the savant Mme du Châtelet. After a period in Prussia he settled in 1755 in a château near Geneva, where he published *Essai sur les mœurs et l'esprit des nations* (1756, trs. as *Essays on the Manners and Spirit of Nations*, 1758) and *Candide, ou l'optimisme* (1759, trs. as *Candide, or All for the Best*, 1759). This was followed by the equally satirical *Dictionnaire philosophique* (1764, trs. as *Philosophical Dictionary*, 1764). He subsequently lived in France, but only returned to Paris shortly before his death, to be hailed as the greatest French champion of the *Enlightenment, and his generation's most courageous spokesman for freedom and toleration.

Philosophically Voltaire imbibed the combination of science, empiricism, and religious awe characteristic of *Newton and *Locke. Although he wrote passionately against the metaphysical speculations of his predecessors, especially *Leibniz, Voltaire was prepared to take refuge in ignorance, for instance of the nature of the soul, or the way to reconcile evil with divine providence. Himself a *deist, he became famous as the implacable opponent of organized Christian religion, whose baleful effects were all too visible in the world of his time. Although his lustre as a philosopher does not match his eminence as a man of letters, poet, and playwright, Voltaire remains a central example of the philosopher as a politically engaged, liberal humanist.

SEE WEB LINKS

- An archive of biographies of Voltaire
- A searchable electronic archive of writings by or on Voltaire

voluntarism Generally a position seeing reason and intellect as subservient to the will: any position sympathizing with *Hume's dictum that reason is and ought to be the slave of the passions. In ethics, voluntarism is the position that it is will or desire that creates values, although this is more commonly called *projectivism or *expressivism. The theological position that all values are traits that become elevated through being chosen by God is also known by the name. Also in theology, voluntarism is a term for the *fideistic position that it is legitimate to believe in things because it is legitimate to want to do so. This position is found in *Pascal, *Kierkegaard, and the pragmatist *James. Finally, the term is applied to the embracing metaphysic of *Schopenhauer that places a blind and all-powerful will at the basis of all nature.

von Neumann machine Named after the mathematician John von Neumann (1903–57), a von Neumann machine is a computer built around (i) a control unit, an arithmetic and logic unit, a memory, and input and output facilities; (ii) a way of storing programs in memory; and (iii) a method whereby the control unit sequentially reads and carries out instructions from the program. A non-von Neumann machine is an architecture without some or all of these elements: the most discussed examples in philosophy are networks implementing parallel distributed processing (*see* CONNECTIONISM).

von Wright, Georg Henrik (1916–2003) Finnish philosopher and successor of *Wittgenstein in his chair in Cambridge. Von Wright was born in Helsinki, and attended the university there. Attracted to *logical positivism, he visited Vienna, but because of the Anschluss settled in Cambridge, studying with both *Broad and Wittgenstein. He taught in Helsinki, but in 1948 returned to Cambridge, holding the chair for three years until Wittgenstein's death, after which he returned to Helsinki. Von Wright was a founder of *deontic logic, and in later years an engaged critic of the modern world and notions of social progress, having shared with Wittgenstein a taste for the pessimism of *Spengler. His works include *An Essay in Modal Logic* (1950) and *A Treatise on Induction and Probability* (1951), *The Varieties of Goodness* (1963), and *Explanation and Understanding* (1971).

vortex *See* DESCARTES.

voters' paradox A problem (not strictly a paradox) in assessing majority preference, published by Edward John Nanson (1850–1936) in *Transactions and Proceedings of the Royal Society of Victoria*, 1882, but anticipated by *Condorcet. Suppose three citizens A, B, C, vote to rank three policies x, y, z. The results are: A: $x > y > z$; B: $y > z > x$; C: $z > x > y$. Then two citizens (a majority) prefer x to y, and two (a majority) prefer y to z, but a majority also prefers z to x. Each voter is consistent but the 'social choice' is inconsistent. This illustrates the difficulty of extracting a social choice from individual preferences. *See also* ARROW'S THEOREM.

Vygotsky, Lev Semenovich (1896–1934) Soviet psychologist. Working largely in isolation from mainstream psychologists in Byelorussia, Vygotsky developed theories of learning similar to those of *Piaget. His works emphasize the socially transmitted knowledge of the teacher and the active engagement of the child in the learning process; they are free of doctrinaire Marxist dogma, and sought a reconciliation between different schools of psychology. His works include *Thought and Language* and *The Crisis of Psychology*; they were only published posthumously, shortly thereafter suppressed, and known in the west only after 1958.

Waismann, Friedrich (1896–1959) Austrian member of the Vienna Circle. Waismann is principally remembered for a defence of *conventionalism in logic and mathematics, and for introducing the notion of 'porosity' or *open texture into the philosophy of language. His most important contributions included *Einführung in das mathematische Denken* (1936, trs. as *An Introduction to Mathematical Thinking*) and *The Principles of Linguistic Philosophy* (1965).

Wang Pi (AD 226–49) Chinese sage who founded a new Taoist movement, known as *hsuan hsueh*, 'the dark learning', or neo-Taoism. He also provided the impulse that would emerge as *tao hsueh*, 'learning of the Truth', or Neo-Confucianism. Opposed to the dead rituals and empty forms of contemporary Confucianism, Wang Pi represented an analytical and philosophical turn to deeper metaphysics. His principal work is a commentary on the *Tao Te Ching*.

Wang Yang-Ming (1472–1529) The most important *Neo-Confucian philosopher of the period corresponding to the Western Middle Ages. Wang Yang-Ming taught a kind of pragmatism, arguing that knowledge and action are inseparable. Purely contemplative ideals presuppose a split between mind and the world; whereas by eliminating selfishness and obscurity, and then through action, the mind is united with the principle (**li*) of things.

war, just *See* JUST WAR.

Ward, James (1843–1925) English philosopher of mind, who established the first psychology laboratory in Cambridge. An opponent of mechanical *associationist psychology, Ward instead highlighted the active powers of the mind, including will and attention. He was the first to hold the Cambridge chair later occupied by *Moore and *Wittgenstein.

warranted assertibility Term introduced by *Dewey for the status a proposition gains when it is warranted through the ongoing, self-correcting processes of enquiry. Dewey held a resolutely dynamic view of these processes, opposing them to the static picture in which propositions gain the title of knowledge through a logical relationship with basic experience. The term is also used in connection with 'assertibility condition' theories of meaning. These are opposed to truth-conditional theories by denying that recognition of the circumstances under which a sentence is true can be fundamental to understanding it. It may be that we cannot display such recognition, since the circumstances may be beyond us (e.g. they may be lost in time, or might require infinite computational powers). Instead, understanding is guaranteed by knowing what would warrant the assertion of the sentence. The idea bears affinities with the *verification principle.

Watson, John Broadus (1878–1958) American psychologist and founder of *behaviourism. His first major work, *Behavior: an Introduction to Comparative Psychology* (1914), established the principles of scientific behaviourism, rejecting any reliance on introspection, consciousness, or intentionality in favour of observation and experiment in laboratory settings. His best-known textbook was *Psychology from the Standpoint of a Behaviorist* (1919). Watson spent the years after 1920 in advertising, perhaps appropriately as he became notorious for an anti-humanist, mechanical, and emotionally arid approach to infant nurture.

Watsuji Tetsuro (1889–1960) Japanese playwright, cultural historian, and moral philosopher. Tetsuro's main philosophical writing is the *Ningengaku toshite no rinrigaku* ('Ethics as Anthropology'), written in the years after 1931. Heavily influenced by *Confucian and *Buddhist elements, and in contrast with the individualistic ethics of the West, he espoused a communal and social view of correct living whereby the individual is absorbed in the larger whole.

wayward causal chain *See* DEVIANT CAUSAL CHAIN.

weakness of the will *See* *AKRASIA*.

Weber, Max (1864–1920) German sociologist and philosopher. Born in Berlin into a liberal legal family, Weber studied law and the history of law at various universities. He had a brief academic career as professor of economics in Freiburg and Heidelberg, before retiring through the onset of ill-health in 1897. Weber is remembered philosophically first for insisting on the distinction between fact and value, and for insisting that the conduct of the social sciences must be value-free. He is remembered secondly for his adherence to the **Verstehen* tradition of *Dilthey. On the first issue, Weber argued that scientific, historical, and philosophical analysis of a period could never by itself provide the criteria necessary for a definitive solution of evaluative questions, including those of politics. The social scientist must strictly distinguish between that which exists, and that which ought to be: the importance Weber attached to this reflects his concern at the increasing power of faceless, impersonal bureaucracy, making evaluative decisions on purely 'scientific' and technological criteria. On the second, connected, issue he recognized that sociological study must recognize that actions have a meaning in the eyes of agents, and no scientific approach to them that ignores that dimension can be adequate. The sociologist must be able to place himself in the mind of those he studies. The subjectivity that this might seem to introduce is avoided by the discipline of describing the 'ideal type', embodying the objective spirit of bureaucracy, Calvinism, capitalism, etc.

Weber insisted that no understanding is complete without including the moral, political, and religious dimension of the concerted activities of human agents. His most famous work, *Die protestantische Ethik und der Geist des Kapitalismus* (1922, trs. as *The Protestant Ethic and the Spirit of Capitalism*, 1930), connected the rise of capitalism with the complacent Protestant desire to find a sign of predestined salvation in worldly success (*see also* ELECTIVE AFFINITY). Weber realized that such studies require comparative analysis of other cultures and times, and much of his writing addresses that problem. Important theoretical works include *Wirtschaft und Gesellschaft* (1922, trs. as *Economy and Society*, 1968) and the collected papers translated in *The Methodology of the Social Sciences* (1949).

SEE WEB LINKS

- A biography of Weber, with links to other resources
- A list of internet resources on Weber, including his writings

Weil, Simone (1909–43) French Jewish mystic. Weil published only articles, and no definitive interpretation of her thought exists. She lived a life of dedicated deprivation, finding a higher purpose in self-imposed affliction. She eventually starved herself to death in England as a kind of symbolic participation in French suffering during the Second World War, although she had also protested against herself being classified as Jewish. Her work was collected in *Cahiers* (3 volumes, 1951–6, trs. as *The Notebooks of Simone Weil*, 1956). It is centred upon the eventual contradictory nature of rational thought, and the resulting need for the way of Platonic mysticism, in which the self becomes annihilated through unification with divine love.

welfare A concept that has frequently taken the place of *utility in political thought, with the idea that the aim of social betterment should be to maximize the welfare of the population. Problems of comparison, measurement, and aggregation dog the notion, and different conceptions of what amounts to genuine welfare abound. *See also* CAPABILITIES, PREFERENCE.

well-being *See* *EUDAIMONIA*, HAPPINESS.

well-formed formula At its most general a formula may be thought of in logical theory as any string of symbols from the lexicon of the theory. A well-formed formula (abbreviated as wff) is one that obeys the formation rules of the system. Since other strings are typically of no interest, well-formed formulae are often simply referred to as formulae.

well-ordering *See* ORDERING RELATION.

Weltanschauung German, a general world view; an overarching philosophy.

Weltschmerz (German, world sorrow) Generalized sentimental pessimism, fashionable in 18th-century *Romanticism.

Wertfreiheit (German, value-freedom) *See* VALUE-FREE.

Westermarck, Edward (1862–1939) Finnish anthropologist who wrote on the diversity of moral systems. Westermarck espoused a kind of *relativism, although without an account of what the truth of a moral statement actually consisted in. He saw the importance of emotion and culture in defining moral systems, without the *Enlightenment or *Kantian confidence either in a universal human nature or a universal reason. Works included *The Origin and Development of Moral Ideas* (1906) and *Ethical Relativity* (1932).

wff Abbreviation for *well-formed formula.

Whewell, William (1794–1866) English philosopher of science and polymath, of whom the essayist Sydney Smith (1771–1845) said 'science is his forte, and omniscience is his foible'. Whewell was a lifelong Fellow of Trinity College, Cambridge. His philosophy of science can be seen as applying *Kant to the scientific enterprise as conceived by *Newton and Francis *Bacon. Thus *The Philosophy of the Inductive Sciences* (1840) begins with the claim that 'Man is the interpreter of Nature, science is the right interpretation'. He analyses scientific theorizing into the decomposition or analysis of facts, the explication of conceptions or attempt to formulate concepts to apply to the facts, and the colligation of facts, whereby facts and conceptions are brought together to give rise to the general propositions of a science (*see also* CONSILIENCE). It is noteworthy that for Whewell the process requires real inventiveness: there is no mechanical or purely logical procedure that guarantees scientific success. In this and other respects his work bears affinities to the later philosophy of science of *Popper. Whewell also noticed the theory-laden nature of observation. His other major work is the *History of the Inductive Sciences* (1837).

Whichcote, Benjamin (1609–83) English liberal theologian. Whichcote was the senior of the *Cambridge Platonists, and through his position as Provost of King's was an influential opponent of the *Calvinism of his time. He published no work in his lifetime, but his teaching emphasized the optimistic reconciliation of reason and faith characteristic of the Platonists.

Whig view of history Term coined by the historian Herbert Butterfield as the title of his book *The Whig Interpretation of History* (1931). The error is that of reading history as a progress, starting in some benighted time and somehow directed upon, or inevitably culminating in, the glorious present. More generally it may include the error of reading present beliefs and attitudes back into the past. *See also* RATIONALIZATION.

Whitehead, Alfred North (1861–1947) English mathematician and philosopher. Whitehead was *Russell's tutor in Cambridge, where he was Fellow of Trinity from 1884 to 1910, when he moved to London, and then to a chair of philosophy at Harvard in 1924. He collaborated with Russell on *Principia Mathematica* (1910–13). His own philosophy is an attempt at a systematic metaphysics built in the light of modern logic and science. Whitehead was impressed by the scientific concept of a flux or field of force and energy. Disliking both the atomism of the Newtonian world view, and that of the Humean analysis of experience into distinct perceptions, he sought to analyse such atoms in terms of overlapping sets of larger processes. His 'method of extensive abstraction' is that of defining an object such as a point in terms of nested volumes of space; similarly events become nested processes. The general ordering of the processes of the world is the primordial nature of God, represented as the principle of concretion whereby actual processes emerge. His *Enquiry Concerning the Principles of Natural Knowledge* (1919) and *The Concept of Nature* (1920) are considerably more accessible than the later *Process and Reality* (1929).

why Many *explanations answer the question why something happened, and one view of good explanations is that the only feature they have in common is that of being satisfactory answers to some why-question, as asked by some person in some situation.

wickedness The *Socratic thesis or paradox that nobody does wrong willingly is challenged by wickedness, which in some moral systems is universal (*see* ORIGINAL SIN), and in others at least occasional. Wickedness is often assimilated to loss of control (*see* AKRASIA), the idea being that full control would put reason back in charge of any unruly or base passions. A 20th-century reversal of this, with roots in de *Sade and *Nietzsche, romantically elevates the freedom that is supposed to come from deliberately flouting (transcending) normal ethics, thought of as an external system of restraints on conduct.

will To have a will is to be able to desire an outcome and to purpose to bring it about. Strength of will, or firmness of purpose, is supposed to be good, and weakness of will or **akrasia* bad. *See also* FREE WILL, GOOD WILL, VOLITION.

William of Auvergne (*c.*1180–1249) Born in Aurillac, William studied in Paris, of which he became Bishop in 1228. He was instrumental in tipping the philosophical balance of the church away from *Augustine towards *Aristotle, and in rescuing Aristotle from what were regarded as misinterpretations by Islamic scholars.

William of Auxerre (1140/50–1231) Theologian and professor at the university of Paris. William was one of three theologians appointed by Pope Gregory IX to prepare amended editions of the physical and metaphysical works of *Aristotle. His principal work was the *Summa Aurea* which is something more than the usual collection of commentaries on the *Sentences* of Peter *Lombard.

William of Champeaux (*c.*1070–*c.*1120) Theologian and teacher first at Paris and subsequently at Châlons-sur-Marne, where he became Bishop in 1114. Philosophically he is remembered for taking the *realist side in a dispute over the nature of *universals with his pupil, the nominalist *Abelard, who defeated him completely.

William of Moerbeke (*c.*1218–1286) Belgian Dominican, and one of the most important men of letters and translators of the 13th century. His translations of *Aristotle into Latin, and of

*Proclus and other mathematical and scientific writings were much admired for centuries after his death.

William of Ockham *See* OCKHAM.

William of Sherwood *See* SHERWOOD.

Williams, Bernard Arthur Owen (1929–2003) English philosopher. Born in Essex, Williams was educated at Balliol College, Oxford, and held fellowships at All Souls and New College. He was professor of philosophy at Cambridge from 1967 to 1979 and Provost of King's College, Cambridge, from 1979 to 1987, when he accepted a chair at Berkeley, returning to the chair of moral philosophy at Oxford in 1990. Williams was known for a subtle *relativistic position in moral philosophy that rejected both *Aristotelian and *Kantian promises that virtue arises from the exercise of rational propensities in the mind. He also rejected *expressive and *projective theories, arguing instead that ethics cannot be what it seems to be, if it is based purely on contingent sentiments and passions. He argued influentially that Kantian ethics, and *utilitarianism, impose an unnatural emphasis on purely impersonal concerns, ignoring the personal projects that necessarily occupy the foreground of people's practical lives (*see also* AGENT-CENTRED MORALITY, INTEGRITY, STOICISM, UNIVERSALIZABILITY). Williams's principal books include *Descartes: The Project of Pure Enquiry* (1978), *Ethics and the Limits of Philosophy* (1985), *Shame and Necessity* (1993), and *Truth and Truthfulness* (2002). Collections of papers include *Problems of the Self* (1973) and *Moral Luck* (1981).

will to believe Term coined by *James in a lecture of the same name (1896) for the claim that he associated with *pragmatism, that what we believe may be determined not just by evidence, but by the *utility of the resulting states of mind. It thus becomes legitimate to believe in *free will or to believe in God, because such states of mind have beneficial effects on the believer. The doctrine caused outrage from the beginning. *See also* PASCAL'S WAGER.

will to power According to *Nietzsche, the fundamental element of human nature. The power in question is not necessarily domination over others, but can be achieved in creative activity: it is associated with self-sufficiency and self-confidence. When this will is frustrated, consolatory myths appear in the shape of unhealthy ethical systems promoting 'virtues' such as charity and humility, which are in fact sublimations of resentment and envy.

Windelband, Wilhelm (1848–1915) German Neo-Kantian and founder of the Baden school of Neo-Kantianism. A historian of philosophy, he is almost entirely remembered for the *idiographic/nomothetic distinction. Works included *Präludien, Ausfsätze und Reden zur Philosophie und ihrer Geschichte* ('Preludes and Conversations on Philosophy and its History', 1884), *Lehrbuch der Geschichte der Philosophie* ('Textbook of the History of Philosophy', 1890), and *Einleitung in die Philosophie* ('Introduction to Philosophy', 1914').

wisdom The traditional goal of philosophy, considered to be some amalgam of knowledge, spiritual profundity, Stoical ability to put up with the evils of the world, and practical ability or **phronēsis*. The *myth of the cave recognizes the difficulty the wise man or philosopher will have in communicating his understanding to those who remain in the cave; the central problem with wisdom is that those who do not have it will be unable to distinguish those who do from false claimants and pretenders. This is particularly so when wisdom is equated with the incommunicable, ineffable contact with a higher world than this one. The so-called wisdom literature of the Bible includes the books Job, Ecclesiastes, Proverbs, and the Song of Solomon.

Wisdom, Arthur John Terrence Dibben (1904–93) British analytical and linguistic philosopher. Wisdom was educated at Cambridge, and after a period in St Andrews returned to Cambridge in 1934, becoming professor in 1952. His work before this time was analytic in direction, and best represented by *Interpretation and Analysis in Relation to Bentham's Theory of Definition* (1931), and the five essays on 'Logical Constructions' published in *Mind* between 1931 and 1933. Under the influence of *Wittgenstein he repudiated the approach, and later works attempt to explore the likenesses and differences between various attitudes to philosophical problems, with the emphasis being on a discursive and relatively open-ended journey around different viewpoints. His collection *Other Minds* (1952) is the most sustained attack on that problem using the new approach. Other works include *Philosophy and Psychoanalysis* (1953).

witchcraft *See* MAGIC.

Wittgenstein, Ludwig (1889–1951) Austrian philosopher. Born the youngest of eight children into a wealthy Viennese industrial family, Wittgenstein originally studied engineering, first in the *Realschule* in Linz, then in Berlin. In 1908 he went to Manchester to study aeronautics. Becoming fascinated by the philosophy of mathematics, in 1911 he visited *Frege, who advised him to study under *Russell in Cambridge. Until the First World War he worked as Russell's protégé and collaborator, on problems in the foundations of logic and mathematics. During the war he served in the Austrian army, and completed the manuscript that was published in 1921 as the *Tractatus Logico-Philosophicus* (trs. into English in 1922). Convinced that he had definitively solved all soluble problems of philosophy, he abandoned the subject for rural school-teaching in Austria, until 1929 when contact with the Vienna Circle (*see* LOGICAL POSITIVISM), mathematical intuitionism, and above all *Ramsey persuaded him that there remained work for him to do, and he returned to Cambridge, where he became professor in 1939. During the Second World War, Wittgenstein worked as a hospital porter at Guy's Hospital in London, and then as a laboratory assistant in Newcastle. He resigned his chair in 1947, and died of cancer in Cambridge. He was undoubtedly the most charismatic figure of 20th-century philosophy, living and writing with a power and intensity that frequently overwhelmed his contemporaries and readers.

It is usual to divide Wittgenstein's work into the early period, culminating in the *Tractatus*, and the late period from 1929 until his death, whose most famous expression is the *Philosophical Investigations*, published in 1953 (the doctrines of the late period were not published in Wittgenstein's lifetime, but collected from notebooks and lecture notes). Both periods are dominated by a concern with the nature of language, the way in which it represents the world, and the implications this has for logic and mathematics. In the early work language is treated in relative abstraction from the activities of human beings, but in the late period concern with the philosophy of mind, the nature of certainty, and even ethics is reintroduced. The early period is centred on the *picture theory of meaning, according to which a sentence represents a state of affairs by being a kind of picture or model of it, containing elements corresponding to those of the state of affairs and a structure or form that mirrors the structure of the state of affairs that it represents. All logical complexity is reduced to that of the *propositional calculus, and all propositions are *truth functions of atomic or basic propositions. Since atomic propositions must therefore be logically independent of one another, the nature of the 'atoms' from which they are constructed remains elusive. For Russell at the time atoms were primitive elements of experience, but although the *Tractatus* was a major influence on logical positivism (which also emphasizes primitive elements of experience) there is no reason to suppose that Wittgenstein makes the same equation. The *Tractatus* moves to a denial of factual or cognitive meaning to sentences whose function does not fit into its conception of representation, such as those concerned with ethics, or meaning, or the self, and ends with the famous repudiation of its own meaningfulness. Doctrines about logical form are amongst the things that can be shown but not said: 'whereof we cannot speak, thereof we must be silent.'

In the later period the emphasis shifts dramatically to the actions of people and the role their linguistic activities play in their lives. Thus whereas in the *Tractatus* language is placed in a static, formal relationship with the world, in the later work Wittgenstein emphasizes its use in the contexts of everyday social activities of ordering, advising, requesting, measuring, counting, exercising concern for each other, and so on. These different activities are thought of as so many '*language games' that together make up a form of life. Philosophy typically ignores this diversity, and in generalizing and abstracting distorts the real nature of its subject-matter: a work like the *Tractatus* is the product of thinking that language has to be one thing or another, whereas the correct method is to look and see what it actually is. When attention to detail is abandoned, the real function of statements is missed, and 'language goes on holiday'. What is needed is therefore a cure for the philosophical impulse, a therapy rather than a theory. Wittgenstein's writing typically deploys analogies, aphorisms, new perspectives, and invitations to look at old phenomena in new ways, rather than conventional linear arguments, in order to cure us of the urge to generalize. In all this Wittgenstein was following the Austrian phenomenological tradition of *Brentano and especially *Husserl, who anticipated the need not to think, but to look, i.e. to pay more attention to the contours of the actual phenomena, and less to preconceptions about what they must be like. Philosophy, for this tradition, also makes no discoveries, strictly speaking, but only reminds us of what we find when we turn our attention in unfamiliar directions.

The most sustained and influential application of these ideas was in the philosophy of mind. Here Wittgenstein explored the role that reports of introspection, or sensations, or intentions, or beliefs actually play in our social lives, in order to undermine the *Cartesian picture that they function to describe the goings-on in an inner theatre of which the subject is the lone spectator. Passages that have subsequently become known as the *rule-following considerations and the *private language argument are among the fundamental topics of modern philosophy of language and mind, although their precise interpretation is endlessly controversial.

In addition to the *Tractatus* and the *Investigations*, collections of Wittgenstein's work published posthumously include *Remarks on the Foundations of Mathematics* (1956), *The Blue and Brown*

Books (1958), *Notebooks 1914–1916* (1961), *Philosophische Bemerkungen* (1964), *Zettel* (1967), and *On Certainty* (1969). There are admirable biographies by Ray Monk and Brian McGuinness.

SEE WEB LINKS

- An online archive of material on Wittgenstein, including an illustrated biography
- An audio discussion of Wittgenstein by three American philosophers

Wolff, Christian (1679–1754) The principal follower and interpreter of *Leibniz. Wolff was primarily a mathematician, but renowned as a systematic philosopher, supposing that all the necessary tenets of metaphysics are derivable from the principle of *sufficient reason and the principle of identity (*Leibniz's law). He was exiled from his university, Halle, in 1723 through the hostile influence of the *pietists, but recalled by Frederick II in 1740. In 1743 he became Chancellor of the university. In his most important work, *Philosophia Prima sive Ontologia* ('First Philosophy or Ontology'), Wolff gave a systematic ontology along *scholastic lines, fusing elements from the systems of Leibniz and *Descartes. His system was enormously influential in Germany until well into the 19th century. *Kant's teacher Martin Knutzen was a Wolffian, and it was only after he had taught Wolff's system for many years that Kant's 'dogmatic slumbers' were shattered by *Hume.

Wollaston, William (1660–1724) English moral philosopher, whose *The Religion of Nature Delimited* (1722) was immensely popular in the first half of the 18th century. It propounded the theory that all vice is a species of lying, or in other words that the fault of a wrong action lies in its tendency to give rise to false belief. The theory had the misfortune to be discussed by *Hume (*Treatise*, Bk III, 1, 1) who first admits that 'a person, who thro' a window sees any lewd behaviour of mine with my neighbour's wife, may be so simple as to imagine she is certainly my own' but goes on to point out that this is hardly my fault, and furthermore 'if I had used the precaution of shutting the windows, while I indulg'd myself in those liberties with my neighbour's wife, I should have been guilty of no immorality; and that because my action, being perfectly conceal'd, would have had no tendency to produce any false conclusion'.

Wollstonecraft, Mary (1759–97) English radical and *feminist. Largely self-taught, in 1787, after the failure of the nonconformist school she had founded, she published *Thoughts on the Education of Daughters*. She became a member of a radical group including *Paine, *Godwin, and the painter Fuseli (1741–1825). In 1796 after a prolonged and unhappy affair with the American Gilbert Imlay, she married William Godwin, by whom she was pregnant, but died ten days after the birth of their daughter, Mary (later Mary Shelley, author of *Frankenstein*). Her most important works were *A Vindication of the Rights of Men* (1790), an answer to *Burke's conservative reaction to the French Revolution, and the ground-breaking *Vindication of the Rights of Women* (1792), a direct challenge to *Rousseau's assumptions of feminine inferiority. Her feminism was deeply founded on a radical nonconformist and egalitarian social philosophy; something of her attitude to manly virtue can be inferred from her description of an army corps as a 'chain of despots, who, submitting and tyrannizing without exercising their reason, become dead weights of vice and folly on the community'. Other works include *The Female Reader* (1789) and *History and Moral View of the Origins and Progress of the French Revolution* (1793).

SEE WEB LINKS

- A brief biography of Wollstonecraft, with a bibliography
- An archive of Wollstonecraft's writings

women in philosophy *See* FEMINISM.

world-soul *See* PANPSYCHISM.

wu-hsing Chinese term meaning 'five phases', fire, earth, wood, metal, and water, which form the structure of change (wood gives birth to fire; fire to earth, earth to metal, water overcomes fire, etc.). Together with *yin* and *yang* these were the basis of Chinese cosmologies in the period 403 BC to AD 220, and could be interpreted in medicine and in ritual and colour.

Wundt, Wilhelm (1832–1920) German psychologist and polymath. Wundt taught physiology at Heidelberg, where he acted as assistant to Helmholtz. In 1875, the same year as William James began experimental philosophy at Harvard, he founded his psychological laboratory in Leipzig, where he was newly professor. He did not confine himself to the experimental study of stimuli and sensations, but wrote widely on philosophy, mythology, cultural practices, rituals, literature, and art. His ten-volume *Völkerpsychologie*, published between 1900 and 1920, delineates stages of cultural development, from the primitive, to the totemic, through the age of heroes and gods, to the age of modern man.

wu wei Chinese term for 'non-action' or absence of government or effort, an ideal which in *Taoism is to be commended both for individuals and for political society. The idea is that in the harmonious soul or state, the right outcomes flow without conscious control.

Wyclif, John (*c.*1320–84) Scholastic philosopher and reformer. Wyclif's major work was the *Summa de Ente*, a collection of two books with six treatises in each. His central preoccupation was the problem of *universals. Wyclif accepts an out-and-out *realism, arguing the Platonic and Augustine position of *universalia ante rem*: universals are prior to the particular in logic and time. They form the way in which God understands creatures; a singular thing partakes of a universal as a kind of projection of the mind of God. It follows that it is incapable of annihilation. Wyclif's views were condemned at the Council of Constance. Politically Wyclif's belief in predestination threatened to remove the rationale for the organized Church of his day, an unpopular consequence, compounded by his view that only those with grace could exercise dominion.

Xanthippe (5th c. BC) The wife of *Socrates.

Xenocrates of Chalcedon (4th c. BC) Greek philosopher who headed the *Academy of Athens from 339 to 314 BC. He enjoyed a distinguished reputation in Athens, but seems to have been less impressive as a philosopher than as a figurehead.

Xenophanes of Colophon (*c.*570–478 BC) Early *Presocratic philosopher. Xenophanes left Ionia at the age of 25, and lived in exile largely in Sicily. He is treated by *Plato as a founder of the *Eleatics. He is philosophically important for his criticism of the anthropomorphic religion of Hesiod and Homer, and the substitution of a single, eternal, and spiritual deity. He is also remembered for his attack on the conventional military and athletic virtues of the time, in favour of those of the intellect. He was hailed as an honourable, semi-sceptical forerunner by later classical *sceptics.

Xenophon (*c.*428–*c.*354 BC) Greek general and historian. Xenophon is remembered philosophically for a number of writings in which he sets out to rehabilitate *Socrates from the various charges that led to his death. His Socrates tends to be a more reasonable kind of chap than that of *Plato; for example, instead of embracing the *Socratic paradox of identifying virtue with knowledge, he is aware that a training of the sentiments may be needed in order to keep knowledge of what one should do vivid in one's mind at the crucial moment.

Xungxi *See* HSÜN TZU.

Yang Chu (*c.*370–319 BC) Maverick Chinese philosopher notable for holding that man's duty is to himself, and the best thing to do with society is to avoid its entanglements in favour of nurturing one's own health and longevity.

Yang Hsiung (53 BC–AD 18) Chinese philosopher known for the sensible doctrine that human nature was a mixture of good and evil, avoiding the extremes of *Mencius and *Hsün Ṭzu.

yi Chinese term denoting fitting or appropriate behaviour or the disposition to settle on it. What this consists in varies according to the different schools.

Yijing *See* I CHING.

yin/yang In Chinese thought the two great opposite but complementary forces at work in the cosmos. *Yin* is the female, cold, dark, passive power; *yang* represents masculinity, light, and warmth. Earth, rain, soft, evil, black, small, and even (numbers) are *yin*; heaven, sunshine, hard, good, white, large, and odd are *yang*. The interplay of the two forces makes up **chi*, or the material principle governing the universe. Their balance is essential to harmony and health. The Yin/Yang school of Chinese philosophy, perhaps founded by Tsou-Yen (*c.*305–240 BC), is an early attempt at a cosmology, based on the opposition of *yin* and *yang* and a doctrine of Five Elements (metal, wood, water, fire, and earth), operating in ordered cycles in the production of nature and history.

Yoga The Hindu school, associated with the school of *Samkhya as the practical method for achieving the understanding of the self. Yoga is the discipline (or 'yoke') necessary for the pure subject to recognize itself, and separate itself from the empirical reality with which it is confused. Various kinds of involvement with the ego and desires and aversions are responsible for 'fluctuations of the mind-stuff' that can only be overcome by training. Yoga includes moral restraints, and spiritual imperatives, as well as the familiar exercises (*asanas*) designed to withdraw consciousness from the senses, focus the mind, and ultimately achieve meditation in which the self is completely and transparently understood (*samadhi*).

Yogacara A *Buddhist school arising in the 3rd to 4th centuries, that denies the existence of any reality independent of consciousness. Like *Berkeley the school acknowledges a supreme consciousness, or *vijnana*, and it is also designated the Vijnanavada or Vijnana school. The supreme consciousness serves as a kind of storehouse for perceptions. By a process of meditation we can come to awareness of the truth, and eliminate the illusory distinction between subject and object.

yu, wu Awkward pair of terms in Chinese philosophy, denoting 'being' and 'non-being' respectively. In some writings they produce each other; in others one of the two is regarded as fundamental.

yung Chinese term meaning 'courage' or 'bravery'. Confucians advocate an ideal form of *yung* guided, naturally, by **yi*.

Zabarella, Jacopo (1533–89) Italian Aristotelian philosopher who taught at Padua. He was important to the development of Aristotelian logic in the direction of natural philosophy, methodology, and theory of knowledge. His works include commentaries on several books of Aristotle, as well as *Opera logica* (1578), *De naturalis scientiae constitutione* (1586), and *De rebus naturalibus* (1590).

Zarathustra *See* ZOROASTRIANISM.

Zen (Sanskrit, *dhyana*, meditation, pronounced chan in Chinese, zen in Japanese) A form of *Buddhism centred upon sitting meditation, and the wordless and silent nature of enlightenment. It claims a history stretching back to the Buddha himself, but its origins are linked with Bodhidharma, a Buddhist who arrived in China in the 5th century, and then allegedly sat motionless for nine years gazing at a wall. A variety of techniques are used to restore identity with the nature of Buddha, including shouting and beating. The discipline, or *zazen*, may be aided by concentration on texts and problems, or **koan*. Since the state of enlightenment is not communicable, it must be manifest in the radiant attitude which the adept can adopt to all the ordinary things of life.

Zeno of Citium (*c.*335–263 BC) The founder of *Stoicism, Zeno was a Phoenician born on Cyprus, who came to Athens in 313 and was said to have been a pupil of *Crates the *Cynic. He turned to Socratic philosophy, and gradually evolved the unified metaphysics, epistemology, and ethics that make up the Stoical system.

Zeno of Elea (*fl.* early 5th c. BC) The pupil and principal defender of *Parmenides, Zeno was called the inventor of dialectic by *Aristotle. His one book, of which we possess only fragments, contained many arguments for the unreality of the pluralistic world that we take ourselves to inhabit. The most famous of these are the four arguments against motion, known as *Zeno's paradoxes. But Zeno also proposed many other *antinomies, showing that objects must be both limited and unlimited in number, like and unlike, one and many, infinitesimally small and infinitely large. Zeno's own attitude to these antinomies, as to his arguments against motion, has been disputed, but he is consistently described as a convinced Parmenidean.

SEE WEB LINKS

- An introduction to Zeno's philosophy
- A biography of Zeno, with links to other internet resources

Zeno's paradoxes *Zeno of Elea's arguments against motion precipitated a crisis in Greek thought. They are presented as four arguments in the form of *paradoxes: (1) the Racecourse, or dichotomy paradox, (2) Achilles and the Tortoise, (3) the Arrow, and (4) the Moving Blocks, or Stadium.

1 Suppose a runner needs to travel from a start S to a finish F. To do this he must first travel to the midpoint, M, and thence to F: but if N is the midpoint of SM, he must first travel to N, and so on *ad infinitum* (Zeno: 'what has been said once can always be repeated'). But it is impossible to accomplish an infinite number of tasks in a finite time. Therefore the runner cannot complete (or start) his journey.

2 Achilles runs a race with a tortoise, who has a start of n metres. Suppose the tortoise runs one-tenth as fast as Achilles. Then by the time Achilles has reached the tortoise's starting-point, the tortoise is n/10 metres ahead. By the time Achilles has reached that point, the tortoise is n/100 metres ahead, and so on *ad infinitum*. So Achilles cannot catch the tortoise.

3 An arrow cannot move at a place at which it is not. But neither can it move at a place at which it is. But a flying arrow is always at the place at which it is. That is, at any instant it is at rest. But if at no instant is it moving, then it is always at rest.

4 Suppose three equal blocks, A, B, C, of width l, with A and C moving past B at the same speed in opposite directions. Then A takes one time, t, to traverse the width of B, but half the time, t/2, to traverse the width of C. But these are the same length, l. So A takes both t and t/2 to traverse the distance l.

These are the barest forms of the arguments, and different suggestions have been made as to how Zeno might have supported them (for one version, *see* BAYLE'S TRILEMMA). A modern approach might be inclined to dismiss them as superficial, since we are familiar with the mathematical ideas (a) that an infinite series can have a finite sum, which may appear to dispose of (1) and (2), and (b) that there is indeed no such thing as velocity at a point or instant, for velocity is defined only over intervals of time and distance, which may seem to dispose of (3). The fourth paradox seems merely amusing, unless Zeno had in mind that the length l is thought of as a smallest unit of distance (a quantum of space) and that each of A and C are travelling so that they traverse the smallest space in the smallest time. On these assumptions there is a contradiction, for A passes C in half the proposed smallest time.

The purely mathematical response only works if we have a satisfactory foundation not only for the arithmetic of infinity but also for the measurement of space and time by its means. The real importance of the paradoxes has lain in the pressure they put on those foundations. For instance, the third paradox suggests that if we are happy to treat a line as made up of extensionless points, and time as made up of instants that occupy no time, then motion is a succession of states of rest. The difficulty with using the fact that an infinite series can have a finite sum as a sufficient solution of the paradoxes has been brought out by considering a lamp set to go on for half a minute, go off for a quarter, on for an eighth .... At the end of the minute, is it on or off? Neither answer is mathematically acceptable, since there is no last member of the series. So it seems that there can be no such lamp, yet it also seems to be an accurate model of Achilles' completed journey.

Zermelo–Fraenkel set theory The first rigorous axiomatization of *set theory was presented by Ernst Zermelo (1871–1953) in 1908, and its development by A. A. Fraenkel (1891–1965), adding the axiom of *replacement, is known as ZF. If the axiom of *choice is added it is known as ZFC. For other axioms *see* CHOICE, EXTENSIONALITY, POWER SET, REPLACEMENT, SELECTION, SUM SET.

Zermelo–König paradox *See* KÖNIG'S PARADOX.

zero-sum game A game in which one player's gain is an equivalent net loss to the other player or players. No overall gain is possible. This contrasts with games in which all players can gain, for example by coordination.

zeugma (Greek, yoke) A figure of speech in which one term links two others in a sentence. This may be perfectly correct ('let me hear the people and their demands') or it may generate a syllepsis, in which case the linking term is only grammatically or semantically appropriate for one of the others ('she went home in a flood of tears and a taxi'). Opponents may charge that certain philosophical positions construct such zeugmas, e.g. if one holds that we see both real daggers and hallucinatory daggers.

Zheng Xuan (127–200) Commentator on the Chinese classics, credited with establishing an authoritative structure of five Confucian texts as the supreme guide to morality, politics, and history.

zhi (Chinese, knowledge) This covers especially knowledge as shown in practical and interpersonal abilities.

Zhu Xi *See* CHU HSI.

Zorn's lemma A proposition in set theory equivalent to the axiom of *choice. Call a set A a chain if for any two members B and C, either B is a subset of C or C is a subset of B. Now consider a set D with the properties that for every chain E that is a subset of D, the union of E is a member of D. The lemma states that D contains a member that is maximal, i.e. which is not a subset of any other set in D.

Zoroastrianism Indo-Iranian religion, founded by Zoroaster or Zarathustra, now generally placed between 1200 and 1000 BC. The dominant religion of Persia until the rise of Islam, Zoroastrianism is now largely confined to the Parsi community of Bombay. Its scriptures are known as the *Avesta*. It maintains a dualistic doctrine, contrasting the force of light and good in the world (*Ahura-mazda*) with that of darkness and evil (*Ahriman*, or *Angra Mainyu*). Offshoots of Zoroastrianism include Mithraism and *Manichaeanism. Zoroastrianism entered the Western tradition as an influence on Judaism, and hence on *Middle Platonism. Zarathustra was the character invested with *Nietzsche's imaginings of a spiritual rebirth and a higher form of humanity in *Also Sprach Zarathustra*. (*See also* ÜBERMENSCH.)

SEE WEB LINKS

- An outline of the main features of Zoroastrianism
- An audio discussion on Zoroastrianism by three experts

zygote (Greek, *zygotos*, yoked together) A cell formed by the union of two reproductive cells, or more broadly the developing organism produced by such a cell. The zygote is mentioned in debates about *abortion as the smallest single 'thing' to which the history of a living individual can be traced.

Appendix: Logical Symbols

Reading logical symbolism frightens many people more than it should. The very term symbolic logic sounds terrifying, and the presence of even a small amount of symbolism may deter many readers from otherwise perfectly intelligible texts. The following explanation introduces the symbolism used in this work, and lists some of the variations that may be encountered in other works. It should be noticed that technical terms used in this appendix are also explained under their own headwords in the body of the dictionary, and cross-references have been given where appropriate.

Lower-case italic letters from this part of the alphabet: *p, q, r*..., are used as propositional *variables. This means that they stand for *propositions or statements. Some logicians dislike these categories, and prefer to call them sentence letters, or sentential variables. In either event, they occur where a sentence can be substituted, just as the *x* and *y* of algebra stand where an expression for a number can be substituted. A statement like 'If someone believes that *p* and *q* then he believes that *p*' says that in any case in which someone believes a conjunction (such as 'It is raining and it is windy'), then that person believes its individual parts (that it is raining). Variations encountered include capitals (P, Q, ...), or italic capitals (*P, Q*, ...).

Lower-case italic letters from the end of the alphabet: *x, y, z*..., are used as object variables. This means that they stand where reference to a person, or a thing, or a number might take place. Using such a variable, the example above could be phrased: 'If *x* believes that *p* and *q* then *x* believes that *p*', where *x* stands for any person. This notation is virtually universal, although the typographical appearance of the variables varies.

As in common mathematical usage, lower case roman letters, especially n, k, j..., are used in a context to refer to specific numbers. From the beginning of the alphabet, a, b, c..., are also individual constants, or terms used in a context to refer to specific things or people. Fa means that some specific thing, a, is F, and is therefore a self-standing sentence, true or false as the case may be. F*x* by contrast is not, because nothing is picked out by the variable *x*.

Capital roman letters, F, G, R, stand for *predicates and relational expressions. Particular instances of these are standard: for instance, identity ($=$), non-identity ($\neq$), greater than and less than ($>$, $<$), and other mathematical relations. The usual convention is for predicate letters to stand before the terms to which they apply. Fn means that n is F; Rab means that a bears the relation R to b. In some works this would be written aRb.

The most simple relations between propositions studied in logic are the *truth functions. These include:

Not. Not-*p* is the negation of *p*. Classically, it is the proposition that is false when *p* is true, and vice versa. In this work it is written not-*p* where the context is informal, and $\neg p$ in more formal contexts. These mean exactly the same. Variations encountered include $-p$ and $\sim p$.

And. *p* and *q* is the conjunction of the two propositions. It is true if and only if they are both true. In this work it is written p & q. Variations encountered include $p \,.\, q$, and, more commonly, $p \wedge q$.

Or. *p* or *q* is the disjunction of the two propositions. It is true if and only if at least one of them is true. In this work it is written $p \vee q$, and this is standard. Exclusive disjunction, meaning that one of *p*, *q* is true, but not both, is sometimes encountered, written $p \veebar q$.

Implication. Logic studies various kinds of implication. The most simple is called *material implication. Here it is written $p \rightarrow q$. The most common variation is $p \supset q$.

Equivalence. If $p \rightarrow q$ and $q \rightarrow p$ then *p* and *q* are said to be equivalent (they have the same *truth-value). Informally this is often expressed as p iff q. It is written $p \leftrightarrow q$. The most common alternative is $p \equiv q$.

This is the basic set of truth functions, in terms of which others are usually defined. In the *predicate calculus the internal structure of propositions, as well as relations between them, is studied. The key notions are the two *quantifiers:

The universal quantifier. In this work this is written $\forall$. $(\forall x)\mathrm{F}x$ means that everything is F. Variations that may be met include $(\mathrm{A}x)$ $\mathrm{F}x$ and $(x)\mathrm{F}x$.

The existential quantifier. In this work this is written $\exists$. $(\exists x)\mathrm{F}x$ means that something is F. The principal variation that may be met is $(\mathrm{E}x)\mathrm{F}x$.

In the predicate calculus numerical quantifiers can be defined, e.g. $(\exists_n x)(\mathrm{F}x)$ means that there are n xs such that $\mathrm{F}x$. The principal variation is $(\exists!x)\mathrm{F}x$ (called E-shriek x), meaning that there is exactly one x such that x is F.

Terms may be defined from definite descriptions. The main examples encountered are $(\iota x)\mathrm{F}x$ (the unique x such that x is F) and $(\mu x)\mathrm{F}x$ (the least x such that x is F).

*Modal logic studies the notion of propositions being necessary or possible. The basic notation is:

Necessarily p. Written $\Box p$. The main variation is Np.

Possibly p. Written $\Diamond p$. The main variation is Mp.

In *metatheory, or the theory of logical systems, formulae and their relations become the topic. In this work capital roman A, B are variables for formulae, with $\mathrm{A}_1 \ldots \mathrm{A}_n$ referring to a sequence of formulae. In other works, Greek in various forms (α, β ...) may be encountered. The principal relations that matter are:

There is a proof of B from A. This is standardly written $\mathrm{A} \vdash \mathrm{B}$.

B is true in all *interpretations in which A is true. This is standardly written $\mathrm{A} \models \mathrm{B}$.

In traditional, or Aristotelian logic, there is not the same array of notions. Sentences are thought of as made up from terms, such as a subject and predicate, or the middle term of a *syllogism. Capital roman letters (S, P, M) are used for these in this work. Set theory introduces a small new range of fundamental terms:

$\{x\text{: F}x\}$ refers to the set of things, x, that meet a condition F. This is now standard. A set may also be referred to by listing its members ('extensionally'): {a, b, c} is the set whose members are a, b, and c.

The set with no members, or null set, is written $\emptyset$. An older variation is $\wedge$.

Sets themselves are denoted by capital roman S, T, etc. There are many typographical variations possible.

$\in$ denotes set-membership. $x \in \mathrm{S}$ means that x is a member of the set S.

$x \in \{y\text{: G}y\}$ means that x is a member of the set of things that is G.

$< \ldots >$ refers to an *ordered n-tuple.

The main notions used to construct sets include:

**Intersection.* S *Union.* $\mathrm{S} \cup \mathrm{R}$ is the set of things that belong either to S or to R. This too is standard.

**Complement.* $\bar{\mathrm{S}}$ is the set of things that do not belong to S.

**Cartesian product.* $\mathrm{S} \times \mathrm{R}$ is the set of ordered pairs whose first member belongs to S, and second belongs to R.

Relations between sets include:

Subset: $\mathrm{S} \subseteq \mathrm{R}$ means that all members of S are members of R (notice that $\mathrm{S} \subseteq \mathrm{S}$).

Proper subset: $\mathrm{S} \subset \mathrm{R}$ means that S is included in R (it is a subset, but not identical with R).

The main non-standard notation that may be encountered is *Polish notation, which is explained in the body of the dictionary, as is *substitutional quantification and its notation.

Chronology

In this chronology broadly 'philosophical' events mentioned in the body of the dictionary are in the second column, surrounding cultural, scientific, or political events are in the third column.

BC		
10,000		Lascaux cave paintings
8000		Earliest city on the site of Jericho
3500		Earliest known (Sumerian cuneiform) writing
2800		Egyptian Old Kingdom, period of the Great Sphinx
2500		Pyramid of Cheops
1500	Beginning of the Vedic period in India	Stonehenge; Minoan and Mycenean culture
1000		Accession of David as King of Israel
900–800		The *Iliad* and *Odyssey* take shape, ascribed to the bard Homer
776		First recorded Olympic games
*c.*630	Zoroaster (d. *c.*553)	
*c.*610	Anaximander (d. *c.*547); Thales of Miletus (d. *c.*545)	
600	Aesop active; rise of Zoroastrianism in Persia; Lao-Tzu, founder of Taoism (d. ?)	
*c.*570	Pythagoras (d. ?)	
*c.*563	Buddha (d. 483)	
*c.*551	Confucius (d. *c.*479)	
*c.*550	Heraclitus (d. ?)	
521		Buddha preaches his first sermon in a deer park in Varanasi
*c.*515	Parmenides (d. ?)	
500	Anaxagoras (d. *c.*427)	Hindu epic the *Ramayana*; birth of Greek sculptor Phidias
496		Sophocles (d. 406)
*c.*493	Empedocles (d. *c.*433)	
490–449		Greek wars against Persia
*c.*490	Zeno of Elea, inventor of dialectic (d. ?); Protagoras (d. *c.*420)	
480		Battle of Salamis, Greeks destroy the Persian fleet
*c.*470	Socrates (d. 399)	
462		Beginning of the age of Pericles in Athens
*c.*460	Democritus of Abdera (d. *c.*370)	Hippocrates, father of medicine
450		Alcibiades (d. 404)

448–433		Rebuilding of the Acropolis at Athens
*c.*435	Aristippus of Cyrene (d. *c.*350)	
433–404		Peloponnesian War between Athens and Sparta
429	Plato (d. 347)	
423		Aristophanes' play 'The Clouds' satirizes Socrates
*c.*400	Diogenes of Sinope (founder of Cynicism, d. 325)	Retreat of the Ten Thousand under Xenophon
BC		
387	Formation of Plato's academy	
384	Aristotle (d. 322)	
371	Mencius (d. 289)	
*c.*365	Pyrrho, (d. *c.*275), originator of Greek scepticism	
356		Alexander the Great (d. 323)
343	Aristotle teaches Alexander the Great	
341	Epicurus (d. 270)	
335	Foundation of the Peripatetic school by Aristotle	
*c.*334	Zeno of Citium, founder of Stoicism (d. 262)	
*c.*331	Cleanthes (d. 232)	
327		Alexander invades India
*c.*323	Euclid's *Elements*	Beginning of the Ptolemaic dynasty in Egypt
*c.*316	Arcesilaus (d. 242)	
287		Archimedes (d. 212)
276		Eratosthenes (d. 194, first scientist to measure the circumference of the earth)
250	Middle Academy of Athens founded by Arcesilaus	
*c.*214	Carneades (d. 129)	
106	Cicero (d. 43)	
88/87	Philo's departure for Rome ends the Athenian academy as an institution; origins of Middle Platonism	
60	Lucretius's poem *De Rerum Natura*	
55		Caesar's invasion of Britain
44		Death of Julius Caesar
*c.*4		Jesus Christ (d. *c.*30)
*c.*2		Ovid, *Ars Amatoria*
AD		
*c.*50	Plutarch (d. *c.*120)	
*c.*55	Epictetus (d. *c.*135)	

65		Earliest possible date of the first Gospel, that according to St Mark
79		Destruction of Pompeii
*c.*100	Rise of the *Nyaya* school of Indian philosophy	
121	Marcus Aurelius (d. 180)	
*c.*175	Aurelius's *Meditations*	
*c.*200	Sextus Empiricus *fl.*; Nagarjuna *fl.* in India	
*c.*205	Plotinus, founder of Neoplatonism (d. 270)	
*c.*285	Porphyry's *Commentaries* on Aristotle's *Categories*	
313		Emperor Constantine establishes toleration of Christianity
354	Augustine (d. 430)	
410		Alaric sacks Rome
411	St Augustine's *City of God*	
436		Romans leave Britain
440	School of Alexandria	
*c.*475	Boethius (d. 524)	
476	Proclus becomes head of the Academy	End of the Roman Empire in the West
AD		
529	Justinian closes the pagan schools	
532–7		Hagia Sophia built in Constantinople
537		Legendary date for the death of King Arthur
570		Mohammed, founder of Islam (d. 632)
597		Conversion of England to Christianity begins
600		Decimal notation in use in India; book printing in China
622		Mohammed's flight from Mecca to Medina. Year 1 of the Moslem calendar
*c.*788	Shankara (d. *c.*820)	
*c.*790		Indian numeral system, including zero, known in the Arab world
*c.*800		Sufism, or Islamic mysticism, begins its influence
*c.*810	Eriugena (d. *c.*877)	
828		Ptolemy's *Almagest* translated into Arabic
*c.*870	al-Farabi (d. 950)	
968		University of Cordoba founded
980	Avicenna (d. 1037)	
1033	St Anselm (d. 1109)	
1059	al-Ghazali (d. 1111)	

1079	Abelard (d. 1142)	
1101	Héloïse (d. 1164)	
1116		Earliest lectures at Oxford
1126	Averroës (d. 1198)	
1135	Maimonides (d. 1204)	
1170		Death of Thomas à Becket
1194–1260		Chartres cathedral
*c.*1200	Albert the Great (d. 1280)	
1214	Roger Bacon (d. 1292)	
1222		Genghis Khan invades Russia
1225	Aquinas (d. 1274)	
1221		Dominicans and Franciscans arrive in England
1265	Dante Alighieri (d. 1321)	
1272		Marco Polo begins his journey to China (72–95)
1273	Aquinas's *Summa Theologica*	
1277	Bishops of Paris and Canterbury condemn 'Averroist' doctrines and assert authority of faith over reason	
1285	William of Ockham (d. 1349)	
*c.*1295	Buridan (d. 1358)	
1307		Dante begins *La Divina Commedia* (1307–21)
1320	John Wyclif (d. 1384)	
1340		Geoffrey Chaucer (d. 1400)
1347		Black Death ravages Europe
1400		Origins of Renaissance art and architecture in Italy
1452		Leonardo da Vinci (d. 1519)
1453		Gutenberg Bible printed at Mainz; Turks capture Constantinople
1466	Erasmus (d. 1536)	
1478	Thomas More (d. 1535)	
AD		
1483		Martin Luther (d. 1546)
1498		Leonardo's *Last Supper*
1504		Michaelangelo's *David*
1512	Machiavelli's *The Prince*	
1516	More's *Utopia*	
1517		Martin Luther posts his 95 theses on the door of the church at Wittenberg
1519		Spaniards arrive in Mexico
1533	Montaigne (d. 1592)	
1534		Henry VIII of England splits with Rome; foundation of the Jesuit order
1535		Execution of Thomas More

1543	Copernicus's *De Revolutionibus Orbium Coelestium*	
1546		Michaelangelo begins the completion of St Peter's
1558		John Knox's *First Blast of the Trumpet Against the Monstrous Regiment of Women*
1561	Francis Bacon (d. 1626)	
1564	Galileo (d. 1642)	William Shakespeare (d. 1616)
1568		Gerardus Mercator designs his cylindrical projection for maps
1571	Johannes Kepler (d. 1630)	
1580	Montaigne's *Essays*	
1588	Hobbes (d. 1679)	
1596	Descartes (d. 1650)	
1605–15		Cervantes's *Don Quixote*
1607		First English settlement in America (Jamestown, Virginia)
1611		Authorized Version (King James Bible)
1612	Arnauld (d. 1694)	
1617	Cudworth, foremost Cambridge Platonist (d. 1688)	
1623	Pascal (d. 1662)	Shakespeare's *First Folio*
1625	Grotius's *The Laws of War and Peace*	
1628		William Hervey's *De Motu Cordis*
1632	Galileo's *Dialogue Concerning the Two Chief World Systems*; Locke (d. 1704); Spinoza (d. 1677)	
1633		Galileo forced to recant the Copernican theory by the Inquisition
1635		Founding of the Académie Française by Richelieu
1638	Malebranche (d. 1715)	
1641	Descartes's *Meditations*	
1642		Civil War in England
1646	Leibniz (d. 1716)	
1647	Pierre Bayle (d. 1706)	
1649		Execution of Charles I
1651	Hobbes's *Leviathan*	
1662		*The Book of Common Prayer*; foundation of the Royal Society
1667		Milton's *Paradise Lost*
1674	Malebranche's *De la recherche de la vérité*	
1675		Leibniz invents the calculus; Wren begins St Paul's cathedral (1675–1710)

1685	George Berkeley (d. 1753)	Composers J. S. Bach (d. 1750); G. F. Handel (d. 1759); D. Scarlatti (d. 1757)
AD		
1687	Newton's *Principia*	
1688		Accession of William of Orange
1689	Locke's Essay; Montesquieu (d. 1755)	
1692	Joseph Butler (d. 1752)	Witchcraft trials condemn nineteen women and one man in Salem, Massachusetts
1694	Voltaire (d. 1778)	
1697	Bayle's *Dictionary*	
1710	Berkeley's *Principles*; Leibniz's *Theodicy*; Reid (d. 1796)	
1711	Hume (d. 1776); Boscovich (d. 1787); Shaftesbury's *Characteristics*	
1712	Rousseau (d. 1778)	
1714	Leibniz's *Monadology*	
1717	Jean D'Alembert (d. 1783)	
1719		Daniel Defoe's *Robinson Crusoe*
1724	Immanuel Kant (d. 1804)	
1725	Vico's *New Science*	
1726		Jonathan Swift, *Gulliver's Travels*
1729	Burke (d. 1797)	Bach's *St Matthew's Passion*
1733–4	Pope's *Essay on Man*	
1739–40	Hume's *Treatise of Human Nature*	
1743	Condorcet (d. 1794)	
1748	Jeremy Bentham (d. 1832); Montesquieu's *On the Spirit of the Laws*; Hume's first *Enquiry* including the essay on Miracles.	
1751	Hume's *Enquiry concerning the Principles of Morals*; Diderot publishes volume 1 of the *Encyclopédie*	
1755		Johnson's *Dictionary of the English Language*; Great Lisbon earthquake upsets the argument to design, by occurring when the churches were full but the brothels empty
1756	Burke's *Origin of Our Ideas of the Sublime and the Beautiful*	Wolfgang Amadeus Mozart (d. 1791)
1759	Adam Smith's *The Theory of Moral Sentiments*; Voltaire's *Candide*	Schiller (d. 1805); Sterne's *Tristram Shandy* (1759–67); Jonathan Harrison's chronometer no. 4 (the first means of determining longitude at sea)
1762	Rousseau's *Social Contract*	

1763	Bayes's theorem revealed to the Royal Society by Richard Price	
1770	Hegel (d. 1831)	James Cook discovers Australia; William Wordsworth (d. 1850)
1774		Goethe's *The Sorrows of Young Werther*; rise of Romanticism
1776	Smith's *An Inquiry into the Nature and Causes of the Wealth of Nations*	American Declaration of Independence; first volume of Gibbon's *Decline and Fall* (1776–88)
1779	Posthumous publication of Hume's *Dialogues Concerning Natural Religion*	Abraham Darby's iron bridge at Coalbrookdale, Shropshire
1781	Kant's *Critique of Pure Reason*	
1786		Mozart's *The Marriage of Figaro*
1788	Schopenhauer (d. 1860)	
1789		French Revolution; William Blake's *Songs of Innocence*
AD		
1790	Burke's *Reflections on the Revolution in France*	
1791	Paine's *The Rights of Man*	Boswell's *The Life of Samuel Johnson*
1792	Mary Wollstonecraft's *Vindication of the Rights of Women*	
1795	Thomas Carlyle (d. 1881)	
1798	Auguste Comte (d. 1857)	Malthus's *Essay on Population*
1802		John Dalton's atomic theory
1806	John Stuart Mill (d. 1873)	
1807	*Hegel's Phenomenology of Spirit*	
1808		Goethe's *Faust*
1809		Charles Darwin (d. 1882)
1813	Kierkegaard (d. 1855); Mme de Staël's *On Germany* published in England, fomenting German Romanticism	Jane Austen's *Pride and Prejudice*
1814	Alexander Bakunin (d. 1876)	
1815		Napoleon's defeat at Waterloo
1817		Ricardo's *Principles of Political Economy*
1818	Marx (d. 1883); Schopenhauer's *The World as Will and Idea*	Mary Shelley's *Frankenstein*
1824		Beethoven's *Ninth Symphony*
1830		Liverpool–Manchester railway
1834		Abolition of slavery in the British Empire
1837		Coronation of Victoria; Thomas Carlyle's *The French Revolution*
1838	Brentano (d. 1917)	
1839	Peirce (d. 1914)	Poe's *Tales of the Grotesque and Arabesque*
1841		The Oxford Movement in full swing

AD		
1842	William James (d. 1910)	
1843	Mill's *System of Logic*; Kierkegaard's *Either/Or*	Ruskin's *Modern Painters* (1843–60)
1844	Nietzsche (d. 1900)	
1845	Engels's *The Condition of the Working Class in England*	John Henry Newman, leader of the Oxford Movement, becomes a Catholic
1846	F. H. Bradley (d. 1924)	
1847	Boole's *Mathematical Analysis of Logic*	
1848	Frege (d. 1925); *The Communist Manifesto*	Revolutions in Paris, Vienna, Venice, Berlin
1850		Clausius formulates second law of thermodynamics, and the kinetic theory of gases
1851		Herman Melville's *Moby Dick*
1854	Boole's *An Investigation of the Laws of Thought*	Georg Riemann's *On the Hypotheses Forming the Foundation of Geometry*
1856	Sigmund Freud (d. 1939)	
1859	Henri Bergson (d. 1941); Husserl (d. 1938)	Darwin's *Origin of Species*
1861	Mill's *Utilitarianism*	American Civil War (1861–5)
1862		Measurement of the speed of light by Léon Foucault
1863–9		Tolstoy's *War and Peace*
1865	Rise of absolute idealism in Britain	Assassination of Abraham Lincoln; 13th Amendment of the US Constitution abolishes slavery; the monk Mendel formulates the laws of heredity; Whymper climbs Matterhorn
1867	Benedetto Croce (d. 1952)	
1870	First volume of Marx's *Capital*	
	Rise of Neo-Kantianism in Germany	Vatican Council formulates the doctrine of Papal infallibility; first performance of Wagner's *Die Walküre*; Lenin (d. 1924)
1873	Russell (d. 1970); Samuel Butler's *Erewhon*	
1874	Moore (d. 1958)	Clausewitz's *On War*
1875	Sidgwick's *Methods of Ethics*	First Impressionist Exhibition, Paris
1876	Bradley's *Ethical Studies*	Tolstoy's *Anna Karenina*
		First complete performance of Wagner's *Ring* at Bayreuth
1879	Frege's *Begriffsschrift*	Aquinas confirmed as the principal orthodox Catholic theologian; rise of Neo-Thomism

AD		
1883	Mach's *The Science of Mechanics*; J. M. Keynes (d. 1946)	
1884	Frege's *Grundlagen der Arithmetik*	
1885	Nietzsche's *Also Sprach Zarathustra*	Karl Benz builds first automobile
1889	Wittgenstein (d. 1951)	
1890		Massacre of American Indians at Wounded Knee, South Dakota ('Custer's last stand')
1891	Cantor's theorem; Rudolph Carnap (d. 1970)	
1897		Durkheim's *On Suicide*
1899	Veblen's *The Theory of the Leisure Class*	Freud's *The Interpretation of Dreams*
1900	Hilbert's programme; Bergson's *Laughter*	
1901	Russell discovers his paradox	
1903	Moore's *Principia Ethica*	
1905	Sartre (d. 1980); Russell's theory of definite descriptions	Einstein's Special Theory of Relativity
1907	William James's *Pragmatism*	
1908	Quine; Zermelo's axiomatization of set theory	
1910–13	Russell and Whitehead's *Principia Mathematica*	
1913		Proust's *A la recherche du temps perdu* (1913–27)
1914	Watson's *Behavior: An Introduction to Comparative Psychology*	First World War (1914–18)
1916	Saussure's *Course in General Linguistics*	Einstein's General Theory of Relativity
1917		October Revolution in Russia; inauguration of communist rule
1918	Spengler's *Decline of the West*	
1920–30	Emergence of the Frankfurt school	
1921	Wittgenstein's *Tractatus Logico-Philosophicus*	
1922	Weber's *The Protestant Ethic and the Spirit of Capitalism*	Dadaist exhibition in Paris; T. S. Eliot's *The Waste Land*; Le Corbusier's *Towards a New Architecture*; James Joyce's *Ulysses*
1924	Founding of the Vienna Circle and logical positivism	Development of quantum mechanics by Louis de Broglie
1925		Hitler's *Mein Kampf*; Kafka's *The Trial*
1927	Heidegger's *Being and Time*	
1928		D. H. Lawrence's *Lady Chatterley's Lover*
1929	Gramsci's *Prison Notebooks*	Wall Street crash ushers in the Great Depression

AD		
1931	Gödel's theorems; Husserl's *Cartesian Meditations*	
1932		Melanie Klein's *The Psychoanalysis of Children*
1933	Tarski's paper 'The Concept of Truth in Formalized Languages'	
1934	Carnap's *Logical Syntax of Language*	
1935	Popper's *Logic of Scientific Discovery*	
1936	Ayer's *Language, Truth, and Logic*	Keynes's *General Theory*
1939–45		Second World War
1943	Sartre's *Being and Nothingness*	
1944		Von Neumann and Morgenstern's *A Theory of Games and Economic Behaviour*
1945	Russell's *History of Western Philosophy*	
1948		Assassination of Mahatma Gandhi
1949	Simone de Beauvoir's *The Second Sex*	
1950	Turing's paper 'Computing Machinery and Intelligence' (*Mind*) inaugurates the philosophy of artificial intelligence	Lévi Strauss's *Elementary Structures of Kinship*
1951		Arendt's *The Origins of Totalitarianism*
1952	Hare's *The Language of Morals*	
1953	Wittgenstein's *Philosophical Investigations*	Crick and Watson construct the double helix model of DNA
1954	Goodman's *Fact, Fiction, and Forecast*	
1957	Chomsky's *Syntactic Structures*	
1959	Strawson's *Individuals* makes metaphysics respectable once again in Britain	
1960	Quine's *Word and Object*	
1962	Kuhn's *The Structure of Scientific Revolutions* begins the trend to less formal, more historical philosophies of science	America enters war in Vietnam (1962–73)
1963		Martin Luther King's 'I have a Dream' speech; assassination of J. F. Kennedy; Betty Friedan's *The Feminine Mystique* galvanizes feminism in the United States
1966		Cultural Revolution in China
1969		Apollo II mission lands on the moon
1970		Germaine Greer's *The Female Eunuch*
1971	Rawls's *A Theory of Justice* inaugurates new interest in political philosophy	

AD		
1980	Kripke's *Naming and Necessity*	
1988		Stephen Hawking's *A Brief History of Time*
1989		Demolition of the Berlin Wall; general retreat of communism as a political system in Eastern Europe ushers in era of nationalistic conflict
1991		First Gulf War
1996	Alan Sokal publishes spoof article 'Transgressing the Boundaries: Towards a Transformative Hermeneutics of Quantum Gravity' in the journal *Social Texts*, striking a blow at postmodernism	Exponential growth of the worldwide web as a source of information
1997		Kyoto protocol on restriction of greenhouse gases
2000		George Bush becomes President of the USA; rise of neo-conservatives and Christian Right
2001		Terrorists destroy World Trade Center in New York
2002	Death of David Lewis	
2003	Death of Donald Davidson	United States and Britain attack Iraq
2004	Death of Jacques Derrida	
2006	Death of Peter Strawson	

Oxford Paperback Reference

The Concise Oxford Companion to English Literature
Margaret Drabble and Jenny Stringer

Based on the best-selling *Oxford Companion to English Literature*, this is an indispensable guide to all aspects of English literature.

Review of the parent volume
'a magisterial and monumental achievement'

Literary Review

The Concise Oxford Companion to Irish Literature
Robert Welch

From the ogam alphabet developed in the 4th century to Roddy Doyle, this is a comprehensive guide to writers, works, topics, folklore, and historical and cultural events.

Review of the parent volume
'Heroic volume ... It surpasses previous exercises of similar nature in the richness of its detail and the ecumenism of its approach.'

Times Literary Supplement

A Dictionary of Shakespeare
Stanley Wells

Compiled by one of the best-known international authorities on the playwright's works, this dictionary offers up-to-date information on all aspects of Shakespeare, both in his own time and in later ages.